BUSINESS AND SOCIETY
Corporate Strategy, Public Policy, Ethics

McGRAW-HILL SERIES IN MANAGEMENT

Fred Luthans and Keith Davis, Consulting Editors

ARNOLD AND FELDMAN: Organizational Behavior

BARTOL AND MARTIN: Management

BERNARDIN AND RUSSELL: HUMAN RESOURCE MANAGEMENT: An Experiential Approach

BOONE AND BOWEN: Great Writings in Management and Organizational Behavior

BOONE AND KURTZ: Management

BOUNDS, YORKS, ADAMS, AND RANNEY: Beyond Total Quality Management: Toward the Emerging Paradigm

BOVÉE, THILL, WOOD, AND DOVEL: Management

CASCIO: Managing Human Resources: Productivity, Quality of Work Life, Profits

DAVIDSON AND DE LA TORRE: Managing the Global Corporation: Case Studies in Strategy and Management

DESS AND MILLER: Strategic Management

DILWORTH: Operations Management: Design, Planning, and Control for Manufacturing and Services

DILWORTH: Production and Operations Management: Manufacturing and Services

DOBLER, BURT, AND LEE: Purchasing and Materials Management: Text and Cases

FELDMAN AND ARNOLD: Managing Individual and Group Behavior in Organizations

FITZSIMMONS AND FITZSIMMONS: Service Management for Competitive Advantage

GAYNOR AND KIRKPATRICK: Introduction to Time Series Modeling and Forecasting for Business Economics

HESS AND SICILIANO: Management: Responsibility for Performance

HODGETTS AND LUTHANS: International Management

HOFFMAN AND MOORE: Business Ethics: Readings and Cases in Corporate Morality

JAUCH AND GLUECK: Business Policy and Strategic Management

JAUCH AND GLUECK: Strategic Management and Business Policy

JAUCH AND TOWNSEND: Cases in Strategic Management and Business Policy

KATZ AND KOCHAN: An Introduction to Collective Bargaining and Industrial Relations

KOONTZ AND WEIHRICH: Essentials of Management

KOPELMAN: Managing Productivity in Organizations: A Practical, People-Oriented Perspective

KURILOFF, HEMPHILL, AND CLOUD: Starting and Managing the Small Business

LEVIN, RUBIN, STINSON, AND GARDNER: Quantitative Approaches to Management

LUTHANS: Organizational Behavior

LUTHANS AND THOMPSON: Contemporary Readings in Organizational Behavior

MILES: Theories of Management: Implications for Organizational Behavior and Development

MILES AND SNOW: Organizational Strategy, Structure, and Process

MILLS: Labor-Management Relations

MITCHELL AND LARSON: People in Organizations: An Introduction to Organizational Behavior

MOLANDER: Responsive Capitalism: Case Studies in Corporate Social Conduct

MONKS: Operations Management: Theory and Problems

NEWSTROM AND DAVIS: Organizational Behavior: Human Behavior at Work

NEWSTROM AND DAVIS: Organizational Behavior: Reading and Exercises

NOORI AND RADFORD: Production and Operations Management: Total Quality and Responsiveness

PEARCE AND ROBINSON: Corporate Strategies: Readings from *Business Week*

PORTER AND MCKIBBIN: Management Education and Development: Drift or Thrust into the 21st Century?

POST, FREDERICK, LAWRENCE, AND WEBER: Business and Society: Corporate Strategy, Public Policy, Ethics

PRASOW AND PETERS: Arbitration and Collective Bargaining: Conflict Resolution in Labor Relations

RICKS, GINN, AND DAUGHTREY: Contemporary Supervision: Managing People and Technology

RUE AND HOLLAND: Strategic Management: Concepts and Experiences

RUGMAN AND HODGETTS: International Business: A Strategic Management Approach

SAYLES: Leadership: Managing in Real Organizations

SCHLESINGER, ECCLES, AND GABARRO: Managing Behavior in Organizations: Text, Cases, and Readings

SCHROEDER: Operations Management: Decision Making in the Operations Function

STEERS AND PORTER: Motivation and Work Behavior

STEINER: Industry, Society, and Change: A Casebook

STEINER AND STEINER: Business, Government, and Society: A Managerial Perspective, Text and Cases

STEINHOFF AND BURGESS: Small Business Management Fundamentals

SUTERMEISTER: People and Productivity

WALKER: Human Resource Strategy

WEIHRICH: Management Excellence: Productivity through MBO

WEIHRICH AND KOONTZ: Management: A Global Perspective

WERTHER AND DAVIS: Human Resources and Personnel Management

WOFFORD, GERLOFF, AND CUMMINS: Organizational Communications: The Keystone to Managerial Effectiveness

YOFFIE AND GOMES-CASSERES: International Trade and Competition: Cases and Notes in Strategy and Management

BUSINESS AND SOCIETY

Corporate Strategy, Public Policy, Ethics

EIGHTH EDITION

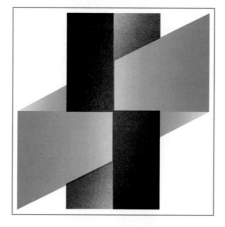

James E. Post
Boston University

William C. Frederick
University of Pittsburgh

Anne T. Lawrence
San Jose State University

James Weber
Duquesne University

McGraw-Hill, Inc.
New York   St. Louis   San Francisco   Auckland   Bogotá   Caracas
Lisbon   London   Madrid   Mexico City   Milan   Montreal   New Delhi
San Juan   Singapore   Sydney   Tokyo   Toronto

To Keith Davis
Author, Scholar, Friend

Pioneer and Creator of the First Edition
of *Business and Society* Three Decades Ago

BUSINESS AND SOCIETY
Corporate Strategy, Public Policy, Ethics

This book is printed on acid-free paper.

2 3 4 5 6 7 8 9 0   DOC   DOC   9 0 9 8 7 6

ISBN 0-07-050494-6

This book was set in Zapf Book Light by Ruttle, Shaw & Wetherill, Inc.
The editors were Lynn Richardson and Dan Alpert;
the production supervisor was Annette Mayeski.
The cover was designed by Joan Greenfield.
Project supervision was done by The Total Book.
R. R. Donnelley & Sons Company was printer and binder.

Library of Congress Cataloging-in-Publication Data

Business and society: corporate strategy, public policy, ethics.—
8th ed. / James E. Post . . . [et al.]
    p.   cm.
  Rev. ed. of Business and society. 7th ed. / William C. Frederick,
James E. Post, Keith Davis, c1992.
  Includes bibliographical references and index.
  ISBN 0-07-050494-6
  1. Social responsibility of business.   I. Post, James E.
II. Frederick, William Crittenden, (date). Business and society.
HD60.F72   1996   95-9391
658.4' 08—dc20

ABOUT THE AUTHORS

James E. Post is Professor of Management and Public Policy at Boston University. His primary areas of teaching and research are business and public policy, corporate public affairs management, and management of environmental and natural resource issues. He is the author or coauthor of such books as *Private Management and Public Policy* (with Lee Preston), *Managing Environmental Issues: A Casebook* (with Rogene Buchholz and Alfred Marcus), and *Research in Corporate Social Performance and Policy*, an international research volume for which he has served as series editor. He has been an adviser to businesses, industry associations, and such non-profit organizations as the National Wildlife Federation's Corporate Conservation Council, the World Health Organization, Rockefeller Foundation, and The Population Council. As an expert witness, he has testified before various committees of the U.S. Senate and House of Representatives. He also served as Director of the Business and Society research program at The Conference Board, a leading business association. A past chairperson of the Social Issues in Management division of the Academy of Management, he has served as an editorial board member or reviewer for many academic journals. In 1989, his book, *Private Management and Public Policy,* was cited by the Academy of Management for "its lasting contribution to the study of business and society."

William C. Frederick is Professor Emeritus of Business Administration at the University of Pittsburgh. Corporate social performance, business ethics, and managerial values are his major areas of scholarly interest and research. Professor Frederick has been credited with helping to found the business and society field of management studies in the United States. He has coauthored five editions of *Business and Society,* and his most recent book is *Values, Nature, and Culture in the American Corporation.* He has been chair of the Social Issues in Management division of the Academy of Management, president of the Society for Business Ethics, president of the Society for Advancement of Socio-Economics, and a member of the editorial board of the *Academy of Management Review.* He has a Ph.D. in economics from the University of Texas.

Anne T. Lawrence is Associate Professor of Organization and Management at San Jose State University. She holds a Ph.D. from the University of California, Berkeley, and completed two years of post-doctoral study at

Stanford University. Her articles, cases, and reviews have appeared in many journals, including the *Academy of Management Review, Administrative Science Quarterly, Journal of Management Education, Case Research Journal, Business and Society Review,* and *Research in Corporate Social Performance and Policy.* Her cases in business and society have also been reprinted in many textbooks and anthologies. She is Associate Editor of the *Case Research Journal* and has served as President of the Western Casewriters Association. At San Jose State University, she was named Outstanding Undergraduate Instructor in the College of Business and received the Dean's Award for Faculty Excellence.

James Weber is Associate Professor and Director of the Beard Center for Leadership in Ethics at Duquesne University. He has a Ph.D. from the University of Pittsburgh and has formerly taught at the University of San Francisco, University of Pittsburgh, and Marquette University. His areas of interest and research include managerial and organizational values, cognitive moral reasoning, business ethics, and ethics training and education. He has published works in numerous management and ethics journals and was recognized by the Social Issues in Management division of the Academy of Management with the Best Paper Award in 1989 and 1994. He is a member of, and has served in various leadership roles, in the Social Issues in Management division of the Academy of Management, the International Association of Business and Society (IABS), and the Society for the Advancement of Socio-Economics (SASE).

CONTENTS

PREFACE   XX

INTRODUCTION AND OVERVIEW   XXV

PART ONE: THE CORPORATION IN SOCIETY

**1   The Corporation, Its Stakeholders,
      and the Twenty-First Century**   3

Key Questions and Chapter Objectives   3

Business—Government—Society: An Interdependent System   6
A Systems Perspective 6

The Stakeholder Concept   8
The "Three-Legged Stool" 9 ▪ *Primary and Secondary
Stakeholders* 10 ▪ *Stakeholder Interests and Power* 14
▪ *Stakeholder Coalitions* 15

Forces Shaping Business-Society Relations   18
Strategic and Social Challenges 19 ▪ *Ethical Expectations and
Public Values* 22 ▪ *Global Economic Change* 24 ▪ *Government
and Public Policy* 26 ▪ *Ecological and Natural Resource
Concerns* 29

Corporate Strategy for the Twenty-First Century   30

Summary Points of This Chapter   31

Key Terms and Concepts Used in This Chapter   31

Discussion Case: Inland National Bank   32
Discussion Questions 33

2   Corporate Social Responsibility   35

Key Questions and Chapter Objectives   35

The Meaning of Corporate Social Responsibility   37
Social Responsibility in Other Nations ▪ 38

How Corporate Social Responsibility Began   41
The Charity Principle 41 ▪ *The Stewardship Principle* 42

Modern Forms of Corporate Social Responsibility   43

The Limits of Corporate Social Responsibility   46
Legitimacy 46 ■ *Costs 48* ■ *Efficiency 48* ■ *Scope and
Complexity 49*

Voluntary Responsibility versus Legal Requirements   49
Enlightened Self-Interest 51 ■ *Voluntary Action versus Legal
Compulsion 52*

Profits and Social Responsibility   53
Long-run Profits versus Short-run Profits 54 ■ *Optimum Profits
versus Maximum Profits 54* ■ *Stockholder Interests versus Other
Stakeholder Interests 54*

Summary Points of This Chapter   55

Key Terms and Concepts Used in This Chapter   56

Discussion Case: Cummins Engine Company   56
Discussion Questions 58

3   **Socially Responsive Management**   59

Key Questions and Chapter Objectives   59

Stakeholder Expectations and Corporate Performance   61
The Peformance-Expectations Gap 61

The Social Climate of the 1960s and 1970s   62

Strategies of Response   63
An Inactive Strategy 64 ■ *A Reactive Strategy 65* ■ *A Proactive
Strategy 65* ■ *An Interactive Strategy 66*

The Public Affairs Function   67

Formulating Socially Responsive Strategies   69
The Macroenvironment of Business 70 ■ *Scanning and
Environmental Analysis 72*

Implementing Social Responsiveness   74
A Model of Corporate Social Responsiveness 74 ■ *Framework
for Social Policy 77*

Making a Social Strategy Work   77
Corporate Culture 77 ■ *Organizational Structure and
Management 78* ■ *Rewards and Evaluation 80* ■ *Public
Disclosure 80*

Conclusion   81

Summary Points of This Chapter   81

Key Terms and Concepts Used in This Chapter   82

Discussion Case: Stride Rite Corporation   82
Discussion Questions 83

PART TWO: THE CORPORATION AND ETHICAL ISSUES

4 Ethical Dilemmas in Business 87

Key Questions and Chapter Objectives 87

The Meaning of Ethics 89
What Is Business Ethics? 90 ■ *Why Should Business Be Ethical?* 90

Types of Business Ethics Issues 94
Face-to-Face Ethics 94 ■ *Corporate Policy Ethics* 95 ■ *Functional-Area Ethics* 96

Why Ethical Problems Occur in Business 101
Personal Gain and Selfish Interest 101 ■ *Competitive Pressures on Profits* 102 ■ *Business Goals versus Personal Values* 103 ■ *Cross-Cultural Contradictions* 104

Global Ethics Issues 105
Efforts to Curtail Unethical Practices 106

Ethics, Law, and Illegal Corporate Behavior 108
Corporate Lawbreaking and Its Costs 109

Summary Points of This Chapter 110

Key Terms and Concepts Used in This Chapter 110

Discussion Case: It's A Short Life, So Go Ahead and Light Up! 110
Discussion Questions 112

5 Ethical Reasoning and Corporate Programs 113

Key Questions and Chapter Objectives 113

The Core Elements of Ethical Reform 114
Managers' Goals and Values 115 ■ *Personal Character and Moral Development* 118 ■ *Corporate Culture and Ethical Climates* 121

Analyzing Ethical Problems in Business 124
Utility: Comparing Benefits and Costs 125 ■ *Rights: Determining and Protecting Entitlements* 126 ■ *Justice: Is It Fair?* 127 ■ *Applying Ethical Reasoning to Business Activities* 128

Making Ethics Work In Corporations 130
"It's OK to Talk about Ethics Here" 130 ■ *Building Ethical Safeguards into the Company* 132 ■ *Comprehensive Programs and Ethics Awards* 136

Summary Points of This Chapter 137

Key Terms and Concepts Used in This Chapter 137

Discussion Case: Organizing for Ethics Reform 138
Discussion Questions 139

PART THREE   THE CORPORATION IN A GLOBAL SOCIETY

6 Managing in Diverse Social Systems   143

Key Questions and Chapter Objectives   143

Doing Business in a Diverse World   145
Diversity and Global Business 146 ■ *A World of Diversity* 147

Basic Types of Socioeconomic Systems   149

Free Enterprise   151
Free Enterprise Ideology 152

Central State Control   156

Mixed State-and-Private Enterprise   159

Militarized Nondemocratic Socioeconomic Systems   160

Systems in Transition: China Faces the Twenty-First Century   161
China's Socioeconomic Pendulum Swings Back and Forth 162

Preparing for the New World Order   165

Summary Points of This Chapter   168

Key Terms and Concepts Used in This Chapter   169

Discussion Case: What Is Hong Kong's Future?   170
Discussion Questions 171

7 Global Challenges to Corporate Responsibility   173

Key Questions and Chapter Objectives   173

The International Imperative   175
Factors Encouraging International Business 175

The Global Business Enterprise   178
Size, Power, and Accountability 178 ■ *Public and Private
Roles* 181 ■ *Multinational Corporations* 182

National Sovereignty and Corporate Power   183
National Sovereignty and the Stateless Corporation 183
■ *Ownership and Control* 185 ■ *Foreign-Owned Business in
the United States* 186

Political and Social Challenges of Doing Business Abroad   188
Political Challenges 188 ■ *Social Challenges* 191 ■ *Questionable
Payments* 194 ■ *Labor Standards* 195

Corporate Social Strategy   197

Summary Points of This Chapter   197

Key Terms and Concepts Used in This Chapter   198

Discussion Case: General Electric in Hungary   199
Discussion Questions 200

PART FOUR   THE CORPORATION AND PUBLIC POLICY

8   The Corporation and Public Policy   203

Key Questions and Chapter Objectives   203

Public Policy   205
What Is Public Policy? 205 ▪ *Powers of Government* 206 ▪ *Elements of Public Policy* 207

Public Policy and Business   208
National Economic Growth 209 ▪ *Taxation Policy* 211 ▪ *Trade Policy* 213 ▪ *Industrial Policy* 215

Social Welfare Policies   215
Health Policy 216 ▪ *Social Security* 218 ▪ *Entitlements* 219

Government Regulation of Business   221
Goals and Objectives 221 ▪ *Types of Regulation* 221

Growth of Regulation   223
Underlying Factors 225 ▪ *The Costs of Regulation* 225 ▪ *Deregulation, Re-regulation, and Recent Trends* 227 ▪ *Reinventing Government* 229

International Regulation   229
Regulation of Imported Products 229 ▪ *Regulation of Exported Products* 231 ▪ *Regulation of International Business Behavior* 231

The Future   232

Summary Points of This Chapter   232

Key Terms and Concepts Used in This Chapter   233

Discussion Case: Meeting the Nation's Health Care Crisis   233
Discussion Questions 235

9   Managing Business-Government Relations   237

Key Questions and Chapter Objectives   237

Evolution of Public Issues   239
From Social Concerns to Public Action 240 ▪ *The Public Issues Life Cycle* 240

Issues Management   246
The Process 246 ▪ *Managing the Single Issue* 249 ▪ *Managing Multiple Issues* 250

Strategic Management of Government Relations   250
Political Involvement 252 ▪ *Business and The Political System* 253

American Politics in the 1990s   254
Critical Problems of the 1990s 256

Responsible Business Politics in a Global World   265

Summary Points of This Chapter   267

Key Terms and Concepts Used in This Chapter   268

Discussion Case: Harry and Louise: A $15 Million Couple   268
  Discussion Questions 270

10 Antitrust, Mergers, and Global Competition   271

Key Questions and Chapter Objectives   271

Corporate Power and Legitimacy   273
  *Corporate Economic Power 274 ■ Corporate Political Power 275
  ■ Corporate Social Power 275 ■ The Dilemma of Corporate
  Power 276*

Antitrust Regulation   277
  *Objectives of Antitrust 278 ■ The Major Antitrust Laws 280
  ■ Enforcing the Antitrust Laws 284 ■ Key Antitrust Issues 285*

Corporate Mergers   286
  The Consequences of Corporate Mergers 289

Global Competition and a Changing Economy   290
  Intellectual Property 292

Summary Points of This Chapter   293

Key Terms and Concepts Used in This Chapter   294

Discussion Case: The Antitrust Case against Microsoft   294
  Discussion Questions 296

PART FIVE   THE CORPORATION AND THE NATURAL ENVIRONMENT

11 Ecology, Sustainable Development, and Global Business   299

Key Questions and Chapter Objectives   299

Ecological Challenges   301
  *The Global Commons 301 ■ Sustainable Development 302
  ■ Threats to the Earth's Ecosystem 303 ■ Forces of Change 305
  ■ The Limits to Growth 307*

Global Environmental Issues   308
  Ozone Depletion 309 ■ Global Warming 310 ■ Biodiversity 313

Response of the International Business Community   316
  *Business Council for Sustainable Development 316 ■ Voluntary
  Business Initiatives 317*

Summary Points of This Chapter   321

Key Terms and Concepts Used in This Chapter   321

Discussion Case: Saving the Malaysian Rain Forest   321
  Discussion Questions 322

12 Managing Environmental Issues   323

Key Questions and Chapter Objectives   323

Role of Government 325
Major Areas of Environmental Regulation 325 ■ *Alternative Policy
Approaches* 331 ■ *Civil and Criminal Enforcement* 335

Costs and Benefits of Environmental Regulation 337

The Greening of Management 340
Stages of Corporate Environmental Responsibility 340 ■ *Elements
of Effective Environmental Management* 342 ■ *Voluntary Initiatives
by Business* 344

Summary Points of This Chapter 345

Key Terms and Concepts Used in This Chapter 346

Discussion Case: Locating a Toxic Waste Facility:
Racism or Opportunity? 346
Discussion Questions 347

PART SIX   **RESPONDING TO PRIMARY STAKEHOLDERS**

13 Stockholders and Corporate Governance 351

Key Questions and Chapter Objectives 351

Stockholders 353
Who Are Stockholders? 353 ■ *Objectives of Stock Ownership* 354

Stockholders' Legal Rights and Safeguards 356
Stockholder Lawsuits 357 ■ *Corporate Disclosures* 357

Corporate Governance 358
The Board of Directors 358 ■ *Top Management* 359 ■ *Creditors* 360
■ *The Process of Corporate Governance* 361

Current Trends in Corporate Governance 362
The Rise of Institutional Investors 362 ■ *Changing Role of the
Board of Directors* 365 ■ *Social Responsibility Shareholder
Resolutions* 365 ■ *Employee Stock Ownership* 367

Executive Compensation: A Special Issue 368

Government Protection of Stockholder Interests 371
Securities and Exchange Commission 371 ■ *Insider Trading* 372

Stockholders and the Corporation 373

Summary Points of This Chapter 374

Key Terms and Concepts Used in This Chapter 374

Discussion Case: Shareholders Walk out at Philip Morris 374
Discussion Questions 376

14 Consumer Protection 377

Key Questions and Chapter Objectives 377

Pressures to Promote Consumer Interests 378
The Anatomy of Consumerism 379 ■ *Reasons for the Consumer Movement 380* ■ *Consumer Advocacy Groups 382*

Leading Consumer Issues of the 1990s 383
Ecological Impacts of Consumption 383 ■ *Nutritional and Safety Concerns 385* ■ *Advertising's Social Dimension 386*

How Government Protects Consumers 389
Goals of Consumer Laws 389 ■ *Major Consumer Protection Agencies 392* ■ *Product Liability: A Special Problem 394*

Positive Business Responses to Consumerism 399
Total Quality Management 399 ■ *Consumer Affairs Departments 400* ■ *Arbitration and Consumer Action Panels 400* ■ *Product Recalls 400*

Consumerism's Achievements 401

Summary Points of This Chapter 402

Key Terms and Concepts Used in This Chapter 402

Discussion Case: General Motors' Pickup Truck 402
Discussion Questions 404

15 **The Employee-Employer Relationship** 405

Key Questions and Chapter Objectives 405

The Employee-Employer Contract 406
The New Social Contract 407 ■ *Government Intervention in the United States 409* ■ *International Alternatives to Employee Layoffs 409*

Equal Job Opportunity 410
Government Policies and Regulations 410 ■ *Corporate Responses 412* ■ *Americans with Disabilities Act 413* ■ *Reverse Discrimination 413*

Workplace Diversity 414
Immigration 415 ■ *Language in the Workplace 415* ■ *Managing a Diverse Workforce 416*

Job Safety and Health 417
Occupational Safety and Health Administration 418 ■ *OSHA in the 1980s and 1990s 418* ■ *Management's Responses 419* ■ *Workplace Violence 420*

Challenging Employees' Privacy 421
Computer Data Banks 422 ■ *Monitoring Employee Activity 422* ■ *AIDS Testing 424*

Employees' Rights and Responsibilities 425

Testing to Control Employees' Actions 425
Employee Drug Use and Testing 426 ■ *Alcohol Abuse at Work 427* ■ *Employee Theft and Honesty Testing 428*

Restricting Employee Behavior 429
Smoking in the Workplace 430 ■ *Whistle-Blowing* 431

Employees as Corporate Stakeholders 432

Summary Points of This Chapter 432

Key Terms and Concepts Used in This Chapter 433

Discussion Case: Responding to AIDS in the Workplace 433
Discussion Questions 435

16 Women, Work, and the Family 437

Key Questions and Chapter Objectives 437

The Status of Women in Society: Historical Background 438
The Women's Movement 440

Why Women Have Entered the Workplace 441

Where Women Work and What They Are Paid 443

Women in Management 444
Where Women Manage 445 ■ *Do Women and Men Managers
Manage Differently?* 447 ■ *The Glass Ceiling* 449 ■ *Women
Business Owners* 450

Government's Role in Securing Women's Workplace Rights 451
Equal Pay and Equal Opportunity 451 ■ *Comparable Worth* 453

What Business Can Do: Policies and Strategies 453
Reforming Personnel Policies 454 ■ *Providing Support Programs
for Work and Family* 454 ■ *Work Flexibility* 457 ■ *Reforming
Attitudes in the Workplace* 458

The Gender-Neutral, Family-Friendly Corporation 460

Summary Points of This Chapter 461

Key Terms and Concepts Used in This Chapter 461

Discussion Case: Johnson Controls and Fetal Protection
in the Workplace 462
Discussion Questions 463

PART SEVEN   SOCIAL ISSUES IN MANAGEMENT

17 The Community and the Corporation 467

Key Questions and Chapter Objectives 467

Community Relations 469
Limited Resources Face Unlimited Community Needs 470 ■
Community Involvement and Firm Size 470 ■ *Community
Support of Business* 473

Strengthening the Community 475

Improving Economic Development 476 ■ *Housing 477* ■ *Education Reform 478* ■ *Technical Assistance to Government 480* ■ *Aid to Minority Enterprise 480* ■ *Environmental Programs 480*

Corporate Giving   481
Corporate Giving in a Strategic Context 483 ■ *Priorities in Corporate Giving 485*

The Role of Volunteerism   486

Corporate Restructuring and Community Relations   487
Social Costs of Restructuring 488 ■ *Community Responses 488* ■ *Company Responses 491* ■ *The Age of Anxiety 491*

The Need for Partnership   492

Summary Points of This Chapter   493

Key Terms and Concepts Used in This Chapter   495

Discussion Case: Abbott Laboratories Helps
Habitat for Humanity   495
Discussion Questions 496

18 Technology and the Media   497

Key Questions and Chapter Objectives   497

Technology as a Social Force   498
Features of Technology 499 ■ *Business Applies Technology 500* ■ *Phases of Technology in Society 500* ■ *Economic Effects of Technology 502*

Social Consequences of Technological Change   503
Social Costs 503 ■ *Genetic Engineering—A New Frontier 504* ■ *Information Technology 505* ■ *Stakeholder Reactions 507*

Role of Government and Business in Technological Change   508
Government Involvement 508 ■ *Business Responsibility for Technological Change 509*

Emergence of the Media as Technological Force   511
Role of the Media in an Information Society 511 ■ *Critical Media Issues 512*

Corporate Media Strategies   520
Public Relations 520 ■ *Crisis Management 520* ■ *Advocacy Advertising 521* ■ *Media Training of Employees 522*

Social Responsibility Guidelines for the Media and
Media Sponsors   523

Summary Points of This Chapter   524

Key Terms and Concepts Used in This Chapter   524

Discussion Case: Media Woes and a Triumph   525
Discussion Questions 527

19 **Business and the Twenty-First Century** 529

Key Questions and Chapter Objectives 529

Corporate Strategy for the Twenty-First Century 531
Population, Technology, and Work Force 531 ■ *The New
Social Contract* 532

Business and Society in the Twenty-First Century 533
Corporate Strategy 533 ■ *Ethics and Public Values* 535 ■ *Global
Challenges* 536 ■ *Political Revolutions of the 1990s* 536
■ *Ecological Challenges* 538

Problems of Community 539

Immigration 539
Barriers to Immigration 540 ■ *U.S.-Mexico Immigration Issues* 541

Violence 543

The Underclass 546

Racism 549

Business Must Be Involved 551

Summary Points of This Chapter 553

Key Terms and Concepts Used in This Chapter 554

Discussion Case: Thinking about the Future 555
Discussion Questions 556

CASE STUDIES IN CORPORATE SOCIAL POLICY

The Tylenol Recalls 558

Bhopal 576

Personal Ethics Dilemmas 587

Crisis and Collaboration in Silicon Valley 592

The Lincoln Savings and Loan Scandal 603

The Merck-Medco Merger Proposal 617

**The Spotted Owl, the Forest Products Industry,
and the Public Policy Process** 628

Doing Business in the Maquiladoras: A Shareholder Challenge 641

Dow Corning and the Silicone Implant Controversy 651

Save Our Cities: Business and the Community 665

GLOSSARY 675

BIBLIOGRAPHY 689

INDEXES

Name Index 694

Subject Index 699

PREFACE

As the world moves toward the twenty-first century, it is strikingly obvious that business operates within complex webs of social relationships. Broad societal forces have become so much a part of modern life that political revolution, global economic forces, and technological transformation of communications and financial transactions have produced networks of social relations that span the globe. Business is conducted—quite literally—twenty-four hours a day, every day, in every nation on earth. In every nation, human beings are affected, directly and indirectly, intentionally and unintentionally, by this extraordinary confluence of commerce and society. And because change produces more change, the prospect of yet greater transformation grows.

Today, the relationship between business and society is evolving in new and sometimes troubling ways:

- In the United States and other advanced nations, businesses are transforming the nature of the employment relationship, abandoning decades-long practices that provided job security to employees, in favor of highly flexible, but less secure, forms of employment.
- The restructuring and redesign of businesses have been driven by intense competition in global markets, continuous pressure to improve the quality of products and services, and information networks that facilitate rapid transfer of economic, social, and political information. The stability and protection that geography, technology, and time once provided are gone.
- Governmental policies toward individual industries and sectors of the economy have reshaped the marketplace for goods and services. Governmental policies toward trade are now critical to the competitive future of businesses everywhere, and to the social well-being of more than 5 billion people that now inhabit the earth.
- Ecological and environmental problems have been catapulted into prominence, forcing governments and businesses to take action. Crises, scientific research, and new knowledge of how normal human activities affect natural ecosystems are producing widespread concern that environmental protection must be integrated with economic growth if development is to be sustainable into the next century.
- Public concern has grown about the ethical and moral behavior of businesses and their employees. In many countries, corruption and

criminal behavior threaten civil society. As moral standards change, corporations are challenged to understand new ethical climates, adjust practices, and reconcile sometimes conflicting ethical messages.

■ Companies are challenged to function as ethical actors in a world community where great differences exist in public values. Religious ferment, ethnic conflicts, and pressure to link human rights practices to trade policies are among the many values challenges confronting business in the mid-1990s.

The eighth edition of *Business and Society* is designed to address this complex agenda of issues and relationships. The development of this new edition began with an effort to build on the proven success of earlier editions. Recent adopters of the book shared their insights and thoughts with the author team, and many of the changes in this edition result from their advice.

The author team is diverse and experienced in the business and society field. Two new coauthors, Anne T. Lawrence and James Weber, add valuable experience and perspectives to the text. Professor Lawrence brings an extensive background of business and society teaching, research, and case development. Professor Weber, like Professor Lawrence, is a contributor of cases and other materials to earlier editions; his research and writing focuses on business ethics, managerial moral reasoning, and organizational values. Professor William C. Frederick is well known for his extensive work on business values and for his dedication to incorporating business ethics and business and society studies into the curricula of modern business schools. Professor James E. Post represents the third generation of business and society scholars to have guided the development of *Business and Society.* His current work focuses on business responses to community issues, management of the corporate public affairs function, and how companies are dealing with the ecological issues of sustainable development.

Since 1966, when Professors Keith Davis and Robert Blomstrom wrote the first edition, *Business and Society* has maintained a position of leadership by presenting the central issues of corporate social performance in a form that students and faculty have found engaging and stimulating. In each edition, the authors and publisher have sought to achieve high quality and market acceptance in the field by identifying the emerging issues that shape the organizational, social, and public policy environments in which students will soon live and work.

Business and Society, eighth edition, builds on this heritage of business and society leadership by examining such *classic* issues as the role of business in society, the nature of corporate responsibility, business ethics, and the complex roles of government and business in the global economic community, Throughout, examples of individuals and companies, large and small, facing these challenges illustrate concepts, theories, research studies, and ideas for each topic.

This edition also addresses *emerging* themes in modern business and society teaching and scholarship. For example, ecological and natural resources problems are becoming central to industry and challenging business and political leaders. In the face of serious ecological threats that accompany industrial activity, how can economic development—vital to the improved life of so many of the world's poor—become sustainable? In a world where time and geographic distance no longer provide a buffer against change, this text addresses how managers can create business strategies that respect the interests of stakeholders, support community development, respect personal values, and can be implemented fairly and be economically successful.

The major changes and improvements in this edition of *Business and Society* can be briefly summarized:

- **The text includes a discussion of the new social contract between employers and employees.** A profound shift has occurred in how employees relate to companies and how managers understand their responsibilities to employees and all stakeholders in the modern competitive environment. This is a critical theme for students to consider in the 1990s.

- **The discussion of global competition and its effects on companies, industries, and nations is incorporated throughout the book.** Important developments such as growth of the European Union, the creation of the North American Free Trade Agreement (NAFTA), and the creation of new international trade communities such as Mercosur (Argentina, Brazil, Paraguay, Uruguay) are discussed.

- **The dramatic shifts in public consensus about the proper role of government are examined in public policy chapters and throughout the book.** These developments, which have occurred in other nations and are now prominent in the United States, promise a major reassessment of which social institutions bear responsibility for addressing critical societal issues.

- **Reflecting the growing importance of ecological issues to businesses and nations, we have expanded our coverage of environmental policy issues.** The need for improved ways of harmonizing economic activity with sustainable environmental practices will create managerial challenges for many years to come. Two chapters now address a range of ecological issues and management responses to the environment.

- **A new chapter has been written on technology and the media.** As the promise of the information superhighway becomes reality, the convergence of technological advances with the central role of the media as a means of communicating about social change will become more central to our lives.

- **A new chapter dealing with such emerging social issues as im-**

migration, violence, and urban revitalization has been added.
The importance of these issues and the likelihood of their continued
significance have been central to the decision to develop this chapter.

■ **New cases have been added but a number of classic cases favored by instructors and students have been retained.** Readers
will notice a greater diversity of case materials. In addition to new cases
prepared by the authors, we have also included several contributions
from leading scholars at other universities.

■ **Improved pedagogical features appear in each chapter.** Each
chapter contains Key Questions and Chapter Objectives, Key Terms
and Concepts, Summary Points linked to Key Questions and Chapter
Objectives, and a Discussion Case keyed to the chapter's major themes.
Illustrative figures help explain major points and are supplemented by
boxed exhibits intended to illuminate especially important perspectives.

■ **The color format and improved artwork not only enhance the
book's attractiveness but also focus attention on major discussion points.** The excellent quality of the design and art serves to enhance the learning process for students.

■ **Supplementary materials have been expanded.** The Instructor's
Manual has been completely revised, with an expanded test bank and
additional teaching resource materials. A McGraw-Hill video package is
also available for use with the book.

ACKNOWLEDGMENTS

This edition has benefited from the skill and collaboration of many professionals. We are pleased to acknowledge the excellent case studies prepared by Jeanne Logsdon (University of New Mexico), Margaret J. Naumes
(University of New Hampshire), and William Naumes (University of New
Hampshire).

For reading portions of the manuscript and offering suggestions for improvement, we thank Ruth Milkman (University of California, Los Angeles), Diana Roose (Oberlin College), Kenneth D. Roose (American Council
on Education, retired), Randall Stross (San Jose State University), and the
following reviewers: Leslie Connelly, University of Central Florida; Craig
P. Dunn, San Diego State University; Joseph W. Ford, Iona College; John F.
Hulpke, California State University–Bakersfield; Roy B. Johnson, Appala-
chian State University; Edwin C. Leonard, Jr., Indiana University–Purdue
University at Fort Wayne; Kenneth R. Mayer, Cleveland State University;
Nina Polok, University of Colorado–Colorado Springs; and Paul L.
Wilkens, Florida State University.

For research assistance we are grateful to Patrick Deegan (Duquesne

University), Lisa Iha (San Jose State University), Andy Kivel (Data Center, Oakland, California), and Brian Walsh (Boston University). For administrative and secretarial support we also thank Sr. Mary Jennings (Boston University).

Textbooks describe the central ideas in a field of study. For this reason, we wish to acknowledge the work of colleagues at colleges and universities in the United States and abroad. Of particular note are the members of the Social Issues in Management division of the Academy of Management, members of the Society for Business Ethics, and members of the International Association for Business and Society (IABS). They are largely responsible for producing the research data and theoretical insights that undergird the study of business and society relations. We hope that we have captured the essence of their work and reflected the continuing efforts of hundreds of scholars who are striving to create a coherent field of knowledge.

The McGraw-Hill editorial team has provided a continuing commitment to publishing excellence. We thank Lynn Richardson, management editor, Dan Alpert, senior associate editor, Annette Bodzin, project supervisor, and Kerime B. Toksu, copyeditor, for their assistance. It has been a pleasure to work with each of them.

James E. Post
William C. Frederick
Anne T. Lawrence
James Weber

INTRODUCTION AND OVERVIEW

In this introduction, we explain the overall design of the book, which is divided into seven major parts and a group of case studies. Each chapter displays several common features designed to enhance student learning, and these are explained, along with additional design elements of the book.

PART ONE: THE CORPORATION IN SOCIETY

Students are introduced to the basic conceptual themes and ideas of the interaction of business and society. Chapter 1 introduces the corporation, its stakeholders, and the role of the firm in its social and political setting. Major forces shaping business and society relations as the twenty-first century approaches are introduced. Chapter 2 describes various models and theories of corporate social responsibility and examines the relationship between voluntary corporate behavior and legally required actions. Chapter 3 discusses the socially responsive behavior of business in a changing social and political environment. This chapter also examines the corporate organizational structures and programs that have been created to respond to a changing social environment.

PART TWO: THE CORPORATION AND ETHICAL ISSUES

Chapters 4 and 5 introduce the ethical concepts, theories, and practical actions that guide business behavior. Importantly, these chapters stress the worldwide ethical responsibility of corporations and of the people who make decisions in those organizations.

PART THREE: THE CORPORATION IN A GLOBAL SOCIETY

Chapters 6 and 7 focus on the powerful changes that are reshaping the business world of the late twentieth century. The influence of multinational corporations, the failure of communism, the emergence of market economies, and the rise of ethnic, religious, and radical forces in the geopolitical world are all influencing global commerce.

PART FOUR: THE CORPORATION AND PUBLIC POLICY

Chapters 8 through 10 discuss the changing role of government in the global economy, especially its role as a strategist for national economic growth and social welfare. The many roles and responsibilities of government in advanced industrial nations are explored in comparative form, and the essential roles of governments in developing and newly industrialized countries are also discussed. Corporate political action, regulatory processes, and the new rethinking of government's proper role are examined. Chapter 10 introduces students to the special issues of competition policy, antitrust, and national competitive strategies.

PART FIVE: THE CORPORATION AND THE NATURAL ENVIRONMENT

Chapters 11 and 12 address the ecological and natural resource issues that have influenced corporate behavior in recent times and are certain to reshape entire industries as the next century unfolds. Population growth, resource depletion, and the mismanagement of scarce global resources are the seeds of complex social and political forces that will inevitably require corporations to adjust to new realities in the economic, social, and political environment.

PART SIX: RESPONDING TO PRIMARY STAKEHOLDERS

The central concepts and themes discussed in earlier chapters are applied to a variety of the corporation's primary stakeholders and to a number of emerging policy areas. Chapter 13 looks at the arena of corporate governance and the powers of ownership in a world of both individual and institutional stockholders. Chapter 14 focuses on consumers and the challenges of consumer protection in the modern global marketplace. Chapter 15 examines employment and workplace issues, including employee-employer relations and trends in extending equal employment opportunity to all. Chapter 16 addresses the special needs, issues, and requirements of women, men, and families in the modern workplace.

PART SEVEN: SOCIAL ISSUES IN MANAGEMENT

The role of the corporation in the community is examined in Chapter 17, including the role of business in education reform, the importance of charitable contributions, and the place of employee volunteerism in community life. Chapter 18 is a new chapter that examines the complex relationships between science, technology, and the media in the so-called age of information. If the information superhighway does emerge, as experts believe it will within the next decade, the careers of future managers will be inextricably entwined with its capabilities. This technological transformation of business and society will alter the role of the media and limit the ability of companies to operate without regard for stakeholders who can readily acquire and share information.

Chapter 19 concludes by dealing with a number of emerging issues and examining the standards of global citizenship that leading corporations are creating as the twentieth century closes. Corporate responses to issues such as violence and the socioeconomic underclass are also addressed.

CASE STUDIES IN CORPORATE SOCIAL POLICY

Ten full-length cases are included in this section. They represent a wide variety of business and society issues that call for responsible corporate social policies. Included are product recalls, doing business across national and cultural boundaries, industrial accidents, environmental issues and responses, community activism, public-private partnerships, ethical dilemmas, and others. These cases represent a range of responses by corporations to changing social and political issues, including positive corporate social performance as well as less desirable outcomes. These case studies can be used in any order by instructors. Each case is linked to two or more chapters in the text.

LEARNING FEATURES OF EACH CHAPTER

Preview Paragraph: The first page of each chapter contains a short paragraph giving a condensed introduction to that chapter's content.

Key Questions and Chapter Objectives: Five or six key questions outline the major issues explored in the chapter.

Opening Examples: Each chapter begins with one or more examples that illustrate the issues, problems, or major themes discussed.

Illustrative Examples: Throughout each chapter, color-highlighted examples from the actual world of business emphasize the relevance of the chapter's concepts to business operations.

Figures: Graphic figures and tables are integrated into the textual material to illustrate relationships and to condense detailed information.

Exhibits: From one to three boxed and color-highlighted exhibits are included in most chapters to reinforce major points by demonstrating their relevance to actual business operations.

Summary Points: The chapter's major content is summarized in several condensed points at the end of each chapter. Each of these summary points matches the Key Questions and Chapter Objectives that appear at the beginning of the chapter.

Key Terms and Concepts: The terms and concepts most important for understanding the chapter's content are listed. For easy identification and review, each of these terms and concepts is printed in **boldface**.

Discussion Case: Each chapter ends with a short case that illustrates the chapter's major themes and demonstrates their application in the business world. Discussion Questions accompany each Discussion Case.

OTHER LEARNING FEATURES

Glossary: A list of technical terms used in the text, together with their definitions, appears after the case studies at the end of the book. This glossary can be used by students to review key meanings as they read through the text and before examinations.

Bibliography: A select bibliography is included for each of the seven major parts of the book. These books and articles can be consulted for additional information, diverse points of view, preparing term papers, and studying for examinations.

Indexes: A name index and a subject index are included to aid in finding a specific topic or person in the text and case studies.

PART ONE

The Corporation in Society

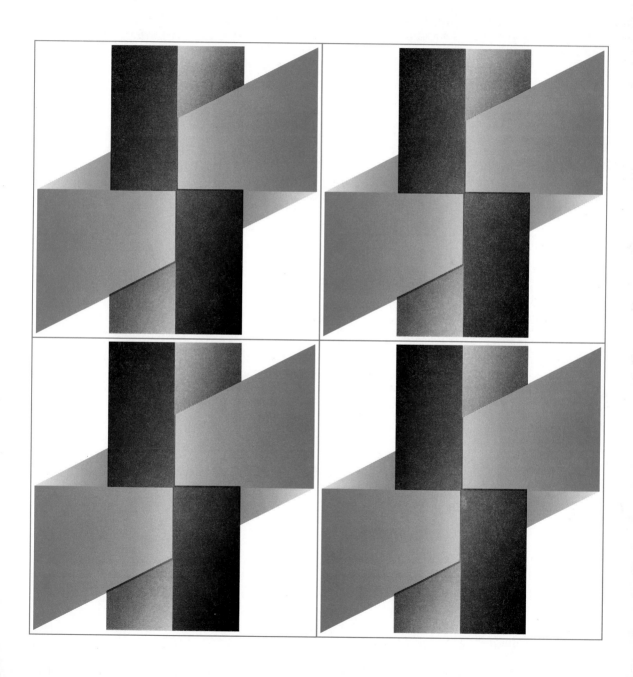

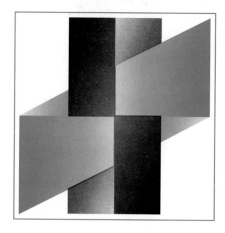

1

The Corporation, Its Stakeholders, and the Twenty-First Century

Business has complex relationships with many segments of society. The existence and power of these segments require careful management attention and action. A company's success can be affected—negatively or positively—by its stakeholders. In an era when business strategies are changing because of such forces as global competition, new political arrangements, shifting public values, and ecological concerns, managers are challenged to achieve good economic results while also considering the needs and requirements of their business's stakeholders.

Key Questions and Chapter Objectives

This chapter focuses on these key questions and objectives:

- Why are business, government, and society an interactive system?
- What kind of involvement does business have with other segments of society?
- Who are a corporation's primary and secondary stakeholders?
- Why are stakeholders important to a corporation, and how can they affect its success?
- What major forces of change are reshaping the business environment for companies?
- How do globalization, ecological concerns, and ethical norms affect corporate stakeholders?

Bell Atlantic is a communications company.[1] It was created in 1982 as part of the breakup of American Telephone and Telegraph (AT&T), the famous "Ma Bell" that traced its roots to Alexander Graham Bell and the invention of the telephone. Bell Atlantic began its life as a regional telephone company whose service area covered the mid-Atlantic region of the United States from Philadelphia to Washington, D.C. Bell Atlantic's chief executive officer from the 1980s to the 1990s was Raymond Smith, a believer in business competition, ethical business behavior, and newly emerging telecommunications technologies.

In the late 1980s, the company launched a joint venture on the other side of the world when the New Zealand government decided to privatize its state-owned telephone company. The franchise was given to a new company, Telecom New Zealand, a company jointly owned by Bell Atlantic and local New Zealand investors. In a few years, Telecom New Zealand became one of the Pacific region's communications leaders.

Bell Atlantic shocked the communications world again in 1993 by announcing its intention to merge with TCI, the largest cable television company in the United States. Raymond Smith and TCI chairman John Malone spoke of how telecommunications and cable television technologies would soon be integrated, and how in the twenty-first century people around the world will be tied together through interactive information technology. News of wars, earthquakes, and political change will be shared instantaneously; business executives in San Francisco will readily communicate with suppliers and customers in Mexico, Ireland, or Khazakistan. In such a world, employees can "telecommute" from Auckland, New Zealand, to Philadelphia.

The merger with TCI eventually collapsed because investors learned that governmental action had changed some of the key financial assumptions. The Federal Communications Commission, a U.S. regulatory agency that sets rates for cable television services, announced a reduction of rates totaling more than 15 percent after the merger was announced. That reduction in revenue sharply affected the value of TCI and the price that Bell Atlantic could reasonably pay to acquire TCI stock. While this merger failed, experts were optimistic that Mr. Smith's vision of merging telecommunications and cable operations would eventually occur.

Bell Atlantic has been a pioneer in other ways as well. AT&T and its local operating companies had a long history of community involvement

---

[1]Based on published material in the *Wall Street Journal*, other business journals, and author's interviews. See, for example, "Bell Atlantic's Acquisition Presented as a Quantum Leap," *New York Times*, Oct. 14, 1993, p. D11; "Why the Mega-Merger Collapsed: Strong Wills and a Big Culture Gap," *Wall Street Journal*, Feb. 25, 1994, pp. A1, A16.

before the 1982 breakup. Bell Atlantic has continued to support local charities, employee volunteer work, and political awareness wherever it does business. As it conducts business in new parts of the world, its managers face the question, "What forms of social responsibility will Bell Atlantic adopt in those settings?" For example, telephone poles are typically made from tree logs that are specially treated with chemicals that prevent rotting of the wood. However, these chemicals can dissipate into the ground over many years and affect the quality of a community's water supply. As Bell Atlantic responds to such ecological issues in the United States, its managers will have to decide whether to continue using wooden telephone poles in other nations where environmental protection laws may be less strict. The ethical implications of such choices are important to employees and to the communities involved.

Global economic, political, and technological change is altering Bell Atlantic from what it once was (a local telephone company) to what it has yet to be ("a global telecommunications, interactive video, digital information business"). Its employees are facing complex and difficult issues that are entwined with being a business enterprise in a global society with numerous governmental laws and regulations, varying ethical standards, and pressing social and economic needs.

Every corporation has complex involvements with other people, groups, and organizations in society. Some of these are intended and desired; others are unintentional and not desired. The people and organizations with which a business is involved have an interest in the decisions, actions, and practices of the firm. Customers, suppliers, employees, owners, creditors, and local communities are among those affected by the profitability and economic success of the business. Their support can be critical to a company's success or failure.

As the 1990s give way to a new decade—and a new century—imagination and opportunity are leading more of the world's people to think about, and be a part of, the business community. The business of the twenty-first century—whatever its size—is going to be part of a global business community, affecting and being affected by social change, events, and pressures from around the world. Whether the company has 50 employees or 50,000, its linkages to customers, suppliers, employees, and communities around the world are likely to be more numerous, diverse, and important to its success. This is why the relationship between business, government, and society is so important to understand as a citizen and as a manager. Whether looked at from outside business—as a member of the community—or from within business—as a manager, entrepreneur, or employee—it is important to see how businesses can blend economic and social purposes together, with minimum conflict and maximum benefits for all.

BUSINESS–GOVERNMENT–SOCIETY: AN INTERDEPENDENT SYSTEM

As the Bell Atlantic example illustrates, business, government, and other elements of society are highly interdependent. Few business actions are without an impact on others in society, just as few actions by government are without direct or indirect impact on business. And, of course, business and government decisions continuously affect all segments of the general public. To manage these interdependencies, corporate managers need a conceptual understanding of the relationships and ideas for responding to issues.

A Systems Perspective

Management thinking has been greatly influenced by general systems theory. According to this theory, all living organisms (systems) interact with, and are affected by, other forces in their host environments. The key to survival is the ability to adapt—to be responsive to the changing conditions in the environment. For an organism such as the modern business corporation, systems thinking provides a powerful tool to help managers appreciate the relationships between their companies and the rest of the world.

Figure 1-1 illustrates the "systems" connections between very broad, abstract ways of thinking about business-government-society relationships and very specific, practical ways of doing so. The broadest view of that relationship is a societal perspective that emphasizes the "systems" connections between a nation's economic activity, its political life, and its culture. Every society is a mixture of economic, political, and cultural influences, each generated by its own "system" of people, institutions, and ideas.[2] In other words, reality for all of us is a mixture of economic, political, and cultural influences.

A somewhat narrower perspective is illustrated in the middle panel of Figure 1-1. "Business" is composed of many segments, industries, and sectors; "government" involves political life at the national, state, local, and, increasingly, international levels; and "society" is composed of many segments, ethnic and other groups, and stakeholders.

Once, it was widely believed that business interacted with others in society only through the marketplace. But that view has long since been replaced by an understanding that business and society have many nonmarket interactions as well. Many social influences on business come from cultural and political forces in society; business also has an influence on the political life and culture of any society.

[2]See, for example, Amitai Etzioni, *The Spirit of Community*, New York: Crown Publishers, 1993. Another discussion is Michael Novak, *The Spirit of Democratic Capitalism*, New York: Simon and Schuster, 1982.

FIGURE 1-1

A range of levels for understanding business, government, society relations.

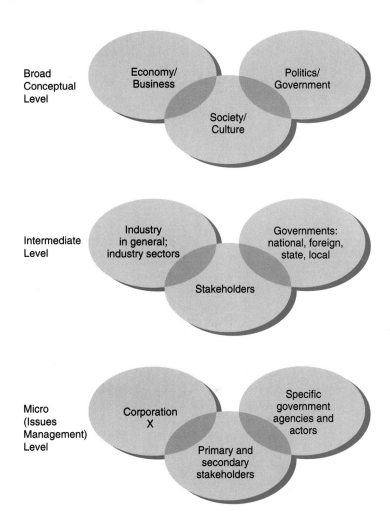

Broad Conceptual Level

Intermediate Level

Micro (Issues Management) Level

Bell Atlantic's joint venture in New Zealand made possible an expanded array of telecommunications services for that nation. Faxes between New Zealanders and others throughout the Pacific grew exponentially; the number of international telephone calls exploded. New Zealanders became more "connected" to the rest of the world despite large geographic distances.

Computer technology has had similarly pervasive effects on culture in societies everywhere. These cultural effects are largely due to the success of computer pioneers such as IBM and Apple Computer in developing technology, marketing it to many types of customers, and encouraging the public to use it for work and entertainment.

One result of this close, inseparable relationship between business and society is that all business decisions have a social impact, much as a pebble thrown into a pond creates ever-widening ripples. Another result is that the vitality and survival of business depend on society's actions and attitudes. Business can be smothered under a heavy blanket of social demands. Taxes can be set at levels that sap funds for capital investment or encourage relocation to communities in countries with lower tax burdens. Environmental regulations may prove too costly or technically impossible to allow certain industries to continue operating, leading to plant closures and job losses. Labor unions can demand wages or working conditions that exceed a company's ability to pay or its ability to compete in the marketplace. So, while business decisions can have both positive and negative impacts on society, the actions of a society can often determine whether a business firm will prosper or die.

That is why business and society, taken together, are an **interactive social system.** Each needs the other; each influences the other. They are entwined so completely that an action taken by one will inevitably affect the other. The boundary line between the two is blurred and indistinct. Business is part of society, and society penetrates far and often into business. They are both separate and connected. And in a world where global communication is rapidly expanding, the connections are closer than ever before. At the beginning of the twentieth century, most travel was done by horse-drawn vehicles, trains, and ships. Fifty years later, autos and airplanes were transforming society. Today, as the twenty-first century approaches, equally momentous transformations are occurring in business and politics, and among the people of the world. Throughout this book are examples of organizations and people who are shaping the business-society relationships of the twenty-first century.

THE STAKEHOLDER CONCEPT

When business interacts so often and so closely with society, a shared interest and interdependence develops between a company and other social groups. When this occurs, corporate stakeholders are created. **Stakeholders** are all the groups affected by, or that can affect, an organization's decisions, policies, and operations. The number of stakeholders, and the variety of interests, that a company's management must consider can make decisions quite complex.

Although the government, a stakeholder, creates conditions that can influence a company to stay in or withdraw from a particular market, the decision is ultimately the company's to make. However, a business cannot act without regard to stakeholder interests. In addition to profit and economic considerations, the company must consider its customers, suppliers, employees, owners, and creditors. Simply stated, good managerial decisions are made by paying attention to the effects of those decisions—pro and con—on the people and interests that are affected. Weighing conflicting considerations such as these is a part of any manager's job.

The "Three-Legged Stool"

Stakeholders and stakeholder relationships have changed over the years. Previously, managers had only to focus their attention on the product-market framework; they could concentrate on bringing products and services to market as efficiently and effectively as possible. The number of stakeholders was limited. Thomas J. Watson, Sr., chairman of IBM in the 1950s, described management's role as one of balancing a "three-legged stool" consisting of employees, customers, and shareholders. To emphasize their equality, he routinely changed the order in which he mentioned the three groups in his talks and speeches. In those days, it could be assumed that these were the important stakeholders. In contrast, the 1990 book about IBM by Thomas J. Watson, Jr., son of the senior Mr. Watson, emphasized the large number and variety of other stakeholders—communities, arts organizations, colleges and universities, foreign governments, and many more—with which the company interacted during the era of the younger Mr. Watson's leadership. And, ironically, John Akers, one of the Watsons' successors as IBM chairman, was deposed as IBM's chief executive in 1993 because he was unable to meet expectations of critical stakeholders such as shareholders and creditors. The multi-legged stool had become unbalanced and cost Mr. Akers his job as the economic stakeholders reasserted their importance and power.

Managers have the challenge of weighing and balancing the interests of the corporate stakeholders. If their concerns are disregarded, the stakeholders may damage or halt the company's operations. The key point about corporate stakeholders is that they may, and sometimes do, share decision-making power with a company's managers. Their justification for seeking a voice is that they are affected by the company's operations. The interest created between a company and its stakeholders can be a powerful aid to business, or it can be turned against a company. When stakeholders demand a voice in decision making and policy making, the company's managers need to respond with great skill if their primary business mission—producing goods and services—is to be achieved.

On the positive side, a corporation's stakeholders can also be enlisted to aid and support a company that is in trouble.

For example, when the Norton Company, an abrasives manufacturer located in Worcester, Massachusetts, received an unsolicited and unwelcome buyout offer from BTR, a British conglomerate, Norton's management asked for the help of employees, community officials, the governor and state legislative leaders, and prominent business leaders. The state legislature passed an anti-takeover law in record time to help prevent the Norton takeover. Fears of lost jobs, closed plants, and a loss of company support for local charities contributed to the prompt response. Norton's stakeholder network was concerned and eager to help the company resist the unwanted purchase by BTR. The state's congressional representatives and senators even called on the President of the United States to invoke a federal law preventing takeovers by foreign companies when the U.S. company is involved in critical defense-related businesses. The pressures eventually succeeded and BTR failed in its bid to acquire Norton.[3]

There are many examples of companies disregarding their stakeholders' wishes, either out of the belief that the stakeholder is wrong or out of arrogance and the attitude that "one unhappy customer, employee, or regulator doesn't matter"! Such attitudes are foolish and often prove costly to the company involved. Today, for example, builders know that they cannot locate a plant in a community that strongly objects. The only way to build a power plant or incinerator, for example, is to work with the community, to respond to concerns, and to invest in creating and maintaining a relationship of trust. John deButts, who served as chairman of AT&T in the late 1970s, commented about the "three-legged stool" in this way: "The only image which recurs with uncomfortable persistence is not a piece of furniture at all. It is a porcupine, with quills reversed!"[4]

Today, many stakeholders have the ability to stick quills into business. Companies need comprehensive approaches that take into account the needs of a larger and more diverse group of stakeholders. Business cannot be done in a social and political vacuum, and good management planning must take into account this web of considerations.

Primary and Secondary Stakeholders

Business interacts with society in a variety of different ways and a company's relations differ with different stakeholders. Figure 1-2 shows business interacting with groups that affect its ability to carry out its primary purpose of providing society with goods and services. Stockholders and creditors provide financial capital to the company; employees contribute their work skills and knowledge; suppliers provide raw materials, energy, and other supplies; and wholesalers, distributors, and retailers help move the product from plant to sales offices to customers. All businesses need customers who are willing to pay for the products or services being produced, and most companies compete against others offering similar products and services in the marketplace. These are the fundamental interac-

---

[3]"Lawmakers Join Foes of Norton Takeover," *Boston Globe*, Apr. 20, 1990, pp. 65–66; "No End in Sight in Norton Battle," *New York Times*, Apr. 19, 1990, p. D2.
[4]John deButts, "A Strategy of Accountability," in William Dill, ed., *Running the American Corporation*, Englewood Cliffs, NJ: Prentice-Hall, 1978, p. 141.

FIGURE 1-2

Relations between a business
firm and its primary stakeholders.

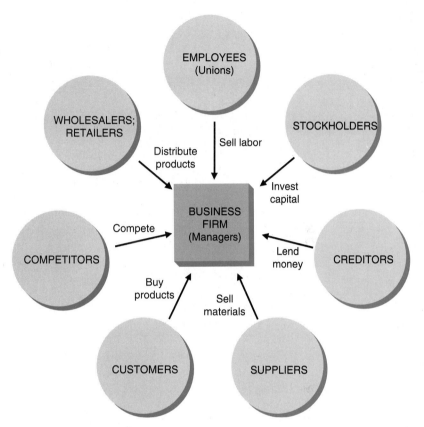

tions every business has with society, and they help us define the primary
economic mission of the company.

A business's primary involvement with society includes all the direct
relationships necessary for it to perform its major mission of producing
goods and services for customers. These interactions normally occur in
the marketplace and involve processes of buying and selling. The primary
involvements shape a company's strategy and the policy decisions of its
managers, and reveal the importance of the stakeholders who are critical
to its existence and activities. These market-driven customers, suppliers,
employees, and investors are its **primary stakeholders.**

However, as Figure 1-3 reveals, a business's relationships go beyond
those primary involvements to others in society. Another level of interaction occurs when other groups express an interest or concern in the organization's activities. A business's secondary involvements are a result of
the impacts caused by the company's primary business activities. **Secondary stakeholders** are those groups in society who are affected, directly or indirectly, by the company's secondary impacts and involvements.

FIGURE 1-3

Relations between a business firm and its secondary stakeholders.

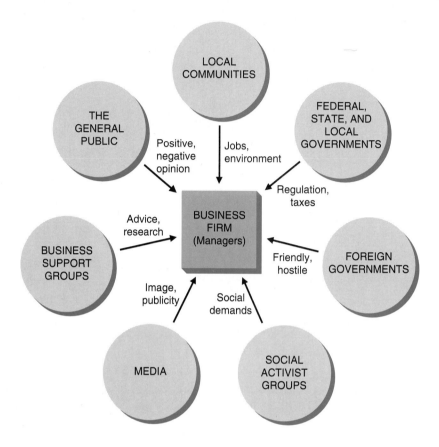

Calling these involvements and stakeholders "secondary" does not mean that they are less important than business's primary relationships with society. It means that they occur as a *consequence* of the normal activities of conducting business. Primary and secondary areas of involvement are not always sharply distinguished; often, one area shades into the other. For example, while the safety or environmental effect of a product (e.g., an automobile) is a *primary* concern to a customer, the cumulative effect of the use of the product may represent a *secondary* safety or environmental concern for the entire community (e.g., smog from automobile emissions).

Combining business's primary and secondary interactions gives an **interactive model of business and society,** as shown in Figure 1-4. Primary interactions conducted through the market are shown on the left. The secondary interactions, which are carried out through nonmarket processes, are shown on the right.

The main lessons that emerge from this interactive model are the following:

■ In making decisions, business is influenced by its primary and secondary stakeholders. The influence of these stakeholders has be-

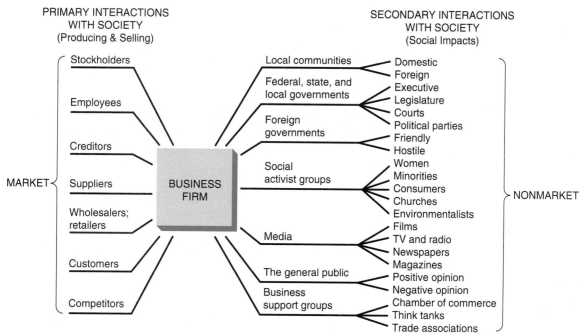

FIGURE 1-4
An interactive model of business and society relations.

come important to all businesses, large and small, domestic and foreign.

- The managers of business firms—especially those responsible for a local store, plant, or business unit—need to become skilled in responding to social and political factors, as well as to the economic factors, involved in their stakeholder relationships.

- A business firm's acceptance by society—its legitimacy as an approved institution—depends upon its performance in both the economic and the social-political spheres. An auto manufacturer may produce reasonably priced cars that make a profit but encounter public disapproval because they are unsafe or environmentally harmful. A local bank may pay current market rates on savings deposits but get into trouble with its depositors because it refuses to reinvest in the neighborhoods where those depositors live.

The interactive model of business and society recognizes the fundamental role of business as an economic contributor to society. But it also suggests that managers must make decisions and take actions that benefit the society as a whole, as well as the company's economic interests. The net effect is to enhance the quality of life in the broadest possible way, as that quality of life is defined by society. Business acts to produce the goods and services that society wants, recognizes the social impacts and effects of its activities, and is concerned with the social and economic effects on society.

Stakeholder Interests and Power

Stakeholder groups exist in many forms, some being well organized, others much less so. This variety makes it more difficult for a company's managers to understand and respond to stakeholder concerns. Each stakeholder has a unique connection with the organization, and managers must understand these involvements and respond accordingly. For example, stockholders have an ownership interest in the organization. The economic health and success of the corporation affect these people financially; their personal wealth is at stake. Customers, suppliers, and retailers have a different interest. Owners are most interested in realizing a return on their investment, while customers and suppliers are most interested in gaining fair value in the exchange of goods and money. Neither has a great interest in the other's stake. And when we recognize that there are different kinds of owners, ranging from large pension funds with large holdings to individual owners with small holdings, the picture grows more complicated.

Governments, public interest groups, and local communities have another sort of relationship with the company. In general, their stake is broader than the financial stake of owners or persons who buy products and sell services to the company. They may wish to protect the environment, assure human rights, or advance other broad social interests. Managers need to track these stakeholder interests with great care.

Different stakeholders also have different types and degrees of power. **Stakeholder power,** in this instance, means the ability to use resources to make an event happen or to secure a desired outcome. Most experts recognize three types of stakeholder power: voting power, economic power, and political power.[5]

Voting power (not referring to political, electoral voting) means that the stakeholder has a legitimate right to cast a vote. For example, each stockholder has a voting power proportionate to the percentage of the company's stock that he or she owns. Stockholders typically have an opportunity to vote on such major decisions as mergers, acquisitions, and other extraordinary issues. Through the exercise of informed, intelligent voting, they may influence company policy so that their investment is protected and produces a healthy return.

Customers, suppliers, and retailers have a direct economic influence on the company. Their power is economic in nature. Suppliers can withhold supplies or refuse to fill orders if a company fails to meet its contrac-

[5]R. Edward Freeman, *Strategic Management: A Stakeholder Approach*, Marshfield, MA: Pitman, 1984.

tual responsibilities. Customers can choose to boycott products or an entire company if they believe the goods to be too expensive, poorly made, unsafe, or inappropriate for consumption. Other customers may refuse to buy a company's products if the company enacts an improper policy.

Government exercises political power through legislation, regulations, or lawsuits. Other stakeholders also exercise political power, using their resources to pressure government to adopt new laws or regulations or to take legal action against a company.

> In a landmark case, a group of citizens in Woburn, Massachusetts, sued W. R. Grace and Company and Beatrice Foods for allegedly dumping toxic chemicals that leaked into underground wells used for drinking water. The deaths and illnesses of family members led the survivors to mobilize political power against Grace and Beatrice. Investigations were conducted by private groups and public agencies. The lawsuits and political pressure helped make toxic dumping and the protection of underground water supplies very important political issues.

Of course, a single stakeholder is capable of exercising more than one type of power. The Woburn families sued the two companies (political power), but they had other powers too. They could have led a boycott of the companies' products (economic power), or purchased shares of stock in the companies and attempted to oust the directors and management through a proxy fight (voting power). Exhibit 1-A illustrates the nature and different types of power of the key stakeholders identified in Figure 1-4.

Stakeholder Coalitions

Stakeholder coalitions are not static. Stakeholders that are highly involved with a company today may be less involved tomorrow. Issues that are most salient at one point in time may be replaced by other issues at another time; stakeholders who are most dependent on an organization at one time may be less dependent at another. To make matters even more complex, the process of shifting coalitions may not occur uniformly in all parts of a large corporation. Stakeholders involved with one part of a large company often have little or no involvement with other parts of the organization.

Groups are always changing their relationships to one another in society. **Stakeholder coalitions** are the temporary unions of stakeholder groups that come together and share a common point of view on a particular issue or problem. There are very broad coalitions whose member organizations span the nation and the world. "Movements" such as the environmental movement or the human rights movement involve hundreds of state, national, and international organizations and may operate with little or no coordination and policy making. Other movements may be very di-

EXHIBIT 1-A

PRIMARY AND SECONDARY STAKEHOLDERS: NATURE OF INTEREST AND POWER

Stakeholder	Nature of Interest— Stakeholder Wishes To:	Nature of Power— Stakeholder Influences Company By:
PRIMARY STAKEHOLDERS		
EMPLOYEES	■ Maintain stable employment in firm ■ Receive fair pay for work ■ Work in safe, comfortable environment	■ Union bargaining power ■ Work actions or strikes ■ Publicity
OWNERS/ STOCKHOLDERS	■ Receive a satisfactory return on investments (dividends) ■ Realize appreciation in stock value over time	■ Exercising voting rights based on share ownership ■ Exercising rights to inspect company books and records
CUSTOMERS	■ Receive fair exchange: value and quality for dollar spent ■ Receive safe, reliable products	■ Purchasing goods from competitors ■ Boycotting companies whose products are unsatisfactory or whose policies are unacceptable
SUPPLIERS	■ Receive regular orders for goods ■ Be paid promptly for supplies delivered	■ Refusing to meet orders if conditions of contract are breached ■ Supplying to competitors
COMPETITORS	■ Be profitable ■ Gain a larger share of the market ■ See the entire industry grow	■ Technological innovation, forcing competitors to "keep up" ■ Charging lower prices
RETAILERS/ WHOLESALERS	■ Receive quality goods in a timely fashion at reasonable cost ■ Offer reliable products that consumers trust and value	■ Buying from other suppliers if terms of contract are unsatisfactory ■ Boycotting companies whose goods or policies are unsatisfactory
CREDITORS	■ Receive repayment of loans ■ Collect debts and interest	■ Calling in loans if payments are not made ■ Utilizing legal authorities to repossess or take over property if loan payments are severely delinquent

SECONDARY STAKEHOLDERS

LOCAL COMMUNITIES	■ Employ local residents in the company ■ Ensure that the local environment is protected ■ Ensure that the local area is developed	■ Refusing to extend additional credit ■ Issuing or restricting operating licenses and permits ■ Lobbying government for regulation of the company's policies or methods of land use and waste disposal
SOCIAL ACTIVISTS	■ Monitor company actions and policies to ensure that they conform to legal and ethical standards, and that they protect the public's safety	■ Gaining broad public support through publicizing the issue ■ Lobbying government for regulation of the company
MEDIA	■ Keep the public informed on all issues relevant to their health, well-being, and economic status ■ Monitor company actions	■ Publicizing events that affect the public, especially those which have negative effects
BUSINESS SUPPORT GROUPS (e.g., trade associations)	■ Provide research and information which will help the company or industry perform in a changing environment	■ Using its staff and resources to assist company in business endeavors and development efforts ■ Providing legal or "group" political support beyond that which an individual company can provide for itself
FOREIGN GOVERNMENTS	■ Promote economic development ■ Encourage social improvements	■ Granting permits to do business ■ Adopting regulations
FEDERAL, STATE, AND LOCAL GOVERNMENTS	■ Raise revenues through taxes ■ Promote economic development	■ Issuing regulations, licenses, and permits ■ Allowing or disallowing industrial activity
THE GENERAL PUBLIC	■ Protect social values ■ Minimize risks ■ Achieve prosperity for society	■ Supporting activists ■ Pressing government to act ■ Condemning or praising individual companies

verse but operate in a coordinated manner through a central policy-making board or group.

Coalitions of stakeholders have become increasingly internationalized as well. Sophisticated communications technology has enabled like-minded people to communicate quickly, irrespective of political boundaries. Fax machines, telephones, and computers have become powerful tools in the hands of activist groups trying to monitor how multinational businesses are operating in different locations around the world.

> Consider the case of the Scott Paper Company, a U.S. multinational corporation headquartered in Philadelphia. In the late 1980s, Scott negotiated an agreement with the government of Indonesia to build a new paper mill and pulp processing plant in Sumatra, one of Indonesia's principal islands. Indonesian environmentalists were outraged at the proposal, however, and fought to prevent it. They feared that the presence of the plant would inevitably lead to destruction of Sumatra's rain forest. In addition, pulp and paper mills are notorious for their air and water pollution. The Indonesian environmentalists contacted friends in the United States, including the Natural Resources Defense Council (NRDC). NRDC staff focused on what kind of pressure they could apply against Scott. They concluded that a national boycott of Scott paper products, including such highly visible consumer products as Scotties tissues, was possible. Once this was communicated to Scott Paper's executives, they recognized the company's vulnerability to a consumer boycott and decided to withdraw from the Indonesia project. The Indonesian government was disappointed, having anticipated tax revenues and the creation of jobs. The government turned to a Japanese company to build and operate the pulp and paper mill.[6]

The combination of improved skills, national and international networks of experienced activists, and media interest in a wide range of local, national, and international issues make coalition development and issue activism an increasingly powerful factor in business.

FORCES SHAPING BUSINESS-SOCIETY RELATIONS

Today's business firms do not operate in a social or political vacuum. They find themselves in a virtual whirlwind of social and political problems and controversies. Business managers are buffeted by complicated and threatening forces, many of them global in scope. These trends now intrude into

[6]Based on an interview by one of the authors with the head of the Indonesian Environmental Federation.

the very core of business operations, thus requiring careful attention and planning. Even small business firms that serve local markets are affected by disruptions in supply, price fluctuations, regional warfare, and uncertainty stemming from international political and economic events. Figure 1-5 illustrates five critical forces that are shaping business-society relations in the 1990s. Each of these forces is introduced below; other chapters in this book discuss each of these topics in further detail.

Strategic and Social Challenges

Throughout the world, companies of all sizes and in all industries are rethinking critical business assumptions about where to compete and how. **Strategic rethinking** has produced major changes in virtually every company in every industry. Many companies have restructured their business operations, often eliminating those activities that seem too distant from the company's strengths or too vulnerable to competitors. Reorganization of business operations occurs frequently as companies have tried to improve the quality of their products and services, reduce costs, and

FIGURE 1-5

Major forces shaping business-society relations in the 1990s.

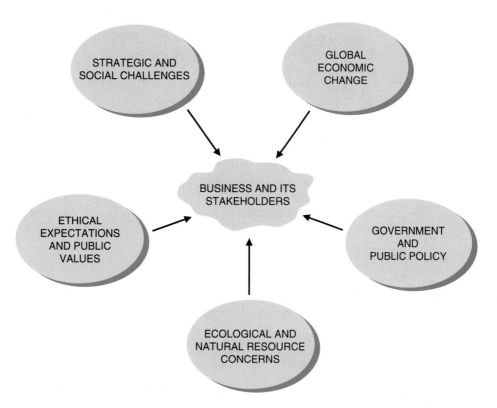

improve the speed with which they respond to customers. This redesign of business operations is also known as **reengineering.**[7]

This broad process of "reinventing the corporation"[8] has many social consequences. Employees are dismissed from jobs that no longer exist in a redesigned manufacturing or service-delivery system. People who have made long-term career commitments to one firm are asked to take an "early retirement" or face dismissal. The impact can be tempered by financial arrangements and efforts to train and relocate former employees in new jobs. But the overwhelming sense of loss that people feel in such circumstances is reflected in social indicators such as increased suicide, alcoholism, mental illness, and child and spouse abuse.

Strategic changes in a company's business affect its relationships with other segments of society. External stakeholders are hurt when a business closes: suppliers, competitors, and other businesses (restaurants, retailers, banks, movie theaters) suffer. A "multiplier effect" of social effects leaves the community short on jobs, tax revenues, and morale.

Traditional concepts of corporate social responsibility are challenged when a company begins to rethink its strategy. One such idea is the **social contract,** an implied understanding between a business and stakeholders as to how they will act toward one another. Social contracts are affected by corporate restructuring, however. Commitments to employees change in bad times. Community involvements decline and reductions in charitable contributions occur when a company encounters severe economic problems. The fact that such events have become common in the 1990s has led some observers to pronounce the "good corporation" dead.[9]

What is emerging in the view of some observers, however, is a "new social contract"[10] between the corporation, its employees, and other stakeholders. As the dynamics of business operations change, relationships with stakeholders also change. The roles and responsibilities a company acknowledges and accepts must necessarily change.

The **new social contract** implies that stakeholders can reasonably expect that managers will acknowledge those relationships, deal with the impacts of their decisions, and respond to the people that are touched by the corporation's activities. That is the essence of "doing the right thing." This new social contract is illustrated by the actions of Chevron and Hewlett-Packard in the following example.

---

[7]Michael Hammer and James Champy, *Reengineering the Corporation,* New York: Harper Business, 1993. An excellent introduction to this area is Kathryn Troy, *Change Management: An Overview of Current Initiatives,* Report No. 1068-94-RR, New York: The Conference Board, 1994.

[8]"Reinventing the Corporation," *Business Week,* Special Issue, July 1992.

[9]Robert J. Samuelson, "R.I.P.: The Good Corporation," *Newsweek,* July 5, 1993, p. 41.

[10]Severyn T. Bruyn, *A Future for the American Economy: The Social Market,* Stanford, CA: Stanford University Press, 1991. See also James E. Post, "The New Social Contract," in Oliver Williams and John Houck, eds., *The Global Challenge to Corporate Social Responsibility,* New York: Oxford University Press, 1995.

Between 1992 and 1994, more than 2 million job reductions were announced by large American companies. Virtually every sector of the economy was affected: manufacturing, financial services, retailing, and transportation. A package of benefits was typically offered to departing employees, including compensation based on years of service, continuation of health care benefits for a period of time (ranging from thirty days to one or more years), and support for retraining or education. Research showed that surviving employees also felt the psychological impact of staff reductions, including fears of how management would act in the future. Companies such as Chevron and Hewlett-Packard recognized the need to "do the right thing" for employees and responded to these concerns by stating in writing the commitments on which continuing employees could count. In some companies, these statements of commitments are called "compacts," "covenants," or "social contracts," symbolizing the special nature of the employee-employer relationship.

Reinventing corporate strategy along these lines is often more a matter of mind and managerial attitude than anything else. It takes a business executive who is willing to look at more than the "bottom line." Social sensitivity is possessed by a manager who realizes that employees are people first and producers second. Employees may take pride in their work, but at the same time they are family members, citizens of communities, members of churches, political adherents, people with aspirations, problems, hopes, and desires who are often emotional, sometimes rational, and frequently confused.

Research has shown that companies with the best social reputations and the best social performance records have top managers who take a very broad view of their company's place in society.[11] In fact, these managers often believe that their companies should take the lead in helping society to solve its problems. Corporations with this attitude generally take a long-run view of the company, rather than focusing exclusively on short-run gains. Social goals, as well as economic goals, are given a high priority in planning the company's future. Such an attitude will not prevent the company from facing the stern pressures of marketplace competition, or enable them to avoid difficult issues of restructuring, reorganizing, and refocusing, but it will help ensure that the interests of the company and all of its stakeholders are integrated into the corporate strategy.

There are many companies, large and small, that are committed to finding ways to operationalize this new social contract. Anita Roddick, founder and managing director (CEO) of The Body Shop International, a company that manufactures and markets natural cosmetics, soaps, and toiletries through franchise stores, expresses a sentiment shared by members of such businesses in this way:

[11]See "America's Most Admired Corporations," *Fortune*, Feb. 7, 1994, pp. 58–95.

. . . (O)ver the past decade, while many businesses have pursued what I call "business as usual," I have been part of a different, smaller business movement—one that has tried to put idealism back on the agenda. We want a new paradigm, a whole new framework, for seeing and understanding [that] business can and must be a force for positive social change. It must not only avoid hideous evil—it must actively do good.[12]

Whether or not this attitude will yield consistent, high levels of economic performance is not yet clear. What is clear is that the business-society relationship is always dynamic; it has been changing very rapidly in recent years and is likely to continue doing so in the next decade. Creating a successful business strategy will require managers who are concerned that business continue to perform a positive role in society. These issues are discussed further in Chapters 2 and 3.

Ethical Expectations and Public Values

Ethical expectations are a vital part of the business environment. The public expects business to make decisions ethically. They want corporate managers to apply **ethical principles**—in other words, guidelines about what is right and wrong, fair and unfair, and morally correct—when they make business decisions. Figure 1-6 charts their importance.

In the global arena, ethical standards—and even what is meant by "ethics"—can vary from one society to another. These kinds of problems and how to deal with them are discussed in Chapters 4 and 5. In spite of differences in ethical meanings, cultural variation does not automatically rule out common ethical agreement being reached among people of different societies. For example, the European Union's Social Charter promotes common job rights and humane workplace treatment among its member nations. The International Chamber of Commerce has promoted a common code of environmental practices and principles to protect natural resources around the world. For many years, great pressure was exerted on political leaders in South Africa to halt racially discriminatory practices of apartheid; more recently, pressures from many sources have focused on alleged abuses of human rights in countries such as China.

The question is not, "Should business be ethical?" Nor is it, "Should business be economically efficient?" Society wants business to be both at the same time! Ethical behavior is a key aspect of corporate social performance. To maintain its public support and credibility—that is, **business legitimacy**—business must find ways to balance and integrate these two social demands: high economic performance and high ethical standards. When a company and its employees act ethically in dealings with other

[12]Anita Roddick, "Corporate Responsibility: Good Works Not Good Words," Speech to the International Chamber of Commerce, Oct. 21, 1993; reprinted in *Vital Speeches of the Day*, vol. 60, no. 7, Jan. 15, 1994, pp. 196–199.

FIGURE 1-6

Society seeks companies with high economic performance and high ethical and social performance.

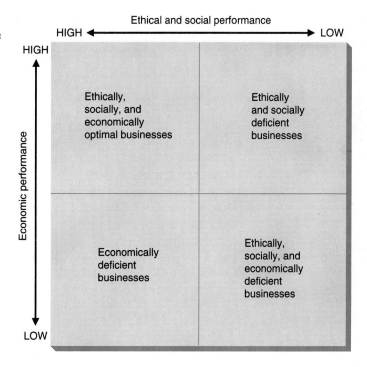

Ethical and social performance

HIGH ◀————————————————————▶ LOW

Economic performance — HIGH

Ethically, socially, and economically optimal businesses

Ethically and socially deficient businesses

Economically deficient businesses

Ethically, socially, and economically deficient businesses

LOW

stakeholders, they are improving the organization's contribution as a social actor. When they fail to act ethically, there is the risk of losing the public support an organization needs to be credible and successful.

For example, in the early 1990s it was disclosed that William Aramony, chief executive officer of United Way of America, a nonprofit organization, was being paid a salary in excess of $400,000 per year, plus other expensive benefits. Moreover, there was alleged evidence that directors and others were misled by Aramony as to the extent of his compensation and spending habits. This was viewed as unethical and scandalous for a nonprofit organization that pays no taxes because it is a charitable institution. The negative publicity resulted in Aramony's dismissal, a shake-up of officers at United Way, and the naming of a new chief executive officer at a significantly lower salary. Most importantly, public support declined and financial contributions to United Way fell dramatically.

Business leaders are faced with the continuing challenge of meeting public expectations which are, themselves, always changing. Yesterday's acceptable behavior may not be tolerated today. Many forms of discrimination and harassment were once common; today, social standards make such actions unacceptable. Public expectations of service and ethical behavior are as relevant to a business as customer expectations regarding products such as automobiles and computers.

Global Economic Change

Foremost among the factors affecting business in the 1990s is **global economic change.** Beginning in the 1970s and continuing unabated into the mid-1990s, dramatic changes have transformed the world's economic scene. Some of the most far-reaching economic developments were Japanese industrial growth, third world economic development, western European economic integration, the experiments of eastern European economies with free markets and competition, and the North American Free Trade Agreement. Global changes of this magnitude create more than just sharper economic competition. As economies have changed, so have established governments, politics, and social systems. As discussed in Chapters 6 and 7, achieving business goals in the midst of such global change requires a keen understanding of interrelated social, economic, political, and cultural trends.

The emergence of Japan as a global economic power dramatically illustrates the nature of global economic change as a force in business-society relations. Best known for the prowess it developed during the 1970s and 1980s in steel, electronics, and automobile production, by the 1990s, no business leader anywhere in the world could afford to ignore Japan's emergence as a leading competitor in major sectors of the global economy. Japan also became a large investor in the economies of other nations. For example, Japanese interests doubled their investment in Europe during the late 1980s and grew from 10 percent of foreign-owned business in the United States in 1985 to more than 20 percent in 1990.[13] They have invested in industrial projects in the developing nations of Asia, Latin America, and Africa and became a primary player in the world's financial markets.

While Japan continued to grow, some of the world's less developed nations also began to make their economic influence felt. Nations that earlier had occupied only the outer margins of the world economy emerged as strong competitors during the 1980s and early 1990s. Korea, Taiwan, Singapore, Brazil, Spain, and Mexico became world-class competitors in clothing, footware, toy, and electronic assembly industries. As they shifted production into basic industries such as steel and other capital intensive manufacturing industries, even poorer countries with lower wage rates began to produce consumer items such as clothing and footware.

The new players in the world economy have greatly intensified compe-

---

[13]U.S. Commerce Department, "Foreign Direct Investment in the United States: An Update," June 1993.

tition. Their competitive success has disrupted social and economic relations in other countries. The jobs that have gone to people willing to work for low wages in other nations have sometimes taken away jobs from workers in the developed countries. By opening plants in the third world, companies have forced the closing of older operations in Europe and North America, creating economic and social distress there. The effects have been dramatic, signaling economic hope for poorer nations but sending a competitive chill into the ranks of companies and leaders in the highly industrialized nations. This new and intense competition from third world countries has helped reshape the economic and social strategies of the advanced industrial nations, as discussed above.

One exceptionally important development has been the opening of societies previously closed to trade and international competition. The opening of the People's Republic of China (PRC) to foreign investment and economic development, for example, stimulated an impressive boom of commercial activity. Billions of dollars of foreign investment have flooded into China to support infrastructure projects such as new roads, power plants, water systems, and investment in industries such as steel, electronics, textiles, and consumer products. With a population of 1.2 billion people, the PRC represents one of the world's largest markets for goods and services and a potential economic colossus as a producer. In 1993, for example, China's gross domestic product grew by 12.1 percent, the highest rate of any nation in the world. Its industrial production soared by 18.9 percent, well above runner-up Malaysia, which had a 12.4 percent rate of increase. By contrast, the U.S. gross domestic product grew by less than 3 percent in 1993.[14] Such success has led other nations that have disdained economic trade with the world to rethink their policies.

Political reorganization and change have also stimulated major economic changes. Western European nations have pursued the opening and integration of their economies. This is a development that was promoted by many European leaders as necessary to create a vibrant economic base that created jobs and well-being for more than 300 million people, a population larger than the combined total of the United States, Canada, and Mexico. The 1980s saw twelve member nations of the European Economic Community (EEC), or "Common Market," agree to integrate their economies more closely with one another by the end of 1992. Declining trade barriers have produced a larger European market; additional countries are seeking to join the renamed European Union (EU).

The remarkable economic, political, and ideological upheavals that occurred in eastern Europe, beginning with the fall of the Berlin Wall and including the breakup of the former Soviet Union, have also created a mixture of opportunities and threats to business. The opening of eastern European nations to democracy and trade with the rest of the world pro-

---

[14]"Emerging Market Indicators," *The Economist,* Jan. 29, 1994, p. 114.

vides economic opportunities, but is also producing social strains as old ways crumble.

The basic lesson for managers is clear: fundamental social and political change pressures business to adjust the way it conducts operations. A firm's economic and financial strategy is vitally affected by political events and changing public attitudes. In these rapidly changing political and social settings, a company's short-term and long-term success may depend greatly on how well its social and economic strategy work together.

Since the end of World War II in 1945, numerous international agreements have been crafted to encourage trade among nations. Much of this effort was coordinated through the General Agreement on Tariffs and Trade (GATT). Many nations have also established trade agreements with nations with whom they are economically interdependent. This drive to open markets and integrate economic activity across national borders in North America started in the late 1980s when the leaders of Canada, Mexico, and the United States began shaping a North American Free Trade Agreement (NAFTA) to remove trade and investment restrictions. The agreement, which went into effect on January 1, 1994, will lower trade barriers among the three nations for the next decade.

The political and economic reorganization of global markets has not occurred without difficulties. People who think of themselves as citizens of France, Germany, the Netherlands, or any other nation will not quickly give up that sense of cultural identity simply because the European Union exists. Former communists will not embrace capitalism just because the new political leadership does. American workers will remain concerned that high-paying jobs are not exported to Mexico by firms seeking to reduce labor costs. While the economic environment might become simpler by establishing free trade and uniform economic standards and regulations, the social and political environment will remain quite complex. Firms planning to do business in this challenging business environment will need a sophisticated understanding of local customs, social institutions, and political systems. That is another way of saying they will need a sound social strategy.

Government and Public Policy

Beginning sometime in the 1960s and 1970s, new winds of change began to blow through many of the world's economic, political, and social institutions. No one knew exactly what had set these new currents of reform in motion. They were not felt with the same strength in all nations. Nor were all kinds of institutions challenged in any one nation. But wherever these currents blew, they seemed to have one trait in common: focal points of centralized power and authority came under attack. Governmental power and, especially, the role of government in society were challenged.

Demands were made to disperse power more widely within many societies and nations. "Power to the people" became a popular rallying cry that captured the essence of this new social force. Leaders in all areas of society discovered that their grip on institutional power was not as secure as it had been in earlier times. The public seemed to be less trusting of its leaders. They wanted a "piece of the action." They believed that too much power had been concentrated at the top of society's major institutions. They demanded reform.

The best known of these political changes are deregulation and privatization in the Western world, ***glasnost*** (openness) and ***perestroika*** (reform, reconstruction, renewal) in the (former) Soviet Union, moves toward freer markets and a more decentralized economic system in China, and the sweeping political upheavals in eastern Europe beginning in the late 1980s. In all of these cases, centralized governmental power was being dispersed and moved out from the center toward the periphery.

What does this global reform movement mean for business? It creates new business opportunities but it also poses new business risks. When free markets open up where none existed before, corporations can take advantage of profit opportunities. European, Japanese, and American business firms flocked to China in the early days of its reform movement. But just as quickly, they became more cautious when government authorities showed signs of reinstalling centralized power over all business decisions. When the (former) Soviet Union and eastern European nations relaxed government controls and welcomed economic ties with Western nations, many corporations crossed over into that formerly forbidden territory, seeking profitable opportunities. The business risks were considerable, though, because these former socialist nations frequently lacked free and open market systems, stable currencies, and competitive traditions.

As eastern Europe struggled to transform its economic and political institutions, its governments faced formidable problems such as inflation, unemployment, and declining national income. Speaking of this difficult period, a Hungarian political scientist said, "The cold war is over, but this will be a very dangerous peace. . . . Conflicts are growing between nationalities, between rich people and poor, between the government and street protesters, between industrialists and laborers."[15] The view was prophetic: ethnic, ideological, and economic conflicts have raged in eastern Europe (Bosnia, Serbia) since the early 1990s, and the political winds have blown in different, often contradictory directions. Indeed, in 1994 Hungarian voters returned socialist political leaders to power.[16]

The global movement toward more freedom and democracy and away from centralized authoritarian governments carries both pluses and minuses for business. Once again, corporations have found themselves facing large measures of uncertainty and risk.

---

[15]"East Europe Offers Investors Big Profits and Big Perils," *Wall Street Journal*, Jan. 11, 1991, p. A6.

[16]Jane Perlez, "Welcome Back Lenin," *New York Times*, May 31, 1994, pp. A1, A9.

Russia has suffered political convulsions since the late 1980s as Mikhail Gorbachev, Boris Yeltsin, and Vladimir Zhiranovsky have contested for power. Chevron Corporation, a U.S.-headquartered multinational oil company, has invested heavily in Kazhakistan, a former Soviet republic. But as the political fortunes of the republics have ebbed and flowed, the political risk facing Chevron has grown. The company knows how bad it can get: In the 1980s, Chevron invested $1 billion in Sudan. But as that nation slid into anarchy, Chevron was forced to abandon its wells, refineries, and pipelines. Although Chevron sees business potential in Kazhakistan it also recognizes that political risk may overwhelm the business opportunity.[17]

These volatile political and ideological forces have become a central part of the world business climate. Corporations and their managers cannot ignore them; to do so could be fatal. Integrating changing political realities into a corporate business strategy has become a basic requirement in the 1990s.

The role of government has also changed in the United States. Beginning in the late 1970s, calls for "deregulation" of segments of the economy created change for the airlines, trucking, and communications. In the 1980s, Presidents Ronald Reagan (1981–89) and George Bush (1989–93) pressed for an approach that would limit the role of the federal government and leave more responsibility with state and local governments to meet public needs. During the 1992 presidential campaign, candidates George Bush, Bill Clinton, and Ross Perot pressed their sharply different views of the role government should play in education, environmental protection, and, most importantly, in creating a healthy economy. The election of President Clinton did not settle the debate, however. Two years later, Republicans swept into Congress on a campaign platform that called for "downsizing" the role of the federal government.

At the outset of the Clinton presidency, the new administration acted to address issues such as reduction of the national deficit, revision of the nation's health care system, and reform of national unemployment insurance. These were but a few of many proposals that would alter the role of government and affect the business community. Like political changes in other nations, these changes required corporate managers to think broadly about the way political and economic change would affect their businesses and their strategies. Because business has a large stake in these matters, it is actively involved in the political process, lobbying for some proposals and against others, and often supporting the election of candidates whose positions will support economic growth and free markets.

The role of government and public policy, including regulation and an-

---

[17]"Chevron Is Plunging into Foreign Projects to Build Oil Reserves," *Wall Street Journal,* Feb. 2, 1994, pp. A1, A6. In May 1994, Chevron announced the termination of its investment in Kazhakistan.

titrust, and the role of business in politics are discussed in Chapters 8, 9, and 10. The importance of these issues in the modern world was succinctly expressed by Milton Friedman, a Nobel Prize–winning economist who has long urged that government not interfere with free markets:

> It is today possible, to a greater extent than at any time in the world's history, for a company to locate anywhere, to use resources from anywhere to produce a product that can be sold anywhere. . . . [The challenge] is to use our influence to make sure governments are not short-sighted and do not short-circuit the process.[18]

Ecological and Natural Resource Concerns

One of the most important social challenges to business is to strike a balance between industrial production and nature's limits. Industrial production, mining, and farming are bound to produce waste and pollution, along with needed goods and services. Waste and pollution are a price society pays for rising populations, urbanization, and more goods and services. All industrial societies—whether the United States, Japan, Germany, Russia, or South Korea—create a disproportionate (relative to population) share of the world's pollution and waste simply because these are the unavoidable by-products of a high level of economic activity. The emerging nations of the third world, with their rapid growth rates and limited pollution controls, also contribute to global ecological problems as their economies become more industrialized.

Consumers too are responsible for much solid waste and pollution because they demand, buy, and use pollution-generating products such as automobiles, refrigerators, air conditioners, and computers. The widespread use of product packaging and the proliferation of toxic products such as cleaners, lawn chemicals, batteries, and antifreeze all contribute to global pollution issues.

Ecological impacts extend far beyond national boundaries. Stratospheric ozone depletion potentially threatens health and agriculture on a worldwide basis. The industrial accident at Chernobyl's nuclear power station spread dangerous radiation across several European nations and sent a radiation cloud around the globe. Oil spills have fouled the oceans and beaches of many nations. The cutting and burning of tropical rain forests has the potential to affect weather climates throughout the world.

Environmental protection, through pollution control, waste minimization, and natural resource conservation, has become a high priority for developing nations as well as the advanced industrialized nations. International agreements have been created to address the most pressing is-

---

[18]Milton Friedman, quoted in Lindley H. Clark, Jr., "The New Industrial Revolution," *Wall Street Journal,* Nov. 23, 1993, p. A16.

sues (e.g., ozone depletion, biodiversity, and global warming). But government and industry leaders recognize that this is just the beginning of what must be done to achieve a sustainable balance between economic activity, which requires the use of resources, and global environmental protection, which requires the preservation of resources. Business leaders, and managers at every level of business activity from the corporate headquarters to the local retail outlet, are being challenged by the need to integrate ecological thinking into their managerial decision making.

As will be discussed in Chapters 11 and 12, companies are learning how to adjust their products, manufacturing processes, purchasing activities, and business strategies to the need for sustainable economic and ecological practices. While much has already been improved, there is no doubt that reducing harmful ecological effects will continue to be a major social challenge for corporate managers in the 1990s and beyond. Pollution and waste cannot be stopped entirely, but their volume can be reduced through improved product designs, better controls, and the recycling of reusable materials. Environmental accidents such as oil spills can be prevented by careful planning, and cleanup efforts can be pursued vigorously with new techniques and technologies. The basic goal is to achieve a livable balance between human needs and nature's limits.

CORPORATE STRATEGY FOR THE TWENTY-FIRST CENTURY

Business, government, and society are interdependent and their relationship is complex in every nation. General systems theory tells us that all organisms or systems are affected by their host environments; thus an organization must be appropriately responsive to changes and conditions in its environment in order to survive and succeed.

This web of interactions between business, government, and society naturally generates a system of stakeholders—groups affected by and influential in corporate decisions and actions. The analysis of these stakeholders—who they are, what power they hold, and the ways in which they interact with one another—helps managers understand the nature of their concerns and needs, and how these relationships are changing. The business of the twenty-first century must have managers who understand the importance of creating business strategies that include these considerations.

The relationship between business and society is also continuously changing. People, organizations, and social activity change; inevitably, new social issues arise and challenge managers to develop new solutions. To be effective, corporate strategy must respond to the biggest and most central questions in the public's mind. As the twentieth century ends, people everywhere expect businesses to be competitive, to be profitable, and to act responsibly by meeting the reasonable expectations of stakeholders. The corporation of the twenty-first century is certain to be affected by global economic and political trends, powerful new technologies, and a global population of stakeholders who will expect that their interests are integrated into the business strategies and thinking of the companies from which they buy goods and services and to which they contribute labor and ideas as well as extend the hospitality and support of their communities.

SUMMARY POINTS OF THIS CHAPTER

- Business, government, and society are an interactive system because each affects and influences the other and because neither can exist without the others. Economic, political, and cultural life are thoroughly entwined with one another in every nation. Together, they are the distinguishing features of a society.
- Every business firm has economic and social involvements and relationships with others in society. Some are intended, some unintended; some are positive, others are negative. Those related to the basic mission of the company are its primary involvements; those which flow from those activities but are more indirect are secondary involvements.
- The people, groups, and organizations that interact with the corporation and have an interest in its performance are its stakeholders. Those most closely and directly involved with a business are its primary stakeholders; those who are indirectly connected are its secondary stakeholders. Stakeholders may exercise their power independently or in coalitions.
- Five key forces are affecting the business-society relationship as companies move into the late 1990s: strategic refocusing and restructuring of businesses; changing ethical expectations and public values; global economic change; a global trend toward rethinking the role of government; and ecological and natural resource concerns.
- To be effective, corporate strategy must take into account the interests, needs, and expectations of all of the company's stakeholders. Companies should have a strategy that combines business goals and broad social interests.

KEY TERMS AND CONCEPTS USED IN THIS CHAPTER

- Interactive social system
- Stakeholders
- Primary and secondary stakeholders

- Interactive model of business
  and society
- Stakeholder power
- Stakeholder coalitions
- Strategic rethinking and reengi-
  neering
- Social contract
- New social contract

- Ethical principles and business
  legitimacy
- Global economic change
- *Glasnost* and *perestroika*
- Environmental protection

DISCUSSION CASE

INLAND NATIONAL BANK

Amy Miller, district manager for community affairs of Inland National Bank (INB), was faced with a problem. As a result of the recent acquisition of another local bank, Home Savings Bank, INB senior management was reorganizing the company's retail banking operations and consolidating some branches. Located in a medium-sized city in the midwestern United States, Inland National Bank had a good reputation for community involvement and solid financial performance. The decision to reorganize the branch banking business made sense financially, but Amy was troubled by the effects on local neighborhoods. Two branches in her district were directly affected by the reorganization.

INB announced just after Labor Day that it planned to close a former Home Savings Bank branch in the Rockdale section of the city. The problem with the branch was obvious: The neighborhood was old and on the decline, and the branch office facility was in a fairly run-down condition. Home Savings Bank had not modernized the facility for many years, and the cost of a major upgrading was not warranted by the financial base in the neighborhood. The other banks that once had Rockdale branches had closed them at least five years ago. In its announcement, INB encouraged customers to use its branch in Culver Heights, about a ten-minute auto or bus ride from Rockdale. According to a mailing INB sent to all Rockdale depositors, the Culver Heights branch was "conveniently located" on a local bus route. Still, Rockdale residents were very upset and organized a group of picketers in front of the Home Savings branch a few days after the announcement. A local television station sent a crew to cover the story. One local resident who was interviewed said, "INB just hates old people and old people is all that lives in Rockdale! They care more about money than people."

The second branch that concerned Amy Miller was in the North Madison section of the city. This was a poor neighborhood, with an average household income that was $3,000 per household lower than any other section of the city. Many of North Madison's residents were on welfare and other forms of public assistance. Home Savings Bank had one branch in this area, and INB also had a branch nearby. To Amy's dismay, INB's senior management had decided to close both branches and replace them with four automatic teller machines located closer to North Madison shopping areas. The move would eliminate a total of twenty jobs at the two branches, with only a few employees being likely to find other jobs within the bank. Amy understood that about half of the employees in the two branches lived in or near North Madison.

INB received angry telephone calls from several city officials immediately after the announcement. Sheila Thomas, an elected member of the city council who represented the North Madison neighborhood, was especially vocal about the bank's plan. She questioned whether the bank was acting in good faith toward all of the city's residents and asked whether it was right for a bank to "cut the heart out of my neighborhood" by replacing people with ATMs. Amy Miller knew and respected Sheila Thomas, but she also recognized the political visibility this issue was providing Ms. Thomas.

Inland National Bank operated under the regulatory supervision of several federal and state banking agencies. The bank had a good record with these authorities, but the branch reorganization plan clouded the picture. Under the federal Community Reinvestment Act, INB had to disclose where its deposits came from and where its deposits were being invested. This was to help ensure that money was being fairly reinvested in communities where depositors lived and worked. The law gave banking officials some leverage to force banks to pay attention to local community needs.

The protests in Rockdale and the criticism by residents of North Madison had caught the attention of banking officials who needed to approve INB's branch closings. The traditional test for banking officials was whether the financial solvency of the bank would be improved or harmed by the proposed action. Now, these communities were raising different issues.

INB's president had been asked by banking regulators to submit a plan to respond to the issues raised by the residents of Rockdale and North Madison. Amy Miller was on the spot to recommend a course of action. Her report was to be given to INB's president by the end of the week.

Discussion Questions

1. Who are the stakeholders in this case? Which are primary, and which are secondary? What influence do they have? How are they related to each other?
2. If INB decides to close the Rockdale and North Madison branches, how will the business-government-society relationship come into play? How might the issue unfold? What considerations must be weighed?

3. What should Amy Miller recommend to INB's president? Are there steps that can be taken to soften the impact of the closings? Should she recommend against closing the branches?
4. Compare the business and social considerations in the Rockdale and North Madison communities. If Amy had to rank the branches on their importance to the community, which one should stay open? Are there any meaningful differences between the two situations?
5. Identify the key terms and concepts in this chapter that apply to this discussion case.

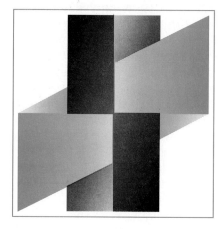

2

Corporate Social Responsibility

Corporate social responsibility challenges businesses to be accountable for the consequences of their actions affecting the firm's stakeholders while they pursue traditional economic goals. The general public expects business to be socially responsible, and many companies have responded by making social goals a part of their overall business operations. Guidelines for acting in socially responsible ways are not always clear, thus producing controversy about what constitutes such behavior, how extensive it should be, and what it costs to be socially responsible.

Key Questions and Chapter Objectives

This chapter focuses on these key questions and objectives:
- What is the basic meaning of corporate social responsibility?
- Where and when did the idea of social responsibility originate?
- What must a company do to be considered socially responsible?
- What are the limits of corporate social responsibility?
- Are laws required to make corporations act in socially responsible ways, or can we count on voluntary corporate actions?
- How does social responsibility affect profits?

"There was an epic debate, almost theological in tone," declared Anthony J. F. O'Reilly, chairman of H. J. Heinz Company.[1] He was speaking of the company's board of directors, who in April 1990 had just announced that its subsidiary, Star-Kist Seafood Company, would no longer buy tuna caught by nets that also kill dolphins. Lobbied by environmentalists, boycotted by many consumers, and facing the threat of new federal regulations to protect dolphins, Heinz and the other two leading tuna producers adopted this new environmental policy. The three companies normally

---

[1]"Lobbying, Research Convinced Heinz 'Dolphin-Safe' Tuna Made Business Sense," *New York Times News Service,* reprinted in *Pittsburgh Post-Gazette,* Apr. 17, 1990, pp. 1, 7.

sell around 70 percent of all tuna in the United States. Each can of the "dolphin-safe" tuna was expected to cost from 2 to 10 cents more. Star-Kist's president said, "We had been uncomfortable with the whole dolphin issue for a long time. Killing dolphins is undesirable for everyone." One financial analyst added, "The negative publicity of doing nothing would probably have harmed Heinz. Heinz would have looked like it was not being run by socially conscious people."

Question: Should Heinz adopt a "dolphin-safe" policy at the insistence of environmental and consumer groups? What if this action required the firm to raise the price of its product, losing customers? How can Heinz balance its environmental social responsibility with its economic goals?

"I'm following the moral convictions of myself, our people, my company and my country. I generally believe in what our government does, but personally I'm embarrassed for our government right now." This comment came from Nick H. Prater, president of Mobay Corporation, a producer of thionyl chloride.[2] Mobay had just refused to fill a U.S. government order for the chemical, which is an ingredient for a lethal chemical weapon, nerve gas. Prater cited a five-year-old company policy against use of its products in chemical weapons. He also criticized the U.S. government for continuing to manufacture these weapons while it was urging other nations to stop making them. The Defense Production Act of 1950 allows the government to force companies to supply materials necessary for national defense. Knowing this, Prater said, "If the Department of Commerce directs us to sell the product, we will do so; but, we will do so under protest."

Question: Should Mobay Corporation follow the government's order for chemical production or follow the company's policy and its president's moral convictions against the production of nerve gas? What is the socially responsible act?

These examples reveal some of the complexities of trying to act in socially responsible ways. In each case, some people believed the company was being socially responsible, while others thought the opposite. The top executives of these companies felt much pressure from those most affected, whether environmentalists or national defense officials. Stockholders, consumers, employees, and government regulators also had a stake in these decisions. These episodes make it obvious that social responsibility involves questions of ethics, legality, economic costs, and management judgment.

In this chapter we discuss the advantages and drawbacks of being socially responsible. Most of all, though, we argue that social responsibility is an inescapable demand made by society. Whether businesses are large or small, make goods or services, operate at home or abroad, willingly try to be socially responsible or fight against it all the way—there is no doubt

---

[2]*Pittsburgh Press,* Mar. 29, 1990, pp. B7–B8; "Defense: A Chemical Reaction," *Newsweek,* Apr. 23, 1990, p. 25; Mobay Corporation news release, Mar. 28, 1990.

about what the public expects. Many business leaders also subscribe to the idea of social responsibility. A 1990 *Business Week*–Louis Harris poll revealed that U.S. top-level corporate executives (69 percent of those polled) and MBA students (89 percent) believe that corporations should become more involved in solving social problems. Similar beliefs were recorded in a study of 107 European corporations, where a majority of CEOs surveyed agreed that addressing social issues, such as substance abuse, health care, and education, was needed.[3]

THE MEANING OF CORPORATE SOCIAL RESPONSIBILITY

Corporate social responsibility means that a corporation should be held accountable for any of its actions that affect people, their communities, and their environment. It implies that negative business impacts on people and society should be acknowledged and corrected if at all possible. It may require a company to forego some profits if its social impacts are seriously harmful to some of the corporation's stakeholders or if its funds can be used to promote a positive social good.

However, being socially responsible does not mean that a company must abandon its primary economic mission. Nor does it mean that socially responsible firms cannot be as profitable as others less responsible (some are and some are not). Social responsibility requires companies to balance the benefits to be gained against the costs of achieving those benefits. Many people believe that both business and society gain when business firms actively strive to be socially responsible. Others are doubtful, saying that business's competitive strength is weakened by taking on social tasks.

The social responsibilities of business grow directly out of two features of the modern corporation: (a) the essential functions it performs for a variety of stakeholders and (b) the immense influence it has on the lives of the stakeholders. We count on corporations for job creation, much of our community well-being, the standard of living we enjoy, the tax base for essential municipal, state, and national services, and our needs for banking and financial services, insurance, transportation, communication, utilities, entertainment, and a growing proportion of health care. These positive achievements suggest that the corporate form of business is capable of performing a great amount of good for society, such as encouraging economic growth, expanding international trade, and creating new technology.

The power and influence of the modern corporation are unmatched, as described by a leading expert:

[3]"A Kinder, Gentler Generation of Executives?" *Business Week,* Apr. 23, 1990, p. 86; and David L. Mathison, "European and American Executive Values," *Business Ethics: A European Review,* Apr. 1993, pp. 97–100.

> The large corporation . . . has become a social institution which embraces the thousands of human beings whose lives are affected by it and which provides an important focus for the employees' social relationships. In the more complex society, with greater mobility, the loosening of community ties, and urban anonymity, the neighborhood social unit has lost its cohesion and the corporation has assumed some of its role. . . . With the expansion of group health insurance programs, pension plans, and personal counselling services, the corporation is further strengthening the areas of its participation in the nonbusiness portion of its employees' lives.[4]

In addition, the modern corporation wields great political and governmental influence, as discussed in Chapters 8, 9, and 10.

Many people are concerned about potential corporate influence. In 1989, two-thirds of a national sample believed that "Business has gained too much power over too many aspects of American life."[5] The focused power found in the modern business corporation means simply that every action it takes can affect the quality of human life—for individuals, for communities, and for the entire globe. With such corporate technology as computers, communications satellites, and television networks drawing the world into a tighter and tighter "global village," the entire Planet Earth has become the corporation's most important stakeholder. All societies are now affected by corporate operations. As a result, social responsibility has become a worldwide expectation.

Social Responsibility in Other Nations

Social responsibility, however, reflects cultural values and traditions and takes different forms in different societies. What may be the accepted custom in the United States, Japan, or South Korea may not be customary practice in Germany, Brazil, Indonesia, or the Ukraine. Drawing the lines as to what is socially acceptable from a global view is often a difficult process.

Japanese firms, for example, have historically not experienced stakeholder protests as have firms in the United States. Victims of environmental disasters have been treated as outcasts when seeking compensation for harm caused by Japanese business. Employment practices which may favor certain groups have been generally accepted as a social practice in Japan.[6] However, as Japanese firms have become more integrated with the international community, corporate social responsibility has begun to emerge. The corporations' goal of seeking profits has been challenged by

---

[4]Phillip I. Blumberg, *The Megacorporation in American Society*, Englewood Cliffs, NJ: Prentice-Hall, 1975, pp. 2–3.

[5]"The Public Is Willing to Take Business On," *Business Week*, May 29, 1989, p. 29.

[6]Richard E. Wokutch, "Corporate Social Responsibility Japanese Style," *The Academy of Management Executive*, May 1990, pp. 56–74; and "Kyosei: Japanese Firms Must Pick Up the Social Tab As Well," *Tokyo Business Today*, Jan.-Feb. 1993, pp. 33–34.

EXHIBIT 2-A

SOCIAL RESPONSIBILITY JAPANESE STYLE

Kuniji Miyazaki, president of Dai-Ichi Kangyo Bank, Ltd., emphasizes that each employee "has a renewed, full awareness of the bank's business doctrine . . . [and] seeks to further improve the system of providing customers with the best of service." According to Miyazaki, contributing to society means: providing customers with ways to save money and thereby help build an asset base for the bank, facilitating economic activity through the bank's intermediary functions of credit creation and settlement of accounts, and carrying out the fair distribution of loans.

SOURCE: Yasuo Inoue, "Dai-Ichi Kangyo Bank Takes Social Responsibility Seriously: Interview with Kuniji Miyazaki, President, The Dai-Ichi Kangyo Bank, Ltd.," *Business Japan,* Oct. 1991, pp. 32–33.

stakeholders' demands for firms to act as both economic and social entities. Japanese business has responded by attempting to develop a positive working relationship with society. An illustration of a Japanese banker's understanding of corporate social responsibility is found in Exhibit 2-A.

Evidence of corporate social responsibility is also demonstrated by Dong Ah Company, a South Korean construction firm. In October 1994, one week after a seventeen-year-old bridge in Seoul, South Korea, collapsed killing thirty-two people, the company pledged to build a new bridge even though the company was not blamed for the accident. (Several Seoul officials were arrested on charges of neglecting to maintain the bridge). The cost of replacing the structure was 150 billion won, or $188.1 million. In addition, the company donated 10 billion won, about $12.5 million, to a program designed to improve South Korean commuters' safety.

Corporate social responsibility assumes a different form in European countries because governments there provide many social services often received as benefits from private employers in the United States. For example, debate by government representatives over social responsibility issues resulted in the adoption of a social policy for the European Union (EU) countries, named the Social Charter. Rather than relying upon private corporate initiatives, governments represented in the EU drafted a public policy which provided incentives and rewards for corporate social actions within the EU.[7]

The Social Charter was approved by 11 of the 12 EU members, but not without controversy. The United Kingdom was an unyielding dissenter, re-

---

[7]A discussion of European public policy involving social responsibility can be found in Terence P. Stewart and Delphine A. Abellard, "Labor Laws and Social Policies in the European Community After 1992," *Law & Policy in International Business,* Spring 1992, pp. 507–591; and Matthew Lynn, "Social Charter: Much Ado about Nothing," *International Management,* Jan. 1992, pp. 44–45. A less socially minded European view is reported in David L. Mathison, "Are Economic Realities Forcing EC Europe to Abandon Social Democracy in the Workplace?" paper presented at the national Academy of Management meeting, 1994, Dallas, Texas.

fusing to sign the Charter. The UK stood fast to its preference for a policy of deregulation regarding employment issues.[8] Embodied within the Social Charter is the Social Action Programme (SAP). The SAP established health and safety guidelines, regulations on working hours, Europe-wide rules for worker consultation, and rules for gender equality at work. Thus, European businesses' response toward social responsibility is actually a matter of compliance with various governmental policy guidelines and program initiatives.

In addition, business leaders' and government officials' attitudes toward social responsibility differ across cultures and countries. Figure 2-1 compares the contrasting attitudes of European and U.S. corporate executives toward two social responsibility issues: testing new employees for AIDS and drug use, and job opportunities for women and minorities.

In many of the world's developing nations where poverty is widespread or civil strife is frequent, economic goals and military activities tend to be given a higher priority than the pursuit of social goals. Environ-

---

[8]The UK position is explained in Samantha Swiss, "Between a Rock and a Hard Place," *International Financial Law Review*, Aug. 1992, pp. 3–5.

FIGURE 2-1

Opinions of corporate executives concerning selected social issues, 1990.

SOURCE: Adapted from David L. Mathison and David Boje, *Have European CEOs' Social and Strategic Priorities Changed with the New Europe? A Methodological Study of France, U.K., and Germany: A Preliminary Report,* unpublished manuscript, Los Angeles, CA: College of Business Administration, Loyola Marymount University, n.d. Used with permission of the authors. See also a survey of 100 U.K. companies reported in Shailendra Vyakarnam, "Social Responsibility: What Leading Companies Do," *Long Range Planning*, Oct. 1992, pp. 59–67.

OPINIONS OF CORPORATE EXECUTIVES CONCERNING SELECTED SOCIAL ISSUES, 1990
(N = 107)

	Percent Answering "Yes"				
	USA	**France**	**UK**	**Scotland**	**West Germany**
Should corporations routinely test new employees for AIDS and drug use, or not?	59	27	8	32	19
Should corporations provide a separate career track for women executives to work part-time so they can continue to pursue a professional career without having to sacrifice the rewards of motherhood, or not?	46	39	52	69	60
Do women and minorities have the same opportunities to advance in [the respondent's country's] business as white males, or not?	44	24	31	7	50

mental protection, for example, may be considered less critical than having a polluting steel plant that creates jobs. In these cases, social responsibility initiatives by business tend to be slow in coming.

HOW CORPORATE SOCIAL RESPONSIBILITY BEGAN

In the United States, the idea of corporate social responsibility appeared around the turn of the twentieth century. Corporations at that time came under attack for being too big, too powerful, and guilty of antisocial and anticompetitive practices. Critics tried to curb corporate power through antitrust laws, banking regulations, and consumer-protection laws.

Faced with this kind of social protest, a few farsighted business executives advised corporations to use their power and influence voluntarily for broad social purposes, rather than for profits alone. Some of the wealthier business leaders—steelmaker Andrew Carnegie is a good example—became great philanthropists who gave much of their wealth to educational and charitable institutions. Others like automaker Henry Ford developed paternalistic programs to support the recreational and health needs of their employees. The point to emphasize is that these business leaders believed that business had a responsibility to society that went beyond or worked in parallel with their efforts to make profits.[9]

As a result of these early ideas about business's expanded role in society, two broad principles emerged. These principles have shaped business thinking about social responsibility during the twentieth century. They are the historical foundation stones for the modern idea of corporate social responsibility.

The Charity Principle

The idea that the wealthier members of society should be charitable toward those less fortunate is a very ancient notion. Royalty through the ages has been expected to provide for the poor. The same is true of those with vast holdings of property, from feudal times to the present. Biblical passages invoke this most ancient principle, as do the sacred writings of other world religions. When Andrew Carnegie and other wealthy business leaders endowed public libraries, supported settlement houses for the poor, gave money to educational institutions, and contributed funds to many other community organizations, they were continuing this long tradition of being "my brother's keeper."

---

[9]Morrell Heald, *The Social Responsibility of Business: Company and Community, 1900–1960*, Cleveland: Case-Western Reserve Press, 1970. For a history of how some of these business philanthropists acquired their wealth, see Matthew Josephson, *The Robber Barons: The Great American Capitalists*, New York: Harcourt Brace, 1934.

This kind of private aid to the needy members of society was especially important in the early decades of this century. At that time, there was no Social Security system, no Medicare for the elderly, no unemployment pay for the jobless, and no United Way to support a broad range of community needs. There were few organizations capable of counseling troubled families, sheltering women and children victims of physical abuse, aiding alcoholics, treating the mentally ill or the physically handicapped, or taking care of the destitute. When wealthy industrialists reached out to help others in these ways, they were accepting some measure of responsibility for improving the conditions of life in their communities. In doing so, their actions helped counteract the critics who claimed that business leaders were uncaring and interested only in profits.

Before long, these community needs outpaced the riches of even the wealthiest persons and families. When that happened, beginning in the 1920s, much of the charitable load was taken on by business firms themselves rather than by the owners alone. The symbol of this shift from *individual* philanthropy to *corporate* philanthropy was the Community Chest movement in the 1920s, the forerunner of today's United Way drives that are widespread throughout the United States. Business leaders gave vigorous support to this form of corporate charity, urging all business firms and their employees to unite their efforts to extend aid to the poor and the needy. Business leaders established pension plans, employee stock ownership and life insurance programs, unemployment funds, limitations on working hours, and higher wages. They built houses, churches, schools, and libraries, provided medical and legal services, and gave to charity.

For many of today's business firms, corporate social responsibility means this kind of participation in community affairs—making paternalistic, charitable contributions. However, charitable giving is not the only form that corporate social responsibility takes. The founders of the doctrine also had another principle in mind.

The Stewardship Principle

Many of today's corporate executives see themselves as stewards, or trustees, who act in the general public's interest. Although their companies are privately owned and they try to make profits for the stockholders, the company is managed and directed by professional managers who believe they have an obligation to see that everyone—particularly those in need—benefits from the company's actions. According to this view, corporate managers have been placed in a position of public trust. They control vast resources whose use can affect people in fundamental ways. Because they exercise this kind of crucial influence, they incur a responsibility to use those resources in ways that are good not just for the stockholders alone but for society generally. In this way, they have become stewards, or trustees, for society. As such, they are expected to act with a special degree of social responsibility in making business decisions.[10]

This kind of thinking eventually produced the modern theory of stakeholder management, which was described in the opening chapter of this book. According to this theory, corporate managers need to interact skillfully with all groups who have a "stake" in what the corporation does. If they do not do so, their firms will not be fully effective economically or fully accepted by the public as a socially responsible corporation. As one former business executive declared, "Every citizen is a stakeholder in business whether he or she holds a share of stock or not, is employed in business or not, or buys the products and services of business or not. Just to live in American society today makes everyone a stakeholder in business."[11]

MODERN FORMS OF CORPORATE SOCIAL RESPONSIBILITY

These two principles—the charity principle and the stewardship principle—established the original meaning of corporate social responsibility. Figure 2-2 shows how these two principles have evolved to form the modern idea of corporate social responsibility. **Corporate philanthropy** is the modern expression of the charity principle. The stewardship principle is given meaning today when corporate managers recognize that business and society are intertwined and interdependent, as explained in Chapter 1. This mutuality of interests places a responsibility on business to exercise care and social concern in formulating policies and conducting business operations. Exhibit 2-B shows a few of the numerous examples of modern day corporate philanthropy.

Figure 2-3 shows a list of social priorities from the early 1970s developed by the Committee for Economic Development (CED), a group of about 200 top-level business executives. These recommendations were some of the first industry-wide suggestions for social responsibility programs.

Most recent surveys identifying areas of corporate social involvement generally reflect the CED's 1971 list. Employment and training expanded to include various health and wellness issues, such as employee fitness, AIDS education and treatment, and dependency upon cigarettes, alcohol, and drugs. Other emerging issues are identified and addressed by Businesses for Social Responsibility, described in Exhibit 2-C.

[10]Two early statements of this stewardship-trustee view are Frank W. Abrams, "Management's Responsibilities in a Complex World," *Harvard Business Review,* May 1951; and Richard Eells, *The Meaning of Modern Business,* New York: Columbia University Press, 1960.
[11]James E. Liebig, *Business Ethics: Profiles in Civic Virtue,* Golden, CO: Fulcrum, 1990, p. 217. For stakeholder theory, see R. Edward Freeman, *Strategic Management: A Stakeholder Approach,* Boston: Pitman, 1984.

FIGURE 2-2
Foundation princi-
ples of corporate
social responsibil-
ity and their mod-
ern expression.

	Charity Principle	**Stewardship Principle**
Definition	Business should give voluntary aid to society's needy persons and groups.	Business, acting as a public trustee, should consider the interests of all who are affected by business decisions and policies.
Modern Expression	■ Corporate philanthropy ■ Voluntary actions to promote the social good	■ Acknowledging business and society interdependence ■ Balancing the interests and needs of many diverse groups in society
Examples	■ Corporate philanthropic foundations ■ Private initiatives to solve social problems ■ Social partnerships with needy groups	■ Stakeholder approach to corporate strategic planning ■ Optimum long-run profits, rather than maximum short-run profits. ■ Enlightened self-interest attitude

EXHIBIT 2-B

CORPORATE PHILANTHROPY IN THE 1990S

Working Assets is a consumer-services company that donates part of its profits to four main areas: economic justice, the environment, peace, and human rights. In co-operation with Boston's State Street Bank, the firm launched its Visa card project. For every customer purchase using a Visa card, Working Assets donated a nickel to support thirty-six nonprofit groups. Donations reached $1.5 million.

When Hurricane Andrew devastated southern Miami in August 1992, Burger King joined several other companies in providing much needed assistance. Food, water, and shelter were supplied to Burger King employees and other homeless people in the disaster area. Other programs included an early distribution of the employees' paychecks and construction crews sent to repair employees' homes.

In November 1993, Hershey Foods launched an eighteen-month, $500,000 eye care project. In cooperation with optometrist Robert Morrison, Hershey sought to provide affordable glasses to millions of the needy at a cost of $1 per pair. Morrison created a lab-on-wheels, where people could have their eyes examined and be fitted for glasses in minutes. In a test run in Perry County, Pennsylvania, about 1,000 people received glasses and Dr. Morrison detected four cases of untreated glaucoma.

FIGURE 2-3
Recommended
social responsibility actions—
Committee for
Economic Development.

SOURCE: *Social Responsibilities of Business Corporations*, New York: Committee for Economic Development, 1971.

BUSINESS ACTIVITIES TO IMPROVE SOCIETY
(Committee for Economic Development, 1971)

- **Economic growth and efficiency**
  - Improving productivity
  - Cooperating with government
- **Education**
  - Giving aid to schools and colleges
  - Assisting in managing schools and colleges
- **Employment and training**
  - Training disadvantaged workers
  - Retraining displaced workers
- **Civil rights and equal opportunity**
  - Ensuring equal job opportunities
  - Building inner-city plants
- **Urban renewal and development**
  - Building low-income housing
  - Improving transportation systems
- **Pollution abatement**
  - Installing pollution controls
  - Developing recycling programs
- **Conservation and recreation**
  - Protecting plant and animal ecology
  - Restoring depleted lands to use
- **Culture and the arts**
  - Giving aid to arts institutions
- **Medical care**
  - Helping community health planning
  - Designing low-cost medical care programs
- **Government**
  - Improving management in government
  - Modernizing and reorganizing government

The Council on Economic Priorities (CEP) is a corporate watchdog organization that reports periodically on the social behavior of large corporations. In 1987 the council began to "accentuate the positive" by citing companies that had demonstrated an outstanding record of socially responsible behavior. A selective list of the CEP award recipients is provided in Figure 2-4. Companies are ineligible for CEP's annual "corporate conscience award" if their charitable contributions are less than 1 percent of pretax earnings, if they have no women or minorities on the board of directors, if they have seriously violated environmental standards, if they make nuclear, chemical, or biological weapons, or if they are among the top ten weapons contractors for the Department of Defense. In addition, companies have been given "dishonorable mentions" for a variety of socially irresponsible actions.

The Business Enterprise Trust, founded in 1989 by prominent leaders in business, academia, labor, and the media, recognizes business leaders and other individuals who have significantly advanced the cause of social responsibility through "acts of courage, integrity, and social vision." The Trust's annual awards have been presented to Merck & Company for developing a drug to combat river blindness, GE Plastics for an employee team-building project which renovated community youth centers, DAKA International—a restaurant and food service business—for pioneering an aggressive AIDS education program, and Julia Stasch for developing the Female Employment Initiative to assist women in the pursuit of careers in the construction industry.[12] The firms honored by the various organizations have a common theme: they did well economically, while "doing good" socially. Firms interested in achieving a balance between economic and social goals might look to these award-winning firms as examples.

THE LIMITS OF CORPORATE SOCIAL RESPONSIBILITY

Social responsibility is widely expected of business, but it has limits. The main limits are legitimacy, cost, efficiency, and scope and complexity. As a result of these constraints, the amounts and kinds of social actions pursued by business are sometimes less than the public wants to see.

Legitimacy

"Is this social problem any of our affair?" is a question worth asking by corporate officials. "Is it seriously affecting our business?" "Do we have the needed in-house talent?" "Can solving it help us, as well as others?" A "Yes"

---

[12]A thorough analysis of the Business Enterprise Trust program can be found in James O'Toole, "Do Good, Do Well: The Business Enterprise Trust Awards," *California Management Review,* Spring 1991, pp. 9–24.

EXHIBIT 2-C

BUSINESSES FOR SOCIAL RESPONSIBILITY

Businesses for Social Responsibility (BSR) is a U.S. trade group seeking to change the basic way business is done by making social, environmental, and worker-friendly practices an integral part of corporate policy making. BSR's fifty-five charter members include Ben & Jerry's, Stride Rite, and Lotus Development. Citing increased consumer interest in green marketing (discussed later in Chapter 12) and social investing (discussed later in Chapter 13), BSR is actively pursuing programs of education and training to help interested companies better address the concerns of their communities, consumers, and employees.

SOURCE: Larry Reynolds, "A New Social Agenda for the New Age," *Management Review,* Jan. 1993, pp. 39–41.

FIGURE 2-4

Social responsibility honored by the Council on Economic Priorities.

SOURCE: *America's Corporate Conscience Awards,* New York: Council on Economic Priorities, 1989–1994.

AMERICA'S CORPORATE CONSCIENCE AWARDS
1989–1994

Charitable Contributions:

U.S. West	Tom's of Maine
H. B. Fuller	Foldcraft
Cummins Engine	Dayton Hudson
Ben & Jerry's	

Community Involvement:

Brooklyn Union Gas	Time Warner
Clorox	Supermarkets General
Prudential Insurance	Holdings
America Works	

Employee Issues:

SAS Institute	Pitney Bowes
Merck	Quad Graphics
Donnelly Corp.	Kellogg
Federal Express	Avon

Environmental Stewardship:

S. C. Johnson	Stmyfield Farm
Digital Equipment	Aveda Corp.
Church & Dwight	Herman Miller
AT&T	

Silver Anniversary Awards:
(recognition for long-term efforts)

Xerox	Shorebank Corp.

answer to these questions might lead a company to an understanding that it has a legitimate obligation to take socially responsible action. If, for example, drug usage is causing serious safety problems in a plant, a company might be justified in spending money on a drug-education and treatment center that can help its employees and others in the community. Or when Eddie Bauer, the sporting goods company, supports the March of Dimes' programs for the physically handicapped, it gives tangible help while exhibiting its own concern.

However, a "No" answer or an "I'm not sure" answer to the questions should cause company executives to think twice. Social expenditures by corporations can be justified, and are considered to be a lawful use of stockholders' funds, if they promote the interests of the company while simultaneously helping society. This legal principle was established in a famous 1951 lawsuit when a judge ruled that corporations were justified in contributing company funds to a university because these corporate gifts benefited the company in the long run. Judgments about the legitimacy of any social activity are usually made by a firm's top-level executives who, in the words of the court, must take "a long-range view of the matter" and exercise "enlightened leadership and direction."[13]

Costs

Every social action is accompanied by costs of one kind or another. A company's contributions to a worthy charity, or establishing a child care center for its employees, or adopting a dolphin-safe tuna-buying policy imposes costs on someone. A United Way contribution could have been paid instead to company stockholders as a dividend. Money spent on a child care center could have been used instead to boost employees' wages. Dolphin-safe tuna is more costly to consumers. Building oil tankers with double hulls to prevent harmful oil spills boosts the price of gasoline. As worthy as some of these social actions may be, they do impose costs either on the business firm or on some groups in society—or both.

Efficiency

The costs of social responsibility, like all business expenses, can potentially reduce a company's efficiency and affect its ability to compete in the marketplace. For example, if a company is pressured by a local community to keep an outmoded, inefficient plant in operation because closing it would mean a big job loss for local people, while its competitors close their old plants and move operations to foreign nations where wage rates are lower, which company is more likely to survive in the long run? The so-

---

[13]See *Barlow, et al. v. A. P. Smith Manufacturing Company* (1951, New Jersey Supreme Court), discussed in Clarence C. Walton, *Corporate Social Responsibility*, Belmont, CA: Wadsworth, 1967, pp. 48–52.

cially responsible managers who care for local employees, even though making what seems to be a socially responsible decision, may not be able to compete with their lower-cost, more efficient competitors.

Scope and Complexity

Some of society's problems are simply too massive, too complex, and too deep-seated to be solved by even the most socially conscientious company or even by all companies acting together.

Examples are environmental problems such as acid rain, ozone depletion in the upper atmosphere, and destruction of rain forests. What is required is joint action by corporations and governments in several nations, as happened when companies producing the chemicals that destroy the planet's high-level ozone layer agreed to phase out production gradually.[14]

Some of today's health problems—AIDS, on-the-job drug abuse, and tobacco use—frequently reflect complex social conditions. While socially responsive businesses can adopt workplace policies and programs regarding these and other health problems, solutions are most likely to be found through joint actions of government, business, community groups, and the individuals involved.

Other social problems are even more persistent. These may include the deep-seated issues of race relations, sex discrimination, and ethnic and religious animosities. No single business firm can be expected to root out these long-standing features of society. The most it can do is to adopt socially responsible attitudes and policies about these issues, being certain that company practices do not make things worse.

These four limits often produce disagreements among those who want corporations to be socially responsible and those who think business is doing enough. The latter group usually declares, "Business cannot do more because of these limits." Their opponents in the debate usually respond by saying, "Business should be socially active in spite of these constraints, because business is obligated to help society solve its problems." Exhibit 2-D gives a flavor of these different viewpoints.

VOLUNTARY RESPONSIBILITY VERSUS LEGAL REQUIREMENTS

Do we need laws and government regulations to ensure socially responsible conduct by business? Or will business, knowing that society expects a high standard of social behavior, decide voluntarily to be socially responsible?

Oddly enough, the answer to both of these questions is "Yes." Business

[14]The Montreal Protocol, the multinational government-business agreement which banned or phased out the use of various materials harmful to the earth's ozone layer, is discussed in Chapter 11.

EXHIBIT 2-D

CORPORATE SOCIAL RESPONSIBILITY = SHAREHOLDER WEALTH

"In a market-based economy that recognizes the rights of private property, the only social responsibility of business is to create shareholder value and to do so legally and with integrity. Yet we do have important unresolved social challenges—from drug abuse to education and the environment—that require collective action. Corporate management however has neither the political legitimacy nor the expertise to decide what is in the social interest. It is our form of government that provides the vehicle for collective choice via elected legislators and the judicial system.

"Whether corporate social responsibility is advocated by political activists or the chief executive officer, the costs of these expenditures, which don't increase the value of the company or its stock, will be passed on to consumers by way of higher prices, or to employees as lower wages, or to shareholders as lower returns."

SOURCE: Alfred Rappaport, "Let's Let Business Be Business," *New York Times,* Feb. 4, 1990, p. F13.

CORPORATE SOCIAL RESPONSIBILITY = ALL STAKEHOLDERS

"Increasingly, responsible corporate behavior is being defined as taking into account the values, concerns, and needs of a wide variety of stakeholders, those parties—including those external to the organization—who have a legitimate stake, or interest, in the organization, its conduct and performance. Traditionally in business, these stakeholders have been identified solely as the company's shareholders, and the objective function of business was tidily summed up as maximizing the shareholders' wealth. . .

"There are too many other competing interests in today's pluralistic society to ignore. Stakeholders other than shareholders have important claims on a business which also must be met if the company is to survive and flourish. Meeting these claims probably means less profit in the short term and may mean some reduction in potential shareholder wealth in the long term. Nonetheless, such outside groups and their demands cannot be ignored."

SOURCE: From *Corporations and the Common Good,* Dickie and Rouner, eds. © 1986 by the University of Notre Dame Press. Used by permission.

---

does need social guidance from laws and public policies.[15] Without them, companies would be uncertain about which social goals they should pursue and in which order of priority. For example, since the early 1970s, the public has signaled clearly that it wants the environment cleaned up, and lawmakers have responded by adopting strong pollution control laws and updating them every few years (e.g., the Clean Air Act of 1990). These new legal rules set standards for business to follow. They tell business that environmental protection is an important social goal with a high priority.

[15]Chapters 8 and 9 in this book discuss public policy in greater detail. For further information, see Rogene A. Buchholz, *Essentials of Public Policy for Management,* Englewood Cliffs, NJ: Prentice-Hall, 1992, chap. 2.

Laws and regulations also help create a "level playing field" for businesses that compete against one another. By requiring all firms to meet the same social standards—for example, the safe disposal of hazardous wastes—one firm cannot gain a competitive advantage over its rivals by dumping its wastes carelessly without the risk of lawsuits, fines, possible jail terms for some of its managers and employees, and unfavorable publicity for the lawbreaking firm.

Businesses that comply with laws and public policies are meeting a minimum level of social responsibility expected by the public. According to one leading scholar of corporate social performance, even legal compliance is barely enough to satisfy the public:

> The traditional economic and legal criteria are necessary but not sufficient conditions of corporate legitimacy. The corporation that flouts them will not survive; even the mere satisfaction of these criteria does not ensure the corporation's continued existence. . . .
>
> Although relatively few corporations have been accused of violating the laws of their nations, they have been increasingly criticized for failing to meet societal expectations and failing to adapt their behavior to changing social norms. Thus, social responsibility implies bringing corporate behavior up to a level where it is in congruence with currently prevailing social norms, values, and performance expectations. . . . [Social responsibility] is simply a step ahead—before the new societal expectations are codified into legal requirements.[16]

Legal and regulatory compliance is the least that the public expects from business performance. However, by being stated in broad general terms, laws and regulations require interpretation to know just how they should be applied. So a company's version of how to comply with, for example, an equal opportunity hiring law may be quite different from how the hiring rules are seen by government regulators. If these differences result in a lawsuit, then the courts may interpret the law in yet another way. This means that business must use its own best judgment in interpreting and honestly trying to comply with the law. One such approach is called "enlightened self-interest."

Enlightened Self-Interest

Being socially responsible by meeting the public's continually changing expectations requires wise leadership at the top of the corporation. Companies with an ability to recognize profound social changes and anticipate how they will affect operations have been shown to be "survivors." They get along better with government regulators, are more open to the needs

[16]S. Prakash Sethi, "A Conceptual Framework for Environmental Analysis of Social Issues and Evaluation of Business Response Patterns," in S. Prakash Sethi and Cecilia M. Falbe (eds.), *Business and Society: Dimensions of Conflict and Cooperation*, Lexington, MA: Lexington Books, 1987, pp. 42, 43.

of the company's stakeholders, and often cooperate with lawmakers as new laws are developed to cope with social problems. Corporate leaders who possess this kind of social vision believe that business should help create social change rather than try to block it. With such an attitude, they know that their own companies will have a better chance of surviving in the turbulent social currents of todays' world.[17]

Companies with this outlook are guided by **enlightened self-interest,** which means that they are socially aware without giving up their own economic self-interest. According to this view, profits are the reward for the firm as it continues to provide true value to its customers, to help its employees to grow, and to behave responsibly as a corporate citizen. These goals are reflective of the fastest-growing most profitable firms in the United States.[18]

An emphasis on social responsibility can attract customers. A poll conducted by Opinion Research Corporation shows that 89 percent of purchases by adults are influenced by a company's reputation. Social responsibility also benefits companies by enabling them to recruit a high-quality labor force. The reputation of the firm and the goodwill associated with socially responsible actions attract talented prospective employees, people seeking an employer for whom they would be proud to work.

Voluntary Action versus Legal Compulsion

Should a company get credit for being socially responsible if its actions are required by law or government regulations? Some people say "No." They argue that the only truly socially responsible corporations are those motivated by a strong desire to do social good and willing voluntarily to "put their money (or their actions) where their mouth is." According to this view, a company that must be legally coerced to act in responsible ways falls short of the true meaning of social responsibility.

> For example, manufacturers of infant formula have been criticized for marketing this product in third world nations where poverty and unsanitary conditions prevent its proper use. The resulting malnourishment, as many mothers give up breast-feeding their babies, contributes to high infant mortality rates in some countries. Only after many years of public protests and boycotts, and the threat of new laws to control marketing practices, were the manufacturers persuaded to modify their selling tactics.
>
> By contrast, in the famous Tylenol product-tampering case of the

[17]Robert H. Miles, *Managing the Corporate Social Environment: A Grounded Theory,* Englewood Cliffs, NJ: Prentice-Hall, 1987.
[18]The relationship between profits and social responsibility is asserted by Charles A. Garfield, "Do Profits and Social Responsibility Mix?" *Executive Excellence,* Mar. 1992, p. 5.

early 1980s, Johnson & Johnson immediately withdrew this product from the shelves and voluntarily took other very costly steps to ensure the safety of consumers using this popular pain reliever. Company executives acted well in advance of legal pressures and collaborated closely with regulatory officials to safeguard the public.

Socially responsible actions frequently occur as a result of mixed motives—partly from a genuine desire to promote worthy social goals, partly from wanting to project a caring image of the company, and partly from the knowledge that government may step in if business fails to act on its own.

PROFITS AND SOCIAL RESPONSIBILITY

Do socially responsible companies sacrifice profits by working conscientiously to promote the social good? Do they make higher profits, better-than-average profits, or lower profits than corporations that ignore or flout the public's desires for a high and responsible standard of social performance? While the arguments in the previous section provide a logical relationship, efforts to discover an observed relationship between a company's financial performance and its social performance have produced mixed results. Some studies seem to demonstrate that a good social performer also has a good record of profit making, which could be an example of "enlightened self-interest." However, other research reports that the relationship between profits and social responsibility is sequential. Once the company is profitable, it can "afford" to be socially responsible in its actions. Others argue that being socially responsible attracts investors to the firm. The relationship between social responsibility and profitability is extremely complex and difficult to prove.[19]

Faced with this kind of uncertainty, corporate executives who favor a positive and proactive approach to social responsibility have developed the following broad principles about how social activities can be reconciled with business's need for profits.

---

[19]The "profits first, then social action" argument is discussed by Jean B. McGuide, Alison Sundgeon, and Thomas Schneeweis, "Corporate Social Responsibility and Firm Financial Performance," *Academy of Management Journal*, vol. 31, no. 4, 1988, pp. 854–872. The "social responsibility attracts investors" argument is supported by research reported in Samuel B. Graves and Sandra A. Waddock, "Institutional Owners and Corporate Social Performance," *Academy of Management Journal*, 1994, pp. 1034–1046. Prior studies investigating this relationship are summarized in Kenneth E. Aupperle, Archie B. Carroll, and John D. Hatfield, "An Empirical Examination of the Relationship between Corporate Social Responsibility and Profitability," *Academy of Management Journal*, June 1985, pp. 449–459.

Long-run Profits versus Short-run Profits

Any social program—for example, an in-company child care center, a drug education program for employees, or the lending of company executives as advisers to community agencies—will usually impose immediate monetary costs on the participating company. These short-run costs certainly have a potential for reducing the company's profits unless the social activity is designed to make money, which is not usually the purpose of these programs. Therefore, a company may sacrifice **short-run profits** by undertaking social initiatives.

But what is lost in the short run may be gained back over a longer period. For example, if a drug education program prevents and reduces on-the-job drug abuse, the firm's productivity may be increased by lower employee turnover, fewer absences from work, a healthier workforce, fewer accidents and injuries, and lower health insurance costs. In that case, the company may actually experience an increase in its **long-run profits,** although it had to make an expensive outlay to get the program started.

Optimum Profits versus Maximum Profits

Maximum profits are the "official" goal of all business activities. Sometimes, however, business judgments are deliberately made that result in less than a maximum return. In these cases, companies seem willing to settle for **optimum profits** rather than maximum profits. An optimum profit is a return that is considered to be satisfactory by the managers or owners of a business. It may be lower than what is actually possible, and it is higher than the minimum return necessary to keep the company in business. An optimum profit may be the best a company can earn when operating in unfavorable economic conditions or under tough government regulations.

Social responsibility decisions may lead to optimum profits by diverting funds that otherwise could be used to drive profits close to the maximum level. For example, the drug education funds might have been used to purchase a more productive computer system. Or a favorable financial opportunity might be avoided in order to escape public protest, as happened to many U.S. firms who withdrew their generally profitable operations from South Africa during the late 1980s.

Stockholder Interests versus Other Stakeholder Interests

Top-level managers, along with a corporation's board of directors, are generally expected to produce as much value as possible for the company's stockholders. This can be done by paying high dividends regularly and by running the company in ways that cause the stock's value to rise. Not only are high profits a positive signal to Wall Street investors that the company is being well run—thereby increasing the stock's value—but those profits make possible the payment of high dividends to stockholders. Low profits have the opposite effects and put great pressure on managers to improve the company's financial performance.

However, stockholders are not the only stakeholder group that management must keep in mind. All the stakeholders must be considered. None can be ignored. The top manager's job is to interact with the totality of the company's stakeholders, including those groups who advocate high levels of social responsibility by business. Management's central goal is to promote the interests of the entire company, not just any single stakeholder group, and to pursue multiple company goals, not just profit goals.

This broader and far more complex task tends to put more emphasis on the long-run profit picture rather than an exclusive focus on immediate returns. It also leads to taking optimum profits rather than maximum profits. When this happens, dividends paid to stockholders may be less than they desire, and the value of their shares may not rise as rapidly as they would like.

These are the kinds of risks faced by corporate managers who have a legal responsibility to produce high value for the company's stockholder-owners but who also must try to promote the overall interests of the entire company. Some of the corporate takeovers that occurred during the 1980s and 1990s were brought on by a low-value, low-dividend record of the target company. Corporate raiders charged management with not producing high economic value for stockholder-owners. Takeovers often ousted one management team and put another in its place.

This dilemma continues to be a puzzle in the 1990s. Putting all of the emphasis on short-run maximum profits for stockholders can lead to policies that overlook the interests and needs of other stakeholders. Social responsibility programs that increase short-run costs also may be downgraded, although it is well known that socially responsible companies are strongly approved by the general public. To handle this problem, an enlightened self-interest point of view may be the most useful and practical approach. That means incurring reasonable short-run costs to undertake socially responsible activities that benefit both the company and the general public. The results might satisfy stockholders' pressures for short-run profits while generating long-run positive public attitudes toward business.

SUMMARY POINTS OF THIS CHAPTER

- Corporate social responsibility means that a corporation should be held accountable for any of its actions that affect people, their communities, and their environment. However, an understanding and expression of this term differs across countries and cultures.

■ The idea of corporate social responsibility in the United States first appeared in the early twentieth century and was adopted by business leaders as a new philosophy of corporate enterprise.

■ The central themes of social responsibility have been charity—which means giving aid to the needy—and stewardship—which means acting as a public trustee and considering all corporate stakeholders when making business decisions.

■ Business is limited in its efforts to be socially responsible by actions that are unrelated to company goals and abilities, are too costly, impair business efficiency, and are highly complex.

■ Social responsibility is a result of both voluntary initiatives taken by business and laws that promote desirable social goals.

■ Social responsibility does not necessarily lower profits but may encourage firms to focus on long-run profits rather than short-run profits, optimum profits rather than maximum profits, and the interests of the entire company and all stakeholders rather than just the stockholders' interest.

KEY TERMS AND CONCEPTS USED IN THIS CHAPTER

■ Corporate social responsibility
■ Charity principle
■ Stewardship principle
■ Corporate philanthropy
■ Enlightened self-interest

■ Short-run profits
■ Long-run profits
■ Maximum profits
■ Optimum profits

DISCUSSION CASE

CUMMINS ENGINE COMPANY

One admirer called it "capitalism at its best." Another said its chief executive officer "believed in superb products, concern for employees, involvement in the community—all those qualities that made American corporations the envy of the world."[20]

But as the 1990s began, this paragon of social responsibility appeared

[20]All quotations are from Robert Johnson, "Survivor's Story: With Its Spirit Shaken but Unbeat, Cummins Shows Decade's Scars," *Wall Street Journal*, Dec. 13, 1989, pp. A1, A6; and Letters to the Editor, *Wall Street Journal*, Jan. 15, 1990, p. A11. See also Rogene A. Buchholz, William D. Evans, and Robert A. Wagley, *Management Response to Public Issues: Concepts and Cases in Strategy Formulation*, Englewood Cliffs, NJ: Prentice-Hall, 1985, pp. 239–249; and "Mr. Rust Belt," *Business Week*, Oct. 17, 1988, pp. 72–83.

to be in trouble. It had lost over $100 million in 1986, almost as much in 1988, and had only a tiny net profit in 1987. It had fended off one British corporate raider at a cost of $72 million but faced another potential hostile takeover by a Hong Kong investor who held around 15 percent of the company's stock.

In spite of shaky profits, the company refused to cut long-term research spending to improve its products or to reduce charitable contributions which were among the highest in industrial America. Neither would company officials listen to those who urged a move from its Midwestern home to nonunion lower-cost areas in the South. When Hurricane Hugo devastated large sections of South Carolina in 1989, the company sent free engines and generators to some of the victims. Near its new factory in Brazil, it helped build a school, a clinic, and a gymnasium in a poor neighborhood. Viewing this situation, one financial analyst declared, "Cummins is one big social slush fund. An incredibly naive attitude exists at the company. . . ."

The subject of all this commentary, both positive and negative, was Cummins Engine Company, a leading maker of heavy-duty diesel engines for trucks. From its founding in 1919, Cummins was known for a benevolent attitude, mainly a result of the religious convictions and social philosophy of Clessie Cummins, the founder. It also was famous for high-quality, reliable, and efficient engines, which earned profits for the company for forty-three straight years until 1980. During the 1980s, Cummins began to feel the combined pressures of foreign competition, a recession, and takeover threats from raiders impatient with a spotty profit picture.

Cummins's long record of social responsibility is well known. Its headquarters town of Columbus, Indiana, is sprinkled with public buildings designed by some of the world's leading architects whose fees were paid by Cummins. The management staff was racially integrated as early as the 1960s, and Cummins became an early leader in reducing pollution caused by its engines. Employees are protected against unwarranted use of personal data in company files, and Cummins's chairman helped develop privacy guidelines for other employers. Many local causes draw upon the company's charitable funds, along with the voluntary help of company executives and employees. Townspeople remained fiercely loyal to the company, even after over 4,000 were laid off during the 1980s. Cummins employees receive good wages and benefits and take much pride in producing high-quality engines.

Faced with the tough competitive environment of 1990, Henry B. Schacht, Cummins's chairman, said, "Some say the company's main goal should be to maximize shareholder value . . . I say no. [The company's goal is] being fair and honest and doing what is right even when it is not to our immediate benefit." Hearing this, a Wall Street skeptic declared that Cummins has been "in a long-term mode for 10 years. . . . Schacht sounds great, but at some point there's got to be a payout for all this spending."

An outside observer responded by saying, "Wall Street stubbornly ignores the success of Japanese industrial enterprises—success achieved in long-term planning for market penetration, in lieu of a consuming emphasis on short-term results. If the financial community would lay off the hounding of public-company managements [like Cummins], allowing them to run their businesses instead of wasting valuable time reacting to the ill-conceived criticisms of these Wall Street gurus, domestic enterprises would be all the better for it." A former chairman of the company summed up his own view: "Cummins has a fantastic future because it isn't just factories, machines and cash. It's outstanding people who take intense pride in their work and their community."

Demonstrating that his social skills are matched by an equal financial ability, Cummins's CEO in mid-1990 sold a 27 percent stake of the company to Ford Motor, Tenneco, and Kubota, a Japanese firm. The deal gave Cummins needed new business for its diesel engines and $250 million to reduce debt and invest in modernization. By the end of 1993, Cummins appeared to be on the way toward economic recovery. The firm reported its second-best third quarter ever, tripling profits to $40.7 million from $13.8 million in 1992. Sales also rose for the firm, from $903.6 million to $988.3 million or 9.4 percent. This trend toward economic health continued into 1994. Cummins Engine Company appears to provide an example that profits and social responsibility can coexist.

Discussion Questions

1. Is Cummins's commitment to social responsibility fair to the company's stockholders? If you were Cummins's CEO, would you cut back on social expenditures so you could pay higher dividends to the company's owners? Would that keep the corporate raiders at bay?
2. Which principle of social responsibility—the charity principle or the stewardship principle—is the basis of Cummins's approach to social responsibility? Give some examples from the case.
3. Of the four major limits to social responsibility discussed in this chapter, which ones seem to apply to Cummins?
4. Is Cummins an example of what this chapter calls "enlightened self-interest?" Explain your answer.

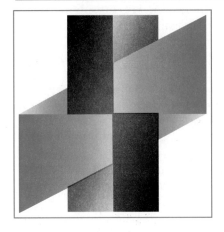

3

Socially Responsive Management

Current business activities and future business plans define the company's key involvements with its stakeholders. The socially responsive corporation considers and carefully plans for the social impacts of its decisions and policies. This chapter discusses how businesses integrate social responsiveness into the management decision process and infuse social responsibility into the organization and its activities.

Key Questions and Chapter Objectives

This chapter focuses on these key questions and objectives:
- What groups and social forces changed the way management responds to the social environment?
- What are four basic strategies of corporate response to the social environment?
- What is the purpose of the corporate public affairs function?
- How can a firm collect and analyze information to formulate a social strategy?
- What changing phases confront a business as it implements a social program? What objectives provide a framework for businesses formulating a social program?

Strategic alliances became common in the 1990s as leading corporations faced an increasing number of social issues. In order to respond to the complex social problems affecting business, companies joined together and with their key stakeholders (government agencies, community or special interest groups, schools, etc.) to form **collaborative partnerships.** By pooling their financial and human resources, a network of organizations could better address the challenges presented by the various social concerns of the 1990s and more effectively achieve their mutual goals.

A partnership among businesses to address various social issues was reflected in the actions taken by a group of companies in September 1992.

This collaboration, simply called the "Partnership of 109 Companies," was "aimed at making major improvements in the quality and supply of child-care and elder-care services nationwide."[1] Working with the businesses were many state, city, and nonprofit organizations. The partnership was committed to the creation of child-care centers and programs, the training of child-care workers, increased services for the elderly, and the expansion of day programs for school-age children. The creation of these programs was acutely relevant to U.S. businesses, as many of these issues directly affected employees' lives and their ability to work. The partnership, which pledged over $25 million, was led by IBM, and joined by American Express, AT&T, Eastman Kodak, Johnson & Johnson, and Motorola. Helen Blank, a child-care expert at the Children's Defense Fund, believed that the collaboration made an "impressive contribution" toward solving serious problems with the nation's dependent-care system.

Another partnership was formed in the late 1980s when businesses in Milwaukee, Wisconsin, realized that dramatic changes required dramatic responses. Gangs, drug dealers, and prostitutes became familiar residents of the Avenues West area, a 100-square block section of the city on the fringe of the downtown business district. Crime in the area was up 22 percent; residential housing was decaying. By 1990, 60 percent of the buildings in the Avenues West area contained twenty or more rental units. Only a small percentage of the housing units were owner-occupied. Absentee landlords frequently let dwellings fall into disrepair or be taken over by drug dealers, becoming "crack houses" where drugs were easily purchased. These and other factors led to a collaborative partnership involving business and its stakeholders in order to seriously address these social challenges. The plan was called "the Campus Circle Project."[2]

Announced in November 1991, the project created a partnership with numerous organizations and community groups to redevelop the Avenues West neighborhood. Four local corporations—Wisconsin Energy Corporation, Wisconsin Bell, Catholic Knights Insurance Company, and Aurora Health Care—pledged nearly $15 million. Marquette University, a Jesuit Catholic college located in the Avenues West area, joined the partnership and committed cash, land, and in-kind contributions worth $9 million. The City of Milwaukee created a special tax structure to help pay for public improvements. Finally, a $20 million, five-year federal grant was received to provide further support for the project.

The multi-phase project of crime prevention, community planning, housing rehabilitation and construction, and economic development for the Avenues West neighborhood continued throughout the mid-1990s.

---

[1]"Partnership of 109 Companies Aims to Improve Care Nationwide for Children and the Elderly," *Wall Street Journal*, Sept. 11, 1992, p. A20.
[2]"Marquette University Leads Urban Revival of Blighted Environs," *Wall Street Journal*, Feb. 1, 1994, pp. A1, A6.

Initial assessments indicate that this type of cooperative partnership between corporate, academic, and governmental institutions may be one alternative to combat high crime and declining housing neighborhoods.

But what gave rise to the change in corporate social responsiveness of the 1980s and 1990s? What events or social movements triggered these changes in stakeholder management analysis and the programs developed from the analysis?

STAKEHOLDER EXPECTATIONS AND CORPORATE PERFORMANCE

One possible reason for a rise in collaborative partnerships with stakeholders is the failure of a corporation's performance to meet the expectations of critical stakeholder groups. Often the first sign of a problem is complaint, objection, or protest from a stakeholder group whose expectations are not being met. For example, a group of residents may object to the odor or smoke from a local plant, or others may protest the use of monkeys or mice for scientific research at a local university. Or an employee may claim that he or she became ill after working in a plant or breathing fumes from hazardous chemicals.

The Performance-Expectations Gap

What has happened in each of these instances is that a gap has developed between the expectations of the stakeholder (person or group) and the actual performance of the corporation. (See Figure 3-1.) Stakeholder expectations are a mixture of the opinions, attitudes, and beliefs of people about what constitutes responsible business behavior. The residents do not believe that air emissions constitute responsible behavior; some people who care about animals do not believe it is morally responsible to inflict pain on animals in the name of scientific research; employees who choke on fumes do not believe it is ethically responsible for a company to endanger their health in this way.

Managers have a responsibility to identify these kinds of beliefs or expectations as early as possible. Failure to understand the concerns of stakeholders and to respond appropriately will permit the performance-expectations gap to grow larger. This gap shows the magnitude of the difference between what the stakeholder expects and the firm's actual performance. The larger the gap, the greater the risk of stakeholder backlash.

The decades of the 1960s and 1970s were times of significant stakeholder protests and challenges. There was an intense focus upon a cluster of social issues. The gap between corporate performance and stakeholder expectations appeared to be at a critical point.

FIGURE 3-1

The performance-expectations gap: a measure of stakeholder wants versus company action over time.

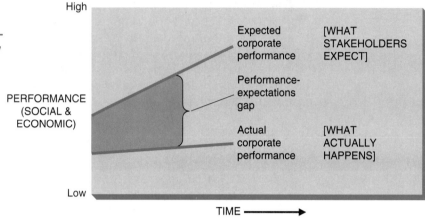

THE SOCIAL CLIMATE OF THE 1960S AND 1970S

The 1960s and 1970s in the United States were turbulent times for businesses and managers. Challenges by corporate stakeholders came from many diverse groups.

- Consumer advocates, spearheaded by Ralph Nader's fight against the U.S. automobile industry for safer vehicles, demanded safe products, accurate information, and competitive pricing of products.
- Environmentalists held the first Earth Days in the 1970s, calling for businesses to be accountable for air and water quality.
- Anti–Vietnam War activists demanded that businesses participating in the Military Industrial Complex abandon conventional and chemical weapons production and convert to the manufacture of peacetime goods.
- African-American groups organized under the civil rights movement and pressed for an end to discriminatory practices in the hiring, promotion, and training of employees.
- Women's groups accused businesses of gender bias and discrimination.
- Workers, of all races and both genders, pushed for safer working conditions.
- Communities protested the use and transportation of toxic materials by businesses, as well as the construction and operation of nuclear energy plants.

These and other corporate stakeholders dramatically altered the business environment within which managers attempted to perform their tasks. Most of the groups mentioned will be discussed in greater detail in the following chapters of the book. The overall contribution of these groups to the collective social movements of the 1960s and 1970s demanded a different response from businesses in addition to those embodied in the notions *of corporate social responsibility*. Firms were now required to develop a sense *of corporate social responsiveness*.

As discussed in the previous chapter, corporate social responsibility is founded upon the principles of charity and stewardship. Expressions of these concepts are seen in corporate philanthropy and the care of the public's resources. However, the basis for corporate social responsiveness does not rely upon the generosity of the firm's senior management or their awareness of their role as trustees of the public's interests. **Corporate social responsiveness** is seen in the way a firm addresses social demands initiated by corporate stakeholders or in the social actions taken by the firm which affect its stakeholders. Firms are no longer in total control of the social interaction between the firm and its stakeholders. Rather, the firm is obligated to respond to stakeholder demands or risk suffering damaging consequences. The contrast between corporate social responsibility and what has been labeled corporate social responsiveness—describing businesses' responses to the social demands of the 1960s and 1970s—is highlighted in Figure 3-2.

STRATEGIES OF RESPONSE

Businesses respond to stakeholder pressures in various ways. Some firms steadfastly adhere to their plans, no matter how strong the opposition or pressure from other actors in society. Some firms change only when

FIGURE 3-2
Contrast between corporate social responsibility and corporate social responsiveness.

	Corporate Social Responsibility	**Corporate Social Responsiveness**
Origin	1920s	1960s
Basis	Principles of charity and stewardship	Demands made by numerous social stakeholder groups
Focus	Moral obligations to society-at-large	Practical responses by businesses to corporate stakeholders
Action	Philanthropy, trustee of the public's interests	Social programs

forced to do so by strong outside pressures. Others actively attempt to move society in directions that will be to the company's advantage. A fourth approach is to try to find ways to harmonize a company's own goals with the changing needs, goals, and expectations of the public. These approaches are referred to, respectively, as an **inactive strategy,** a **reactive strategy,** a **proactive strategy,** and an **interactive strategy** of response to the environment. They are shown in Figure 3-3.

An Inactive Strategy

Many managers are apt to respond initially by resisting, altering their policies only as pressure and criticism mount. Occasionally, however, a company will absolutely refuse to change its behavior in response to the concerns of others.

For example, Quarex Industries, a publicly traded company that the President's Commission on Organized Crime reported had ties to organized crime, repeatedly failed health inspections by authorities in New York, paid small fines, and continued to "short weight" customers, sell unfit food, and operate some of the most unsanitary supermarkets in New York State. For such companies, nothing less than a government edict, court order, or imprisonment of managers will force a modification of behavior. A well-publicized example occurred in 1990 when Eastern Airlines was charged with criminal violations of airline safety rules. The indictment charged that during the late 1980s Eastern's man-

FIGURE 3-3
Four basic strategies of social response.

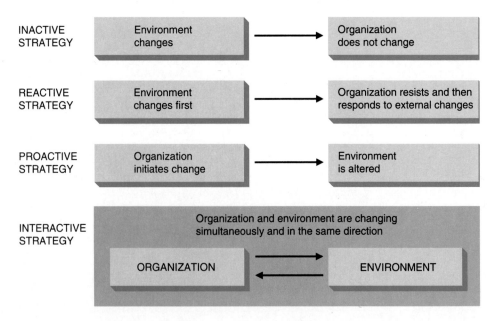

agement failed to implement mandated safety procedures and falsified safety records. This occurred in defiance of federal safety regulations and rules. In 1994, Eastern Airlines ex-Chief Executive Officer Frank Lorenzo was denied permission to start another airline due to the failure to address the safety problems which existed during his leadership of the firm.

A Reactive Strategy

Utilizing a reactive strategy, a firm resists an unanticipated change in its environment after the significant change is under way. Often, company practices will be modified only as strong pressures are applied.

Consider the actions of the makers of aerosol spray products. Scientists discovered in the mid-1970s that chemical propellants, once released into the air, posed a threat to the protective ozone layer in the earth's atmosphere. Without this protection, the earth would be exposed to harmful solar radiation that can cause skin cancer and mutations in plants and animals. The manufacturers initially attempted to defend their products, but after mounting public pressure, they acceded to a 1978 government regulation banning the use of damaging aerosols.

In the mid-1980s, the controversy again heated up, as a large "hole" in the ozone layer was discovered over Antarctica. Pressure was exerted to have chlorofluorocarbons (CFCs), widely used as refrigerants and industrial solvents, banned. Environmental groups pushed for an international agreement of nations to ban the damaging substances, resulting in the Montreal Protocol of 1987, discussed in Chapter 11. A large number of companies that manufactured or used CFCs in their products began to switch to non-CFC alternatives. Although costly, there was a sense that it was necessary to react to new evidence and mounting political pressure.

A Proactive Strategy

Companies utilizing proactive strategies are a step ahead of those that merely react, because they understand the need to get ahead of changes that are occurring in their environments.

Midas International, an automobile repair store, attempted to address the alarming increase in infant and child mortalities and injuries caused during auto accidents. In May 1993, all 1,800 Midas shops participated in launching Project Baby Safe. Each store offered child car seats at a wholesale price of $42. This offer was not tied to any other purchase or service provided by Midas. After the seats were no longer needed, consumers returned them for a certificate good for $42 worth of service. Midas donated used seats to needy families or hospitals. "I can't think of a cause more important than protecting infants and children from accidents," said John R. Moore, Midas's president and chief executive officer.[3]

An Interactive Strategy

When a company is able to anticipate environmental change and blend its own goals with those of the public, it has adopted an interactive strategy. An interactive strategy promotes harmonious relations between a firm and the public by reducing the gap between public expectations and business performance. This is often accomplished through a serious management commitment to dialogue with its stakeholders.

As concerns for protection of the natural environment have grown, for example, many people have criticized the fast food industry for promoting a "throw-away" culture that ignores the ecological consequences of such practices. McDonald's Corporation, the largest fast food company in the world, faced a major strategic challenge. The company's business strategy has rested on speed, service, quality, and consistency. Recycling laws, new packaging, and other ecological issues could seriously affect the way the company does business. To enhance the search for creative solutions, McDonald's reached an agreement with the Environmental Defense Fund (EDF), a leading environmental organization, to cooperate in finding practical options for dealing with the environmental dimensions of McDonald's business. The heart of the agreement is the company's commitment to a continuing dialogue.[4]

Research has demonstrated that, under various conditions, the inactive, reactive, and proactive response strategies may produce temporary, short-run successes for companies. However, evaluations of longer-term successes strongly suggest that an interactive approach brings greater, more lasting benefits for both business and society.[5] Exhibit 3-A describes an organization of companies that is pursuing an interactive strategy with leading environmentalists.

A strategy of response to the social and physical environment depends

---

[3]"Midas Shops Will Offer Child Car Seats at Cost," *Wall Street Journal*, Apr. 22, 1993, p. C20.

[4]"McDonald's Waste Study Planned," *New York Times*, Aug. 2, 1990, p. D18; Peter Nulty, "Recycling Becomes a Big Business," *Fortune*, Aug. 13, 1990, pp. 81–86; "Big Mac Joins with Big Critic to Cut Trash," *Wall Street Journal*, Aug. 3, 1990, p. B1.

[5]James E. Post, *Corporate Behavior and Social Change*, Reston, VA: Reston, 1978; Robert Miles, *Managing the Corporate Social Environment: A Grounded Theory*, Englewood Cliffs, NJ: Prentice-Hall, 1987.

EXHIBIT 3-A

CORPORATE CONSERVATION COUNCIL

As the pressure of a growing concern for environmental issues has increased on business, some companies have sought new ways to break out of the old adversarial relationship with environmental groups. One such effort was begun in 1982 when the Corporate Conservation Council (CCC) was formed.

The council is a division of the National Wildlife Federation (NWF), an environmental organization with nearly 6 million members. Jay Hair, president of NWF, believed that a dialogue with members of industry could occur and would further the cause of conservation and the wise use of natural resources. With a group of corporate leaders from companies such as Du Pont, Dow Chemical, ARCO, Weyerhauser, and USX (formerly U.S. Steel), the Corporate Conservation Council set out to expand the dialogue between industry and the environmental community. Beginning with quarterly meetings at which candid "off the record" discussions were held on key environmental issues such as waste reduction and global warming, the council has expanded into developing policy statements on such problems as hazardous waste and wetlands protection.

In 1988, the council used its Outreach Program to begin a program to create environmental education for business and management students. By 1991, environmental courses were being taught and case studies were being used in universities and colleges in the United States, Europe, and Asia. The commitment to dialogue and the search for "win-win" solutions continues among the current CCC members, including many leading U.S. companies. According to the council's executive director, Barbara Haas, the objective is to use the council as a forum for dialogue.

on how well a manager understands that the environment is changing and that a strategic approach is needed to respond to it. Only then can any of these specific responses be employed. As one author says: "Major strategic shifts in the business environment require conceptual shifts in the minds of managers."[6] Thus managers need to reexamine their assumptions and think about the present and future environment in a way that is accurate, practical, and up-to-date.

THE PUBLIC AFFAIRS FUNCTION

Public pressure on corporations and demands by stakeholders have led many companies to create specialized staff departments to manage stakeholder relationships. The emergence of the corporate **public affairs function** has been a major innovation in U.S. management, replacing and often combining the specialized departments such as government rela-

[6]R. Edward Freeman, *Strategic Management: A Stakeholder Approach*, Marshfield, MA: Pitman, p. 24.

tions, community affairs, media relations, and public relations. This trend is also globally evident as Australian and European firms have also created corporate public affairs departments.[7]

According to one group of experts:

> [T]he essential role of public affairs units appears to be that of a *window out* of the corporation through which management can perceive, monitor, and understand external change, and simultaneously, a *window in* through which society can influence corporate policy and practice. This boundary-spanning role primarily involves the flow of information to and from the organization. In many firms it also involves the flow of financial resources in the form of political contributions to various stakeholder groups in society.[8]

Between 1970 and 1980 more than half (58 percent) of 400 corporations in a Boston University study had established a public affairs unit; an update of that study showed that the trend toward establishing public affairs continued into the 1990s.[9] Today, medium-sized and small businesses are joining larger companies in using the public affairs function as a means of coordinating political, social, and economic initiatives. Figure 3-4 summarizes a broad range of activities that are normally associated with public affairs management. Governmental relations (at the federal, state, and local levels), community relations, and political action account for much of the activity. Yet, many companies also recognize the need to include corporate (charitable) contributions, issues management, and media and public relations.

Many companies have developed a public affairs function that meshes with the company's decision-making system in three key ways. First, public affairs often is responsible for collecting, analyzing, and preparing political and social intelligence for top management. Issues are identified, trends forecasted, and the environment analyzed. Second, public affairs is responsible for communicating important information to a variety of other management groups within the company. Special reports may be prepared for the board of directors, the chief executive officer, strategic planners, and operating managers in different product divisions.[10] Third, public affairs is responsible for developing and executing action programs that target key external stakeholders. Thus a public affairs department

[7]For example, a survey of Australian public affairs departments is in James E. Post and the Australian Centre for Public Affairs, "Australian Public Affairs Practice: Results of the 1992 National Public Affairs Survey," *Research in Corporate Social Performance and Policy*, Greenwich, CT: JAI Press, vol. 14, 1993, pp. 93–103.

[8]Boston University Public Affairs Research Group, *Public Affairs Offices and Their Functions: A Summary of Survey Results*, Boston, MA: Boston University School of Management, 1981, p. 1.

[9]James E. Post and the Foundation for Public Affairs, "The State of Corporate Public Affairs in the United States," *Research in Corporate Social Performance and Policy*, Greenwich, CT: JAI Press, vol. 14, 1993, pp. 81–91.

[10]Thomas G. Marx, "Strategic Planning for Public Affairs," *Long-Range Planning*, Feb. 1990, pp. 9–16.

FIGURE 3-4
Public affairs functions, 1993.

SOURCE: Adapted from James E. Post and the Foundation for Public Affairs, "The State of Corporate Public Affairs in the United States," *Research in Corporate Social Performance and Policy,* Greenwich, CT: JAI Press, vol. 14, 1993, pp. 81–91.

WHAT ACTIVITIES FALL WITHIN YOUR ORGANIZATION'S PUBLIC AFFAIRS FUNCTION?
(N = 159 U.S. firms)

Activity	Percentage of Respondents Saying "Yes"
Federal government regulation	86.8
State government regulation	84.9
Local government regulation	79.9
Community relations	79.2
Political action committee	77.4
(Charitable) contributions	74.8
Grassroots lobbying	73.0
Issues management	73.0
Media relations	71.1
Public relations	67.9

may have a media contacts program, community affairs operations, and federal government lobbying activities. The public affairs organization chart depicted in Figure 3-5 shows how these programs and functions are arranged at a large global company.

Two-thirds of the companies responding to the Boston University study have drafted a public affairs mission statement to define their department's purpose and focus. Most companies have appointed a senior management executive to lead the public affairs department, providing a direct voice or access to the company's major strategy and policy decisions. The size of the department and the support staff provided vary widely across companies. To promote the public affairs function, some companies assign employees from other departments to help plan, coordinate, or participate in public affairs activities. The formulation and implementation of the policies and programs developed by a company's public affairs function are discussed in the following section.

FORMULATING SOCIALLY RESPONSIVE STRATEGIES

Before a social strategy can be formed a corporation must skillfully analyze various influences and forces and then weigh the information collected. This section discusses the multiple environments which impact business and the techniques available to analyze them.

FIGURE 3-5
Public affairs
organization for a
global corporation.

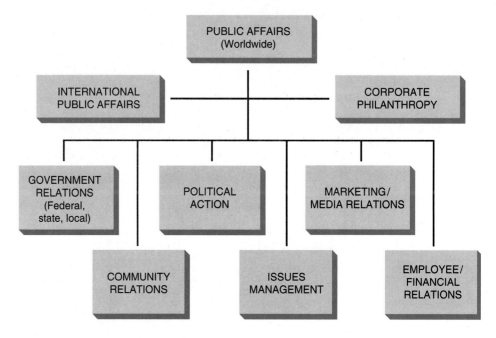

The Macroenvironment of Business

In order to begin formulating a socially responsive strategy, a framework of environmental information is needed. Managers must understand what is occurring in many sectors of the external world. According to two authorities, the environment that is relevant for businesses and their managers consists of four distinct segments: social, economic, political, and technological.[11] This **macroenvironment of business** consists of an almost unlimited amount of information, including facts, trends, issues, and ideas. Each of these segments represents a focused area of information, some of it important and relevant to the business. The Campus Circle Project, described at the beginning of this chapter, is used to illustrate each of the four segments of the macroenvironment of business, shown in Figure 3-6.

The **social segment** focuses on information about (1) demographics, (2) life-styles, and (3) social values of a society. Managers have a need to understand changes in population patterns, characteristics of the population, emergence of new life-styles, and social values that seem to be in or out of favor with the majority of the population.

The social environment of the Avenues West neighborhood was quickly deteriorating. Housing decay and increases in drug traffic, prosti-

---

[11]Liam Fahey and V. K. Narayanan, *Macroenvironmental Analysis for Strategic Management*, St. Paul, MN: West, 1986, pp. 28–29.

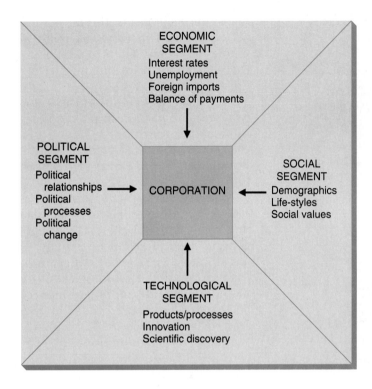

FIGURE 3-6
The macroenvironment of business.

tution, and violent crimes began to challenge the business community's lack of social involvement in the neighborhood. The direct impact of these social conditions upon the viability of business and its stakeholders (local community, customers, employees) was a critical motivation in the formulation of a socially responsive strategy.

The **economic segment** focuses on the general set of economic factors and conditions confronting industries in a society. For example, information about interest rates, unemployment, foreign imports, and many other such factors is relevant to virtually all businesses. The economic segment obviously has a large impact on all business organizations.

This impact was also central to the Campus Circle Project. The conditions in the neighborhood contributed to the overall economic decline in the area. Businesses were considering relocating to a safer, more prosperous suburban Milwaukee industrial park. The costs of doing business near the Avenues West area increased as safety programs were created to protect employees as they walked from the parking lot to work. The economic segment of the macroenvironment of business was central to the project's strategic focus. The socially responsive strategy had to deal with the economic objectives and needs of those involved in the partnership, as well as the social ones.

The **political segment** deals with specific political relationships in society, changes in them, and the processes by which society makes political decisions. Changes in the tax code, for example, redistribute income and tax burdens. This involves political relationships between various segments of society. The creation and dissolution of regulatory institutions that set standards for business behavior are examples of changes in the political process.

A critical participant in the Campus Circle Project was the City of Milwaukee. The partnership relied on a special tax structure to help pay for numerous public improvements to the Avenues West area. Another political relationship was evident on the federal level, as the Campus Circle Project secured a $20 million, five-year grant to supplement the private funding for the project.

The **technological segment** is concerned with the technological progress and potential hazards that are taking place in society. New products, processes, or materials, including any negative social impacts; the general level of scientific activity; and advances in fundamental science (e.g., biology) are the key concerns in this area.

Although the technological segment is often understood in terms of manufacturing development or processes, the Campus Circle Project utilized a somewhat unique technology: urban planning. Extensive drafting and revisions were made to plans calling for housing demolition, construction, or rehabilitation. The relocation of numerous businesses into a centrally located mall was carefully planned and coordinated with the business owners. The city was petitioned to close a stretch of a major avenue that cut through the Avenues West area to ensure greater safety for the residents and to create a buffer between the residential neighborhood and the downtown business district.

The macroenvironment, as presented in Figure 3-6, is a system of interrelated segments, each one connected to and influencing the others. In the Campus Circle Project, social decay had economic consequences for businesses and other organizations in the neighborhood. In order to turn around the Avenues West area, a collaborative partnership of business, government, and educational organizations was formed. This group had to integrate the social, economic, political, and technological segments of their macroenvironment to formulate a socially responsive strategy to address the challenge facing them.

A manager must understand each of these segments, their interrelationships, and those facts which are of direct importance to the corporation. This knowledge will improve his or her understanding of the relevant environment in which strategies must be formulated.

Scanning and Environmental Analysis

In order to effectively formulate socially responsive strategies, managers must learn about the company's external environment. **Environmental scanning** is a managerial process of analyzing the external social, economic, political, and technological environments. Scanning can be done informally or formally, and by individual managers or by teams. It is largely an information collection, analysis, and processing activity, and it is a valuable first step in building a socially responsive strategy for an organization.

Generally, scanning can be done by focusing on one or more of the following: trends that are occurring in government, society, or segments of each; issues that are emerging in one's industry, sector of the economy, or nations where the company conducts business; and stakeholders who are important to the organization currently or who appear to be potentially important in the future.

Trend analysis attempts to understand and project the implications and consequences of current trends into the future. Companies whose products or services have particularly long life spans have a special need for understanding long-term trends. The life insurance industry, for example, regularly enters into individual contracts that have a life span of twenty, thirty, or even fifty years. Policyholders may pay premiums on a life insurance policy for decades before the company is required to make payment on the policy. Trends such as increasing life spans and more active lifestyles also can alter the calculation of how many years an insurer may have to pay out on a pension plan or annuity. The failure to understand such trends and their implications can result in poor financial planning that injures the company and the insurance beneficiary or pension recipient.

Issues analysis involves a careful assessment of specific concerns that are having, or may have, an impact on the company. In many companies, public affairs managers do detailed tracking and monitoring of taxation proposals in state legislatures and the Congress. Because tax proposals frequently involve highly technical and specific aspects of a company's business (e.g., depreciation rates for different types of equipment), it is often crucial for a company's top management to know the specific dollar effects of proposed bills or regulations. In manufacturing and natural resource industries, for example, it is not unusual for companies to have one or more specialists whose entire job is to track the development of such proposals and assess each one's impact on the company. This analysis becomes the basis for the company's lobbying or other political activities.

Stakeholder analysis places the scanner's focus on the people, groups, and organizations that populate the external environment. By trying to understand the issues that are of concern to the company's primary and secondary stakeholders, managers are better able to predict what types of demands are going to be made in the months ahead. There are many ways to collect such information, ranging from professional reporting services that track leaders of activist groups to direct contacts and discussions with stakeholder representatives. Informal discussions with union leaders or local environmentalists can go a long way toward providing managers with an understanding of what is critical to these groups and why.

IMPLEMENTING SOCIAL RESPONSIVENESS

Companies do not become socially responsive overnight. The process takes time. New attitudes have to be developed, new routines learned, and new policies and action programs designed. Once a company is prepared to implement a social strategy, it must follow specific guidelines to achieve its social objectives. Many obstacles must be overcome in implementing socially responsive strategies. Some are structural, such as the reporting relationships between groups of managers; others are cultural, such as a historical pattern of only men or women in a particular job category.

A Model of Corporate Social Responsiveness

An early model of how large corporations effectively implement socially responsive policies is illustrated in Figure 3-7. There are three stages to the responsiveness process depicted in this model. Each is discussed below.

The policy stage

The first stage of social responsiveness involves being aware of which part of the surrounding environment needs to be responded to and acted upon by the company. Awareness may occur after stakeholder expectations change, or it may result from a systematic environmental analysis. Whether or not stakeholder pressure exists, a company's management

FIGURE 3-7

A three-stage model of corporate social responsiveness.

SOURCE: Adapted from Robert W. Ackerman and Raymond A. Bauer, *Corporate Social Responsiveness: The Modern Dilemma*, Reston, VA: Reston, 1976.

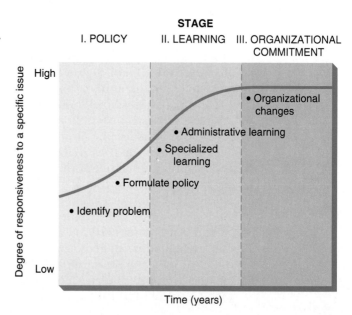

may think, based on the company's own environmental analysis, that a response is needed to emerging issues, concerns, or social trends.

> For example, a group of Boston businesses announced a $6 million program designed to guarantee financial aid to all graduates of the city's public high schools who get into college and to provide jobs for those who complete their education. This effort was taken in reaction to a dramatic increase in the dropout rate among Boston-area high school students. In addition to the funds provided, 350 Boston-area companies pledged to help provide jobs to high school graduates, and many offered to help pay for guidance counselors in the schools. This commitment served two purposes: the students and schools were helped, and the companies ensured themselves a future pool of applicants for entry-level jobs.[12]
>
> A continued awareness of the crisis in education and its impact on business is apparent in the 1990s. The Edison Project, a for-profit education firm, has assumed the management of three Boston-area schools. A dozen additional elementary and high schools have been turned over to Boston companies. By 1994, eight states had "charter schools," educational institutions owned and operated by for-profit companies and ten more states are considering this opportunity.[13]

Social responses need to be guided by policies that are carefully and deliberately developed by top management and the board of directors. Those policies provide a framework for shaping other aspects of the organization's response. New production policies, for example, may result in better quality control for consumer products, may remove job hazards, and may reduce water pollution all at the same time.

The learning stage

Once a social problem—for example, excessive numbers of high school dropouts—has been identified, and once a general policy—for example, an educational opportunity policy—has been adopted, the company must learn how to tackle the problem and make the new policy work. Two kinds of learning are needed: specialized learning and administrative learning.

Specialized learning occurs when a "sociotechnical" expert—for example, an inner-city educator who is thoroughly familiar with the culture, life-styles, motivations, and special problems of high school youth—is em-

---

[12]Fox Butterfield, "Funds and Jobs Pledged to Boston Graduates," *New York Times,* Sept. 10, 1986, p. D25.

[13]"Private Groups to Run 15 Schools in Experiment by Massachusetts," *New York Times,* Mar. 19, 1994, pp. 1, 8. Business involvement in public school education is discussed in detail in "Breaking the Mold: The Private Sector's Accelerating Role in Public Education," *Business Week,* Oct. 17, 1994, pp. 122–153.

ployed to advise company officers and managers. The kind of specialized knowledge that the sociotechnical expert brings to the company is particularly helpful in the early stages of social responsiveness when the company is dealing with an unfamiliar social problem, whether it is high school dropouts, prejudice against minorities in hiring practices, excessive pollution, or toxic chemical hazards.

Administrative learning occurs when a company's supervisors and managers—those who administer the organization's daily affairs—become familiar with new routines that are necessary to cope with a social problem. A technical expert can assist the company in taking its first steps to solve a problem but cannot do the whole job alone. Social responsiveness requires the full cooperation and knowledge of line managers as well as staff experts. Personal involvement is essential.

> Managers of businesses involved in supporting the education systems in their cities have had to learn many new skills. For example, Dianne Sullivan, the president of Miraflores Designs in New York, pledged to help sixty East Harlem students. Then, the day before school started in September, she learned that they did not know which junior high school they were supposed to attend. Sullivan immediately telephoned the local school superintendent and worked to solve the problem. Had she not done so, many of the students might have missed the program's beginning.[14]

The organizational commitment stage

One final step is needed to achieve full social responsiveness: an organization must "institutionalize" its new social policy.[15] The new policies and routines learned in the first two stages should become so well accepted throughout the entire company that they are considered to be a normal part of doing business. In other words, they should be a part of the company and its standard operating procedures. For example, when managers respond to the needs of the local education system or to the students without having to rely upon special directives from top management, the socially responsive policy can be considered to be institutionalized.

The normal organizational pressures to resist change mean that both effort and time are needed to improve a corporation's responsiveness. In the past, it took large corporations an average of six to eight years to progress from the first stage to the third stage on any given social issue or problem such as equal employment opportunity or pollution control. Yet some firms are more flexible than others, and some social problems are easier to handle than others, so the time involved may vary considerably. It is clear, however, that a combination of internal factors, especially man-

---

[14]Jane Perlez, "Public Schools and the Private Sector," *New York Times*, Sept. 14, 1986, p. 14.
[15]Robert Ackerman, "How Companies Respond to Social Demands," *Harvard Business Review*, July–Aug. 1973, pp. 88–98.

agement willpower, and external factors, especially continued stakeholder action on the problem, is necessary for effective change to occur.[16]

Framework for Social Policy

After reaching the organizational commitment stage the company must develop specific guidelines to direct the strategic social policy. Two scholars in the strategic management field have created a set of guidelines to enhance the success of a business's social policy. They believe that social policies should:

- "... concentrate action programs on *limited objectives.* No company can take significant action in every area of social responsibility. It can achieve more if it selects areas in which to concentrate its efforts. ...
- "... concentrate action programs on *areas strategically related to the* present and prospective *economic functions* of the business. ...
- "... begin action programs *close at home* before spreading out or acting in far distant regions. ...
- "... *facilitate employee action* which they can take as individuals rather than as representatives of the company. ..."[17]

MAKING A SOCIAL STRATEGY WORK

Countless obstacles impede effective implementation of management policy in the modern corporation. As illustrated in Figure 3-8, top management often targets those factors that can influence change: corporate culture, organizational structures, evaluation and reward systems, and public disclosure. Companies that have demonstrated significant success in being socially responsive to their stakeholders and the environment have recognized that new attitudes, as well as new structures and new incentives, are needed.

Corporate Culture

The culture of an organization—that is, its traditions, customs, and values—affects employees and the company's stakeholders. In companies with a strong commitment to social strategy, top management uses a variety of

---

[16]Miles, op. cit.
[17]From Archie B. Carroll and Frank Hoy, "Integrating Corporate Social Policy into Strategic Management," *Journal of Business Strategy,* Winter 1984, pp. 48–57, emphasis added. Also see Craig Smith, "The New Corporate Philanthropy," *Harvard Business Review,* May–June 1994, pp. 105–116.

FIGURE 3-8
Influences on a corporate social strategy.

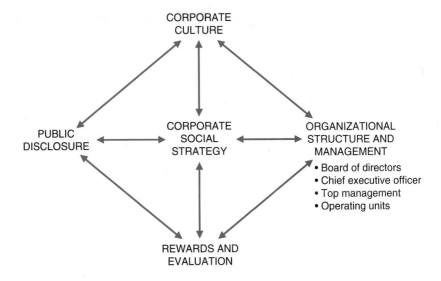

tools to encourage a climate of respect for social values and stakeholder interests. These may include a demonstrated personal commitment by top-level managers to desirable social goals, symbolic company actions (such as developing and enforcing a code of conduct) to dramatize a strong social commitment, and training programs that teach employees and managers how to respond positively to stakeholders' demands.

As illustrated in Figure 3-8, a corporation's culture is directly, and critically, linked to the social strategy top management is trying to achieve. Moreover, it is indirectly but clearly connected to the organization's structure, rewards and evaluation activities, and willingness to disclose information. All of these areas of organizational life contribute to the development of a corporation that "stands for something" in the eyes of the employees, customers, community members, and other stakeholders. The corporate culture is the practical means that managers have for translating their social "vision" into actions that reach all of the corporation's stakeholders.

Organizational Structure and Management

A corporation cannot achieve any strategy if it is organized improperly. An organization's structure is the "architecture" that helps determine how it will look to others and how it will perform for its stakeholders. The most important organizational components are examined next.

Board of directors

Corporate response often begins with the board of directors. The board is responsible for the basic policy and strategy of the firm. Many corporate social actions are major ones that require board approval. The board needs to improve its interaction with the environment in order to gain more social understanding. The directors need to learn what is happening in the social world in the same way that they historically have sought to know what is happening in the economic world.

One way to increase social inputs to the board is to increase the number of outside members, as compared with insiders who also are top managers of the company. Outside directors generally have a broader perspective and sometimes may possess specialized social knowledge. Another suggestion is to appoint stakeholder representatives as board members: minorities, women, consumers, environmentalists, labor union representatives, and others who might contribute distinctive social viewpoints to corporate policies.

Many large corporations have a public responsibility committee within the board of directors. The job of such a committee is to monitor the social environment, identify social and political issues most likely to affect the firm, and make recommendations to the full board for appropriate actions.

Chief executive officer

The chief executive officer (CEO) is the link between the board's policies and the top management group that must put policies into action. CEOs often spend substantial amounts of time on external affairs that affect their companies. An active and socially alert CEO can keep both the board and top management well informed, thereby increasing the firm's chances of responding meaningfully to external pressures.

Top management

While the board of directors and the CEO can work together to establish general social policies for a company, the company's upper-level managers should translate these broad guidelines into operational plans and programs. For example, the board of directors of a large food manufacturer wanted to demonstrate the company's concern for members of the city's poorer neighborhoods. Top officers of the company, after consulting with production and marketing departments, decided to donate excess inventories of canned goods to selected community agencies. The costs of the program were absorbed by the public affairs department. In this way, a policy favored by the public affairs managers became a practical reality through top management planning. The participation of many business firms in such major activities as elder care, literacy, and antidrug education efforts was implemented in similar ways.

Operating units

Change eventually affects operating departments, and usually its impact is greatest there. Since traditional ways of work must be revised to conform with new programs, change always brings some operating costs, regard-

less of the benefits that eventually may occur. In the case of social involvement, there often are high beginning costs, while the benefits are long
range, often indirect, and sometimes not very evident to an individual department. As a result, from a department's point of view a cost-benefit
analysis may be negative; therefore, management faces an additional task
of providing resources that can help departments to develop a long-term
perspective. Nevertheless, it is in the plant, the office, the mine, and the
field location—where a company actually conducts its business—that top-
level social policies and goals either succeed or fail.

Rewards and Evaluation

Success or failure in social programming generally depends on the same
kinds of factors that operate in normal business situations. Is there
enough money allocated for the program? Is a qualified person in charge?
Is there proper follow-up and review? And, most importantly, are managers and employees motivated to be socially responsive? Peter Jones, former senior vice president and corporate counsel of Levi Strauss, a company that has often appeared among lists of the most socially responsive
companies in America, stated the problem succinctly: "The key to getting
the desired type of behavior in the modern corporation is providing
enough countervailing pressures—either incentives or sanctions—to overcome the incentives to behave in the undesired way."[18]

When Du Pont's chief executive, E. S. Woolard, committed the company
to become a leader in corporate environmentalism, the compensation of
all managers was tied to the speed and effectiveness of their environmental program. This approach is a vital way of convincing operating managers that the policy is not mere "window dressing"; if they wish to receive
their "normal" bonuses, they must make environmental improvement
part of their normal performance.[19]

Public Disclosure

Public disclosure of information by a firm is an important component to
ensure a successful social strategy. At one time, only financial performance data were presented in annual reports. By 1990, however, the pressure for greater disclosure of social performance information had led 90
percent of the top 500 corporations to include information about their social activities in the company's annual report to shareholders. A few com-

---

[18]Peter R. Jones, "Sanctions, Incentives and Corporate Behavior," in R. B. Dickie and L.
Rouner, eds., *Corporations and the Common Good*, South Bend, IN: University of Notre Dame
Press, 1986, pp. 118–137.
[19]E. S. Woolard, Address to National Wildlife Federation/Corporate Conservation Council,
Jan. 30, 1990.

panies, such as General Motors, Bank of America, and Atlantic Richfield, published special yearly reports detailing the company's efforts to be a socially responsible member of the community. In the insurance industry, the Clearing House for Corporate Social Involvement has collected and published reports about member companies' performance in such socially important areas as equal employment opportunity, inner-city investments, and charitable contributions.

Public disclosure of social strategies in general is done on a mostly voluntary basis in the United States, but it is required in nations such as Germany, France, and Spain.[20] Social performance reporting is more highly advanced in Europe because of the commitment of both government and companies to its implementation, and because of pressure from activist trade unions and national political parties.

CONCLUSION

The true measure of a company's social responsiveness is how well its core activities reflect a concern for stakeholders. Companies display basic strategies for responding to these issues. This chapter has focused on the relationship between a company's business and social strategies, their interconnections, and the actions needed to infuse social responsibility into the organization and its activities.

SUMMARY POINTS OF THIS CHAPTER

- Due to performance-expectations gaps confronting business, borne out by the changing social climate evident in the 1960s and 1970s, managers have recognized the need to develop formal social response strategies and programs.
- Businesses respond to stakeholders' demands through an inactive strategy, reactive strategy, proactive strategy, or interactive strategy.
- The public affairs function is the mechanism many companies use to organize and manage their responses to social challenges and other external relationships.
- By addressing the social, economic, political, and technological segments which make up the macroenvironment of business, social response strategies can develop positive business-stakeholder relationships. Environmental scanning is an important part of these strategies.

[20]Meinolf Dierkes and Ariane Berthoin Antal, "Whither Corporate Social Reporting: Is It Time to Legislate?" *California Management Review*, Spring 1986, pp. 106–121.

- The implementation of socially responsive strategies and policies is a major challenge to business. The objective is to build a corporate culture that encourages and rewards socially responsible behavior. Managers can use structure, rewards and evaluation, and public disclosure to improve corporate social responsiveness.

KEY TERMS AND CONCEPTS USED IN THIS CHAPTER

- Collaborative partnerships
- Corporate social responsiveness
- Inactive strategy
- Reactive strategy
- Proactive strategy
- Interactive strategy
- Public affairs function
- Macroenvironment of business: social, economic, political, and technological segments
- Environmental scanning

DISCUSSION CASE

STRIDE RITE CORPORATION

The challenge of acting responsibly in both the social and economic environments is illustrated by the actions taken by Stride Rite Corporation. Senior management was committed to being responsive to its social stakeholders, while also being sensitive to their obligations to company stockholders.[21] These two objectives left people wondering: Was Stride Rite successful in being a socially responsive company as well as an economically viable enterprise?

Stride Rite had been at the forefront of corporate social responsiveness for decades. The firm received numerous public service awards and consistently allocated 5 percent of pre-tax profits to the firm's foundation for charitable contributions. In addition to cash contributions, Stride Rite provided sneakers to children in Mozambique, paid Harvard graduates to work in Cambodian refugee camps, and made available to inner-city youths scholarships to attend Harvard University. Employees at Stride Rite participated in the firm's social programs as tutors to disadvantaged children. In response to employees' requests, the firm became a corporate leader in the integration of its on-site day-care and elder-care programs at many of its facilities. Elderly people at the company centers assisted in providing day-care to the children of Stride Rite employees. In 1992, Stride

[21]Much of the corporate information was taken from "Social Responsibility and Need for Low Cost Clash at Stride Rite," *Wall Street Journal,* May 28, 1993, pp. A1, A4.

Rite joined fifty-four other companies to form the Businesses for Social Responsibility, a group of U.S. corporations committed to various social programs (presented in Chapter 2, Exhibit 2-C).

This list of exemplary corporate social activities certainly portrayed Stride Rite as a socially responsive business. Yet, there was another picture to consider—that is, the economic side of Stride Rite.

Beginning in the 1980s, Stride Rite made a number of corporate decisions based on economic grounds which had significant social consequences. In 1981, the company moved its corporate headquarters from Boston's rough inner-city and economically depressed Roxbury to Cambridge. During the next six years Stride Rite scaled down its operations at the Roxbury plant, which had employed 2,500 workers. By 1994, the plant was completely closed and Stride Rite had significantly contributed to the rising level of unemployment in Roxbury.

Over a dozen plant closings within the Stride Rite system of operations had severe consequences for its workers and local communities. Each of these decisions was based upon strong economic grounds. Moving operations out of the Northeast was financially justified since operations in Asian countries were established with substantially lower labor costs. Distribution centers located in the Midwest were more economical than centers operating in the Northeast due to the Midwest's proximity to the majority of Stride Rite's customers in the Midwest and South. A distribution site in Louisville, Kentucky, eliminated 800 to 1,200 miles of traveling on some routes, increasing delivery time by two to five days. One Stride Rite distribution site in Kentucky received $24 million in tax breaks over ten years, compared to the $3 million offered in tax breaks if Stride Rite had stayed in Massachusetts.

Stride Rite demonstrated a keen concern for the social welfare of various domestic and global stakeholders. The company committed financial and human resources, as well as products, to those in need. At the same time, the firm made a number of tough business decisions based on economic criteria which had severe impacts upon their workers and local communities. Stride Rite was a firm which tried to satisfy both its social commitments and its economic obligations. And, as we can see, this was indeed a difficult task.

Discussion Questions

1. What qualifies a company to be called "socially responsive"? Was Stride Rite a socially responsive firm? What facts would support your answer?
2. How far can a socially responsive firm be expected to go? How does a firm balance its social commitments with its economic obligations? Did Stride Rite do a reasonable job in maintaining this balance between social and economic goals? Give reasons to support your answer.

3. Should Stride Rite maintain an economically inefficient plant for the sake of maintaining employment in an economically depressed community?

4. Does a firm have to sacrifice some social obligations to remain competitive? How does a company draw the line? Did Stride Rite draw the line correctly?

5. Using the Key Terms and Concepts list for this chapter, explain which terms and concepts apply to this discussion case. Be specific and give reasons.

PART TWO

The Corporation and Ethical Issues

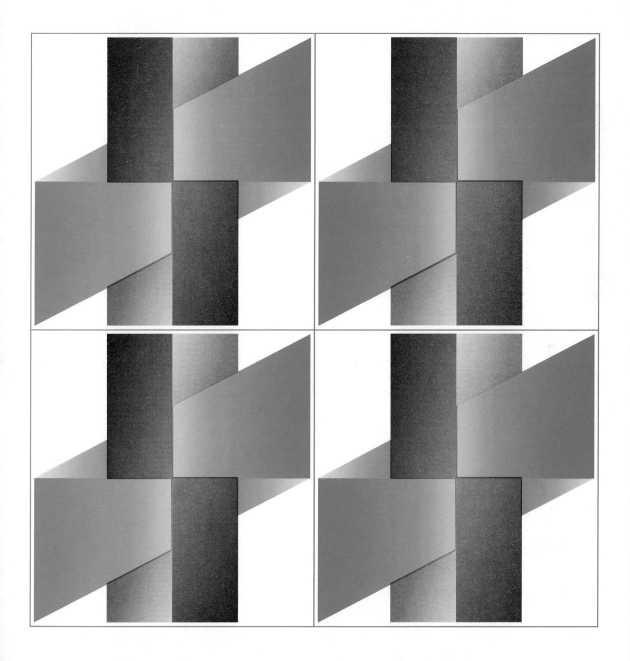

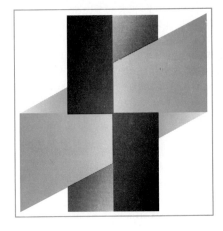

4

Ethical Dilemmas in Business

People who work in business—managers and employees alike—frequently encounter and must deal with on-the-job ethical issues. Learning how to recognize the different kinds of ethical dilemmas and knowing why they occur is an important business skill. The costs to business and to society of unethical and illegal behavior are very large. A business firm is more likely to gain public approval and social legitimacy if it adheres to basic ethical principles and society's laws.

Key Questions and Chapter Objectives

This chapter focuses on these key questions and objectives:

■ What is ethics? What is business ethics?
■ Why should business be ethical?
■ What major types of ethical issues are found in business?
■ Why do ethics problems occur in business?
■ Do similar ethical issues arise globally?
■ Are ethical behavior and legal behavior the same?

Roger Worsham had just graduated as an accounting major with an MBA degree and had landed a job with a small regional accounting firm in northern Michigan. Working there would give him the experience he needed to qualify as a certified public accountant (CPA). He, his wife, and their two small children settled in to enjoy small-town life. Roger's employer was experiencing tough competition from large accounting firms that were able to offer more varied services, including management consulting, computerized data processing services, and financial advice. Losing a big client could mean the difference between staying open or closing down one of the local offices.[1]

During one of his first audit assignments of a local savings and loan (S&L) company, Roger uncovered evidence of fraud. The S&L was restricted by law at that time to mortgages based on residential property, but it had loaned money to a manufacturing company. To conceal this illegal loan from Roger, someone had removed the file before he began the audit. Roger suspected that the guilty party might have been the S&L president, who, in addition to being the largest owner of the manufacturing firm, was also a very influential lawyer in town.

Roger took the evidence of wrongdoing to his boss, expecting to hear that the accounting firm would include it in the audit report, as required by standard accounting practices. Instead, he was told to put the evidence and all of his notes through a shredder. His boss said, "I will take care of this privately. We simply cannot afford to lose this client." When Roger hesitated, he was told, "You put those papers through the shredder or I'll guarantee that you'll never get a CPA in Michigan, or work in an accounting office in this state for the rest of your life."

Question: If you were Roger, what would you do? If you were Roger's boss, would you have acted differently? What is the ethical thing to do?

Roger Worsham is not alone in grappling with an ethical dilemma at work. Imagine you are employed at the European Bank for Reconstruction and Development. The primary mission of the bank is to assist in financing the reconstruction of eastern Europe. The bank reports that it is unable to fulfill its mission at this time. However, the bank has been able to find $85 million to fund an interior decoration project for its corporate offices, including over $1 million to change the marble in a reception area. Despite rising furor over the situation, the bank president refuses to apologize. Only later does he resign.[2]

Question: As an employee at the bank, what would you do as you witnessed the elaborate redecoration project while the basic corporate mission remained unfulfilled? If the bank president fails to assume responsibility, do you as an employee have any obligation to correct this injustice? What is the ethical thing to do?

Ethical puzzles like these occur frequently in business. They are troubling to the people involved. Sometimes, a person's most basic ideas of fairness, honesty, and integrity are at stake. This chapter explores the meaning of ethics, identifies the different types of ethical problems that occur in business, and tells why these dilemmas arise. A discussion of cor-

---

[1]More details about this episode are in LaRue Tone Hosmer, *The Ethics of Management,* 3d. ed., Homewood, IL: Irwin, 1991, pp. 164–168. See also "Big Eight Firms Woo Little Guy in an Effort to Grow," *Wall Street Journal,* Jan. 17, 1989, p. B2.

[2]Eugene Robinson, "Europe's Aid Bank Helps Itself First," *Washington Post,* Apr. 23, 1993, p. A1; and Richard W. Stevenson, "European Bank Chief Quits Amid Criticisms of Spending," *New York Times,* June 26, 1993, p. A35.

porate crime illustrates the relationship of law and ethics. Chapter 5 then tells how ethical performance in business can be improved by providing some tools for grappling with on-the-job ethical dilemmas.

THE MEANING OF ETHICS

Ethics is a conception of right and wrong conduct. Ethics tells us when our behavior is moral and when it is immoral. Ethics deals with fundamental human relationships—how we think and behave toward others and how we want them to think and behave toward us. Ethical principles are guides to moral behavior. For example, in most societies lying, stealing, deceiving, and harming others are considered to be unethical and immoral. Honesty, keeping promises, helping others, and respecting the rights of others are considered to be ethically and morally desirable behavior. Such basic rules of behavior are essential for the preservation and continuation of organized life everywhere.

These notions of right and wrong come from many sources. Religious beliefs are a major source of ethical guidance for many. The family institution—whether two parents, a single parent, or a large family with brothers and sisters, grandparents, aunts, cousins, and other kin—imparts a sense of right and wrong to children as they grow up. Schools and schoolteachers, neighbors and neighborhoods, friends, admired role models, ethnic groups—and of course, the ever-present television—influence what we believe to be right and wrong in life. The totality of these learning experiences creates in each person a concept of ethics, morality, and socially acceptable behavior. This core of ethical beliefs then acts as a moral compass that helps to guide a person when ethical puzzles arise.

Ethical ideas are present in all societies, all organizations, and all individual persons, although they may vary greatly from one to another. Your ethics may not be exactly the same as your neighbor's, or one particular religion's notion of morality may not be identical to another's, or what is considered ethical in one society may be forbidden in another society. These differences raise the important and controversial issue of **ethical relativism,** which is the question of whether ethical principles should be defined by various periods of time in history, a society's traditions, the special circumstances of the moment, or personal opinion. If so, the meaning given to ethics would be relative to time, place, circumstance, and the person involved. In that case, there would be no universal ethical standards on which people around the globe could agree. For companies conducting business in several societies at one time, this question can be vitally important, and we discuss those issues in more detail later in this chapter.

For the moment, however, we can say that, in spite of the diverse systems of ethics that exist within our own society and throughout the world, all people everywhere do depend on ethical systems to tell them whether their actions are right or wrong, moral or immoral, approved or disapproved. Ethics, in this sense, is a universal human trait, found everywhere.

What Is Business Ethics?

Business ethics is the application of general ethical ideas to business behavior. Business ethics is not a special set of ethical ideas different from ethics in general and applicable only to business. If dishonesty is considered to be unethical and immoral, then anyone in business who is dishonest with employees, customers, stockholders, or competitors is acting unethically and immorally. If protecting others from harm is considered to be ethical, then a company that recalls a dangerously defective product is acting in an ethical way. To be considered ethical, business must draw its ideas about what is proper behavior from the same sources as everyone else. Business should not try to make up its own definitions of what is right and wrong. Employees and managers may believe at times that they are permitted or even encouraged to apply special or weaker ethical rules to business situations, but society does not condone or permit such an exception. People who work in business are bound by the same ethical principles that apply to others.

Figure 4-1 shows what executives from 300 U.S. and non-U.S. corporations consider to be ethical issues in business. Nearly half (45 percent) of the issues involve employee relations—in other words, the way people interact with each other and are treated on the job. About one-fifth of the issues deal with customer relations. Community ethical concerns account for another one-fifth of the list.

These same executives, when asked to name the ethical issues they believed would be very important in the following years, identified six as particularly important: environmental issues (86 percent said it would be a serious or critical issue), product safety (78 percent scored it serious or critical), employee health screening (77 percent), security of company records (73 percent), shareholder interests (70 percent), and workplace safety (70 percent). These are the ethical challenges in business, as they see them.[3] All of these issues are given special attention in later chapters of this book.

Why Should Business Be Ethical?

Why should business be ethical? What prevents a business firm from piling up as many profits as it can, in any way it can, regardless of ethical considerations? For example, what is wrong with Roger Worsham's boss

[3]Ronald E. Berenbeim, *Corporate Ethics,* New York: The Conference Board, 1987, pp. 3–4.

IS THIS AN ETHICAL ISSUE FOR BUSINESS?

The Views of 300 Corporate Executives
in the United States, Canada, Europe, Japan, and Australia

Issue	Percent Saying "Yes"
Widespread Agreement (High majority)	
Employee conflicts of interest	91
Inappropriate gifts to corporate personnel	91
Sexual harassment	85
Unauthorized payments	84
Affirmative action	84
Employee privacy	84
Environmental issues	82
Moderate Level of Agreement (High to moderate majority)	
Employee health screening	79
Conflicts between company's ethics and foreign business practices	77
Security of company records	76
Workplace safety	76
Advertising content	74
Product safety standards	74
Corporate contributions	68
Shareholder interests	68
Corporate due process	65
Whistle-blowing	63
Employment at will	62
Disinvestment (e.g., from South Africa)	59
Government contract issues (e.g., overcharging)	59
Financial and cash management procedures	55
Plant/facility closures and downsizing	55
Political action committees	55
No Consensus (Less than a majority)	
Social issues raised by religious organizations	47
Comparable worth (of men's and women's jobs/salaries)	43
Product pricing	42
Executive salaries	37

telling him to destroy evidence of a client's fraudulent conduct? Why not just shred the papers, thereby keeping a good customer happy (and saving Roger's job, too)? Figure 4-2 lists the major reasons why business firms should promote a high level of ethical behavior.

We mentioned one reason when discussing social responsibility in Chapter 2. *The general public expects business to exhibit high levels of ethical performance and social responsibility.* Companies that fail to fulfill this public demand can expect to be spotlighted, criticized, curbed, and punished.

FIGURE 4-2
Why should
business be
ethical?

REASONS FOR BUSINESS TO BE ETHICAL

- Fulfill public expectations for business
- Prevent harming others
- Improve business relations and employee productivity
- Reduce penalties under the U.S. Corporate Sentencing Guidelines
- Protect business from others
- Protect employees from their employers
- Promote personal morality

Measuring up to public expectations of high ethical behavior is one way for business to gain widespread public approval. It means that business and society, working together in partnership, have found ways to enjoy the economic benefits of business while adhering to ethical principles of conduct.

A second reason why businesses and their employees should act ethically is to *prevent harm to the general public and the corporation's many stakeholders.* One of the strongest ethical principles is stated very simply: "Do no harm." A company that is careless in disposing of toxic chemical wastes that cause disease and death is breaking this ethical injunction. Many ethical rules operate to protect society against various types of harm, and business is expected to observe these commonsense ethical principles.

Some people argue that another reason for businesses to be ethical is that it pays, since ethical behavior is related to *better business relations and productivity in the workplace.* Being ethical imparts a sense of trust which promotes positive alliances among business partners. If this trust is broken, the unethical party may be shunned and ignored. This situation occurred in 1994 when Malaysian government officials gave the "cold shoulder" to French executives. When asked why they were being unfriendly, a Malaysian dignitary replied: "Your chairman is in jail!"[4] The nurturing of an ethical environment and the development of ethical safeguards, discussed in the next chapter, can be critical incentives for improving business relations and employee and organizational productivity.[5]

The U.S. Corporate Sentencing Guidelines provide a strong incentive for businesses to promote ethics at work. The sentencing guidelines come

---

[4]"Scandals Crimp Business for French Firms," *Wall Street Journal,* Oct. 20, 1994, p. A20.
[5]Frances Burke and Amy Black, "Improving Organizational Productivity: Add Ethics," *Public Productivity and Management Review,* vol. 14, no. 2, 1990, pp. 121–133; and Marion M. Staples, "The Quality-Ethics Connection," *Quality Progress,* June 1994, pp. 73–75.

into play when an employee of a firm has been found guilty of a criminal wrongdoing. To determine sentencing a federal judge computes a "culpability (or degree of blame) score" under the equations contained in the guidelines. The score is significantly affected if a firm's ethics program monitors and aggressively responds to reported criminal violations at work. Under the sentencing guidelines, corporate executives found guilty of criminal activity could receive lighter penalties if their firm has developed a strong ethics program.[6]

A fifth reason for promoting ethical behavior is to *protect business firms from abuse by unethical employees and unethical competitors.* Security experts estimate that one out of every three employees has stolen from their employer. Employee theft and embezzlement cost U.S. businesses $40 billion annually.[7] For the retail industry, it is a larger cost to store owners than customer shoplifting. One of the reasons for the magnitude of the problem is the difficulty of detecting the crime. Store owners admit that they are often at the mercy of the employees to act honestly. A startling example of employee theft was discovered in 1994 involving an MCI Communications employee. The employee was arrested by U.S. Secret Service agents after it was alleged that he stole more than 60,000 telephone-card numbers which were sold on the international black market. More than $50 million in revenues was lost by the four major telephone carriers.[8]

High ethical performance also *protects people who work in business.* Employees resent invasions of privacy (such as unjustified polygraph tests) or being ordered to do something against their personal convictions (such as falsifying an accounting report) or being forced to work in hazardous conditions (such as entering unventilated coal mines or being exposed to dangerous agricultural pesticides in the fields). Businesses that treat their employees with dignity and integrity reap many rewards in the form of high morale and improved productivity. It is a win-win-win situation for the firm, its employees, and society.

A final reason for promoting ethics in business is a personal one. *Most people want to act in ways that are consistent with their own sense of right and wrong.* Being pressured to contradict their personal values creates much emotional stress. Knowing that one works in a supportive ethical climate contributes to one's sense of psychological security. People feel good

[6]For a thorough discussion of the U.S. Corporate Sentencing Guidelines, see Jeffrey M. Kaplan and William K. Perry, "The High Cost of Corporate Crime," *Management Accounting,* Dec. 1991, pp. 43–46; and Dan R. Dalton, Michael B. Metzger, and John W. Hill, "The 'New' U.S. Sentencing Commission Guidelines: A Wake-up Call for Corporate America," *Academy of Management Executive,* vol. 8, no. 1, 1994, pp. 7–13.

[7]"Businesses Lose Billions of Dollars to Employee Theft," *Wall Street Journal,* Oct. 5, 1992, p. 32; and Joan Delaney, "Handcuffing Employee Theft," *Small Business Reports,* July 1993, pp. 29–31.

[8]"MCI Worker Charged in U.S. Investigation of Phone-Card Fraud," *Wall Street Journal,* Oct. 4, 1994, p. B7.

about working for an ethical company because they know they are protected along with the general public.

TYPES OF BUSINESS ETHICS ISSUES

Not all ethics issues in business are the same. Some occur as people interact with each other on the job. These are everyday face-to-face ethical
dilemmas related to people's jobs. Ethics issues at this level often have a
very human, personal dimension. Other ethics issues deal with large-scale
problems such as oil spills, hazardous waste disposal, and a company's attitudes about honesty in advertising or sponsoring television programs
that feature violence. These companywide problems are focused at a
higher level of organizational authority and require top-management
policy decisions. Still other kinds of ethical puzzles appear in the different
operational areas of business, such as accounting, marketing, finance,
information systems, and others. These three types of ethics issues—**face-
to-face ethics, corporate policy ethics,** and **functional-area ethics**—
are depicted in Figure 4-3 and discussed next.

Face-to-Face Ethics

Problems having an ethical dimension appear frequently in most business
firms. That is because there is a human element in most business transactions. For example, it is normal for a supervisor who works with a group
of employees on a day-to-day basis to get to know something about their
personal lives, whether they have children or elderly parents, what their
professional goals are, and the various kinds of personal and family crises
they encounter. The same kind of personal relationship may develop between a purchasing agent and the sales representative who sells supplies
to a company; they frequently know one another on a first-name basis,
have lunch together, and talk often on the telephone. A company's best
customers may be well known to people in the production department; it
helps to ensure that the company's products fit the customers' needs. And
every business firm has an informal network or "grapevine" that links employees together into small groups whose members interact closely with
one another.

  Because business is composed of these human interactions, it should
not be surprising that face-to-face ethics issues occur from time to time.
Studies have shown that managers and employees commonly encounter
these "everyday moral issues" as they go about their work. Many of these
ethical issues are listed in Figure 4-1. Observations of unethical acts by a
predominantly female group of employees are shown in Figure 4-4. Exhibit 4-A lets managers tell in their own words how they view some of
these situations.

FIGURE 4-3
Diverse types of
ethics in business.

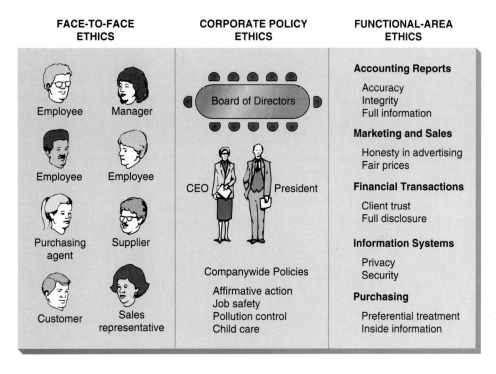

| FACE-TO-FACE ETHICS | CORPORATE POLICY ETHICS | FUNCTIONAL-AREA ETHICS |

As mentioned earlier, managers and employees face conflicts when their own personal standards differ from job demands. Particularly difficult are the giving of gifts and kickbacks to gain business, unfair discrimination in dealing with others, unfair pricing, and firings and layoffs that harm people. The unethical practices that one group of business executives most wanted to eliminate included unfair pricing, gift giving, cheating customers, and unfairness to employees.[9]

Corporate Policy Ethics

Companies are sometimes faced with ethical issues that affect their operations across all departments and divisions of the firm. Top managers and the board of directors then are faced with establishing companywide policies to cope with the issues, such as the following:

- Should our company adopt a drug abuse policy, including required screening of employees for drug use and a remedial program for abusers? Will this policy violate our employees' privacy rights?
- When some of our employees who are members of National Guard units are called up for active duty as peacekeepers in the world's

[9]Scott J. Vitell and Troy A. Festervand, "Business Ethics: Conflicts, Practices and Beliefs of Industrial Executives," *Journal of Business Ethics*, vol. 6, 1987, pp. 115–116.

FIGURE 4-4
Face-to-face
ethical issues and
the groups most
often involved.

SOURCE: Adapted from
R. Sandroff, "How Ethical Is American Business?" *Working Woman*, Sept. 1990, p. 116.

UNETHICAL ACTS PERSONALLY OBSERVED BY READERS OF *WORKING WOMAN*

	Percent Observing Action		Percent Observing Action
Fairness Violations		**Dishonesty**	
Favoritism or nepotism	70	Violating confidentiality	64
Taking credit for others' work	67	Lying to employees	52
		Lying to make a sale	31
Doing business with sexist clients	52		
Discrimination	47	**Sexual Trading**	
Sexual harassment	41	Flirting to make a sale	43
		Sexual intimacy with boss	29
Stealing		Sex with coworker on company time	19
Expense-account abuses	52	Sex with client to make a sale	10
Bribery	5		

trouble spots or to maintain order after a natural disaster, should we have a policy that continues their pay and guarantees them their jobs back when they return? If so, will this practice lower our efficiency by having to rely on temporary replacements? What would be ethical?

■ Even though our company is not a government contractor and does not receive any federal government funds, should we voluntarily develop an affirmative action program to hire and promote Hispanics, Native Americans, African Americans, and women of all races? Are we ethically obligated to promote social goals that are not required by law?

The ethical burden of deciding corporate policy normally rests on a company's leaders. The top managers and directors are responsible for making policies and seeing that they are carried out. The ethical content of their policies can have enormous influence throughout the company. It can set an ethical tone and send a forceful message to all employees as well as to external stakeholders.

Functional-Area Ethics

Because business operations are highly specialized, ethics issues can appear in any of the major functional areas of a business firm. Each function tends to have its own particular brand of ethical dilemmas, as discussed next.

EXHIBIT 4-A

MANAGERS TALK ABOUT ETHICS

Regarding Employees

"We have a lot of people in my company who don't know where they stand. Half-truths or incomplete pictures are drawn in performance appraisals. The truth is bent and the employee is not dealt with in a forthright and honest fashion with respect to his performance and his prospects."

"We go out of our way to help an employee hit with a personal problem (e.g., drinking, financial crisis); we have intervened with creditors, negotiated better pay-check terms, all on a confidential basis."

Regarding Customers

"We have been forced to compromise quality in order to remain competitive. We secretly cheapen a product and keep selling it as if it met the standards of the original product and rationalize it as 'good enough for the application.' "

"We don't buy business but we do offer use of our ski chalet, fishing camp and Florida condo to our customers. It's a question of secretiveness and level of recipient. In our case we only offer it to top executives."

Regarding Suppliers

"I took over as works manager and discovered a great deal of 'patronage,' e.g., suppliers subsidizing parties, providing contracting services to the management club, tire suppliers providing tires to several foremen, etc.; I told the group that they had till the end of the month for 'confession' and that the practices were to stop immediately."

"Shades of truth are required in negotiating with suppliers. One may offer me a product at $3.50/unit and I tell him I have a promotion and need it at $3.00. After he says okay, I tell him hold on and then go out to look for a promotion."

(Selected quotations from James A. Waters, Frederick Bird, and Peter D. Chant, "Everyday Moral Issues Experienced by Managers," *Journal of Business Ethics*, vol. 5, 1986, pp. 376–378. Reprinted by permission of Kluwer Academic Publishers.)

Accounting ethics

The accounting function is a critically important component of every business firm. Accounting reports tell owners and managers whether the firm is doing well or poorly. Company managers, external investors, government regulators, tax collectors, and labor unions rely on accounting data to make key decisions. Honesty, integrity, and accuracy are absolute requirements of the accounting function. No other single issue is of greater concern to accountants in industry and public accountancy than ethics. Roger Worsham's dilemma, discussed at the beginning of this chapter, highlights the importance of honest accounting.

Professional accounting organizations—such as the American Institute of Certified Public Accountants and the Financial Accounting Standards Board—have developed generally accepted accounting principles whose purpose is to establish uniform standards for reporting accounting and auditing data. Spurred by the increasing threat of liability suits filed against accounting firms and the desire to reaffirm professional integrity, these standards go far toward ensuring a high level of honest and ethical accounting behavior. Failure to observe them, however, can produce the kinds of ethical issues shown in Figure 4-5. Such problems also occur in other nations; and member nations of the European Union have discussed the desirability of adopting uniform accounting rules that would apply to all members.[10] The **U.S. Foreign Corrupt Practices Act** requires U.S. companies with foreign operations to adopt accounting procedures that ensure a full disclosure of the company's relations with sales agents and government officials; the purpose is to prevent bribery and other legally questionable payments.

Marketing ethics

Relations with customers tend to generate many ethical problems. Pricing, promotions, advertising, product information, relations between advertising agencies and their clients, marketing research—all of these are potential problem areas. To improve the marketing profession, the American Marketing Association in 1987 adopted a code of ethics for its members. The AMA code advocates professional conduct guided by ethics, adherence to applicable laws, and honesty and fairness in all marketing activi-

[10]Andrew Likierman, "Ethical Dilemmas for Accountants: A United Kingdom Perspective," *Journal of Business Ethics*, vol. 8, 1989, pp. 617–629. For several excellent examples of ethical dilemmas in accounting, see Steven M. Mintz, *Cases in Accounting Ethics and Professionalism*, New York: McGraw-Hill, 1990; and "Battle of the Books: Audit Firms Are Hit by More Investor Suits for Not Finding Fraud," *Wall Street Journal*, Jan. 24, 1989, pp. A1, A12.

FIGURE 4-5
Ethical issues in the accounting profession.
SOURCE: Don W. Finn, Lawrence B. Chonko, and Shelby D. Hunt, "Ethical Problems in Public Accounting: The View from the Top," *Journal of Business Ethics*, vol. 7, 1988, p. 609. Reprinted by permission of Kluwer Academic Publishers.

ETHICAL ISSUES IN THE ACCOUNTING PROFESSION
(Responses of 332 Practitioner Members of the American Institute of Certified Public Accountants)

Rank	Issue	Frequency Mentioned
1	Client proposals of tax alteration and tax fraud	47%
2	Conflict of interest and independence	16%
3	Client proposals of alteration of financial statements	12%
4	Fee problems (billing, collection, contingent fee problems, or competitor bids)	10%
5	Other issues	15%
		100%

ties. The code also recognizes the ethical responsibility of marketing professionals to the consuming public and specifically opposes such unethical practices as misleading product information, false and misleading advertising claims, high-pressure sales tactics, bribery and kickbacks, and unfair and predatory pricing. These code provisions have the potential for helping marketing professionals translate general ethical principles into specific working rules.[11]

Financial ethics

Finance produced some of the most spectacular ethics scandals of the 1980s and 1990s. Wall Street financiers were found guilty of insider trading, illegal stock transactions, and various other financial abuses. Officers at the Bank of Credit and Commerce International fraudulently spent over $20 billion of its investors' deposits to support the financing of illegal arms sales, nuclear weapon production, and money-laundering of drug trade profits. Executives involved in the fraud were sentenced to as many as fourteen years in prison and fined $9.13 billion. Prudential Insurance improperly sold partnerships without appropriate licenses through a commission-sharing scheme with its subsidiary, Prudential-Bache Securities. From 1983 to 1990, Prudential received $777 million in partnership fees while ignoring warning signs that partnerships may be a highly risky venture. Hundreds of savings and loan associations failed after their managers misused their depositors' funds, rewarded themselves and family members with lavish salaries and "perks," misled bank examiners, published false accounting reports, and left U.S. taxpayers to pay the cost of the largest corporate bailout in the nation's history.

Several other kinds of financial transactions are potential ethical minefields: investment banks that finance hostile corporate takeovers that threaten employees' jobs and local communities; trust departments that are charged with safely investing funds entrusted to them; money market managers who must vote on shareholder resolutions dealing with controversial ethical issues; banks that must decide whether to side with a corporation's management team that has been a good customer even though management's policies cause damage to the company's stockholders; and stockbrokers' relationships with clients who seek sound investment advice.[12]

---

[11]The AMA Code for Market Researchers and a discussion of numerous marketing ethics issues can be found in Gene R. Laczniak and Patrick E. Murphy, *Ethical Marketing Decisions,* Boston: Allyn and Bacon, 1993. Other ethics issues in marketing are presented in Ralph M. Gaedeke, Craig A. Kelley, and Dennis H. Tootelian, "Practitioners' Perceptions of Ethical Standards in Marketing: An Empirical Investigation," *Journal of Professional Services Marketing,* vol. 8, no. 2, 1993, pp. 11–26.

[12]For several good examples of these and other areas, see John L. Casey, *Ethics in the Financial Marketplace,* New York: Scudder, Stevens & Clark, 1988; James B. Stewart, *Den of Thieves,* New York: Simon and Schuster, 1991; and Larry Alan Bear and Rita Maldonado-Bear, *Free Markets, Finance, Ethics, and Law,* Englewood Cliffs, NJ: Prentice-Hall, 1994.

Information Systems ethics

One of the fastest growing areas of business ethics is in the field of information systems. Exploding in the 1990s are ethical challenges involving invasions of privacy; the collection, storage, and access of personal and business information; confidentiality of communications over the telephone, electronic mail, and facsimile machine; copyright protection regarding software copying; and numerous other related issues. In response to calls of business people and academics for an increase in ethics in the information system field, professional organizations have developed or revised professional codes of ethics.[13]

Other functional areas

Production and maintenance functions, which may seem to be remote from ethics considerations, can be at the center of some ethics storms. Dangerously defective products can injure or kill innocent persons, and toxic production processes may threaten the health of workers and the general public. Flawed manufacturing and lack of inspection of aircraft fuse pins, which hold the engines to the wing on Boeing 747 jet airplanes, were suspected in some accidents endangering the lives of airlines passengers as well as innocent bystanders. Fuse pin defects may have contributed to the December 1991 crash of a China Airlines flight in Taiwan and an October 1992 crash of an El Al plane in Amsterdam, killing more than fifty people as the Boeing 747 crashed into an apartment complex. Union Carbide's pesticide plant in Bhopal, India, was allegedly not properly maintained, and this failure was believed to be a contributing cause of the tragic leak that killed over 2,000 people.

Ethics issues also arise in purchasing departments. A recent survey by the National Association of Purchasing Management reported common ethics problems: exaggerating a problem to receive a better price from a supplier; providing preferential treatment to a supplier who is also a good customer; allowing personal friendships to enter into selection decisions; providing information to a competing supplier; accepting promotional prizes or purchase volume incentives; accepting trips, meals, or entertainment; and giving special treatment to vendors preferred by higher management.[14]

These examples make one point crystal clear: all areas of business, all people in business, and all levels of authority in business encounter ethics dilemmas from time to time. Ethics issues are a common thread running through the business world.

---

[13]For further discussion of ethics in information systems see Ernest A. Kallman and John P. Grillo, *Ethical Decision Making and Information Technology*, New York: McGraw-Hill, 1993; and Effy Oz, "Ethical Standards for Computer Professionals: A Comparative Analysis of Four Major Codes," *Journal of Business Ethics*, vol. 12, 1993, pp. 709–726.

[14]Renee Florsheim and Eduardo S. Paderon, "Purchasing Practices in a Hospital Environment: An Ethical Analysis," *Hospital Material Management Quarterly*, vol. 13, no. 4, 1992, pp. 1–10. Also see Stanley J. Modic, "Many Purchasers Rationalize Ethics," *Purchasing World*, Mar. 1990, pp. 69–70.

WHY ETHICAL PROBLEMS OCCUR IN BUSINESS

Obviously, ethics problems in business appear in many different forms. While not common or universal, they occur frequently. Finding out just what is responsible for causing them is one step that can be taken toward minimizing their impact on business operations and on the people affected. Some of the main reasons are summarized in Figure 4-6 and are discussed next.

Personal Gain and Selfish Interest

Personal gain, or even greed, causes some ethics problems. Business sometimes employs people whose personal values are less than desirable. They will put their own welfare ahead of all others, regardless of the harm done to other employees, the company, or society. In the process of hiring employees there is an effort to weed out ethically undesirable applicants, but ethical qualities are difficult to anticipate and measure. The embezzler, the expense account padder, the bribe taker, and other unethical persons can slip through. Lacking a perfect screening system, business is not likely to eliminate this kind of unethical behavior entirely. Moreover, business has to proceed carefully when screening applicants, taking care not to trample on individuals' rights in the search for potentially unethical employees.

A manager or an employee who puts his or her own self-interest above

FIGURE 4-6
Why ethical problems occur in business.

WHY ETHICAL PROBLEMS OCCUR IN BUSINESS

Reason	Nature of Ethical Problem	Typical Approach	Attitude
Personal Gain and Selfish Interest	Selfish interest vs. others' interests	Egoistical mentality	"I want it!"
Competitive Pressures on Profits	Firm's interest vs. others' interests	Bottom-line mentality	"We have to beat the others at all costs!"
Business Goals vs. Personal Values	Boss's interests vs. subordinates' values	Authoritarian mentality	"Do as I say, or else!"
Cross-Cultural Contradictions	Company's interests vs. diverse cultural traditions and values	Ethnocentric mentality	"Foreigners have a funny notion of what's right and wrong!"

all other considerations is called an **ethical egoist.** Self-promotion, a focus on self-interest to the point of selfishness, and greed are traits commonly observed in an ethical egoist. The ethical egoist tends to ignore ethical principles accepted by others, or to believe that "ethical rules are made for others." **Altruism**—which is acting for the benefit of others when your own self-interest is sacrificed—is seen to be sentimental or even irrational. "Looking out for Number One" is the ethical egoist's motto.[15]

Competitive Pressures on Profits

When companies are squeezed by tough competition, they sometimes engage in unethical activities in order to protect their profits. This may be especially true in companies whose financial performance is already substandard. Research has shown that poor financial performers and companies with lower profits, as compared with those with higher profits, are more prone to commit illegal acts.[16] However, a precarious financial position is only one reason for illegal and unethical business behavior, because profitable companies also can act contrary to ethical principles. In fact, it may be simply a single-minded drive for profits, regardless of the company's financial condition, that creates a climate for unethical activity.

Price-fixing is a practice that often occurs when companies compete vigorously in a limited market. Besides being illegal, price-fixing is unethical behavior toward customers, who pay higher prices than they would if free competition set the prices. Companies fix prices to avoid fair competition and to protect their profits, as happened in the following cases.

> Over forty dairy companies were convicted or pleaded guilty to federal criminal charges of price-fixing and bid-rigging in 1993. Executives from the firms conspired to rig bids on milk products sold to schools and military bases in at least twenty states. These practices artificially inflated profits for the dairy companies.
>
> In another case, Japan's Fair Trade Commission demonstrated its aggressiveness toward uncovering unfair trade practices in two separate incidents. In May 1993, eight Japanese plastic food wrapping companies were fined between $54,225 and $72,300 and several executives

---

[15]For a compact discussion of ethical egoism, see Tom L. Beauchamp and Norman E. Bowie, *Ethical Theory and Business*, 3d ed., Englewood Cliffs, NJ: Prentice-Hall, 1988, pp. 18–21.

[16]For a discussion, see Peter C. Yeager, "Analyzing Corporate Offenses: Progress and Prospects," in William C. Frederick, ed., *Business Ethics: Research Issues and Empirical Studies*, Greenwich, CT: JAI Press, 1990, pp. 168–171; Philip L. Cochran and Douglas Nigh, "Illegal Corporate Behavior and the Question of Moral Agency: An Empirical Examination," in William C. Frederick, ed., *Research in Corporate Social Performance and Policy*, Vol. 9, Greenwich, CT: JAI Press, 1987, pp. 73–91; and Michael K. McCuddy, Karl E. Reichardt, and David L. Schroeder, "Ethical Pressures: Fact or Fiction?" *Management Accounting*, vol. 74, no. 10, 1993, pp. 57–61.

were suspended for conducting an elaborate price-fixing cartel. Later that year, the commission raided the nation's largest electronic companies to uncover evidence of bid-rigging. Close ties between Japanese businesses and government officials had effectively shut out foreign competition in bidding for public works projects.[17]

Price-fixing among competing companies is not the only kind of unethical behavior that can occur. Senior Honda executives pleaded guilty in 1994 to accepting bribes and expensive gifts from U.S. dealers as a condition of providing them with an adequate supply of the most popular cars. Dozens of dealers contend that the corruption began in the 1970s but dramatically escalated in the 1980s when Honda automobiles were in great demand but import quotas limited supply.[18]

Other kinds of unethical behavior also occur under competitive pressures. Suppliers can be coerced into lowering their prices due to nonmarket pressures by companies, thereby receiving less than a fair price. When company officials have a strict "bottom-line mentality" shaped almost exclusively by market competition, they may overlook the ethical claims of their stakeholders. Doing so has the unfortunate and needless effect of pitting business against society.

Business Goals versus Personal Values

Ethical conflicts in business sometimes occur when a company pursues goals or uses methods that are unacceptable to some of its employees. "Whistle-blowing" may be one outcome, if an employee "goes public" with a complaint after failing to convince the company to correct an alleged abuse. Another recourse for employees caught in these situations is a lawsuit. This option has become less of a financial and professional risk for employees in recent years due to various governmental protection acts.

Paul Blanch blew the whistle on his employer, Connecticut's Northeast Utilities. Blanch identified safety lapses in plant operations. Shortly after his complaints, Blanch was subjected to negative job evaluations and harassing internal audits. Seeking government protection, the Nuclear Regulatory Commission imposed a $100,000 fine upon Northeast Utilities for its actions against Paul Blanch.

Former GE employee Chester Walsh sued General Electric for over-

[17]Diane B. Henriques and Dean Baguet, "Evidence Mounts of Rigged Bidding in Milk Industry," *New York Times,* May 23, 1993, p. A1; "Japan's Court Fines Eight Firms," *Wall Street Journal,* May 24, 1993, p. A6; and Jathon Sapsford, "Japanese Electronics Firms Are Raided by Agency on Suspicion of Bid-Rigging," *Wall Street Journal,* Nov. 16, 1993, p. A15.

[18]Doron P. Levin, "Honda's Ugly Little Secret," *New York Times,* May 2, 1993, sec. 3, p. 1; and Krystal Miller, "Former Honda Executives Plead Guilty to Charges Tied to Bribes from Dealers," *Wall Street Journal,* Mar. 15, 1994, p. A8.

charging the government on aircraft parts destined for Israel. After GE agreed to settle the suit for $39.5 million, a federal judge ordered the firm to pay $11.5 million to Walsh.[19]

The protesting employees in these companies were not troublemakers. They tried to work through internal company procedures to get the problems corrected. The ethical dilemma arose because the company's goals and methods required the employees to follow orders that they believed would harm themselves, other employees, customers, the company, and the general public. As far as they were concerned, they were being asked or ordered to do something unethical. Their own internal ethical compass was at odds with the goals and methods of their company.

Cross-Cultural Contradictions

Some of the knottiest ethical problems occur as corporations do business in other societies where ethical standards differ from those at home. Today, the policymakers and strategic planners in all multinational corporations, regardless of the nation where they are headquartered, face this kind of ethical dilemma. Consider the following situations:

> U.S. sleepwear manufacturers discovered that the chemicals used to flameproof childrens' pajamas might cause cancer if absorbed through the child's skin. When these pajamas were banned from sale in the United States, some manufacturers sold the pajama material to distributors in other nations where there were no legal restrictions against its use.

> *Question: Although the foreign sales were legal, were they ethical? Is "dumping unsafe products" ethical if it is not forbidden by the receiving nation?*

> When Honda began building automobile plants in Ohio, it located them in two mostly white rural areas and then favored job applicants who lived within a 30-mile radius of the plant. This policy excluded African Americans who lived in Columbus, the nearest big city. Earlier, Honda also had agreed to pay nearly half a million dollars to settle an age-discrimination suit brought by older job applicants who had been refused work there.

> *Question: Were Honda's job-hiring policies, which would have caused few problems in Japan, unethical in Ohio?*

---

[19]Matthew L. Ward, "Regulator Says Connecticut's Largest Power Company Harassed Worker," *New York Times*, May 5, 1993, p. B6; and Amal Kumar Naj, "Whistle-Blower at GE to Get $11.5 Million," *Wall Street Journal*, Apr. 26, 1993, p. A3, A4.

These episodes raise the issue of ethical relativism, which was defined earlier in this chapter. Should ethical principles—the ones that help chart right and wrong conduct—take their meaning strictly from the way each society defines ethics? Are Japanese attitudes toward job opportunities for minorities, older workers, and women as ethically valid as U.S. attitudes? Were the children's pajama makers on solid—or shaky—ethical ground when they sold the cancer-risky pajama cloth in countries where government officials did not warn parents about this possible health risk? Who should assume the ethical responsibility? What or whose ethical standards should be the guide?

As business becomes increasingly global, and as more and more corporations penetrate overseas markets where cultures and ethical traditions vary, these questions will occur more frequently. Employees and managers need ethical guidance from clearly stated company policy if they are to avoid the psychological stresses mentioned earlier. One U.S. corporate executive emphasized this point by saying that he and his company

> recognize that the world consists of a wide array of races, religions, languages, cultures, political systems and economic resources. We accept these differences as legitimate and desirable; we recognize that each country must determine its own way. . . . However, we must not use local custom as an excuse for violating applicable laws or corporate policies. We regard observing local law to be the minimum acceptable level of conduct; PPG's own standards frequently oblige us to go beyond that legal minimum and to conduct our affairs according to a higher standard.[20]

GLOBAL ETHICS ISSUES

Examples of unethical conduct by business employees are reported from nearly every country. The challenge to perform in an ethical manner is clearly a global issue. Questionable or unjust payments to ensure or facilitate business transactions are found in nearly every sector of the global marketplace. For example, incidents of bribery were reported in China, India, Nigeria, and Venezuela during the past few years. Instances of kickbacks were reported in Japan involving the sale of medical diagnostic equipment, in Israel where the United States sought to sell military weapons, and in Argentina concerning the importation of wheat. Far-reaching corruption probes conducted in Italy unearthed systemic unethical corruption practices throughout the Italian financial community. After initial denials of any wrongdoing, five Fiat executives have confessed to paying kickbacks on a bus contract to political parties through a Swiss bank account. This Italian business scandal may be only the tip

[20]Vincent A. Sarni, chairman, PPG Industries, Inc., *Worldwide Code of Ethics*, Pittsburgh, PA, n.d.

of the iceberg concerning instances of unethical business practices in Europe.[21]

Olivetti, an Italian manufacturer, admitted paying $7 million over four years to government officials to secure telecommunication contracts. Olivetti's president, Carlo DeBenedetti, argued that "I only gave in [to pressure from political parties] when I found it necessary to defend the survival of the company and the interests of tens of thousands of workers and of shareholders." DeBenedetti claimed that people and acts must be judged in their historical context. The Italian judicial system disagreed, as evidenced by the prosecution of DeBenedetti's actions.[22]

Unfair treatment of a company's business partners, or clients, is evident throughout the global marketplace. Fraud involving the sale of automobiles to the handicapped was found in Argentina, mail fraud was reported in Nigeria, and securities fraud occurred in Germany, Japan, Thailand, and the United States. Thailand's Securities and Exchange Commission uncovered a multimillion dollar stock manipulation conspiracy involving thirty people. The individuals were charged with stock market manipulation of three companies' stocks, with many well-known and wealthy Thais included in the group, although some defendants have been acquitted of criminal charges. These practices send a clear message that unethical business activity has a global presence.[23]

Efforts to Curtail Unethical Practices

Numerous efforts are underway to curb unethical business practices throughout the world. The most common control is through government intervention and regulation. By enacting stiff legislative controls or empowering government agencies with more authority, efforts to address the problem of unethical business behavior often begin with the national government. Many governments are attempting to establish a moral minimum as a guide for proper behavior or to draw the line to control unethical action. For example, Germany's government has pledged to more carefully monitor white collar crime and, in 1994, passed a strict anti-insider trading law. The "teeth of the law" lie in the creation of a securities regulatory agency and the power of the agency to impose fines and prison terms for violations. Similarly, Japan is committed to investigating accusations of

[21]"Corruption Sinks European Businesses," *Pittsburgh Post-Gazette,* June 19, 1994, p. E1; Lisa Bannon, "Fiat Officer Faces Warrant for Arrest in Bribery Probe," *Wall Street Journal,* Apr. 8, 1993, p. C9; and Peter Gumbel, "As Corruption Scandals Mount, France Fears Becoming Like Italy," *Wall Street Journal,* June 6, 1994, p. A8.

[22]"Olivetti President Concedes That Firm Paid Bribes," *Wall Street Journal,* May 17, 1993, p. A12; and Lisa Bannon, "DeBenedetti Says Political Bribes Were Commonplace in the 1980s," *Wall Street Journal,* May 20, 1993, p. A15.

[23]"30 Thais Face Charges of Manipulating Stocks," *Wall Street Journal,* Apr. 23, 1993, p. A11; and Paul Sherer, "Thailand Court Acquits 12 Defendants in SEC's First Stock-Manipulation Case," *Wall Street Journal,* June 28, 1994, p. A13B.

price-fixing and to increasing penalties for securities violations. The Venezuelan government threatened to overregulate industries if necessary to eliminate instances of unethical and illegal activities.

Various international organizations, such as the International Labor Organization or the United Nations, have attempted to develop an international code of conduct for multinational corporations. These efforts have emphasized the need for companies to adhere to universal ethical guidelines when conducting business throughout the world. These codes and the ethical issues they address are shown in Figure 4-7.

Some businesses have joined their governments in efforts to control unethical employee behavior. As discussed in the next chapter, corporate codes of ethics have been drafted or recently revised to cover instances of undesired practices in the global marketplace. Businesses located in the United States, Europe, and Australia are more likely to address unethical behavior in this way, although a Japanese firm reported an effort to model itself after IBM—including the development of a code of ethics.

Some people question the effectiveness of governmental legislation or corporate policies. Rather than establishing rules, businesses are trying to educate and motivate their employees worldwide to both respect the customs of other nations and adhere to basic ethical principles of fairness, honesty, and a respect for human rights. Some who study international

FIGURE 4-7

International ethics codes and ethics issues addressed in these codes.

SOURCE: This chart is adapted from William C. Frederick, "The Moral Authority of Transnational Corporate Codes," *Journal of Business Ethics,* vol. 10, 1991, pp. 165–177, particularly table 1, p. 168; and Kathleen A. Getz, "International Codes of Conduct: An Analysis of Ethical Reasoning," *Journal of Business Ethics,* vol. 9, 1990, pp. 567–577.

ISSUES COVERED IN INTERNATIONAL ETHICS CODES FOR MULTINATIONAL CORPORATIONS

Ethics Issues Addressed	International Ethics Codes			
	ICC	OECD	ILO	UN/CTC
Economic Development	X	X	X	X
Technology Transfer	X	X	X	X
Regulatory Action	X	X		X
Employment	X	X	X	
Human Rights			X	X
Environmental Protection	X	X		X
Consumer Protection		X		X
Political Action		X		X

Key for the international codes of conduct:
ICC   =   International Chamber of Commerce code (1972)
OECD   =   Organization for Economic Cooperation and Development code (1976)
ILO   =   International Labor Organization code (1977)
UN/CTC =   United Nations Commission on Transnational Corporations code (1984)

business ethics say that such higher standards of ethics already exist. Thomas Donaldson, a leading ethics scholar, has outlined a set of fundamental human rights—including the right to security, to freedom of movement, to subsistence income, and other rights—that should be respected by all multinational corporations. These standards and other ethical values are at the core of the development of transnational codes of conduct promoted by the United Nations and other international organizations.[24]

ETHICS, LAW, AND ILLEGAL CORPORATE BEHAVIOR

Before discussing specific ways to improve business's ethical performance (in the next chapter), we want to consider the relationship of law and ethics. Some people have argued that the best way to assure ethical business conduct is to insist that business firms obey society's laws. However, this approach is not as simple as it seems.

Law and ethics are not quite the same. Laws are similar to ethics because both define proper and improper behavior. In general, laws are a society's attempt to formalize—that is, to reduce to written rules—the general public's ideas about what constitutes right and wrong conduct in various spheres of life. However, it is rarely possible for written laws to capture all of the subtle shadings that people give to ethics. Ethical concepts—like the people who believe in them—are more complex than written rules of law. Ethics deals with human dilemmas that frequently go beyond the formal language of law and the meanings given to legal rules. The following situation demonstrates that there is not always a perfect match between the law and important ethical principles.

In 1994, educators and parents voiced their concern over the significant increase in sexually explicit language and violence depicted in video games and computer software. Congress joined in the criticism and called for a system of warnings for consumers. The Interactive Digital Software Association, which represents video game makers, established a five-category system which was voluntarily adopted by the industry. The labeling system informed consumers of the intended target audience: early childhood (three years old and up), children to adults (ages six and up), teenagers (thirteen and over), mature audience (seventeen and up), and adults only. The video game industry also agreed to provide content warnings, such as "mild profanity," and to use warning symbols: a hand grenade means violence, a hand partly

---

[24]For a discussion of global ethics, see Joanne B. Ciulla, "Why Is Business Talking About Ethics?: Reflections on Foreign Conversations," *California Management Review*, vol. 34, no. 1, 1991, pp. 67–86, and the July 1990 issue *of Journal of Business Ethics*. For a complete list of fundamental human rights, see Thomas Donaldson, *The Ethics of International Business*, New York: Oxford University Press, 1989.

covering an eye indicates sexual scenes, and an exclamation point warns of foul language.[25]

This example suggests that legality cannot always define when something is believed to be ethical or unethical. Although laws attempt to codify a society's notions of right and wrong, they are not always able to do so completely. Obeying the law is usually one way of acting ethically, and the public generally expects business to be law-abiding. But at times, the public expects business to recognize that ethical principles are broader than the law. Because of the imperfect match between law and ethics, business managers who try to improve their company's ethical performance need to do more than comply with the law. Society will generally insist that they heed ethical principles *and* the law.

Corporate Lawbreaking and Its Costs

Although estimates vary, lawbreaking in business is not unusual and may cause serious financial losses.

> A Department of Justice estimate puts the total annual loss to taxpayers from reported and unreported violations of federal regulations by corporations at $10 to $20 billion. The Chamber of Commerce of the United States, a conservative probusiness organization, has estimated that various white-collar crimes cost the public some $41 billion a year. One of the most thorough attempts to calculate the financial loss to the country from corporate crimes was that of a U.S. Senate subcommittee which put the cost of corporate crime at between $174 and $231 billion a year. Compared to even the lesser of these estimates, the $3 to $4 billion annual loss to street crime—robbery, burglary, assault, etc.—represents only a small proportion of the economic cost of crime.[26]

Beyond these dollar costs of illegal behavior are the physical and social costs. Over 100,000 deaths each year are attributed to occupational diseases, and most of these are a result of violations of health and safety laws. During 1992, over 6,000 workers were killed due to on-the-job injuries. This amounts to an average of nearly seventeen workplace deaths each day. Tragically, many of the deaths might have been avoided if employers and workers were informed about the risks and complied with established safety and health regulations.[27]

[25]"Games Industries Introduce Voluntary Ratings System," *Wall Street Journal,* July, 29, 1994, p. B3.
[26]See Jeffrey S. Hornsby, Donald F. Kuratko, and William Honey, "Emerging Growth Companies and the At-Risk Employee: The Viability of Pre-Employment Honesty Testing," *SAM Advanced Management Journal,* vol. 54, no. 4, 1992, pp. 24–29.
[27]An extensive analysis of the U.S. census data on workplace fatalities is in Guy Toscano and Janice Windau, "Fatal Work Injuries: Results from the 1992 National Census," *Monthly Labor Review,* Oct. 1993, pp. 39–48.

SUMMARY POINTS OF THIS CHAPTER

- Ethics is a conception of right and wrong behavior, defining for us when our actions are moral and when they are immoral. Business ethics is the application of general ethical ideas to business behavior.
- Ethical business behavior is expected by the public, prevents harm to society, fosters business relations and employee productivity, reduces criminal penalties, protects business against unscrupulous employees and competitors, protects business employees from harmful actions by their employer, and allows people in business to act consistently with their personal ethical beliefs.
- Business ethics issues usually appear in three different forms: face-to-face personal interactions on the job; corporate policy ethics involving companywide ethical concerns; and functional-area ethics in accounting, marketing, finance, information systems, and other core business functions.
- Ethics problems occur in business for many reasons, including the selfishness of a few, competitive pressures on profits, the clash of personal values and business goals, and cross-cultural contradictions in global business operations.
- Similar ethical issues arise throughout the world and many national governments are actively attempting to minimize such actions—although international codes and principles may be more effective.
- Although law and ethics are closely related, they are not the same; ethical principles tend to be broader than legal principles. Illegal behavior by business and its employees imposes great costs on business and the general public.

KEY TERMS AND CONCEPTS USED IN THIS CHAPTER

- Ethics
- Ethical relativism
- Business ethics
- Face-to-face ethics
- Corporate policy ethics
- Functional-area ethics
- U.S. Foreign Corrupt Practices Act
- Ethical egoist
- Altruism
- Law

DISCUSSION CASE

IT'S A SHORT LIFE, SO GO AHEAD AND LIGHT UP!

"You can't turn around to a guy who is going to die at age 40 and tell him that he might not live two years extra at age 70," said a British tobacco company executive. He was defending cigarette sales to smokers in poor third world nations where average life expectancy is much lower than in advanced nations.[28]

The world's tobacco companies in the last quarter century have turned to overseas sales to bolster profits made at home. These foreign markets are especially important for their long-term survival. Numerous scientific studies link smoking to many life-threatening diseases such as cancer, stroke, and heart disease. Governments in North America, western Europe, and other advanced regions began restricting tobacco sales in the 1960s and 1970s. Health warnings are required on cigarette packages and in tobacco advertisements; television ads for tobacco products are banned in the United States and several other nations; sports figures may not be depicted in cigarette ads in Israel; nonsmoking seating arrangements are required in many restaurants, public buildings, and entertainment centers, or smoking may be completely prohibited; by 1990 most globe-straddling airlines banned all smoking except on the longest flights; and city ordinances often attempt to make cigarette vending machine sales to minors especially difficult.

Third world markets are an especially attractive prospect for the tobacco companies. A large and youth-weighted population there is growing rapidly, government smoking regulations are absent or less onerous, and in some nations an expanding middle class is eager to identify itself with the symbols of wealth and success that are seen as typical of life in advanced countries. The third world "is where the growth is," according to one expert on the tobacco industry; estimates put third world sales at about one-third of the world total. In most of these nations, no health warnings are required and radio and television advertising is not restricted.

Because average incomes are low, individual cigarettes are sold. Even so, tobacco use burdens family budgets. In Bangladesh, according to a British medical journal, people spend about 20 percent of their incomes on tobacco, thereby threatening the family's dietary needs.

Cigarette ads are appealing. An Ambassador cigarette billboard in Zaire was labeled "La classe" and showed a business-suited man stepping from a chauffeured Mercedes. Another promotion for Graduate cigarettes in Nigeria featured a university student in cap and gown. The Gold Leaf brand depicted a lawyer in the traditional British white wig, claiming Gold Leaf to be "a very important cigarette for very important people."

Defending these ads, one tobacco company representative said, "Every cigarette manufacturer is in the image business. [In these countries] a lot of people can't understand what is written on the ads anyway, so you'll zero in on the more understandable one and usually on a visual image."

As these ads take hold in the third world, smokers there get a bigger

---

[28]Except when otherwise noted, quotations and examples used in this case are from Steve Mufson, "Smoking Section: Cigarette Companies Develop Third World as a Growth Market," *Wall Street Journal,* July 5, 1986, pp. 1, 19. Reprinted by permission of the *Wall Street Journal,* © 1986 Dow Jones & Company, Inc. All rights reserved worldwide.

dose of tar and nicotine than smokers in the advanced nations. "These people are used to smoking their own locally made product, which might have several times as much tar and nicotine," said a spokesperson for B.A.T., the London-based manufacturer. "It's a black lie that we sell higher tar and nicotine in the third world," countered a Philip Morris vice president; but a study of Benson & Hedges Special Filter cigarettes showed tar and nicotine content ranged from 31 to 83 percent higher in some developing nations.

Speaking of the lax regulatory attitude toward tobacco use in poorer nations, one tobacco industry representative said, "If there is no ban on TV advertising, then you aren't going to be an idiot and impose restrictions on yourself. If you get an order and you know they've got money, no one is going to turn down the business."

Third world governments are usually strapped for funds to meet the crushing burdens of their large populations, so they are glad to get the revenues from tobacco sales. China, which welcomed R. J. Reynolds in a joint venture to make cigarettes, takes in $5 billion each year from its state-owned tobacco industry. During the 1980s Japan, South Korea, and Taiwan succumbed to threats of trade retaliation and significantly liberalized imports of U.S. tobacco products. The Soviet Union struck a deal in 1990 with Philip Morris and RJR Nabisco to import 34 billion cigarettes to help overcome a shortage caused by that nation's transition toward a market-directed economy. A tobacco company representative said, "We think our American-blend cigarettes will be very popular there—this is a wonderful opportunity for us." Bowing to pressure from U.S. tobacco companies, Thailand's cabinet decided to allow legal imports of cigarettes. Imported tobacco is subjected to the same conditions as domestic companies—a 55 percent tax on their products and a ban on all cigarette advertising in the mass media.[29]

Discussion Questions

1. Do you believe that tobacco companies have an ethical problem when selling their products in third world nations? Defend your answer.
2. Of the four reasons given in this chapter for ethical problems occurring in business, which one or more may be operating in this situation? Which do you consider to be the most important?
3. Does this case illustrate face-to-face ethical problems, corporate policy ethical problems, or functional-area ethical problems? Give examples from the case to illustrate your answer.

---

[29]"Smokeless Soviets Say 'Da' to Philip Morris and RJR," *Wall Street Journal,* Sept. 14, 1990, pp. B1, B7; and Helen E. White, "Thailand, Bowing to Foreign Pressure, Will End Its Ban on Cigarette Imports," *Wall Street Journal,* Oct. 12, 1990, p. B5C.

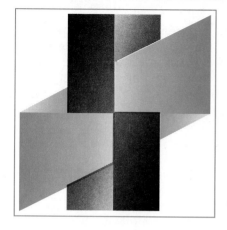

5

Ethical Reasoning and Corporate Programs

Tangible steps can be taken by business to improve its ethical performance. The most important components leading to ethical reform are corporate values and the personal character of the employees, especially managers. Corporate ethical action can be improved by creating and/or revising various organizational safeguards, such as codes of ethics, ethics committees, employee ethics training, and so on. These programs enable employees to improve their ethical reasoning by emphasizing a concern for achieving the greatest good for all those affected by the action while respecting peoples' rights and striving for a just and fair solution.

Key Questions and Chapter Objectives

This chapter focuses on these key questions and objectives:
- What are managers' major goals and values? How do they affect a company's ethical performance?
- What role does personal character play in business ethics?
- How do a company's culture and work climate influence the ethical views of managers and employees?
- When analyzing ethics issues, how much weight should be given to harms and benefits, to human rights, and to social justice?
- What are the strengths and weaknesses of ethics codes, ethics training programs, ethics "hot lines," and similar reform efforts?

"Here's an up-from-the-ranks guy who's now head of the division and suddenly running into profit problems. He's seen what had happened to his former boss, and he's scared." The government prosecutor was referring to the vice president of AEL Industries, a Philadelphia defense contractor. Earlier in his career when the vice president was a junior manager, he had been demoted and his boss had been fired when their division lost money on a contract.[1]

Now, AEL's Emtech division had landed two jobs, one to develop radar equipment for the U.S. army and a similar contract with South Korea. The U.S. army contract was profitable, but the Korean one was not. Knowing that top management frowned on poor financial performance, Emtech's vice president allegedly directed clerks to change entries on the time cards of 26,000 employees during a three-year period. These falsely inflated costs—amounting to $1.6 million—were then charged to the government. When auditors uncovered the scheme, the vice president was sent to jail for six months and AEL paid a fine of $2.66 million.

Around the company, the vice president was known as a "kind and conscientious" person. He was admired for working his way up the hard way—going to night school and then moving through the ranks. A Pentagon defense official had been impressed with his "honest good deeds" after he had saved the government money by recommending a cost-saving material. His own attorney, referring to the time when the young manager and his boss had been penalized for the money-losing contract, said, "It does not require a psychiatrist's insight to sense the impact of that decision on the defendant."

This episode raises some disturbing questions: Can top-down pressure for profitable performance corrupt middle-level managers and employees, causing them to take dishonest actions in order to save their jobs? Can it happen even when those who feel the pressures have a good personal character?

More importantly, what steps can companies take to guard against such ethical abuses? Following the court action, AEL agreed to appoint an ethics director and to tighten up its accounting systems. During the 1980s and 1990s, several other leading defense contractors who were charged with similar ethical lapses began ethics training programs and wrote or revised their ethics codes.

In this chapter, we examine ways to improve business's ethical performance. The keys to success are a blend of managers' values, personal character, a company's culture and ethical climate, the tools available for analyzing moral dilemmas, and practical changes in company procedures that permit high ethical performance along with profitable operations.

THE CORE ELEMENTS OF ETHICAL REFORM

Whether a company improves its ethical performance depends on three core components: the goals and values of its managers; the personal char-

---

[1]"Pressure for Profits: Tough Goals Put a Strain on Honesty," *Los Angeles Times*, June 27, 1986, p. 24.

acter of its managers and other employees; and the traditions, attitudes, and business practices built into the company's culture. Good ethical practices not only are possible but they become normal with the right combination of these three components.

Managers' Goals and Values

Managers are one of the keys to whether a company will act ethically or unethically. As major decision makers, they have more opportunities than others to create an ethical tone for their company. The values held by these managers, especially the top-level managers, will serve as models for others who work there.

Figure 5-1 shows that U.S. managers' value orientations in the 1990s are pretty much what one would expect. Most managers emphasize a self-focus and a concern for being competent, placing importance on values such as having a comfortable life, living an exciting life, and being capable, intellectual, and responsible. Some managers show a strong concern for values which include others, evident in the values of living in a world at peace or seeking equality among people. One out of four managers emphasize the other set of values—moral values. These managers place greater importance upon the value of forgiving others, being helpful, and acting honestly.

Do managers' values change over time? The value orientations of U.S. managers in 1990 appear to be similar to the value approaches underlying managers' decision making in 1975. The pragmatic approach exhibited by U.S. managers fifteen years later is consistent with the emphasis upon a competency and self-focus manifested by managers today. Having a practical, work-oriented, individualistic, and achievement-focused set of values

FIGURE 5-1

Important values for managers influencing their decision making at work.

SOURCE: Adapted from James Weber, "Managerial Value Orientations: A Typology and Assessment," *International Journal of Value Based Management,* vol. 3, no. 2, 1990, pp. 37–54, particularly table 5, p. 49. Reprinted by permission of Kluwer Academic Publishers.

VALUE ORIENTATIONS OF U.S. MANAGERS IN 1990
Percent of Managers Emphasizing a Value Focus (N = 413)

	Goal-Oriented Values		
	Self-focus	(vs.) Other-focus	Totals
Means-Oriented Values			
Competency focus	53.5%	21.8%	75.3%
(vs.)			
Moral focus	18.4%	6.3%	24.7%
Totals	71.9%	28.1%	

is a characteristic trait of most U.S. managers. However, this emphasis can vary from nation to nation.

England's classic 1975 study reported that almost six of every ten U.S. managers approach a decision by asking, "Will what I am about to do produce practical results?" Only three of the ten begin by asking, "Is it right or ethical?" In both Australia and India, this pragmatic tendency is less pronounced, while Japanese managers are far more practical-minded than others.[2]

Current discussions about effective organizational leadership often center around individuals' values. For example, a charismatic leader exhibiting strong moral character is capable of positively influencing an entire department or organization. While there are risks associated with assuming this "higher moral ground," ethical charismatic leaders, described in Figure 5-2, are seen as "other-centered" visionaries who bring out the best in their followers. Although varying from the predominant value orientations of managers in the 1970s and 1990s, the moral standards of the ethical manager may enable business leaders to better address the difficult moral decisions encountered at work; some of these standards are listed in Figure 5-3.

How managers' values can promote ethics reform

Managers are authority figures and role models in their companies. By setting a personal example of high ethical behavior, they can influence others around them. Repeated studies over the years have arrived at the same conclusion: *the behavior and ethical attitudes of an employee's boss are seen*

---

[2]For additional information about variations in ethical viewpoints in different societies, see Helmut Becker and David J. Fritzsche, "Business Ethics: A Cross-Cultural Comparison of Managers' Attitudes," *Journal of Business Ethics*, vol. 6, 1987, pp. 289–295.

FIGURE 5-2
Qualities of an ethical charismatic leader.

SOURCE: Adapted from Jane M. Howell and Bruce J. Avolio, "The Ethics of Charismatic Leadership: Submission or Liberation?" *Academy of Management Executive*, vol. 6, no. 2, 1992, p. 45.

The ethical charismatic leader:

- Uses power to serve others
- Aligns vision with followers' needs and aspirations
- Considers and learns from criticisms
- Stimulates followers to think independently and to question the leader's view
- Fosters open, two-way communication
- Coaches, develops, and supports followers
- Shares recognition with others
- Relies upon internal moral standards to satisfy organizational and societal interests

FIGURE 5-3

Moral standards used by managers.

Source: Adapted from Froderick Bird and James A. Waters, "The Nature of Managerial Moral Standards," *Journal of Business Ethics*, vol. 6, 1987, pp. 1–13.

MORAL STANDARDS USED BY MANAGERS
(33 Managers from 10 Different Organizations)

Standard	Percent of Cases in Which Standard Was Used
Fair treatment of employees, customers, suppliers, coworkers, and other managers	30.1
Fair competition regarding pricing, dealing with suppliers and customers, and avoiding favoritism	29.5
Honesty in communications regarding job evaluations, advertising, labeling, expense accounts, and public relations	25.9
Organizational responsibility that promotes efficiency, reduces waste, and advances the organization	21.2
Special consideration regarding personal problems of employees, handicapped employees, long-term customer and supplier relationships, and similar unique situations	15.0
Respect for law, including obeying both the spirit and letter of the law	9.3
Social responsibility regarding community impacts, environmental pollution, hazardous consumer goods, and corporate philanthropy	5.7

as the most important factors determining whether the employee will behave unethically on the job.[3]

Managers can be a powerful force for improving a company's ethical performance. To be one, they need to be keenly aware of—and on guard against—their tendencies to put the company's interests before all other considerations. Being sensitive to the ethical perspectives of others, particularly the company's many diverse stakeholders, is a step in the right direction.

Another step toward better ethics is simply acknowledging that an ethical outlook has become central to the job of managing today's complex, global corporation, as noted by a leading ethics scholar:

---

[3]However, a recent study looked at the influence upon managers by functional area and reported that influences may differ depending upon whether managers are in the personnel, marketing, manufacturing, or finance departments of the company. See Barry Z. Posner, W. Alan Randolph, and Warren H. Schmidt, "Managerial Values in Personnel, Marketing, Manufacturing, and Finance: Similarities and Differences," *International Journal of Value Based Management*, vol. 6, no. 2, 1993, pp. 19–30.

Few kinds of decision making are exempt from moral or social factors. The issue is whether the manager has chosen to deal with the factors. Moral issues in management are not isolated and distinct from traditional business decision making but right smack in the middle of it. . . . *Moral* competence is an integral part of *managerial* competence. . . . [T]he moral manager sees every evolving decision as one in which an ethical perspective must be integrated. This view to the future is an essential executive skill.[4]

Personal Character and Moral Development

Clarence Walton, a seasoned observer of managerial behavior, says that personal character is one of the keys to higher ethical standards in business. "People of integrity produce organizations with integrity. When they do, they become moral managers—those special people who make organizations and societies better."[5]

Others agree, including one long-time business executive who did an in-depth study of twenty-four business managers who were notable for high-quality ethical standards in their companies. He emphasizes the close connection between personal character and a person's belief system or values.

Virtuous leaders are persons of honesty, integrity and trust. As popularly defined in business literature today, they are concerned about excellence. Facing the rough-and-tumble of competition, and its ancillary temptations, they must exhibit moral courage. But virtue requires more than techniques and personal integrity. Virtue requires the acceptance of equity in human relationships and a commitment to act accordingly. It involves that core element, the belief system of a person.[6]

The most important formative influences discovered by this particular study were a person's religious upbringing, critical events or crises that brought forth what the person really believed in, and seeing the actions and absorbing the beliefs of inspirational role models such as family members, church leaders, teachers, friends, and others. Personal character was forged over a long period of many years and depended largely on the contacts and experiences of each of the managers.[7]

Business schools play a part in educating students about ethical behavior. In a review of recent studies looking at whether ethics education influences students, James Glenn concludes that there is an influence. The teaching of ethics helps students to better recognize ethical issues and resolve ethical dilemmas, although the power of an ethics course may be

---

[4]Archie B. Carroll, "In Search of the Moral Manager," *Business Horizons,* Mar.–Apr. 1987, p. 14.
[5]Clarence C. Walton, *The Moral Manager,* Cambridge, MA: Ballinger, 1988, p. 33 and part III, "The 'Ethic' of Character."
[6]James E. Liebig, *Business Ethics: Profiles in Civic Virtue,* Golden, CO: Fulcrum, 1990, p. 5.
[7]Ibid., pp. 196–197.

short-lived. The firm employing the former business student quickly assumes a significant role as an influence upon the individual's values and behavior.[8]

Managers' moral development

Personal character and personal values—taken together—exert a powerful influence on the way ethical work issues are treated. Since people have different personal histories and have developed their character and values in different ways, they are going to think differently about ethical problems. This is as true of corporate managers as it is of other people. In other words, the managers in a company are liable to be at various **stages of moral development.** Some will reason at a high level, others at a lower level.

A summary of the way people grow and develop morally is diagramed in Figure 5-4. From childhood to mature adulthood, most people move steadily upward from stage 1. Over time, they become more developed and advanced in moral reasoning. At first, they are ego-centered, fixed on avoiding punishment and obediently following the directions of those in authority. Slowly and sometimes painfully, the child learns that what is considered to be right and wrong is pretty much a matter of reciprocity: "I'll scratch your back, if you'll scratch mine." As adolescence comes along the individual enters a wider world, learning the give-and-take of group life among small circles of friends, schoolmates, and similar close-knit groups. Studies have reported that interaction within groups can provide an environment which improves the level of moral reasoning.[9]

This process continues into early adulthood. At this point, pleasing others and being admired by them are important clues to proper behavior. Most people are now "other-directed" rather than "me-directed." Upon reaching full adulthood—the late teens to early twenties in the United States—most people accept the society's customs, traditions, and laws as the proper way to define what is right and wrong. Stages 5 and 6 in Figure 5-4 lead to a special kind of moral reasoning, because people begin to get

[8]A table summarizing past studies on business ethics education can be found in James R. Glenn, Jr., "Can a Business and Society Course Affect the Ethical Judgment of Future Managers?" *Journal of Business Ethics*, vol. 11, 1992, pp. 217–223. An outline for teaching ethics is presented by Thomas R. Piper, Mary C. Gentile, and Sharon Daloz Parks, *Can Ethics Be Taught? Perspectives, Challenges and Approaches at Harvard Business School*, Boston: Harvard Business School, 1993. A study looking at students' ethics and their ethical values four years after graduation is reported by Peter Arlow and Thomas A. Ulrich, "Business Ethics and Business School Graduates: A Longitudinal Study," *Akron Business and Economic Review*, Spring 1985, pp. 13–17.

[9]See Janet M. Dukerich, Mary Lippitt Nichols, Dawn R. Elm, and David A. Vollrath, "Moral Reasoning in Groups: Leaders Make a Difference," *Human Relations*, vol. 43, no. 5, 1990, pp. 473–493; and Donald Nelson and Tom E. Obremski, "Promoting Moral Growth Through Intra-Group Participation," *Journal of Business Ethics*, vol. 9, 1990, pp. 731–739.

FIGURE 5-4

Stages of moral development and ethical reasoning.

SOURCE: Adapted from Lawrence Kohlberg, *The Philosophy of Moral Development*, New York: Harper & Row, 1981.

STAGES OF MORAL DEVELOPMENT AND ETHICAL REASONING

Age Group	Development Stage and Major Ethics Referent	Basis of Ethics Reasoning
Mature adulthood	**Stage 6** UNIVERSAL PRINCIPLES Justice, fairness, universal human rights	Principle-centered reasoning
Mature adulthood	**Stage 5** MORAL BELIEFS ABOVE AND BEYOND SPECIFIC SOCIAL CUSTOM Human rights, social contract, broad constitutional principles	Principle-centered reasoning
Adulthood	**Stage 4** SOCIETY AT LARGE Customs, traditions, laws	Society-and-law centered reasoning
Early adulthood, Adolescence	**Stage 3** SOCIAL GROUPS Friends, school, coworkers	Group-centered reasoning
Adolescence, Youth	**Stage 2** REWARD SEEKING Self-interest, own needs, reciprocity	Ego-centered reasoning
Childhood	**Stage 1** PUNISHMENT AVOIDANCE Punishment avoidance, obedience to power	Ego-centered reasoning

DIRECTION OF MORAL DEVELOPMENT ↑

above and beyond the specific rules, customs, and laws of their own societies. They base their ethical reasoning on broad principles and relationships, such as human rights and constitutional guarantees of human dignity, equal treatment, and freedom of expression. In the highest stage of moral development, the meaning of right and wrong is defined by universal principles of justice, fairness, and the common rights of all humanity.[10]

Research has demonstrated that most people, including managers, get only as far as stages 3 and 4. Their ethical horizons are defined by their family, close friends, neighborhood groups, and society's laws and customs. For managers, who typically reason at stages 3 and 4, the company's

[10]For details and research findings, see Lawrence Kohlberg, *The Philosophy of Moral Development*, San Francisco, CA: Harper & Row, 1981; and Anne Colby and Lawrence Kohlberg, *The Measurement of Moral Judgment, Volume I: Theoretical Foundations and Research Validations*, Cambridge, MA: Cambridge University Press, 1987.

rules and customary ways of doing things become their main ethical compass. While at work, the company is their ethical reference group. For them, the right way to do business depends upon what the boss and one's coworkers accept as right and wrong (this is stage 3 reasoning), as long as everyone also shows a respect for society's laws (this is stage 4 reasoning).[11]

Another way to think about the development of moral character has been developed by Carol Gilligan. She suggests that men's and women's personal characters are distinct because boys and girls are raised differently. Boys and young men learn that fairness and justice result from obeying rules and principles. For them, being ethical means adhering to rules laid down by parents, teachers, friends, and society's customs and laws. Girls and young women follow a somewhat different path in their moral development. Their ethical orientation is toward responsibility to others, caring for others' well-being, being involved in and wanting to preserve close relationships, and valuing direct actions over dependence on rules when facing an ethical dilemma. Corporate managers with this more caring attitude about others would have an important impact on the way companies cope with on-the-job ethical issues.[12]

The development of a manager's moral character—regardless of whether it arises from a rule-based ethics or a caring-based ethics—can be crucial to a company. Some ethics issues—an example is the defense-contractor vice president's dilemma mentioned at the beginning of this chapter—require managers to move beyond selfish interest (stages 1 and 2), beyond company interest (stage 3 reasoning), and even beyond sole reliance on society's customs and laws (stage 4 reasoning). Needed is a manager whose personal character is built on a caring attitude toward others, recognizing others' rights and their essential humanity (a combination of stage 5 and 6 reasoning and care-based reasoning). The moral reasoning of upper-level managers, whose decisions affect companywide policies, can have a powerful and far-reaching impact both inside and outside the company.

Corporate Culture and Ethical Climates

Personal values and moral character play key roles in improving a company's ethical performance. However, they do not stand alone, because personal values and character can be affected by a company's culture.

Corporate culture is a blend of ideas, customs, traditional practices,

---

[11]James Weber, "Managers' Moral Reasoning: Assessing Their Responses to Three Moral Dilemmas," *Human Relations*, vol. 43, 1990, pp. 687–702. See also Robert Jackall, *Moral Mazes: The World of Corporate Managers*, New York: Oxford University Press, 1988.

[12]The "ethic of care" was first presented by Carol Gilligan, *In a Different Voice*, Cambridge, MA: Harvard University Press, 1982. This theme continues in her more recent work, Carol Gilligan, Janie V. Ward, Jill M. Taylor, and Betty Bardige, eds., *Mapping the Moral Domain*, Cambridge, MA: Harvard University Press, 1990.

company values, and shared meanings that help define normal behavior for everyone who works in a company. (This concept was briefly discussed in Chapter 3.) Culture is "the way we do things around here." Two experts testify to its overwhelming influence:

> Every business—in fact every organization—has a culture . . . [and it] has a powerful influence throughout an organization; it affects practically everything—from who gets promoted and what decisions are made, to how employees dress and what sports they play. . . . When [new employees] choose a company, they often choose a way of life. The culture shapes their responses in a strong, but subtle way. Culture can make them fast or slow workers, tough or friendly managers, team players or individuals. By the time they've worked for several years, they may be so well conditioned by the culture they may not even recognize it.[13]

Hewlett-Packard, the California-based electronics manufacturer, is well known for a culture that stresses values and ethics. Called "The HP Way" by employees, the most important values of the culture are confidence in and respect for people, open communication, sharing of benefits and responsibilities, concern for the individual employee, and honesty and integrity. "Particular values, defining ethical and human concerns, have driven all the Company's relationships with its employees, its customers, its suppliers, and the communities in which it has operated. These values have been integrated into and are central to the company's strategy, its objectives and its self-image."[14] The impact of this ethics-oriented culture is evident to managers and employees alike. A Hewlett-Packard manager commented that "It is not easy to get fired around HP, but you are gone before you know it if it is an ethics issue." Another manager said, "Somehow, the manipulative person, the person who is less open and candid, who shaves the truth or the corners of policies, doesn't last. They either get passed over for promotion or they just don't find this a comfortable environment."

Ethical climates

In most companies, a "moral atmosphere" can be detected. People can feel the way the ethical winds are blowing. They pick up subtle hints and clues that tell them what behavior is approved and what is forbidden. This unspoken understanding among employees is called an **ethical climate.** It is the part of corporate culture that sets the ethical tone in a company.[15]

---

[13]Terrence E. Deal and Allan A. Kennedy, *Corporate Cultures: The Rites and Rituals of Corporate Life*, Reading, MA: Addison-Wesley, 1982, pp. 4, 16.

[14]Kirk O. Hanson and Manuel Velasquez, "Hewlett-Packard Company: Managing Ethics and Values," *Corporate Ethics: A Prime Business Asset*, New York: The Business Roundtable, Feb. 1988, p. 75.

[15]Karen N. Gaertner, "The Effect of Ethical Climate on Managers' Decisions," in Richard M. Coughlin, *Socio-Economic Perspectives 1990*, Armonk, NY: M. E. Sharpe, 1990; and Mary E. Guy, *Ethical Decision Making in Everyday Work Situations*, New York: Quorum Books, 1990, chap. 5.

FIGURE 5-5

The components of ethical climates.

SOURCE: Adapted from Bart Victor and John B. Cullen, "The Organizational Bases of Ethical Work Climates," *Administrative Science Quarterly,* vol. 33, 1988, p. 104.

THE COMPONENTS OF ETHICAL CLIMATES

Ethical Criteria	Focus of Ethical Concern		
	Individual Person	**Company**	**Society**
Egoism (Self-centered approach)	Self-interest	Company interest	Economic efficiency
Benevolence (Concern-for-others approach)	Friendship	Team interest	Social responsibility
Principle (Integrity approach)	Personal morality	Company rules and procedures	Laws and professional codes

One way to view ethical climates is diagramed in Figure 5-5. Three different types of ethical yardsticks are egoism (self-centeredness), benevolence (concern for others), and principle (respect for one's own integrity, for group norms, and for society's laws). These ethical yardsticks can be applied to dilemmas concerning individuals, or one's company, or society at large. For example, if a manager approaches ethics issues with benevolence in mind, he or she would stress friendly relations with an employee, emphasize the importance of team play and cooperation for the company's benefit, and recommend socially responsible courses of action. However, if the manager used egoism to think about ethical problems, he or she would be more likely to think first of self-interest, promoting the company's profit, and striving for efficient operations at all costs. A company's ethical climate depends on which combination it has of these nine possibilities.

Research has demonstrated that different companies have different ethical climates. The pioneering study diagramed in Figure 5-5 discovered five types of corporate ethical climates.[16]

- *A caring climate.* A benevolence yardstick was predominant here. Employees said such things as, "The most important concern is the good of all the people in the company as a whole."
- *A law-and-code climate.* A principles yardstick produced a positive attitude toward society's laws and professional codes. A typical em-

[16]Bart Victor and John B. Cullen, "The Organizational Bases of Ethical Work Climates," *Administrative Science Quarterly,* vol. 33, 1988, pp. 101–125.

ployee statement here was, "People are expected to comply with the law and professional standards over and above other considerations."

- *A rules climate*. Company rules and regulations were the principles emphasized here. In this climate, employees agreed that "Successful people in this company go by the book."
- *An instrumental climate*. An egoism yardstick was typical in this climate, and it was focused on the self-interest of the company and of employees. Employees agreed that "People are expected to do anything to further the company's interests, regardless of the consequences." They also said, "In this company, people are mostly out for themselves."
- *An independence climate*. People in this climate preferred a yardstick that put the emphasis on personal beliefs. A typical attitude was "In this company, people are guided by their own personal ethics."

The researchers concluded that "Employees were more satisfied with the ethics of their company when they observed greater levels of caring . . . and lower levels of instrumentalism. . . ."[17]

Ethical impact of corporate culture and ethical climates

By signaling what is considered to be right and wrong, corporate cultures and ethical climates can put much pressure on people to channel their actions in certain directions desired by the company. Among over 1,000 U.S. corporate managers, four out of ten supervisory managers said they had to compromise their personal principles to conform to company expectations, and about seven out of ten managers at all levels believed that such pressures were strong.[18]

This kind of pressure can work both for and against good ethical practices. In a caring ethical climate, the interests of the company's employees and external stakeholders most likely would be given high priority. But in an instrumental ethical climate, employees and managers might be encouraged to disregard any interests other than their own.

ANALYZING ETHICAL PROBLEMS IN BUSINESS

Business managers and employees need a set of guidelines that will shape their thinking when on-the-job ethics issues occur. The guidelines should

---

[17]Ibid., p. 117.
[18]Barry Z. Posner and Warren H. Schmidt, "Values and the American Manager: An Update," *California Management Review*, Spring 1984, p. 211.

help them (a) identify and analyze the nature of an ethical problem, and (b) decide which course of action is likely to produce an ethical result. The following three methods of ethical reasoning can be used for these analytical purposes, as summarized in Figure 5-6.

Utility: Comparing Benefits and Costs

One approach to ethics emphasizes the utility—the overall amount of good—that can be produced by an action or a decision. Should a company close one of its older plants and move production to its modern facility in another part of the country (or world)? The answer would depend on how much good is produced by the move, compared to the harm that could result. If those affected are better off after the move than before, then they would claim that the move was ethical because more good than harm resulted.

This ethical approach is called **utilitarian reasoning.** It is often referred to as cost-benefit analysis because it compares the costs and benefits of a decision, a policy, or an action. These costs and benefits can be economic (expressed in dollar amounts) or social (the effect on society at large) or human (usually a psychological or emotional impact). After adding up all the costs and all the benefits and comparing them with one another, the net cost or the net benefit should be apparent. If the benefits outweigh the costs, then the action is ethical because it produces "the greatest good for the greatest number" of people in society. If the net costs

FIGURE 5-6
Three methods of ethical reasoning.

Method	Critical Determining Factor	An Action Is Ethical When ...	Limitations
Utilitarian	Comparing benefits and costs	Net benefits exceed net costs	Difficult to measure some human and social costs Majority may disregard rights of minority
Rights	Respecting rights	Basic human rights are respected	Difficult to balance conflicting rights
Justice	Distributing fair shares	Benefits and costs are fairly distributed	Difficult to measure benefits and costs Lack of agreement on fair shares

are larger than the net benefits, then it is probably unethical because more harm than good is produced.

The main drawback to utilitarian reasoning is the difficulty of accurately measuring both costs and benefits. Some things can be measured in monetary terms—goods produced, sales, payrolls, and profits—but other items are trickier—employee morale, psychological satisfactions, and the worth of a human life. Human and social costs are particularly difficult to measure with precision. But unless they can be measured, the cost-benefit calculations will be incomplete, and it will be difficult to know whether the overall result is good or bad, ethical or unethical.

Another limitation of utilitarian reasoning is that the rights of those in the minority may be overridden by the majority. Since utilitarian reasoning is primarily concerned with the end results of an action, managers using this reasoning process often fail to consider the means taken to reach the end. Closing an outmoded plant may produce "the greatest good for the greatest number," but this good outcome will not change the fact that some workers left behind may be unable to find decent jobs. The problem is especially difficult for older workers or those not well educated or members of minority groups. A utilitarian solution may leave them in the lurch. They will not agree that this method of reasoning produces an ethical outcome.

In spite of these drawbacks, cost-benefit analysis is widely used in business. Because this method works well when used to measure economic and financial outcomes, business managers sometimes are tempted to rely on it to decide important ethical questions without being fully aware of its limitations or the availability of still other methods that may improve the ethical quality of their decisions. One of these other methods is to consider the impact of business decisions on human rights.

Rights: Determining and Protecting Entitlements

Human rights are another basis for making ethical judgments. A right means that a person or group is entitled to something or is entitled to be treated in a certain way. The most basic human rights are those claims or entitlements that enable a person to survive, to make free choices, and to realize one's potential as a human being. Denying those rights or failing to protect them for other persons and groups is normally considered to be unethical. Respecting others, even those with whom we disagree or whom we dislike, is the essence of human rights, provided that others do the same for us. This approach to ethical reasoning holds that individuals are to be treated as valuable ends in themselves just because they are human beings. Using others for your own purposes is unethical if, at the same time, you deny them their goals and purposes. For example, a union that denies a group of women employees an opportunity to bid for all jobs for which they are qualified is depriving them of some of their rights. Or a company that carelessly disposes of hazardous wastes may be guilty of ignoring the rights of others and simply using the environment for its own selfish purposes.

The main limitation of using rights as a basis of ethical reasoning is the difficulty of balancing conflicting rights. For example, an employee's right to privacy may be at odds with an employer's right to protect the firm's cash by testing the employee's honesty. Some of the most difficult balancing acts have occurred when minorities and women have competed with white males for the right to hold jobs in business and government. Rights also clash when U.S. multinational corporations move production to a foreign nation, causing job losses at home but creating new jobs abroad. In such cases, whose job rights should be respected?[19]

In spite of this kind of problem, the protection and promotion of human rights is an important ethical benchmark for judging the behavior of individuals and organizations. Surely most people would agree that it is unethical to deny a person's fundamental right to life, freedom, privacy, growth, and human dignity. By defining the human condition and pointing the way to a realization of human potentialities, such rights become a kind of common denominator of ethical reasoning, setting forth the essential conditions for ethical actions and decisions.

Justice: Is It Fair?

A third method of ethical reasoning concerns **justice.** "Is it fair or just?" is a common question in human affairs. Employees want to know if pay scales are fair. Consumers are interested in fair prices when they shop. When new tax laws are proposed, there is much debate about their fairness—where will the burden fall, and who will escape paying their fair share?

Justice (or fairness) exists when benefits and burdens are distributed equitably and according to some accepted rule. For society as a whole, social justice means that a society's income and wealth are distributed among the people in fair proportions. A fair distribution does not necessarily mean an equal distribution. The shares received by people depend on the society's approved rules for getting and keeping income and wealth. These rules will vary from society to society. Most societies try to consider people's needs, abilities, efforts, and the contributions they make to society's welfare. Since these factors are seldom equal, fair shares will vary from person to person and from group to group.

Determining what is just and unjust is often a very explosive issue be-

[19]For a discussion of employee rights, see Patricia H. Werhane, *Persons, Rights, and Corporations*, Englewood Cliffs, NJ: Prentice-Hall, 1985.

cause the stakes are so high. Since distributive rules usually grant privileges to some groups based on tradition and custom, sharp inequalities between groups can generate social tensions and demands for a fairer system. An "equal opportunity" rule—that is, a rule that gives everyone the same starting advantages in life (to health, to education, and to career choices)—can lead to a fairer distribution of society's benefits and burdens.

Justice reasoning is not the same as utilitarian reasoning. A person using utilitarian reasoning adds up costs and benefits to see if one is greater than the other; if benefits exceed costs, then the action would probably be considered ethical. A person using justice reasoning considers who pays the costs and who gets the benefits; if the shares seem fair (according to society's rules), then the action is probably just. Is it ethical to move a factory from Boston to Houston? The utilitarian would say "Yes" if the net benefits to all parties are greater than the costs incurred by everyone. A person using justice reasoning would say "Yes" if the benefits and costs caused by the move were fairly borne by all parties affected by the move. The utilitarian reasoner is interested in the net sum. The justice reasoner is interested in fair shares.

Applying Ethical Reasoning to Business Activities

Anyone in the business world can use these three methods of ethical reasoning to gain a better understanding of ethical issues that arise at work. More often than not, all three can be applied at the same time. Using only one of the three methods is risky and may lead to an incomplete understanding of all the ethical complexities that may be present. It also may produce a lopsided ethical result that will be unacceptable to others.

Figure 5-7 diagrams the kind of analytical procedure that is useful to employ when one is confronted with an ethical problem or issue. Two general rules can be used in making such an analysis.

The unanimity rule

If you want to know whether a decision, a policy, or an activity is ethical or unethical, you first ask the three questions listed in Figure 5-7. As shown in step 2 of the figure, if the answers to all three questions are "Yes," then the decision or policy or activity is probably ethical. If answers to all three are "No," then you probably are looking at an unethical decision, policy, or activity. The reason why you cannot be absolutely certain is that different people and groups (1) may honestly and genuinely use different sources of information, (2) may measure costs and benefits differently, (3) may not share the same meaning of justice, or (4) may rank various rights in different ways. Nevertheless, any time an analyst obtains unanimous answers to these three questions—all "Yeses" or all "Noes"—it is an indication

FIGURE 5-7
An analytical approach to ethical problems.

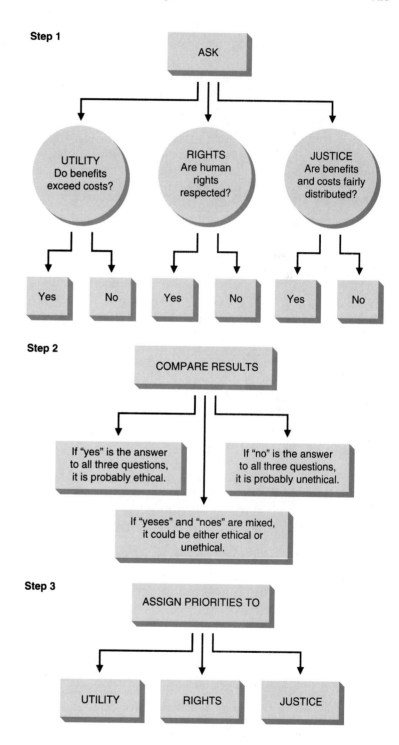

that a strong case can be made for either an ethical or an unethical conclusion.

The priority rule

What happens when the unanimity rule does not apply? What if there are two "Yeses" and one "No," or another combination of the various possibilities? In that case, a choice is necessary. As shown in step 3 of Figure 5-7, a corporate manager or employee then has to assign priorities to the three methods of ethical reasoning. What is most important to the manager, to the employee, or to the organization—utility? rights? or justice? What ranking should they be given? A judgment must be made, and priorities must be determined.

These judgments and priorities will be strongly influenced by a company's culture and ethical climate. A company with an instrumental ethical climate—or one with a rules ethical climate—would probably assign high value to a utilitarian approach that calculates the costs and benefits to the company. A caring ethical climate will bring forth a greater respect for the rights of employees and the just treatment of all stakeholders. Obeying the law would be a top priority in a law-and-code ethical climate.

The type of ethical reasoning chosen also depends heavily on managers' values, especially those held by top management, and on the personal character of all decision makers in the company. Some will be sensitive to people's needs and rights, while others will put themselves or their company ahead of all other considerations.

MAKING ETHICS WORK IN CORPORATIONS

Any business firm that wishes to do so can improve the quality of its ethical performance. Doing so requires two fundamental steps. The first step is to legitimize moral discourse or "ethics talk." The second step requires a company to build ethical safeguards into its everyday routines.

"It's OK to Talk about Ethics Here"

The language of ethics—that is, talking about utility, rights, justice, honesty, integrity, and fairness—is a foreign language in most business firms. Some of the reasons are depicted in Figure 5-8. Study after study has made the same point. Managers

> did not feel much support from others for making moral choices. . . . As moral actors they were on their own. . . . Because managers do not feel able to discuss moral issues with peers and superiors, they often experience the stress of being morally on their own. . . . In a very real sense, morality needs to be brought "out of the organizational closet" and collectively recognized as an important dimension of an organization's culture and as an important aspect of everyday managerial life.[20]

FIGURE 5-8

Why managers are reluctant to talk about ethics.

SOURCE: Frederick Bird and James A. Waters, "The Moral Muteness of Managers." Copyright 1989 by the Regents of the University of California. Reprinted from the *California Management Review*, vol. 32, no. 1, 1989. By permission of the Regents.

WHY MANAGERS ARE RELUCTANT TO TALK ABOUT ETHICS

Moral talk is viewed as creating these negative effects . . .	. . . because of these assumed attributes of moral talk.
■ Threat to Harmony	■ Moral talk is intrusive and confrontational and invites cycles of mutual recrimination.
■ Threat to Efficiency	■ Moral talk assumes distracting moralistic forms (praising, blaming, ideological) and is simplistic, inflexible, soft, and inexact.
■ Threat to Image of Power and Effectiveness	■ Moral talk is too esoteric and idealistic and lacks rigor and force.

Until people in business feel comfortable "talking ethics," progress may be slow in making ethics work in corporations.

Overcoming the ethics language barrier is almost entirely in the hands of a company's senior-level managers. Recent surveys have reported that much of the responsibility for promoting ethics in corporations rests with human resource professionals.[21]

By injecting ethics into their policy statements, by insisting that ethics problems be brought out into the open, and by setting a personal example through their own behavior, company leaders signal others in the company that "it's OK to talk about ethics here." This approach can extend to special ethics training programs and workshops, where the real ethics dilemmas that come up every day can be aired. Lower-level managers and supervisors can be encouraged—and rewarded for doing so—to be more open with their subordinates when ethics problems emerge. When this kind of ethics dialogue occurs, the manager and employee need not feel alone and isolated in grappling with a tough ethics problem. "Talking it out" is the beginning of corporate ethics reform.

Attention given to promoting ethics at work appears to be growing. The Center for Business Ethics surveyed the *Fortune* 1,000 industrial and service companies and reported that companies making efforts to "instill ethi-

[20]James A. Waters and Frederick Bird, "The Moral Dimension of Organizational Culture," *Journal of Business Ethics*, vol. 6, 1987, p. 18. For similar findings, see Barbara Toffler, *Tough Choices: Managers Talk Ethics*, New York: Wiley, 1986; and Kathy E. Kram, Peter C. Yeager, and Gary E. Reed, "Decisions and Dilemmas: The Ethical Dimension in the Corporate Context," James E. Post, ed., *Research in Corporate Social Performance and Policy*, Vol. 11, Greenwich, CT: JAI Press, 1989.

[21]See Joseph A. Petrick and Ellen B. Pullins, "Organizational Ethics Development and the Expanding Role of the Human Resource Personnel," *Health Care Supervisor*, vol. 11, no. 2, 1992, pp. 52–61.

cal values into their firms' routine operations" increased from 80 percent in 1984 to 93 percent in the 1992 study.[22]

Building Ethical Safeguards into the Company

Managers and employees need guidance on how to handle day-to-day ethical situations; their own personal ethical compass may be working well, but they need to receive directional signals from the company. Several organizational steps can be taken to provide this kind of ethical awareness and direction.

Top management commitment and involvement

When senior-level managers signal employees that they believe ethics should receive high priority in all business decisions, a giant step is taken toward improving ethical performance throughout the company. By personal example, through policy statements, and by willingness to back up words with actions, top management can get its message across. Johnson & Johnson's famous Credo—a twenty-four point statement of the company's basic beliefs—is used in just this way. Managers are expected to be familiar with the Credo and to use it in decision making. Failure to follow it can lead to reprimand or dismissal.[23]

Codes of ethics

Surveys show over 90 percent of all large U.S. corporations have **ethics codes.** Their purpose is to provide guidance to managers and employees when they encounter an ethical dilemma. A typical code discusses conflicts of interest that can harm the company (for example, guidelines for accepting or refusing gifts from suppliers, hiring relatives, or having an interest in a competitor's firm). Rules for complying with various laws, such as antitrust, environmental, and consumer protection laws, also are popular code provisions. The most effective codes are those drawn up with the cooperation and widespread participation of employees. An internal enforcement mechanism, including penalties for violating the code, puts teeth into the code. A shortcoming of many codes is that they tend to provide more protection for the company than for employees and the general public. They do so by emphasizing narrow legal compliance—rather than taking a positive and broad view of ethical responsibility toward all company stakeholders—and by focusing on conflicts of interest that will harm the company.[24]

[22]Center for Business Ethics, "Instilling Ethical Values in Large Corporations," *Journal of Business Ethics,* vol. 11, 1992, pp. 863–867.

[23]Laura L. Nash, "Johnson & Johnson's Credo," *Corporate Ethics: A Prime Business Asset,* New York: The Business Roundtable, Feb. 1988, pp. 77–104.

[24]Center for Business Ethics, op. cit., p. 864; and M. Cash Mathews, *Strategic Intervention in Organizations: Resolving Ethical Dilemmas,* Newbury Park, CA: Sage Publications, 1988, chaps. 4 and 5.

Ethics codes are more popular in U.S. corporations than among foreign-based companies. The Conference Board revealed in a 1987 study of 200 companies worldwide that only 30 percent of non-U.S. corporations reported having an ethics code. About one-half of large Canadian companies were found to have a code, while a survey of British corporations turned up just 42 percent with codes. These results are generally compatible with a survey of 189 British, French, and West German business firms, where only 41 percent relied on codes of ethics, compared with the over 90 percent of U.S. companies. Most of the European codes were introduced in the mid-1980s, about a decade later than U.S. experience. A big difference also appears in topics covered in the European and U.S. codes. Employee conduct was included in all of the European business codes but in only 55 percent of U.S. company codes, and local community and environmental affairs were more frequently mentioned in European codes (65 percent) than in U.S. codes (42 percent). However, U.S. companies seemed to be more attentive to customers, suppliers, and contractors than the Europeans. The authors of this comparative study concluded that corporate ethics codes vary considerably from country to country, reflecting differences in political, governmental, and social approaches to business ethics issues.[25]

Ethics committees

Nearly half of all companies surveyed from the *Fortune* 1,000 list of companies have created **ethics committees** or appointed an **ethics officer** to give guidance on ethics matters. It can be a high-level committee of the board of directors, usually chaired by an outside board member (to create an arm's-length relationship with top management). In other cases, the committee's members or the ethics officer are drawn from the ranks of top management. Nearly one-third of all ethics officers are selected from the vice presidential level in the organization or higher. For example, "Boeing's Ethics and Business Conduct Committee is chaired by . . . a senior vice president. It also includes staff vice presidents for finance and human resources, as well as the heads of the company's three operating divisions—commercial, computers, and military."[26]

These committees field ethics questions from employees, help a company establish policy in new or uncertain areas, advise the board of directors on ethics isues, and sometimes oversee ethics training programs.

---

[25]Ronald E. Berenbeim, *Corporate Ethics,* New York: Conference Board, 1987, chap. 3; Leonard J. Brooks, "Corporate Codes of Ethics" [in Canadian companies], *Journal of Business Ethics,* vol. 8, 1989, pp. 117–129; Bodo B. Schlegelmilch and Jane E. Houston, "Corporate Codes of Ethics in Large UK Companies, *European Journal of Marketing,* vol. 23, no. 6, 1989, pp. 7–24; and Catherine C. Langlois and Bodo B. Schlegelmilch, "Do Corporate Codes of Ethics Reflect National Character? Evidence from Europe and the United States," *Journal of International Business Studies,* vol. 21, no. 4, 4th quarter 1990, pp. 519–539.

[26]Quoted from "The Ethics Committee: 'A Vehicle to Keep the Process Moving,'" *Ethikos,* Sept.–Oct. 1990, p. 6. For a discussion of ethics officers, see Rorie Sherman, "Ethicists: Gurus of the '90s," *The National Law Journal,* Jan. 24, 1994, pp. 1, 30–31.

Ethics advisers, advocates, and directors

Pacific Bell, once part of American Telephone and Telegraph, sailed into rough ethical waters when on its own. It was charged with abusive, high-pressure sales tactics, it was sued for allowing dial-a-porn companies to use its telephone lines, and consumers charged that their privacy was violated when Pacific Bell announced plans to sell lists of its customers to telemarketers and direct mail firms. As part of its response, the company established an "ombudsman" office. Its function is to give a private and confidential hearing to ethics complaints of employees who might be reluctant to report their concerns to their immediate supervisor. The staff then investigates and acts as a go-between. "We're trying to create an environment where employees feel safe raising [ethics] issues, trying to create a support system within the company," according to the company's director of external affairs.[27] The use of ethics directors or outside ethics consultants dramatically increased in the early 1990s.

Ethics hot lines

In some companies, when employees are troubled about some ethical issue but may be reluctant to raise it with their immediate supervisor, they can place a call on the company's "ethics hot line." These hot lines have become more common—estimated to be in over 100 companies—since the passage of the U.S. Corporate Sentencing Guidelines in 1991. The ethics director or perhaps a member of the ethics committee receives the confidential call and then quietly investigates the situation. Elaborate steps are taken to protect the identity of the caller, so as to encourage more employees to report ethically questionable activities. In other words, ethics hot lines encourage internal whistle-blowing, which is better for a company than to have disgruntled employees take their ethical complaints to the media. However, some employees react negatively to the implementation of hot lines, citing their distrust of the promise of anonymity and the threat of retaliation by management.[28]

Ethics training programs

Over half of all companies provide ethics training for their managers and employees. After all, firms frequently train their employees in accounting methods, marketing techniques, safety procedures, and technical systems, so why not also give them training in ethics?

This question was answered in the affirmative by many companies that developed ethics training programs in the early 1990s. Union Pacific Railroad, Dunn and Bradstreet, Donnelly Corporation, NYNEX, and Levi Strauss all developed extensive training programs in ethics for their em-

---

[27]"Pacific Bell: Dial E for Ethics," *Ethikos*, May–June 1990, p. 5.
[28]Marcy Mason, "The Curse of Whistle-Blowing," *Wall Street Journal*, Mar. 14, 1994, p. A14. For an example of a company hotline program, see "Bell Helicopter Seeks a Safe Landing for Ethical Employees," *Ethikos*, July–Aug. 1990, pp. 6–8.

ployees. Other firms, such as Honeywell, Northrup, Hughes Aircraft, and Harris Corporation, made significant revisions to update their existing ethics training programs during this time. Cummins Engine Company established ethics as a critical focus within their employee training program, as shown in Exhibit 5-A.

The two most common approaches for establishing a training program in ethics are: (1) developing employee awareness of ethics in business, and (2) drawing attention to ethical issues to which an employee may be exposed. Nearly all ethics training programs include messages from the chief executive officer, discussion of codes of ethics, and procedures for discussing or reporting unethical behavior.

Numerous approaches are used to promote ethical awareness and decision making: case studies, corporate rules or guidelines, decision frameworks (such as the Golden Rule or ethical principles), and approaches which attempt to develop higher stages of moral reasoning. Most of the corporate ethics training programs are permanent modules in the employee training curriculum, with a majority offered to all managerial employees.[29]

Ethics audits

The **ethics audit** system at Hewlett-Packard (HP) emphasizes accountability and communications.

> During the annual audit, the auditor is required to note any deviations from HP's [ethics] standards that become evident during the audit and bring them to the attention of the audit supervisor. In addition, the managers of each operating entity must make a report to the auditor on the corrective action they have taken to deal with any deviations from the standards that emerged in the prior year's audit. Managers must also report on the written procedures they have established for informing new employees of the standards and for providing

[29]Adapted from Susan J. Harrington, "What Corporate America Is Teaching about Ethics," *Academy of Management Executive,* vol. 5, no. 1, 1991, pp. 21–30. Also see John Kohls, Christi Chapman, and Casey Mathieu, "Ethics Training Programs in the Fortune 500," *Business and Professional Ethics Journal,* vol. 8, no. 2, n.y., pp. 55–72.

EXHIBIT 5-A

CUMMINS ENGINE COMPANY ETHICS TRAINING PROGRAM

Cummins Engine Company has established a model for ethical business management, similar to efforts taken by other companies, such as Allied, Chase Manhattan, Citibank, and General Electric. The company conducts a two-day workshop, divided into three phrases: (1) discussion of the social context of management ethics, (2) introduction of conceptual models for ordering and analyzing ethical issues, and (3) analyses of cases and situations brought to the workshop by the participants.

SOURCE: Ronald Nelson, "Training on Ethics: Cummins Engine Company," *Journal of Management Development,* vol. 11, no. 4, 1992, pp. 21–33.

ongoing review of the standards with other employees. If a manager is deficient in either of these areas, an appropriate comment is placed on the manager's letter of evaluation.

In addition, the auditing team must interview the top managers of each entity (in Marketing entities this includes the General Manager, the Business Manager, the Sales Manager, and the Support Manager; in manufacturing entities this includes the General Manager, the Marketing Manager, the Manufacturing Manager, the R&D Manager, and the Controller). During the interview each manager is asked [both general and detailed] questions....

Upon completion of the audit, the auditor is required to sign the following statement: "As a result of the audit tests and procedures performed during the audit of the entity, I did not detect any violations of HP Standards of Business conduct policies, except for those referenced above."[30]

Comprehensive Programs and Ethics Awards

The critical component in installing an effective ethics program is the integration of various appropriate ethics safeguards into a comprehensive program. In an interview, A. W. Clausen, head of BankAmerica Corporation's Executive Committee, described a comprehensive approach to building ethical safeguards at the bank. This program is shown in Exhibit 5-B.

Firms have been honored for their efforts at creating an ethical climate and improving ethical performance. Business Ethics Awards, sponsored by *Business Ethics* magazine, were awarded from 1989 to 1991 and honored Herman Miller Company, Johnson & Johnson, H. B. Fuller, Stoneyfield Yogurt, Patagonia, Monsanto, Polaroid, and other companies for their commitment to ethics and exemplary ethics programs.

In March 1994, *Forbes* magazine published the first annual American Business Ethics Awards (ABEA). Merck and Company was one of the four recipients of the ABEA due to its commitment to provide life-saving medicine to those in need regardless of their ability to pay. Texas Instruments

---

[30]Kirk O. Hanson and Manual Velasquez, "Hewlett-Packard Company: Managing Ethics and Values," in *Corporate Ethics: A Prime Business Asset,* New York: The Business Roundtable, Feb. 1988, pp. 72–73.

EXHIBIT 5-B

BANKAMERICA'S ETHICS PROGRAM

The bank has established an office of insider-trading compliance and integrated ethics in the management training program. Management emphasizes that moral strength and a willingness to forego short-term results in order to achieve long-term goals are essential for ethical performance. Bank management is required to make the following commitments in order to have an ethical impact: lead associates by example, communicate expected ethical standards, and enforce the ethical code.

Source: "BankAmerica Takes a Stand on Ethics," *Banker's Magazine,* vol. 174, no. 4, 1991, pp. 9–13.

also received an ABEA in 1994 for its maintenance of an ethics office, ethics training program, ethics hot line, and other efforts aimed toward enabling its employees to act ethically. Hanna Andersson annually donated five percent of its company profits to charity and created a program to provide clothing to needy children. These efforts at promoting ethical action were recognized in 1994 as the company received the ABEA. Levi Strauss was likewise awarded an ABEA. The exemplary ethical culture at Levi Strauss, reflected in the company's code of ethics and management cycle of caring for its employees' needs and concerns, was honored.

These and other award-winning firms provide the foundation for a collection of corporate ethics role models. The firms' commitment to ethical values and efforts toward establishing effective ethics programs demonstrate that firms can be financially successful and ethically focused.

SUMMARY POINTS OF THIS CHAPTER

- Improving a company's ethical performance depends on the values and goals of its managers, the personal character of employees and managers, and the company's culture and ethical climate. Managers' on-the-job values tend to be company-oriented, assigning high priority to company goals.
- The quality of personal character and moral development varies within any company; moral courage and principled reasoning can greatly assist in coping with ethical dilemmas.
- A company's culture and ethical climate tend to shape the attitudes and actions of all who work there, sometimes resulting in high levels of ethical behavior and at other times contributing to less desirable ethical performance.
- People in business can analyze ethics dilemmas by using three major types of ethical reasoning: utilitarian reasoning, rights reasoning, and justice reasoning.
- Companies can improve their ethical performance when top management leads the way and when organizational safeguards are adopted, such as ethics codes, ethics committees, ethics training programs, and ethics audits.

KEY TERMS AND CONCEPTS USED IN THIS CHAPTER

- Stages of moral development
- Corporate culture
- Ethical climate
- Utilitarian reasoning
- Human rights
- Justice
- Ethics codes
- Ethics committees
- Ethics officer
- Ethics audit

DISCUSSION CASE

ORGANIZING FOR ETHICS REFORM

In the mid-1980s, General Dynamics, headquartered in St. Louis, was one of several U.S. defense contractors charged with fraudulent accounting practices and overbilling the government. Until it had made certain management changes, the U.S. Secretary of the Navy suspended all of General Dynamics' contracts with the navy. One of the changes demanded was the establishment and enforcement of "a rigorous code of ethics for all General Dynamics officers and employees with mandatory sanctions for violation."[31]

Within three months, General Dynamics initiated a comprehensive ethics program, which the company described as follows:[32]

> The organization of the Ethics Program begins with the Board Committee on Corporate Responsibility. The Committee has broad oversight responsibility for company programs and policies in relation to employees, customers, suppliers, shareholders, and community. The Committee consists entirely of outside directors. . . .
>
> In addition to the Board Committee, a Corporate Ethics Steering Group, made up of the heads of major functional departments within the corporation, has responsibility for providing policy guidance and general administrative direction for the Ethics Program corporatewide. Similar groups at some of the divisions provide divisonwide direction for the program. Company attorneys, at both the Corporate Office and at each division, support the Ethics Program with legal counsel concerning the laws, regulations, and government rules that lie behind the specific guidelines for conduct found in the Standards booklet. Corporate and division counsel also play important roles in investigations concerning violations of the Standards.
>
> At the Corporate Office, and at each division, subsidiary, and major location, there are Ethics Program Directors responsible, on a day-by-day basis, for assisting management in the implementation and maintenance of the Ethics Program. The Ethics Program Directors provide advice to employees with questions about the application of the Standards, and they are responsible for screening allegations concerning possible violations of the Standards. Many of the directors maintain hotlines.
>
> Altogether, at the close of 1986, there were 39 individuals serving as Ethics Program Directors around the corporation. There is a full-time Corporate Ethics Program Director at the Corporate Office who reports to the Chairman and Chief Executive Officer. There are full-time directors at each of the defense division headquarters. These persons report directly to their General Manager or President. The directors at the commercial subsidiaries serve on an added-task basis but are available full-time if necessary. As Ethics Program Directors,

[31]Andrew Singer, "General Dynamics Corporation: An Ethics Turnaround?" *Ethikos,* Mar.–Apr. 1990, pp. 1–5, 11.
[32]Reported in Ronald E. Berenbeim, *Corporate Ethics,* New York: Conference Board, 1987, p. 29. Reprinted with permission.

they report directly to their President. At any of the satellite locations of the divisions, there are individuals serving on a part-time basis as Ethics Program Directors. In their capacity as Ethics Program Directors, they report directly to the Manager of their facility.

General Dynamics is a corporation where leadership is most visibly and effectively exercised through line management. Line management has been particularly important in the implementation of the Ethics Program and integration of the Standards. Line management defines expectations and sets the example. Ethical conduct depends on alertness and information. It is not a product of a specialized skill and requires no expert knowledge of philosophy, theology, psychology, law or other academic disciplines. It depends heavily on commitment. "You gotta wanna," as the phrase goes, and in the area of employee attitude, management—up and down the line—has a special responsibility for setting an example. Functional departments also play an important supporting role, especially Human Resources, Legal, Security, and Internal Audit. In the midst of all this, the role of the Ethics Program Director is to assist management in its leadership role and to assist employees generally in their understanding and application of the Standards to daily business conduct.

Discussion Questions

1. Using the major ideas of this chapter, evaluate the strengths and weaknesses of General Dynamics' ethics program. In doing so, identify the specific organizational reforms introduced into the company's routines.
2. What factors that contribute to a company's ethical performance (and which are discussed in this chapter) are not included in this description of General Dynamics' ethics program? How important do you consider their omission to be? Could it make the difference between a high level of ethical conduct and something less desirable?
3. Discuss possible reasons why General Dynamics did not begin their ethics program prior to the navy's suspension of its contracts. In your discussion, refer to Chapter 4 as well as the material in this chapter.

PART THREE

The Corporation in a Global Society

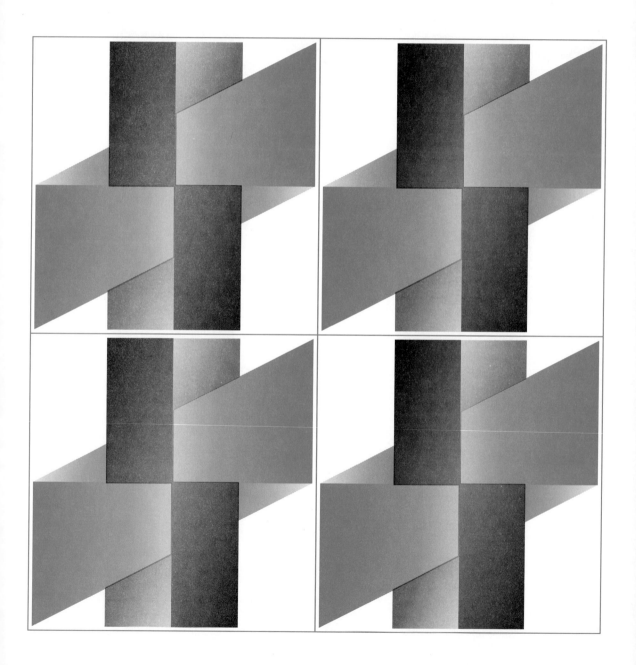

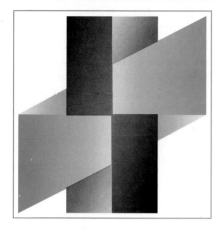

6

Managing in Diverse Social Systems

The globalization of business has affected companies of all sizes and types. This means that modern managers often interact with people from other cultures and socioeconomic systems. In recent years, the social and political systems of free enterprise, central state control, and mixed state-and-private enterprise have undergone enormous change in many countries. Modern managers must understand the nature of these socioeconomic systems, what they permit and forbid, and how they are changing as a "New World Order" evolves at the end of the twentieth century.

Key Questions and Chapter Objectives

This chapter focuses on these key questions and objectives:

- What is the difference between an ethnocentric and a geocentric view of the world?
- How does the social, political, and cultural diversity of nations affect their economies?
- What are the critical differences among systems of free enterprise, central state control, and mixed state-and-private enterprise?
- What major changes occurred in the world's socioeconomic systems in the late 1980s and early 1990s?
- Is it possible for systems of central state control to transform themselves into free enterprise societies?

In May and June 1989, student demonstrations in Tiananmen Square in Beijing produced a worldwide awareness of the democracy movement in China. When the Chinese military intervened, television enabled the world to see the raw power of soldiers, tanks, and armored personnel vehicles being used to inflict death and imprisonment on hundreds of students and other demonstrators. The outrage and anger felt by people in democratic nations forced governments to condemn China's actions and call for the release of imprisoned protestors. China refused to buckle to the pressure and a "war of political wills" began as countries moved to impose sanctions on China for destroying the political rights of dissidents.

In the United States, anger against China escalated and President George Bush was pressured to take strong steps, especially to cut off trade with China. A former ambassador to China, Mr. Bush believed that such actions would backfire and only harden the position of Chinese leaders. A few months later, during his campaign for reelection to a second term as president, Mr. Bush was regularly assailed for a weak "China policy" by his opponent, Bill Clinton. When Clinton won the election, he promised that human rights would guide U.S. policy toward China, and that trade restrictions would follow unless China improved its human rights record. The point of leverage would be the renewal of China's "Most Favored Nation" trading status with the United States which had to be renewed in the spring of 1994, close to the fifth anniversary of the Tiananmen Square protests.[1]

China's economy had been growing rapidly in the 1980s as the government sought to strengthen what is potentially one of the world's great economies.[2] To do so, trade with other nations is essential. Under international law, the United States could grant China a special right to import and export with U.S. businesses free of tariffs, duties, and other trade restrictions. This designation gives a country a **Most Favored Nation (MFN) trading status.** U.S. law requires that this special status be renewed every year. President Clinton's decision to tie MFN renewal to China's human rights record was applauded by various human rights groups, but criticized by many business groups that believed it a great diplomatic mistake to connect commerce and human rights.

As the deadline neared in 1994, President Clinton was pressured on all sides. China refused to cooperate, make concessions, or change its position. Human rights groups put pressure on businesses that had commercial investments and plans to do business in China. One full-page advertisement in national newspapers called on business leaders to ask the president to support human rights in China. Pressures mounted on all sides until the president finally announced that China's MFN would be renewed despite its poor record on human rights.[3] The president said:

> Our relationship with China is important to all Americans. We have significant interests in what happens there and what happens between us. China has an atomic arsenal and a vote and veto in the U.N. Security Council. It is a major fac-

[1]See "The Road from Tiananmen," *The Economist,* June 4, 1994, pp. 19–21. The decision regarding Most Favored Nation status was also covered extensively in newspapers such as the *Wall Street Journal, New York Times,* and *USA Today,* and business journals such as *Fortune* and *Business Week.*

[2]See, for example, "China: The Making of an Economic Giant," Special Report, *Business Week,* May 17, 1993, pp. 54–69.

[3]The decision was announced on May 26, 1994, at a White House press conference. The following excerpt is from the president's statement. See "Clinton's Call: Avoid Isolating China," *New York Times,* May 27, 1994, pp. A1, A8.

tor in Asian and global security. We share important interests, such as in a nuclear-free Korean peninsula and in sustaining the global environment. China is also the world's fastest growing economy. Over $8 billion of United States exports to China last year supported over 150,000 American jobs. . . . I have decided that the United States should renew Most Favored Nation trading status toward China. This decision, I believe, offers us the best opportunity to lay the basis for long-term sustainable progress in human rights and for the advancement of our other interests with China. Extending M.F.N. will avoid isolating China and instead will permit us to engage the Chinese with not only economic contacts but with cultural, educational and other contacts, and, with a continuing aggressive effort in human rights—an approach that I believe will make it more likely that China will play a responsible role, both at home and abroad.

The presidential decision received mixed reviews. While many political and business leaders praised the decision as the best under difficult circumstances, some newspaper headlines (e.g. "Profit Motive Gets the Nod," "Back to Business on China Trade," and "Clinton Eats Some Crow Over China") implied that the United States was backing away from democratic principle. Other commentators pointed to the U.S. need for China's assistance in dealing with the threat of North Korea's nuclear arms as a factor that ultimately shaped the decision.

The decision regarding China's MFN status demonstrates how difficult a "good" decision can be when economic, political, and social interests are entwined. But such complexity is increasingly the case in the modern world. Global interconnections abound and commercial and political interdependencies are becoming more intricate. Businesses of all sizes, large and small, are knitted together in increasingly complex international relationships. Governments and businesses both need to manage this complicated spiderweb of relations with great skill. This can only be done when the people involved understand the key features, differences, and workings of socioeconomic systems. As we move toward the twenty-first century, it seems certain that doing business in diverse social and political systems will become more complicated. The need will grow for managers who understand the dynamics of doing business in a global system.

DOING BUSINESS IN A DIVERSE WORLD

Doing business in other nations is much more than a step across a geographical line. It is also a step into different social, educational, political, and cultural settings. Even businesses operating in one nation cannot function successfully without taking into account a wide variety of stakeholder needs and interests. When companies do business in several countries, the number of stakeholders that must be considered increases even more.

Historically, companies that operated internationally often reflected an **ethnocentric perspective.** This perspective views the home nation as the major source of the company's capital, revenues, and human resource talent. The home country's laws are viewed as dominant, and the company "flies the flag" of its home nation.

Today's businesses have discovered that they must consider the world, not just one nation, as their "home." Companies which have such a **geocentric perspective** adapt their practices to different cultures and environments while maintaining their worldwide identity and policies. They develop managers at all levels from a worldwide pool of talent and seek to use the best people for all jobs regardless of their country of origin.

Companies such as IBM, General Electric, and Exxon have long histories of bringing their managers from around the world to meetings and workshops for the purpose of broadening everyone's understanding of the world in which their company operates.[4] Dow Chemical, for example, manufactures many of its chemical-based products in several plants located around the world. Technical specialists from each plant are "connected" through electronic mail and come together several times a year to discuss advances in science and technology. European corporations such as Nestle (Switzerland), Asea Brown Boveri (Sweden-Switzerland), and Unilever (Great Britain-Netherlands) have led the way toward corporate boards with diverse national membership.

Small companies also develop a geocentric perspective when they do business across borders and among different cultures. Managers throughout the southwestern United States speak Spanish, understand much about Mexico, and engage in cross-border commerce. Citizens of Maine, New York, Michigan, and Washington understand the importance of business with Canadians and are likely to better understand the significance of such Canadian issues as Quebec's desire for independence from Canada.

Diversity and Global Business

As managers participate in the flow of ideas and commerce across national boundaries, they become increasingly geocentric in their outlook and perspective. It is not farfetched for today's students to imagine themselves being citizens of the United States working for a European-owned corporation negotiating an agreement with an Indonesian company to form a joint venture that will manufacture products in Malaysia for sale in Australia. That is a reality many managers are facing today.[5]

---

[4]See, for example, Vladimir Pucik, Noel Tichy, and Carole Barnett, eds., *Globalizing Management: Creating and Leading the Competitive Organization,* New York: John Wiley & Sons, 1992.
[5]Robert B. Reich, "Who Is Us?" *Harvard Business Review,* Jan.–Feb. 1990, pp. 53–64.

The more geocentric managers become in their outlook, the more they are likely to prize cultural, racial, and other forms of diversity in their organization. **Diversity** recognizes the qualities that distinguish people from one another, yet emphasizes the common bonds of understanding, values, and objectives that they share. Companies are often in the lead on these issues, especially if they do business in many cultural settings. (Diversity is also discussed in Chapter 15.)

Andrew Young, former U.S. civil rights leader, UN ambassador, and Mayor of Atlanta, Georgia, has served as an adviser to companies. One company could not get permission to do business in an African country. The company had sent its white, male lawyers to negotiate with the country's authorities. Finally, at Young's suggestion, it sent a female lawyer of color to speak to the officials. She succeeded in negotiating the permissions, in part because of a common cultural connection that her predecessors did not possess.[6] The point, according to Young, is that to succeed in a world of diverse races and religions, companies must be diverse in their people and multicultural in their outlook.

The development of a multicultural perspective that recognizes the importance of diversity is a natural outgrowth of a geocentric approach to doing business in the 1990s. In a world of nearly 200 nations, with thousands of ethnic groups and growing religious diversity, there really is no other way for managers to conduct global business.

A World of Diversity

Business opportunities depend greatly on the size and wealth of a population. As shown in Figure 6-1, the world's population is growing around the world, but at rates that are quite different. Birth rates in Africa, Latin America, and South Asia, for example, are two or three times greater than birth rates in Europe and North America. For companies that sell consumer products such as packaged food, clothing, and even automobiles, there is a need to "go where the people live." Eventually, fast food restaurants, telecommunications, entertainment, and other consumer products and services will find their way to all the world's people.

To do business in world markets, a company must be capable of designing a business plan that fits with the cultural, competitive, and political realities of diverse societies. Societies are defined by cultural features such as language, customs, religion, and traditions. Sociological and anthropological experts who study the fine points of difference among the world's societies recognize that factors such as geography, climate, and the contacts that one society has with others will affect the people, values, organizations, and behavior of that society. Societies also differ greatly in the way

[6]Remarks of Ambassador Andrew Young to the Annual Meeting of the Academy of Management, Social Issues in Management Division, Atlanta, Georgia, August 1993.

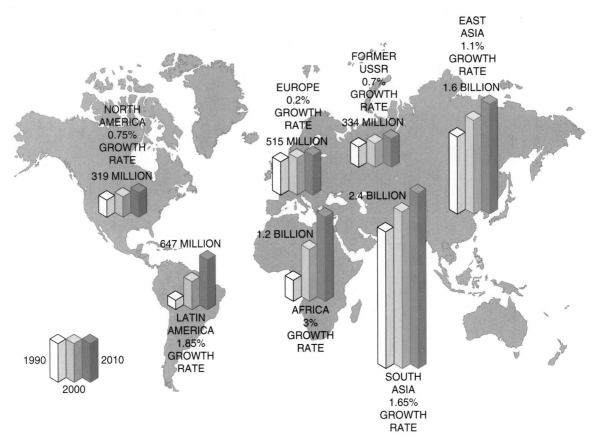

FIGURE 6-1
Global population and its annual growth rates, 1990, 2000, 2010.

their political affairs are organized. For centuries, many European societies were monarchies. Kings, queens, and feudal lords held great power over the population, often through military power. Countries in Africa and Latin America, by contrast, had different cultural histories, with tribal organization giving way—often violently—to colonialism. Today, colonialism has been abandoned and there are only a few monarchies in the world. Political power is held in other forms such as elected democracies or totalitarian systems of state control.

Ideas about the way political power should be organized and held in society ultimately affect the way modern economic activity is conducted. Societies differ greatly in their preferences for cooperation versus competition for example. They also differ in their views about who owns property, who sets the rules for using common resources (e.g., water), and who must approve social investments in technology, public works projects, and caring for people. Because these societal systems integrate and blend decisions about social, political, and economic matters, they are called **socio-**

economic systems. Several basic types of socioeconomic systems are predominant in the modern world and are discussed below.

BASIC TYPES OF SOCIOECONOMIC SYSTEMS

The world's peoples, faced with solving their economic and social problems, generally organize themselves according to one of three basic systems: **free enterprise, central state control,** and **mixed state-and-private enterprise.** In each system, there is some combination of private efforts and government controls, although the balance differs quite greatly. As shown in Figure 6-2, varying amounts of freedom and coercion are present in each system. Some systems are politically democratic and socially open, while others are dominated by a single political party that controls the government and centralizes economic and social decisions.

The socioeconomic system of any nation depends greatly on that nation's history and cultural experience. Strong ties between business and government in Japan, for example, result from a long tradition of close co-

FIGURE 6-2
Basic types of socioeconomic systems.

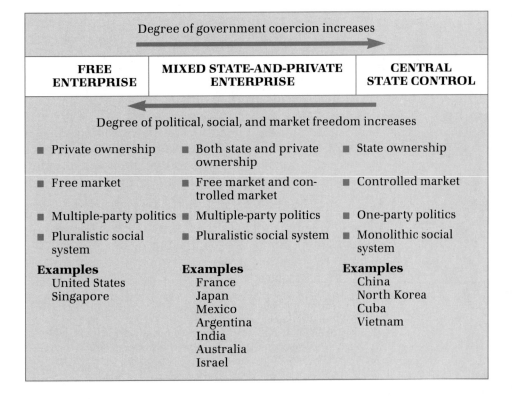

	Degree of government coercion increases →	
FREE ENTERPRISE	**MIXED STATE-AND-PRIVATE ENTERPRISE**	**CENTRAL STATE CONTROL**
← Degree of political, social, and market freedom increases		
■ Private ownership	■ Both state and private ownership	■ State ownership
■ Free market	■ Free market and controlled market	■ Controlled market
■ Multiple-party politics	■ Multiple-party politics	■ One-party politics
■ Pluralistic social system	■ Pluralistic social system	■ Monolithic social system
Examples United States Singapore	**Examples** France Japan Mexico Argentina India Australia Israel	**Examples** China North Korea Cuba Vietnam

operation between public authorities and private merchants. In China, historical traditions of showing respect for a male-dominated family, an honorable standing for elderly persons, a rigid bureaucratic system of government, and a custom of relying on a strong central authority figure in most areas of life still influence Chinese society, commerce, and politics. Fifty years ago, these traditions supported the rise of the Chinese Communist Party and its ascendance to control of government.[7]

But history is not the whole story. Socioeconomic systems can, and do, change, sometimes with dramatic speed. The best example is the collapse of the Soviet Union, and the turning out of communist regimes in eastern Europe in the late 1980s. South Africa provides another dramatic example of change. Following decades of conflict, racial separatism began to give way in the 1990s to a more integrated, and politically democratic, way of life.

Business leaders know that the grounds on which they do business are constantly shifting. As more of the world's commerce becomes global, involving customers, suppliers, and competitors from other nations, cultures, and political systems, it is important that managers understand how diverse socioeconomic systems affect the working of markets and the social-political environment for business. Businesses of all sizes have a stake in understanding these issues.

> The small business in Michigan that sells machine parts to customers in Canada, or the insurance agency in San Antonio, whose customers speak Spanish and have relatives and relationships in Mexico, are also part of the international business community. Under the trade laws that will apply as the United States moves into the twenty-first century, small businesses are expected to greatly expand the number and value of international transactions.

Their understanding of cultural differences, social and political factors, and how these factors affect economic life, is as important to their companies as to the giant businesses that operate around the world. This diversity is already the operating terrain for many international businesses.

To understand the dynamics of socioeconomic change in the world today, it is important to understand the basic features of the dominant socioeconomic systems. The following sections review the central features of each.

---

[7]"China: The Making of an Economic Giant," Special Report, *Business Week*, May 17, 1993, pp. 54–68; Merle Goldman, *Sowing the Seeds of Democracy in China: Political Reform in the Deng Xiaoping Era*, Cambridge, MA: Harvard University Press, 1994; and Oiva Nelson, *Management in China During and After Mao in Enterprises, Government, and Party*, Berlin: Walter deGruyter, 1988, pp. 330 ff.

FREE ENTERPRISE

A free enterprise economy is based on the principle of voluntary association and exchange. People with goods and services to sell take them voluntarily to market, seeking to exchange them for money or other goods or services. Other people with wants to satisfy go to market voluntarily hoping to find the things they want to buy. No one forces anybody to buy or to sell. Producers are drawn voluntarily to the market by their desire to make a profit. Consumers likewise go willingly to the marketplace in order to satisfy their many wants. The producer and the consumer then make an economic exchange in which normally both of them receive an economic benefit. The producer earns a profit, and the consumer has a new good or service that satisfies some want or desire.

As Figure 6-3 suggests, in such a market economy, production is for profit and consumption is for the satisfaction of wants. People try to promote their own interests in the marketplace. To make the system work fairly, competition must be present. For example, a supermarket operator has to sell at prices close to those of its competitors or run the risk of losing customers and profits to the stores offering lower prices. All prices in such a situation are the result of completely impersonal forces of supply (by producers) and demand (by buyers). When these conditions exist, producers are led to produce what consumers want at prices that are low yet allow for a fair profit. The power of consumers and producers in such a system is approximately equal in the marketplace. When governments

FIGURE 6-3

Basic components of a free market system.

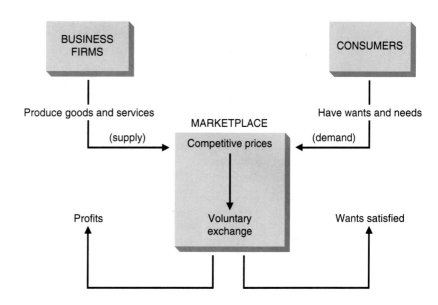

make decisions about production or price, or when either the producer or buyer has disproportionate power relative to the other (e.g., only one supplier of a product or service), the market is not able to work its "magic." In free competitive markets, the consumer is "king" or "queen" because producers must obey the wishes and demands of consumers if they want to make a profit.

In this kind of market system, the members of society satisfy most of their economic wants through these voluntary market transactions. Business firms (like the supermarket) that sell goods and services to consumers for a profit are, at the same time, also fulfilling a social or public need. Consider American society's needs for automobiles, housing, energy, and entertainment. All are produced mostly by private enterprise. Usually there is a very large overlap between society's needs and business's efforts to provide those needs through profit-making activities.

Of course, some serious problems can occur in this kind of socioeconomic system. If people cannot earn an adequate income, for whatever reason, they will not be able to satisfy their wants very well. Large numbers of such persons can create a serious poverty problem for a society. Other difficulties can arise if some business firms find ways to charge noncompetitive prices, if labor unions manage to drive wages to unfair levels, or if government regulations impose unnecessary costs.

Very few economic systems conform strictly to the ideal conception of a free enterprise system. The United States comes the closest of any of the major industrial powers, partly because its historical traditions have favored free markets and partly because the American public prefers the economic and social freedom as well as the less centralized government typical of free enterprise. The economies of Singapore and Hong Kong also exhibit many of the features of "pure" free enterprise.

Free Enterprise Ideology

All socioeconomic systems have an **ideology**—a guiding philosophy—that explains and justifies the way economic activities are organized. This philosophy shapes the attitudes and general outlook of corporate managers and government officials. It channels their thinking about how economic problems should be approached and solved.

Free enterprise ideology originated over 200 years ago in Great Britain. Adam Smith, the Scottish philosopher, first outlined the main components of this capitalist philosophy in 1776 when he wrote *An Inquiry into the Nature and Causes of the Wealth of Nations*. This book, often referred to by the shortened name, *The Wealth of Nations*, has guided business thinking in free market nations ever since. Although its basic principles have been ignored or rendered impractical in many cases, and some people have argued that it has lost much of its relevance for today's business needs, its ideals have drawn a resurgence of interest as eastern European nations have broken away from the domination of the Soviet Union and have struggled to build democratic societies characterized by the core elements of free enterprise ideology.

In free enterprise societies, special attention is given to the major economic role that should be played by private business. Government is assigned the tasks that cannot be undertaken by the private sectors of society. Government is also expected to maintain civil order, protect national security, and enforce the business "rules of the game," such as free competition and private property.

The advocates of a free enterprise system build their case on several basic ideas. These ideas form a core of principles that guide the thinking and actions of business, government, and the public. The following ideas make up the core of this free enterprise ideology.

- *Individualism.* The individual person is considered to be more important than society or its institutions. Social institutions exist to protect and promote the interests of individuals. The opposite is true in a collectivist state, where individuals are subordinate to the powers of government, the military, or organized religion.
- *Freedom.* All individuals must be free to promote and protect their own personal interests. This means that they must have freedom to own property, to choose a job and career, to move freely within a society and to other societies, and to make all of life's basic decisions—where to live, whom to marry, personal life-style—without being coerced by others. In business affairs, it means that companies should be free to pursue profits, and markets should be free of government intervention.
- *Private property.* The bedrock institution on which free enterprise is founded is private property. Unlike socialist states, where government owns the productive system, private property is held by individuals or companies in a free enterprise system. The ownership and use of property allows one to control one's own destiny, rather than to have important decisions made by others.
- *Competition.* Competition is an indispensable part of free enterprise thinking. It encourages the most skilled, the most ambitious, and the most efficient to succeed. Competition is society's way of encouraging high levels of economic performance from all of its citizens. The behavior of firms and individuals is regulated in a system of competition by what Adam Smith called an "invisible hand," rather than the "visible hand" of government regulation. In this way, competition signals business to do its best, or else a competitor will win customers away with a better product or service.
- *Profit.* Profit is a gain made by owners who use their property for productive purposes. Although profits are sometimes made by using property inappropriately (e.g., illegal drug sales), or by not using property at all (e.g., subsidies for not using farmland), a free enter-

prise economy tends to draw all property into productive uses because that is the way to make profits. Profits are a reward for making a productive contribution to society. They act as a powerful incentive to produce goods and services that are of value to a society.

These core beliefs of free enterprise ideology are shown in Figure 6-4. The attraction of a system that is built on principles of individualism, freedom, private property, competition, and profit remains very powerful in the 1990s. People for whom freedom was a distant hope have struggled against great odds to relocate to free enterprise economies. In the mid-1990s, the United States found that it was very hard to draw meaningful distinctions among the economic and political motives of immigrants from Haiti and Cuba who, in great numbers, sought to reach American soil.

Free enterprise systems have incorporated other principles into their ideology. Foremost among these is the belief in *limited government.* The founders of free enterprise generally believed that "that government is best which governs least." Beyond protecting private property, enforcing contracts, and providing for public security, the government is expected to do little. A hands-off policy toward business—often called *laissez faire*—is a preferred ideal of free enterprise theory, although many things have changed since that theory was first advanced.

A second principle is that of *equal opportunity.* Equality of opportunity has long been an element of free enterprise thinking. Although some free enterprise economies have less equal opportunity than others, there is in general a tendency to create a "level playing field" on which all people begin. No special advantages in education, access to jobs, or treatment at work should be allowed to tip the scales in favor of one person over another. Although no nation is able to provide an exactly equal opportunity to every citizen, this ideal remains a powerful element of free enterprise thinking.

FIGURE 6-4

Central elements of today's U.S. business ideology.

- Free enterprise ideals
  - individualism
  - freedom
  - private property
  - competition
  - profit
- More free market, less government intervention
- Socially responsive corporations
- Government-business cooperation in social problem solving
- Promotion of free trade and development of U.S. competitive strength

The *work ethic* is another idea that is central to the working of free enterprise systems. Most Americans have been raised in the belief that work is desirable, good for one's health and self-esteem, necessary if society is to reach high levels of productivity, and even a fundamental right that should not be denied. This work ethic has fluctuated from period to period but remains an important strand in the fabric of free enterprise thought. In the older Calvinist version of the work ethic, work was considered to be a way of using God-given talents to improve oneself. Eventually, this quasi-religious notion of work helped justify the pursuit of worldly wealth by merchants, financiers, and others in business. Today, the interpretation of the work ethic seems to be changing again as companies restructure and reorganize themselves, sometimes eliminating thousands of jobs. In the view of some modern thinkers, work is becoming a "privilege," and the meaning of the work ethic continues to be transformed by new generations.

Business ideology in the United States retains much of the flavor of Adam Smith's views, but with a recognition that changing times have seen new uses of free enterprise philosophy (see Exhibit 6-A). The traditional U.S. business belief system, which was based on pure free enterprise principles, has given way partly to the idea of socially responsive corporations run by socially aware business leaders. This view is especially popular

EXHIBIT 6-A

MARKETS AND FREEDOM GO TOGETHER

One of the most influential books of modern times is a thin little volume by Friedrich von Hayek called *The Road to Serfdom.* Originally published in 1944, the book recently celebrated its fiftieth anniversary with a special commemorative edition.[1] The book has often been quoted by conservative political leaders in the United States and other nations. Professor von Hayek is now deceased, but his words and ideas still shape the debate about the proper role of collective control versus individual control in the modern world. As eastern European nations began their experiments with democracy and capitalism in the 1980s, von Hayek's ideas have been central to the reform effort.

Milton Friedman, a Nobel Prize winner in Economics, was invited to write the introduction to the fiftieth anniversary edition of *The Road to Serfdom.* Assailing those who want government to step in and create "collective" solutions to problems ranging from urban deterioration to environmental harm to health care availability, Professor Friedman summed up his argument this way:

> [Individual values] require an individualistic society. They can be achieved only in a liberal order in which government activity is limited primarily to establishing the framework with which individuals are free to pursue their own objectives. The free market is the only mechanism that has ever been discovered for achieving participatory democracy.[2]

[1]Friedrich von Hayek, *The Road to Serfdom,* Chicago: University of Chicago Press, 1994.
[2]Milton Friedman, "Once Again: Why Socialism Won't Work," *New York Times,* Op-Ed, Aug. 13, 1994.

among leaders of large corporations, while leaders of small businesses and entrepreneurial companies have often questioned how far such social responsiveness can be carried. A larger and more active government that works in close partnership with business has been accepted as necessary for handling some of society's bigger problems, including policies that promote greater trade and U.S. competitive strength. There is disagreement about the range of social problems that government should be responsible for addressing. Some business leaders of the past have favored wide-ranging government involvement, but many others—especially in the 1990s—see the need for government to pare back and limit its role. Corporate stakeholder groups may place curbs and regulations on the private enterprise system, but business believes these should be kept to a minimum because of the costs they impose on business and the public. The business community prefers a free enterprise system based on profits and one where government intervention in business is not allowed to lower efficiency and productivity. The older ideals of freedom, equal opportunity, and the right to make one's own decisions remain at the core of today's business ideology.[8]

CENTRAL STATE CONTROL

Corporations doing business under a system of central state control encounter an entirely different set of rules. In such a system, most economic and political power is concentrated in the hands of government officials and political authorities. The central government owns most property that can be used to produce goods and services. Private ownership may be forbidden or greatly restricted, and most private markets are illegal. Citizens are required to get government permission to move from one job to another. Wages and prices are strictly controlled by government planners and bureaucrats. Foreign corporations, if permitted to operate at all, may find it difficult or impossible to take their profits out of the country.

The political system is also different. Usually, only one political party is authorized to nominate candidates for public office. Not all citizens are permitted to join this one party, so the party's members may form a privileged elite of powerful people. With no political opposition, elections are only a formality, used by the nation's leaders to reinforce their control over politics, government, and other spheres of society. These leaders also set the terms and conditions under which any businesses, including foreign corporations, are permitted to operate. This means that the business

---

[8]For a more detailed discussion, see Gerald F. Cavanaugh, *American Business Values*, 3d ed., Englewood Cliffs, NJ: Prentice-Hall, 1992. Another discussion of the differences between American ideology and that of other nations is George C. Lodge, *The New American Ideology*, New York: Alfred A. Knopf, 1984.

owners, or the corporation's managers, must be skilled in political negotiations with government officials. Since government bureaucracies are often slow moving, corporations must exercise great patience as they wait for decisions to be made by government agencies.

In this type of socioeconomic system, government is the central actor, making decisions about what social and economic needs should be met, and how. Very often, governments in central state control systems resort to elaborate "five-year plans" that spell out what goods are to be produced by state-managed factories, in what volume, and what services (e.g., health care) will be available through what institutions (e.g., hospitals, clinics). Government bureaucrats then allocate budget resources to those factories, hospitals, and other organizations and oversee the way in which they meet their goals. All of the key functions performed by individual companies and managers in a free enterprise system—deciding what will be produced; allocating resources to factories, stores, and farms; and determining wages, costs, and prices—are performed by government in a centrally controlled state system.

> For many years in the former Soviet Union, top officials in government and in the Communist Party chose to emphasize military strength and basic industrial development in their five-year plans. Consumer goods and services were deliberately downgraded or ignored in their overall priority system. Steel, rubber, and chemicals were used to produce tanks, missiles, airplanes, and other weapons rather than to satisfy consumer desires for refrigerators, cars, and televisions. This centralized planning system dominated the Soviet Union's economy until the 1990s, when reforms were introduced.

Government goals in this kind of system can include deliberate attempts to solve social problems. For example, when Fidel Castro and his followers seized power in Cuba in the 1950s, they set about creating a system that provided primary health services to the entire population. The system was very expensive, however, and its continuation depended on Cuba's sale of sugar cane to the Soviet Union and Castro's willingness to shift resources away from other activities. The collapse of the Soviet Union meant the end of the sugar cane subsidy to the Castro government. By the mid-1990s, the Cuban economy had grown steadily weaker because of the costs of such social programs and the government's inability to generate income from exports or other economic activity.

Under central state control, a political ideology usually guides government planners and party leaders in setting production targets and social priorities. The official ideology may promote the broad interests of the masses of workers, or it may warn against the external threats from unfriendly neighbors, or it may praise the virtues of the traditional ways unique to its own people. Production goals of China's economy for many years reflected the priorities of Chairman Mao Zedong that the Chinese people should make themselves secure from foreign attacks. The workforce was exhorted to exceed production quotas in order to carry forward the Chinese "people's revolution." All social goals and economic goals were determined by Mao's political ideology.

Under such circumstances, government planners and party leaders may decide economic production is more important than safe factories, clean air and water, and healthy workers. Central state control, exercised through the party or other means, gives them the power to make such decisions. Coercion is the dominant feature of this type of system, as shown in Figure 6-5. Although large numbers of the population may accept the dominant political ideology, they can do little to change it if they do not like it. The government and the party have a monopoly on economic and social decision making.

Figure 6-5 also contrasts a "top-down" system typical of central state control with the "bottom-up" decision making in a free enterprise system. In a system of central state control, government and party planners at the top decide what and how much consumers will get, in contrast to the free enterprise system in which customers very often shape the system through their decisions to buy, or not to buy, in a competitive marketplace. Every society faces the challenge of designing a system that fits with its peoples' needs, customs, culture, and preferences. The tension between free enterprise and central state control is real, and has been evident in the United States as well as other countries. There is every reason to be-

FIGURE 6-5
Comparison of "top-down" versus "bottom-up" decision making under central state control and in a free market system.

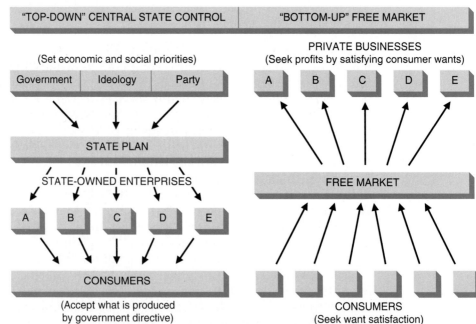

lieve that the tug and pull of social and political forces will continue to require that managers watch, participate in, and make business decisions
with an eye on these important elements of change.

MIXED STATE-AND-PRIVATE ENTERPRISE

Standing between the extremes of free enterprise and central state control is another type of socioeconomic system that combines some elements of both of those systems. Not all, but some portion of the industrial
and financial sectors is owned and operated by the government. This may
include the central bank through which the country's overall monetary
policies are determined; the railroads, bus lines, and airline companies;
public utilities such as telephone, water, electric, and gas companies; and
basic industries such as steel, auto manufacturing, coal mining, nuclear
power, and health care.

In spite of these government-controlled business activities, many mixed
systems provide opportunities for private sector business activity. These
private businesses compete alongside the state enterprises and transact
business according to free market principles; they make profits for their
owners or stockholders, serve consumers, and face the normal business
of failure if the market does not value their products and services.

This type of socioeconomic system is popular in many parts of the
world. As illustrated in Figure 6-2, many countries have developed
economies with a mixture of private and state-owned businesses. These
countries tend to provide a degree of economic and political freedom far
greater than the central state control systems. Political elections are open
and free, and the social system tends to be pluralistic and diverse. However, when compared with free enterprise systems, the amount of market
freedom is considerably less.

As with all socioeconomic systems, the benefits and costs need to be
balanced against each other in judging the system's effectiveness. Japan
and the former West Germany have achieved spectacular economic
growth and productivity rates through such mixed state-and-private enterprise systems. However, their record of social problem solving has not always matched their economic performance. Both countries have had serious environmental pollution problems, a consequence of state policies
that permitted "dirty" industries to operate with less than state-of-the-art
technologies to control emissions.

Mexico's government has committed to a program of change that will
expand private sector activities in an increasingly free enterprise environment. The government has refused to allow competition to challenge its state-owned petroleum industry. The state-owned oil industry
has long been a source of Mexico's wealth, and a matter of national

pride. Fears that competition would damage this national treasure have led political leaders to insist on maintaining the state enterprise. It is noteworthy that this industry has been among Mexico's worst environmental offenders.

The nations of eastern Europe have evolved away from communism toward a form of mixed state-and-private enterprise in the 1990s. These nations include Poland, Hungary, Czechoslovakia (which became two nations, the Czech Republic and Slovakia), and East Germany, which joined with West Germany to form a single German nation. While moving toward free enterprise in some areas, these nations have preserved parts of their former socialist regimes by maintaining government-sponsored health plans, retirements, pension plans, housing, and other social services. Some have found it difficult to abandon price controls, subsidies to farmers, and other forms of state assistance. Railroads, airlines, and other public utilities have also continued under state-enterprise management in many of these nations. Still, the freeing of large portions of their economies to private economic activity signals a turn toward a mixed system of state control and private enterprise. [9]

MILITARIZED NONDEMOCRATIC SOCIOECONOMIC SYSTEMS

Military regimes—in the form of dictatorships or strong military factions—operate in many countries of the world. Central America, for example, has been the scene of powerful military rulers and attempted takeovers in nations such as Panama, Nicaragua, and El Salvador. A small, wealthy class is sometimes allied with the military government, with its members serving in high-level government posts. Human rights and democratic freedoms may be severely curtailed by the government. The press and media are normally government controlled and used for propaganda purposes. Labor unions, religious organizations, and some professional groups (e.g., artists, teachers, writers) are watched carefully by government authorities to keep them from becoming vocal political opponents.

Outwardly, the socioeconomic system may appear to be a mixed system of private and state enterprise. Private markets may be tolerated and many large privately owned businesses may exist. The government may welcome foreign investment and foreign corporations. There may be opposition political parties, although the opposition is unlikely to win in elections, which are usually controlled by the government and military.

[9]See "A Future For Socialism?" *The Economist,* June 11, 1994, pp. 11–12; and "The Left in Western Europe," loc. cit., pp. 17–19.

Military-political regimes have appeared with unfortunate frequency during the last half of the twentieth century. Sometimes they have been pawns of the superpowers as they engaged in skirmishes in different parts of the world. (Iran's military rulers were long supported by the United States and its allies as a way of keeping Iran's oil resources away from the Soviet Union.) Sometimes they have been the result of the ambition of local military officers, impatient with other forms of democratic self-government (e.g., North Korea under Kim IL Sung was the preeminent example until Kim's death in 1994; Myanmar—formerly Burma—is one of the world's most restrictive military regimes in the mid-1990s).

Military-political regimes present a serious ethical and strategic problem for business leaders. In an effort to attract business activity, such regimes may be willing to make attractive deals to companies. Low taxes, low wages, guaranteed freedom from criticism in the press, and weak environmental rules and regulations are among the attractions that a military regime can create through its power. Still, if a company knows that human rights are suppressed, that military leaders are lining their own pockets with money that should go to the country, and that corruption and abuse of power are typical of the regime, business leaders must pause and think about long-term consequences. The strategic business question is an ethical question: Are the benefits of doing business in such a system worth the economic, human, and social costs?

SYSTEMS IN TRANSITION: CHINA FACES THE TWENTY-FIRST CENTURY

Socioeconomic systems change over time. In the past ten years, for example, some of the world's most important economies have shifted their position on the scale shown in Figure 6-2. Poland, Romania, Hungary, and other eastern European nations, for example, moved away from central state control toward greater reliance on market forces. Others have shifted away from free markets and toward more government involvement: France nationalized key industries in the 1980s; Japan elected a socialist prime minister in 1994. The United States debated creating a national health care plan, but the public recoiled and voted for political representatives who favored more traditional free market solutions.

When changes like these occur, business is affected and must adjust to the new conditions. Opportunities may be created in some instances, while threats to profitable ways of doing business may appear in others. Whether good or bad for business, one conclusion stands out: a company's strategy will always be affected. This happens because a company's relations with its stakeholders—for example, government, labor, and local communities—are often changed in significant ways.

China's Socioeconomic Pendulum Swings Back and Forth

China provides an important example of the ways in which socioeconomic systems change, and how these shifts in direction can affect corporate economic and social strategy. Since 1949, when Mao Zedong founded the Communist People's Republic of China (PRC), a one-party system of political power has prevailed. The communists abolished private ownership of businesses and farms, and by the 1960s, all industrial output was produced by state-owned and collectively owned firms.

Faced with the enormous task of feeding a rapidly expanding population, Chinese planners wanted to stimulate economic development for their country. One early attempt in the late 1950s, called the Great Leap Forward, was a dismal failure. Then, in the late 1960s, Mao launched the Great Proletarian Cultural Revolution, which proved to be an even greater disaster. China adopted a "go it alone" policy with a vengeance. Ideological purity and loyalty to the Communist regime were elevated to the status of a quasi-religion. Doctors, engineers, university professors, and many other professional and technical persons were sent to the countryside to help with farming chores. Plant managers were subject to the whims of unskilled and inexperienced Communist Party officials and members of the youth-oriented radical Red Guards. Scientific education was severely restricted, and Chinese experts were denied opportunities to make contacts with experts in other nations. Athletes were also banned from international competition. Anyone thought to have a favorable opinion of capitalism was in danger of being jailed, often being called a "capitalist roader" or a "running dog of capitalism." (Deng Xiaoping, who succeeded Mao as China's leader, was himself labeled a "capitalist roader" during this period and was accused of having a "lust for foreign technology and equipment, blatantly opposing the principles of independence and self-reliance.") In spite of official Communist Party enthusiasm for Mao's two big economic programs, they did not succeed in their goals of converting China into a modern industrial nation.

Mao died in 1976 and was succeeded by Deng Xiaoping in 1978. Deng's attitude toward economic development and capitalism was strikingly different from Mao's. Deng and his supporters took a pragmatic view of relations with free enterprise systems. China needed technology, foreign capital, an infusion of up-to-date scientific and technical knowledge, and a renewal of contacts with other industrial nations. The United States, Europe, and even former archenemy Japan were invited to explore possible trade, scientific, and educational exchanges. Management know-how was sought from American business schools, and Chinese students were sent to universities and technical schools in the West.

Deng also loosened a number of centralized controls. Plant managers were allowed to set their own production targets rather than take orders from government planners, and some plants were permitted to keep and invest some of their profits rather than give them back to the central government. Small entrepeneurs—for example, the owner of a noodle stand in Canton or of a small restaurant in Chongqing—no longer had to risk jail for owning property and making small profits. In the all-important countryside, farmers could raise crops and sell them in private markets, a forbidden practice that could have led to jail during Mao's regime. Deng broke up China's state-owned airline into five companies in order to promote efficiency and service.

One important innovation was the creation of **Special Economic Zones** along China's coast. These carefully restricted regions are industrial areas reserved for foreign corporations that wish to do business in China. Corporations are able to take advantage of Chinese labor costs (low), productivity (high), and easy access to a market of more than 1 billion consumers. Major consumer products companies such as Johnson & Johnson and Procter & Gamble, along with dozens of high-technology manufacturers, set up shop inside the zones. The Special Economic Zones enabled China to have its centrally planned economic cake and eat it too (with free enterprise advantages). Figure 6-6 shows how China and foreign corporations benefited from the zones.

Just as China appeared to be adopting some free enterprise practices, the pendulum swung back toward central state control. In 1989, the student democracy movement was seen to threaten the supremacy of one-party control by the Communists. The military moved into Tiananmen Square and crushed the protestors. Also, Deng's economic reforms had worked unevenly: some created inflation and income disparities and encouraged political corruption. Relaxed controls over farm and regional industries made it harder for central planners to meet their goals. "Recentralization"—which meant drawing power back to the central government

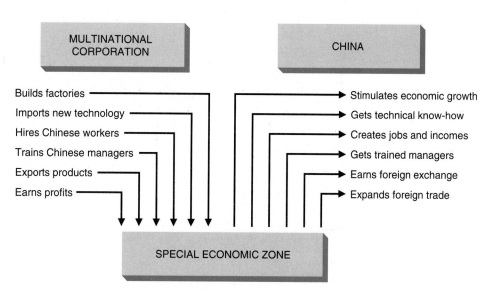

FIGURE 6-6
Benefits of China's Special Economic Zones.

MULTINATIONAL CORPORATION

CHINA

Builds factories — Stimulates economic growth
Imports new technology — Gets technical know-how
Hires Chinese workers — Creates jobs and incomes
Trains Chinese managers — Gets trained managers
Exports products — Earns foreign exchange
Earns profits — Expands foreign trade

SPECIAL ECONOMIC ZONE

and Communist Party officials—became the new policy. Price controls, which had been relaxed, were tightened. The selling of some state enterprises to Chinese citizens and workers was halted. Some semiprivate rural factories were closed. State-owned industries were given preferential treatment and subsidies. Profit-sharing plans between provincial governments and factories were no longer encouraged. Over 2 million private enterprises were closed.

The changes were disastrous for business. The shift was widely viewed as the end of a decade-long economic and political reform movement. Democratic governments condemned China's lurch back toward central state control, and companies that had invested in China were suddenly facing huge risks.

> For example, Givaudan Far East., Ltd., a Swiss company, found it harder to sell chemicals to shampoo and soap factories in China because the government restrictions had slowed the factories' supplies of working capital. The loss of business cost Givaudan nearly 40 percent of its business.

PepsiCo had the same kind of experience, although its bottling plant was in one of the privileged Special Economic Zones. Its explosive growth was halted when Chinese central planners stopped issuing permits for Chinese distributors to buy Pepsi. The planners preferred to direct entrepreneurial efforts toward other purposes. Foreign corporations that had been doing business in consumer products and light-industry sectors found their business and profits drying up as China moved back toward central state control.

However, China's leaders recognized the need to keep up the pace of economic reform and re-instituted procedures that enabled business to function more efficiently. By 1993 and 1994, China was once again booming with business opportunities for foreign companies.[10] The Chinese economy was once again trying to digest the change brought about by political shifts and economic progress. Yet by 1995, an aged Deng Xiaoping was rumored to be near death; speculation about his successor was rampant in Beijing and business board rooms throughout China. Moreover, business losses and related difficulties were souring business executives on China. Familiar obstacles were arising again: Automobile companies, for example, were ordered to make parts in China, rather than import them as a condition of receiving an assembly plant license. The government insisted on majority control of operations, regardless of how much the other joint venture partners invested.[11]

---

[10]See "The Road from Tiananmen," *The Economist*, June 4, 1994, pp. 19–21; and "China: The Making of an Economic Giant," Special Report, *Business Week*, May 17, 1993, pp. 54–69.
[11]See "After the Initial Ardor, China and Foreigners Argue about Money," *Wall Street Journal*, Dec. 2, 1994, pp. A1, A5.

As China faces the twenty-first century, two realities stand out. First, this nation will almost surely become one of the largest economies in the world within twenty years. A research study by the World Bank projected China to be the largest economy in the world by 2020, significantly larger than the United States or Japan.[12] Its population, resources, and demonstrated ability to be productive will enable China to challenge the most successful economies. Second, the historical tensions and the shifting political fortunes of Chinese leaders will continue to tug and pull at the nation's leadership and influence its direction. This will create some uncertainty about China's political future. Businesses will continue to be drawn to China because of the opportunities to enter large markets, produce goods at low cost, and achieve quality and productivity standards. But China's socioeconomic system is not settled, and the future seems certain to contain significant elements of risk.

PREPARING FOR THE NEW WORLD ORDER

Political leaders in the 1990s often use the phrase **New World Order** to describe the relationships that are emerging among nations that are no longer facing the threats of the cold war. From the 1940s to the 1990s, governments around the globe organized into communist and noncommunist political blocs. Organizations such as the Warsaw Pact and the North American Treaty Organization (NATO) were created to deter nations from military actions and geo-political threats. Today, the New World Order is emerging more around economic interests than ideology or politics.

Economic relationships are redrawing the map of the world shown in Figure 6-1. As illustrated in Figure 6-7, the European Union (EU) has emerged as a coalition of nations that is trying to establish a framework for more trade and commerce on the European continent. The North American Free Trade Agreement (NAFTA) will help to integrate the economies of Canada, Mexico, and the United States. In 1994, Chile was admitted to NAFTA; other Latin American and Caribbean nations—including such economic giants as Brazil and Argentina—are likely to seek admission before the end of the 1990s.[13]

In the Asia-Pacific region, there are many dynamic economies, ranging from nations with large land mass such as China, Australia, and Indonesia to the smaller, dynamic economies of Taiwan, Thailand, Singapore, Malaysia, Korea, and others. Figure 6-8 shows the configuration of South-

[12]See "The Global Economy: War of the Worlds," Special Survey, *The Economist,* Oct. 1, 1994, p. 4.
[13]David E. Sanger, "Chile Is Admitted as North American Free Trade Partner," *New York Times,* Dec. 12, 1994, p. A8.

FIGURE 6-7

(a) Countries of the European Union (EU)

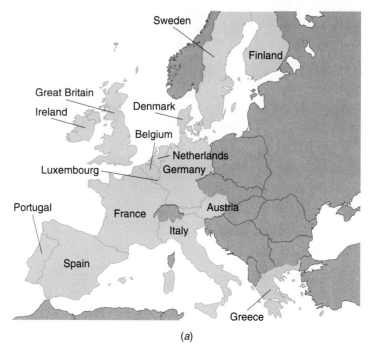

(a)

(b) Countries of the North American Free Trade Agreement (NAFTA) shown in light blue and Mercosur in dark blue.

(b)

FIGURE 6-8
The nations of Southeast Asia.

east Asian countries that are beginning to comprise a significant regional economy. According to a report by a leading business research organization, Southeast Asia represents one of the world's most promising economic regions for the twenty-first century. The members of the Association of Southeast Asia Nations (ASEAN)—Brunei, Indonesia, Malaysia, the Philippines, Singapore, and Thailand—have cooperated to lower trade barriers and create an integrated market of 330 million people with a gross domestic product that is growing at more than 7 percent a year.[14]

The socioeconomic systems represented by the nations of the EU, NAFTA, ASEAN, and other important trade blocs are diverse. These nations do not see the world in the same way, and each nation's policies and political systems reflect its unique cultural and historical experiences. As illustrated in Exhibit 6-B, the results of compromise are often quite surprising.

It is likely that nearly every reader of this book will travel on business to some of the nations mentioned in this chapter in the decade ahead. Whether they travel to nations such as Mexico and Canada, which are

[14]Gerrit W. Gong and Keith Eirinberg, *The Southeast Asian Boom,* Global Business White Paper No. 13, New York: The Conference Board, 1994, p. 6.

EXHIBIT 6-B

BUSINESS, POLITICS, AND CHEESE

Vermont. Wisconsin. France. Switzerland. These are among the world's best known producers of cheese, one of the world's most popular dairy products. Cheese is produced in many countries; virtually any nation that raises dairy cattle has a cheese processing industry. Cheese production is directly tied to milk production, in part because cheese can be stored and preserved for longer periods of time than milk. So, along with milk powder and butter, cheese is one of the world's leading dairy products.

As more of the world's nations establish dairy industries, however, the increased world supply of milk will tend to drive down prices if milk can be transported across national borders. But because dairy farmers are often politically influential, there is resistance to allowing "foreign" milk into a country. Thus, many nations have created trade barriers to prevent imported milk from entering their country and threatening their domestic dairy industries.

Several years ago, when national governments began negotiating the so-called Uruguay Round of the General Agreement on Tariffs and Trade (GATT), cheese became an important issue. Canada, Norway, Finland, Poland, and others wanted to maintain high tariffs on dairy products to protect their dairy industry. Other nations wanted to lower tariffs on all products, including dairy products. France, however, had a more complex concern: it might benefit as an exporter of cheese but also feared a flood of less expensive, lower quality cheese would undermine its domestic cheese market.

What to do? For years, delegates from the nations debated the cheese provision. Finally, they settled on a formula: On January 1, 1995, countries must offer imports access to at least 3 percent of total cheese consumption. Six years later (January 1, 2001), the import access will rise to 6 percent of total consumption. GATT economists estimate that this change will lead to a 50 percent increase in cheese exports by all nations. As we look at the twenty-first century, it seems likely that the world will be eating considerably more cheese.

SOURCE: "GATT Sees Uruguay Round Settlement Lifting Cheese Exports by 50 Per Cent," *The Financial Times*, Dec. 6, 1994, p. 28.

---

close to U.S. borders, or to such distant locations as China, Germany, or Japan, managers of the future will need to recognize and appreciate the social, political, and economic differences and similarities that characterize each society. In the end, these features will affect the willingness of others to do business and shape the manner in which those transactions will occur.

SUMMARY POINTS OF THIS CHAPTER

- An ethnocentric perspective on the world views the home nation as the major source of the company's capital, revenues, and human resource talent. The home country's laws are viewed as dominant, and the company "flies the flag" of its home nation. A geocentric perspective leads companies to adapt their practices to different cultures and environments while maintaining their worldwide identity and policies.

■ Social, political, and cultural diversity influence a society's outlook and its economic relations, including trade with other nations. History, customs, and traditions are reflected in the way governments shape economic and social policy.

■ Free enterprise, central state control, and mixed state-and-private enterprise differ from one another in the amount of freedom permitted for making economic choices, including how much government coercion and regulation is present.

■ Free enterprise ideology emphasizes individualism, freedom, private property, competition, profit, and limited government involvement in the economy.

■ A system of central state control favors central planning by government officials, state-owned property, strong allegiance to the government and nation, and one-party political control.

■ Mixed state-and-private enterprise systems have features of both central state control and free enterprise. Government retains an important and central role in such mixed systems, but freedom grows and markets are allowed to reign in parts of the economy.

■ The major changes that occurred in the world's socioeconomic systems in the late 1980s and early 1990s involved a shift away from central state control in the direction of free enterprise. As a result, many mixed systems are emerging.

■ The experience of China reveals that systems of central state control can be reformed to be more like free enterprise systems, but the transition is difficult, occurs unevenly, and may take many years, including attempts to return to central state control.

■ As the so-called New World Order evolves, managers can be most successful in achieving business goals if they have an understanding of the world's socioeconomic systems and the influences that are shaping the global business environment.

KEY TERMS AND CONCEPTS USED IN THIS CHAPTER

■ Most Favored Nation (MFN) trading status
■ Ethnocentric perspective
■ Geocentric perspective
■ Diversity
■ Socioeconomic systems
■ Free enterprise

■ Central state control
■ Mixed state-and-private enterprise
■ Ideology
■ Free enterprise ideology
■ Special Economic Zones
■ New World Order

DISCUSSION CASE

WHAT IS HONG KONG'S FUTURE?

Hong Kong is one of the world's most exciting cities. It is a commercial and financial center of extraordinary vigor with thriving businesses, a stock market, and banking. It is a center of financial wealth, much of it derived from investments made throughout the Asian Pacific area. But in 1997, Great Britain will end more than a century of political presence in East Asia by turning the governance of Hong Kong over to the People's Republic of China (PRC).

The British decision to return Hong Kong to Chinese political control was long in coming. After World War II, as a new international order came into being, China asserted its historical claims to Hong Kong, whose population is overwhelmingly Chinese and has family ties to Chinese citizens just across the border. The British viewed Hong Kong as a prize jewel in the colonial empire created in earlier centuries. Hong Kong's wealth was great because of its harbor and, in part, because of its entrepreneurial population.

As communism prevailed in the PRC, the British were reluctant to cede Hong Kong to a communist power. For decades, the issues were not negotiated in any meaningful way. China, however, had given the British a ninety-nine-year lease of Hong Kong. The lease expires in 1997.

Britain knew China had a legal right that would be enforced in the World Court, and China's position would surely be supported by other nations. The British government made the decision to negotiate with the Chinese government for the return of Hong Kong.

One of the fears Hong Kong residents harbored about a return to China was the effect on their freedoms of a communist political system. Britain bargained hard to lock in the political rights of the Hong Kong population. The right to a free press, for example, was at issue in 1994 when China imprisoned a journalist for disclosing "state secrets." The "state secrets" involved China's plan to sell gold, raise interest rates, and support the exchange rate, matters routinely reported on by the media in the United States, Japan, and Britain. Economic rights to own property, engage in business, make a profit, and so forth were also at stake.

During the negotiations, many Hong Kong residents began to consider relocating to other countries. Among the favored destinations were Britain, the United States, Canada, and Australia. But these countries all feared the effects of a massive influx of immigrants. Canada adopted a relatively liberal entry policy, and Vancouver, British Columbia, became Canada's center for the Hong Kong Chinese community. Many wealthy Hong Kong business people relocated to Vancouver, buying real estate, establishing businesses, and moving their families. Vancouver has known boom times in the 1990s as the infusion of people, talent, and wealth has improved the business climate.

Companies with operations in Hong Kong face an equally difficult set of choices. Hong Kong is attractive to foreign investment, and the country has attracted many foreign businesses for decades. Many U.S. companies have established offices, factories, and business operations in Hong Kong. American hotels, such as Hyatt, are prominent in the city, and U.S. airlines have helped to make Hong Kong a popular destination for U.S. tourists as well as business travelers. All of these businesses face hard choices as 1997 nears. Should they stay in Hong Kong? Should their investment, which may amount to billions of dollars in plants, facilities, and equipment, be liquidated? Who would buy the assets? Where should they relocate to if the decision is made to leave Hong Kong? And, to add to the complexity, many companies are seeking to expand their businesses in the PRC itself. Would the decision to leave Hong Kong jeopardize their reputations as good citizens with whom Beijing would like to continue doing business?[15]

Discussion Questions

1. How can a business executive who is responsible for an office and staff in Hong Kong decide whether it is best to leave or stay?
2. Develop two alternative scenarios of what may happen in Hong Kong in 1997. What assumptions must be made about the political and economic climate?
3. How might the Chinese (PRC) government "reform" Hong Kong's free enterprise system? What parts of Hong Kong's economy are likely candidates for state control? Refer to concepts in this chapter.
4. Suppose you were the manager of the Hyatt hotel in Hong Kong. Would you be seeking prospective buyers for the hotel? Would you be willing to recommend a sale to Hyatt's top management, even if it was for less than the fair market value of a hotel in a country with a strong free enterprise system?

[15]See "Hong Kong: Things to Come," *The Economist*, Apr. 23, 1994, p. 34.

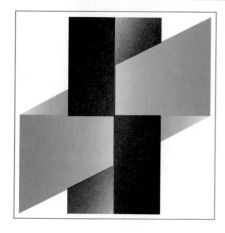

7

Global Challenges to Corporate Responsibility

As business becomes increasingly global, managers are confronted with new social and political challenges. The diversity of cultural values and the differing ways in which political systems treat economic activity require managers to have a more sophisticated view of the world. The rise of multinational corporations, which are becoming more numerous and influential, tests the sovereignty of national governments and requires government leaders to have a more sophisticated view of the world as well. Governments and corporations have a stake in seeing concepts of global corporate responsibility become more widely adopted.

Key Questions and Chapter Objectives

This chapter focuses on these key questions and objectives:

- What factors lead companies to be more involved in international business?
- Why is the multinational corporation one of the most prominent actors in international commerce?
- What distinguishes the multinational corporation from other types of business enterprise?
- Why is there a conflict between national sovereignty and global economic activity?
- How is foreign investment occurring in the United States and with what effects?
- What do host countries and home countries do to encourage, or discourage, multinational companies from doing business?
- What political and social pressures do companies and their managers face as they engage in international business transactions?
- How does corporate social strategy help companies deal with global corporate responsibility challenges?

In 1994, Nelson Mandela, leader of the African National Congress and a former political prisoner, was elected president of South Africa. Following years of international pressure on the government of South Africa to abandon the policy of racial separation known as "apartheid," free elections had successfully transferred power from the minority white population to the majority black population. Among Mr. Mandela's first acts as president was to call upon foreign businesses, which had left South Africa as part of the international campaign for change, to return and provide the jobs and economic activity that are crucial to South Africa's future.

In the 1980s, PepsiCo, the global beverage (Pepsi Cola) and food product (Frito-Lay) giant, had withdrawn from South Africa. Along with many other U.S. multinational companies, PepsiCo had faced continued pressure from shareholders, activists, and other stakeholders to join the economic campaign against apartheid. That pressure eventually succeeded and South Africa returned to a democratic form of government. Now that Mr. Mandela's election was a reality, PepsiCo's management was considering whether it should return to South Africa.

Question: Should PepsiCo return to South Africa under the new government? If so, should its hiring and business development policies favor supporters of the new South African government?

The Chrysler Corporation announced a joint venture with Renault to build small recreational vehicles called "Junior Jeeps" (JJs).[1] The announcement brought joy to the people of Valladolid, Spain, where the manufacturing operation was to be located. The prospect of jobs, increased local income, and other economic benefits was good news for the town, which is about 100 miles north of Madrid.

In the months that followed, joy turned to disappointment as the companies encountered serious problems in their planning. Finally, Chrysler and Renault announced a joint decision to terminate the JJ venture. The companies had been unable to overcome various business problems. For the citizens of Valladolid there would be no jobs and no improvement in their town's economic future.

Question: Do Chrysler and Renault have responsibilities to the citizens of Valladolid? If so, what are they? If not, why?

When British conglomerate Grand Metropolitan acquired U.S. food giant Pillsbury, a corporation headquartered in Minneapolis, Minnesota, business and civic leaders were concerned. Pillsbury had long been an active participant in a variety of arts, education, and development activities sponsored by the Minneapolis-St. Paul ("Twin Cities") business community. Many Twin Cities citizens and organizations worried that Grand Met's acquisition would affect Pillsbury's role as a corporate citizen.[2] Other voices expressed concern that foreign interests were acquiring too

---

[1]"Chrysler-Renault Project Is Ended," *New York Times*, June 13, 1990, p. D1.
[2]See David Logan, *The Community Involvement of Foreign-Owned Companies in the United States*, New York: The Conference Board, 1994.

many U.S. business assets.[3] Twin Cities leaders prepared a letter to Grand Met's chief executive, expressing their concerns and asking Grand Met to make a public statement that it would honor Pillsbury's commitments to the Twin Cities community and that it would continue that tradition of community action.

Question: Should Grand Met make the public statement to continue Pillsbury's corporate citizenship role? If so, why? If not, what, if anything, should the company do to respond to community concerns?

These examples illustrate the complexity of global business relationships and responsibilities. Most businesses can no longer consider just one country as their whole sphere of operations. As companies conduct business with parties in many other nations, their policies and practices have an impact on all of the countries in which the company does business. The incidents described above suggest some of the complex economic, political, and social issues that managers deal with when operating outside of their home country. Issues arise involving stakeholders, business strategies, and corporate power. These are challenges to corporate responsibility at home and abroad.

THE INTERNATIONAL IMPERATIVE

Nearly all large businesses, and many small and medium-sized businesses, are drawn to doing business across national borders in the 1990s. The list of industries that are affected by global competitive forces grows longer each day, and even small retailers—such as those that surround college campuses—are affected by the global production and sales practices of companies that manufacture, import, and sell the clothing, CDs, snack foods, and books. Many U.S. companies have subsidiaries, affiliates, and joint venture partners in other countries. In some instances, the number of foreign employees may actually exceed those from the company's home nation. Exhibit 7-A, for example, demonstrates how much business is done in foreign countries by some well-known U.S. corporations. For many of these companies, more than 50 percent of their revenue comes from sales to customers outside the United States.

Factors Encouraging International Business

Only a few decades ago, the opportunities for global business were limited. International communications systems were much slower; travel and shipping took longer and were more expensive. Today, people can get to virtually any place on the globe in a day or less, and international commu-

---

[3]Ibid; and Martin Tolchin, "Foreign Investors Hold $2 Trillion in U.S. in '89," *New York Times,* June 13, 1990, p. D1.

EXHIBIT 7-A

FOREIGN SALES ARE IMPORTANT TO LEADING U.S. CORPORATIONS

Foreign sales are an important part of the revenues of many well-known U.S. companies. Listed below are ten large U.S. companies, each with substantial sales outside the United States.

1993 Rank	Company	Foreign Revenue*	Total Revenue*	Foreign Revenue as Percent of Total
1	Exxon	$75.6	$ 97.8	77.3%
2	General Motors	38.7	138.2	28.0
3	Mobil	38.5	57.0	67.5
4	IBM	37.0	62.7	59.0
5	Ford Motor	32.9	108.5	30.3
6	Texaco	24.2	45.3	53.5
7	Citicorp	20.7	32.1	64.5
8	E.I. DuPont de Nemours	16.8	32.6	51.4
9	Chevron	16.6	40.3	41.1
10	Procter & Gamble	15.8	30.4	52.1

Some other well-known U.S. corporations also have large foreign sales. For example, in 1993, 67 percent of Coca Cola's $13.9 billion of worldwide sales came from outside the United States; American Express received 29.5 percent of its revenues ($14.1 billion) from foreign sales; Aflac, an insurance carrier, received a whopping 82.5 percent of its $5 billion in revenues from foreign countries; Gillette received 67.5 percent of its $5.4 billion of sales from outside the United States; and McDonald's garnered 46.9 percent of its $7.4 billion of sales from its foreign business operations.

*Revenue in billions of U.S. dollars.
SOURCE: "Getting the Welcome Carpet: The 100 Largest Multinationals," *Forbes*, July 18, 1994, pp. 276–277.

nication is almost instantaneous. It is possible to manage and control business operations in many countries simultaneously, and it can be done effectively and profitably. Resources are sometimes more plentiful and less costly in other countries; labor may be cheaper; taxes may be lower. In some cases, it may even be beneficial if the weather is better.

In the 1990s, several factors are encouraging the internationalization of business.

- *Trade barriers are falling.* As discussed in Chapter 6, western Europe's democratic nations have agreed to move toward integration of their economies; the European Union (EU) is a market of fifteen nations and more than 300 million consumers. Liberalization of trade through actions such as the North American Free Trade

Agreement (NAFTA) and expansion of the General Agreement on Tariffs and Trade (GATT) are producing new opportunities for doing business with more of the world's population. See Figure 7-1.

■ *Social and political reforms have opened nations that were once closed to international business.* The former communist nations of eastern Europe, for example, are now open to doing business with companies from around the world. Millions of people who live in these countries are now able to take advantage of the goods and services that global commerce provides in an open and free marketplace. The political reunification of East and West Germany and the integration of their economies is creating an extraordinarily strong global competitor.

■ *New regions of the world are becoming dynamic competitors in global markets.* A great wave of change has occurred in the Pacific region since the 1980s. The rise of Japan as a leading economic power in the 1980s has been accompanied by the economic dynamism of other Asian nations, including Taiwan, South Korea, Malaysia, Thailand, and Indonesia. China, the world's most populous nation, holds great economic promise because of its size and need to modernize. In the view of many experts, the economies of the Pacific are likely to

FIGURE 7-1

Actions that have opened the door to more global trade.

Action	Impact
Creation and expansion of European Union (EU)—formerly the European Economic Community	Creates a market of more than 300 million people; lowers trade barriers ranging from inspection permits to taxes
Expansion of General Agreement on Tariffs and Trade (GATT)—since World War II, the basic mechanism for nations to discuss liberalization of trade	Provides a framework for nations to lower trade barriers and expand all types of commercial relationships
Creation of North American Free Trade Agreement (NAFTA)—Canada, Mexico, and the United States (Chile admitted 1994); agreement to open borders to free commercial movement	U.S. expands its sales of goods and products in Mexico by more than $50 billion in the first 6 months; Mexico sells an equal amount in the U.S.; many companies set up operations in Mexico; non-U.S. companies establish operations in Mexico as a way to enter U.S. and Canadian markets
Creation of Asian Pacific Economic Council (APEC)—group of nations bordering on c` part of Pacific region; agreemer` to reduce trade barriers	Develops long-term plan to lower trade barriers among APEC nations; sets timetable of dates for action from 1995 to 2020

grow at faster rates than those of any other region of the world. For companies that seek to be where the "economic action" is, countries with large populations—China, India, and Brazil—and countries that are likely to contribute new technologies, products, and services to world markets are "must" locations.

THE GLOBAL BUSINESS ENTERPRISE

Today, much of the world's commerce is done through corporations that operate beyond one country's borders. It has been estimated that more than 37,000 such corporations now do business around the world. The most central fact is that each of these companies does business *across* the borders of two or more nations. This is why UN agencies use the name *transnational corporation (TNC)* to describe such a business. Other experts prefer to use **multinational corporation (MNC)**, *multinational enterprise (MNE)*, or *global corporation.*[4] (See Exhibit 7-B.) Some people prefer to use or emphasize one or another of these terms. However, there is no common agreement as to which is best. Throughout this book, the terms are used interchangeably unless otherwise noted.

Irrespective of the name used to describe them, corporations that do business across national borders are growing larger and are very important to the global economy. As illustrated in Figure 7-2, some of these companies are so large that their annual revenues from worldwide sales exceed the gross national products of very significant nations. For example, General Motors' sales in 1993 exceeded the entire gross national product of Denmark; Wal-Mart had a gross revenue greater than the entire GDP of Poland. In this context, the chief executives of General Motors and Wal-Mart are responsible for economic activities equal to or greater than those managed by the political leaders of Denmark and Poland, respectively.

Size, Power, and Accountability

As their companies become more global in their operations, the leaders of many of these corporations recognize the importance and necessity of harmonizing global business goals with other responsibilities everywhere they operate. In much of the world, business organizations are the powerful engines through which economic growth occurs.

Overall, corporations account for an enormous share of the wealth created in the global economy. While there may be many more proprietorships and partnerships in a country, the economic wealth created by

---

[4]Christopher Bartlett and Sumantra Ghoshal, *Managing Across Borders: The Transnational Solution,* Boston: Harvard Business School Press, 1989.

EXHIBIT 7-B

WHAT'S IN A NAME?

There is a debate about what to call a company whose business ranges across national borders, tying together home and host countries through corporate policies and practices. Here are some of the terms used to describe these companies:

Transnational Corporation (TNC)

Because companies "transcend" or operate across national borders, some experts prefer the term "transnational corporation," or TNC. The United Nations favors this term and has created a Research Center for the Study of Transnational Corporations.

Multinational Corporation (MNC)

The fact that companies operate in multiple countries has led some experts to adopt the term "multinational corporation," or MNC. This term is very popular in the business press and in textbooks. It seems to be the most generic name to describe corporations operating around the world.

Multinational Enterprise (MNE)

Because some of the international giants are state-owned enterprises, rather than corporations, the term "multinational enterprise," or MNE, has entered the vocabulary of international trade.

Global Corporation

This term has become very popular in the 1990s. The term seems to have first been used to describe a small number of companies whose business was conducted in dozens of—perhaps more than 100—nations. Hence, Nestle has long been described as "truly global" because the scope of its operations extends to more than 150 nations around the globe. The term is often applied to companies who do business in several areas of the world (e.g., Europe, Latin America, Asia-Pacific, and North America).

---

them is only a small fraction of that created by corporations. However, small businesses (which are more often proprietorships and partnerships) often account for many more jobs than do the more capital-intensive corporations. The companies listed in Figure 7-2, for example, tend to have more capital investment per employee than typical small businesses. Thus, they may generate fewer jobs per million dollars of investment than a smaller business. Still, very large amounts of capital investment are necessary to build and operate auto plants, steel mills, electric utilities, and other large-scale businesses.

As many governments also take steps to turn state-owned enterprises into competitive businesses through **privatization,** the power of these new corporations is added to that of the private sector. (For an example of how this process works, see the Discussion Case at the end of this chapter.)

FIGURE 7-2

Comparison of multinational corporations' revenues and the gross national product of selected nations.

Source: Company data are derived from "The Forbes Foreign Rankings," *Forbes*, July 18, 1994, pp. 220ff (numbers reflect 1993 revenues); country data are derived from table 3, "Structure of Production, World Bank, *World Development Report*, 1992, New York: Oxford University Press, 1992, pp. 222-223 (numbers reflect 1990 GNP estimates).

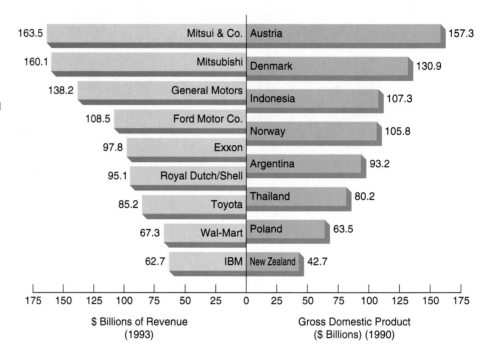

Despite the size and power that corporations possess in the modern world, the legal concept of the corporation remains quite simple: in law, the corporation is an "artificial legal person" with the same rights and powers given to other persons except as modified by the laws of the nation. In the United States and most industrialized nations, a corporation can own property in its own name, buy and sell goods and services, employ others, pay taxes, incur legal obligations, and do everything else that is needed to run a business. Among the things a corporation cannot do are vote in elections and participate as a "citizen" in political activities except as allowed by special laws that are discussed in Chapter 9.

Corporate accountability and responsibility are fundamental aspects of this legal existence. All nations, including the United States, have laws to establish the responsibilities of corporations. If a corporation fails to meet its legal responsibilities, it can be disciplined by financial penalties, be ordered to comply with the law, or even lose its right to exist. This obligation to comply with the law of each nation can pose ethical dilemmas for managers as the following example illustrates.

In the 1970s and 1980s, the white apartheid government of South Africa enacted a number of laws that forced businesses to cooperate with the government's policy of racial separation. Polaroid Corporation, for example, was ordered to sell its instant camera technology to the government for use in issuing identification cards with photos to all citizens. This was a practice used to force nonwhite South Africans to stay in specified areas. Polaroid's management, forced to comply with the South African law, decided to stop doing business in the country. The company closed its operations and withdrew.

There are often disagreements between corporations and governments over the exact terms of legal responsibility. Not surprisingly, many of these involve money.

For example, beginning in the 1970s the State of California sought to impose taxes on the many multinational corporations that were headquartered in the state. Many of those companies argued that it was improper for the State of California to impose a so-called unitary income tax on revenues earned outside of the United States. The disagreement involved years of discussion, lawsuits, and lobbying by business and other interests. The issue was finally resolved by the United States Supreme Court in 1994, when it ruled that California has the right to impose such obligations on corporations that wish to do business there.[5]

Public and Private Roles

Every society tries to strike a balance between business's role as a generator of wealth and its role as an employer of large numbers of people, a seller of goods to customers, and a resource in the communities in which it operates. This public role must be acknowledged by corporate managers and creatively linked to private, wealth-generating activities.

Three ideas guide much of the modern understanding about a corporation's private and public roles, whether it is operating at home or in foreign countries.

First, it is generally accepted that a business is responsible for the consequences that flow directly from its business activities. Thus, a company is accountable for the chemicals it discharges into local rivers, the quality of its products, and the safety of its operations. When a company fails to meet these expectations—as Union Carbide did at its Bhopal, India, plant where leaking chemical vapors killed more than 2,000 residents in 1984—the government is entitled to take action to hold the corporation "to account."

Second, these responsibilities are not unlimited. At some point, for example, the chemicals discharged by a local plant cannot be distinguished from chemicals discharged by dozens of other facilities. At that point, government is required to correct the collective problem and allocate the costs among all businesses. In Bhopal, Union Carbide was the only com-

[5]"California Taxing Method Is Upheld," *Boston Globe,* June 21, 1994, pp. 34, 37.

pany involved. But when dealing with air pollution in Mexico City, for example, there are so many contributors to the pollution that government must find a fair way to set standards and allocate pollution costs.

Third, business should reconcile and integrate its private, profit-seeking activities with its public responsibilities. In most cultures, a person is believed to bear a responsibility for oneself, one's family, and the community. No society holds the view that human beings are accountable only for themselves. Societies cannot function when such ideas prevail. Thus, when the corporation or a business enterprise is part of a community anywhere in the world, the leaders of that business are expected to assume responsibility for the community's well-being. Managers are thereby expected to find ways to harmonize the company's public responsibilities with its private, profit-seeking objectives.

Multinational Corporations

Nowhere is the reconciliation of public and private roles more important, or more at issue, than with the multinational corporation (MNC). The MNC functions in more than one or two countries, establishes ownership of affiliate or subsidiary firms in each nation, and controls those firms through the design of a common strategy. In practice, this means that a group of managers in one country can make decisions that affect thousands, perhaps millions, of people in dozens of countries around the world. Understandably, people in these countries are anxious to know that their interests are being helped, not harmed, by those decisions. That is why governments are often especially active in negotiating terms of entry for MNCs and establishing rules of conduct to guide their behavior in the foreign nation.

The very largest multinational corporations operate in more than 100 nations around the world. Petroleum companies such as Exxon (United States), British Petroleum (United Kingdom), and Shell (Netherlands) conduct exploration, refinery operations, and the marketing of oil products throughout the world. Consumer products companies such as Nestle (Switzerland), Unilever (Anglo-Dutch), and Philip Morris (United States) sell familiar brand names in mind-boggling quantities to people in nearly every corner of the earth. For example, one out of five of all of the world's adult males use a Gillette razor and razor blade to shave each day! Such global brand identification simply underscores the success these companies have known in establishing their identity marketing presence in a world of many cultures and values. Coca-Cola soft drinks, Fuji film, Canon cameras, Siemens electronics, American Express traveler's checks, and Mercedes Benz automobiles are familiar products throughout the world.

The multinational corporation gains its competitive advantage in several ways. First, it sells to customers on a worldwide basis. Second, it draws supplies and raw materials from worldwide sources. And, third, it seeks cost advantages by finding the best places in the world to produce its products. Each industry has a different combination of needs and requirements, but taken as a whole, managers in multinational businesses think globally about customers, suppliers, and operations.

> Electronics and textile manufacturers have turned to countries with low labor costs (e.g., Thailand, Malaysia, Taiwan, Mexico) as the best place to establish manufacturing operations; consumer products companies have balanced low manufacturing costs with access to important markets (e.g., China); and software development companies have tended to locate in countries with better educated populations for their skilled workforce.

As more companies develop a global business outlook and think about their suppliers, employees, and customers in this way, there are fewer assumptions about where a business will be located, or how a particular product will be produced and marketed. But such economic strategies also have impacts and effects on many other stakeholders. The decision to move a business from Michigan to Mexico, for example, affects stakeholders in both locations; expansion of a production facility in Arizona or Argentina will affect employees, customers, and communities in either location. In the 1990s, a corporation's stakeholders are often located in many different parts of the world, and its managers must recognize the responsibilities and challenges involved in such activities. Managers need to think in global terms about every aspect of their business.

NATIONAL SOVEREIGNTY AND CORPORATE POWER

The expansion of global business has created a number of problems. Because global business activity creates new relationships and new forms of activity, existing rules and institutions of government are sometimes inadequate in responding. Among the key problems facing nations are how to protect national sovereignty, how to assure a proper balance between foreign ownership and local ownership, and how to assure citizens that business will behave responsibly. The United States also faces these issues. Each of these issues is discussed below.

National Sovereignty and the Stateless Corporation

Foremost among the challenges facing nations are threats to the **national sovereignty principle.** This principle holds that a nation is a sovereign state whose laws, customs, and regulations must be respected. It means that the government of any nation has the power to create laws, rules, and regulations regarding the conduct of business within its borders. Nations exist by exercising political power over those who live and operate within their borders. Those borders can be protected by military power and by the mutual recognition of borders by other governments.

The second principle that shapes business-government relations in most nations is the **business legitimacy principle.** This principle holds that a company's behavior is legitimate if it complies with the laws of the nation and responds to the expectations of its stakeholders. In theory, the principles of national sovereignty and business legitimacy are not in conflict. In practice, however, there are times when conflicts occur.

> For example, the government of India had a long and difficult struggle with foreign corporations such as Coca-Cola to establish terms that the country and the company could live with. In 1977, Cola-Cola was forced to leave India for refusing to disclose the secret of its product formula. It was not until 1989 that Coca-Cola was able to renegotiate entry into India by setting up a bottling plant in one of the country's export processing zones (free trade zone). The plant would ship 75 percent of its production outside India and 25 percent within India. The exports would help India's foreign trade balance.[6]

As multinational corporations reach across national borders, their global operations may exceed the regulatory influence of any single nation.[7] This has raised concerns that what is emerging is a **stateless corporation.**[8] These are corporations whose facilities, ownership, and customers are everywhere. Therefore, they seem to owe loyalty to no single nation and are able to organize and reorganize around the globe. There are economic and political advantages for being, or appearing to be, "stateless."

> For example, when countries impose trade bans on products from another nation, a company may be able to continue its business if it operates through a subsidiary that is incorporated in a nation that is not the target of the ban. Taiwan and South Korea had banned automobiles from Japan as part of their trade policy. But because Honda Motor Co. had U.S. operations in Marysville, Ohio, it was able to circumvent the restrictions by shipping Honda autos from the United States to Taiwan and South Korea. For the purpose of such trade, Honda was considered a U.S. corporation.

[6]Sanjoy Hazarika, "Effort by Coke Challenged in India," *New York Times,* Feb. 6, 1989, p. D10.
[7]See Richard J. Barnet and John Cavanaugh, *Global Dreams: Imperial Corporations and the New World Order,* New York: Simon & Schuster, 1994. The classic statement of this problem was made by Richard J. Barnet and Ronald E. Muller, *Global Reach: The Power of the Multinational Corporation,* New York: Simon & Schuster, 1974.
[8]"The Stateless Corporation," *Business Week,* May 14, 1990, pp. 98–106.

Statelessness allows a company's management to avoid various political problems, regulatory hurdles, and powerful labor unions. But statelessness does not eliminate corporate responsibilities. As the chief executive officer of SmithKline Beecham, a leading pharmaceutical company, noted, a company must recognize its obligations to stakeholders wherever it does business.

> The rapid flow of technology and the means of production around the globe and the clear trend from many companies to gear their strategies and management attitudes to the global market all point to the emergence of new global enterprises. Indeed, our company, SmithKline Beecham, is a prototype of [such a company].... But I object to the term stateless in describing companies such as ours. The dictionary describes stateless as "without political community." The new global companies—I prefer to call them transnational companies—are not "unfettered from their home countries."... As our corporations become globalized, we assume more responsibility, not less. In the process, we help to define the world market and become a major force for global interdependence, wealth creation, and higher and increasingly common standards for the quality of life.[9]

Global corporations face serious questions of how to operate in legitimate ways in many nations while both respecting the sovereignty of those nations and achieving their economic objectives. Corporate codes of conduct, policy statements and guidelines, and education and training programs are all used by companies to help employees understand that the corporation is a guest in each host country.

Ownership and Control

A related problem for governments and society is the consolidation and concentration of power in the hands of a small number of global firms in key industries. For many years, the petroleum industry was the classic example of an area of economic activity that was dominated and controlled by less than a dozen companies. The power of such companies as Exxon, British Petroleum, Shell, Texaco, Standard Oil of Ohio, and Amoco was greater than that of the governments of nations that produced oil and needed those revenues or nations that depended on oil for military fuel.[10] In the 1990s, the power of financial institutions and global manufacturing industries, such as automobiles and computers, has been challenged as rivaling that of governments themselves.[11] Moreover, as the twenty-first century approaches, many experts are concerned that global communications, media, and entertainment industries will converge to dominate the

---

[9]Harry Wendt (Chairman, SmithKline Beecham, Philadelphia), "Letters to the Editor," *Business Week,* July 9, 1990, p. 8.
[10]See Daniel Yergin, *The Prize,* New York: Simon and Schuster, 1990.
[11]See Barnet and Cavanaugh, op. cit.

so-called information superhighway. The global media empires of such modern entrepreneurs as Rupert Murdock and Ted Turner have been important vehicles for knitting the world together through modern technologies. But fears exist that the personal biases of such strong-willed people may ultimately affect what the world's citizens see and hear through their televisions, computers, and other communications devices.

Managers of global corporations and national governments need to address these problems. Business seeks economic growth and governments usually seek improvement in the standard of living for their citizens. There is much common ground. But fears about concentration of power in multinational companies is understandable. It is the responsibility of business leaders and government leaders to find appropriate ways to reconcile global business imperatives with national sovereignty. Ownership of foreign enterprises is one way governments of host nations try to protect national interests.

Companies cannot operate in a nation without the permission of government. Thus, as in the case of Coca-Cola and India, extensive negotiations may occur regarding the ownership of the business and other terms and conditions. Governments often exert great power as they privatize former state-owned enterprises (e.g., telephone companies and electric utilities), demanding that significant ownership be shared with citizens through the sale of stock and that other terms and conditions be met. Companies and governments also cooperate in developing plans for industries that are critical to the future. Many business-government partnerships exist in the global telecommunications industry, so that the "information superhighway" will encourage technological development while respecting national interests.

Foreign-Owned Business in the United States

Foreign ownership is also a concern for nations that are home countries for many of the world's multinational corporations. For example, foreign-owned businesses have a significant presence in the United States, itself the home of many multinational firms. Figure 7-3 illustrates the presence of foreign-owned businesses in the United States. Notice that the United Kingdom, Canada, Japan, and France led the foreign investment parade in terms of number of foreign-owned manufacturers operating in the United States, but investors from many other nations have also established or acquired businesses in the United States. And immigrants, who often retain strong ties to their native countries, are another segment of the American population most likely to start new businesses, frequently using funds received from relatives or investors outside the United States. These businesses are typically small, but employ many people in the aggregate, often from the family of the entrepreneur. In many cities, immigrants and business persons of foreign extraction operate many of the retail shops, restau-

FIGURE 7-3

Foreign manufacturing businesses in the United States, 1990.

SOURCE: Ned G. Howenstine and William J. Zeile, "Characteristics of Foreign-Owned U.S. Manufacturing Establishments," *Survey of Current Business*, Jan. 1994, pp. 34–62. Derived from table 4, p. 38.

Country of Origin	Number of Establishments	Number of Employees	Value of Shipments (in billions)	Percent of Foreign Company Totals		
	(1)	(2)	(3)	(1)	(2)	(3)
Canada	1,538	269,000	$58.9	12.9%	13.4%	14.1%
France	1,217	178,000	36.1	10.2	8.9	8.7
Germany	1,045	229,000	40.5	8.8	11.4	9.7
United Kingdom	3,219	456,000	80.6	27.6	22.8	19.3
Mexico	64	n/a	n/a	0.5	1.0	n/a
Australia	497	36,000	10.4	4.2	1.8	2.5
Japan	1,356	291,000	65.7	11.4	14.5	15.7
Korea	20	4,000	1.1	0.2	0.2	0.3
Taiwan	37	5,800	1.3	0.3	0.3	0.3

rants, and personal service businesses that serve the community. Although there are occasional problems of ethnic conflict, such businesses are most often real economic assets to a community.

During the 1980s, foreign investment appeared to increase significantly in the United States. A number of highly publicized business acquisitions were made by Japanese investors, including Mitsubishi's 1989 purchase of the famous Rockefeller Center property in New York City. The media coverage helped set off a wave of anger toward foreign (especially Asian) investors and calls from political and business leaders for tolerance of a normal commercial investment. Ironically, American investment in other nations has often sparked the fear that "imperialistic foreigners" were gobbling up national assets. Many countries have created **foreign investment review boards** to analyze and evaluate proposed acquisitions. In the 1970s, Canada, for example, established such a board and required that it review and approve any foreign acquisition of Canadian business. Although the United States decided not to establish such a board, a variety of government agencies, including the Attorney General and the Federal Trade Commission, typically scrutinize such acquisitions for their projected impact on workers, communities, investors, and other national interests.

In 1994, for example, Sprint, a U.S. telecommunications company, agreed to sell a 20 percent stake in the company to the national telecommunications companies of Germany (Deutsche Telekom) and France (France Telecom) for $4.2 billion. The money would be used to expand technology development. Two of Sprint's competitors, AT&T and MCI Communications, immediately expressed concerns about foreign interests being able to compete in the United States while they are blocked from competing in Germany and France. AT&T and MCI asked the Justice Department to investigate and the Attorney General indicated that an inquiry would be launched.[12]

People often have difficulty understanding the facts surrounding foreign investment. As shown in Exhibit 7-C, the facts surrounding foreign ownership of business in the United States illustrate the conflicting interpretations that can be drawn about foreign ownership.

POLITICAL AND SOCIAL CHALLENGES OF DOING BUSINESS ABROAD

Business and society are challenged by multinational business in the political and social arenas. The multinational firm, the host nation, and the company's home country have important stakes in harmonizing one another's goals and objectives. Still, there are significant areas of conflict, which forces managers to decide how to conduct their business activities in light of these challenges to economic and ethical decision making.

Political Challenges

International business is affected by political and governmental factors on two levels. First, in the broadest sense, business operates in an environment shaped by the relationships between governments (home country and host country), which may range from friendly to hostile. Second, even in an atmosphere of normal relations between governments, companies must recognize that host governments are powerful political actors who set the "rules of the game" by which they will operate in the foreign country.

Intergovernmental relations

The relations between national governments have a great deal of influence on international businesses. If two countries are at war, for example, there will be no trade between them.

When Great Britain and Argentina went to war over ownership of the Falkland Islands, for example, British companies such as Unilever, a large consumer products company, found themselves in a real dilemma. Unilever subsidiaries conducted business in Argentina but were barred by the government from doing business with the

---

[12]"Sprint Deal Raises Specter of Trade Flap," *Wall Street Journal,* June 15, 1994, p. B3.

EXHIBIT 7-C

FOREIGN OWNERSHIP OF BUSINESS IN THE UNITED STATES: A REASON FOR CONCERN?

In 1990, there were 11,900 foreign-owned manufacturing establishments in the United States. They employed 2 million workers and shipped over $400 billion of goods. These firms accounted for about 13 percent of all value-added by U.S. manufacturing establishments. More than one-half of this value-added came from four industries: chemical and allied products ($40 billion); food and related products ($20 billion); electronic and other electric equipment ($17 billion); and industrial machinery and equipment ($14 billion).

What do these data suggest? Are there too many foreign-owned businesses in the United States? Do they account for too many jobs, too much economic activity? If these companies were not doing business in the United States, would either the jobs or the production of goods occur?

Clear answers are difficult to draw from such statistics. The share of total U.S. production accounted for by foreign-owned manufacturers was largest in chemicals (32 percent), stone, clay, and glass products (25 percent), and primary metals (19 percent). But foreign-owned companies accounted for less than 5 percent in apparel and textile products, lumber and wood products, furniture and fixtures, and transportation equipment. A reasonable conclusion may be that nothing can be concluded from this information alone!

In judging the effect of foreign ownership, it is important to look at the actual behavior of the companies involved. For example, how do they do in meeting American expectations regarding workplace conditions, wages, product quality, and the discharge of their corporate citizenship responsibilities. Without this information, the picture remains very incomplete.

SOURCE: Data derived from Ned G. Howenstine and William J. Zeile, "Characteristics of Foreign-Owned U.S. Manufacturing Establishments," *Survey of Current Business*, Jan. 1994, pp. 34–62.

"enemy," Great Britain. Similarly, Great Britain ordered all British companies to cease commercial transactions with the "enemy," Argentina. Unilever was therefore under orders from the warring governments not to send or receive messages between its headquarters and its Argentinean businesses. The dilemma facing Unilever's managers was eventually resolved when it was determined that the headquarters and business units could report to Unilever's office in a neutral country (e.g., Brazil) without violating the "dealing with the enemy" rules of the combatants.

But even in the absence of military hostilities, international transactions may be influenced by the political relations of home and host country governments.

Japan and the United States have had a strong but difficult relationship in the past several decades. After World War II, the United States encouraged rebuilding of the war-torn Japanese economy. Much of that nation's industrial base had to be rebuilt: steel, ship building, automobiles, and others. But huge investments and hard work eventually succeeded. By the 1970s, Japan had become a powerful industrial empire, and it used its great production efficiencies to its advantage in the international market. By first exporting steel, then automobiles, to the huge U.S. market, Japanese companies established a base of business in North America.

At first, the United States did not object. Then, as the shares of U.S. firms declined in these markets, business leaders argued that Washington needed to act. Charges of Japanese "dumping"—selling below real costs—to dominate U.S. competitors became familiar and the U.S. government held numerous meetings with Japanese officials. Congress threatened legislative action; lawsuits were brought by companies and government agencies. The result has been that for twenty years, from the 1970s to the 1990s, the United States and Japan have had countless trade negotiations while trying to preserve an uneasy peace.

The shifts in U.S. relations with Japan are mirrored by its changing relationships with other countries such as China, Russia, and the United Kingdom. Economic relations are affected, for better or worse, by political change. Export-oriented industries such as agriculture and high-technology equipment are especially vulnerable to the consequences of such change. As global markets have developed, however, business and government have become much closer partners in achieving political and economic goals. When the United States reestablished economic relations with Nicaragua in 1990, for example, not only did the United States remove economic sanctions previously in force but it pledged $500 million to assist in restoring a stagnant economy. Much of the aid was in the form of credits to buy products and services from U.S. companies.

Host government influence

When a multinational firm enters another country, it is usually subject to a variety of ownership regulations, controls, licenses, and foreign exchange rules imposed by the government. This web of bureaucratic restrictions can be complicated and burdensome for a company. It may be so difficult, in fact, that companies conclude they cannot do business in the nation. Such a situation can actually be counterproductive for countries that are seeking economic development.

The host government may use a variety of sanctions and incentives ("sticks and carrots") to shape and regulate foreign investment, attempting simultaneously to lure investors and prevent excessive manipulation by them.[13] The host government often faces a dilemma of weighing the tech-

---

[13]The stages through which nations develop in dealing with multinational investors is well-presented in William A. Stoever, "The Stages of a Developing Country Policy Toward Foreign Investment," *Columbia Journal of World Business,* Fall 1985, p. 3.

nology, jobs, and tax revenues that foreign investment can bring versus the power that the foreign investor will acquire.

> For example, in 1989 British Airways sought to acquire a significant ownership interest in United Airlines, one of the largest U.S. airlines. The leaders of British Air and United believed the ownership stake would help facilitate the creation of a highly successful international air carrier. But the U.S. government, fearing that such an investment might mean the end of a major U.S.-owned air carrier, decided to invoke an American law that forbids foreign corporations from owning more than 25 percent of any U.S. airline. The deal was stopped. (British Air later bought a significant stake in US Air, a regional air carrier, and in 1994, United Airlines became an employee-owned company.)

National governments often create laws, rules, and regulations to ensure that companies do not engage in certain types of conduct. These standards usually apply to all companies in a nation, or in a specific industry. In some countries, however, national governments may single out multinational businesses for special treatment.

The most extreme form of host government interference occurs when a government insists that it become a partial owner of the foreign business, especially a basic or natural resources industry. This has frequently happened in natural resources industries such as petroleum and mining. Resource-rich nations, such as Brazil, Chile, Papua New Guinea, and Indonesia, have often insisted that foreign mining and exploration firms share ownership with the government. For many years, state-owned enterprises—such as Mexico's national petroleum company—were the rule; then, shared ownership followed. Only in recent times have these countries been willing to allow full foreign ownership of the resources that are viewed as national assets.

In situations of social upheaval or changes in government control, a country may nationalize or expropriate the assets of a company or plant. That is, the government will take ownership and control of the property and may or may not pay for what it takes. In 1960, Fidel Castro nationalized several billion dollars of assets of U.S. firms in Cuba; in 1990, Iraq seized all of Kuwait's assets, including its oil fields. Still, such expropriations are relatively rare and are estimated at no more than about 5 percent of all total foreign-owned assets. More common, by far, is the taking of assets from local owners—especially the political opposition—when a government changes hands or an ethnic war or revolution occurs.

Social Challenges

The social and cultural differences among nations present formidable challenges for the multinational firm, its managers, and their families. Differences in language, physical surroundings, and values of the population can create important business and human conflicts. Business has discovered that social and cultural differences may pose difficult problems in establishing a productive and capable workforce in its foreign affiliates.

Cultural distance

The wide variations in culture among people and nations make each business setting unique. There are important variations in prevailing concepts of human rights, equality among sexes, races, and ethnic groups, and corporate responsibilities. The amount of difference between two social systems is called **cultural distance,** and in many situations it can be very significant. Extensive cultural distance can make it difficult for employees and their families to adapt to foreign job assignments. One researcher has noted that in several studies of foreign job assignments, the failure rate exceeded 30 percent.[14] This has led companies to make great efforts to ease the transition from one culture to another and, equally important, to place people in job assignments that are short-term, or that do not stretch the cultural distance too far.

> Southern China is industrializing and developing at an explosive rate. In Guangzhu province, change is staggering: construction sites are everywhere, with companies racing to get their businesses under way. There are many problems, but the one most often identified by managers in 1994 was "people." U.S. companies such as Procter & Gamble, Motorola, and Johnson & Johnson are highly respected for their human resources practices. But they cannot get enough of the people they would like to staff their Chinese operations. U.S. managers face family pressures since housing, schools, and amenities seem very limited. Chinese managers with the proper skills are so scarce that they are regularly recruited away from one employer to another for much more money and job responsibility. What is the answer? Managers who were interviewed from many different firms agreed: "There is no easy answer."[15]

Inadequate facilities may lead a company to build housing, establish schools, and create transportation systems to ease the difficulties for employees. International business needs not only a proper physical infrastructure of airports, telephones, and fax machines, but a social infrastructure as well. Whether the project is in the remote highlands of Papua New Guinea, the deep jungle of Zaire, or the desert city of Amman, Jordan,

[14]Rosalie L. Tung, "Corporate Executives and Their Families in China: The Need for Cross-Cultural Understanding in Business," *Columbia Journal of World Business*, Spring 1986, pp. 21–25.
[15]Interviews conducted by Fred K. Foulkes (Director, Human Resources Policy Institute, Boston University) in China during the summer 1994.

there are certain requirements that the host country environment must provide for the business to be successful. There must be a system of law that ensures that contracts will be honored; a system of essential civil services, such as fire and police protection; and a social tolerance for people from different nations and cultures. If the government is unable to provide them, it may be necessary for the company to do so or to conclude that it cannot do business in the host country.

Cultural conflicts

Adherence to a host country's cultural norms may also be complicated by the multinational's home country values. Stakeholders in the home nation will be watching the company's conduct abroad: if they find some policy or method of operation unacceptable, there will be pressure on the company to change.

> When U.S. companies conducted business in South Africa during the 1970s and 1980s, the nation's apartheid system of racial separation offended many U.S. citizens. A campaign was organized to force individual companies to practice racial integration in South Africa, despite the country's public policy, or to withdraw and stop doing business in that setting. Pressures grew, and in 1986 the U.S. Congress passed a law imposing economic sanctions on South Africa that pressured some U.S. companies to close their South African operations.

In the case of South Africa, a nearly worldwide consensus was reached that condemned the system of apartheid. Many situations are less clear. The Arab-Israeli conflict, for example, demonstrates how U.S. companies are confronted with opposing host and home country values and laws.

> In 1987, NCR Corporation, a U.S. computer manufacturer, was fined $381,000 for allegedly cooperating with an Arab boycott against Israel. The U.S. Commerce Department charged that nine NCR subsidiaries disclosed information to Arab League members on their ties to Israeli companies. This information could have been used by Arab League members to discriminate against companies having business relations with Israel. U.S. law forbids such disclosure, on the grounds that firms doing business with Israel could be disadvantaged. In addition to NCR, companies such as Citibank and Safeway stores have also been investigated and fined for their alleged participation in the Arab boycott.

Conflicts between the home country and the host country arise for many different reasons. Often, the cultural and political practices of the home country simply are not applied in the host nation. Two examples are familiar to virtually any company doing business around the world: questionable payments and labor standards.

Questionable Payments

Questionable payments by business are those that raise significant questions of ethical right or wrong in the host or home nation. Some people condemn all questionable payments as bribes, but real situations are not that simple. Managers of a foreign subsidiary may find themselves forced to choose between the host country's laws or customs and the policies of corporate headquarters.

The Foreign Corrupt Practices Act regulates questionable payments of all U.S. firms operating in other nations. It was passed in 1977 in response to disclosure of a number of questionable foreign payments by U.S. corporations. The law has the following major provisions:

- It is a criminal offense for a firm to make payments to a foreign government official, political party, or candidate for political office to secure or retain business in another nation.
- Sales commissions to independent agents are illegal if the business has knowledge that any part of the commission is being passed to foreign officials.
- Government employees "whose duties are essentially ministerial or clerical" are excluded, so expediting payments to persons such as customs agents and bureaucrats are permitted.
- Payments made in genuine situations of extortion are permitted.
- Companies whose securities are regulated by the Securities Exchange Act must establish internal accounting controls to assure that all payments abroad are authorized and properly recorded.

It can be seen that the basic purposes of the law are (1) to establish a worldwide code of conduct for any kind of payment by U.S. businesses to foreign government officials, political parties, and political candidates, and (2) to require proper accounting controls for full disclosure of the firm's transactions. The U.S. law applies even if a payment is legal in the nation where it is made. The intention is to assure that U.S. businesses meet U.S. standards wherever they operate.

Many business leaders have criticized the efforts of the U.S. Congress to impose such regulations. Their complaint is that companies from other nations do not have to operate in similar ways and can make payments that tip the competitive scales against U.S. firms. The counterargument, according to proponents of such standards, is that the United States should not slip to the lowest competitive level and should prove its superiority in product quality, service, and other factors, not questionable payments. There is merit to both positions and this is, therefore, a debate not likely to be resolved in the near future.

Labor Standards

Labor standards refer to those conditions that affect a company's employees, or those of its suppliers, subcontractors, or others in the commercial chain. For example, in some countries, sweatshop conditions exist in which women and children labor long hours in extreme heat for very little money and with virtually no safety protection.

> In 1991, Levi Strauss, a U.S. company which has a reputation for progressive social responsibility programs, was accused of using an unethical contractor in Saipan. The contractor was accused of keeping some workers as virtual slaves. Wages were below the island's legal minimum, and conditions were wretched and unsafe. Levi fired the contractor and formed a committee of senior managers to review procedures for hiring contractors. In 1992, the company became the first multinational to adopt a wide-ranging set of guidelines for its hired factories. The guidelines cover the treatment of workers and the environmental impact of production. Levi now sends inspectors who conduct audits of work and safety conditions at all of its contractors. Deficiencies must be corrected promptly or Levi will cancel the contract.[16]

There is growing pressure to ensure that workers who are willing to work for low wages in many developing countries, where social and economic conditions are often quite desperate, not be exploited by unscrupulous businesses. When the North American Free Trade Agreement (NAFTA) was being debated in the United States, organized labor opposition focused on the abuses that could occur as higher paying jobs in the United States became low-paying jobs in Mexico. The creation of labor standards and business commitments to honor them could ease some of this concern. However, as the following example suggests, implementation of such commitments has been uneven in recent years.

> Sony Corporation, Honeywell, and General Electric were among the first companies alleged to have broken U.S. labor laws under NAFTA. In 1994, Sony (Japanese) and the two U.S. companies were accused of actions to stifle union organizing campaigns at their plants in Mexico. Several activist organizations filed a complaint with the National Administrative Office, a U.S. agency established to enforce the terms of the agreement. The group claimed that Sony and Mexican authorities failed to enforce laws that give workers in Sony's plant in Nuevo Laredo, along the U.S. border, rights to hold union elections. The company was charged with making workers work beyond the 48-hour maximum under Mexican law, harassing employees who favored unions,

---

[16]G. Pascal Zachary, "Exporting Rights: Levi Tries to Make Sure Contract Plants in Asia Treat Workers Well," *Wall Street Journal,* July 28, 1994, pp. A1, A9.

and creating dangerous working conditions. Although Sony denied the charges, the complaints foretell a continuing battle to create standards that all stakeholders will support.[17]

Human rights codes of conduct are the newest development in this area of concern. Companies such as Reebok International have created codes of conduct that will be applied to all of its suppliers (see Exhibit 7-D). Some business leaders doubt whether such individual company codes can stop labor abuses in other nations, in part because foreign competitors may not abide by similar standards. This has led some experts to call on the U.S. Congress to create a labor standards law similar to the Foreign Corrupt Practices Act that would set the global labor standards for all U.S. companies, wherever they do business in the world.[18] Despite some political interest in such action, the Congress has thus far declined to develop such legislation.

The best evidence that human rights codes have an impact is found when individual companies take actions based on their codes. For example, Reebok acted on the code principles described in Exhibit 7-D when it threatened one of its Chinese contractors, Yue Yuen International (Holdings), Ltd., with cancellation of orders if workers were not moved out of unsafe dormitories and into safer housing. A story in the *Asian Wall Street Journal* described hundreds of women working in conditions that were unsafe and violated labor regulations in Guangdong Province. After Reebok's protests, Yue Yuen relocated 800 workers from the unsafe dormitories to newer, safer facilities.[19]

[17]Asra Q. Nomani, "SONY Is Targeted in Rights Action Based on NAFTA," *Wall Street Journal,* Aug. 18, 1994, p. A2.
[18]Peter Behr, "Can U.S. Firms Do Well Abroad and Do Good?" *Washington Post,* July 8, 1994, pp. F1, F3.
[19]"Reebok Compels Chinese Contractor to Improve Conditions for Workers," *Wall Street Journal,* Aug. 16, 1994, p. A9.

EXHIBIT 7-D

REEBOK'S HUMAN RIGHTS PRODUCTION STANDARD

The company will only do business with firms that:

1. Do not discriminate in hiring and employment on grounds of race, color, national origin, gender, religion or political or other opinion.
2. Do not require more than 60-hour work weeks on a regularly scheduled basis, except for appropriately compensated overtime in compliance with local laws.
3. Do not use forced labor, including labor that is required as a means of political coercion or punishment. It also will not purchase materials produced by forced prison or other compulsory labor and will terminate business relationships with any sources found to utilize such labor.

SOURCE: Reebok International, company documents and interview. See also, Peter Behr, "Can U.S. Firms Do Well Abroad and Do Good?" *Washington Post,* July 8, 1994, pp. F1, F3.

CORPORATE SOCIAL STRATEGY

Doing business in international settings presents many challenges to businesses and their managers. There is no magic solution to meeting these issues as they arise. Understanding why issues arise and bringing imagination and thoughtful action to bear on them is the best solution. But managers and companies can prepare for the type of challenges discussed in this chapter by asking basic questions and designing a **global corporate social strategy** that matches and balances the company's economic strategy. The following questions are a good place to start the process:

- *Are we being socially responsible in all that we do?* Are we meeting the expectations of our host country as well as our home country? Are there stakeholders in either country who would question our actions?
- *Are we responsive to all of the stakeholders in each country where we do business?* Do we treat employees, customers, suppliers, local communities, and other stakeholders in a fair and just way?
- *Do we see the emerging issues, as well as the immediate social issues, in the countries and communities where we operate?* Are we anticipating change rather than just reacting to it?
- *Do we respect and abide by host government regulations and policies?* Do we have good systems for ensuring that all of our employees and the agents who represent us follow our corporate policies?
- *Do we conduct our business in ways that respect the values, customs, and moral principles of each society, recognizing that there may be times when they may be in conflict with principles of other societies?* Are we prepared to address these conflicts in thoughtful, positive ways?

Companies that address these questions before trouble strikes are better prepared to meet global challenges to corporate responsibility. They are better prepared to prevent crises, anticipate change, and avoid situations that compromise the values and principles for which the company stands. A corporate social strategy always helps managers achieve both the economic and social goals of the company. In the world of global business challenges, it is the management equivalent of the Boy Scout motto: *Be prepared!*

SUMMARY POINTS OF THIS CHAPTER

- Companies are drawn to international business by their search for global customers, suppliers, employees, and cost-effective business operations. Falling trade barriers, socioeconomic and political reforms in many nations, and the new competitiveness of Asian nations are propelling this growth.

- The global business enterprise, or multinational corporation (MNC), is a powerful actor in the world economy. The size and wealth of the largest of these companies rival that of nations. Governments seek to impose legal controls on these companies to ensure responsible corporate behavior.
- The multinational corporation is distinguished by the global perspective of its managers and employees and the ways in which it integrates its private interests with the economic and social aspirations of host nations.
- National sovereignty is challenged in a world where economic interdependence, global communications, and human mobility are increasing and political barriers are more difficult for nations to enforce. Their ability to span national boundaries has led some to refer to MNCs as "stateless" corporations.
- Foreign investment is also increasing in the United States. Large companies from Europe and Asia are locating facilities in the United States and immigrant entrepreneurs are starting small businesses that employ thousands of people.
- Home countries and host countries often encourage international business but structure the "rules of the game" in ways that benefit their citizens. Laws and regulations are created to protect national interests as global business expands.
- Businesses face the challenge of maintaining ethical norms and standards when operating in other nations. Host country customs, traditions, and ways of conducting business may conflict with home country standards in the workplace and in dealing with government officials.
- Global corporate social strategy is a means of assisting management in dealing with complex global responsibility issues in areas such as questionable payments, human rights, and labor standards.

KEY TERMS AND CONCEPTS USED IN THIS CHAPTER

- Multinational corporation (MNC)
- Privatization
- National sovereignty principle
- Business legitimacy principle
- Stateless corporation
- Foreign investment review boards

- Cultural distance
- Questionable payments
- Labor standards
- Human rights codes of conduct
- Global corporate social strategy

DISCUSSION CASE

GENERAL ELECTRIC IN HUNGARY

In 1989, after the iron curtain fell, the General Electric Company, a U.S.-based multinational company with operations around the world, made a major investment in Hungary when it purchased Tungsram, a maker of lighting products. Tungsram was one of Hungary's leading state-owned companies under communist rule. Under Hungary's new democratic government, however, state-owned enterprises were to be privatized. Foreign investment and management experience were sought for these companies that would now have to compete in competitive market environments. The Hungarians wanted to learn how to compete, and General Electric was eager to have Tungsram as a part of its global business.

Things quickly turned unpleasant. Tungsram was losing large amounts of money on its operations. The equipment was old, work practices were inefficient, communication was poor, and a lackadaisical attitude permeated the workforce. General Electric discovered that a business strategy that looked good on paper ran into serious problems when its managers tried to implement it among Tungsram's workers. GE's strategy was to use Tungsram as an entry point into the eastern European markets that had been closed to its products. It intended to bring product quality, high standards of customer service, and aggressive pricing to the marketplace. By using GE management principles, manufacturing quality could be improved; by using the company's marketing experience, customers could be satisfied and profits could be made. Virtually every aspect of the strategy ran into problems.

Costs had to be reduced and quality improved if Tungsram's products were to be competitive. When markets were controlled under communist regimes, neither cost nor quality seemed very important. If plants ran at an operating deficit, the government subsidized the operation. With GE, that was to change. First, GE's analysis showed that Tungsram had far too many workers for the volume of production. The workforce would have to be cut. GE designed a plan to lay off those who were nearest retirement. Employees received nine months of wages, considerably more than Hungarian law required. But many women who were on leave under Hungary's generous three-year maternity leave were not rehired. In 1992 and 1993, as GE's productivity goals became more ambitious, more employees were dismissed.

Workers who remained had to undergo a changed "mindset" about Tungsram and their work habits. GE adapted its American system of "action workouts" at Tungsram to improve productivity. These "workouts" involve teams of workers who tackle specific problems. Results typically involve changing work routines, altering the mix of people and machines, and finding better ways to achieve goals. Communication is critical and requires a common language and commitment to the company's goals. At

Tungsram, workers had to attend English classes and were forced to read a GE book containing many of Chairman Jack Welch's favorite sayings, including "If we're not No. 1 or No. 2 in a business, improve it, close it or sell it!" A culture change was underway. Progress was slow and difficult to achieve.

In 1993, GE announced that it effectively lost all of the $150 million it had invested when it bought 50.1 percent of Tungsram in 1989. Much more money was required to achieve results. GE had now invested more than $550 million in Tungsram. The strategy that had looked so appealing in 1989 looked very costly for five years.

By 1994, however, great progress was achieved. Tungsram became a successful competitor in the European lighting business. Costs were brought in line with the best lighting manufacturers in the world, and Hungarian scientific expertise has helped produce innovative new products that are selling well and innovative new processes that are making Tungsram's plants more efficient. But workers' pay has not kept pace with Hungary's inflation rate and about one-third of Tungsram's workers live close to the poverty line. Still, GE claims that Tungsram's wages average more than $300 per month, an amount that is in the top 25 percent in each of the eight towns where the company has plants.[20]

Discussion Questions

1. What business objectives could have led General Electric to invest in Hungary in 1989? Why would they invest when there were so many uncertainties?

2. What challenges confronted General Electric when it started the process of changing Tungsram into a competitive enterprise?

3. Assess General Electric's decision to lay off workers. Why would they pay more than Hungarian law required to departing employees?

4. In the United States, GE's home country, they would be required to rehire women on maternity leave. In Hungary, however, they have not done so. Is it proper for GE to operate with different standards in different countries?

5. Did GE have a corporate social strategy for its business in Hungary? Using the questions on page 197, explain what GE could have done to anticipate the problems it encountered.

[20]This case is based on interviews and published information, including annual reports of the General Electric Company. See also Jane Perlez, "G.E. Finds Tough Going in Hungary," *New York Times*, July 25, 1994, pp. D1, D8; Letters to the Editor, "G.E. Succeeded with Hungary Venture," *New York Times*, Aug. 1, 1994, p. A14.

PART FOUR

The Corporation and Public Policy

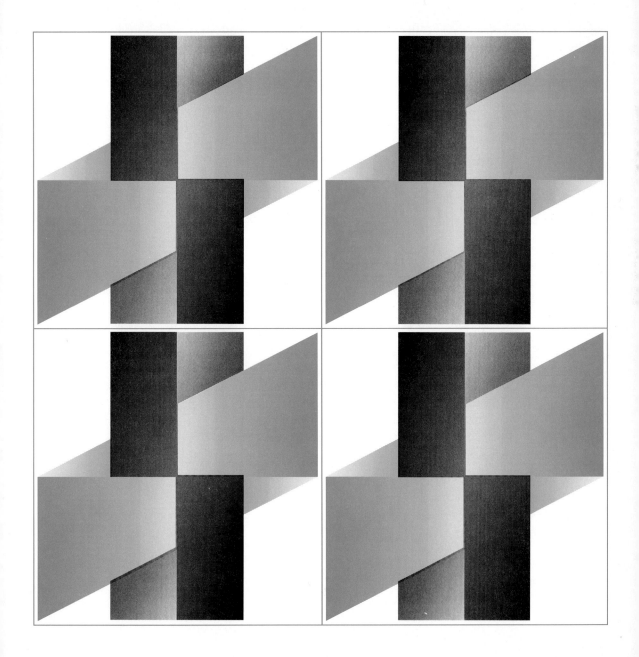

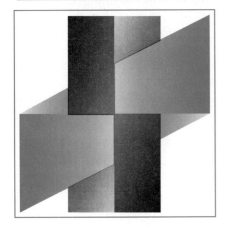

8

The Corporation and Public Policy

Business decision making and political decision making are closely connected. Business decisions affect politics; political decisions affect business. Government's actions are an expression of a nation's public policy and shape the business environment in important ways. Managers must understand the public policy process in every nation in which their corporation operates, and be prepared to participate in that process in an ethical and legal manner.

Key Questions and Chapter Objectives

This chapter focuses on these key questions and objectives:
- What is public policy?
- What are the key elements of the public policy process?
- What major areas of economic policy affect business in every nation?
- How do social welfare policies affect business?
- What are the major forms of government regulation of business?
- What factors have driven the growth of regulation in many industrial nations, including the United States?
- What is meant by deregulation and re-regulation?
- How is international regulation emerging, and how does it work?

September 1994 was an important time for William Clay Ford. The board of directors of the Ford Motor Co. named him to the position of chairman of the management committee, a very senior position in the company's hierarchy. The appointment placed the thirty-seven-year-old Mr. Ford in a critical position of responsibility for the company his great-grandfather had founded in the early 1900s. Industry observers and the media speculated that in naming Mr. Ford to his new position, the board of directors was signaling their intention to see him emerge as the company's future chief executive officer, perhaps by the end of the 1990s.

The Ford Motor Co. has had four generations of "Mr. Fords" leading it in the course of its history. Each has faced great challenges in building and growing a world-class automobile manufacturer. Not the least of those challenges has involved the role of government in the economy.

In 1903, when Henry Ford organized the Ford Motor Co. and developed the mass production systems that made it possible to produce huge numbers of automobiles at prices that were affordable for common people, his relationship with government was relatively simple. There was only one antitrust law on the books, and his business was too small to be bothered by it. The federal government did not tax the income of the company or its employees or their capital gains. Although there were rival car makers in this country, Ford faced no foreign competition. No unions were permitted in Ford plants, and government regulations about wages, hours, working conditions, and safety and health were unheard of. The government exacted no payments for employee retirement and pension plans for the simple reason that none existed. The company faced no problems of a polluted environment, energy shortages, or consumer complaints about auto safety, all of which in later years would bring the wrath of government down on the Ford company. His main worry in those days was a patent infringement suit brought against him by competitors, but he eventually won the suit in the courts.

In the 1970s Henry Ford II, the founder's grandson and the chief executive officer of the company, faced a different world. He could scarcely make a move without government taking an active hand or peering over his shoulder. That single antitrust law known to his grandfather had grown into a tangle of antitrust laws and court rulings regulating competition, pricing practices, mergers, and acquisitions. Labor laws legalized unions and controlled wages, hours, working conditions, safety and health, and employee discrimination. Federal, state, local, and foreign governments levied taxes on company income, plants and equipment, capital gains, auto and truck sales, and salaries.

In the 1990s William Clay Ford faces yet another major set of changes. Foreign competition has increased in the United States, and Ford competes in dozens of countries around the world. The company's workforce exists across the globe and includes people of many races and nationalities. In many industries, government and business are cooperating, even jointly planning how to compete in this global economy. In a little more than ninety years, the leaders of Ford Motor Co. have seen their relationship with all levels of government become much more complex and change from one of adversaries to potential partners.

As the newest Mr. Ford looks to the year 2000 and beyond, the Ford Motor Co. is designing automobiles that are powered by new fuel sources, are environmentally clean, and are controlled by computers in traffic networks that help avoid accidents, traffic congestion, and hazards. In all of this, government policy—public policy—plays an increasingly important role in the success and operation of the company.

This chapter focuses on government as an important reality with which all businesses must reckon. In no country in the world does business have an absolute right to exist and pursue profits; its rights are always conditioned on compliance with appropriate laws and public policy.

Government imposes major costs on business through taxes and regulations, and holds the power to grant or refuse permission for many types of business conduct and activity. Even the largest multinational companies—like Ford Motor Co.—operating in dozens of nations, must obey the laws and public policies of those nations if they are to retain the right to conduct business.

The topics in this chapter are closely related to some of the major ideas in earlier chapters, including the interactive model of business and society (Chapter 1), corporate stakeholders (Chapter 1), the relationship of business strategy to social strategy (Chapter 7), and how changing public values and ethical expectations influence governments to define business responsibilities (Chapters 2, 3, and 6).

One of the main features of the interactive model of business-society relations is the involvement of business with government. Stakeholders have persuaded governments to regulate business activities in order to promote or protect social interests. Public policy is also used to encourage business to meet social challenges such as drug use, education, and job creation. Global business competition has sharpened the understanding of U.S. business and political leaders about alternative ways that government and business can relate to one another. As a result, business and government are interacting more often in the public policy process and in new ways. The relationship between corporations and government, like that between business and all of society, is dynamic.[1]

PUBLIC POLICY

What Is Public Policy?

Public policy is a plan of action undertaken by government to achieve some broad purpose affecting a substantial segment of a nation's citizens. Or, as Senator Patrick Moynihan is reported to have said: *Public policy is what a government chooses to do or not to do.* In general, these ideas are consistent. Governments generally do not choose to act unless a substantial segment of the public is affected and some public purpose is to be achieved.

---

[1]A very readable treatment of this theme in American business history is Louis Galambos and Joseph Pratt, *The Rise of the Corporate Commonwealth: United States Business and Public Policy in the 20th Century,* New York: Basic Books, 1988. See also George Lodge, *Comparative Business-Government Relations,* Englewood Cliffs, NJ: Prentice-Hall, 1990.

This is the essence of what is meant by the concept of government acting in the *public interest.*

The role of government is broad in many modern economies. Although there are vigorous debates in the United States and other nations about the size and specific actions of government, there is much less disagreement that government has *some* appropriate role to play in modern life. As world population increases, individual nations have more citizens whose needs have to be met and whose interests and concerns have to be reconciled into reasonable plans of action. These are the roles that government—whatever its specific form—plays in the modern world. Public policy, while differing in each nation, is the basic set of goals, plans, and actions that each national government follows in achieving its purposes.

Powers of Government

The power to make public policy comes from a nation's political system. In democratic societies, the power of government is derived from the public through the electoral process: citizens elect political leaders who, in turn, can appoint others to fulfill defined public functions ranging from municipal services (e.g., water supplies, fire protection) to national services, such as public education or national defense.

Democratic nations often enumerate and spell out the powers of government in the country's constitution. The U.S. Constitution, for example, is one of only two sources of governmental power in the United States, the other being the history of common law. English common law, the original basis of the American legal system, gave government the right to regulate human affairs in order to achieve fairness and justice. The U.S. Constitution embodies these common law principles and is now the primary legal foundation for government's power.

In nondemocratic societies, the power of government may derive from and be controlled by a monarchy (e.g., Saudi Arabia), a military dictatorship (e.g., Saddam Hussein's Iraq), or religious authority (e.g., the mullahs' Iran). In many nations, several of these sources of power may interact, creating a balance of civilian and military authority. The balance of authority and power is often expressed in the form of a constitution or document that forms the "rules of order" for government and society. As discussed in Chapter 6, the political systems of China, Russia, Hungary, and South Africa have undergone profound changes in the past decade. And even in democratic nations such as Canada, individual regions (e.g., Quebec) may seek to become independent nations in order to exercise the powers of a sovereign state.

Shifts in political power and changes in the political system occur throughout the history of every nation. In the United States, for example, disagreements about state sovereignty and governmental powers prompted the Revolutionary War in the 1700s, the Civil War in the 1800s, and great debates about expanding (the New Deal) or limiting (the "Reagan revolution") the powers of government in the twentieth century. A nation's public policy reflects all of these forces and influences.

Elements of Public Policy

The governmental action of any nation can be understood in terms of several basic **elements of public policy.** As shown in Figure 8-1, these are the basic building blocks of government action and can guide managers in their understanding of how public policy is formed.

Many factors, or **inputs,** influence the development of public policy. Government may determine its course of action on the basis of economic or foreign policy concerns, domestic political pressure from constituents and interest groups, technical information, and ideas that have emerged in national politics. Public policy also may be influenced by technical studies of complex issues such as taxation or the development of new technologies such as fiber optic electronics. All of these inputs can help shape what the government chooses to do and how it chooses to do it.

Public policy **goals** can be lofty and high-minded or narrow and self-serving. National values, such as freedom, democracy, and equal opportunity for citizens to share in economic prosperity—that is, high-minded public policy goals—have led to the adoption of civil rights laws, liberal immigration laws, and assistance programs for those in need (e.g., the poor, aged, disabled, or refugees). Narrow, self-serving goals are evident when nations negotiate trade agreements or decide how tax legislation will allocate the burden of taxes among various interests and income

FIGURE 8-1

The key elements of public policy.

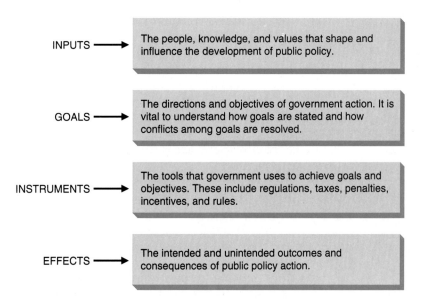

INPUTS ⟶ The people, knowledge, and values that shape and influence the development of public policy.

GOALS ⟶ The directions and objectives of government action. It is vital to understand how goals are stated and how conflicts among goals are resolved.

INSTRUMENTS ⟶ The tools that government uses to achieve goals and objectives. These include regulations, taxes, penalties, incentives, and rules.

EFFECTS ⟶ The intended and unintended outcomes and consequences of public policy action.

groups. In short, public policy goals may vary widely, but it is always important for citizens and managers to inquire, "What public policy goals are being served by this action?"

Governments use different public policy tools, or **instruments,** to achieve their policy goals. In budget negotiations, for example, much discussion is likely to focus on alternative ways to raise revenue—higher tax rates for individuals and businesses, reduced deductions, new sales taxes on selected items (e.g., luxury automobiles, tobacco, gasoline, alcohol). In general, the instruments of public policy are those combinations of incentives and penalties that government uses to stimulate citizens, including businesses, to act in ways that achieve policy goals. As discussed later in this chapter, government's regulatory powers are broad and constitute one of the most formidable instruments for accomplishing public purposes.

Public policy actions always have **effects.** Some are intended; others are unintended. Because public policies usually affect many people, organizations, and other interests, it is almost inevitable that government actions will please some and displease others. Regulations may cause business to improve the way toxic substances are used in the workplace, thus reducing health risks to employees. Yet it is possible that other goals may be obstructed as an unintended effect of compliance with such regulations. For example, when health risks to pregnant women were associated with exposure to lead in the workplace, some companies removed women from those jobs. This action was seen as a form of discrimination against women that conflicted with the goal of equal employment opportunity. The unintended effect (discrimination) of one policy action (protecting employees) conflicted head-on with another public policy goal (equal opportunity).

In assessing the action of government, it is important for managers to find answers to these four questions:

- What inputs will affect the public policy?
- What goals are to be achieved?
- What choices will be made about the instruments to be used?
- What effects, intended and unintended, are likely to occur?

These questions are a foundation for understanding any nation's public policy actions.

PUBLIC POLICY AND BUSINESS

Governments significantly influence business. National governments attempt to manage economic growth, using fiscal and monetary policy; state governments shape the business environment through a variety of regional economic policies; local governments affect business through policies that involve operating permits, licenses, and zoning requirements. The following sections discuss national-level policies that nearly all countries pursue. Various state and local policies are also discussed throughout the chapter and in Chapter 17.

The role of government as "manager" of the modern economy has become widely accepted in the twentieth century. Political and business leaders recognize that government can create—or destroy—the basic conditions necessary for business to compete and for citizens to prosper. This is not a new idea. Historically, for example, the governments of Spain, France, England, and other European nations during the seventeenth, eighteenth, and nineteenth centuries tried to build strong domestic economies through the colonization of distant lands (North America, Africa, East Indies). Raw materials were brought back to Europe, manufactured goods were sold to settlers in the colonies, and the wealth of the colonies became the wealth of the home country. But history teaches that misguided policies of government can destroy economies: excessive taxation of the colonies, for example, produced anger, resentment, and political revolt. In recent times, the nations of eastern Europe suffered greatly as communist governments mismanaged those economies. One of the great lessons of the twentieth century is that governments must manage the economy in ways that do not destroy economic initiative and enterprise.

Today, the role of government in the national economy is executed through a series of macroeconomic policies. Just as the social environment of the colonial era was tied to the underlying economic conditions and roles of business and government, so too is the social environment of the 1990s tied to the effectiveness of government in creating conditions for growth of the modern economy. Business and society are profoundly affected by what governments do and how well, or poorly, they do it.

National governments normally influence business through public policy in key areas such as economic growth, government spending and taxation, monetary policy, and trade. Nations that create a proper mix of policies in these areas can enjoy economic success, while those that set contradictory or self-defeating policies will suffer.

National Economic Growth

National governments generally accept the view that a key role of government is to create public policy that promotes economic growth. After World War II, for example, the U.S. Congress created the Full Employment Act which established targets for economic growth and unemployment. But as experience proved, healthy economic growth is affected by many factors, thereby requiring continuing efforts by government to manage the macroeconomy. Economic growth is stimulated by government policies that encourage investment (e.g., inviting foreign investors to locate facilities in the country); foster technology development (e.g., patent protection); provide key services (e.g., roads, sanitation, and police protection); and create a capable workforce through education. Each year, dozens of laws are proposed by legislators to improve the nation's "business climate" and promote economic growth.

In the mid-1990s, the United States is the world's largest economy but it is not among the world's fastest growing economies. This means that new opportunities are not being created as rapidly in the United States as in other, faster-growing nations. Economists generally suggest that a mature economy like that of the United States should have about a 3 percent growth rate to meet the needs of population growth. In contrast, the economic growth rate of developing countries is significantly higher (e.g., People's Republic of China was 11 percent in 1994; Malaysia was more than 8 percent). Ultimately, economic growth affects a nation's capacity to direct resources to social needs, which impacts on the environment in which businesses operate.

Low economic growth can contribute to a nation's social problems, including high unemployment, costly welfare programs, and pressures to raise taxes. An expanding economy can mean job opportunities for trained workers but also higher labor costs for businesses. On balance, political leaders favor economic growth because it creates increased national wealth.

Governments spend money on many different types of activities. Local governments employ teachers, trash collectors, police, and fire fighters. State governments typically spend large amounts of money on roads, social services, and park lands. National governments spend large sums on military defense, international relationships, and hundreds of public works projects. **Fiscal policy** refers to those patterns of government spending and taxing in an economy that are intended to stimulate or support the macroeconomy. During the Great Depression of the 1930s, governments learned that public works projects were an effective way to employ large numbers of people, put money into their hands, and stimulate consumption of goods and services through such "pump priming." In the 1990s, governments still use fiscal policy as the primary way to achieve economic growth and prosperity. As the following example shows, public works projects such as roads and airports remain among the most popular means of creating employment while achieving other public goals.

The largest public works project in the United States in the mid-1990s is called the "Big Dig." It is a decade-long construction project, employing more than 15,000 people, to create a tunnel beneath Boston harbor that will connect the city with its airport. The project also involves tearing down an elevated roadway known as the Central Artery that passes through the downtown area and replacing the entire highway with an underground roadway. The project will ease traffic congestion and add acres of usable land for development in Boston's high-priced financial district. The benefits do not come cheaply, however. Cost estimates for the Central Artery/Third Harbor Tunnel project are in excess of $7 billion, an amount which is being shared by the federal and state governments. User fees and general tax revenues will pay for the project. Some critics believe costs of the project will exceed $10 billion by 1999. All agree that at a cost of $1 billion per mile for each of the seven miles of roadway that will be built, the Big Dig will be the most expensive roadway per mile ever built in the United States.[2]

Taxation Policy

Actions by government to raise or reduce taxes on business directly affect how much money firms have to invest in new plants, equipment, and people. The same is true of taxes on individuals: after-tax household income affects spending for food, housing, automobiles, and entertainment. Tax rates also affect the money available for savings and reinvestment in the economy. Even "minor" rules can have large effects: rules about the tax deductibility of at-home offices affect nearly 20 million at-home businesses in the United States.

Tax policies are often a consequence of other goals that government seeks to achieve and the cost of meeting those goals. Governments may feel forced to raise taxes because other needs or commitments are great and the pressures of stakeholders to get government to act exceed the pressures of taxpayers.

When nations are at war, for example, tax rates are raised, new taxes are created, and collection of taxes becomes more aggressive because of the government's need to pay the costs of soldiers, military equipment, and munitions. Peacetime spending priorities also affect tax policies. Large social welfare programs can involve major government spending requirements that need tax support. President Bill Clinton's proposal to create a national health care system with universal health coverage for all Americans encountered heavy opposition because of the costs such a plan might create. Estimates of the new taxes needed to finance such a plan ranged from $10 billion to more than $100 billion. Opposition to increased taxes was one of the key reasons the Clinton health care proposal was defeated.

A nation's **monetary policy** affects the supply, demand, and value of a nation's currency. The value of a nation's currency is affected by the strength of its economy relative to the economies of other nations. The amount of

---

[2]"The Big Dig," 3-part series, *Boston Globe,* Sept. 11, 12, 13, 1994, pp. 1ff.

money in circulation and the level of demand for loans, credit, and currency influence inflation, deflation, and government objectives.

In the United States, the Federal Reserve Bank, an independent agency whose members are appointed by the president but whose policies are set by the bank's board of governors, plays the role of other countries' central banks. By raising and lowering the interest rates at which private sector banks borrow money from "The Fed," the board of governors is able to influence the size of the nation's money supply and the value of the dollar relative to other national currencies.

Managing a nation's monetary policy is exceedingly difficult. A healthy economy requires a supply of money and credit that is sufficient to enable people and businesses to maintain economic growth, but not so great as to stimulate overbidding for economic resources (i.e., inflation). Too small a supply of money produces the opposite problem, deflation, which involves too few dollars chasing available goods and services. The following examples illustrate the challenge to government.

> In the late 1970s and early 1980s, inflationary pressures in the United States led the Federal Reserve Bank to raise interest rates as high as 20 percent in order to discourage people and companies from spending. By the early 1990s, inflation was very low and interest rates had fallen to 5 percent. Spending and economic growth were stimulated by the low interest rates. In contrast, when Ernesto Zedillo Ponce de Leon was inaugurated as the new president of Mexico in 1994, he inherited an economy that was in desperate condition. Inflation was rampant, workers were pressing for higher wages, and the government was running huge budget deficits. Creditors from the international investment community were demanding payment of interest on their loans. President Zedillo's minister of finance recommended that the government devalue the peso by letting it "float" against other currencies in the free market. By refusing to defend the value of the peso, the government allowed it to fall in value relative to other currencies, losing nearly 50 percent of its buying power. Government leaders defended the devaluation as a way to improve Mexico's economy, but pressure from the public, whose wages now bought much less than before, and pressure from foreign investors, whose investments were similarly reduced in value, mounted. The international business community was deeply concerned that the new Mexican government did not have a clear sense of where it was steering the economy.[3]

The worth, or worthlessness, of a nation's currency has serious effects on business and society. It affects buying power, the stability and value of

[3]See Anthony DePalma, "Peso Down; Mexican Stocks Fall," *New York Times,* Jan. 5, 1995, pp. D1, D10; also, James Brooke, "Warning for Brazil in Mexican Crisis," *New York Times,* Jan. 5, 1995, pp. D1, D10.

savings, and the confidence of people within the country and outside of it about the nation's future. It also affects the ability of the nation to borrow money from other nations. Businesses are very much affected by the strength or weakness of the national currency as they conduct trade with other nations.

> When Mexico devalued the peso, Mattel Inc., a U.S. toy manufacturer, suffered a $20 million loss. The company had a manufacturing plant in Mexico that had been under repair following a fire. To serve customers in what is Mattel's fifth largest foreign market, the company sent toys from its U.S. plants to Mexico. It billed its customers in 1994 pesos but they paid in post-devaluation pesos. Moreover, the devaluation made the U.S. manufacturer's goods more expensive in Mexico. Mattel's toy's cost nearly twice as many pesos after the devaluation.[4]

The volume of business transacted across international borders in the 1990s forces buyers and sellers to continuously assess whether it is more advantageous to do business within a country or across borders. In a global economy, the manner in which monetary policy is managed has great implications for both business and society.

Trade Policy

Trade policy refers to those actions of government that are taken to encourage or discourage commerce with other countries. Many countries favor trade with others. Nations with large amounts of natural resources such as oil, timber, coal, minerals, and agricultural products tend to favor trade because it creates markets for their goods and helps them achieve economic growth. Nations that are cost-efficient producers of clothing, electronic equipment, and computers also tend to favor international trade because they can offer better prices to customers than their less efficient competitors. But there are social consequences for a nation that opens its borders to trade.

Countries that are not rich in natural resources, or do not have highly efficient manufacturing industries, may find trade to be less beneficial for their citizens. Trade may enable wealthy citizens to spend money on foreign produced goods and services, but citizens who are unemployed will not find jobs if local businesses cannot match the cost efficiencies of foreign firms. The results can be socially explosive: relatively few people control a large percentage of the national wealth while a large number of people suffer in poverty.

Wealthy nations may also find international trade to be of questionable

---

[4]"Peso Reduces Mattel's Profit," *New York Times,* Jan. 5, 1995, p. D10.

value. When the North American Free Trade Agreement (NAFTA) was adopted, U.S. labor leaders feared that jobs would be lost to lower-priced labor in Mexico, creating unemployment and causing social damage to American communities. Environmentalists were concerned that Mexico's more permissive laws would encourage U.S. companies to lower their environmental costs by operating in Mexico rather than the United States.

Such considerations lead some countries to favor open markets and free trade, while others favor protected markets and restricted trade. As the following example suggests, some countries favor free trade in certain sectors while restricting it in others.

> Japan has tended to favor free trade in industries where it has a competitive advantage based on cost or innovative technology. The Japanese government has pressed other nations to open their economies to Japanese steel, consumer electronics, and computers. But Japan has resisted opening its economy to trade with nations whose goods and services are less expensive or technologically advanced. U.S. computer companies, construction firms, and automobile manufacturers have had great difficulty getting permission to sell their products in Japan. Producers of fast food, cigarettes, and designer clothing have had a much easier time getting permission to do business in Japan. But the most difficult U.S. product to get into Japan was one that affected millions of Japanese farmers, namely, rice. For years, the government refused to permit imported rice into Japan. Only an acute shortage of domestic rice, plus intense pressure from the U.S. government to persuade Japanese officials, succeeded in creating an opportunity for U.S. rice imports in Japan.[5]

Nations often seek to be self-sufficient in some areas of economic activity, such as farming, in order to preserve traditions and national values, or in industries that employ many people and are, therefore, vital to the social fabric of the economy. For example, Japan, France, and Italy are among the nations that have sought to protect their traditional family-based agricultural industry from highly efficient foreign competitors. And many nations have sought to protect declining industries which could not meet world-class production efficiencies but employed many thousands of employees. These pressures may force governments to create *trade barriers* by imposing extra charges (tariffs) on imported goods or strict quality requirements that force the seller to raise the price of the products if they can be sold at all.

---

[5]See S. Lenway, K. Rehbein, and L. Starks, "The Impact of Protectionism on Firm Wealth: The Experience of the Steel Industry," *Southern Economic Journal,* 1990, pp. 1079–1093; also, K. A. Rehbein and L. Starks, "The Wealth Effect of U.S. Trade Policy on Japanese Firms," *Japan and the World Economy,* forthcoming.

Industrial Policy

Many national governments have attempted to direct economic resources toward the development of specific industries within the country. This is known as **industrial policy.** A nation that has oil resources, for example, may structure tax and other policies in order to encourage exploration and production of oil fields. Many nations have also encouraged industries such as steel, automobiles, textiles, and other large employers through public policy. In the widest application of industrial policy, governments can invest in new technologies (e.g., fiber optics) directly, by creating a state-owned enterprise, or indirectly, by creating rules and conditions that encourage others to invest in new businesses (e.g., casino gambling). Beginning in the 1980s, a vigorous debate occurred in the United States as to whether government should "pick winners and losers" through industrial policy.[6] In the mid-1990s, U.S. political leaders have generally favored using the power of government to create the *conditions* for new businesses to grow rather than picking specific industries for growth.

As illustrated in Figure 8-2, a nation's economic growth is entwined with its fiscal, monetary, and trade policies. They, in turn, shape and influence other public policies that governments make. All public policy has a direct or indirect impact on business by shaping the climate in which companies do business within the nation and across national borders.

SOCIAL WELFARE POLICIES

The economically advanced industrial nations have typically developed elaborate systems of social services for their citizens. As Figure 8-3 shows, social welfare policies affect the workplace, the marketplace, and business profitability.

[6]See, for example, M. Dertouzos, R. Lester, and R. Solow, *Made in America: Regaining the Productivity Edge (Report of the MIT Commission on Industrial Productivity)*, Cambridge, MA: MIT Press, 1989.

FIGURE 8-2
National economic policies affecting business.

Economic Policy →	Economic Effects
Economic growth	Employment/unemployment, welfare assistance
Fiscal policy	Government spending, taxation
Monetary policy	Currency value, interest rates
Trade policy	Exports/imports (balance of trade), trade barriers (e.g., tariffs)
Industrial policy	Support of priority industries

FIGURE 8-3
Social welfare
policies affecting
business.

Policies affecting the workplace:

- Child labor laws
- Wages, hours, and working conditions
- Safety and health standards
- "Right to know" disclosure rules

Policies affecting the marketplace:

- Consumer protection safety rules
- Government subsidies to poor, disabled, and other needy segments of society

Policies affecting profitability:

- Social Security tax payments
- Mandatory retirement benefits
- Disability and unemployment compensation rules
- Health insurance coverage and benefits

Health Policy

Health care is among the most essential of social services, in part because public health problems can affect all of a nation's population. Even less industrialized nations tend to devote significant resources to providing basic health care to the population.

In 1994, doctors in the Indian city of Surat discovered that they were dealing with an outbreak of pneumonic plague, a deadly communicable disease. The discovery of the plague in Surat led the Indian government to mobilize its resources to fight the epidemic which killed more than forty people within two weeks and afflicted hundreds—perhaps thousands—of others. The worst problem, however, was the prospect of the epidemic spreading to other cities in India and, potentially, to other countries around the world. The World Health Organization worked with the Indian government to organize public health resources to deal with the plague in Surat, Bombay, and New Delhi, hundreds of miles away. Thousands of health workers—doctors, nurses, and paramedics—were organized to deal with plague victims.

While advanced industrial societies rely on hospitals, medical technology, and sophisticated pharmaceutical products, many other nations emphasize meeting basic health care needs through local clinics, community education, and reliance on locally available medicines. Investment in such "primary" health care tends to produce significant improvement in indicators such as infant mortality, illness rates of small children, and vaccination of the population against disease.

According to a survey of national health care systems conducted by the World Bank, the United States has a technologically advanced health care system that produces the largest number of sophisticated procedures, such as heart transplants, but it ranks below the other nations in ensuring primary health care through programs such as child vaccinations.[7] The relationship between health care expenditures and health care benefits has been hotly debated for years in many nations. As shown in Figure 8-4, industrial nations vary in their expenditures on health care and in the outcomes, or indicators of success, resulting from that spending. The United States, for example, spends more of its income (gross domestic product [GDP]) on health care than any other nation, yet people in other countries live longer than Americans. In general, the prevailing view among experts is that by viewing a population as a national resource, capable of creating new wealth for a nation through imagination and creative work, health expenditures are investments in "human capital."

[7]World Bank, *World Development Report, 1993,* New York: Oxford University Press, 1993, pp. 1–25.

FIGURE 8-4

Comparative health care costs and benefits.

Source: United Nations, *1994 Human Development Report,* New York: United Nations Development Program, 1994. Data is derived from various tables in Appendix A.

Countries in Order of Life Expectancy	Life Expectancy at Birth (in years, 1992)	Population (in millions, 1992)	Real GDPs (per capita, 1991)	Total Expenditures on Health (percent of GDP)
1. Japan	78.6	124.5	$19,390	6.8%
2. Sweden	77.7	8.6	17,490	8.8
3. Spain	77.4	39.1	12,670	6.5
4. Greece	77.3	10.2	7,680	4.8
5. Canada	77.2	27.4	19,320	9.9
6. Netherlands	77.2	15.2	16,820	8.7
7. Australia	76.7	17.6	16,680	8.6
8. France	76.6	57.1	18,430	9.1
9. Israel	76.2	5.1	13,460	4.2
10. United Kingdom	75.8	57.7	16,340	6.6
11. Germany	75.6	80.2	19,770	9.1
12. United States	75.6	255.2	22,330	13.3
13. Ireland	75.0	3.5	11,430	8.0

Health policy has moved from a "soft" area of public policy to a "hard" area as health costs have grown relative to GDP. In the early 1990s, experts said that U.S. health care costs would rise from approximately 13 percent of GDP to as much as 20 percent of GDP by 2010. This sparked fear of a runaway cost spiral that would do much damage to the rest of the American economy. Government officials were pressed to "get control" of health costs. This produced the type of pressure that led President Bill Clinton to develop health care legislation and many health maintenance organizations (HMOs), hospitals, and health care companies to merge.

Health issues are also entwined with other important areas of public policy. For example, environmental policy is often shaped by the need to protect human health from harmful pollutants. This has been influential in the creation of clean water and clean air legislation, and in the development of toxic dump site regulations. Similarly, education has been influenced by health considerations such as the need to teach children and teens about sexually transmitted diseases, including AIDS. But the costs of such policies do sometimes provoke criticism and calls for change.[8]

> The Committee for Economic Development (CED), a business organization of about 250 large corporations, has called for an end to efforts to incorporate mentally and physically handicapped children in regular classrooms and has urged that schools move away from providing social services like pregnancy counseling and AIDS education. In their view, these programs deter from educational quality and do not serve the business community's needs for well-trained employees.[9] But educators strongly disagree, arguing that such programs are crucial to helping all students become adults who understand how to function in communities that are filled with risks, challenges, and diversity.

As such examples suggest, the business community has a large stake in the extent to which health policy objectives and costs are imposed on economic activity. Corporations must monitor such developments because of the immediate and longer term consequences. The consequences may be positive or negative, depending on the nature of the proposal, the costs involved, and the benefits to business and to society.

Social Security

National governments have traditionally developed various mechanisms for meeting the needs of special segments of the population who are in

---

[8]For a critique of these requirements, see Committee for Economic Development (CED), *Putting Learning First,* New York: Committee for Economic Development, 1994.
[9]Catherine S. Manegold, "Study Says Schools Must Stress Academics," *New York Times,* Sept. 23, 1994, p. A22.

need. In the 1800s, orphan children and poor families often required such assistance; in modern times, children, the elderly, the disabled, and homeless members of society comprise a large and needy population. To respond to these social welfare needs, many countries have created government-run social security systems that provide guaranteed economic assistance to needy segments of the population.

In the United States, Social Security has been a national commitment since the 1930s, when the Social Security Act was passed (1934). The legislation created a Social Security fund into which working Americans paid a small amount of money from each paycheck. The fund grew as worker contributions grew and the proceeds were used to make monthly Social Security payments to retirees. For decades the system was very successful. However, the system is subject to two problems in the 1990s. First, as the population has aged and people live longer, retirement payments tend to drain increasing amounts from the Social Security fund. Second, the base of younger workers contributing to the Social Security fund is not increasing as fast as the payouts to retirees. The result has been a series of increases in Social Security taxes and strong pressure to reduce the rate of benefits paid from the Social Security fund. Despite several attempts by the U.S. Congress to stabilize the Social Security fund by balancing inflows of tax revenue with outflows of payments, the Social Security system remains troubled. According to some experts, the conflict surrounding Social Security reflects a larger problem of **intergenerational equity,** in which one generation of citizens (those born between 1970 and 1990) will be asked to bear a heavier tax burden to support the generations of their parents and grandparents (see Exhibit 8-A). The equity issue involves fairness: how much should one generation (older or younger) be required to give in order to support another generation? No society has yet found the ideal answer to this crucial public policy question.

Entitlements

As nations expand the range of social welfare programs for their citizens, pressures may grow to increase levels of support and assistance. Once programs have been in place for a reasonable period of time, citizens begin to expect that benefits of such programs will be available if, and when, the need arises. This creates an **entitlement** mentality, in which there is the widespread belief that the political system (government) will deliver social assistance when the need arises.

Entitlements create dilemmas for political leaders. Pressures can arise to expand the number of beneficiaries of social welfare programs and to ensure that benefits are spread generously among the population. Costs inevitably rise under such pressures, and that creates the dilemma of balancing the interests of taxpayers against the interests of recipients. Resent-

EXHIBIT 8-A

THE "TIME BOMB" OF INTERGENERATIONAL TAXATION

The federal government has started estimating the total tax burden that different generations pay over their lifetime. In the following chart, the government has estimated the amount of federal, state, and local taxes that people born at different times will pay, minus payments like Social Security that people get back from government. This creates a "net tax burden" over a person's lifetime.

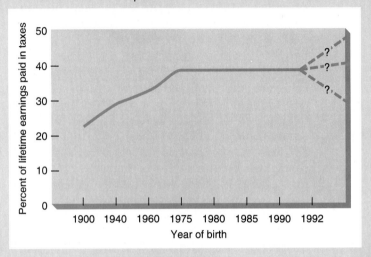

People born in 1975, for example, will pay more than 35 percent of their lifetime earnings in taxes. Rates have risen with successive generations, in part because government is engaged in more activities, and in part because it is borrowing money on which later generations must pay interest.

SOURCE: *1995 Economic Report of the President,* Washington, D.C.: Government Printing Office, 1995, chapter 1. See also, Keith Bradsher, "Large Tax Burden for Young Is Seen," *New York Times,* Feb. 9, 1994, p. A17.

ment often rises when the public learns of incidents in which people or businesses that do not really need social or economic benefits receive them. The media may portray these as examples of waste, fraud, and abuse.[10] In this area, too, few nations have found effective and lasting solutions to the dilemma of how to provide benefits to those who are truly needy at a cost to taxpayers that is perceived as fair.

[10]Mickey Kaus, "The Welfare Mess—How It Got That Way," *Wall Street Journal,* Sept. 12, 1994, p. A16; "Entitlement Politics, R.I.P.," *Wall Street Journal,* Sept. 28, 1994, p. A18. The cost of entitlements is discussed in Robert Eisner, *The Misunderstood Economy: What Counts and How to Count It,* Boston, MA: Harvard Business School Press, 1994.

GOVERNMENT REGULATION OF BUSINESS

Goals and Objectives

Societies rely on government to establish rules of conduct for citizens and organizations. Such regulation is done for a "public purpose," such as maintaining public order or ensuring that citizens can depend on the quality of goods and services. Because government operates at so many levels (federal, state, local), the modern business faces complex webs of regulations. Companies often require staffs of lawyers, public affairs specialists, and government relations managers to monitor and manage the interaction with government (see Chapter 3). The constitutional powers forming the basis for most government regulation of business in the United States are (1) the power to regulate interstate and foreign commerce; (2) the power to tax and spend; (3) the power to borrow; and (4) the power to promote the general welfare. State regulation must conform to state constitutions and federal laws.

Economic objectives characterize some government regulations, while social goals are paramount in others. One economic argument that supports government regulation is the **market failure** argument—that is, the marketplace fails to adjust the product price for the true costs of a firm's behavior. There is no market incentive, for example, for a company to spend money on pollution control equipment if customers do not demand it. The market "fails" to incorporate the social cost (harm) of pollution into the economic equation. Government can use regulation to force all competitors in a business to prevent pollution, thereby incorporating the social cost to the environment into the product price.

There is often an ethical rationale for regulation as well. As discussed in Chapter 5, for example, there is a "utilitarian" ethical argument in support of safe working conditions: it is costly to train and educate employees only to lose their services because of accidents that are preventable. There are also "fairness" and "justice" arguments for government to set standards and develop regulations to protect employees, consumers, and other stakeholders. Debates about regulation often feature advocates for and against regulatory proposals using both economic and ethical arguments to support their views.

Types of Regulation

Government regulations come in different forms. Some are directly imposed; others are more indirect. Some are aimed at a specific industry (e.g., banking) while others, such as those dealing with job discrimination or pollution, apply across the board to all industries. Some have been in existence for a long time—the Interstate Commerce Commission (ICC) was created in 1887—while others, such as those governing state lotteries and other forms of legalized gambling, are of recent vintage in many states.[11]

Industry-specific economic regulations

Our oldest form of regulation by government agency is directed at specific industries such as the railroads, telephone companies, and banks. Regulations of this type are primarily economic in nature and are deliberately intended to modify the normal operation of the free market and the forces of supply and demand. Such modification may come about because the free market is distorted by the size or monopoly power of companies, or because the social side effects or consequences of actions in the marketplace are thought to be undesirable. Under such conditions, government regulators substitute their judgment for that of the marketplace in such matters as price setting, capital expansion, quality of services, and the entry of new competitors. For example, railroads were not permitted to raise most rates to shippers without permission from the ICC, nor could they abandon costly service to a community as a free market firm would do. Nor could telephone companies increase their charges to customers, expand into related lines of business, or deny service to customers without first getting the approval of various local, state, and federal agencies.

Many industries have evolved through various "stages" of government regulation during the past century. Airlines, natural gas, telecommunications, and banking, for example, have gone through periods of rising regulation designed to correct abuses and problems, followed by periods of consolidation and implementation of regulation. When regulatory programs become ineffective, as command-type regulations often do, pressures to deregulate or otherwise reform the industry arise. Views change regarding how much regulation, and of what type, is required. For example, petroleum was regulated during the 1930s to stabilize a volatile oil marketplace that suffered from gluts and excesses of oil. Regulations were followed until the 1970s, when oil prices rose sharply. New regulatory controls were tried, but reformers concluded that oil prices should be deregulated to encourage exploration and development of oil supplies. Regulation always faces problems of staying current with changes that shape the underlying dynamics of an industry.

All-industry social regulations

All-industry social regulations are aimed at such important social goals as protection of consumers, the environment, and providing workers with safe and healthy working conditions. Equal employment opportunity, protection of pension benefits, and health care for employees are other important areas of social regulation. Unlike the economic regulations mentioned above, social regulations are not limited to one type of business or industry. Laws concerning pollution, safety and health, and job discrimi-

[11]Richard McGowan, *State Lotteries and Legalized Gambling: Painless Revenue or Painful Mirage*, Westport, CT: Praeger/Quorum Books, 1994, chapter 6.

nation apply to all businesses; consumer protection laws apply to all relevant businesses producing and selling consumer goods.

Social regulations typically benefit large segments of society. Critics argue that costs are shared by a narrow segment of society, business and its customers. If the agencies that enforce social regulations do not consider the overall financial impact of their actions on firms or industries, businesses may experience losses and even be forced to close, leaving workers without jobs, communities without tax revenues, and customers without products. This argument does not excuse socially irresponsible conduct, however. In recent years, more political leaders have recognized that the effect of regulations on an industry's economic health is connected to the public interest. [12]

Functional regulations

Certain operations or functions of business have been singled out for special attention by government regulators. Labor practices, for example, are no longer left to the operation of free market forces. Government sets minimum wages, regulates overtime pay, sets the rules for labor union campaigns, and mediates serious and troublesome labor-management disputes, including, in recent years, strikes by airline pilots, flight attendants, school teachers, and even professional baseball players!

Competition is another business function strongly affected by regulation. Antitrust laws and rules, discussed in Chapter 10, attempt to prevent monopolies, preserve competitive pricing, and protect consumers against unfair practices.

Functional regulations, like social regulations, may cut across industry lines and apply generally to all enterprises, as they do in the case of antitrust and labor practices. Or they may, as in the case of regulations governing stock exchanges and the issuance of corporate securities, be confined to specific institutions such as the stock markets or the companies whose stocks are listed on those exchanges.

Figure 8-5 depicts these three types of regulation—economic, social, and functional—along with the major regulatory agencies responsible for enforcing the rules at the federal level in the United States. Only the most prominent federal agencies are included in the chart. Individual states, some cities, and other national governments have their own array of agencies to implement regulatory policy.

GROWTH OF REGULATION

Government regulation is used to perform many tasks and serve many different purposes. Some are economic, others political, legal, and cultural. The shapes and forms of U.S. regulation are so numerous that inconsisten-

---

[12]See Murray Weidenbaum, *Business, Government, and the Public,* 2d ed., Englewood Cliffs, NJ: Prentice-Hall, 1994.

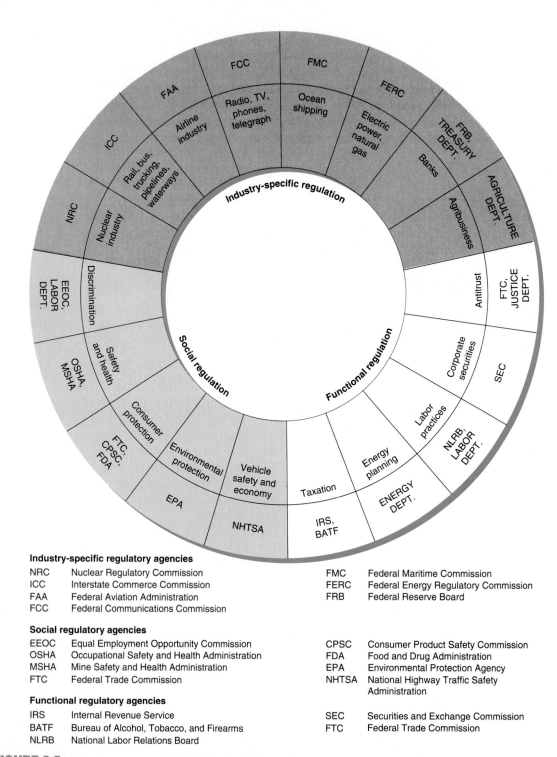

FIGURE 8-5
Major federal regulatory agencies arranged by type of regulation.

Industry-specific regulatory agencies

NRC	Nuclear Regulatory Commission
ICC	Interstate Commerce Commission
FAA	Federal Aviation Administration
FCC	Federal Communications Commission
FMC	Federal Maritime Commission
FERC	Federal Energy Regulatory Commission
FRB	Federal Reserve Board

Social regulatory agencies

EEOC	Equal Employment Opportunity Commission
OSHA	Occupational Safety and Health Administration
MSHA	Mine Safety and Health Administration
FTC	Federal Trade Commission
CPSC	Consumer Product Safety Commission
FDA	Food and Drug Administration
EPA	Environmental Protection Agency
NHTSA	National Highway Traffic Safety Administration

Functional regulatory agencies

IRS	Internal Revenue Service
BATF	Bureau of Alcohol, Tobacco, and Firearms
NLRB	National Labor Relations Board
SEC	Securities and Exchange Commission
FTC	Federal Trade Commission

cies sometimes appear. Regulation is a tool of government that policymakers have long used to address important problems throughout the history of the United States. Other nations have designed comparable regulatory systems in response to their own histories, unique problems, and political cultures.

Underlying Factors

Why do societies turn to more regulation as a way to solve problems? Part of the explanation lies in changes that have occurred in nations in recent times. For example, as science and technology have enabled nations to meet many of their economic needs, social concerns have received more attention. Smokestacks that once signaled industrial jobs and prosperity became negative symbols of environmental damage as people shifted their concerns from economic growth to the health effects of pollution.

Another reason for the expansion of business regulation is the number of advocates who speak for other interests. Environmental groups urge government officials to halt pollution; organizations representing minorities and women seek expansion of equal employment opportunity rules in the workplace; consumer groups advocate government regulations that ensure product quality and safety; and labor unions lobby regulators to set rules that will protect employees from workplace hazards and health risks.

Media attention to environmental disasters, protests, and confrontations between business and the public also help convince government officials that action is necessary. Throughout history, protests have helped pressure governments into action; in the late twentieth century, as the news media literally connect communities around the globe so that events are seen as they happen, the public as well as government officials "see" social needs that should be met. It is hard to resist pressures to act under such conditions.

The Costs of Regulation

The call for regulation may seem irresistible to government leaders and officials, but there are always costs to regulation. In recent years, much more attention has been given to the costs, as well as the benefits, of government regulation. An old economic adage says, "There is no free lunch." Someone eventually has to pay for the benefits created. This is the **rule of cost,** and it applies in all socioeconomic systems, whether free market or central state control.

An industrial society such as that of the United States can "afford" almost anything, including social regulations, if it is willing to pay the price. Sometimes, the benefits are worth the costs; sometimes the costs exceed the benefits. The test of **cost-benefit analysis** helps the public understand what is at stake when new regulation is sought.

When Congress debated the Clinton administration's national health care proposals, strong opposition arose when it was determined that the plan would impose large regulatory costs. Although the exact cost was debated vigorously, Congress realized that the American public did not want the benefits *at just any cost;* they wanted them at little or no cost.

Figure 8-6*a* illustrates the costs of federal regulation in the United States over the past twenty-five years. The cost of economic regulation has

FIGURE 8-6

The costs of regulation, 1970–1995.

SOURCE: Center for the Study of American Business, Washington University. Derived from the Budget of the United States Government and related documents, various fiscal years. Used with permission.

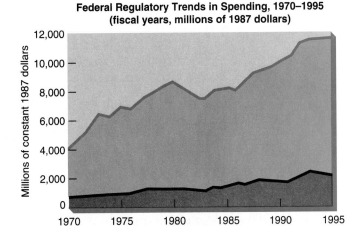

Federal Regulatory Trends in Spending, 1970–1995
(fiscal years, millions of 1987 dollars)

(*a*)

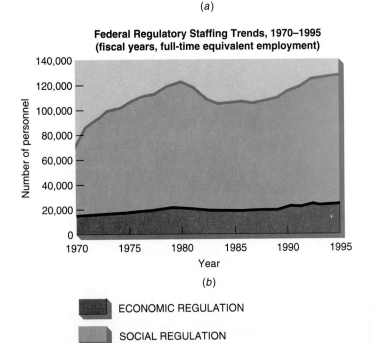

Federal Regulatory Staffing Trends, 1970–1995
(fiscal years, full-time equivalent employment)

(*b*)

ECONOMIC REGULATION

SOCIAL REGULATION

grown more slowly (about a 100 percent increase over twenty-five years) than social regulation (about a 300 percent increase over 25 years). Costs of state and local regulation have also risen greatly over this period.

The growth in federal regulatory programs is not a new phenomenon. As scholars at the Center for the Study of American Business have documented, the growth pattern has been interrupted only briefly during the past three decades. In the early 1980s, President Ronald Reagan led a campaign to cut government regulation. In 1980, 122,000 people staffed federal regulatory agencies; Reagan's budget cuts reduced the number to 102,000 in 1985. But under President George Bush, staff increases began to push the numbers higher. By 1992, regulatory personnel equaled the 1980 number, and by 1994 federal regulatory personnel grew to more than 130,000 (see Figure 8-6*b*).[13]

Deregulation, Re-regulation, and Recent Trends

Deregulation is the removal or scaling down of regulatory authority and regulatory activities of government. In the 1990s, politicians such as Representative Newt Gingrich symbolize the public's revolt against the activist role of government and the growing role of regulation. But deregulation pressures have existed for many years. President Ronald Reagan symbolized this theme in the early 1980s, when he campaigned on the promise to "get government off the back of people." Major deregulatory laws were enacted beginning in 1975 when Gerald Ford was president and continued through the administrations of Jimmy Carter, Ronald Reagan, and George Bush. These laws loosened the grip of the federal government on a number of industries and markets in the following ways.

> In the petroleum industry, all price controls on domestic oil were abolished in 1981. Prices of natural gas were gradually decontrolled until all controls ended in 1987. A phased deregulation of commercial airlines removed government supervision of rates and allowed domestic airlines to enter domestic routes more easily and to make mergers and acquisitions with less delay and oversight. The Civil Aeronautics Board (CAB), the chief airline regulatory agency since the 1930s, was abolished in 1985. Intercity trucking companies were permitted to charge lower prices and provide wider services. More competitors entered the industry. Railroads, which were tightly regulated for a century, were deregulated and given the freedom to set rates in some parts of their business and to compete in new ways. Financial institutions were allowed to be more flexible in setting interest rates on loans and, most

[13]Melinda Warren, *Reforming the Federal Regulatory Process: Rhetoric or Reality?* Occasional Paper 138, St. Louis: Washington University, Center for the Study of American Business, 1994, p. 5.

importantly, to compete across state lines in what is known as "interstate banking."

But deregulation does not always succeed. Commercial radio broadcasting was deregulated in the early 1980s, and Congress relaxed the licensing process for radio and television stations. Steps were planned to promote more competition in the entire telecommunications industry—telephone service, electronic information transfer, and cable television broadcasting. But as the development of new technologies advanced, restrictions on the businesses in which regional telephone companies could compete still existed. In 1994, Congress tried to enact a comprehensive communications law that would set the rules for future competition in the telecommunications industry. The complexity of the problems and the concerns of various special interests, however, proved too much of an obstacle to overcome. The proposed deregulatory communications law died without being enacted.[14]

Deregulation can be achieved in various ways. In addition to changing the laws that govern specific industries, such as telecommunications, deregulation can be achieved by cutting back staff and budgets for regulatory agencies. Some experts have argued that such cutbacks are, in fact, the best way to achieve deregulation.

Pressures favoring deregulation always contend with the public's desire to see government "solve problems." This produces cross-currents in which government is trying both to deregulate in some areas and to introduce new regulation in others. **Re-regulation** is the increase or expansion of government regulation, especially in areas where the regulatory activities of government had previously been reduced. In the United States, the Clinton administration has moved toward re-regulation in areas where too little government regulation may be dangerous. Since the early 1990s, the federal government has taken action to toughen worker safety standards, establish new environmental protection standards, set curbs on insider trading of corporate securities, fix requirements for airline collision avoidance equipment, and impose drug testing of train engineers, airline pilots, and others.[15]

Re-regulation has occurred in areas such as securities and stock market oversight to prevent scandals such as those in the 1980s involving well-known Wall Street figures Ivan Boesky, Michael Milken, and Dennis Levine, all of whom were convicted of securities law violations.

Deregulation in banking led to cutbacks in financial inspection by government officials during the 1980s, and has been associated with

---

[14]Edmund L. Andrews, "Bill to Revamp Communications Dies in Congress," *New York Times*, Sept. 24, 1994, pp. 1, 43.

[15]See, for example, Kenneth Labich, "Should Airlines Be ReRegulated?" *Fortune*, June 19, 1989, pp. 82–89.

bank collapses and the savings and loan scandals. (See Lincoln Savings and Loan case study, pp. 603–616).

Reinventing Government

A recent trend toward streamlining government, making its operations more efficient, is called **reinventing government.**[16] This idea draws heavily upon business success in reengineering corporations and instituting total quality management systems. It operates on the principle that greater efficiency can be achieved if programs are reengineered to eliminate unnecessary procedures, processes, and people—that is, it is possible to do more with less resources. In 1994, Vice President Al Gore headed a federal government effort to "reinvent government" in this way. The government report detailed a lengthy list of ways in which federal agencies, including regulatory agencies, could "do more with less" and save taxpayers' dollars while meeting important needs.[17]

INTERNATIONAL REGULATION

International trade has tied people and businesses together in new and complicated ways. U.S. consumers regularly buy food, automobiles, VCRs, and clothing from companies located in Europe, Canada, Latin America, Australia, Africa, and Asia. Citizens of other nations do the same. As these patterns of international commerce grow more complicated, governments see the need to establish rules that protect and serve the public interest of their own citizens. No nation wants to accept dangerous products manufactured elsewhere that will injure local citizens. No national government wants to see its economy damaged by unfair competition from foreign competitors. These concerns are the reasons for a rapidly growing set of international regulatory agreements and actions. Three types of such regulation are discussed below and illustrated in Figure 8-7.

Regulation of Imported Products

Every nation has the power to set standards for products to be sold in the country. When a child in Chicago receives a Christmas toy made in Taiwan, for example, that toy has met the product safety standards set by the

---

[16]David Osborne and Ted Gaebler, *Reinventing Government: How the Entrepreneurial Spirit Is Transforming the Public Sector,* Reading, MA: Addison-Wesley, 1992.
[17]Al Gore, *From Red Tape to Results: Creating a Government that Works Better and Costs Less: Report of the National Performance Review,* Washington, DC: Government Printing Office, 1993.

FIGURE 8-7
Forms of
international
regulation.

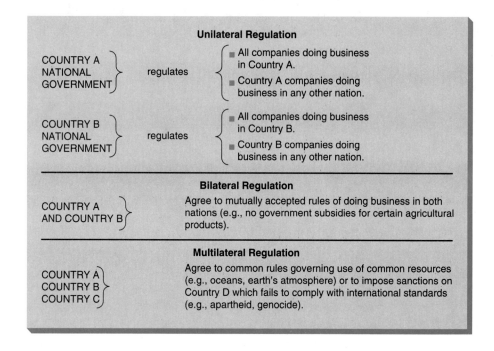

Consumer Product Safety Commission, an agency of the U.S. government. This is a legitimate use of governmental authority. But there can be a temptation for policymakers to set standards for foreign products that are unjustifiably higher or more difficult to meet than those for locally produced goods. If the Consumer Product Safety Commission were to set one standard for U.S. companies and a more demanding standard for foreign toy companies, the result would help U.S. companies and hurt foreign competitors. Because the standard would discriminate against foreign manufacturers, the practice would likely be deemed a trade barrier in violation of international trade agreements. This could make the United States liable for damages to the foreign toy producers. Governments, however, are under pressure from other interests, including local companies, labor organizations, and communities, not to open local markets to foreign sellers. These stakeholders may feel threatened by foreign competitors and seek to block them from selling to a "safe" market of customers.

As discussed in Chapters 6 and 7, political and economic arrangements, such as the European Union, tend to favor greater free trade and discourage protective regulation. This trend is growing but is not easy to achieve. The desire to expand competition, improve consumer choices, and build healthy economies places pressures on governments and businesses to use regulation to promote and protect a broad spectrum of stakeholders.

Regulation of Exported Products

Governments have a real interest in knowing what types of products their businesses are exporting to the rest of the world. The federal government is understandably concerned that products that say "Made in America" are of good quality. U.S. companies have sometimes exported products to other nations that were banned from sale at home because of safety concerns. In addition, the government is concerned that U.S. companies not sell military technology to unfriendly nations. In the 1980s, a number of cases arose in which U.S. and West German businesses illegally sold sophisticated technology with potential military applications to Libya, Iran, and Iraq. These transactions violated U.S. laws that restrict the sale of classified military technology to only those customers approved by the Defense Department. For example, EG&G, a U.S. manufacturer of specialized electronic equipment for military uses, discovered that some of the triggering devices it manufactured for nuclear weapons were being sold to Iraq. The company cooperated with U.S. officials, and a shipment of such devices was traced through a series of intermediaries to a destination in Europe from which they were to go to Baghdad. With the cooperation of foreign officials and EG&G, the illegal exporters were caught and arrested.

Regulation of International Business Behavior

Nations also have sought to standardize trade practices through various international organizations. United Nations agencies such as the World Health Organization have worked with the pharmaceutical industry to create data bases on the side effects of drug product characteristics, establish quality standards, and resolve conflicting manufacturing and marketing practices that might harm the public. Elaborate processes of consultation between leaders of business, governmental, and nongovernmental organizations (e.g., consumer groups) are required to make such changes because of the vast number of stakeholders involved. The World Health Organization's international marketing code for infant formula products, for example, required nearly three years of meetings and consultations before a suitable code was ready for adoption by national governments.[18]

National governments sometimes create special organizations to keep the discussions moving forward. For example, the General Agreement on Tariffs and Trade (GATT) is a set of international agreements among nations on acceptable trade practices. Periodically, nations agree to another "round" of negotiations to be hosted in a particular nation. In the early 1990s, the "Uruguay Round" of talks focused on such issues as government

---

[18]S. Prakash Sethi, *Multinational Corporations and the Impact of Public Advocacy on Corporate Strategy*, Hingham, MA: Kluwer, 1994.

subsidies to agriculture that prevent fair competition from occurring. Lengthy and complex negotiations produced a new international body—the World Trade Organization (WTO)—to enforce the new international trade laws.

Nations work together to establish standards for the use of resources not owned by any nation. Multilateral international agreements govern ocean fishing, the protection of sea mammals such as dolphins and whales, the protection of the ozone layer of the earth's atmosphere, and the dumping of hazardous chemical wastes in oceans. In each case national governments recognize the need to address a problem that cannot be solved through the actions of one nation alone. The result is a framework of international agreements, standards, and understandings that attempts to harmonize business activity and the public interest.[19]

THE FUTURE

Whether maintaining extensive state control of industry or permitting the operation of free markets, government involvement with business is a central feature of the socioeconomic system. In the United States, government economic policy has shaped the macrobusiness environment and regulation has influenced business behavior. The pendulum of regulation has swung back and forth for nearly a century, sometimes favoring more control, sometimes less. Pressures to reduce the role of government contend with pressures for government to solve problems in cost-efficient ways. The nations of Europe, Africa, Latin America, Asia, and the Pacific region face these choices. All seek an optimal solution to the challenge of harmonizing economic growth with the social welfare of citizens. Public policy is the tool used by government to meet this challenge. It shapes the business environment for companies wherever they operate and helps define the social issues that confront business leaders. The repercussions of these choices are felt throughout business and society. For these reasons, if no other, business has a significant stake in the making of public policy.

SUMMARY POINTS OF THIS CHAPTER

- Public policies are government actions intended to achieve a broad public purpose.
- The key elements of public policy are inputs, goals, instruments to achieve those goals, and effects, both intended and unintended.

[19]William C. Frederick, "The Moral Authority of Transnational Corporate Codes," *The Journal of Business Ethics*, vol. 10, 1991, pp. 165–177.

- Key national policies affecting business in every nation include economic growth, taxation, government spending, the value of money, international trade, and industrial policy.
- Social welfare policies affect business both directly (e.g., workplace rules) and indirectly (e.g., government spending) and express the social priorities of a nation. Health care, Social Security, and education are among a nation's most important social welfare policies.
- Government regulation of business is a mechanism for implementing public choices. Economic, social, and functional regulation of business exists in most countries.
- The role of government has grown—and regulation of business has grown—because society demands and expects more of government.
- Government regulation is costly and society pays these costs in the form of higher prices, slowed product innovation, and higher taxes. This has fueled pressure to deregulate and reduce the role of government. In some areas where deregulation has been tried, pressures have grown for government to re-regulate in the public interest.
- International regulation is emerging as global business activity creates problems that cannot be solved by any one nation's government. As nations recognize their needs to cooperate in controlling business activities that cross national borders, international regulations are focusing on imports, exports, and business practices. Agreements among national governments are the key to developing effective international standards.

KEY TERMS AND CONCEPTS USED IN THIS CHAPTER

- Elements of public policy: inputs, goals, instruments, effects
- Fiscal policy
- Monetary policy
- Trade policy
- Industrial policy
- Intergenerational equity

- Entitlement
- Market failure
- Rule of cost
- Cost-benefit analysis
- Deregulation
- Re-regulation
- Reinventing government

DISCUSSION CASE

MEETING THE NATION'S HEALTH CARE CRISIS

When Bill Clinton was elected president of the United States in November 1992, he promised voters that he would launch a major effort to respond to public demands to reform the national health care system. Clinton's campaign advisers, including James Carville, recognized the rising importance of the health care issue many months earlier when Harris Wofford won an election in Pennsylvania to fill a vacant U.S. Senate seat against a popular former governor of the state. Wofford's campaign rested heavily on his promise to "do something" about rapidly rising health care costs. Clinton's advisers, including Carville, calculated that the concerns of Pennsylvania's voters were shared by voters all across America. Mr. Clinton's successful campaign relied heavily on public fears that health care costs were "out of control" and would soon claim 20 percent of the annual gross national product.

Following his inauguration in January 1993, President Clinton announced that the First Lady, Hillary Rodham Clinton, would chair a task force on health care reform. The task force was large—more than 100 members—but secretive. Meetings were held behind closed doors; leaks to the press were plugged. For a long time, even the membership was kept secret to minimize the ability of special interests to pressure members toward specific views. The task force gathered enormous amounts of information from experts, government agencies, and public hearings held around the country. No aspect of the huge American health care system was immune from inspection and assessment. As months passed, the process of information gathering developed its own momentum and the task force's deadline was extended.

When the task force issued its report in January 1994, it called for sweeping reforms in the delivery of health services to citizens. First, it proposed a system of universal coverage that would ensure every American man, woman, and child access to health services. Second, it favored a system of financing that would place burdens on all employers, large and small, to pay for the health insurance coverage of employees and their families. Insurance companies would have to change their way of doing business, including the elimination of varying types of insurance forms. Paperwork reduction was assumed to be an important source of savings. More savings would be achieved as health care providers—hospitals, health maintenance organizations, and individual providers—banded together in a system of health care alliances which would be big enough to place real cost pressures on suppliers of drugs and pharmaceutical products, medical equipment, and related services. Firms in these industries had been among America's most prosperous businesses for decades, and the task force concluded that an important way of controlling rising health care costs was to pressure these suppliers through the marketplace by creating larger, more powerful customers through the health care alliances.

Reforming health care proved to be one of the most complicated public policy processes in recent years. Everyone seemed to have a stake in changing, or preserving, part of the system. Hundreds of interest groups talked to legislators, urging them to act for some provisions and against others. The Clinton administration's bill was large and comprehensive, incorporating dozens of suggestions from Hillary Rodham Clinton's task force. But the scope of the proposed changes was so great that many citizens and legislators worried that good parts of the health care system might also be destroyed by changes. Small businesses worried about the cost of providing health benefits for all employees; large businesses worried about the implementation of managed care proposals; physicians, nurses, and other health care providers worried about job losses as hospitals became "more efficient" through consolidation.

The president offered compromise to those who found fault in his plan. Other versions of health care legislation were drafted by members of Congress. Each new idea seemed to spark more objections. Polls showed that Americans wanted some of the features of the health plans being proposed but were worried and skeptical about other aspects, including costs.

In August, members of the Congress went home on vacation. Discussions with constituents sealed the fate of health care reform. By the time the Congress reconvened in September, health care reform had officially been declared dead.

Elections were coming in November and a new, powerful concept emerged in the public consciousness, the Republican party's "Contract with America."[20] A group of 367 Republican candidates for congressional office signed their names to a ten-point program that included proposals for a balanced budget, welfare reform, fairness for seniors, and reduction of taxes. If elected, they promised to propose legislation on each item in the "contract" within 100 days. The "contract" had no health care provision but captured the public imagination. Led by Representative Newt Gingrich, architect of the idea, Republican candidates were swept into office, establishing majority control of the House of Representatives and the Senate. In January 1995, just as the new Republican leaders were being sworn into office, public opinion polls showed the American public was looking for quick action on a host of issues included in the Republican contract. Ironically, the polls also showed strong public support for an issue that was not part of the contract, namely, health care reform. The problems of the health care system had not gone away and the American public knew it.

Discussion Questions

1. What elements of public policy are evident in the health care debate? How did the issue get on to the policy agenda? What inputs shaped the debate? What goals and instruments were discussed?

[20]Ed Gillespie and Bob Schellhas, eds., *Contract with America: The Bold Plan by Rep. Newt Gingrich, Rep. Dick Armey, and the House Republicans to Change the Nation,* New York: Random House/Times Books, 1994.

2. Discuss the role of the task force headed by Hillary Rodham Clinton. Why might the president prefer to create a separate group rather than use existing government agencies to organize the health care plan?
3. Consider the task force's proposal to control rising health care costs by encouraging the creation of health care alliances to place cost pressures on health product manufacturers. Is this likely to be an effective instrument of public policy?
4. What forms of regulation did the Clinton health care plan propose to use to achieve its goals? Was this a policy area that could be helped by deregulation? By re-regulation?
5. How might the politics of health care change for insurance companies and health care product manufacturers with Republican legislators in control of the Congress? Given the problems of the system as detailed in the task force report, is health care reform likely to remain a dead issue? What might reinvigorate the issue?

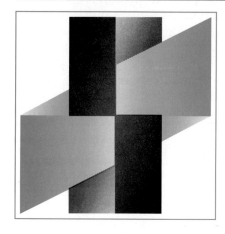

9

Managing Business-Government Relations

Businesses face complex challenges in managing their relationships with government and the public policy process. Managers must recognize public issues as they emerge and know how to respond. The dynamics of the public policy process demand political understanding and impose on companies a need for issues management that has a strategic focus. But political pressures produce ethical dilemmas that often demand careful judgment. The world of politics operates by different rules than business, so managers must bring an ethical and pragmatic perspective to government relations. Managers have a large stake in ensuring that their company is perceived as one of the government's stakeholders, whose interests should be carefully weighed when government officials make decisions.

Key Questions and Chapter Objectives

This chapter focuses on these key questions and objectives:
- What is the public issues life cycle and what does it suggest about the way social concerns become public policy issues?
- How do corporations engage in issues management?
- What forms does corporate political activity take?
- What role does business play in electoral politics?
- What does strategic management of business-government relations mean?
- Why is it important for business to be involved in public policy decision making?
- How do the 1990s problems of the American political system affect business?

Dow Chemical, one of the world's largest and most successful chemical manufacturers, was founded nearly a century ago in Midland, Michigan. Located near Detroit, Dow grew by supplying chemical products to automobile and other industrial manufacturers. The company used research and development in chemistry to create such new products as Saran Wrap, the popular plastic wrap. Plastics based on sophisticated chemical formulations are produced in large-scale manufacturing plants and are used for many purposes. Chemistry has been Dow's core business technology.

The chemical industry has created many products used by the military. In the 1960s and 1970s, Dow became embroiled in a controversy surrounding "Agent Orange," a chemical product containing dioxin that was used by the U.S. military as a defoliant in Vietnam. The effects of dioxin on living organisms, including human beings, can be quite horrible. Dioxin has been called the most toxic substance ever created by humans, and researchers have linked dioxin to cancer in human beings. Dow was criticized for supplying dioxin to the war effort, but the company argued that it had an obligation to assist the U.S. government if asked to do so.

The controversy surrounding the war in Vietnam took years to subside and Dow continued to have its critics. Then, as public concern for the environment rose during the 1980s, scientific attention turned again to dioxin and its effect on humans. Officials in the United States and other countries were under pressure from environmental activists to set more stringent regulations on dioxin exposure. The problem was made more difficult, however, by the extensive industrial use of chlorine, which contains dioxin. In the paper industry, for example, chlorine is used to bleach dark colored wood pulp into white paper. A residue of chlorine is typically discharged into the water from rivers and streams used by pulp and paper mills. Fish and other aquatic life ingest the dioxin, and human beings are exposed to dioxin when they drink the water or eat the contaminated fish.

Dow Chemical is a major producer of chlorine. Its scientists have actively researched many issues involved in the debate about the chlorine-related risks, including dioxin exposure. Many inside the company have felt that the public does not understand the facts about chlorine and dioxin. Environmental activists have focused on the many risks presented to humans, livestock, and crops by chemical exposures, and the public has developed what some call "chemophobia" or fear of chemicals. The result has been many new laws, public pressures, and scientific research to better understand the truth about risks. So extensive and intense is public concern that industry officials feel the entire future of the chemical industry is at stake when government acts.

In 1990, Dow Chemical published a unique message on the cover of its annual report for the preceding year. The statement read: "One issue more than any other will affect our company's prospects in the 1990s and beyond. That issue is the environment." The statement signaled a major effort by the company to shed its Vietnam-era image and position itself within the environmental risk debates of the 1990s. First, David Buzzeli, president of Dow Canada, the Canadian subsidiary, was named vice president and corporate director of environment, health, and safety for Dow's worldwide business. Next, Dow created a strategy of improved environmental performance, employee involvement, strong public communications, systematic efforts to know the "public pulse" at all times, and commitment to actively participate in the public policy process. Political issues management is now a key concept for dealing with the realities of Dow's business environment.

This chapter focuses on managing government and political issues. In no country in the world does business have an absolute right to exist and pursue profits; these rights depend on business compliance with appropriate laws and public policy. As discussed in Chapter 8, public policy is shaped by many factors and influences. Public issues, such as dioxin and chlorine, force companies to monitor public concerns, respond to government inquiries, and participate in the political process. This chapter discusses how businesses and managers can meet the challenge of managing business-government relations.

EVOLUTION OF PUBLIC ISSUES

Government policy is formulated and implemented in several distinct stages. The process differs in each country, of course, especially because of different political cultures and institutions. Still, Figure 9-1 reasonably describes a process that occurs in most nations. Managers must understand this process in order to know what to do and when to do it.

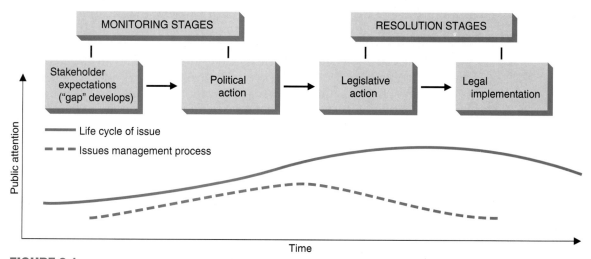

FIGURE 9-1

The public issues life cycle.

From Social Concerns to Public Action

In the United States and many other nations, it is widely believed that government exists to serve the needs and interests of citizens. This principle, deeply rooted in history, means that individuals, groups, and organizations have the right to petition government—federal, state, or local—to respond to perceived problems and needs. As public pressure builds, elected officials and government appointees pay more attention to citizens' concerns and demands. A **public issue** exists, then, when there is a gap between stakeholders' expectations of what institutions should do and the actual performance of those businesses, government agencies, or nonprofit organizations.

> In Times Beach, Missouri, citizens discovered that their dirt roads had been sprayed with a substance that contained dioxin. The company that did the work used waste oil products for the spraying that included dioxin-laced oil. When the new road surface was exposed to rain and snow, some of the dioxin seeped into the ground, affecting groundwater supplies used by residents. The fear of dioxin-induced illness created a near panic in Times Beach. State and federal officials conducted many investigations and eventually decided that the best course of action was for the government to buy the entire town and evacuate the community: 2,200 residents moved out and every building in the town was demolished and removed. A chain-link fence was used to close off a two-mile area along Interstate Route 44.[1]

Times Beach is an extreme example of a process that happens in communities every day. A group of neighbors worry that an intersection is particularly dangerous for children to cross because no traffic signal or stop signs are present. A small town's residents are concerned that a proposed chain store or restaurant will affect the character of the town and destroy its peace and quiet. People who live and work in an urban area worry that crime has made it unsafe to walk to parking lots after dark. In such cases, people may argue that government "must" take action and respond to these concerns.

The Public Issues Life Cycle

Social concerns generally evolve through a series of phases which, because of their natural evolution, can be thought of as a **public issues life cycle.** By recognizing the pattern through which issues evolve, and spot-

---

[1]Debbie Howlett and Rae Tyson, "Toxicity of Times Beach 'No Longer in Doubt,' " *USA Today,* Sept. 13, 1994, p. 1.

ting the early warning signs, managers can anticipate problems and work to resolve them before they reach crisis proportions. As shown in Figure 9-1, the public issues life cycle includes four phases: the changing of stakeholder expectations; political action; legislative action; and legal implementation. Each phase is discussed below.

Stakeholder expectations

Public issues develop as stakeholder expectations of how business or government should behave are not met. This failure can take many forms, ranging from small groups of residents objecting to a local manufacturer's fouling of the air to the concern of animal lovers for the welfare of monkeys being used in scientific research in a laboratory or the anger of voters at officials who raise taxes. As discussed in Chapter 3, once a gap develops, the seeds of a public issue have been sown.

> Few industries have faced as large a legitimacy gap in the 1990s as the American tobacco industry. The industry has had to battle against an increasingly pervasive antismoking climate. For decades, smoking was considered to be glamorous and sophisticated. Advertisements during the 1940s featured movie stars dressed in military garb, which gave the impression that smoking was not only glamorous but patriotic. The perception of smokers and smoking is very different today. The public has increasingly defined smoking as unacceptable. Although the industry has argued that smokers are being unfairly turned into "social pariahs," public health leaders argue that the public is demanding the right to live free from smoke—the right to life, liberty, and the pursuit of happiness *without smoke*. So serious is the pressure that cities, states, and even the federal government have taken steps to ensure that nonsmokers are free of unwanted smoke. In 1993, for example, antismoking advocates introduced legislation (the Smoke-Free Environment Act) in both houses of Congress to prohibit smoking in any building (other than private homes) that is regularly used by ten or more workers a week.[2]

Cigarette manufacturers, such as Philip Morris and R. J. Reynolds, have lived with the health effects issue for many years. As criticism has mounted, the companies have identified segments of the population that oppose, as well as support, smoking restrictions. Although nonsmokers want restrictions, the companies have effectively argued that "smokers have rights too." By campaigning heavily on this theme, the companies have tried to frame the debate in terms of nonsmokers "reasonable" expec-

[2]Investor Responsibility Research Center (IRRC), "Tobacco Divestment: Is the Movement Spinning Its Wheels?" *News for Investors*, Oct. 1994, pp. 1, 4. See also, Richard McGowan, "Public Policy Measures and Cigarette Sales," in J. E. Post, ed., *Research in Corporate Social Performance and Policy*, Vol. 11, Greenwich, CT: JAI Press, 1989, pp. 151–179.

tations, "balancing" the rights of smokers and nonsmokers, and finding ways to create "accommodation."[3]

What does it take to put a problem on the public policy agenda for action by government? The agenda of public issues on which officials are asked to act is enormous. But not all public issues warrant action by government. Of the thousands of issues to which government is asked to respond each year, most fail to get needed support.

Strong and effective leadership is always needed to capture enough public attention to lead a reform movement. The American civil rights movement, for example, had charismatic leadership in Dr. Martin Luther King Jr. during the 1960s. Dr. King was a brilliant public speaker whose speeches attracted large audiences and media coverage, and who served to build powerful support for the expansion of equal opportunity to citizens of all races. Other movements have had leaders with very different personalities. Ralph Nader's fight for automobile safety won public support with detailed technical analyses of dangerous products, including his famous book, *Unsafe at Any Speed.*[4] Gloria Steinem and Betty Friedan were effective writers and advocates for women's rights. Cesar Chavez, a quiet, determined leader of the 1970s, drew attention to the plight of farm workers through hunger strikes and product boycotts. Each of these leaders used his or her personality and knowledge to keep issues in front of the American public and its political leaders. And there are times when a reform movement's leadership comes from within the political system itself, such as U.S. Representative Newt Gingrich's political crusade to reduce the power of the federal government in the 1990s.

Dramatic events can also prompt government to act. Environmental crises such as the nuclear power plant accident at Three Mile Island, the tragedy at Union Carbide's chemical plant in Bhopal, India, or the discovery of chemical dangers in places such as Love Canal (Niagara Falls, New York) or Times Beach, Missouri, all served to generate public pressure on government to strengthen environmental protection laws.

Interest groups may signal the emergence of an issue by swinging into action to protect members by advocating government action. Managers must understand what others are asking government to do and be prepared to ask government to act on behalf of their business. In the 1990s, international trade conflicts have prompted American companies to ask the federal government to challenge the "unfair trade practices" of foreign competitors.

[3]Philip Morris and R. J. Reynolds developed advertising campaigns using the accommodation theme. In one RJR-sponsored advertisement, three picture captions read, respectively, "The Berlin Wall Crumbles," "Russia Approves New Constitution," and "Democracy's Victory in South Africa." The fourth caption provided a contrast: "Nationwide, Reins on U.S. Smokers' Freedom Tightens." The title to the ad read: "Where Exactly *Is* the Land of the Free?" See *New York Times*, Oct. 25, 1994, p. A17. For a discussion of cigarette companies' business strategies see, Richard McGowan, *Business, Politics, and Cigarettes*, Westport, CT: Praeger/Quorum Books, 1995.

[4]Ralph Nader, *Unsafe at Any Speed*, New York: Grossman, 1965.

U.S. auto manufacturers sought the assistance of the federal government in getting Japan to allow more U.S. vehicles to be sold in that country. The unwillingness of Japan to open its domestic market to the sale of more General Motors, Ford, and Chrysler automobiles contrasted sharply with the U.S. market where Japanese auto companies have established major market positions with their Toyota, Nissan, and Honda vehicles. U.S. firms claimed Japanese governmental policy was behind the closed market. Hence, only the U.S. government could move Japan to change.

Political action

It may take months or even years for a concerned group of stakeholders to build a base of support sufficient to challenge a corporation. If an issue persists, however, the group may organize formally and campaign for its point of view through pamphlets, newsletters, posters, and other forms of communication. They may attract the attention of the media, which will result in newspaper, television, or radio coverage. This moves the issue from one of citizen concern to one of political importance.

> The political drive against passive smoking took off in 1973 when the Civil Aeronautics Board ruled that smokers had to be separated from nonsmokers on airline flights. Political developments included the formation of various antismoking groups, including Group Against Smoking Pollution (GASP). GASP received calls from people complaining of illness caused by "passive smoke"—smoke from other people's cigarettes. They assisted companies that wished to establish smoking restrictions. Antismoking activists attribute corporate willingness to set up such policies to dozens of legal cases in which nonsmokers have sued companies for failing to protect them from passive smoke. The Environmental Protection Agency issued statistics that showed passive smoke kills thousands of people each year, and courts have increasingly sided with nonsmokers in passive-smoking lawsuits. Governments have also sued tobacco companies for the costs of smoking-related disease. Since 1994, Florida has sued tobacco product manufacturers to recover the costs of treating the tobacco-related illnesses of Florida Medicaid patients.[5]

Politicians are interested in citizens' concerns and often are anxious to advocate action on their behalf. The government officials become new stakeholders with different types of power to use in closing the gap between public expectations and business performance. The "tobacco lobby" once had the support of a powerful coalition of elected representatives and senators in Washington. But as antismoking pressures have

---

[5]IRRC, op. cit.

grown, more elected officials and political candidates have spoken in favor of antismoking laws. Some have become outspoken critics of the tobacco lobby. The involvement of political actors creates more stakeholders and, hence, makes the issue more complex for the company and its managers.

As interested groups begin to build support for a particular position or viewpoint, *policy formulation* begins to occur. Consensus among participating groups can move government toward decision. If consensus cannot be reached, the issue may drop off the agenda or another effort may be made in the future to resurrect the issue and build more political support.[6] Business's stake in policy formulation is high. Government officials often seek the support of the business community for policies they are trying to enact. During the 1994 debate on health care legislation, for example, the Clinton administration campaigned vigorously for the support of business organizations such as the Business Roundtable, an association of large corporations and small business groups such as the National Federation of Independent Businesses. Support—or lack of support—by such organizations and their member companies, each with thousands of employees, customers, and shareholders, can spell life or death for a policy proposal.

Legislative action

As more people are drawn into a political conflict, ideas may emerge about how to use the law or regulation to solve the problem. When legislative proposals or draft regulations emerge, the public issue moves to a new level of action.

> Much legislative action has been taken in favor of antismoking activists during the past decade. Antismoking legislation has been enacted nationally and in many states and cities. The federal government has required that health warnings on cigarette labels be in larger print and that messages be rotated quarterly to provide more effective warnings. Many communities set limits on the areas in restaurants that can be used by smokers, and nonsmokers in the workplace can legally declare their "immediate work area" a no-smoking zone. Some cities have even outlawed smoking entirely in office buildings, restaurants, and public buildings.

Companies involved in legislative actions are usually represented by lawyers, lobbyists, and professional political consultants. Top manage-

[6]See Philip B. Heyman, "How Government Expresses Public Ideas," in Robert B. Reich, ed., *The Power of Public Ideas,* Cambridge, MA: Ballinger Publishing, 1988, pp. 85–107. The classic reference of agenda building and policy formulation is Roger W. Cobb and Charles D. Elder, *Participation in American Politics: The Dynamics of Agenda-Building,* Boston: Allyn & Bacon, 1972.

ment may be called to testify before government committees or regulatory agencies; corporate lawyers and lobbyists decide what proposals are best and worst for the company; efforts are made to slow or alter legislative proposals to serve a company's interests.

> Tobacco companies have hired dozens of lobbyists, lawyers, and political advisers to fight antismoking efforts. Individually, and through the Tobacco Institute, an industry association, they have challenged scientific findings and worked to defeat antismoking proposals. Two powerful counterarguments have been used: first, that 50 million U.S. smokers are citizens who also have rights, including the personal freedom to smoke; and second, that taxes on tobacco products are an important source of revenue for cities and states, accounting for many millions of dollars. Legislators who might vote for an antismoking law are sometimes stopped by fears of what it will mean for government to lose tobacco tax revenue or to have angry smokers campaigning against them in the next election.

A *policy decision* occurs when a government body either authorizes, or fails to authorize, a course of action. Failing to act can be a policy decision as, for example, when the city council votes against a proposal to borrow money, or Congress votes down a proposed law. Not surprisingly, many pressures are brought by interested parties on decision makers. Business, like other interests, often attempts to persuade decision makers toward a particular position and uses a variety of political techniques to do so.

Legal implementation
Making a public policy decision does not mean that the public policy will be carried out automatically. The validity of new laws and regulations is often challenged through litigation. Once the issue is settled, however, and the company acts to implement the law, other levels of management whose efforts are needed to meet the new requirements will be involved.

Stakeholder interest in an issue tends to plateau or even decline as a new law or regulation is implemented. New laws often spark lawsuits to test the interpretation and limits of the statute. Once the test cases are over, affected parties will normally abide by the law and compliance will reduce public interest in the issue. If the law is violated or ignored, however, the issue may reemerge, as a new gap develops between stakeholder expectations and the corporation's actual performance.

Business still has a chance to influence how the public policy is implemented at this stage of the process. A company may negotiate with a regulatory agency for extending compliance deadlines, as steel companies have often done in introducing pollution control technologies, and auto manufacturers have done in introducing air bags and other safety devices. Legal steps can sometimes be taken to appeal the law or regulation. Or an industry may play off one branch of government against another: presidential actions can sometimes be checked by congressional objections and pressure.[7]

Continuing issues

Debates about some public issues continue long after the implementation of policy. Advocacy groups may keep the issue alive, knowing that new government officials may be receptive to changing the law or interpreting it differently. Therefore, *policy evaluation* becomes an important activity. Groups that were opposed to a policy may work to document its negative effects; sponsors may try to document the positive effects of the policy, while downplaying or minimizing the negative effects. Government officials may try to find out whether the benefits have been worth more than the costs, and whether the policy goals could have been achieved in other, more efficient or less expensive ways.

Costs and benefits are often quite difficult to measure, and difficult to trace to only one policy action. For example, many initiatives have been taken to reduce drug use among the population. If a community's drug abuse admissions to hospitals and clinics decline, is it possible to trace the effect to a single action? Probably not. Interaction among public policy actions often occurs. We know, for example, that children do better in school if they start the day with a nutritionally sound breakfast. So, if reading scores go up in school, is it the breakfast program or new teaching techniques that are responsible?

Public issues often overlap and interweave with one another, creating a complex web of advocacy groups, coalitions, government policies, programs, laws, regulations, court orders, and political maneuvers. Something is always happening in each stage, often involving issues of concern to the company and its management. For business, or for any other interest group, this means that public policy is constantly being made and that it is critical to monitor the social and political environment.

ISSUES MANAGEMENT

The Process

Issues management is a structured way for companies to respond to those public issues that are of greatest importance to the business. Companies rarely have control of a public issue because of the many factors involved. But it is possible for an organization to create a management system that monitors issues as they emerge and involves managers in action to mini-

---

[7]See Hedrick Smith, *The Power Game: How It Works*, New York: Random House, 1988; and David Vogel, *Fluctuating Fortunes—The Political Power of Business*, New York: Basic Books, 1989.

mize the negative effects of a public issue or to maximize the positive effects for the organization's advantage.

> According to its executives, Dow Chemical created an issues management system to provide an "early warning/early response" capability so that a public issue's positive potential can be encouraged and enhanced, and its negative potential can be discouraged or inhibited. "The objective is to identify issues in the early stages of development before options are narrowed and liabilities expanded. The difference between issues management and crisis management is timing!"[8]

Managers have less influence on a public issue as it evolves. That is another way of saying that the sooner a company can become involved in managing an issue, the more likely it is that it can shape an outcome that is acceptable to the organization and others. The **issues management process** is a basic tool used to achieve this objective. Figure 9-2 illustrates the components of a typical issues management system.

Issues identification
This involves the active scanning of newspapers, other media, experts' views, and community concerns to identify issues of concern to the pub-

[8]Tony Jacques, Public Affairs Manager, Dow Chemical (Australia) Limited, presentation at Public Affairs Institute, Melbourne, Australia, July 1994.

FIGURE 9-2
The issues management process.

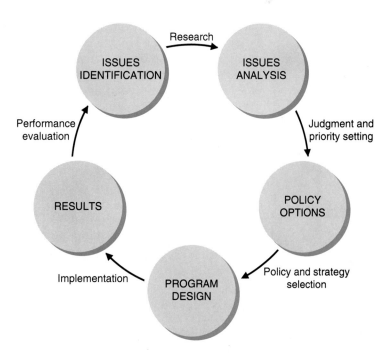

lic. Because there are many ways to spot emerging issues, managers must decide how best to focus their efforts. Companies often use electronic data bases, including the Internet, to track ideas, themes, and issues that may be relevant to their public policy interests.

Issues analysis

Once identified, the facts and implications of the issue must be analyzed. For example, an analysis of the dioxin issue would show that there is much discussion among scientists as to the chemical process of dioxin exposure, and debate as to whether, or how, dioxin contamination can be cleaned up. Similarly, tobacco companies have invested in having researchers examine every study that claims a link between passive smoking and health effects. Issue analysis is guided by management's need to answer two basic questions: (1) what impact can this issue have on our business? and (2) what is the probability that this issue will evolve into later stages of the public issue life cycle?

Policy options

An issue's impact and probability of occurrence tell managers how significant the issue is for the company. It does not tell management what to do. Developing policy options involves creating choices. It requires complex judgments that incorporate ethical considerations, the company's reputation and good name, and other nonquantifiable factors. Management may decide to change internal practices, operating procedures, or even the product itself. Companies in the pulp and paper industry, for example, have invested in developing new bleaching technologies in order to eliminate chlorine from their manufacturing processes.[9] Management may also focus on changing the views of officials, the public, or the media. "Do nothing" may also be an option if an issue is not ripe for immediate action. Research organizations, such as "think tanks," can be useful sources of ideas about alternative policy options. These groups issue papers on many public policy topics, including environmental practices, taxation, minimum wages, and regulation.[10]

Program design

Once the policy option has been chosen, the company must design and implement an appropriate program. For example, tobacco companies made a policy choice to fight antismoking proposals in every city, state, and political district in which such proposals are made. Their program is designed to ensure that no antismoking law is created without efforts by the indus-

[9]"Paper Companies Shape Environmental Futures around New Process Options," *Pulp and Paper,* Sept. 1994, and individual company profiles, for example, "Champion Adds New Bleaching Technology to OD100 Process," pp. 56–57.
[10]See David M. Ricci, *The Transformation of American Politics: The New Washington and the Rise of Think Tanks,* New Haven, CT: Yale University Press, 1993.

try to shape, influence, or kill the proposal. This "fight on every front" policy requires a very expensive program, but it has been an integral part of the tobacco companies' strategy for years.

Early issues identification enables a company to build "political capital" before it is needed. Good will is often created by helping other organizations which, in time, can become your company's allies.

> For many years, Philip Morris has been a patron of the arts. Millions of its dollars have supported museums, art galleries, and performing arts organizations across the nation. In 1994 Philip Morris, which has its corporate headquarters in New York, faced the prospect of a complete ban on cigarettes in restaurants and other public places under an ordinance proposed by the New York City Council. Philip Morris executives telephoned arts institutions that had benefited from the company's grants and asked them to put in a good word with the city council. The company said it would have to move away from New York if such a ban were passed, with inevitable loss of support for the arts organizations. The arts groups were asked to tell the city council how much that would mean to their organizations.[11]

Results

Once an issues management program has been tried, it is important that the results be studied and adjustments made if necessary. Because political issues may take considerable time to evolve, it is important that the manager entrusted with a particular issue regularly update senior managers as to the actions and effectiveness of other stakeholders. The company may reposition or even rethink its approach to the issue.

Managing the Single Issue

Traditionally, public issues have been managed exclusively by the company's public affairs or government relations staff (see Chapter 3). A new trend is for responsibility of managing an issue to be placed in the hands of managers from the area of the business most affected by the problem. For example, an issue involving tax rates or depreciation schedules would be assigned to an *issues manager* from the company's tax department; an issue involving local protests of truck traffic at a plant in Tulsa, Oklahoma, would properly be assigned to the plant manager of the Tulsa facility. TRW, a global manufacturer of defense and industrial products, pioneered the management of issues by operating managers when it created its "quarterback system" in which one manager coordinated the efforts of a team of people from across the company.

---

[11]Maureen Dowd, "Philip Morris Calls in I.O.U.'s in the Arts," *New York Times,* Oct. 5, 1994, pp. A1, C14.

When an issue involves several areas of a company's business, an *issues management team* may be created to deal with the issue. Building on the "quarterback" concept, these teams are led by a manager from the area most directly affected by the problem. She or he will "own" the issue and be responsible for ensuring that the company is acting appropriately to manage the problem. Experts from other areas within the company will be included in the team as needed. Through the use of electronic mail and other technologies, teams can be organized from personnel at different locations.

> For example, Dow Chemical created a global issues management team to deal with the chlorine issue. Members were drawn from the United States, Europe, and Asia-Pacific, and included scientists, plant managers, and managers from Dow's manufacturing businesses that would be impacted by any changes in the availability of chlorine. The global issues management team analyzed scientific studies of chlorine, followed government actions across the world, coordinated research into various aspects of the problem, and worked with lobbyists and government relations staff to ensure Dow spoke with "one voice" when talking about chlorine.

Issues management teams usually exist only as long as the issue is a high priority for the company. This coincides with the modern management trend to use task forces and other temporary team assignments to manage issues in companies. Rather than create large staffs and costly bureaucracies, companies have learned that flexibility is the key to managing public issues as well as other aspects of the business.

Managing Multiple Issues

Companies facing many public issues need to set priorities about which issues will receive the most attention. Many companies use an *issues priority matrix* such as that shown in Figure 9-3. The number of issues that a company can actively work on is limited by resources. If resources are limited, only high priority issues (greatest impact on the firm and highest chance of occurring) will be assigned for managers to work on; the company may use trade associations or consultants to follow less important issues.

STRATEGIC MANAGEMENT OF GOVERNMENT RELATIONS

There is a serious debate between those who favor and those who oppose business involvement in government. This debate involves the question of whether, and to what extent, business should legitimately participate in

FIGURE 9-3

The issues priority matrix.

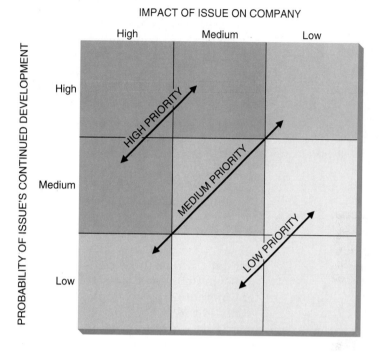

IMPACT OF ISSUE ON COMPANY

the political process. As shown in Figure 9-4, some people believe business should stay out of politics. However, business and politics are increasingly entwined in all nations, a fact that makes it practically impossible for business to stay out of politics. Gradually, business leaders have come to recognize that the survival and prosperity of their businesses are connected to political decisions. Although this clear trend toward expanded business involvement in political debate and discussion is not without critics, managers find it unrealistic and unwise to stand on the sidelines while political leaders make decisions with far-ranging consequences for the economy and competitiveness of businesses.[12]

The techniques used by business to participate in governmental politics are similar to those of other interest groups. Many large corporations place a full-time representative and staff in Washington to keep abreast of developments in government that may affect the company and to exert influence on members of Congress and other officials. Company lobbyists may be active in city halls and state capitals as well. Many companies join *trade associations* such as the National Federation of Independent Businesses (small businesses), the National Association of Manufacturers (manufacturers only), or the U.S. Chamber of Commerce (broad, diverse mem-

[12]A classic discussion of corporate political action is Edwin M. Epstein, *The Corporation in American Politics,* Englewood Cliffs, NJ: Prentice-Hall, 1969.

FIGURE 9-4
The case for and
against political
involvement by
business.

Reasons why business *should* be involved:

- ■ A pluralistic system invites many participants
- ■ Economic stakes are high
- ■ Business counterbalances other social interests
- ■ Business is a vital stakeholder of government

Reasons why business *should not* be involved:

- ■ Executives are not qualified
- ■ Business is naive about politics
- ■ Business is too big, too powerful
- ■ Business risks its credibility in partisan politics

bership), where they count on strength of numbers and a centralized staff to promote their interests with government officials.[13] The U.S. Chamber of Commerce, for example, has a membership of 200,000 companies, operates with a large annual budget, publishes a widely circulated business magazine, and has a satellite television network to broadcast its political messages. Ad hoc political *coalitions* bringing diverse business groups together to lobby for or against particular legislation have also proved effective. In 1990, proposed federal laws establishing day-care programs and strengthening affirmative action programs were defeated, in part, by the work of ad hoc business coalitions. Ad hoc coalitions also combined to defeat health care legislation.

Political Involvement

Business executives must decide on the appropriate level of political involvement for their company. As shown in Figure 9-5, there are multiple levels of involvement and ways to participate. To be successful, a business must think strategically about objectives and how specific political issues and opportunities relate to those objectives.

For example, a software company that designs and manufactures products for use in computer systems around the world has a long-term and strategic interest in encouraging copyright laws and other intellectual

---

[13]Patricia C. Kelley, "Factors that Influence the Development of Trade Associations' Political Behavior," in J. E. Post, ed., *Research in Corporate Social Performance and Policy,* Vol. 12, Greenwich, CT: JAI Press, pp. 63–142.

FIGURE 9-5
Levels of business
political involve-
ment.

Example

Level 1: Financial Involvement

- Formation of political action committee (PAC)
- Trade association support

Level 2: Organizational Involvement

- Lobbying
- Employee "grassroots" involvement
- Shareholder and customer communications

Level 3: Strategic Public Policy Involvement

- Executive participation
- Involvement with industry working groups and task forces
- Policy position development

property protection that prevent piracy of ideas and products. The time to start lobbying for such laws is not when the company's hot new product is introduced—that is much too late. Years in advance of the product introduction, the company must be working with others in the political process to secure the intellectual property protection it will need for future generations of its products. It may need domestic laws and the government's commitment to negotiate such protection with foreign governments.

Strategic interests may be indirect as well as direct. Many businesses have sought to persuade state, local, and national governments to improve public education. Some do so out of the belief that it is "immoral" for students to leave schools without skills to survive in the modern economy. Others have a longer-term business view: future workers who do not have sound education will create a shortage of critical skills and, hence, a problem for companies that will need those skills.

Business and the Political System

Business has a stake in the political system of each nation as well as in the outcome of individual issues. Politics is the way a society makes decisions about who shall have power to make important decisions (who governs), and for what purposes and in what ways that power will be used (toward what ends). Business has a stake in the outcome of discussions of whether free enterprise, central state control, or mixed state-and-private enterprise shall prevail. Apart from expressing a preference for free enterprise, business is sometimes called to play a more substantial role in the political reform of a nation.

> In eastern Europe, for example, business has been a source of capital for newly privatized industries, a source of expertise for creating market systems, and an influential mechanism through which ideas have flowed from the capitalist world to former communist countries. Asea Brown Boveri (ABB), a jointly owned Swiss and Swedish engineering firm, has been involved in construction projects to improve eastern European nations' physical infrastructure. Siemens, Germany's electronics, computer, and equipment giant, has been a partner with the government and banking leader, Deutschebank, in steps to integrate economically disadvantaged East Germany with prosperous West Germany.

AMERICAN POLITICS IN THE 1990s

Business cooperation with government has occurred in the United States for much of the nation's history. Since the 1930s, the federal government has been an "activist" in efforts to guide the economy toward growth, full employment, and social welfare. Activist government emerged during the Great Depression, when most people agreed that government should do all that it could to restore economic prosperity. But fifty years of activist government produced a powerful backlash by the 1980s, when President Reagan effectively portrayed government as the problem, not the solution to America's problems. "Too much government at too high a cost" was a message that resonated in American communities from California to New Hampshire, North Dakota to Texas.

The 1990s are a politically turbulent time in America. Many Americans believe that the nation's economic and social problems require government to set the course and create the framework for prosperity. But many Americans also believe that high taxes are unfair to most families, depriving them of income necessary to make private choices, while feeding "big government" that is out of touch with its citizens. **Political cynicism** refers to a climate of public distrust about politics and politicians. America is suffering from serious political cynicism in the 1990s. Voters are angry with a system that seems unable to deliver on its promises. Voter turnout is low in most elections, and even presidential races draw barely more than 50 percent of registered voters in most states. (In 1992, Minnesota had the highest participation rate, 64 percent). Candidates for political office often engage in *negative campaigning*, in which one candidate attacks the positions and personal qualities (e.g., truthfulness) of his or her opponent.[14] "Attack ads" are used to damage the image of opponents because the public responds to them—political advertising has become a highly specialized world of polling, focus groups, and audience responses. As a result, public respect for all candidates is declining. The public seems to distrust long-serving incumbents; media-wise, "slick" new candidates who advocate change; and media campaigns in general. Such negative attitudes ultimately affect how public policy is made and what ideas become law.

There is a long-standing debate among political experts about how politics and public policy interrelate. Marxists believe that those who control the economic system also will control the political system. Pluralists, on the other hand, think that many different interests compete for influence in the political system. Others believe that the bureaucracy of government itself dominates the political system and that other interests are secondary in impact to the civil servants and entrenched interests within government.[15] A fourth view holds that a social elite, including business leaders and others, make key decisions without much regard to popular wishes. The American political scene seems to offer some evidence—and counterevidence—for each of these views.

There is no clear answer to the debate about whether it is the political system or current issues that account for the problems of American politics in the 1990s. Individual issues often produce contradictory evidence. The United States in the mid-1990s remains a mostly pluralistic political system. Interest groups abound and they have a powerful effect on political life. Because there are so many different interests in modern America, coalitions have to be formed to advance certain ideas, specific legislation, or regulations. According to some experts, all areas of modern political life reflect coalition politics, which means that no special interest is ever powerful enough, by itself, to determine how an issue should be resolved.[16] Others argue that coalitions are formed so rapidly, and with such resources, as to create a type of political gridlock in which action cannot occur. Others disagree, citing the extent to which a few special interests—especially Wall Street and Washington insiders (named the "Beltway Bandits" because they tend to be located within the road that circles the nation's capital)—dominate the political agenda.[17]

[14]See, for example, Tim Curran, "Late, Outside Money Begins to Flow through Independent Expenditures," *Roll Call*, vol. 40, no. 30, Oct. 24, 1994, pp. 1, 12.

[15]Kevin Phillips, *Arrogant Capital: Washington, Wall Street, and the Frustration of American Politics*, Boston: Little, Brown & Company, 1994. See also, Jeffrey Birnbaum, *The Lobbyists: How Influence Peddlers Get Their Way in Washington*, New York: Random House/Times Books, 1992.

[16]Thomas J. Eagleton, *Issues in Business and Government*, Englewood Cliffs, NJ: Prentice-Hall, 1990, p. 5.

[17]Kevin Phillips, op. cit. See also, Peter H. Stone, "Friends, After All," *National Journal*, Oct. 22, 1994, pp. 2240–2445.

Political parties are a vital part of a pluralistic society, representing "grand coalitions" of individuals and interest groups seeking to promote their own welfare through political action. Although political parties are not mentioned in the U.S. Constitution, they have long been an important part of the system of representative government. Not only do they make the electoral process possible by providing a means for proposing candidates for public office, they serve as a rallying point for individuals and groups to work with others who hold similar ideas about how to run the government.[18]

However, political parties have steadily lost their power to hold together diverse political interests and to keep government running. "Third party" presidential campaigns in 1980 (when John Anderson ran against Jimmy Carter and Ronald Reagan) and 1992 (when Ross Perot ran against George Bush and Bill Clinton) have symbolized the inability of the traditional political parties to speak for all voters at the federal level. Between 1992 and 1994, when the Democratic party had majority control of the House of Representatives and the Senate, President Bill Clinton failed to achieve much of his legislative agenda because the members of the Democratic party would not vote with their leaders. Newt Gingrich, who became Republican Speaker of the House of Representatives in 1995, had some success holding his majority but experts questioned how long this unity would last. At state and local levels, political parties seem to command more loyalty, although there is considerable variation from state to state, with large numbers of voters registered as independents and more candidates running outside conventional party designations.

Critical Problems of the 1990s

Business is entangled in a 1990s American political system that is rife with issues, conflicts, and problems. Political scientists disagree whether the system has ever been more embattled, but it is paradoxical that at a time when other nations are looking to the United States as a democratic model, pressures are building for major reforms of this system. Business is not immune from these issues. As a regular participant in the political process, it has a large stake in ensuring that the system operates in a manner that is consistent with the ideals of democracy. Several central problems are discussed below.

Money and campaign financing

American politics is very expensive. Candidates for public office at every level of government—from local government officials to the president of the United States—are forced to spend money to get elected. Costs range from a few thousand dollars in local elections to tens of millions of dollars

[18]One prize-winning analysis of the role of political parties is Arthur M. Schlesinger Jr., *The Cycles of American History*, Boston: Houghton Mifflin, 1986.

for high federal government positions. One estimate is that more than $20 billion was spent by candidates trying to get elected at every level of government in 1994.[19]

This dependence on money for campaigns forces candidates to raise money from potential donors. Many elected officials, such as representatives to Congress, face campaigns every two years and begin campaigning for their *next* term of office on virtually the day they start their current term. This has been called the problem of the **perpetual political campaign.** At the core of the problem is the issue of raising funds.

Business is involved in campaign financing in several ways. Direct contributions by corporations to political candidates for federal offices are forbidden by federal law; some, but not all, states also place restrictions on corporate contributions to candidates in state elections. Since the mid-1970s, companies have been permitted to spend company funds to organize and administer **political action committees (PACs).** PACs are separately incorporated organizations that can solicit contributions from stockholders and employees and then channel the funds to those seeking political office. Companies that have organized PACs are not permitted to donate *corporate* funds to the PAC or to any political candidate; all donations to company-organized PACs must come from individuals. Labor union and other interest group PACs also raise money and support candidates. One notable example is Emily's List, a PAC that supports women candidates (see Exhibit 9-A).

As Figure 9-6 shows, PACs have proved to be very popular with business as well as with other groups. Corporate PACs are the most numerous, accounting for over 40 percent of more than 4,100 PACs, and are among the biggest money raisers and spenders. But as illustrated in Figure 9-7, trade and membership organizations (e.g., National Rifle Association, American Medical Association), labor groups, and nonconnected organizations (e.g., National Association of Realtors) also ranked high in money raised and spent. Labor unions are among the biggest contributors, although as a whole they represent less than 10 percent of all PACs. Interestingly, the number of PACs seems to have peaked in the late 1980s, although the amount of money raised has continued to reach new high levels throughout the 1990s.

The Federal Election Commission has established rules to regulate PAC activities. For example, PACs are not allowed to give more than $5,000 to a single candidate for each election, although the winner of a primary election may be given another $5,000 for the general election. These limits were imposed on all PACs to reduce the role of concentrated wealth in determining the outcome of elections to public office. But new ways are being found to get around the rules. For example, donors took advantage of loopholes that allowed them to spend as much as they wanted indirectly on candidates so long as they did not cooperate or consult with candidates or their campaigns. Thus PACs spent money on television commer-

[19]Based on data reported in *The National Journal,* Sept. 10, 1994, p. 12.

EXHIBIT 9-A

EMILY'S LIST: EARLY MONEY IS LIKE YEAST

Emily's List is a political action committee (PAC). In fact, it is the third largest PAC in the nation, and it raised $5.9 million for the 1994 election. Most importantly, Emily's List is a PAC created by women for the benefit of women candidates. And Emily's List is popular: the organization has about 34,000 members, three-quarters of whom are women.

Emily is not a woman, but an acronym. It means "*Early Money Is Like Yeast:* It makes the dough rise." The PAC was formed in 1986 by a group of women who knew that women were often stopped from becoming candidates for elected office by lack of money. The concept was to provide money to women candidates who showed great promise and, most importantly, to make the donation *early* in a campaign when funds are badly needed and least available to nonincumbents. "Early money," as it is called, also helps candidates raise additional money from sources that are not willing to spend until the candidate proves her ability to raise money from others. In other words, the type of early money Emily's List provides is "yeast" for the candidacies of women.

Because the group started with a relatively small amount of money, it set tough criteria for its support. Candidates had to be knowledgeable, have a good "story" to share with voters, and be extremely committed to expanding the role of women in the political process. In 1986, Emily's List raised and donated $350,000. In 1990, it had grown to $1.5 million raised from 3,500 donors. But in 1992, after the hearings in which the all-male members of the Senate Judiciary Committee approved the Supreme Court nomination of Clarence Thomas despite Anita Hill's sexual harassment charges, women flocked to support Emily's List. Donations in 1992 soared to more than $6 million, raised from 24,000 members. The group invested in fifty-five election races, helping to elect four women to the Senate and twenty-one to the House of Representatives.

SOURCE: Based on Rick Wartzman, "Power of the Purse: Women Are Becoming Big Spenders in Politics and on Social Causes," *Wall Street Journal*, Oct. 17, 1994, pp. A1, A7.

cials, telephone banks, and mass mailings in addition to funds they were permitted to contribute directly to the candidate.[20]

As illustrated in Exhibit 9-B, one consequence of this "money game" is the candidacy for public office of extremely wealthy individuals whose personal fortunes can be used without restriction in support of their political campaigns.

Lobbying and the power of special interests

Since the end of World War II, the federal government has become the focus of both social policy and economic management of the national economy. Special interests have grown in number and political power.

[20]See *Almanac of Federal PACs, 1994–95,* Washington, DC: Congressional Research Service, 1994; Michael Oreskes, "The Trouble with Politics," *New York Times*, Mar. 18, 1990, p. 11; and "GOP 'Soft Money' Topped $16 Million in 2 Months," *Wall Street Journal*, Jan. 11, 1995, p. A6.

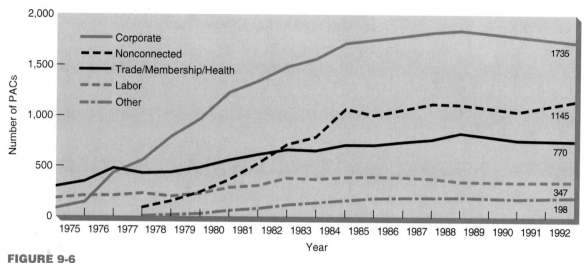

FIGURE 9-6

Profile of PACs, 1975–1992.

SOURCE: Federal Election Commission. Reported in *Almanac of Federal PACs, 1994–95,* Washington, DC: Congressional Research Service, 1994, pp. 377–381.

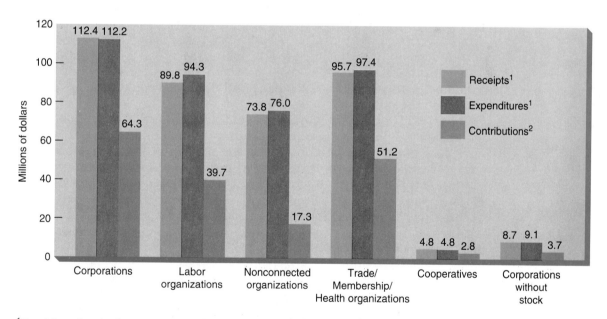

[1]Receipts and expenditures do not include funds transferred between affiliated committees.

[2]Includes contributions to committees of 1990 House and Senate candidates and all federal candidates (for House, Senate, and presidency) campaigning in future elections or retiring debts of former campaigns.

FIGURE 9-7

Financial activity of PACs.

SOURCE: Federal Election Commission. Reported in *Almanac of Federal PACs, 1994–95,* Washington, DC: Congressional Research Service, 1994, pp. 377–381.

EXHIBIT 9-B

THE COSTS OF DEMOCRACY KEEP RISING

The costs of gaining elected office keep rising. In 1990, for example, the Republican National Committee (RNC) raised $38 million in support of candidates across the country. In 1994, the RNC spent more than $60 million in support of about the same number of candidates. Democratic candidates received $12 million from the Democratic National Committee (DNC) in 1990. With President Bill Clinton leading the party's fundraising efforts, the DNC had more than $60 million to spend in 1994.

According to the Center for Responsive Politics, a Washington watchdog organization, the average cost of campaigning for a seat in the House of Representatives has increased by 196 percent between 1976 and 1992. The cost of trying for a Senate seat increased by 154 percent in the same time period.

In 1994, Michael Huffington, the Republican party's candidate for a U.S. Senate seat from California, spent more than $25 million of his own fortune in support of his campaign. Wealthy candidates like Huffington and billionaire Ross Perot who spent an estimated $15 million of his money to run for the U.S. presidency in 1992, are prepared to put their money and hard work into political campaigns. Expert political observers believe this trend will continue and that it is only a matter of time before another wealthy candidate exceeds Huffington's record in pursuit of political office. But money alone does not guarantee success: Huffington lost the Senate race to Diane Feinstein, the incumbent.

Most importantly, these interests—groups as diverse as gun owners represented by the National Rifle Association, and poor and needy children represented by the Children's Defense Fund—have learned to use the tools of political influence.

Many tools are used by business and other interests to directly influence the development of public policy. Most involve efforts to transmit information, express a point of view, or communicate a "message" to an official or regulator.[21] **Lobbying** involves direct contact with a government official to influence the thinking or actions of that person on an issue or public policy. It is usually done through face-to-face contact, sometimes in lengthy discussions, or in meetings that may last only minutes. **Grassroots programs** are organized efforts to get voters to influence government officials to vote or act in a favorable way. Many companies have asked their shareholders to participate in grassroots efforts to persuade their congressional representatives to reduce capital gains taxes and thereby make stock purchases and other investments more lucrative. These programs send a strong message to elected officials that the desired action is supported by voters.

[21]See John Mahon, "Shaping Issues/Manufacturing Agents: Corporate Political Sculpting," and Kathleen Getz, "Selecting Corporate Political Tactics," both in Barry M. Mitnick, ed., *Corporate Political Agency: The Construction of Competition in Public Affairs,* Newbury Park, CA: Sage, 1993; and Robert L. Heath and Richard Alan Nelson, *Issues Management: Corporate Public Policymaking in an Information Society,* Beverly Hills, CA: Sage, 1986.

Direct forms of political action also include letter writing campaigns, "fax attacks," telegrams, and telephone calls to register approval or disapproval of an official's position on an important issue. Businesses often invite government officials to make visits to local plant facilities, give speeches to employees, attend awards ceremonies, and participate in activities that will improve that official's understanding of management and employee concerns. These activities help to "humanize" the distant relationship that can otherwise develop between government officials and the public. Democracy requires citizen access and communication with political leaders. In the United States, with 260 million individuals and millions of businesses, the challenge of maintaining open, balanced communications between officials and the public is becoming complicated and expensive.

Role of the media

The 1990s have produced an explosion of media outlets, including television and radio talk shows, public affairs programming, and noninterpretive outlets such as C-Span, which carries live coverage of congressional debates. In many states and local communities, cable television stations provide live coverage of hearings, debates, and votes. Critics claim that the enormous growth of these media forms has led to excessive attention to the personalities and styles of government officials, devaluing the content of their ideas and the substance of their actions. The range of approaches that help shape public opinion is illustrated by three media "stars" of the 1990s.

Ted Koppell is the founding host of the popular ABC network late night program, *Nightline*. Since the late 1970s, this program has focused on the major news stories of each day, often bringing together opponents on major political issues. Koppell's interviewing is direct and challenging, featuring a form of "traditional" journalism.

Larry King has become a media star by broadcasting his talk show from Washington, D.C., five nights a week on Cable News Network (CNN). An aggressive style has won him a loyal following of viewers who expect tough questions and clever talk from the program's host. King's own positions are not disguised, and he has become a "voice" that sometimes advocates as well as reports.

King's advocacy pales by comparison to that of Rush Limbaugh, whose radio and television personality leave no doubt about his biases, prejudices, and points of view. Articulate and persuasive, Limbaugh has become one of the most powerful media voices in the new politics of the 1990s. While the Clinton administration's national health care proposals were being debated, for example, Limbaugh staged a vigorous assault against President and Mrs. Clinton in personal and policy terms. Supporters credit Limbaugh as an influential force that helped Republicans win control of the House of Representatives and Senate in the 1994 elections.

People's tastes vary, and different segments of the television viewing audience—that is, the *public*— favor each of these stars and their programs. These stars have a powerful effect on how Americans understand the public policy issues facing government and make decisions about whom to believe and whom to trust. Defenders of the media claim this is precisely what democracy was envisioned to be, a contest among a multitude of views and opinions. To these analysts, the solution is to present even *more* views in more ways. They consider 500-channel cable television stations, interactive media, and a public that is more involved in "talk show democracy" as positive developments. In California, a "Democracy Network" was created as a multimedia, on-line service for voters who wanted to compare the views, finances, and positions of the candidates for governorship.[22]

Critics point to excesses and poor taste as reasons to place restraints or limitations on the way media treat political issues. Many nations limit the media's freedom to report on political issues and the political process. But the U.S. Constitution protects citizens' freedom of speech and freedom of the press. Courts, including the Supreme Court, have interpreted these constitutional rights in ways that minimize what can be done to control the content of media programs, although it seems certain that the Constitution's drafters never foresaw television, Internet, or the information superhighway. Excesses are unlikely to stop unless the public changes its listening and viewing habits.

Transparency of the political process

The openness, or transparency, of America's political system creates opportunities for people to closely observe what decisions are being made, and in what way. "Washington is a giant fishbowl," according to one veteran lobbyist, and the result is too much accountability, not too little. As another lobbyist said, "These representatives can't blow their noses without having to answer to someone."[23] Some scholars argue that government officials are "agents" acting on behalf of people who elected or appointed them (the "principals"). This view, called **corporate political agency theory,** holds that conditions that enable citizens to observe how elected officials behave will promote action that serves those that put them in office.[24]

Another view is that while elected officials are sent to office to represent their constituents, they are also sent to act in the broad public interest. Sometimes elected officials have to look beyond the interests of voters in their districts and take action—such as approval of new taxes—that will be unpopular but are in the broad public interest. The problem in the current political climate, according to this view, is that officials are unwilling

---

[22]Frederick Rose, "Democracy Goes On-Line in California," *Wall Street Journal,* Oct. 26, 1994, p. B1.
[23]Author's interviews during the national health care debate, Washington, July 1994.
[24]See Mitnick, op. cit.

to do so when this occurs in the glaring spotlight of attention to each vote, issue, and constituency. "Vote against your constituents," said a twenty-year member of the House of Representatives, "and pay the price of never being able to vote against them again!"[25]

One remedy is to have more "closed door" sessions in which votes can be taken without being recorded or reported.[26] However, such a view runs counter to the mood of public distrust: legislators might do in private what they dare not do in public. It is doubtful that this approach will solve problems of transparency without adding to public cynicism. When Republicans took power in Congress after the 1994 elections, the new leaders of the Senate and House of Representatives promised to "open the process." They soon discovered the need to work behind closed doors to get things done!

Incumbents and appointed officials

Public anger with the political process is often fueled by the people involved. Incumbent politicians and officials who seem to be appointed for life sometimes act in crude, arrogant, and self-serving ways designed to perpetuate power.[27] This may include doing favors for constituents, directing public works money to local communities, and acting on behalf of local companies caught in regulatory snarls and problems. The greater the seniority of elected officials, the more likely they are to exercise real power in government affairs. This makes them targets of political influence, which, in turn, helps them as fund-raisers and facilitates their reelection and continuation in positions of power.

To minimize abuses of power, experts have offered a number of proposals. One of the most popular ideas is **term limits,** a device that would permit elected officials to serve for a maximum number of years. This would weaken the power of long-serving members of Congress, for example, some of whom have served for more than thirty-five years. It would open committee assignments, create opportunities for new members, and still provide a broad base of experience in the legislature. Term limit opponents argue that limits would deprive voters and communities of free electoral choice and the benefits of experience, including the knowledge, contacts, and credibility that are won with experience.

Although there are signs that voters are dissatisfied with elected officials in general, there are contradictions in public attitudes. Voters often reelect officials for many terms, despite campaigns that focus on the virtues of change. Business faces such dilemmas too. Many business leaders favor term limits in principle, but then seek the favor of elected officials and provide assistance and support to reelection campaigns. Why?

---

[25]Author's interview, see note 23.
[26]"More Power to Speaker," *Roll Call,* Oct. 24, 1994, p. 4.
[27]Jeffrey H. Birnbaum, *The Lobbyists: How Influence Peddlers Get Their Way in Washington,* New York: Random House/Times Books, 1992.

The concept of limited terms may seem attractive, but businesses, like other special interests, recognize that incumbents can be very helpful in meeting their needs and solving their problems. This is one reason that PAC spending so often favors incumbents, rather than challengers.

Referendum politics

The complexity of government decision making processes can frustrate efforts to transform a popular idea into law. Government committees, procedures, and compromises often stop, delay, or deflect proposals that seem to have broad public support. To counter these bureaucratic obstacles, advocates of change sometimes use a **public referendum,** or popular vote, to force a public ballot on the question of how government should act on a particular issue.

Many states have adopted laws permitting *citizens' initiatives* to be placed on the ballot of a general election. The initiative process usually requires that a number of citizens (usually 1 to 5 percent of registered voters) sign a petition asking that the initiative resolution or question be placed on the ballot. If the resolution is adopted by a majority of voters, the legislature is obligated to turn the resolution into law.

California is among the states that have broad experience with citizens' initiatives. One scholar who studied all of the initiatives placed on California's ballot from 1976 to 1988 concluded that it is one of the most important policy arenas in that state.[28] In 1988 alone, for example, Californians faced eighteen ballot questions in their general election! Californians have sought to use the initiative process to establish tax limits on property taxes (Proposition 3) in the early 1980s, environmental protections and warning (the "Big Green" Proposition), and tough restrictions on education and welfare benefits to the state's large population of illegal immigrants (Proposition 187 in 1994). Each had broad support and reflected public concerns affecting politics in California and other states.

Research shows that the initiatives often propose actions that business interests oppose. A 1992 California ballot initiative sought to change the pricing of automobile insurance rates. Industry claimed it would be badly hurt by such a law and vigorously opposed the proposition. In Massachusetts, a 1994 ballot proposition launched by a tax reform coalition sought to change the state's 5.95 percent "flat tax" on earned income into a "graduated tax" that would set higher rates for higher levels of income. The governor, a former U.S. senator, and business leaders opposed it, saying it was "poisonous" to impose such taxes on small businesses that are the source of new jobs.[29]

---

[28]See Tom Thomas, "Campaign Spending and Corporate Involvement in the California Initiative Process, 1976–1988," in J. E. Post, ed., *Research in Corporate Social Performance and Policy*, Vol. 12, Greenwich, CT: JAI Press, 1991, pp. 37–61.

[29]Chris Reidy, "Grad Tax Foes Muster 'All-Star' Support," *Boston Globe*, Oct. 25, 1994, pp. 39, 41.

Politics is the "art of the possible." It involves working together, compromising in order that everyone's interests are taken into account, and recognizing that no interest can win—or should win—all the time. Referendum politics appeals to people frustrated at losing in the political process; it is a way of fighting the "system."

Citizens' initiatives are expensive to launch and sustain, however. Tom Thomas, who studied California's initiative history, concluded that campaign spending affected voting results in the California initiative process, especially in cases where nonbusiness groups sought to impose new regulations or costs on business. By heavily outspending proponents of the initiative, business was often successful in defeating ballot initiatives.[30]

RESPONSIBLE BUSINESS POLITICS IN A GLOBAL WORLD

Political action by business—whether to influence government policy or the outcome of elections—is natural in a democratic, pluralistic society. In the United States, business has a legitimate right to participate in the politi-

[30]Thomas, op. cit., p. 59.

EXHIBIT 9-C

TEN THOUSAND LOBBYISTS IN BRUSSELS

Lobbying is not just an American practice. Companies all around the world are learning new ways to "connect" with government officials. In short, whenever a government body controls a resource that business needs—permits, licenses, subsidies—or sets rules that affect what business can do, lobbying is bound to follow.

The European Union (EU) is composed of 15 nations that are integrated in economic and political ways. The European Commission is the legislative and administrative body for the EU and has its headquarters in Brussels. According to a 1994 study, there are more than 3,000 groups in Brussels employing more than 10,000 lobbyists to communicate with the commission's officers and staff.

The lobbyists speak for many interests. Nearly all big European corporations, trade groups, and labor unions have lobbyists; so too do Japanese trade associations and companies. American companies are represented by the U.S. Chamber of Commerce and some companies also have their own lobbyists in Brussels. Because the European Commission is setting rules for the way competition will be conducted in Europe's big marketplace, the stakes are very high.

Lobbyists operate differently in Brussels than in the United States. They can, for example, provide technical help to commission bureaucrats and collaborate more openly with insiders. Learning to "Euro-lobby" effectively takes time, money, and people. By 1999, the number of lobbyists in Brussels is expected to grow to as many as 20,000!

SOURCE: Based on Ronald Facchinetti, "Viewpoint: Why Brussels Has 10,000 Lobbyists," *New York Times*, Aug. 21, 1994, sec. 3, p. 9.

cal process, just as consumers, labor unions, environmentalists, and others do. The rules differ in other nations where restrictions may affect business political activities. Exhibit 9-C shows that lobbying is extensive in the European Union.

This is not true in Japan, however.

> American companies have not had a high political profile in Japan. Japanese companies long ago learned how to organize special interests, employ lobbyists, and leverage high-level contacts into coherent—and successful—political strategies in Washington. U.S. companies did not even have a significant trade association working on their behalf until late 1994 when the U.S. Chamber of Commerce organized meetings with Japanese party leaders and cabinet ministers, including Japan's prime minister. "This is an attempt to go directly to people at the political level who make policy," said a chamber official. American companies will not be making campaign contributions, however; the Foreign Corrupt Practices Act forbids U.S. companies from making donations to foreign politicians.[31]

One danger arising from corporate political activity is that corporations may wield too much power. As business operates in different local communities, and in different global communities, it is important that ethical norms and standards guide managers as they deal with political factors. If corporate power "tips the scales" against other interests in a society, both business and society may lose. A careful use of business influence is therefore an ideal to be sought. This is also true of union power, religious power, consumer power, or any concentrated power that may exist in a democratic society.

Political reform spawns many proposals. Some involve absolute limitations on lobbying, political spending, and fund-raising by business. Others involve a system of public financing (total or matching funds) that would serve to level the campaign playing field. A number of political leaders have offered proposals to require television networks and stations to provide free time for candidates' advertising. As shown in Figure 9-8, other democratic nations utilize a combination of such ideas to reduce the impact of money on electoral politics. In Japan, for example, the U.S. Chamber of Commerce initiative is not expected to have immediate results because, as one analyst commented, "This isn't an American-lobbyist straightforward type of relationship. It isn't so easy to get fruits out of this kind of meeting." Whether in electoral politics or more traditional lobbying, business leaders must address the issues of how to manage relationships with government and special interests in society in ethically sound

---

[31]Michael Williams, "U.S. Business Lobby in Japan Launches First Campaign Aimed at Policy Makers," *Wall Street Journal,* Oct. 19, 1994, p. A17.

FIGURE 9-8
What other countries do to control money in politics.
SOURCE: Michael Oreskes, "The Trouble with Politics: Running versus Governing," *New York Times,* Mar. 21, 1990, pp. A1, A22.

	Public Financing	Limits on Fund-Raising or Spending	Television
U.K.	No	Yes	Free time based on party's strength in previous election
France	Reimburse candidates based on votes received	Yes	Free and equal time to candidates
Japan	No	Yes	Candidates given some free time for speeches; no negative advertising
Germany	Reimbursement to parties according to votes received	No	Free time to candidates on public stations

ways. Ultimately, business has an important long-term stake in a healthy, honest political system.

SUMMARY POINTS OF THIS CHAPTER

- Stakeholder expectations can, if unmet, trigger action to transform social concern into pressure on business and government. The existence of a gap between what is expected and actual performance stimulates the formation of a public issue.
- Corporations engage in issues management by systematically identifying, analyzing, and acting on emerging issues in the social and political environment. Effective issues management leads companies to monitor emerging issues, take action on current issues, and implement policy on issues that have passed through the process.
- Strategic management of government relations involves understanding how a business's long-term economic and social interests are entwined with government policy and then acting to support that relationship.
- Corporate political activity is focused on governmental policies and decision making and on electoral politics. Political action committees, lobbying, and grassroots programs are among the most popular types of corporate political activities.
- Business plays a role in electoral politics by providing campaign funds and other forms of support to candidates. It takes positions on

campaign issues, lending its support to ideas that support business interests and opposing ideas it believes are harmful.

■ Business needs to be involved in public policy decision making for several reasons: it has a large stake in government actions and it is a voice that should be heard on many economic and social policy issues.

■ Business has a stake in the critical issues facing the American political system in the 1990s. Campaign financing, the power of special interests, the media's role, incumbency, and referendum politics are among the issues prompting calls for political reform. The way managers conduct their companies' governmental relations will be influenced by changes in these areas.

KEY TERMS AND CONCEPTS USED IN THIS CHAPTER

■ Public issue
■ Public issues life cycle
■ Issues management process
■ Political cynicism
■ Perpetual political campaign
■ Political action committees (PACs)

■ Lobbying
■ Grassroots programs
■ Corporate political agency theory
■ Term limits
■ Public referendum

DISCUSSION CASE

HARRY AND LOUISE: A $15 MILLION COUPLE

In the legislative and political battle over national health care that occurred in 1993 and 1994, a most unusual couple came to prominence. Their names were Harry and Louise, and they became the unexpected stars of a media campaign by the health insurance industry to cast doubt on various national health care proposals. Sitting at their kitchen table, talking about various health care proposals, they became synonymous with "reasonable people who had reasonable doubts" about health care reform. Their story says a lot about corporate political action in the 1990s.

As the health care debate was heating up in 1993, officials at the Health Insurance Association of America (HIAA), one of the insurance industry's largest trade associations, were deeply concerned about what was shaping up as the industry's biggest public policy battle in more than thirty years. They knew, for example, that two issues—the cost of health care and the number of Americans who were without health care insurance—would produce heavy criticism of their industry. The number, and variety, of administrative forms used by the association's more than 300 members was an area that many experts felt could yield big cost savings by creating standardized administrative systems. In addition, the industry was the target of critics who accused it of refusing to insure people with significant health risks or pricing others out of the market, thereby making the need for universal coverage even more serious.

At a meeting of industry executives to plot strategy for the forthcoming legislative battle, Bill Gradison, president of HIAA, commented that he thought the health care debate would be decided by couples sitting around their kitchen tables, trying to figure out how the various proposals would affect their families. Also present at the strategy meeting was Ben Goddard, head of an advertising agency that was under contract to work with HIAA. Gradison's comment "clicked" with Ben Goddard as a theme for the industry's advertising.

Once it was decided that a media campaign should be created, the Goddard agency began developing program themes: celebrities were tried as spokespersons, different messages were tried with focus groups, and assessments were made about the relative power and value of print and electronic media forms. A media strategy was taking shape, and when "the couple at the kitchen table" was tried with focus groups, it scored high marks. The Goddard agency began turning the idea into a delivery mechanism for the health care industry's messages.

HIAA raised $15 million from its members to support the media campaign. This was only a small part of the total spending by health insurance companies, but it proved to be a very important element. The advertising experts had determined that there was a segment of the Clinton plan coalition that was a potential target for the health insurance industry's basic message that the entire system ought not to be destroyed because some elements were not working as well as they could. The audience with whom such messages might resonate was, surprisingly to some, women over the age of thirty. Research had shown that this audience had "both the desire to fix the system and the intelligence to understand that it had to be fixed right or we could end up with unintended consequences that made things worse." These became known as "Women like Louise."

Harry and Louise became part of the health care "soap opera." They talked about key issues as the legislative battle waged: employer mandates, universal coverage, costs of care, and so on. The advertising was delivered in a way that kept audiences coming back for the next round of Harry and Louise on health care. For HIAA, the media campaign was a dual success: polls showed that women over thirty did indeed begin to have more doubts about sweeping reform proposals as the months passed, and, in addition, Harry and Louise became "credible" voices for an industry that had been branded as one of the "bad guys" in the early going.[32]

[32]See Robin Toner, "Harry and Louise and a Guy Named Ben," *New York Times,* Sept. 30, 1994, p. A22.

Discussion Questions

1. The health insurance industry used a variety of tactics in the national health care debate. Compare the advantages of the Harry and Louise media strategy to lobbying or grassroots tactics. What are the pluses and minuses of each tactic from the industry's view?

2. Discuss how the health insurance industry could integrate its lobbying and other political actions with the Harry and Louise campaign.

3. What kind of issues management activities discussed in this chapter could the health insurance industry have done at an earlier time to shape the debate or prevent health care reform from getting to Congress? Use Figures 9-1 and 9-2 to answer this question.

4. Was the Harry and Louise campaign an ethical form of political action by health care insurance companies? What arguments can be made that it was not a responsible business action? What arguments can be made that it was ethical? Refer to ethics concepts in Chapters 4 and 5 in your answer.

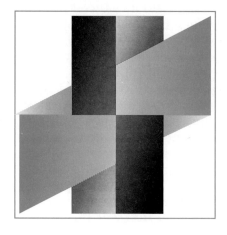

10

Antitrust, Mergers, and Global Competition

All socioeconomic systems face the problem of deciding how much power should be held by leading enterprises, whether they are privately owned or controlled by the state. In the United States, antitrust laws have long been used to curb corporate power, to preserve competition, and to achieve various social goals. As the economy has changed, however, new factors have raised policy issues concerning business competitiveness. These trends have presented public policy makers and corporate leaders with a need to reconcile corporate power, shareholders' interests, and social responsibility with new realities.

Key Questions and Chapter Objectives

This chapter focuses on these key questions and objectives:

- What dilemma does corporate power present in a democratic society?
- What are the objectives of the antitrust laws, and how are they enforced?
- What have been recent key issues in antitrust policy?
- How have the mergers of the 1980s and 1990s affected business-society relations?
- How has the rise of global competition affected antitrust policy?
- Why are intellectual property issues so important to competition policy?

When AT&T, the United States' largest long-distance phone company, announced its intention to acquire McCaw Cellular Communications for over \$12 billion, the merger promised a new era of communications in which voice and electronic messages could be transmitted "anytime, anywhere." But the proposed deal soon faced a number of antitrust hurdles. After a review lasting nearly a year, the U.S. Justice Department in 1994 approved the merger, provided that McCaw continue to give AT&T's competitors in the long-distance business equal access to its network. But a federal judge balked, saying that the deal violated the 1984 antitrust agreement that broke up AT&T and the regional "Baby Bell" companies. Because the McCaw network was partly owned by some of the regional Bells, the judge feared that the merger might suppress competition.

In October 1993, a judge in Arkansas ruled that Wal-Mart, the largest chain of discount stores in the United States, had illegally sold merchandise below cost in order to drive its competitors out of business. Wal-Mart had been sued by three small drugstores, who argued that the discounter's "predatory pricing" had hurt their sales of everyday products like toothpaste, mouthwash, and nonprescription medicines. Predatory pricing is illegal in the United States under both federal and state antitrust laws. Wal-Mart's spokesperson called the decision "anticonsumer," saying that it would result in higher prices. Others believed, however, that the decision would help the consumer in the long run by preventing Wal-Mart from gaining a monopoly in local markets.

When Guardian Industries, a glassmaker based in Michigan, tried to sell its products in Japan, the company "ran into a wall of exclusionary business practices," one of their executives claimed. Guardian Industries went to the Justice Department, complaining that a group of leading Japanese glass companies had shut them out by threatening retaliation against allied firms that did business with the Americans—a charge the Japanese vigorously denied. U.S. regulators were uncertain how to proceed in this and other similar cases. Should the government bring suit against foreign companies that violate U.S. antitrust laws in ways that hurt American exporters? Or would these issues be better addressed through trade negotiations?[1]

These examples of competitive conflicts—involving private businesses, the government, and the courts, in both the United States and abroad—illustrate how anticompetitive practices can arise in the free market system. This chapter looks at how the United States has traditionally sought to preserve and enhance competition through antitrust and related policies. The 1990s present new challenges to traditional approaches according to some observers. As U.S. business competes in global markets, as services outgrow manufacturing, and as research and development become more vital to industry, antitrust and other competition policies are being reexamined.

[1]"AT&T Blocked from McCaw Deal," *New York Times,* Apr. 6, 1994, pp. A1, C5; "AT&T's Bid for McCaw Wins Key Approval," *Los Angeles Times,* July 16, 1994, pp. D1, D8; "AT&T's Bold Bet," *Business Week,* Aug. 30, 1993, pp. 26–30; "Wal-Mart's Pricing on Drugstore Items Is Held to Be Illegal," *New York Times,* Oct. 13, 1993, pp. A1, C5; "Wal-Mart Loses a Case on Pricing," *Wall Street Journal,* Oct. 13, 1993, pp. A3, A8; and "Commerce Cops: Can Justice Open Up Foreign Markets?" *Business Week,* Dec. 13, 1993, pp. 69–70.

CORPORATE POWER AND LEGITIMACY

By almost any measure used, the world's largest business enterprises are impressively big, as shown in Figures 10-1 and 10-2. Size can be measured in several ways—by annual sales, assets, profits, and shareholders' equity—and a company's rank will vary depending on the measurement used. Ranked by sales, the "big five" in 1993 in the United States were General Motors, Ford, Exxon, AT&T, and IBM. Among the biggest non-U.S. companies listed in Figure 10-2, an oil company, a telecommunications firm, an automobile manufacturer, and a number of banks dominate the top levels. Nine of the ten are Japanese.

The ten U.S. corporations shown in Figure 10-1 generate more sales an-

FIGURE 10-1

The ten largest U.S. industrial and service corporations, 1992–1993.

SOURCE: *Fortune*, Apr. 18, 1994, pp. 209–313; *Fortune*, Aug. 22, 1994, pp.180–208. Fortune and Service 500, copyright 1994, Time, Inc. All rights reserved.

Rank	By Sales (billions)	By Assets (billions)	By Profits (billions)	By Shareholders' Equity (billions)
1.	General Motors $133.6	General Electric $251.5	Exxon $5.3	Exxon $34.8
2.	Ford Motor 108.5	Ford Motor 198.9	General Electric 4.3	General Electric 25.8
3.	Exxon 97.8	General Motors 188.2	LTV 4.3	IBM 19.7
4.	AT&T 67.2	Exxon 84.1	Philip Morris 3.1	Mobil 16.5
5.	IBM 62.7	IBM 81.1	Ford Motor 2.5	Ford Motor 15.6
6.	General Electric 60.8	AT&T 60.8	General Motors 2.5	Shell Oil 14.6
7.	Mobil 56.6	Philip Morris 51.2	Intel 2.3	Chevron 14.0
8.	Philip Morris 50.6	Chrysler 43.8	Coca-Cola 2.2	AT&T 13.9
9.	Chrysler 43.6	Mobil 40.6	Merck 2.2	Amoco 13.7
10.	Texaco 34.4	Xerox 38.8	Mobil 2.1	Philip Morris 11.6

Company	Home Nation(s)	Market Value (billions)
1. Nippon Telegraph and Telephone	Japan	$128.9
2. Royal Dutch/Shell Group	Neth./ Britain	91.9
3. Mitsubishi Bank	Japan	77.1
4. Toyota Motor	Japan	75.1
5. Industrial Bank of Japan	Japan	73.3
6. Sumitomo Bank	Japan	67.5
7. Fuji Bank	Japan	67.0
8. Sanwa Bank	Japan	63.2
9. Dai-Ichi Kangyo Bank	Japan	59.6
10. Sakura Bank	Japan	47.3

nually than the entire national output of Australia, Brazil, Canada, China, India, Italy, Mexico, or Nigeria. The employees of these same ten companies, if living together in one location, would make up the seventh or eighth largest metropolitan area in the United States—about the size of greater Boston or greater Washington, D.C.

These giant enterprises are not completely representative of business in the United States or other nations. The overwhelming number of business firms are owned by individual proprietors or by small groups of partners. Only one of every five business firms in the United States is a corporation, and many of these corporations are small. The largest firms at the top of the business pyramid are the focus of so much attention because of their size, power, and influence, not because they represent the entire business community.[2]

Corporate Economic Power

Sheer size alone does not account for the economic significance of large corporations. **Corporate power** arises from the critical tasks society expects these organizations to perform. These functions as performed in the United States were described by one expert in the following way.

[2]Bureau of the Census, *Statistical Abstract of the United States, 1990,* table 859.

Large American business corporations, although "private" enterprises, perform the great majority of essential economic tasks, which, due to their very essentiality, are in many countries undertaken by the state, either directly or through closely affiliated "public" entities. In this country, business corporations produce and distribute all forms of energy, process all ferrous and non-ferrous metals and derivative products, provide air, sea, motor, and for the most part, intra-urban and inter-city rail transportation, maintain radio, television, telephone, and intercontinental satellite broadcasting services, and, finally, service virtually all of the essential financial needs of the nation.[3]

By entrusting large private corporations with these central economic functions, society has granted business much economic influence. By amassing physical assets, employing and training thousands of persons, attracting huge pools of capital, engaging in research and development on a large scale, and reaching throughout the world for resources and markets, the largest corporations are the central economic institutions of industrial nations.

Corporate Political Power

The political influence of business, discussed in Chapter 9, tends to increase with the size of the business firm. One experienced observer of the corporate world confirms this relationship.

Large corporations . . . have . . . moved a long way toward rivaling or surpassing the power of government on issues that are of special importance to them. . . . [In a sense,] the large corporation becomes a piece of government. This is the real character of the large companies that constitute a major part of the economic base of this country [the United States], a nation that still contains the greatest concentration of economic power in the world. In the real economy, where companies are unrecognized parts of the government, we must consider how such companies are governed and how they relate to the political structure within which they move and exercise their enormous capacity.[4]

Corporate Social Power

A corporation's social influence is felt in two kinds of ways: one is external and the other is internal.

Externally, a company's actions can influence how clean the community's air is, how adequate the local tax base is for civic improvement,

[3]Edwin M. Epstein, "Societal, Managerial, and Legal Perspectives on Corporate Social Responsibility: Product and Process," in S. Prakash Sethi and Carl L. Swanson, *Private Enterprise and Public Purpose,* New York: Wiley, 1981, p. 84. Originally published in *The Hastings Law Journal,* May 1979.

[4]Alfred C. Neal, *Business Power and Public Policy,* New York: Praeger, 1981, p. 126.

whether voluntary nonprofit community agencies will be well funded, and the general tone of community relations, including local pride in community accomplishments.

A corporation's internal social influence is felt by employees who spend most of their waking hours in the service of their employer. The result, in the words of one expert, is that

> [t]he large corporation generally—and the megacorporation in particular—has become a social institution which embraces the thousands of human beings whose lives are affected by it and which provides an important focus for the employees' social relationships. In the more complex society, with greater mobility, the loosening of community ties, and urban anonymity, the neighborhood social unit has lost its cohesion and the corporation has assumed some of its role.[5]

The Dilemma of Corporate Power

Neither size nor power alone is bad, when it comes to corporate performance. A big company may have definite advantages over a small one. It can command more resources, often produce at a lower cost, plan further into the future, and weather business fluctuations somewhat better. Big companies make tougher competitors against foreign firms. Many communities have benefited from the social initiatives and influence of large firms.[6]

Most questions of corporate power concern how business uses its influence, not whether it should have power in the first place. Most people want to know if business power is being used to affirm the broad public-purpose goals, values, and principles considered to be important to the nation as a whole. If so, then corporate power is considered to be legitimate, and the public accepts large size as just another normal characteristic of modern business. As we have stated earlier, organizations are legitimate to the extent that their activities fit and reflect the goals and values of the society in which they function. The loss of public confidence is destructive to any organization, and legitimacy is perhaps the major element in the long-term survival of all social institutions.[7] Therefore, the crucial questions about corporate power are:

- *Will corporate economic power be used to promote the interests of the general public, including small business competitors and local commu-*

---

[5]Phillip I. Blumberg, *The Megacorporation in American Society,* Englewood Cliffs, NJ: Prentice-Hall, 1975, pp. 2–3.
[6]For several examples, see *1993 Social Report of the Life and Health Insurance Business: The Record of Corporate Public Involvement,* Washington, DC: Center for Corporate Public Involvement, 1993.
[7]See Edwin M. Epstein and Dow Votaw, eds., *Rationality, Legitimacy, Responsibility: Search for New Directions in Business and Society,* Santa Monica, CA: Goodyear, 1978, p. 72.

nities? For example, large-scale computer systems may increase the productivity of big banks, but this development might jeopardize smaller banks. Or, a cost-saving relocation of a plant from a New England town to Southeast Asia may bring severe economic distress to the community that is left behind.

■ *Will corporate political power be used wisely to preserve the pluralistic balance of power among a society's interest groups?* Where large corporations have rivaled or surpassed the power of some governments, concern is justified that corporate influence may be abused.[8]

■ *Will corporate social power respect the integrity and dignity of individuals, as well as the traditions and needs of the corporation's host communities?* For example, corporate drug-testing programs and sudden plant shutdowns, while considered important for business purposes, may be seen as unacceptable and socially undesirable by those affected.

These three basic questions assume special meaning in Western societies with democratic traditions, representative political institutions, and a strong respect for the individual. In such nations, concentrated power of any kind—whether corporate, governmental, religious, scientific, or military—seems out of place. Reconciling corporate power with an open, free way of life is the crux of the problem. If large corporations can be made to fit into the webbing of an open, pluralistic society, their legitimacy—that is, their public acceptance—will be assured.

U.S. antitrust laws, highly controversial and far from perfect, stand as a monument to society's efforts to cope with the various dilemmas of corporate power. For more than a century, since the first federal antitrust law was enacted, U.S. public policy has sought to balance economic power with social control. As antitrust policy enters its second century, the new realities of global competition and global economic power are forcing a reexamination of how power and social control are best balanced. We examine these issues after outlining antitrust goals and major federal laws.

ANTITRUST REGULATION

Someone once remarked that antitrust is as American as apple pie. Certainly it is an article of faith deeply embedded in the minds of many people. U.S. **antitrust laws** originated in the late nineteenth century in the wake of some spectacular competitive abuses by big business leaders and their companies. An aroused public feared the uncontrolled growth of big business. The first antitrust laws were passed in this climate of fear and

[8]Neal, op. cit., p. 136.

mistrust of big business. Since those early years, other antitrust laws have been enacted, and the first laws have been amended. The result is a formidable tangle of laws, regulations, guidelines, and judicial interpretations that present business with a need to carefully manage relationships with competitors and government antitrust officials.

Objectives of Antitrust

Antitrust laws serve multiple goals. Some of these goals—such as preserving competition or protecting consumers against deceptive advertising—are primarily economic in character. As one authoritative source states: "The U.S. antitrust laws are the legal embodiment of our nation's commitment to a free market economy."[9] Other goals, though, are more concerned with social and philosophical matters, such as a desire to curb the power of large corporations or even a nostalgic wish to return to the old Jeffersonian ideal of a nation of small-scale farmers and businesses. The result is multiple, overlapping, changing, and sometimes contradictory goals.

The most important economic objectives of antitrust laws are the following.

First, *the protection and preservation of competition* is the central objective. This is done by outlawing monopolies, prohibiting unfair competition, and eliminating price discrimination and collusion. The reasoning is that customers will be best and most economically served if business firms compete vigorously for the consumer's dollar. Prices should fluctuate according to supply and demand, with no collusion between competitors, whether behind the scenes or out in the open. An important 1994 case illustrates this feature of antitrust regulation.

Six of the largest airlines in the United States were charged by the Justice Department with violating antitrust laws for colluding to set ticket prices between 1988 and 1992. The government said that the airlines used a sophisticated computerized fare information system, called ATP, to carry on a "detailed electronic dialogue" that allowed them to "signal" each other about changes in ticket prices. For example, an airline would post a proposed fare on a particular route, and then receive counterproposals from other airlines electronically until a consensus was reached. A Justice Department official said, "Although [the airlines'] method was novel, the conduct amounted to price fixing, plain and simple." The six companies—American, Delta, Northwest, Continental, TWA, and Alaska Airlines—agreed in 1994 to

[9]Bureau of National Affairs (BNA), *Antitrust and Trade Regulation Report,* Vol. 55, Washington, DC: Bureau of National Affairs, 1988, p. 5-4.

stop using the ATP system to exchange information about scheduled fare changes.[10]

A second objective of antitrust policy is *to protect the consumer's welfare by prohibiting deceptive and unfair business practices.* The original antitrust laws were aimed primarily at preserving competition, assuming that consumers would be safeguarded as long as competition was strong. Later, though, it was realized that some business methods could be used to exploit or mislead consumers, regardless of the amount of competition. Consider the following hypothetical situations.

A company supplying plastic parts for electrical appliances bribed the purchasing agent for the appliance maker to buy the company's parts, even though they were priced higher than those made by a competitor. As a result, the consumer paid more for the appliances. This type of commercial bribery would be forbidden by the antitrust laws because it takes unfair advantage of innocent consumers.

A distributor of compact discs sent purchasing club members more CDs than they had ordered and then demanded payment, substituted one CD for another in some orders, and delayed prepaid orders of some customers for several months. Such practices would be considered to be unfair by antitrust authorities.

A third objective of antitrust regulation is *to protect small, independent business firms from the economic pressures exerted by big business competition.* As shown in the Wal-Mart example at the beginning of this chapter, antitrust laws prohibit predatory pricing—the practice of selling below cost in order to drive rivals out of business. The objective of these laws is to protect small companies from unfair competition. In other cases, small businesses may be undersold by larger ones because manufacturers are willing to give price discounts to large volume buyers. For example, a tire maker wanted to sell automobile and truck tires to a large retail chain at a lower price than it offered to a small gasoline station. The antitrust laws prohibit such discounts given exclusively to large buyers unless it can be proved that there is a genuine economic saving in dealing with the larger firm.

In promoting the interests of small business over large business in these ways, antitrust regulations disregard both competition—because big businesses are not permitted to compete freely—and consumer welfare—because big firms could sell at a lower price than small firms. This inconsistency occurs because these laws serve the multiple and sometimes contradictory goals of many different groups.

A fourth objective of antitrust policy is *to preserve the values and cus-*

---

[10]"Six Airlines Settle Price Fixing Charges," *Corporate Crime Reporter,* Mar. 21, 1994, p. 7.

toms of small-town America. A strong populist philosophy has been part of the antitrust movement from its beginning. Populists favored small-town life, neighborly relations among people, a democratic political system, family-operated farms, and small business firms. They believed that concentrated wealth posed a threat to democracy, that big business would drive small local companies out of business, and that hometown merchants and neighboring farmers might be replaced by large impersonal corporations headquartered in distant cities. Antitrust restrictions on big business, populists believed, might further these social and political goals. One hundred years later, however, these populist goals often conflict with business views of what is required in a world of global competition.[11]

The Major Antitrust Laws

Today's antitrust laws are the outcome of many years of attempting to make American business fit the model of free market competition. Many people have pointed out how unrealistic it is to expect a modern, high-technology, diversified, worldwide corporation to conform to conditions that may have been considered ideal a century ago when both business and society were simpler. The challenge of applying existing antitrust legislation to the technological, financial, political, and social environment of the late twentieth century begins with an understanding of the major antitrust laws.

Rather than trying to present all of the many detailed provisions of these laws and the history of each one, we concentrate here on four main federal antitrust statutes and give a brief summary of each. Figure 10-3 identifies the purposes of these four laws and the major components of the enforcement process. States also have antitrust laws with similar goals and purposes.

The Sherman Act

Although several states enacted antitrust laws before the federal government did, the Sherman Act of 1890 is considered to be the foundation of antitrust regulation in the United States. This law:

- Prohibits contracts, combinations, or conspiracies that restrain trade and commerce (e.g., collusion among a group of producers to set, or "fix," prices)
- Prohibits monopolies and all attempts to monopolize trade and commerce
- Provides for enforcement by the Justice Department, and authorizes penalties, including fines and jail terms, for violations

---

[11]A lucid historical account may be found in Louis Galambos and Joseph Pratt, *The Rise of the Corporate Commonwealth: Business and Public Policy in the Twentieth Century,* New York: Basic Books, 1988.

FIGURE 10-3
Antitrust laws and
enforcement at the
federal level.

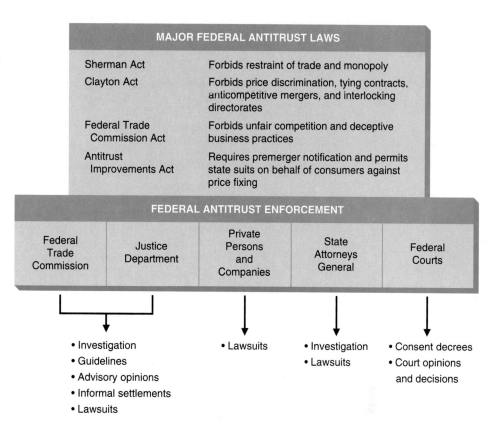

A recent case that involved possible collusion among a group of colleges to fix the cost of higher education is profiled in Exhibit 10-A.

The Clayton Act

Originally passed in 1914 to clarify some of the ambiguities and uncertainties of the Sherman Act, the Clayton Act, as amended, now:

- Prohibits price discrimination by sellers (as illustrated by the tire maker who was forbidden to sell lower-priced tires to a chain store while selling at a higher price to a smaller independent store)
- Forbids tying contracts that require someone to buy a related and perhaps unwanted product in order to get another one produced by the same company (e.g., it would be illegal for a computer company to force hardware purchasers to accept an unwanted maintenance contract as a condition of sale)
- Prohibits companies from merging through purchase of shares or assets if competition is lessened or a monopoly is created (as illustrated by the Justice Department's review of the proposed merger between AT&T and McCaw Cellular)

EXHIBIT 10-A

DID THE IVY LEAGUE COLLEGES AND MIT VIOLATE ANTITRUST LAW?

When antitrust regulators address the issue of price-fixing, they usually deal with the prices of tangible products or services—like computers, medicine, or airplane tickets. But an important 1993 case looked at price-fixing in an unusual area: higher education.

Between the late 1950s and the early 1990s, representatives of nine universities on the East Coast—comprised of the eight Ivy League colleges and the Massachusetts Institute of Technology (MIT)—met every spring for a series of negotiations. Officers from each school, known as the overlap group, came with a list of students accepted for admission, along with a proposal for the amount of financial aid each student would be offered. Where an individual student had been accepted at more than one institution, the officers would negotiate until they agreed on a common figure. Students would find, when they opened their mail on April 15, that the cost of attending all overlap schools where they had been accepted was virtually identical.

In 1990, the Justice Department began an antitrust investigation of these practices, charging that the overlap group was, in effect, illegally fixing the price of a college education and preventing consumers—talented students—from soliciting competing offers of financial aid.

The colleges defended their practices on the grounds that they had "social welfare" benefits that offset possible restraint of trade. The overlap meetings allowed the schools to distribute aid on the basis of need, rather than on the basis of academic or athletic merit. The schools said they were cooperating in the "charitable act of providing financial aid," not price-fixing.

In 1993, the Justice Department settled out of court with MIT (it had earlier settled with the eight Ivy League schools). The agreement, a compromise, allowed MIT to continue to award financial aid strictly on the basis of need and to cooperate with other colleges, so long as it did not negotiate over individual students and present them with fixed aid offers.[1]

[1]"MIT, U.S. Settle Case Alleging Price-Fixing in Student Aid Offers," *Washington Post,* Dec. 21, 1993; "In Trial, M.I.T. to Defend Trading Student-Aid Data," *New York Times,* June 24, 1992, p. A15.

■ Outlaws interlocking directorates in large competing corporations (e.g., Chevron and Mobil Oil would not be permitted to have a single person serve as a member of the board of directors of both companies at the same time)

The Federal Trade Commission Act

This act, too, became law in 1914 during a period when populist sentiment against big business was very strong. In addition to creating the Federal Trade Commission to help enforce the antitrust laws, it prohibited all unfair methods of competition (without defining them in specific terms). In later years, the act was amended to give more protection to consumers by forbidding unfair and deceptive business practices, such as misleading advertising, bait-and-switch merchandising, and other consumer abuses.

The Antitrust Improvements Act

All of the important additions made to the antitrust laws during the 1930s and 1950s were incorporated into the three major laws as summarized above. But in 1976, Congress put a new and separate law on the books. The Antitrust Improvements Act strengthens government's hand in enforcing the other three laws. This law:

- Requires large corporations to notify the Justice Department and the Federal Trade Commission about impending mergers and acquisitions so that the regulators can study any possible violations of the law that may be caused by the merger (e.g., the merger of two large steel companies was delayed by the Justice Department until two of the steel mills were sold in order to preserve competition)
- Expands the Justice Department's antitrust investigatory powers
- Authorizes the attorneys general of all fifty states to bring suits against companies that fix prices and to recover damages for consumers

Exemptions

Not all organizations are subject to these four antitrust laws. Major league baseball, for example, has been exempt from antitrust regulation since 1922. This exemption has been criticized for permitting baseball owners to collude to restrict the number of teams, drive up ticket prices, and force concessions from cities eager to attract or keep a major league team.[12] Also not covered by U.S. antitrust laws are labor unions that attempt to monopolize the supply of labor; agricultural cooperatives that sometimes engage in anticompetitive behavior; insurance companies, which are regulated by state, not federal, laws; and some business transactions related to national defense and cooperative research and development (R&D) efforts.

One of the most important exemptions is the National Cooperative Research Act of 1984. This law clarifies the application of U.S. antitrust laws to joint R&D activities. When companies collaborate on research and technology development, the collaboration may have anticompetitive impacts on others in the industry. Congress sought to balance the positive effects of cooperative R&D with the preservation of competition by instructing the courts to use a "rule of reason" in assessing individual cases. Companies that wish to form joint R&D activities that may have anticompetitive effects are required to submit notice of their plans to the U.S. Attorney General and Federal Trade Commission. If approved, the companies may

---

[12]For a critique of baseball's antitrust exemption, see Andrew Zimbalist, *Baseball and Billions: A Probing Look inside the Big Business of Our National Pastime,* New York: Basic Books, 1992; and Frank Dell'Apa, "Do Pro Sports Take Advantage of Their Fans?" *Public Citizen,* May–June 1993.

share information and cooperate in ways that would otherwise violate antitrust standards.

Enforcing the Antitrust Laws

The two main antitrust enforcement agencies shown in Figure 10-3 are the Antitrust Division of the U.S. Department of Justice and the Federal Trade Commission. Both agencies may bring suits against companies they believe to be guilty of violating antitrust laws. They also may investigate possible violations; issue guidelines and advisory opinions for firms planning mergers or acquisitions; identify specific practices considered to be illegal; and negotiate informal settlements out of court. Under the Clinton administration, antitrust regulators became more activist, especially in prosecuting price fixing, blocking anticompetitive mergers, and dealing with foreign companies that violate U.S. laws on fair competition.[13] At the same time, regulators tried to be sensitive to the impact of antitrust policy on the competitiveness of U.S. firms internationally. The settlement of antitrust charges against Microsoft Corporation, profiled in the discussion case at the end of this chapter, illustrates the Clinton administration's approach to antitrust enforcement.

Antitrust suits also can be initiated by private persons or companies who believe themselves to have been damaged by the anticompetitive actions of a business firm and who seek compensation for their losses. Nearly 95 percent of all antitrust enforcement actions are initiated by private parties, not government officials, as illustrated by the following example.

> In 1993, Nestle USA initiated an antitrust lawsuit against two infant formula manufacturers—Abbott Laboratories (makers of Similac) and Bristol-Myers Squibb (makers of Enfamil)—and the American Academy of Pediatrics. Nestle charged that the three organizations had conspired to prevent Nestle's Carnation brand product from entering the lucrative infant formula market. The Pediatrics group has long advocated a ban on the advertising of infant formula, arguing that it could discourage mothers from breast-feeding. But Nestle claimed that the real point of the advertising ban was to give an unfair advantage to infant formula products, like Enfamil and Similac, already established in the market. During the 1980s, the Pediatrics group received millions of dollars in contributions from Abbott and Bristol-Myers Squibb.[14]

Attorneys general of the various states also may take action against antitrust violators, not only to protect consumers from price-fixing (under

[13]"Annie Gets Her Antitrust Gun," *Business Week*, Aug. 23, 1993, p. 23; and "The Game of Anti-Monopoly," *San Francisco Examiner*, July 29, 1994, pp. B1, B4.
[14]"Battle for Baby Formula Market," *New York Times*, June 15, 1993, pp. C1, C15.

the Antitrust Improvements Act) but also to enforce the antitrust laws of their own states. The National Association of Attorneys General has a special section on antitrust laws, and state officials often cooperate in the investigation and prosecution of cases. In 1993, for example, the New York State Attorney General sued to block Kraft's acquisition of RJR Nabisco's cold cereals, saying that the move would lessen competition and contribute to "soaring [cold cereal] price increases, far out of line with other food products."[15]

Finally, the courts usually have the last word in enforcement, and the outcome is never certain. Cases may be tried before a jury, a panel of judges, or a single judge. The Supreme Court is the court of final appeal, and its opinions carry great weight. Antitrust regulators and businesses alike often appeal their cases to this final forum because the stakes are so high and the judicial precedents created by the high court are so important in the long-run development of antitrust regulation.

Key Antitrust Issues

The business community, government policymakers, and the general public have to seek answers to several key issues if the nation's antitrust laws and regulations are to serve both business and society well. Some of the most important issues are briefly discussed.

Corporate size

The key question here is: Is large size evidence of monopoly or a threat to competition? In general, the courts have said that absolute size by itself is not a violation of the antitrust laws. If, however, a firm uses its larger size to take advantage of rivals through price discrimination, collusion with others, or other specific actions banned by the antitrust laws, then it may be found guilty. Corporations have increased in size for over a century, and the antitrust laws have neither prevented nor significantly slowed their growth.

Economic concentration

The key question here is: Does domination of an industry or a market by a few large corporations violate the antitrust laws? Or, as some ask: Should the biggest firms in each industry be broken up? Many major industries and markets are dominated by a handful of mammoth companies—examples are automobiles, tires, computers, chemicals, insurance, steel, some food and beverage products, paper, and others. Where this kind of concentration exists, competition changes. Companies tend to compete less by underpricing their rivals and more by making their products appear distinctive, servicing their customers, building reliability into products and parts, developing brand-name loyalty in customers, and advertising.

---

[15]"Waking up to Higher Cereal Prices," *New York Times*, Aug. 10, 1993, pp. C1, C5.

Critics claim that economic concentration eliminates effective price competition, reduces consumer choices, causes firms to grow too large to be efficient, inhibits innovation, and concentrates profits in too few hands. The best solution, they say, is to break up the giants into smaller units. Others counter by claiming that big firms have become dominant because they are more efficient; price competition still occurs; today's firms give consumers more, not fewer, choices of goods and services; large companies can finance more innovation than small business; and profits are distributed widely to an increasing number of stockholders. Breaking up large corporations would deprive society of these benefits, say the defenders, and should not be done.

Efficiency versus competition

Another antitrust issue is efficiency versus competition. The key question here is: Is big business efficiency more important than preserving competition? Many big companies claim that their large size makes possible many operating economies. Today's complex technology, far-flung markets, complicated financial systems, and transnational competition make bigness essential for survival and efficient operation. Some bigness is required to compete successfully against state-owned and state-subsidized foreign companies. Placing restrictions on today's corporate growth just to preserve a competitive ideal formed during the eighteenth and nineteenth centuries seems to make little economic sense. On the other hand, others point out that competition stands at the heart of private enterprise ideology and that small businesses, consumers, and workers should be protected against big business expansion even though it may mean a loss of efficiency.

Two other issues in antitrust policy, the impact of global competition and intellectual property rights, are discussed at the end of this chapter.

CORPORATE MERGERS

The mid-1990s have witnessed a wave of **corporate mergers,** echoing in some respects the extended merger boom of the mid-1980s. As Figure 10-4 shows, merger and acquisition activity, after falling dramatically in the early 1990s, was up sharply again in 1993 and 1994, leading one expert to predict "the start of the next great merger wave."[16] These new mergers raised, once again, important questions about the social and economic impact of such corporate consolidation. Not surprisingly, antitrust officials were deeply involved in deciding which mergers were acceptable and which were not.

Students of corporate mergers usually distinguish between three different types of business combinations, as depicted in Figure 10-5. A **vertical merger** occurs when the combining companies are at different stages

---

[16]"Same Old Feeding Frenzy, Different Bait," *Business Week,* Aug. 8, 1994, pp. 22–23.

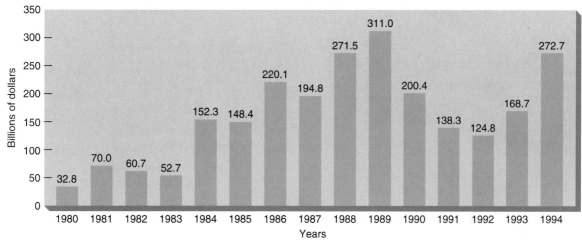

FIGURE 10-4

Value of mergers and acquisitions, 1980–1994.

SOURCES: Data for 1980–1983 are from the Bureau of the Census, *Statistical Abstract of the United States, 1990*, Washington, DC, table 883. Data for 1984–1993 are based on the mergers and corporate transactions data base and are drawn from "1993 M&A Profile," *Mergers and Acquisitions*, May–June 1994, p. 48. Data for 1994 are from the mergers and corporate transactions data base, personal communication with the author. Used by permission of *Mergers and Acquisitions*.

of production in the same general line of business. For example, a rubber tire manufacturer may combine with a company owning rubber plantations and with a chain of auto parts dealers that sells the tires. Production "from the ground up" is then brought under a single management umbrella, so it is referred to as a vertical combination. A **horizontal merger** occurs when the combining companies are at the same stage or level of production or sales. For example, if two retail grocery chains in an urban market tried to combine, antitrust regulators probably would not permit the merger if the combined firms' resultant market share appeared to lessen competition in that area.

A **conglomerate merger** occurs when firms that are in totally unrelated lines of business are combined. Gulf & Western (G&W), for example, a well-known conglomerate of the 1970s, merged under its corporate umbrella firms that manufactured pipeline equipment, auto and truck parts, cigars, chocolate candy, steel mill equipment, pantyhose, and paperback books; other units ran racetracks, distributed educational films, and staged the Miss Universe and Miss USA beauty pageants! Proponents argue that a conglomerate's pooled resources make it more capable of responding to the ups and downs of the business cycle than a company based on a single product or service, and enable it to provide many centralized managerial, technical, and financial services to small business units that otherwise would be unable to afford them.

Corporate mergers seem to occur in waves at different periods of history, each wave with its own distinctive characteristics. The 1950s and

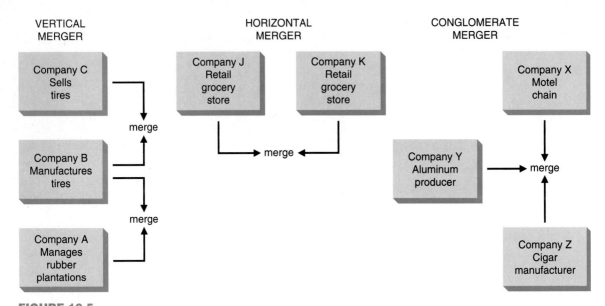

FIGURE 10-5

Three different types of corporate mergers.

1960s saw much activity, culminating in 6,000 mergers during 1969. Many of these mergers produced conglomerates and may have been motivated in part by strict antitrust enforcement that made vertical and horizontal mergers more difficult. Most observers seem to agree that one factor stimulating the 1980s surge, by contrast, was the government's general philosophy of deregulation and a more relaxed attitude toward enforcement of the nation's antitrust laws. This philosophy and approach placed a greater degree of faith in the private enterprise system to preserve competition, protect consumers, and ensure high levels of productivity than the opposite philosophy of curbing corporate power by strong antitrust regulations. In this general climate of greater permissiveness, the number of corporate mergers ballooned.

The 1980s brought large numbers of all types of mergers. Some were designed to improve a company's share of the market in particular industries, while others emphasized vertical integration or financial diversity. Much of the activity in the 1980s and 1990s has emphasized breaking up conglomerates created in the past that did not achieve hoped-for results. Many business leaders have concluded that it is important for a company to be more carefully focused on those activities it performs well. By selling parts of the business that are performing poorly or are not related to the core capability of the firm, money can be raised to invest in the core business.

In the most recent wave, many mergers of the 1990s have been driven by technological or regulatory changes. AT&T's $12 billion buyout of McCaw Cellular, mentioned in the opening example of this chapter, was just one of several blockbuster mergers in telecommunications and media, where major companies jockeyed for a favorable position on the information superhighway. In health care, several big mergers—including Merck's acquisition of Medco Containment Services and Eli Lilly's acquisition of PCS Health Systems—were spurred by anticipated regulatory changes in the delivery of health care.

The challenge faced by the Clinton administration in balancing the sometimes contradictory goals of health care reform and antitrust enforcement is profiled in Exhibit 10-B.

The Consequences of Corporate Mergers

When the smoke has cleared from the corporate mergers of the 1980s and 1990s, what will the results be? What stakeholders will have been helped, and what stakeholders hurt? No one knows that final story, but some results are already observable. The megamergers created enormously larger corporations, thus continuing a trend toward bigger and bigger

EXHIBIT 10-B

HEALTH CARE REFORM AND ANTITRUST LAW

Collusion to fix prices and anticompetitive mergers violate antitrust law. But what if price-fixing—or monopolies—are in the public interest? Government policymakers faced this dilemma in the mid-1990s, as they considered proposals for health care reform.

A key element of President Clinton's proposed health care reform was holding the line on the cost of prescription medicines. To meet this goal, the administration called for voluntary price restraint by the pharmaceutical industry, coupled with government review of the prices of some new drugs.

In response, the drug companies asked the Justice Department for an exemption from antitrust laws, to permit them to coordinate their pricing strategies. The pharmaceutical industry argued that it was, in effect, being asked by the government to break the law! A health care lawyer said, "To accomplish [voluntary price restraint] . . . may require a bunch of competitors to coordinate their activities. That's a fine goal for the While House. But another arm of the government could allege in court that such coordinated action violates federal antitrust statutes."

The antitrust issues potentially went beyond price-fixing. The Clinton health reform plan would require doctors and hospitals to join together in broad networks to provide care. Would mergers or cooperative alliances in the health care industry violate the antimonopoly provisions of the Sherman and Clayton Acts?

Internal documents circulated by the president's task force, headed by Hillary Rodham Clinton, acknowledged that health care reform might require significant modification of the nation's antitrust laws.

SOURCE: "Drug Manufacturers to Ask for Antitrust Exemption," *New York Times,* Mar. 10, 1993, p. A16; "Drug Industry Is Battling Image for Price Gouging," *New York Times,* Mar. 7, 1994, pp. A1, A12.

business units. Employees often lost their jobs when companies merged, as duplicate staffs were combined, and local communities suffered when a large company moved out or shifted its activities to other regions. A surprising number of mergers simply have not worked out as planned, resulting eventually in the breakup of the newly formed company after the expenditure of immense sums of money on a failed effort. Some acquired companies, often called "cash cows," were milked of their cash by the parent corporation, thus weakening that part of the newly formed company or preventing it from plowing the money back into modernization and growth.

One unfortunate result of many 1980s mergers, particularly among those companies that ended up with huge debt loads, was a management focus on short-run profits in order to pay the debt's interest charges. This often mean that long-run investments in improving productivity were sacrificed. This issue has been of less concern in the 1990s, as more recent acquisitions have been paid for in stock, rather than with borrowed capital.

The results of mergers are mixed for stockholders. Share values often are driven up when a takeover struggle begins. The implication is that the company is not being managed to yield maximum value for the stockholders. In that case, shareholders would gain from a takeover. Shareholders also may benefit in the long run from "synergies" between two merged firms—for example, if McCaw's cellular network gives AT&T a much longer reach, AT&T earnings and stock price may rise. But shareholders can also be hurt by mergers, particularly where an acquisition is overpriced or not well thought out. The stock price of Eli Lilly, for example, initially dropped after its acquisition of PCS, suggesting that shareholders thought the deal was a poor bet.

There will remain a need for economic restructuring in the decades ahead, so mergers and acquisitions will continue. They can serve as a dynamic stimulus, producing gains for shareholders and the entire economy from improved efficiency and market pressure. When carried to excess, however, experience has shown that such business combinations can be costly in economic and social terms for some stakeholders.[17] Social control, expressed through antitrust policy, will continue to seek the best balance between competition and other social goals.

GLOBAL COMPETITION AND A CHANGING ECONOMY

The application of antitrust law to mergers is part of the broader debate over how to improve the ability of U.S. firms to compete effectively in the global economy, enhancing the **national competitiveness** of the United

[17]J. Fred Weston and Kwang S. Chung, "Takeovers and Corporate Restructuring: An Overview," *Business Economics*, Apr. 1990, pp. 6–11. See also J. Fred Weston et al., *Mergers, Restructuring and Corporate Control*, Englewood Cliffs, NJ: Prentice-Hall, 1990.

States. Policymakers have focused on two issues in particular: permitting cooperative activities among U.S. firms that can strengthen their competitiveness in the global economy, and protecting U.S. firms from abusive and anticompetitive practices by firms from other nations.

On one hand, the U.S. Justice Department has tried to loosen the rules that affect how companies cooperate on research and development, and increasingly, on joint production agreements where there may be important economies of scale.[18] Joint manufacturing and marketing deals between U.S. and foreign firms are becoming more frequent, often without serious antitrust objections being raised by government. Hewlett Packard, for example, has formed strategic alliances with Samsung (Korea), Northern Telecom (Canada), and Japanese firms including Sony, Hitachi, Canon, and Yokogawa. The joint manufacturing plant set up by General Motors and Toyota in California also was approved by antitrust authorities. Such a joint venture between GM and either Ford or Chrysler surely would have drawn antitrust objections on traditional grounds.[19]

At the same time, the government is concerned about possible violations of antitrust law by foreign companies that may compete in unfair ways with U.S. firms. In the Guardian Industries example at the beginning of this chapter, antitrust regulators considered how best to protect U.S. glassmakers from the anticompetitive practices of Japanese firms. In a similar incident, the Justice Department in 1994 settled a case against a British firm, Pilkington, also a glassmaker, for monopolizing the technology for making sheet glass. The Justice Department said it had jurisdiction in the case because Pilkington is part owner of an American glass company. Since many international companies do business in the United States by setting up operations or buying a subsidiary, this case may signal a new strategy by regulators to prosecute foreign firms under U.S. antitrust laws.[20]

Although in many instances antitrust policies in the United States are more stringent than those of its global competitors, other nations have their own versions of antitrust laws, often referred to as "competition policies." The European Union (EU), for example, recently adopted a set of competition policies that reflect the newly integrated European economy. In 1994, the European Commission, the EU's executive branch, fined a group of carton-board manufacturers about $165 million for fixing prices—the EU's largest fine ever.[21] Similar antitrust regulations—for example, between the United States and the member countries of the EU—help create a level playing field among competing national economies.

Antitrust policymakers are wrestling with the new realities of global business competition. The days of the self-contained U.S. economy are

---

[18]Robert B. Reich, "Who Is Us?" *Harvard Business Review,* Jan.-Feb. 1990, pp. 53–64.
[19]"Trust the Trust, or Bust the Trust?" *The Economist,* Sept. 2, 1989, pp. 63–64.
[20]"U.S. Sues British in Antitrust Case," *New York Times,* May 27, 1994, pp. A1, D2.
[21]"EU Fines 19 Carton-Board Companies Record $164.9 Million for Price Fixing," *Wall Street Journal,* July 14, 1994, p. A6.

gone. Virtually all businesses are touched, directly or indirectly, by the world marketplace. Cooperation among U.S. firms and foreign competitors often makes economic sense. But the need for some form of social control on the excesses of business behavior has not disappeared, both in the United States and abroad. The optimal "fit" between antitrust protection and the global marketplace is not easily achieved.

Intellectual Property

The foundations of U.S. antitrust policy were created in the late nineteenth century when railroads were the leading technology of the day and when control of natural resources—land, oil, minerals—was the surest way to wealth. More than 100 years later, the foundations of the U.S. economy are quite different. Services now equal or exceed manufacturing of consumer and industrial goods as an employer of workers and as a source of economic growth. Manufacturing itself is highly dependent on new technologies and innovation to remain competitive in world markets. According to one observer, "The most valuable resource in the modern economy is the human mind." The point is that innovation, research and development, and global competitiveness depend greatly on new ideas. These ideas are often referred to as **intellectual property,** and the protection of ideas is one of the most central issues for business, government, and society in designing competition policies for the 1990s.

The dilemma that intellectual property presents for antitrust and competition has three parts:

- First, the creator of an idea or invention should be entitled to the benefits that flow from that original creation if it can be proved that they came from that person or organization.
- Second, the right to get special economic advantage from such inventions should not exist forever. At some point, ideas enter the public domain and can be used by others. Thomas Edison was entitled to get some advantage from inventing the electric light bulb, but this advantage should not require everyone who has ever used a light bulb to pay something to Edison or his heirs.
- Third, the right of a person or organization to withhold new ideas or inventions for the purpose of injuring a competitor can be anticompetitive and damaging to the public interest.

Intellectual property is protected through a number of special laws and public policies, including copyright and patent laws. A society that is scientifically and artistically creative has a big stake in such laws. In a global economy where information and knowledge are valuable resources, these forms of intellectual property are economically valuable. Global competition will soon alter the shape of the arts and sciences as well as the manufacture of products. A number of U.S. entertainment companies were bought by foreign businesses in the early 1990s for the purpose of acquiring copyrighted and trademarked property such as films, recordings, and books.

Many temptations can arise for businesses and individuals to use other people's ideas without permission. Patents, copyrights, and other intellectual property are sometimes "infringed"—or wrongfully used—by those who see an opportunity for quick profit. For example, Levi Strauss discovered that many imitation "Levi's" were being manufactured in the Far East, imported into the United States, and sold to unsuspecting buyers. Of course, the buyers were paying for the "Levi's" name and the quality it represents. To protect its reputation for quality, Levi Strauss had to aggressively pursue the "pirate" businesses that wrongfully used the company name. Many lawsuits and governmental actions were required before the pirates halted their practice.

A great deal of "pirating" occurs in industries such as computer software and hardware, industrial machinery, printing and publishing, and designer clothing. Because some governments do not curb such practices, businesses who create ideas are injured. One estimate is that U.S. companies lose more than $60 billion in sales each year because of infringement by non-U.S. competitors. The U.S. government has made such intellectual property issues part of its international trade negotiating position.

The 1990s are a decade when many new ideas will be developed and will lead to new commercial development in such fields as bioengineering, computer software, fiber optics, and medicine to name but a few. Such developments can affect the competitiveness of particular firms, industries, and nations.[22] The employees who work for those companies have an important stake in the fair use of ideas, as do customers who license the technology or buy the products. In addition, issues of ethics, public policy, and business strategy can arise over the use of other people's ideas.

SUMMARY POINTS OF THIS CHAPTER

- The world's largest corporations are capable of wielding much influence because of the central functions they perform in their respective societies and throughout the world. Their economic, political, and social power raises questions about the largest corporations' legitimacy, especially in societies with strong democratic traditions.

[22]Susan S. Samuelson and Thomas A. Balmer, "Antitrust Revisited—Implications for Competitive Strategy," *Sloan Management Review*, Fall 1988, pp. 79–87. See also Thomas A. Stewart, "Brain-power: How Intellectual Capital Is Becoming America's Most Valuable Asset," *Fortune*, June 3, 1991, pp. 44–60.

- In the United States, antitrust laws have been used to curb the influence of corporations and to protect consumers, small business competitors, and others affected unfairly by noncompetitive practices.
- Courts and regulators have generally maintained in recent years that large size and domination of an industry by a few firms do not in themselves constitute a violation of antitrust laws. Also important are the actual impacts of size and market dominance on efficiency and competitiveness.
- The mid-1990s witnessed a fresh wave of mergers and acquisitions. Some believed that it was good for stockholders, while others expressed concern about the long-run effects such mergers would have on both business and society.
- The emergence of global competition in many industries has led business and political leaders to adjust antitrust rules to help the United States better compete in the world economy, for example, by permitting joint R&D efforts where appropriate and by blocking anticompetitive practices by foreign firms.
- As services and knowledge-based manufacturing have grown in economic importance, efforts have expanded to protect intellectual property. Copyright and patent policies are being balanced and integrated with antitrust considerations by business and political leaders in the 1990s.

KEY TERMS AND CONCEPTS USED IN THIS CHAPTER

- Corporate power: economic, political, social
- Antitrust laws
- Corporate mergers

- Vertical, horizontal, and conglomerate mergers
- National competitiveness
- Intellectual property

DISCUSSION CASE

THE ANTITRUST CASE AGAINST MICROSOFT

On July 15, 1994, the Justice Department announced that it had reached a settlement with Microsoft Corporation, culminating a series of antitrust investigations by the U.S. government lasting over four years. The European Commission, which had also been probing Microsoft, reached a nearly identical agreement with the company.

Microsoft Corporation is one of the success stories of the information age. Founded in 1975 by Bill Gates, a computer whiz who dropped out of Harvard, the company first made its mark by developing MS-DOS, an "operating system" that directs a computer's inner workings. When IBM adopted MS-DOS for use in its personal computers (PCs), the program quickly became the industry standard. Microsoft later introduced an improved operating system, Windows, and branched out into applications software, developing word processing, spreadsheet, and other desktop programs.

By the early 1990s, Microsoft controlled 80 percent of the market for all PC operating systems, was earning profits of over $1 billion a year on revenues of close to $5 billion, and had become as big as its next four largest rivals combined. Its success contributed significantly to U.S. domination of the global market for software. A partner in a technology investment partnership said of Microsoft, "They are the Energizer Bunny on steroids. They keep going and going and going."

The government's antitrust investigation focused on two central issues. The first allegation was that Microsoft gave discounts to computer makers who agreed to pay a fee to Microsoft for each computer sold, rather than for each MS-DOS or Windows program installed. This licensing arrangement gave computer manufacturers a huge incentive to install Microsoft operating systems in all their units, and disadvantaged companies, like Novell and IBM, that made competing programs.

The second allegation was that Microsoft used its dominance in the market for operating systems to hurt rivals in the applications business. For example, Microsoft could use its advance knowledge of upcoming changes in MS-DOS or Windows to get a head start on developing compatible word processing or spreadsheet software. Or Microsoft could deliberately design features into its operating systems that would make them incompatible with competitors' applications products. Adobe Systems, a maker of typefaces, for example, complained that Windows had been designed so that Microsoft's own typefaces would run at twice the speed of Adobe's products.

The final agreement—known as a consent decree because the company voluntarily consented to it without going to a court trial—addressed only the licensing issue. Microsoft, without admitting wrongdoing, agreed to stop basing fees on the number of units sold. This freed computer makers to offer customers a choice of operating systems. Government regulators backed off on the second allegation, saying only, "We brought the case there was to bring."

Reactions to the settlement were mixed. Microsoft described the settlement as "reasonable," saying it had not violated the law and had settled only to avoid a protracted contest with the government. U.S. Attorney General Janet Reno said that the settlement "levels the playing field and opens the door for competition."

But Microsoft's competitors were less impressed. "It doesn't seem like anything has changed at all," said the chief executive of Symantec, a software company. Rival firms still had the option of pursuing private legal action against Microsoft, possibly jointly. But one competitor's attorney said, off the record, "This industry is not going to win against Microsoft by suing, but by being better than Microsoft."

In the wake of the settlement, the chairman of Sun Microsystems charged in a newspaper op-ed column that Microsoft's control of "a critical information-communications tool"—the dominant PC operating system—had effectively crippled competition and limited choices for consumers. "It is time," he said, "for Congress to take a fresh look at whether our antitrust laws are adequate to meet the novel challenges of the information age."

Meanwhile, Microsoft moved ahead aggressively with plans to market its newest operating system, known as Windows 95. The program, which combined features of MS-DOS and Windows in new ways, was expected to bring in $1 billion in revenue in 1995—and to make many rivals' software applications obsolete.

Then, on February 14, 1995, a federal judge stunned both Microsoft and the Justice Department by rejecting the proposed settlement, saying it had not gone far enough to curb Microsoft's anticompetitive practices. Although the Justice Department promptly announced it would appeal, the judge's decision cast uncertainty over Microsoft's future direction, including its plans to acquire Intuit, a maker of personal finance software, and to develop programs to access on-line services.[23]

Discussion Questions

1. In what ways have Microsoft's actions promoted the public interest? In what ways have they harmed the public interest?
2. Which objectives of antitrust policy discussed in this chapter were central to the government's investigation of Microsoft? Which objectives were addressed in the final settlement?
3. What is the best solution to Microsoft's market dominance: (a) breakup into smaller companies, (b) strict legal enforcement of applicable antitrust laws, or (c) increased competition from rivals?
4. The basic antitrust laws were written in an era when the economy was dominated by manufacturing firms, and business competition was primarily national or regional in scope. Do you think these laws are relevant to high technology companies that emerged in the late twentieth century? If not, in what ways should antitrust policy be changed?

---

[23]This case is based on the following sources: "Did Microsoft Shut the Windows on Competitors?" *Business Week,* Sept. 28, 1992, pp. 32-33; "The FTC vs. Microsoft," *Business Week,* Dec. 28, 1992, pp. 30–31; "The Microsoft Probe Looks Like a Bust for Trustbusters," *Business Week,* May 3, 1993, p. 32; "A Winning Deal: Microsoft Will Remain Dominant Despite Pact in Antitrust Dispute," *Wall Street Journal,* July 18, 1994, pp. A1, A5; "Antitrust's Bingaman Talks Tough on Antitrust Case," *Wall Street Journal,* July 19, 1994, pp. B1, B5; Scott McNealy, "Window(s) on Monopoly," *Wall Street Journal,* July 27, 1994, p. A14; "Microsoft Antitrust Pact Rejected by Federal Judge," *Wall Street Journal,* Feb. 15, 1995, pp. A3, A6; and "Sorry Bill, the Deal Is Off," *Business Week,* Feb. 27, 1995, pp. 38–40.

PART FIVE

The Corporation and the Natural Environment

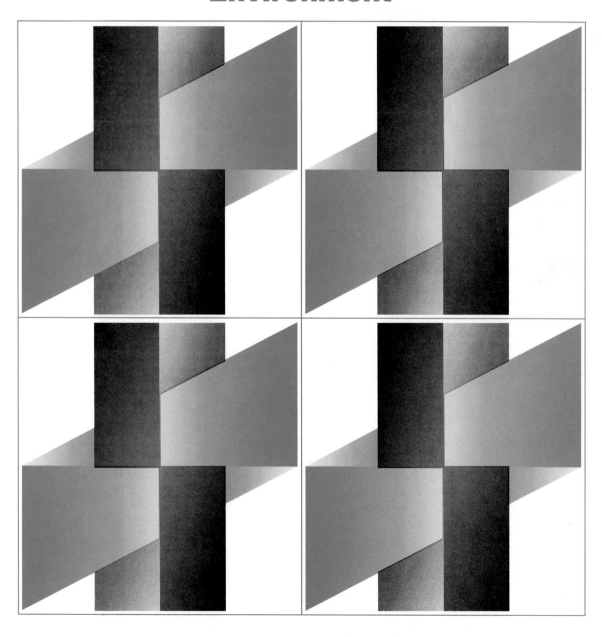

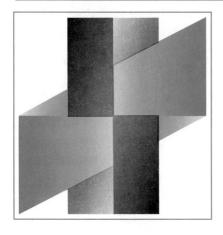

11

Ecology, Sustainable Development, and Global Business

The world community faces unprecedented ecological challenges in the twenty-first century. Many political and business leaders have embraced the idea of "sustainable development," calling for economic growth without destroying the natural environment or depleting the resources on which future generations depend. Yet the concept has remained controversial, and implementation has been difficult. The task for policymakers and corporate leaders will be to find ways to meet both economic and environmental goals in the coming decades, without sacrificing either.

Key Questions and Chapter Objectives

This chapter focuses on these key questions and objectives:

- How and why has ecological damage become a major global issue for business?
- What is sustainable development? What are the obstacles to its adoption as policy?
- What steps has the world business community taken to reduce ecological damage and promote sustainable development?

The Aral Sea, located high in the steppes of central Asia, was once the world's fourth largest freshwater lake and a thriving ecosystem. In the 1960s, central planners in the former Soviet Union decided to divert water from the two major rivers feeding the Aral Sea to irrigate the surrounding plains. Agriculture flourished, but results for the lake were disastrous. By the 1980s, the Aral Sea, cut off from its water sources, had lost 60 percent of its volume and was three times as salty as normal. Fishing boats, stranded by the retreating water, lay topsy-turvy on the seabed. The fishing industry, which supported 60,000 jobs in the 1950s, shut down because all the fish disappeared. In the early 1990s, the five newly formed republics in the Aral basin were faced with deciding what to do. Any meaningful effort to restore the ecological health of the Aral Sea would certainly require international aid.[1]

Astronauts orbiting the earth in the *Discovery* spacecraft in 1993 were startled to observe huge plumes of black smoke rising from the South American continent, drifting high into the atmosphere. The smoke they saw was coming from tropical rain forests, being deliberately burned to clear land for cattle ranching, farming, and housing. During the 1980s, Brazil lost on average about 5 million acres of rain forest a year. This development came at great cost. Many species were destroyed, and widespread burning injected carbon into the atmosphere, contributing to global warming. Some economists believed that the long-term value of the rain forest would be much greater if it were preserved and sustainably harvested for nuts, rubber, and other forest products than if it were cleared.[2]

In the early 1990s, hundreds of thousands of tons of waste, much of it hazardous, were exported from the United States. Some was loaded on ships bound for the Far East. One destination was the Guo Fu smelter, a scrap-metal processing facility near Zhuhai City in southern China. Here, workers earned $2 a day dismantling old car batteries, electrical motors, transformers, and even used computers. The Chinese government welcomed the project, a joint venture with a U.S. firm, because it provided jobs and earned valuable foreign exchange when recycled copper, aluminum, and steel were shipped out of the country. But in a ravine behind the facility, unusable materials—including polychlorinated biphenyls (PCBs), lead, and other heavy metals—were carelessly dumped, threatening the long-term health of residents in the area.[3]

Scenes like these point to the difficult dilemmas faced by world leaders as they gathered in June 1992 in Rio de Janeiro for the UN-sponsored Conference on Environment and Development, popularly known as the **Earth Summit**. On one hand, these leaders faced the growing dangers of environmental degradation. On the other, they also faced an urgent need for economic development in the world's poorer nations. Would it be possible, they asked, to foster economic growth sufficient to lift the majority of the world's people out of poverty, without compromising the ability of future generations to meet their own needs? Maurice Strong, secretary

---

[1] Sandra Postel, *Last Oasis: Facing Water Scarcity,* New York: W. W. Norton, 1992; Al Gore, *Earth in the Balance,* Boston: Houghton Mifflin, 1992; "Disaster Struck Sea Has a Chance of Returning to Life," *Financial Times,* Oct. 28, 1993, p. 8.

[2] "Efforts to Save Rain Forests Raise Suspicions in Brazil," *Washington Post,* Oct. 11, 1993, pp. A1, A23.

[3] Center for Investigative Reporting and Bill Moyers, *Global Dumping Ground: The International Traffic in Hazardous Waste,* Washington, DC: Seven Locks Press, 1990; BNA Environment Daily, "EPA Asks Senate Support for Treaty to Control International Waste Shipments," July 29, 1991; "Dumping on Our World Neighbours," *Green Globe Yearbook 1992,* New York: Oxford University Press, pp. 93–104.

general of the conference, put the matter starkly when he stated, "We now face the ultimate management challenge—that of managing our own future as a species."

ECOLOGICAL CHALLENGES

Humankind is now altering the face of the planet, rivaling the forces of nature—glaciers, volcanoes, asteroids, and earthquakes—in impact. Human beings have literally rerouted rivers, moved mountains, and burned forests. By the 1990s, human society has transformed about half of the earth's ice-free surface and has had a major impact on most of the rest. In many areas, as much land is used by transportation systems as by agriculture. Although significant natural resources—fossil fuels, fresh water, fertile land, and forest—remain, exploding populations and rapid industrialization threaten a day when the demands of human society will exceed the "carrying capacity" of the earth's ecosystem.

The Global Commons

Throughout history, communities of people have created "commons." A commons is a shared resource, such as land, air, or water, that a group of people use collectively. The paradox of the commons is that if all individuals attempt to maximize their own private advantage in the short term, the commons may be destroyed, and all users—both present and future—lose. The only solution is restraint, either voluntary or through mutual agreement.[4] The "tragedy of the commons"—that "freedom in a commons brings ruin to all"—is illustrated by the following parable.

> There was once a village on the shore of a great ocean. Its people made a good living from the rich fishing grounds that lay offshore, the bounty of which seemed inexhaustible. Some of the cleverest fishermen began to experiment with new ways to catch more fish, borrowing money to buy bigger and better equipped boats. Since it was hard to argue with success, others copied their new techniques. Soon fish began to be harder to find, and their average size began to decline. Eventually, the fishery collapsed altogether, bringing economic calamity to the village. A wise elder commented, "You see, the fish were not free after all. It was our folly to act as if they were."[5]

[4] Garrett Hardin, "Tragedy of the Commons," *Science,* vol. 162, Dec. 1968, pp. 1243–1248.
[5] Abridgement of "The Story of a Fishing Village," from *1994 Information Please Environmental Almanac.* Copyright © 1993 by World Resources Institute. Reprinted by permission of Houghton Mifflin Co. All rights reserved.

We live on a **global commons**, in which many natural resources, like the fishing grounds in this parable, are used collectively. The image of the earth as seen from space—a blue and green globe, girdled by white clouds, floating in blackness—shows that we share a single, unified ecological system, or ecosystem. **Ecology** is the study of how living things—plants and animals—interact with one another in such a system. Damage to the ecosystem in one part of the world often affects people in other locations. Depletion of the ozone layer, destruction of the rain forests, and species extinctions have an impact on all of society, not just particular regions or nations. Preserving the global commons and assuring its continued use is a new imperative for governments, business, and society. As we approach the twenty-first century, this challenge is more formidable and more critical than at any time in human history.

Sustainable Development

The World Commission on Environment and Development, including leaders from many industrialized and developing nations, described the need for balance between economic and environmental considerations as **sustainable development**. This term refers to development that "meets the needs of the present without compromising the ability of future generations to meet their own needs."[6] It includes two core ideas.

- *Poverty is an underlying cause of environmental degradation.* People who lack food, shelter, and basic amenities misuse resources just to survive. For this reason, protecting the environment will require providing a decent standard of living for all the world's citizens.
- *Economic development must be accomplished sustainably,* that is, in a way that conserves the earth's resources for future generations. Growth cannot occur at the expense of degrading the forests, water, and air that must continue to support life on this planet.

In short, the idea of sustainable development encompasses a kind of puzzle. It challenges government and business leaders to eradicate poverty and develop the world economy but to do so in a way that does not degrade the environment or plunder natural resources.

Sustainable development is an appealing idea but also a very controversial one, as shown by the debates at the Earth Summit. In order for sustainable development to work, rich nations like the United States and Japan would have to consume fewer resources and dramatically cut pollution, without simply exporting environmental stresses to other countries. Some less developed nations, such as China or Pakistan, for their part,

---

[6] World Commission on Environment and Development, *Our Common Future,* Oxford: Oxford University Press, 1987, p. 8.

would have to use less destructive agricultural practices, cut birth rates, and industrialize more cleanly. This would only be possible with the aid of money, technology, and skills from the developed nations. No wonder there has been so much resistance to the idea of sustainable development from rich and poor nations alike, as illustrated in Exhibit 11-A.

Threats to the Earth's Ecosystem

Sustainable development requires that natural resources be used by human society at a rate that can be continued over an indefinite period of time. Biologists distinguish between renewable resources—such as fresh water or forests—that can be naturally replenished, and nonrenewable resources—such as fossil fuels (oil, gas, and coal)—that, once used, are gone forever. Many natural resources, both renewable and nonrenewable, are now being depleted or polluted at well above sustainable rates. Consider the following examples:

Water resources

Only 3 percent of the water on the earth is fresh, and most of this is underground or locked up in ice and snow. Only about one tenth of 1 percent of the earth's water is in lakes, rivers, and accessible underground supplies—and thus available for human use. Water is, of course, renewable: moisture evaporates from the ocean and returns to earth as freshwater precipitation, replenishing used stocks. But in many areas, humans are

EXHIBIT 11-A

WHO WILL PAY FOR THE GOALS OF AGENDA 21?

The Earth Summit of 1992 produced a detailed plan for protecting the environment, known as Agenda 21 (named for the twenty-first century). In order to meet the goals of Agenda 21, developed countries would have to more than double their foreign aid to poor nations. The conference did not agree on who would pay, or when. Fundamental differences between the developed countries, who favored environmental protection, and the developing countries, who favored economic development, made agreement impossible.

The main agency for financing international environmental projects is the Global Environmental Facility (GEF), a pilot program set up by the World Bank and the United Nations in 1990. The rift between developed and developing countries has already surfaced in GEF. Since GEF operates under World Bank rules, big donors currently make the fund's major decisions. But poor countries want a one country–one vote structure and more influence over what projects are funded.

The Earth Summit agreed on many goals without agreeing on how to reach them—or who would pay.[1]

[1]"Environment in Asia," *Far Eastern Economic Review,* Oct. 28, 1993, pp. 47–58.

using up or polluting water faster than it can be replaced or naturally purified, threatening people and businesses that depend on it.

> One of the most important aquifers (underground water sources) in the United States is the Ogallala formation, stretching from South Dakota to Texas. The Ogallala is the source of almost a third of all groundwater used for irrigation in the United States. In some areas, as much as a quarter of the aquifer has been depleted by unsustainable pumping, threatening local businesses such as farms and cattle ranches.[7]

By one estimate, if society were able to eliminate all pollution, capture all available fresh water, and distribute it equitably—all of which are unlikely—demand would exceed the supply within a hundred years. In the 1990s, regional shortages had already caused the decline of local economies and in some cases had contributed to regional conflicts.[8]

Fossil fuels

Fossil fuels, unlike water, are nonrenewable. Human society used 60 times as much energy in 1985 as it did in 1860. Most of this came from the burning of fossil fuels; 80 percent of all commercial energy in the 1980s came from the combustion of coal, oil, and natural gas. The amount of fossil fuel burned by the world economy in one year took about a million years to form! No one knows how long present supplies will last, because many reserves remain to be discovered. But some estimates suggest that oil and gas will begin to run out in about forty and sixty years, respectively. Coal reserves are more plentiful, and could last three to four more centuries (although coal is more polluting than either oil or natural gas). Eventually, however, many fossil fuel reserves will be depleted, and the world economy will need to become much more energy efficient and switch to renewable energy sources, such as those based on water, wind, and sunshine.

Arable land

Arable (fertile) land is necessary to grow crops to feed the world's peoples. Land, if properly cared for, is a renewable resource. Although the productivity of land increased through much of the twentieth century, by the 1990s much of the world's arable land was threatened with decline. About half of irrigated farmland in developing countries required reclamation because of salinization (excess salt) or poor drainage. In other areas, poor

---

[7] Sandra Postel, "Carrying Capacity: Earth's Bottom Line," in Lester R. Brown, ed., *State of the World 1994*, New York: W. W. Norton, 1994, p. 33.
[8] Donella H. Meadows, Dennis L. Meadows, and Jorgen Randers, *Beyond the Limits: Confronting Global Collapse, Envisioning a Sustainable Future*, Post Mills, VT: Chelsea Green Publishing Co., 1992, p. 56.

farming practices had caused previously arable land to turn into desert. Other areas had become contaminated by agricultural chemicals, or ruined by overly intensive farming practices. In all, productive lands covering an area as large as India and China put together have been significantly degraded since the mid-1940s.[9]

Forces of Change

Pressure on the earth's resource base is becoming increasingly severe. Three critical factors have combined to accelerate the ecological crisis facing the world community and to make sustainable development more difficult. These are population growth, world poverty, and the rapid industrialization of many developing nations.

The population explosion

A major driver of environmental degradation is the exponential growth of the world's population. (A population that doubled every fifty years, for example, would be said to be growing exponentially. Many more people would be added during the second fifty years than during the first, even though the rate of growth would stay the same.) Just 10,000 years ago, the earth was home to no more than 10 million humans, scattered in small settlements. For many thousands of years, population growth was gradual. Around 1950, as shown in Figure 11-1, the world population reached 2.5

[9] World Resources Institute with the United Nations, *World Resources 1992–93,* New York: Oxford University Press, chap. 8.

FIGURE 11-1

World population growth.

SOURCE: United Nations Population Fund estimates.

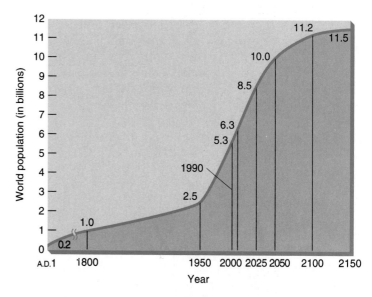

billion, then more than doubled to 5.5 billion by 1993. The United Nations estimates that the population will eventually level out at 11.5 billion around 2150. To gain some perspective on these figures, consider that in the course of a single human lifetime—that of someone born in 1950 who lived to be seventy-five years old—the world population will increase by 6 billion people!

This growth will not be distributed equally. In the industrialized countries, especially in Europe, population growth has already slowed down. About 95 percent of the world's population growth over the next thirty years is predicted to be in less developed countries, especially in Africa, Latin America, and Asia.

The world's burgeoning population will put increasing strain on the earth's resources. Each additional person uses raw materials and adds pollutants to the land, air, and water. The world's total industrial production would have to quintuple over the next forty years just to maintain the same standard of living that people have now. Protecting the environment in the face of rapid population growth is very difficult. For example, in some parts of western Africa, population growth has put great pressure on available farmland, which is not allowed to lie fallow. Because much of the available firewood has already been cut, people use livestock dung for fuel instead of fertilizer. The result has been a deepening cycle of poverty, as more and more people try to live off less and less productive land.[10]

World poverty

A second important cause of environmental degradation is poverty, and the inequality between rich and poor countries. According to estimates by the United Nations, in 1992 around 1.3 billion people lived in "absolute poverty," below the level needed for a nutritionally adequate diet and other basic necessities of life. These people—most of them in low-income countries in sub-Saharan Africa, South and East Asia, and Haiti, Nicaragua, and Guyana in the Americas—lived very near the margin of subsistence. They had only a tiny fraction of the goods and services enjoyed by those in the industrialized nations. Many suffered from hunger, including 192 million children under the age of five.[11]

Some of the most extreme poverty is found on the outskirts of rapidly growing cities in developing countries. In many parts of the world, people have moved to urban areas in search of work. Often, they must live in slums, in makeshift dwellings without sanitation or running water. In Bangkok, Thailand, a sprawling city of 8 million, 35 percent of the population now lives in such areas. In Manila in the Philippines, thousands live in a garbage dump called Smokey Mountain.[12]

[10] Postel, op. cit., p. 7.
[11] United Nations Development Programme, *Human Development Report 1994,* New York: Oxford University Press, 1994, tables 2 and 3, pp. 132–135.
[12] "Warning: All Roads Lead to Asian Cities," *Los Angeles Times,* Nov. 30, 1993, pp. 1, 4.

The world's income is not distributed equally among nations. As Figure 11-2 shows, in 1991 the richest fifth of the world's nations received about 85 percent of all income, while the poorest fifth received less than 2 percent. Japan's national income, to cite one example, was roughly on a par with that of the entire developing world, which had about 37 times as many people. Inequality is an environmental problem because countries (and people) at either extreme of income tend to behave in more environmentally destructive ways than those in the middle. People in the richest countries consume far more fossil fuels, wood, and meat, for example. People in the poorest countries, for their part, often misuse natural resources just to survive.

Industrialization

Parts of the third world are industrializing at a rapid pace. This is a positive development, because it holds out the promise of reducing poverty and slowing population growth. But industrialization has also contributed to the growing ecological crisis. Industry requires energy, much of which is secured from combustion that releases pollutants of various types. The complex chemical processes of industry produce undesirable by-products and wastes that pollute land, water, and air. Its mechanical processes often create dust, grime, and unsightly refuse. More recently, the agricultural "green" revolution—although it has greatly increased crop yields in many parts of the world—has produced overkill with pesticides, herbicides, chemical fertilizers, and refuse from cattle-feeding "factories."

The Limits to Growth

Some observers believe that the earth's rapid population growth, peoples' rising expectations, and the rapid industrialization of less developed countries are heading for a collision with a fixed barrier: the limited carrying capacity of the earth's ecosystem. According to *Beyond the Limits* by

FIGURE 11-2
Global income distribution, 1960–1991.
Source: United Nations Development Programme, *Human Development Report 1992, 1994,* New York: Oxford University Press.

Year	Share of Global Income (%) Richest 20 Percent	Poorest 20 Percent	Ratio of Richest to Poorest
1960	70.2	2.3	30 to 1
1970	73.9	2.3	32 to 1
1980	76.3	1.7	45 to 1
1991	84.7	1.4	61 to 1

Donella Meadows and her colleagues, human society is now overshooting the carrying capacity of the earth's ecosystem. Just as it is possible to eat or drink too much before your body sends you a signal to stop, so too are people and businesses using up resources, and emitting pollution, at an unsustainable rate. But because of delays in feedback, society does not understand the consequences of its actions until the damage is done.

If human society does not make a correction, a collapse may occur, possibly within the lifetimes of many who are alive today. What kind of collapse? Meadows and her colleagues developed several computer models to predict what would happen under different scenarios. If the world continued on its present course, with no major technical or policy changes, they predicted that by the year 2015, food production would begin to fall, as pollution degraded the fertility of the land. Around 2020, nonrenewable resources such as oil would begin to run out, and more and more resources would be needed to find, extract, and refine what remained. By midcentury, industrial production would begin to collapse, pulling down with it the service and agricultural sectors. Life expectancy and population would fall soon after, as death rates were driven up by lack of food and health care.[13]

Critics of the **limits to growth hypothesis** suggest that these "doomsday" predictions are unnecessarily bleak, because there are important offsets to these limits. Market forces are one such offset. For example, as natural resources such as oil and gas become more scarce, their prices will rise, and people and businesses may be motivated to use natural resources more efficiently or to find substitutes. Another offset is technology. Technological advances may slow environmental degradation by developing more reliable birth control, more productive crops through genetic engineering, or nonpolluting sources of energy such as solar-powered engines. The authors of *Beyond the Limits* acknowledge these offsets but stick to their conclusion that if human society does not adopt sustainable development, economic and social catastrophe is just a matter of time.[14]

GLOBAL ENVIRONMENTAL ISSUES

Some environmental problems are inherently global in scope and require international cooperation. Typically these are issues pertaining to the global commons—resources shared by all nations. Three global problems that will have major consequences for business and society—all of which were extensively discussed at the Earth Summit—are ozone depletion, global warming, and biodiversity.

---

[13] Meadows, Meadows, and Randers, op. cit.
[14] For a classic critique of an earlier version of the limits to growth hypothesis, see Robert M. Solow, "Is the End of the World At Hand?" *Challenge*, Mar.–Apr. 1973, pp 39–50.

Ozone Depletion

Ozone is a bluish gas, composed of three bonded oxygen atoms, that floats in a thin layer in the stratosphere between eight and twenty-five miles above the planet. Although poisonous to humans in the lower atmosphere, ozone in the stratosphere is critical to life on earth by absorbing dangerous ultraviolet light from the sun. Too much ultraviolet light can cause skin cancer and damage the eyes and immune systems of humans and other species.

In 1974, scientists first hypothesized that chlorofluorocarbons (CFCs)—manufactured chemicals widely used as refrigerants, insulation, solvents, and propellants in spray cans—could react with and destroy ozone. Little evidence existed of actual ozone depletion, however, until 1985, when scientists discovered a thin spot, or "hole," in the ozone layer over Antarctica. Studies showed that the hole was indeed the work of CFCs. In the upper atmosphere, intense solar rays had split up CFC molecules, releasing chlorine atoms that had reacted with and destroyed ozone. In 1991, scientists for the first time reported evidence of ozone depletion in the northern latitudes over the United States and Europe during the summer, when the sun's ultraviolet rays are the strongest and pose the greatest danger.

World political leaders moved quickly in response to scientific evidence that CFCs posed a threat to the earth's protective ozone shield. In 1987, a group of nations negotiated the **Montreal Protocol,** agreeing to cut CFC production and use by 50 percent by 1999. In 1992, the deadline for phasing out manufacture of CFCs completely was moved up to January 1, 1996, in view of evidence that the ozone layer was being depleted even faster than feared earlier. Developing countries were given until 2010 to ban the chemicals. The United States separately set a 1995 deadline for CFC phase-out.

Many businesses moved to eliminate CFC use in advance of the ban. IBM Corporation's San Jose, California, facility, for example, eliminated all CFC use in manufacturing in 1992, well ahead of the U.S. government's deadline. IBM replaced its CFC-based machines with an innovative cleaning process that produced virtually no pollution. The company's new cleaners took up less space, required no air abatement equipment, and were less costly to operate.[15]

Within a week of the U.S. ratification of the Montreal Protocol, Du Pont Corporation, the inventor of commercial CFCs and the world's largest producer, decided to stop making CFCs completely as soon as a substitute could be developed; in 1993, the company announced it had moved up its

[15] Anne T. Lawrence, "The Pollution Prevention Honor Roll: Leading-Edge Environmental Management in the Silicon Valley," *Northern California Executive Review,* Winter/Spring 1994, pp. 1–8.

timetable for phase-out to 1995. Many other manufacturers have followed suit.

Unfortunately, even the complete phase-out of CFC use in 1996 by signatories of the Montreal Protocol will not solve the problem for many years to come. Many countries, including India and China, have not yet signed the treaty, citing their need for access to inexpensive refrigeration and solvents. Moreover, CFCs are remarkably stable and can persist in the atmosphere for as long as fifty years, so CFCs released in the early 1990s may still be reaching the upper atmosphere as late as the 2040s. CFCs will also continue to be released from products manufactured before the ban took effect. Another problem is that a number of other ozone-depleting chemicals, including some used as substitutes for CFCs, are not yet fully regulated by treaty. Ironically, even though world leaders and businesses have moved aggressively to eliminate CFCs, ozone depletion will likely get worse before it gets better.

Global Warming

Another difficult problem facing the world community is the gradual warming of the earth's atmosphere. Although uncertainty remains about the rate and cause of **global warming,** business and governments are beginning to respond to the issue.

The earth's atmosphere contains carbon dioxide and other trace gases that, like the glass panels in a greenhouse, prevent heat reflected from the earth's surface from escaping into space, as illustrated in Figure 11-3. Without this so-called greenhouse effect, the earth would be too cold to support life. Since the industrial revolution, which began in the late 1700s, the amount of greenhouse gases in the atmosphere has increased by as much as 25 percent, largely due to the burning of fossil fuels such as oil and natural gas. Measurements of temperature over time show that the earth has already warmed by between 0.3 and 0.6 degrees Celsius over the past century (1 degree Celsius equals 1.8 degrees Fahrenheit, the unit commonly used in the United States). Some scientists believe that accelerating levels of greenhouse gases could warm the climate by as much as 5 degrees Celsius more by the mid-twenty-first century.

There are many possible causes of global warming. The burning of fossil fuels, which releases carbon dioxide, is the leading contributor. But consider the following additional causes.[16]

- ■ *Deforestation.* Trees and other plants absorb carbon dioxide, removing it from the atmosphere. Deforestation—cutting down and not replacing trees—thus contributes to global warming. Burning forests to

---

[16] Stephen H. Schneider, *Global Warming: Are We Entering the Greenhouse Century?* San Francisco: Sierra Club Books, 1989.

FIGURE 11-3
Global warming.

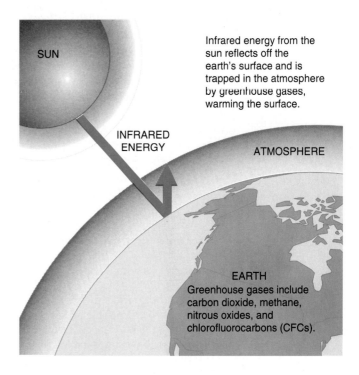

Infrared energy from the sun reflects off the earth's surface and is trapped in the atmosphere by greenhouse gases, warming the surface.

SUN

INFRARED ENERGY

ATMOSPHERE

EARTH
Greenhouse gases include carbon dioxide, methane, nitrous oxides, and chlorofluorocarbons (CFCs).

clear land for grazing or agriculture, mentioned in an opening example in this chapter, also releases carbon directly into the atmosphere as a component of smoke. Large-scale deforestation thus contributes in two ways to global warming.

- *Beef production.* Methane, a potent greenhouse gas, is produced as a by-product of the digestion of some animals, including cows. Large-scale cattle ranching releases significant amounts of methane.
- *Population growth.* Human beings produce carbon dioxide every time they breathe. More people means more greenhouse gases.
- *CFCs,* in addition to destroying the ozone, are also greenhouse gases. The Montreal Protocol will have the unintended beneficial consequence of slowing global warming.

Some scientists believe unless governments and businesses take action now to limit greenhouse gas emissions, the atmosphere will continue to warm. If this occurs, the world may experience extreme heat waves, air pollution crises, and damaging wildfires in the twenty-first century. The polar ice caps may partially melt, raising sea levels and causing flooding in low-lying coastal areas like Florida, Bangladesh, and the Netherlands. It may become as difficult to grow wheat in Iowa as it is now in arid Utah. Such climate change could devastate many of the world's economies and destroy the habitats of many species. These conclusions, however, remain the subject of debate within the scientific community. Some of the arguments against the global warming alarm are presented in Exhibit 11-B.

Whatever the outcome of this debate, many businesses have realized that improving their energy efficiency can make them more competitive—as well as cut down emissions of greenhouse gases.

Hundreds of U.S. companies have signed up for the Environmental Protection Agency's voluntary Green Lights program, which encourages installation of more efficient lighting. Studies have shown that if busi-

EXHIBIT 11-B

GLOBAL WARMING: SOME DISSENTING VOICES[1]

Most scientists agree that the earth has warmed somewhat over the past century. However, not all believe that the situation warrants policies to curb greenhouse gas emissions by business. The following are some dissenting arguments.

The observed warming may not be due to human activity.
There are other possible explanations (besides emissions of greenhouse gases) for the warming of the past century, including natural cycles of warming and cooling (such as those that caused the Ice Age).

Technological solutions may be at hand.
Human society will develop new technologies to slow global warming, ranging from substitutes for carbon-based fuels to more exotic solutions, like reflective material launched into orbit around the earth to deflect the sun's rays.

Scientific uncertainty prevents action now.
Much is unknown about global warming, including the ability of the oceans to absorb heat from the sun. More carbon in the atmosphere might produce cloudier weather, partially offsetting the warming effect of greenhouse gases.

Global warming may benefit some.
The pain caused by global warming would not be evenly distributed among the nations and regions of the earth. In fact, some might benefit. The growing season would be extended in colder climates, such as those of Canada or Siberia.

Restrictions on greenhouse gas emissions are too expensive.
The costs to the global economy and individual businesses of big cutbacks in the use of fossil fuels would be too great, when compared with possible benefits to society.

[1]For arguments against the global warming alarm, see Patrick J. Michaels, *Sound and Fury: The Science and Politics of Global Warming,* Washington, DC: CATO Institute, 1992. Arguments in favor of policy intervention to slow global warming may be found in Stephen H. Schneider, *Global Warming: Are We Entering the Greenhouse Century?* San Francisco: Sierra Club Books, 1989. Christopher D. Stone, in *The Gnat Is Older than Man: Global Environment and Human Agenda* (Princeton, NJ: Princeton University Press, 1993), attempts to summarize and evaluate this debate.

nesses used superefficient light bulbs and other available technologies, electricity used for commercial lighting could be cut in half, reaping large savings on utility bills. The fact that using less electricity—and hence burning less fossil fuel—also reduces global warming is an added benefit.

At the Earth Summit of 1992, world leaders negotiated a Convention on Climate Change that proposes to cut back emissions from the burning of fossil fuels. Under this treaty, industrialized countries agreed to limit emissions of greenhouse gases, eventually capping them at 1990 levels. In 1993, the Clinton administration committed the United States to rolling back emissions of greenhouse gases to 1990 levels by the year 2000. Economists are uncertain what effect these policies will have on business. Limiting the use of fossil fuels will certainly impose additional costs. But one study by the U.S. Environmental Protection Agency found that the gross national product would be helped, not hurt, by curbs on greenhouse emissions. This is because the curbs would force businesses to become more energy-efficient, freeing up capital for investment.[17]

Biodiversity

Biodiversity refers to the number and variety of species and the range of their genetic makeup. To date, approximately 1.4 million species of plants and animals have been named and described. Many scientists believe these are but a fraction of the total. The earth contains at least 10 million species, and possibly as many as 100 million.

Biological diversity is now at its lowest level since the disappearance of the dinosaurs some 65 million years ago. Somewhere between 10 and 100 species of plants and animals are lost every day. The eminent biologist Edward O. Wilson has eloquently stated the costs of this loss:

> Every species extinction diminishes humanity. Every micro-organism, animal and plant contains on the order of from one million to 10 billion bits of information in its genetic code, hammered into existence by an astronomical number of mutations and episodes of natural selection over the course of thousands or even millions of years of evolution. . . . Species diversity—the world's available gene pool—is one of our planet's most important and irreplaceable resources. . . . As species are exterminated, largely as the result of habitat destruction, the capacity for natural genetic regeneration is greatly reduced. In Norman Myers' phrase, we are causing the death of birth.[18]

---

[17] "New Studies Predict Profits in Heading Off Warming," *New York Times,* Mar. 17, 1992, pp. C1, C9. For an alternative view, see "Greenhouse Economics: Count Before You Leap," *The Economist,* July 7, 1990, pp. 21–24.

[18] Edward O. Wilson, "Threats to Biodiversity," in *Managing Planet Earth: Readings from Scientific American Magazine,* New York: W. H. Freeman and Co., 1990, pp. 57–58.

Genetic diversity is vital to each species' ability to adapt and survive and has many benefits for human society as well. By destroying this biological diversity, we are actually undermining our survivability as a species.

Ethicists have recently given greater attention to the responsibilities of humans to conserve the natural environment and to prevent the extinction of other species of plants and animals. This emerging philosophical perspective is profiled in Exhibit 11-C.

A major reason for the decline in the earth's biodiversity is the destruction of rain forests, particularly in the tropics. Rain forests are woodlands that receive at least 100 inches of rain a year. They are the planet's richest areas in terms of biological diversity. In the mid-1990s, rain forests covered only around 7 percent of the earth's surface but accounted for somewhere between 50 to 90 percent of the earth's species. Only about half of

EXHIBIT 11-C

THE EMERGENCE OF ENVIRONMENTAL ETHICS

Environmental ethics is concerned with the ethical responsibilities of human beings toward the natural environment. In much of Western philosophy, there exists a fundamental dualism, or separation, between humans and nature. Some Western philosophers have believed that the purpose of civilization was to dominate and control the environment (or nature) and other living things. This perspective may be contrasted with an emerging philosophical view that human society is part of an integrated ecosystem and that humans have ethical obligations toward nature. The following quotations are drawn from proponents of the latter view.

"A thing is right when it tends to preserve the integrity, stability, and beauty of the biotic community [of living things]. It is wrong when it tends otherwise."

—Aldo Leopold

"The well-being and flourishing of human and non-human Life on Earth have value in themselves. . . . These values are independent of the usefulness of the non-human world for human purposes."

—Arne Naess

"What is proposed here is a broadening of value, so that nature will cease to be merely 'property' and become a commonwealth. . . . If we now universalize 'person,' consider how slowly the circle has enlarged . . . to include aliens, strangers, infants, children, Negroes, Jews, slaves, women, Indians, prisoners, the elderly, the insane, the deformed, and even now we ponder the status of fetuses. Ecological ethics queries whether we ought to again universalize, recognizing the intrinsic value of every ecobiotic [living] component."

—Holmes Rolston

Source: The first two quotations are from Susan J. Armstrong and Richard G. Botzler, eds., *Environmental Ethics: Divergence and Convergence*, New York: McGraw-Hill, 1993, pp. 382, 412; the third quotation is from Roderick Nash, *The Rights of Nature*, Madison: University of Wisconsin Press, 1989, pp. 3–4.

the original tropical rain forests still stand, and at the rate they are currently being cut, all will be gone or severely depleted within thirty years. The reasons for rain forest destruction include commercial logging, cattle-ranching, and conversion of forest to plantations to produce cash crops for export. Overpopulation also plays a part, as landless people clear forest to grow crops and cut trees for firewood.

The destruction of the rain forest is ironic, because to some it has more economic value standing than cut. Rain forests are the source of many valuable products, including foods, medicines, and fibers. The pharmaceutical industry, for example, each year develops new medicines based on newly discovered plants from tropical areas. The U.S. National Cancer Institute has identified 1,400 tropical forest plants with cancer-fighting properties. As rain forests are destroyed, so too is this potential for new medicines.

> Madagascar, the fourth largest island in the world, located off the eastern coast of Africa, is widely regarded as a biological treasure trove. Researchers discovered, for example, that the rosy periwinkle plant, found in the island's tropical rain forest, contained a unique genetic trait that was useful in the treatment of Hodgkin's disease, childhood leukemia, and other cancers. Over 90 percent of Madagascar's rain forest has been cleared, destroying perhaps half of the 200,000 species of plants and animals found there.[19]

One of the issues discussed at the Earth Summit was the right of nations, such as Madagascar, to a fair share of profits from the commercialization of genetic material for which they are the source. Until a few years ago, drug companies, for example, often collected genetic samples from foreign countries without compensation. In most cases, source countries are now more aware of the commercial value of their biological resources and have required the payment of royalties when genetic material is developed commercially. Partnerships have also developed between business firms and source nations that respect the unique contribution of each.

> Shaman Pharmaceuticals, founded in 1990 by Lisa Conte, a biochemist with a graduate degree in business and a strong commitment to the environment, is a small U.S.-based company that specializes in developing medicines from rain forest plants. The company employs a group of field researchers who live and work alongside traditional healers, known as shamans, in the rain forests of Central America. When the re-

---

[19] Jeremy Rifkin, *Biosphere Politics: A New Consciousness for a New Century,* New York: Crown Publishers, 1991, p. 67; and *1994 Information Please Environmental Almanac,* Boston: Houghton Mifflin, 1994, p. 356.

searchers identify a plant that is used medicinally in at least three villages, it is sent to a laboratory for analysis. Some have shown considerable commercial promise. Conte's goal is to donate a portion of the company's profits to an organization dedicated to preserving tropical folk medicine.[20]

The Earth Summit produced a treaty, the Convention on Biological Diversity, which by 1995 had been ratified by 114 countries. The treaty commits these countries to draw up national strategies for conservation, protect ecosystems and individual species, and take steps to restore degraded areas. The convention also allows countries to share in the profits from sales of products derived from their biological resources.

RESPONSE OF THE INTERNATIONAL BUSINESS COMMUNITY

The international business community has undertaken many initiatives to put the principle of sustainable development into practice.

Business Council for Sustainable Development

As part of the preparations for the Earth Summit, the Business Council for Sustainable Development (BCSD), a group of around fifty top corporate executives from around the world, was formed in 1990. Headed by a Swiss industrialist, the group set out to stimulate the involvement of the international business community. Over a two-year period, the group sponsored over fifty conferences in more than twenty countries—especially in the developing nations of Asia, Africa, and Latin America. Their aim was to develop a global business perspective on economic development and the environment.

The BCSD's report, published in 1992 under the title *Changing Course*, analyzed the implications of the global ecological challenge for business.[21] The report called for a new approach to management that would manufacture and distribute products more efficiently, consider their lifelong impact, and recycle components. The group concluded that the most eco-efficient companies—those that added the most value with the least use of resources and pollution—were more competitive as well as more environmentally sound.

[20] David Riggle, "Pharmaceuticals from the Rainforest," *In Business*, Jan.–Feb. 1992; "Drug Wars: Extracting Patents and Profits from the Rain Forest's Medicinal Plants," *Village Voice*, July 21, 1992; "Drug Companies Going Back to Nature," and "More Incentives to Save Vanishing Rain Forests," *New York Times*, Mar. 5, 1992.

[21] Stephan Schmidheiny, *Changing Course: A Global Business Perspective on Development and the Environment*, Cambridge, MA: MIT Press, 1992.

Eco-efficiency is only possible, the Business Council for Sustainable Development concluded, in the presence of open, competitive markets in which prices reflect the true cost of environmental as well as other resources. Accordingly, the group made several specific recommendations. These included:

- **Full-cost pricing.** The price of goods must accurately reflect their full environmental costs. In the past, environmental costs have not been fully accounted, for example, in calculating measures of national production such as the gross national product (GNP). One study showed, for example, that when the true costs of depletion of timber, oil, and topsoil were included, the economic growth rate of Indonesia from 1971 to 1984 was not 7 percent—as officially calculated—but only 4 percent.[22] The BCSD recommended adopting full-cost pricing and revising systems of national accounting to include the costs of environmental damage.
- **Polluter pays principle (PPP).** This would require economic policies based on the principle "the polluter pays," so that the price of goods in the marketplace would reflect their true environmental costs. The price of a product would reflect not only the cost of production, but also any associated environmental damage. For example, a detergent would cost more if its packaging could not be recycled. If the polluter pays principle were adopted, markets would encourage the choice of more sustainable alternatives.

Several other groups, in addition to the BCSD, have given serious attention to the idea of sustainable development and its implications for business. Exhibit 11-D profiles the efforts of several important national and international business organizations to develop codes of environmental conduct.

Many individual businesses and industry groups have also undertaken voluntary initiatives to improve their environmental performance. These are the subject of the next section.

Voluntary Business Initiatives

Many firms around the world have tried to determine how sustainable development translates into actual business practice. Some of the more important voluntary initiatives undertaken by businesses include the following:

Life-cycle analysis involves collecting information on the lifelong environmental impact of a product, all the way from raw material extraction and manufacturing through its distribution, use, and ultimate disposal.

---

[22] Robert C. Repetto et al., *Wasting Assets: Natural Resources in the National Income Accounts,* World Resources Institute, 1989.

EXHIBIT 11-D

INTERNATIONAL CODES OF ENVIRONMENTAL CONDUCT

A number of national and international business organizations have developed codes of environmental conduct. Among the most important ones are the following.

International Chamber of Commerce (ICC)
The ICC developed the "Business Charter for Sustainable Development," sixteen principles that identify key elements of environmental leadership and call on companies to recognize environmental management as among their highest corporate priorities.

Global Environmental Management Initiative (GEMI)
A group of over twenty companies dedicated to fostering environmental excellence, GEMI developed an environmental self-assessment program that helps firms assess their progress in meeting the goals of the Business Charter for Sustainable Development.

Keidanren
This major Japanese industry association in 1991 proposed a "Global Environmental Charter" that sets out a code of environmental behavior.

Chemical Manufacturers Association (CMA)
This U.S.-based industry association developed "Responsible Care: A Public Commitment," that commits its member companies to a code of management practices, focusing on process safety, community awareness, pollution prevention, safe distribution, employee health and safety, and product stewardship. The group is working for the international adoption of these principles.

International Standards Organization (ISO)
ISO 9000 is a series of voluntary quality standards developed by the ISO, an international group based in Geneva, Switzerland. In 1993, ISO began work on a new set of standards that would permit companies to be certified as meeting global environmental performance standards.

SOURCE: "Business Becomes Certifiable," *Resources,* June, 1993, pp. 10–12; Morton L. Mullins, "Responsible Care: A Case Study," in Rao V. Kolluru, ed., *Environmental Strategies Handbook,* pp. 216–229, New York: McGraw-Hill, 1994; and original materials provided by these organizations.

The aim of life-cycle analysis is to minimize the adverse impact of a particular product at all stages. One of the initial pioneers of life-cycle analysis was Procter & Gamble, the U.S.-based consumer products maker. After conducting a life-cycle analysis of a liquid fabric softener, for example, the company introduced a triple-strength version, refillable plastic containers made with recycled material, and paperboard refill cartons. The result was greatly reduced packaging waste.

Industrial ecology refers to designing factories and distribution systems as if they were self-contained ecosystems. For example, businesses can save materials through "closed loop" recycling, use "wastes" from one process as raw material for others, and make use of energy generated as a by-product of production.

> An example of industrial ecology may be found in the town of Kalundborg, Denmark, where several companies have formed a cooperative relationship that produces both economic and environmental benefits. The local utility company sells excess process steam—which had previously been released into a local fjord (waterway)—to a local pharmaceutical plant and oil refinery. Excess fly ash (fine particles produced when fuel is burned) is sold to nearby businesses for use in cement making and road building. Meanwhile, the oil refinery removes sulfur in the natural gas it produces—to make it cleaner burning—and sells the sulfur to a sulfuric acid plant. Calcium sulfate, produced as a residue of a process to cut smoke emissions, is sold to a gypsum manufacturer for making wallboard. The entire cycle both saves money and reduces pollution.[23]

Design for disassembly. Companies using this approach design products so that at the end of their useful life they can be disassembled and recycled. At Volkswagen, the German carmaker, engineers design cars for eventual disassembly and reuse. At the company's specialized auto recycling plant in Leer, built in 1990, old cars can be completely taken apart in just three minutes. Plastics, steel, precious metals, oil, acid, and glass are separated and processed. Many materials are used again—in new Volkswagens.[24]

Technology cooperation. Sustainable development will require the development of long-term partnerships between companies in developed and developing countries to transfer environmental technologies, as shown in the following two examples.

> Since the mid-1960s, Nippon Steel, a major Japanese steel producer, has had a partnership with Usiminas, a Brazilian firm, to develop and run a basic steel industry in the state of Minas Gerais in southeastern Brazil. Modern environmental technology has been part of the project from the start. For example, the Japanese helped introduce energy-efficient continuous casting and a system to clean and recover basic oxygen furnace emissions. The result is a third world steel industry as clean as the most advanced in the world.
>
> The leather tanning industry traditionally generates large amounts of noxious waste. In Kenya—a major leather producer—a Leather Development Centre has been established with funds from the United Nations and Germany. The Centre has developed a model tannery that

---

[23] Arthur D. Little, "Industrial Ecology: An Environmental Agenda for Industry," 1991; "Growth vs. Environment," *Business Week*, May 5, 1992, p. 75.
[24] Schmidheiny, op. cit., pp. 305–308.

uses the most environmentally advanced methods and trains Kenyan tanners in their application.[25]

Although many companies around the world have undertaken valuable experiments, the idea of sustainable development remains controversial in the business community. Nevertheless, one study showed that the proportion of senior executives who believe environmental issues are "extremely important" increased threefold in a two-year period in the early 1990s, and many were taking action to improve the ways their firms managed environmental risk.[26]

Protecting the environment and the well-being of future generations is, as the head of the Business Council on Sustainable Development put it, "fast becoming a business necessity and even an opportunity."[27] Environmental regulations are getting tougher, consumers want cleaner products, and employees want to work for environmentally conscious companies. Finding ways to reduce or recycle waste saves money. The most successful global businesses in coming years may be those, like the ones profiled in this chapter, that recognize the imperative for sustainable development as an opportunity for competitive advantage.

SUMMARY POINTS OF THIS CHAPTER

- The world ecological crisis—including depletion of nonrenewable resources such as oil and coal, air and water, pollution, and the degradation of much arable land—has become worse in recent years. Population growth, poverty, and rapid industrialization in many parts of the world have contributed to these problems. The limits to growth hypothesis maintains that human society will soon exceed the carrying capacity of the earth's ecosystem, unless changes are made now.

- Many world leaders have supported the idea of sustainable development—economic growth without depleting the resources on which future generations will depend. International agreements have been developed addressing ozone depletion, global warming, and biodiversity. But implementation remains a challenge, and the community of nations has not yet worked out who will pay.

- Global businesses have begun to put the principles of sustainable development into action, through such innovative actions as life-cycle analysis, industrial ecology, design for disassembly, and technology

[25] Ibid., pp. 206–209, 224–228.
[26] Study by Booz, Allen, and Hamilton, cited in "Hope for the Future," Special Advertising Section, *Business Week*, Dec. 30, 1991, p. 83.
[27] Stephan Schmidheiny, "The Business Logic of Sustainable Development," *Columbia Journal of World Business*, vol. 27, no. 3–4, 1992, pp. 19–23.

cooperation. But many believe that voluntary actions by business cannot solve environmental problems without supportive public policies, such as ones promoting full-cost pricing and the polluter pays principle.

KEY TERMS AND CONCEPTS USED IN THIS CHAPTER

- Earth Summit
- Global commons
- Ecology
- Sustainable development
- Limits to growth hypothesis
- Ozone
- Montreal Protocol
- Global warming

- Biodiversity
- Full-cost pricing
- Polluter pays principle (PPP)
- Life-cycle analysis
- Industrial ecology
- Design for disassembly
- Technology cooperation

DISCUSSION CASE

SAVING THE MALAYSIAN RAIN FOREST

Malaysia is a federation of several former British territories: Malaya, located on the Malay peninsula in Southeast Asia; and the states of Sarawak and Sabah, located on the northern side of the island of Borneo across the South China Sea. In the 1970s and 1980s, the Malaysian economy grew rapidly, fueled in part by direct foreign investment by many Western firms drawn to the country by tax breaks and low-wage labor.

Malaysia has many natural resources, including tin, oil, and rubber. One of the richest, however, is timber—particularly tropical hardwoods found in the rain forests of Sarawak and Sabah. During the 1980s, the Malaysian rain forest was logged at an astonishing rate. Although Malaysia contained only about 3 percent of the world's tropical forests, the country accounted for 30 percent of all tropical wood harvested in 1991. According to one account, "Malaysia is stripping its Borneo provinces of trees at a breakneck pace. Work in some operations continues around the clock, with gigantic floodlights illuminating the forests. [The result is the] ruin of local ecosystems, the destruction of indigenous homelands, and the economic folly of mining a potentially renewable resource."[28]

Some environmental groups in the West were highly critical of Malaysian forest policy. They charged that rain forests were being harvested at rates as much as four times higher than could be sustained, threatening the loss of one of the world's most biologically diverse areas. Moreover, native peoples—such as the Penan, hunters and gatherers who

---

[28] Worldwatch Institute, *State of the World 1994*, New York: W. W. Norton, 1994, p. 38.

had lived in the Bornean rain forest for centuries—were being displaced from their ancestral lands, and their cultures were being destroyed. Some environmentalists called for a boycott of products made of Malaysian hardwood.

Many Malaysians, however, disputed these criticisms. Timber exports provided a significant source of foreign exchange. Forest products were also important to the government's economic plan, which sought to promote manufacturing by supporting the development of furniture, plywood, and other wood-related industries. By providing jobs and income, the timber industry had reduced poverty and maintained political stability. Some Malaysian officials argued that the United States and other developed countries had overexploited their own forests and that Western criticisms were hypocritical at best—and at worst a disguised attempt to promote their own forest product industries at the expense of Malaysia's.

In 1990, the UN-affiliated International Tropical Timber Organization (ITTO) undertook a study of logging in Sarawak. The group recommended that log output be cut in half, in order to achieve a more sustainable rate of harvest. The Sarawak state government surprised many when it agreed in 1992 to abide in principle by the ITTO's recommendations. Many environmentalists, however, feared that the government's move was too little, too late. They were concerned, moreover, by the lack of enforcement mechanisms and by continued close ties between the Malaysian political elite and timber concession–holders. "In many ways it's an intractable problem," commented an ITTO economist. "Producing countries say it's basically a problem of poverty, and that's a compelling argument."[29]

Discussion Questions

1. What stakeholders are helped by the logging of the Malaysian rain forest? What stakeholders are hurt by it?
2. How does logging the Malaysian rain forest relate to the issues of global warming and biodiversity discussed in this chapter?
3. What political and economic steps would be necessary in order to develop an effective and enforceable plan for the sustainable development of the Malaysian rain forest?

---

[29] This case is based on the following sources: Stan Sesser, "Logging the Rainforest," *The New Yorker,* May 27, 1991, pp. 42–67; Forest Reinhardt, "Forest Policy in Malaysia," Harvard Business School Case 9-792-099, 1992; "The Quagmire of Rain Forest Logging," *L.A. Times,* Dec. 21, 1992, pp. D1, D6; Michael Vatikiotis, "Malaysian Forests: Clearcut Mandate," *Far Eastern Economic Review,* Oct. 28, 1993, pp. 54–55; and Worldwatch Institute, *State of the World 1994.*

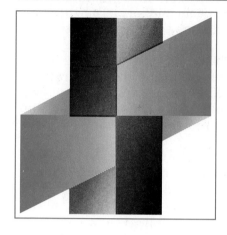

12

Managing Environmental Issues

Growing public interest in protecting the environment has prompted political and corporate leaders to become increasingly responsive to environmental issues. In the United States, policy-makers have moved toward greater reliance on market-based mechanisms, rather than command and control regulations, to achieve environmental goals. At the same time, many businesses have become increasingly proactive and have pioneered new approaches to effective environmental management.

Key Questions and Chapter Objectives

This chapter focuses on these key questions and objectives:

- What are the main features of U.S. environmental laws?
- What are the costs and benefits of environmental regulation?
- Through what stages do business firms progress as they become more proactive with respect to environmental issues?
- How can businesses manage environmental issues most effectively?

Los Angeles, California, is one of the most smog-ridden cities in the United States. On many days, the city is covered by a dense blanket of orange haze, and residents cannot catch even a glimpse of the lovely San Gabriel mountains just a few miles to the east. In 1993, southern California air quality regulators, frustrated with old approaches, tried something new—a market-driven plan called *RECLAIM*. This plan required major overall reductions in smog-producing chemical emissions but permitted individual businesses to buy and sell pollution "credits." Many businesses hailed the program as a less burdensome and costly way to reduce urban smog.[1]

In the early 1990s, the Environmental Defense Fund (EDF), a leading environmental advocacy organization, believed that its old strategy of

[1]"Hard Times Dilute Enthusiasm for Clean-Air Laws," *New York Times,* Nov. 26, 1993, pp. A1, A12.

suing companies and lobbying legislators was not working well enough. Instead, the group tried a cooperative approach, joining McDonald's Corporation to study the issue of fast-food packaging waste. After just a few months, McDonald's agreed to abandon its "clamshell" foam hamburger box, replacing it with a paper wrapper. In 1993, encouraged by this and other successes, EDF joined in an ambitious partnership with a group of major companies—including Time Warner, Johnson & Johnson, and Prudential Insurance—to study the use of ecologically safe paper. Their ultimate goal was to convince paper manufacturers to process recycled material rather than trees.[2]

Dow Chemical Corporation in 1986 initiated a wide-ranging program called Waste Reduction Always Pays—WRAP for short. The idea was that it would be more efficient (and less expensive) for the company to prevent pollution in the first place than to treat and dispose of pollutants at the "end of the pipe." The company reduced the use of hazardous chemicals in production, in order to cut down on waste. Where this was not possible, the company tried to recycle waste by-products. By the mid-1990s, WRAP had cut hazardous emissions by over 50 percent, saving the company $10.5 million annually. The company's president concluded that "the most compelling actions industry can take with respect to environmental protection are voluntary."[3]

In the 1990s, many political leaders, corporate executives, and environmental advocates—like those profiled in these examples—became increasingly concerned that old strategies for promoting environmental protection were failing and new approaches were necessary. In the United States, policymakers moved toward greater reliance on market-based mechanisms, rather than command and control regulations, to achieve environmental goals. Environmentalists engaged in greater dialogue with industry leaders. Many businesses pioneered new approaches to effective environmental management, including pollution prevention and waste minimization programs.

The challenge facing government, industry, and environmental advocacy organizations alike, as they tried out new approaches and improved on old ones, was how to further economic growth in an increasingly competitive and integrated world economy while at the same time promoting sustainable and ecologically sound business practices.

---

[2]"Environmentalists Try to Move Markets," *New York Times,* Aug. 22, 1993, p. E5; "An Alliance of Six Big Consumers Vows to Use More Recycled Paper," *New York Times,* Aug. 19, 1993, p. A1; and Jackie Prince and Richard Denison, "Developing an Environmental Action Plan for Business," in Rao V. Kolluru, ed., *Environmental Strategies Handbook: A Guide to Effective Policies and Practices,* pp. 239–258, New York: McGraw-Hill, 1994.

[3]Frank Popoff, "Pollution Prevention: No Longer a Pipe Dream," *Business Week,* Dec. 30, 1991; "Dow Chemical: Making Waste Reduction Pay," in Stephan Schmidheiny, *Changing Course: A Global Business Perspective on Development and the Environment,* pp. 265–270, Boston: MIT Press, 1992; "Dow Chemical: Environmental Policy and Practice," in Rogene A. Buchholz, Alfred E. Marcus, and James E. Post, eds., *Managing Environmental Issues: A Casebook,* pp. 211–225, Englewood Cliffs, NJ: Prentice Hall, 1992.

ROLE OF GOVERNMENT

The U.S. government has been involved in regulating business activities in order to protect the environment at least since the late nineteenth century, when the first federal laws were passed protecting navigable waterways. The government's role in environmental protection began to increase dramatically, however, around 1970, which marks the beginning of the modern environmental era.

Government has a major role to play in environmental regulation. Business firms have few incentives to minimize pollution, if their competitors do not. A single firm acting on its own to reduce discharges into a river, for example, would incur extra costs. If its competitors did not do the same, the firm might not be able to compete effectively and could go out of business. Government, by setting a common standard for all firms, can take the cost of pollution control "out of competition." It also can provide economic incentives to encourage businesses, communities, and regions to reduce pollution, and it can offer legal and administrative systems for resolving disputes.

Figure 12-1 summarizes the major federal environmental laws enacted by Congress since 1969. In adopting these laws, Congress was responding to strong public concerns and pressures to save the environment from further damage.

Accompanying these laws were new regulatory agencies and a strengthening of the powers of some existing government departments. Figure 12-2 diagrams the jurisdictional authority of several major federal agencies and departments relative to different types of environmental problems. The nation's main pollution control agency is the **Environmental Protection Agency (EPA).** It was created in 1970 to coordinate most of the government's efforts to protect the environment. Other government agencies involved in enforcing the nation's environmental laws include the Nuclear Regulatory Commission (NRC), the Occupational Safety and Health Administration (OSHA), and various regional, state, and local agencies.

Major Areas of Environmental Regulation

The federal government regulates in three major areas of environmental protection: air pollution, water pollution, and land pollution (solid and hazardous waste). This section will review the major issues and the laws in each, and briefly consider the special problem of cross-media pollution that cuts across all three areas.

Air pollution

Air pollution occurs when more pollutants are emitted into the atmosphere than can be safely absorbed and diluted by natural processes. Some pollution occurs naturally, such as smoke and ash from volcanoes

FIGURE 12-1
Leading U.S. environmental protection laws.

1969	National Environmental Policy Act	Created Council on Environmental Quality to oversee quality of the nation's environment.
1970	Clean Air Act	Established national air quality standards and timetables.
1972	Water Pollution Control Act	Established national goals and timetables for clean waterways.
1972	Pesticide Control Act	Required registration of and restrictions on pesticide use.
1973	Endangered Species Act	Conserved species of animals and plants whose survival was threatened or endangered.
1974	Safe Drinking Water Act	Authorized national standards for drinking water.
1974	Hazardous Materials Transport Act	Regulated shipment of hazardous materials.
1976	Resource Conservation and Recovery Act	Regulated hazardous materials from production to disposal.
1976	Toxic Substances Control Act	Established national policy to regulate, restrict, and (if necessary) ban toxic chemicals.
1977	Clean Air Act Amendments	Revised air standards.
1980 & 1986	Comprehensive Environmental Response Compensation and Liability Act (Superfund)	Established superfund and procedures to clean up hazardous waste sites.
1987	Clean Water Act amendments	Authorized funds for sewage treatment plants and waterways cleanup.
1990	Clean Air Act	Required cuts in urban smog, acid rain, greenhouse gas emissions; promoted alternative fuels.
1990	Pollution Prevention Act	Provided guidelines, training, and incentives to prevent or reduce pollution at the source.

and forest fires. But most air pollution today results from human activity, especially industrial processes and motor vehicle emissions. Air pollution degrades buildings, reduces crop yields, mars the beauty of natural landscapes, and harms people's health.

In 1994, the American Lung Association estimated that 115 million Americans, 45 percent of the population, were breathing unsafe air. According to one study, air pollution caused by particulate matter—such

FIGURE 12-2
Regulatory and
monitoring
jurisdiction of
major federal
pollution control
agencies.

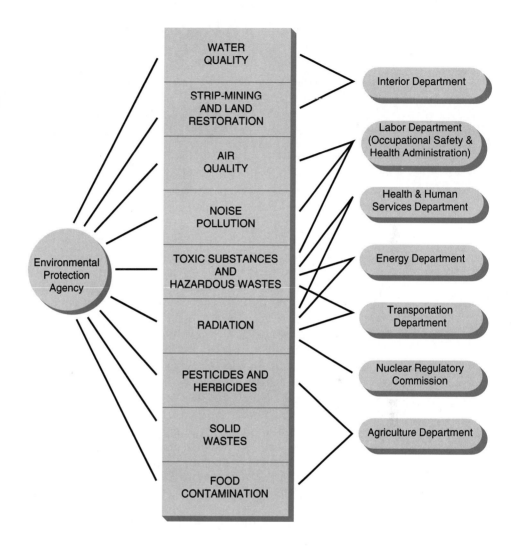

as emissions and dust from cars, trucks, smokestacks, mining, and construction activity—was responsible for as many as 60,000 premature or unnecessary deaths annually.[4]

EPA has identified seven criteria pollutants, relatively common harmful substances that serve as indicators of overall levels of air pollution. These are lead, carbon monoxide, hydrocarbons, total suspended particu-

[4]American Lung Association, "The Perils of Particulates," pamphlet, New York: Mar. 1994; and "Air Pollution and Your Health," pamphlet, New York: 1992; "Studies Say Soot Kills up to 60,000 in U.S. Each Year," *New York Times,* July 19, 1993, pp. A1, A16. EPA data for various pollutants are reported in Environmental Protection Agency, "National Air Pollution Emissions Trends 1900–1992," Washington, DC: Oct. 1993.

lates, sulfur dioxide, nitrogen dioxide, and ozone. (Ozone at ground level is a dangerous component of smog.) In addition, the agency also has identified a list of toxic air pollutants that are considered hazardous even in relatively small concentrations. These include asbestos, benzene, chloroform, dioxin, vinyl chloride, and radioactive materials. Emissions of toxic pollutants are strictly controlled.

A special problem of air pollution is **acid rain.** Acid rain is formed when emissions of sulfur dioxide and nitrogen oxides—by-products of the burning of fossil fuels by utilities, manufacturers, and motor vehicles—combine with natural water vapor in the air and fall to earth as rain or snow that is more acidic than normal. Acid rain can damage the ecosystems of lakes and rivers, reduce crop yields, and degrade forests. Structures, such as buildings and monuments, are also harmed. Within North America, acid rain is most prevalent in New England and eastern Canada, regions that are downwind of coal-burning utilities in the Midwestern states. Acid rain is especially difficult to regulate, because adverse consequences often occur far—often, hundreds of miles—away from the source of the pollution, sometimes across international borders.

The major law governing air pollution is the Clean Air Act, first passed in 1970 and most recently amended in 1990. The 1990 Clean Air Act toughened standards in a number of areas, including stricter restrictions on emissions of acid rain–causing chemicals.

Water pollution

Water pollution, like air pollution, occurs when more wastes are dumped into waterways than can be naturally diluted and carried away. Water can be polluted by organic wastes (untreated sewage), by the chemical by-products of industrial processes, and by the disposal of nonbiodegradable products (that do not naturally decay). Heavy metals and toxic chemicals, including some used as pesticides and herbicides, can be particularly persistent. Like poor air, poor water quality can decrease crop yields, threaten human health, and degrade the quality of life.

In April 1993 around 370,000 people in Milwaukee, Wisconsin, contracted diarrhea. The cause of the mass outbreak was discovered to be a parasite that had contaminated the municipal water supply, and residents were told to boil their water until the problem could be corrected. Health authorities suspected the source of the parasites might have been runoff of water from upstream farms with infected cattle.[5]

In the United States, regulations address both the pollution of rivers, lakes, and other surface bodies of water and the quality of the drinking water.

[5]World Resources Institute, *1994 Information Please Environmental Almanac,* Boston: Houghton Mifflin, pp. 67–70.

The nation's main law governing water pollution is the Water Pollution Control Act (also known as the Clean Water Act). This law aims to restore or maintain the integrity of all surface water in the United States. The Water Pollution Control Act requires permits for most *point* sources of pollution, such as industrial emissions, and mandates that local and state governments develop plans for *nonpoint* sources, such as agricultural runoff or urban storm water. The Pesticide Control Act specifically restricts the use of dangerous pesticides, which can pollute groundwater.

Drinking water quality is regulated by another law, the Safe Drinking Water Act of 1974, most recently amended in 1986. This law sets minimum standards for various contaminants in both public water systems and aquifers that supply drinking wells.

Land pollution

The third major focus of environmental regulation is the contamination of land by both solid and hazardous waste. The United States produces an astonishing 650 million tons of solid waste each year. About 250 million tons, 38 percent of the total, is considered hazardous and requires special treatment. Improperly disposed waste can leach into groundwater or evaporate into the air, posing a danger to public health. Many businesses and communities have established programs to recycle certain kinds of solid waste. Some of these programs are described in Exhibit 12-A.

Several federal laws address the problem of land contamination. The

EXHIBIT 12-A

RECYCLING: HOW SUCCESSFUL?

Recycling paper, steel and aluminum cans, and plastic and glass containers is becoming increasingly popular. In 1992, 5,400 U.S. communities had curbside recycling programs—five times as many as just four years earlier. At many college campuses, businesses, and government offices across the country, people are asked to separate out their trash for disposal in brightly marked containers. But what happens to all this carefully sorted trash? Unfortunately, the demand for recycled materials has not kept up with the supply. Two of the largest waste hauling companies, Waste Management Inc. and Browning-Ferris Industries, reported in 1993 that they were losing money on recycling. These companies spent $175 a ton to collect and sort recyclables but could sell them for only $44 a ton. Solutions to this problem will involve a combination of new technologies, government incentives, and private initiatives to develop new markets for used paper, glass, plastic, and metals. A promising development is the Buy Recycled Business Alliance, a group of companies—including American Airlines, Coca-Cola, and Rubbermaid—that has committed to increasing purchases of recycled materials.

SOURCE: World Resources Institute, *1994 Information Please Environmental Almanac*, Boston: Houghton Mifflin, pp. 93–98; David Biddle, "Recycling for Profit: The New Green Business Frontier," *Harvard Business Review*, Nov.–Dec. 1993, pp. 145–156; "Recycling: Is It Worth the Effort?" *Consumer Reports*, Feb. 1994, pp.92–98.

Toxic Substances Control Act of 1976 requires EPA to inventory the thousands of chemicals in commercial use, identify which are most dangerous, and, if necessary, ban them or restrict their use. For example, polychlorinated biphenyls (PCBs), dangerous chemicals formerly used in electrical transformers, were banned under this law. The Resource Conservation and Recovery Act of 1976 (amended in 1984) regulates hazardous materials from "cradle to grave." Toxic waste generators must have a permit, transporters must maintain careful records, and disposal facilities must conform to detailed regulations. All hazardous waste must be treated before disposal in landfills.

A promising new regulatory approach to waste management, sometimes called **source reduction,** was taken in the Pollution Prevention Act of 1990. This law aims to reduce pollution at the source, rather than treat and dispose of waste at the "end of the pipe." Pollution can be prevented, for example, by using less chemically intensive manufacturing processes, recycling, and better housekeeping and maintenance. Source reduction often saves money, protects worker health, and requires less abatement and disposal technology. The 1990 law provides guidelines, training, and incentives for companies to reduce waste.

The major U.S. law governing the cleanup of existing hazardous waste sites is the **Comprehensive Environmental Response, Compensation, and Liability Act (CERCLA),** popularly known as **Superfund,** passed in 1980. This law established a fund, supported primarily by a tax on petroleum and chemical companies who were presumed to have created a disproportionate share of toxic wastes. EPA was charged with establishing a National Priority List of the most dangerous toxic sites. Where the original polluters could be identified, they would be required to pay for the cleanup; where they could not be identified or had gone out of business, the Superfund would pay.

> An example of a hazardous waste site on EPA's list is the Brio Superfund site, two former waste disposal plants located near the Southbend subdivision outside Houston, Texas. Local wells have been polluted by dangerous chemicals like xylene, and a black tar-like substance has bubbled into driveways and garages. Air pollution is suspected as a possible cause of a rash of birth defects, and children have contracted leukemia and other serious illnesses. The once thriving community of 2,800 is now largely boarded up.[6]

Remarkably, one in four U.S. residents now lives within four miles of a Superfund site. The 1,200 or so sites originally placed on the National Priority List may be just the tip of the iceberg. Congressional researchers have said that as many as 10,000 other sites may need to be cleaned up.

Although Superfund's goals were laudable, it has been widely re-

[6]"Toxic Dumps," *Time,* Sept. 13, 1993, pp. 63–64.

garded as a public policy failure. Only slightly over 200 listed waste sites—about 17 percent of the total—had been cleaned up by 1994. Although little had been accomplished by the mid-1990s, the costs of the program had escalated dramatically. Some analysts estimated that the entire cleanup could cost as much as $1 trillion and take half a century to complete. In a debate on possible Superfund reforms, some policymakers argued that companies should be required to pay only for cleaning up the proportion of a waste site they were actually responsible for, with shares determined by a neutral arbitrator. Others called for clearer priorities for cleanup efforts, focusing attention first on sites posing the greatest risk to public health and those most amenable to remediation with currently available technology.[7]

Cross-media pollution

Cross-media pollution refers to pollution that cannot easily be blamed on any specific source, or medium. For example, hazardous wastes disposed in a landfill might leach out, contaminating groundwater, or evaporate, causing air pollution. The migration of pollutants has apparently become more frequent and severe in recent years. Unfortunately, cross-media pollution (also called multimedia pollution) is especially difficult to control, because laws and regulatory agencies tend to focus on particular kinds of pollution, such as air or water. Several states have experimented with an integrated approach designed to better control pollution from multiple sources. One place this approach has been tried is the Great Lakes region.

> Pollution in the Great Lakes comes from many sources, including discharge of waste into the lakes, airborne toxics, pesticide runoff from farmland, and landfill leaching. In the 1980s and early 1990s, regulators experimented with new approaches. For example, agencies responsible for these different pollutants have developed joint remedial plans for several contaminated "hot spots."[8]

New institutional arrangements like these will be needed to achieve integrated regulation of cross-media pollution.

Alternative Policy Approaches

Government can use a variety of policy approaches to control air, water, and land-based pollution. The most widely used method of regulation historically has been to impose environmental standards. Increasingly, how-

[7]"Can Clinton Clean Up the Superfund Morass?" *Business Week,* Feb. 14, 1994, p. 41; "Not So Super Superfund," *New York Times,* Feb. 7, 1994, p. A10.
[8]Barry G. Rabe and Janet B. Zimmerman, "Cross Media Environmental Integration in the Great Lakes Basin," *Environmental Law,* Fall 1992, pp. 253–279.

ever, government policymakers have relied more on market-based and voluntary approaches, rather than command and control regulations, to achieve environmental goals.

Environmental standards

The traditional method of pollution control is **environmental standards.** Standard allowable levels of various pollutants are established by legislation or regulatory action and applied by administrative agencies and courts. This approach is also called **command and control regulation,** because the government "commands" business firms to comply with certain standards and often directly "controls" their choice of technology.

One type of standard is an environmental-quality standard. In this approach a given geographical area is permitted to have no more than a certain amount or proportion of a pollutant, such as sulfur dioxide, in the air. Polluters are required to control their emissions to maintain the area's standard of air quality. A second type is an emission standard. For example, the law may specify that manufacturers can release into the air no more than 1 percent of the ash (a pollutant) they generate. Each business would then be required to install control equipment that removes at least 99 percent of the airborne ash. Emission standards, with some exceptions, are usually set by state and local regulators who are familiar with local industry and special problems caused by local topography and weather conditions.

A variation of this approach, used since the late 1970s, is the **bubble concept.** A large industrial plant may have many potential sources of pollution from numerous smokestacks, manufacturing processes, and pipes. At one time, environmental rules required that each one of these pollution sources conform to mandated standards. However, under the bubble concept, regulators treat an entire plant as if it were surrounded by an invisible plastic bubble, and they measure only the total pollution coming out of the top of the bubble. One or more smokestacks or discharge pipes may emit more pollutants than the law allows, but as long as the entire plant's total emissions do not violate air or water quality standards, it is considered to be in compliance.

To sum up, federal regulators decide how clean the air and water should be by establishing environmental-quality standards. Local regulators then impose direct emissions controls on polluting sources in order to achieve the federally mandated standards. Some people believe that businesses should be given more flexibility in how they meet government environmental standards. An example of how this might work is shown in Exhibit 12-B.

Market-based mechanisms

In recent years, regulators have begun to move away from command and control regulation, favoring increased use of market-based mechanisms.

EXHIBIT 12-B

> ### GIVING BUSINESSES MORE FLEXIBILITY IN COMPLYING WITH ENVIRONMENTAL REGULATIONS
>
> In the past, many businesses have criticized federal environmental regulations for being too rigid and not providing enough flexibility to meet environmental goals in the most efficient way.
>
> In Yorktown, Virginia, for example, Amoco Corporation was required under the 1990 Clean Air Act to rebuild its waste water treatment plant, at a cost of $31 million, to prevent the evaporation of benzene, a toxic chemical. But the major source of benzene at the refinery was actually not the waste water plant at all, but the York River terminal where oil was unloaded and gasoline was loaded onto ships. Controlling benzene at the terminal would have cost only $6 million. Bu the federal government at the time had no regulations requiring cleanup at marine loading terminals! The company's manager of environmental health and safety at the refinery commented, "Give us a goal to meet rather than all the regulations telling us what controls to put on what sources of pollution."
>
> In 1993, EPA began an effort to make it simpler and less expensive for businesses to comply with environmental rules. Its aims were to consolidate all the rules governing a particular industry into a single operating manual and to give businesses more flexibility in meeting broad objectives, such as reducing benzene emissions.
>
> SOURCE: "Unbending Regulations Incite Move to Alter Pollution Laws," *New York Times*, Nov. 29, 1993, pp. A1–A11.

This approach is based on the idea that the market is a better control than extensive standards that specify precisely what companies are to do.

One approach that has become more widely used is to allow businesses to buy and sell the right to pollute, as shown in the opening example of this chapter. The Clean Air Act of 1990 incorporated the concept of **tradable allowances** as a key part of its approach to pollution reduction. The law established emission levels and permitted companies that achieved emissions below the standard to sell their "rights" to the remaining permissible amount to other firms whose emissions were above the standard, and hence faced a penalty. Over time, the government would reduce permissible emission levels. The system would therefore gradually reduce overall emissions, even though individual companies might continue to pollute above the standard. Companies would have the flexibility to comply with the law in the most economical way, either by reducing their pollution or by buying allowances from others.

In 1992, the Tennessee Valley Association (TVA), an electric utility, purchased the right to emit 10,000 tons of sulfur dioxide, a chemical that causes acid rain, from Wisconsin Power and Light. The price was around $3 million. The transaction gave the TVA additional time to comply with the 1990 Clean Air Act. Wisconsin Power and Light, for its part, was able to profit from "overcomplying" with federal regulations.[9]

Although it may seem to contradict environmental goals, a market in pollution allowances may work well as a means of improving air and water quality at lower overall cost than would otherwise have been possible.

Another market-based type of pollution control is establishment of **emissions charges** or **fees.** Each business is charged for the undesirable waste that it emits, with the fee varying according to the amount of waste released. The result is, "The more you pollute, the more you pay." In recent years, both federal and state governments have experimented with a variety of so-called green taxes or eco-taxes that levy a fee on various kinds of environmentally destructive behavior. In some cases, the revenue from these taxes is specifically earmarked to support environmental improvement efforts.

In addition to taxing "bad" behavior, the government may also offer various types of positive incentives to firms that improve their environmental performance. For example, the government may decide to purchase only from those firms that meet a certain pollution standard, or it may offer aid to those that install pollution control equipment. Tax incentives, such as faster depreciation for pollution control equipment, also may be used.

In short, the trend in the 1990s is toward using more flexible, market-oriented approaches—tradable allowances, pollution fees and taxes, and incentives—to achieve environmental objectives where possible.

Information disclosure

Another approach to reducing pollution that became more widely used in the late 1980s and 1990s is popularly known as "regulation by publicity" or "regulation by embarrassment." The government encourages companies to pollute less by publishing information about the amount of pollutants individual companies emit each year. In many cases, companies take steps voluntarily to reduce their emissions, to avoid public embarrassment.

The major experiment in regulation by publicity has occurred in the area of toxic gas and liquid emissions. The 1986 amendments to the Superfund law (called "SARA") included a provision called the Community Right-to-Know Law, which requires manufacturing firms to report, for about 300 toxic chemicals, the amount on site, the number of pounds released, and how (if at all) these chemicals were treated or disposed of. EPA makes this information available to the public in the *Toxics Release Inventory*, or *TRI*, published annually.

From 1988 to 1991, reporting manufacturers in the United States cut their emissions of hazardous chemicals by 30 percent, according to *TRI*

---

[9]"Utility Is Selling Right to Pollute," *New York Times*, May 12, 1992, pp. A1, C5; and "New Rules Harness Power of Free Markets to Curb Air Pollution," *Wall Street Journal*, Apr. 14, 1992, pp. A1, A12.

data. Some of the biggest cuts were made by the worst polluters. These dramatic results were especially surprising to regulators, because many of the hazardous chemicals were not covered under clean air and water regulations at the time. The improvements, in many instances, had been completely voluntary. Apparently, fear of negative publicity had compelled many companies to act. "We knew the numbers were high, and we knew the public wasn't going to like it," one chemical industry executive explained.

The apparent success of this law prompted EPA in 1994 to expand the toxics release reporting program to include utilities, mines, and large recyclers as well as manufacturers, and to expand the list of chemicals that must be reported. In 1993, EPA tried a similar approach when it published its risk management program rule, requiring about 140,000 businesses to publish "worst case scenarios" and their plans to minimize risk. The agency's intention was to use public concern to force businesses to be more proactive in managing environmental risk.[10]

The advantages and disadvantages of alternative policy approaches to reducing pollution are summarized in Figure 12-3.

Civil and Criminal Enforcement

Traditionally, companies that violate environmental laws have been subject to civil penalties and fines. Increasingly, however, regulators have turned to the use of criminal statutes to prosecute companies and their executives who break these laws. Proponents of this approach argue that the threat of prison can be an effective deterrent to corporate "outlaws" who would otherwise degrade the air, water, or land. Since 1989, about 100 individuals and companies have been found guilty of environmental crimes each year. In 1992, for example, the owner of a Chicago metal plating factory was sentenced to fifteen months in prison. His crime was ordering a worker to pour 4,000 gallons of cyanide and cadmium waste down a floor drain. The toxic chemicals had killed 20,000 fish in the Chicago River and forced authorities to temporarily shut down a branch of the city sewer system.

In 1994, the U.S. Sentencing Commission, a government agency responsible for setting uniform penalties for violations of federal law, established new guidelines for sentencing environmental wrongdoers. Under these rules, penalties would reflect not only the severity of the offense but also a company's demonstrated environmental commitment. Businesses that have an active compliance program, cooperate with government investiga-

[10]EPA, *1991 Toxics Release Inventory,* Washington, DC: May 1993; David Hanson, "Toxic Release Inventory: Firms Make Strides in Cutting Emissions," *Chemical and Engineering News,* May 31, 1993; "An Embarrassment of Clean Air," *Business Week,* May 31, 1993, p. 34; "Industry Faces More Public Pressure," *Environmental Manager,* Nov. 1993.

FIGURE 12-3
Advantages and
disadvantages of
alternative policy
approaches to re-
ducing pollution.

Policy Approach	Advantages	Disadvantages
Environmental Standards	■ Enforceable in the courts ■ Compliance mandatory	■ Across-the-board standards not equally relevant to all businesses ■ Requires large regulatory apparatus ■ Older, less efficient plants may be forced to close
Market-Based Mechanisms		
Tradable allowances	■ Gives businesses more flexibility ■ Achieves goals at lower overall cost ■ Saves jobs by allowing some less efficient plants to stay open ■ Permits the government and private organizations to buy allowances to take them off the market	■ Gives business a "license to pollute" ■ Allowances are hard to set ■ May cause regional imbalances in pollution levels ■ Enforcement is difficult
Emissions fees and taxes	■ Taxes "bad" behavior (pollution) rather than "good" behavior (profits)	■ Fees are hard to set ■ Taxes may be too low to curb pollution
Government incentives	■ Rewards environmentally responsible behavior ■ Encourages companies to exceed minimum standards	■ Incentives may not be strong enough to curb pollution
Information Disclosure	■ Government spends little on enforcement ■ Companies able to reduce pollution in the most cost-effective way	■ Does not motivate all companies

tors, and promptly assist any victims would receive lighter sentences than others with no environmental programs or that knowingly violate the law. These guidelines provided an incentive for businesses to develop active compliance programs to protect themselves and their officers from high fines or even prison if a violation should occur.[11]

COSTS AND BENEFITS OF ENVIRONMENTAL REGULATION

One of the central issues of environmental protection is costs, and how these are balanced by benefits. In the quarter century or so since the modern environmental era began, the nation has spent a great deal to clean up the environment and keep it clean. Some have questioned the value choices underlying these expenditures, suggesting that the costs—in terms of lost jobs, reduced capital investment, and lowered productivity—exceeded the benefits. Others, in contrast, point to significant gains in the quality of life and to the economic payoff of a cleaner environment.

As a nation, the United States has invested heavily in cleaning up the environment. Figure 12-4 shows how much has been spent on pollution control in the United States in recent years and how much will be spent in the year 2000. According to a study by the Environmental Protection Agency,

[11]"A Warning Shot to Scare Polluters Straight," *Business Week,* Nov. 22, 1993, p. 60; *Final Report of the Advisory Working Group on Environmental Offenses,* Washington, DC: United States Sentencing Commission, Nov. 1993; and World Resources Institute, *1994 Information Please Environmental Almanac,* Boston: Houghton Mifflin, p. 26.

FIGURE 12-4
How much has been spent on pollution control in the United States and how much will be spent in the year 2000.

SOURCE: EPA, *Environmental Investments: The Cost of a Clean Environment,* 1990.

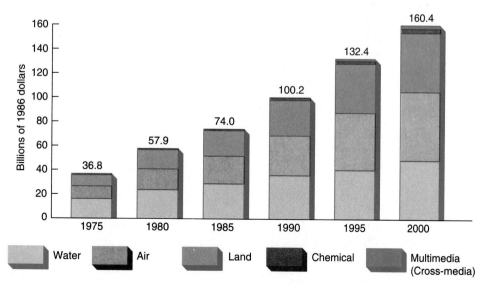

by 1990 environmental spending exceeded $100 billion a year, about 2 percent of the nation's gross national product. Pollution control expenditures were predicted to reach around $160 billion annually by the year 2000. Business spending to comply with environmental regulation has diverted funds that might otherwise have been invested in new plants and equipment, and sometimes strict rules have led to plant shutdowns and loss of jobs. One economist estimated that the U.S. economy will be nearly 3 percent smaller in the year 2000 than it would have been if the environmental laws enacted between 1970 and 1990 had never been passed.[12]

Some regions and industries, in particular, have been hard hit by environmental regulation, especially those with high abatement costs, such as paper and wood products, chemicals, petroleum and coal, and primary metals. Economists often find it difficult, however, to sort out what proportion of job loss in an industry is attributable to environmental regulation, and what proportion is attributable to other causes. For example, the oil industry witnessed a net loss of tens of thousands of jobs in the 1980s. Some economists blamed environmental regulations, such as restrictions on drilling off-shore and in the Alaskan wilderness. But others pointed to declining oil prices on the world market and increased drilling costs as more important factors. No one knew for sure.

The costs of environmental regulation must be balanced against the benefits. In many areas, the United States has made great progress in cleaning up the environment, as these figures show.

- Emissions of nearly all major pollutants in the United States have dropped substantially since 1970, when the Environmental Protection Act was passed. EPA estimated that by 1988, for example, carbon monoxide in the air was just 43 percent of what it would have been without controls; particulates, 30 percent; and volatile organic compounds (that cause smog), 58 percent. Lead in the air was just 3 percent of what it would have been without regulations. Peak levels of ground-level ozone have dropped to a quarter of what they were in 1955 in Los Angeles, despite huge increases in population and vehicle traffic.
- Water quality has also improved. For example, industrial discharges of several damaging pollutants dropped over 90 percent during the first decade the Water Pollution Control Act was in effect. Many lakes and riverways were restored to ecological health. The Cuyahoga River in Ohio, for example, which at one time was badly polluted by industrial waste, by the mid-1990s had been restored to the point where residents could fish and even swim in the river.

[12]Dale W. Jorgenson and Peter J. Wilcoxen, "Impact of Environmental Legislation on U.S. Economic Growth, Investment, and Capital Costs," *U.S. Environmental Policy and Economic Growth: How Do We Fare?* Washington, DC: American Council for Capital Formation, 1992.

Of course, it is hard to measure the value of benefits like cleaner air, rivers, and lakes. One approach, developed by regulators in the early 1990s, is called **contingent valuation.** In this approach, public opinion surveys are conducted to assess the relative value of intangible benefits to the public. The results can be used to help guide government policymakers or to assess liability. For example, the state of Alaska commissioned a study in which a random sample of 1,000 Americans were asked how much they would be willing to pay to avoid an accident similar to the 1989 wreck of the oil tanker *Exxon Valdez,* which caused significant environmental damage to the Alaskan coastline. The average answer was about $30. State attorneys planned to use the results in court to help establish the magnitude of Exxon's liability.[13]

Environmental regulations also stimulate some sectors of the economy. The environmental services and products industry, for example, has grown dramatically since the mid-1980s. While jobs are being lost in industries like forest products and coal mining, others are being created in areas like environmental consulting, asbestos abatement, instrument manufacturing, waste management equipment, and air pollution control. Other jobs are saved or created in industries like fishing and tourism when natural areas are protected or restored. In some cases, regulation prompts innovation. Some companies have been able to commercially exploit technologies developed to comply with environmental regulations, as illustrated by the following example.

> At its huge copper smelter outside of Salt Lake City, Utah, Kennecott Corp. engineers devised an ingenious method to capture sulfur in processed ore, cutting emissions of acid-rain producing sulfur dioxide by a dramatic 96 percent. Kennecott managers hope to sell the innovative process to other companies, particularly in Latin America, where governments have begun to toughen environmental regulations.[14]

Moreover, environmental regulations can stimulate the economy by compelling businesses to become more efficient by conserving energy.

Because of the complexity of these issues, economists differ on the *net* costs and benefits of environmental regulation. In some respects, government controls hurt the economy, and in other ways they help, as summarized in Figure 12-5. What is clear is that choices in the area of environmental regulation reflect underlying values, expressed in a democratic society through an open political process. Just how much a society is prepared to pay—and how "clean" it wants to be—are political choices, reflecting the give and take of diverse interests in a pluralistic society.

[13]"Polls May Help Government Decide the Worth of Nature," *New York Times,* Sept. 6, 1993, pp. A1, A20.
[14]"Escape from Dante's Inferno," *Business Week,* Dec. 21, 1992, p. 86A.

FIGURE 12-5
Costs and benefits
of environmental
regulations.

Costs	Benefits
■ $160 billion a year spent by business and individuals in the United States by 2000	■ Emissions of nearly all pollutants have dropped since 1970
■ U.S. economy 3 percent smaller in 2000 than it would have been without environmental laws passed since 1970	■ Air and water quality improved, some toxic waste sites cleaned; improved health; natural beauty preserved or enhanced
■ Competitiveness of capital-intensive, "dirty" industries adversely affected	■ Growth of other industries, such as environmental products and services, tourism, and fishing

THE GREENING OF MANAGEMENT

Environmental considerations touch all aspects of a business's operations. Modern environmental problems affect the management of a company's operations, marketing, human resources, and other activities. Strategic and operational decisions about such matters as where to locate facilities, what product lines to develop, and environmental, health, and safety standards are all affected by environmental considerations. How a firm fuels its fleet of cars or trucks (with gasoline or alternative fuels), designs energy efficiency into its facilities, organizes employee transportation services, minimizes toxics in manufacturing, and communicates about all of these to communities and government officials affect its environmental profile.

Even such areas as finance and accounting are directly influenced by these issues. For example, courts have ruled that the purchaser of real estate—such as a site of a former gas station contaminated by leaking tanks—assumes the full environmental liability for that property. Companies that merge or acquire other businesses are thus buying potential environmental liabilities as well as assets. In an era when media, government officials, and the general public are interested in these matters, environmental performance has become a focal point for management.

Stages of Corporate Environmental Responsibility

Although environmental issues are forcing all businesses to manage in new ways, not all companies are equally "green," meaning proactive in their response to environmental issues. Researchers have identified five stages of environmental responsibility, depicted in Figure 12-6.

FIGURE 12-6

A five-stage model of corporate environmental responsibility.

Commitment of Organization			
Developmental Stage	**General Mindset of Corporate Managers**	**Resource Commitment**	**Support and Involvement of Top Management**
Beginner	Environmental management is unnecessary	Minimal resource commitment	No involvement
Fire Fighter	Environmental issues should be addressed only as necessary	Budgets for problems as they occur	Piecemeal involvement
Concerned Citizen	Environmental management is a worthwhile function	Consistent, yet minimal budget	Commitment in theory
Pragmatist	Environmental management is an important business function	Generally sufficient funding	Aware and moderately involved
Proactivist	Environmental management is a priority item	Open-ended funding	Actively involved

According to this model, companies pass through five distinct stages in the development of **"green" management** practices. At the *beginner* level, managers ignore potential liability and dismiss the need for specialized environmental programs. Environmental responsibility, if addressed at all, is added onto other programs and positions. Beginners might include older firms established before the modern environmental era, small firms that feel they cannot afford specialized programs, or simply companies in industries where regulatory oversight is perceived to be minimal. *Fire fighters,* companies at the next developmental stage, address environmental issues only when they pose an immediate threat, such as when an unexpected accident or spill occurs. Environmental management is seen as an exception to "business as usual."

Companies as *concerned citizens,* at the third stage, believe environmental protection is worthwhile and may even have specialized staff but devote few resources and little top management attention to "green" issues. *Pragmatists* actively manage environmental issues, have well-funded programs, and evaluate risk as well as immediate problems. In addition to having all the programmatic elements of pragmatists, *proactivists*—companies in the final stage of development—also have senior executives who champion environmental responsibility, extensive training, and strong links between environmental staff and other parts of the organization.

Research shows that most firms are still in the early stages in their development of "green" management practices, with no more than 10 to 25 percent of all companies in the United States now at the proactivist stage. A majority of corporations are now in transition, with many moving from lower to higher stages in the developmental sequence.[15]

Elements of Effective Environmental Management

Companies that have been successful in their environmental management have learned that new structures, processes, and incentives are often needed. Some of the organizational elements that many proactive "green" companies share are the following.[16]

Top managers with environmental responsibilities

One step many companies have taken is to give environmental managers greater authority and access to top levels of the corporation. By 1991, 49 of the *Fortune* 100 companies had a vice president for environmental affairs. These individuals often supervised extensive staffs of specialists and coordinated the work of managers in many areas, including research and development, marketing, and operations.

Dialogue with stakeholders

Environmentally proactive companies also engage in dialogue with external stakeholders, such as environmental organizations. Dow Chemical Corporation, for example, has set up a Corporate Environmental Advisory Council, a group of outside environmental advocates who are regularly invited to the company's headquarters for discussions with top executives and board members about environmental issues facing the company. Many local Dow Chemical facilities have established community advisory panels.

[15]Kurt Fischer and Johan Schot, *Environmental Strategies for Industry: International Perspectives on Research Needs and Policy Implications*, Washington, DC: Island Press, 1993; James E. Post and Barbara W. Altman, "Models of Corporate Greening: How Corporate Social Policy and Organizational Learning Inform Leading-Edge Environmental Management," *Research in Corporate Social Performance and Policy*, vol. 23, 1992, pp. 3–29.

[16]J. Ladd Greeno, "Corporate Environmental Excellence and Stewardship," in Rao V. Kolluru, ed., *Environmental Strategies Handbook: A Guide to Effective Policies and Practices*, pp. 43–64, New York: McGraw-Hill, 1994; Patricia S. Dillon and Kurt Fischer, *Environmental Management in Corporations: Methods and Motivations*, Medford, MA: Tufts University Center for Environmental Management, 1992; Anne T. Lawrence and David Morell, "Leading-Edge Environmental Management: Motivation, Opportunity, Resources, and Processes," *Research in Corporate Social Performance and Policy*, supp. 1, 1995, pp. 99–127.

Line manager involvement

Environmental staff experts and specialized departments are most effective when they work closely with the people who carry out the company's daily operations. For this reason, many "green" companies involve line managers and workers directly in the process of change. At the Park Plaza Hotel in Boston, "green teams" of employees make suggestions ranging from energy-efficient windows to refillable bottles of soap and shampoo.

Codes of environmental conduct

Environmentally proactive companies put their commitment in writing, often in the form of a code of conduct that spells out the firm's environmental goals.

Cross-functional teams

Another organizational element is the use of ad-hoc, cross-functional teams to solve environmental problems, including individuals from different departments. These teams pull together key players with the skills and resources to get the job done, wherever they are located in the corporate structure. At Lockheed Missiles and Space Corporation's facility in Sunnyvale, California, a Pollution Prevention Committee includes representatives from each of the five major business areas within the company. Each year, the committee selects about a dozen projects from among many proposed from each area. Interdivisional, cross-functional teams are set up to work on approved projects, such as one to recycle waste water.

Rewards and incentives

Business people are most likely to consider the environmental impacts of their actions when their organizations acknowledge and reward this behavior. The "greenest" organizations tie the compensation of their managers—including line managers—to environmental achievement and take steps to recognize these achievements publicly.

Environmental audits

"Green" companies closely track their progress towards environmental goals. Some have full-blown **environmental audits** (comparable to the ethics audits discussed in Chapter 5) that periodically review environmental initiatives. National Semiconductor Corporation, for example, initiated a new audit protocol in 1993 that scores company facilities in such areas as air pollution control, water pollution control, hazardous waste management, and groundwater protection. Audits can assess progress and also help spread good ideas across a company. At least two dozen major U.S. firms now publish annual environmental progress reports.

Interorganizational alliances

Many firms have formed alliances with others to promote mutual environmental goals. For example, the Chemical Manufacturers Association started a program called Responsible Care, committing its member companies to work together to respond to public concerns about chemicals.

Many of these programmatic elements represent specific applications of the general model of corporate social responsiveness presented in Chapter 3. This model describes how companies identify a social problem (in this case, environmental degradation), learn how to tackle it, and finally institutionalize procedures to address the problem on an ongoing, routine basis.

Voluntary Initiatives by Business

In recent years, many U.S. businesses have taken voluntary steps to manage in an ecologically sound way. Figure 12-7 presents the "top ten" best-managed U.S. firms, from an environmental perspective, according to the editors of *Fortune* magazine.

- Herman Miller, a maker of office furniture, was cited for its recycling efforts. The company sells fabric scraps to the auto industry for use as car linings; leather trim to luggage makers for attache cases; and vinyl to stereo makers for sound-deadening material. Herman Miller also buys back its used furniture from businesses, so it can refurbish and resell it. Tropical woods are purchased only from suppliers using sustainable forestry practices.

FIGURE 12-7
What companies are most proactive with respect to their environmental management?

THE TOP TEN ENVIRONMENTAL LEADERS, 1993

Company[1]	Industry
Apple Computer	Computers
AT&T	Telecommunications
Church & Dwight	Cosmetics and soaps
Clorox	Cosmetics and soaps
Digital Equipment	Computers
Dow Chemical	Chemicals
H. B. Fuller	Chemicals
Herman Miller	Furniture
IBM	Computers
Xerox	Office equipment

[1]Companies are arranged in alphabetical order.

- The Sun Company (parent of Sunoco), although not on the top ten list, was praised by *Fortune* as one of the most improved companies it studied. Sun was the first major company to sign the CERES Principles developed by the Coalition for Environmentally Responsible Economies. (These were formerly known as the Valdez Principles.) The CERES Principles are a corporate code that calls for management commitment to sound environmental policy and sustainable use of natural resources.
- Xerox, a company that makes copy machines and other office equipment, redesigned many products to be more earth-friendly, introducing such features as double-sided copying (to save paper), recyclable cartridges, and energy-saving devices. An extensive waste minimization program cut almost three-quarters of the company's hazardous waste over a seven-year period.

Fortune's top ten companies, like many other U.S. businesses, have found ways to run their businesses in more ecologically sound ways, while remaining competitive in the global marketplace.

SUMMARY POINTS OF THIS CHAPTER

- The United States regulates in three major areas of environmental protection: air pollution, water pollution, and land pollution. Environmental laws have traditionally been of the command and control type, specifying standards and results. New laws have added market incentives to induce environmentally sound behavior and have encouraged companies to reduce pollution at the source.
- Environmental laws have brought many benefits. Air, water, and land pollution levels are in many cases lower than in 1970. But some improvements have come at a high cost. A continuing challenge is to find ways to promote a clean environment and sustainable business practices without impairing the competitiveness of U.S. firms.
- Companies pass through five distinct stages in the development of "green" management practices. Many businesses are now moving from lower to higher stages.
- All business functions are affected by environmental issues, especially manufacturing, marketing, and product development. Effective environmental management thus requires an integrated approach that involves all parts of the business organization. Many companies have taken voluntary steps to manage in an ecologically sound way.

KEY TERMS AND CONCEPTS USED IN THIS CHAPTER

- Environmental Protection Agency (EPA)
- Acid rain
- Source reduction
- Superfund (CERCLA)
- Cross-media pollution
- Environmental standards
- Command and control regulation
- Bubble concept
- Tradable allowances
- Emissions charges or fees
- Contingent valuation
- "Green" management
- Environmental audits

DISCUSSION CASE

LOCATING A TOXIC WASTE FACILITY: RACISM OR OPPORTUNITY?

In November 1993, two of the nation's largest waste management companies, Hughes Environmental Systems (a subsidiary of General Motors) and USPCI (a subsidiary of Union Pacific Corporation), announced plans to build jointly a toxic waste disposal facility in Noxubee County, Mississippi. The proposal immediately became the focus of a rancorous controversy.

Noxubee County, located in east-central Mississippi, is one of the poorest in the state. The county also has the state's highest proportion of black residents—70 percent—and one of the highest rates of unemployment. If approved, the disposal facility would be one of the biggest in the South, capable of processing 200,000 tons a year of toxic waste, much of it imported from other states.

The community itself was deeply divided. One group supported the proposed disposal facility. "We have an opportunity to develop minority-owned businesses," said this group's leader, an African-American political organizer. "We can give our young people something to help them. When you're poor and got nothing, you're willing to live with a little more risk."

Others were opposed, however, arguing that racism had been a factor in the company's decision to site the facility in a predominantly minority community. A group called African Americans for Environmental Justice came out against the project. Protect the Environment of Noxubee County, a multiracial group that included local fishery operators, also sought to block the waste disposal site.

The companies involved vigorously defended themselves against charges of racism, arguing that the geology of Noxubee County—which lies on a layer of impermeable chalk that could serve as a natural barrier of toxic chemicals—was well suited to their purposes.

The controversy in Noxubee County was part of a larger debate in the nation as a whole. Studies by EPA, the General Accounting Office, and the United Church of Christ showed that waste sites were most often located in black or Hispanic communities. The same month that Hughes and USPCI made their proposal, EPA announced it would investigate whether state permits for hazardous waste sites violated civil rights laws. This announcement cast uncertainty over many siting decisions, including the one in Noxubee County.[17]

Discussion Questions

1. The term "environmental racism" has been used to describe the deliberate siting of hazardous waste sites near predominantly minority communities. Do you believe that this case represents an example of environmental racism? Why or why not?
2. If you were a resident of Noxubee County, what factors would influence your decision either to support or oppose the proposed waste facility?
3. If you were the manager of one of the waste management companies involved in this case, what factors would you take into consideration in selecting a new facility site? What steps would you take to deal with this particular controversy?
4. Are the waste management companies acting ethically, being socially responsible, showing a socially responsive management style, and/or being environmentally responsible? Use concepts from this and other chapters in answering.

[17]"Plan for Toxic Dump Pits Blacks against Blacks," *New York Times,* Dec. 13, 1993, p. A7; "U.S. to Weigh Blacks' Complaints about Pollution," *New York Times,* Nov. 18, 1993, p. A16; Christopher Boerner and Thomas Lambert, "Environmental Justice?" Center for the Study of American Business, Occasional Paper 136, Apr. 1994, pp. 1–29.

PART SIX

PART SIX

Responding to Primary Stakeholders

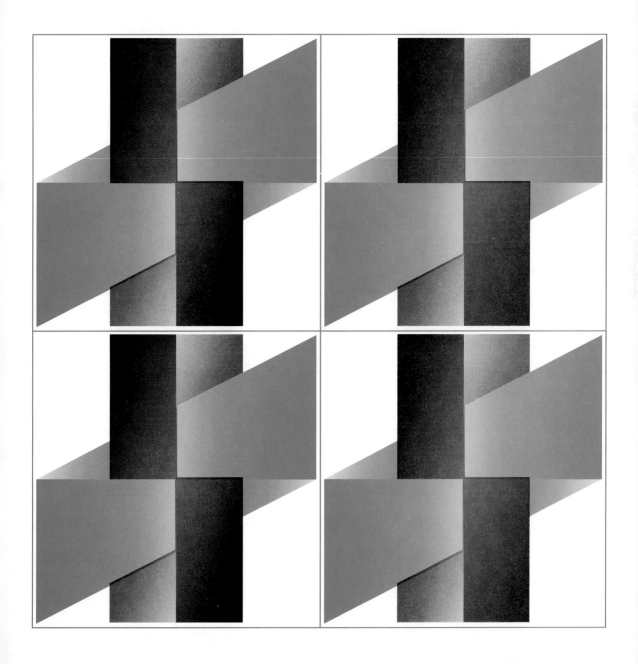

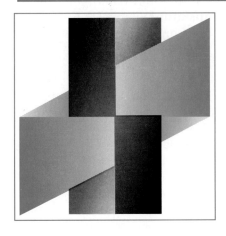

13

Stockholders and Corporate Governance

Stockholders occupy a position of central importance in the corporation because they are the company's legal owners and because they expect high levels of economic performance. But the corporation is not always run solely for their benefit, so they contend with management and the board of directors for control of company policies. Recent changes in corporate governance have strengthened the influence of stockholders and increased the attention given to this stakeholder group by managers and boards of directors.

Key Questions and Chapter Objectives

This chapter focuses on these key questions and objectives:

- Who are stockholders and what are their goals and legal rights?
- Who controls the corporation?
- How has the power of stockholders, relative to that of boards of directors and managers, shifted in recent years?
- What have social activist investors done to change corporate policies?
- What are the pros and cons of employee ownership of corporations?
- Are top corporate executives paid too much?
- How are stockholders affected by insider trading, and how does the government protect against stock market abuses?

In January 1993, American Express (Amex) bowed to pressure from its largest shareholder, J. P. Morgan (a bank), and forced the resignation of its chairman and CEO. The bank, along with several mutual funds that also owned big blocs of stock, had been meeting with Amex's board of directors for several months to voice their dissatisfaction with management. The dramatic ouster was just the latest in a string of such events. The very same week, IBM and Westinghouse Electric also announced the resignations of their top executives, after unhappy institutional investors—including big pension funds like the California Public Employees Retirement System (Calpers)—had clamored for change. "Shareholders have suddenly pulled together as a power base," said the head of a company that assisted companies conduct shareholder votes.

Sisters of the Blessed Sacrament, a small Catholic religious order based in Philadelphia, placed a resolution on the 1992 shareholder ballot of Procter & Gamble, seeking information about its executives' compensation. The nuns, who owned 100 shares of stock in the large consumer products company, were part of a broad coalition of social activist investors. Although the ballot measure received only 17 percent of the vote, Procter & Gamble sent one of its vice presidents to meet with the Sisters. The company agreed to release additional information to the public, and the religious order said it would withdraw its resolution from the following year's ballot. "It's a win-win type of thing," said the chairwoman of the order's Justice Commission. "We were all pleased with the dialogue."

In Mexico, a steel company called *Tubos de Acero de México* made an offer to sell stock that favored a large Argentine stockholder. The State of Wisconsin Investment Board—a state employees' pension fund and the second largest stockholder in the company—objected vigorously and sent a mailing in Spanish to other shareholders stating its case. The pension board lost the vote, but its attorney said that it had "sent a message to the Mexican market that foreign shareholders expect to be treated fairly." This incident was part of what many observers saw as a spread of shareholder activism from the United States to other countries, following the growing globalization of stock trading.[1]

What motivates a major institutional investor like J. P. Morgan or Calpers to challenge the top management of companies like American Express or IBM? Why do managers of big companies pay attention to the wishes of investors such as the Sisters of the Blessed Sacrament? How have foreign companies responded to challenges from stockholders from both the United States and other countries? Each of these examples and the questions they raise involve the complex relationship between the corporation and its legal owners, the stockholders. Management and boards of directors face very difficult issues in responding to corporate owners and balancing their demands with other company goals. This chapter addresses this important set of issues and relationships.

---

[1] "Shareholders Exercise New Power with Nation's Biggest Companies," *New York Times*, Feb. 1, 1993, pp. A1, C5; "They Heard the Order, and Obeyed: How 300 Nuns Got Procter & Gamble to Reveal Its Rationale on Executive Pay," *Washington Post*, Aug. 27, 1993, pp. B1–B2; and "Exporting Shareholder Activism," *New York Times*, July 16, 1993, pp. C1–C2.

STOCKHOLDERS

Stockholders (or shareholders, as they also are called) are the legal owners of business corporations. By purchasing a "share" of the company's stock, they become part owners of the company. For this reason, stockholder-owners have a big stake in how well their company performs. The firm's managers must pay close attention to their needs and assign a high priority to their interests in the company.

Who Are Stockholders?

Two types of stockholders own shares of stock in U.S. corporations: individual people and institutions.

Individual investors

As early as the 1920s, the public at large became significant owners of corporate stock. By 1990, their numbers had grown to over 51 million individuals. Two in every five households now include at least one shareholder. People from practically every occupational group own stock: professionals, managers, clerks, craft workers, farmers, retired persons, and even unemployed adults. Although men make up almost two-thirds of all active investors, individuals buying stock for the first time are now equally split between men and women.[2]

Institutional investors

In addition to the many individuals who have direct ownership in corporations, tens of millions more are indirect owners through personal savings and investments in insurance companies, pension funds, mutual funds, churches, and university endowments. These institutions then invest their funds by buying shares of stock in corporations. Like individual shareholders, the institutions then become direct owners, and the individual savers are indirect owners. The New York Stock Exchange estimates that over one-half of the U.S. population has an indirect ownership interest in corporations. Generally, anyone who owns a life insurance policy, participates in a pension or deferred profit-sharing plan, or buys mutual fund shares may be considered an indirect shareowner. Thus, many millions of people have a direct or indirect stake in the performance of business corporations.

Since the 1960s, the growth of **institutional investors** has been phenomenal because more and more people have purchased insurance policies, invested in mutual funds, and joined pension funds for their retirement years. Studies by the securities industry showed that in 1993,

[2]New York Stock Exchange, "Shareownership, 1990."

institutions accounted for 51 percent of the value of all equities (stocks) owned in the United States, worth a total of $3.1 *trillion*—more than three times the value of institutional holdings a decade earlier.[3]

Figure 13-1 shows the relative stock holdings of individual and institutional investors from the mid-1960s to 1993. It shows the growing influence of the institutional sector of the market over the past three decades.

Objectives of Stock Ownership

Individuals and institutions own corporate stock for a number of reasons.

Economic objective
Foremost among these reasons is the goal of receiving an economic gain or return on investment. Since such money could have been placed in a bank where interest would be earned with relatively little risk, investors

[3]Securities Industry Association, "Holdings of U.S. Equities Outstanding," New York: 1994. These data are based on analysis of the Federal Reserve Bank's "flow of funds" accounts.

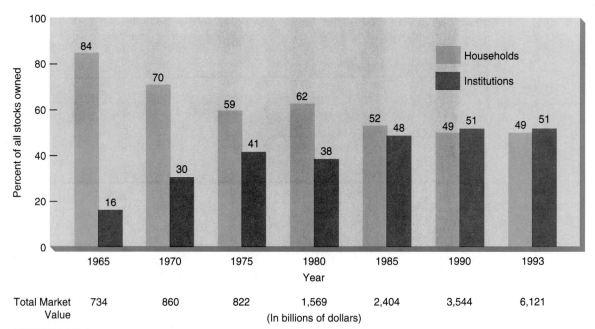

FIGURE 13-1

Individual household vs. institutional ownership of stock in the United States, 1965–1993.

SOURCE: Securities Industry Association, based on Federal Reserve Flow of Funds Accounts. Used by permission.

choose stocks because they believe stocks will produce a gain greater than could be had from placing the funds in a bank. Different types of corporate ownership produce varying levels of return through dividends and an increase in the stock price. A company that pays a relatively high dividend (6 to 7 percent) is not likely to have rapid price appreciation. Conversely, a company with good growth prospects and whose stock is likely to appreciate in price can choose to pay a lower dividend, if any at all, and still attract investors. Investors are thereby free to choose companies that are less speculative or more speculative depending on their personal goals and willingness to assume risk.

Social objective

Some investors use stock ownership to achieve a social or ethical objective. A growing number of mutual funds and pension funds screen companies in which they invest, weeding out ones that pollute the environment, discriminate against their employees, or make dangerous products like tobacco or weapons. In 1992, according to the Social Investment Forum, $200 billion in the United States was invested in mutual funds or pensions using social responsibility as an investment criterion, up from $40 billion just eight years earlier.[4] Social criteria may also be used when selling stocks. In the 1970s and 1980s, many individuals and institutions sold stocks of companies that did business in South Africa because of that country's discriminatory racial policies. With South Africa's transition to multiracial democracy in 1994, many bans on investment there were lifted, and the attention of social investors shifted to other countries. Some called for "divestment" (sale of stock) from companies that had operations in China, where some products were made by forced labor, and Burma, where a repressive military regime had been accused of human rights abuses.[5]

Mixed objectives

Many investors, whether individuals or institutions, invest with both economic and social objectives in mind. They are interested in receiving a good return but also want to invest in socially responsible companies. Such investors require their stockbrokers or investment advisers to apply both social and economic criteria they regard as important to the purchase and sale of stock. Some managers of mutual funds that apply social criteria in selecting stocks have argued that this approach may increase economic returns, since socially responsible companies may perform better in the long term.

[4]"Do-Good Investing Often Results in Good Profits Too," *San Jose Mercury News,* Mar. 22, 1993, p. 12F.
[5]Simon Billenness, "Beyond South Africa: New Frontiers in Corporate Responsibility," *Business and Society Review,* Summer 1993, pp. 28–31.

Corporate control

There are other reasons for investing in corporate stock. Some investors—including corporate "raiders"—are interested in gaining control of the corporation. This may be for the purpose of merging it with another firm or selling its assets to buyers who will pay more for the parts than for the whole company. Many of the takeovers of the 1980s were of this type. Such investments also may have a long-term economic purpose, but the immediate objective is to take control of the company and its assets. Other investors may purchase stock in order to influence management strategy, perhaps by gaining a seat on the board of directors.

STOCKHOLDERS' LEGAL RIGHTS AND SAFEGUARDS

In order to protect their financial stake in the companies whose stocks they hold, stockholders have several legal safeguards. Specific rights of stockholders are established by law. Stockholders have the following legal rights, and these vary somewhat among states: They have the right to share in the profits of the enterprise if dividends are declared by directors. They have the right to receive annual reports of company earnings and company activities, and they have the right to inspect the corporate books, provided they have a legitimate business purpose for doing so and that it will not be disruptive of business operations. They have the right to elect directors and to hold those directors and the officers of the corporation responsible for their acts, by lawsuit if they want to go that far. Furthermore, they usually have the right to vote on mergers, some acquisitions, and changes in the charter and bylaws, and to bring other business-related proposals before the stockholders. And finally, they have the right to sell their stock. Figure 13-2 summarizes the major legal rights of stockholders.

Many of these rights are exercised at the annual stockholders' meeting, where directors and managers present an annual report and shareholders have an opportunity to approve or disapprove of management's plans.

FIGURE 13-2
Major legal rights of stockholders.

- To receive dividends, if declared
- To vote on: Members of board of directors
                 Major mergers and acquisitions
                 Charter and bylaw changes
                 Proposals by stockholders
- To receive annual reports on the company's financial condition
- To bring shareholder suits against the company and officers
- To sell their own shares of stock to others

Approval is generally expressed by reelecting incumbent directors, and disapproval may be shown by attempting to replace them with new directors. Because most corporations today are large, typically only a small portion of stockholders attend to vote in person. Those not attending are given an opportunity to vote by absentee ballot (called a "proxy"). The use of proxy elections by stockholders to influence corporate policy is discussed later in this chapter.

Stockholder Lawsuits

If stockholders think that they or their company have been damaged by actions of company officers or directors, they have the right to bring lawsuits in the courts. These **shareholder lawsuits** can be of two kinds.

If stockholders are directly and personally damaged by actions of the company's officers, they can sue in court to recover their losses. Such *individual* shareholder lawsuits are intended to reimburse stockholders directly and personally. (These lawsuits may be brought either by individual shareholders or by a group of individuals in a class action.) For example, shareholders of Seagate Technology, a California-based maker of hard-disk drives for personal computers, filed several lawsuits after the company's stock price dropped suddenly. Stockholders said that management failed to disclose information that could adversely affect the value of their holdings, and asked for monetary damages.[6] On the other hand, in a shareholder's *derivative* lawsuit, damages are awarded to the corporation. In these lawsuits, disgruntled stockholders are trying to protect the corporation's assets and not just their own personal investments. Shareholder suits are initiated to check many abuses, including insider trading, an inadequate price obtained for the company's stock in a buyout or takeover, lush executive pension benefits, or fraud committed by company officials.

Corporate Disclosures

Giving stockholders more and better company information is one of the best ways to safeguard their interests. The theory behind the move for greater disclosure of company information is that the stockholder, as an investor, should be as fully informed as possible in order to make sound investments. By law, stockholders have a right to know about the affairs of the corporations in which they hold ownership shares. Those who attend annual meetings learn about past performance and future goals through speeches made by corporate officers and documents such as the company's annual report. Those who do not attend meetings must depend pri-

---

[6]"Firms Seek Protection from Class Action Lawsuits," *San Jose Mercury News,* Jan. 31, 1994, pp. D1–D2.

marily on annual reports issued by the company and the opinions of independent financial analysts.

Historically, management has tended to provide stockholders with minimum information. But prompted by the Securities and Exchange Commission and by professional accounting groups, companies now disclose more about their affairs, in spite of the complicated nature of some information. A few corporations go further than required and publish financial information from the detailed "10-K" section of their official reports to the SEC. Stockholders therefore can learn about sales and earnings, assets, capital expenditures and depreciation by line of business, and details of foreign operations.

Corporations also are required to disclose detailed information about directors, how they are chosen, their compensation, conflicts of interest, and their reasons for resigning in policy disputes with management. New rules, discussed later in this chapter, also require companies to publish information about the compensation of their executives.

CORPORATE GOVERNANCE

The term **corporate governance** refers to the overall control of a company's actions. Several key stakeholder groups are involved in governing the corporation.

- *Managers* occupy a strategic position because of their knowledge and day-to-day decision making.
- The *board of directors* exercises formal legal authority over company policy.
- *Stockholders*, whether individuals or institutions, have a vital stake in the company.
- *Employees*, particularly those represented by unions or who own stock in the company, can affect some policies.
- *Government*, through laws and regulations, also is involved, as are *creditors*, who hold corporate debt.

The following discussion concentrates on the roles of three groups that traditionally govern the corporation in addition to stockholders: the board of directors, top management, and creditors.

The Board of Directors

The board of directors is a central factor in corporate governance because corporation laws place legal responsibility for the affairs of a company on the directors. The board of directors is legally responsible for establishing corporate objectives, developing broad policies, and selecting top-level personnel to carry out these objectives and policies. The board also reviews management's performance to be sure that the company is well run and stockholders' interests are protected.

Corporate boards are legally permitted to vary in size, composition, and structure so as to best serve the interests of the corporation and the shareholders. A number of patterns do exist, however. Corporate boards average twelve members, with the largest boards in banks and financial institutions, and the smallest in small and mid-sized firms. Of these members, it is likely that about three-quarters will be "outside" directors (not managers of the company), including chief executives of other companies, retired executives of other firms, investment bankers, academics, attorneys, and representatives of constituencies such as environmentalists or community leaders. Two-thirds of all companies have at least one woman on the board, and about two-fifths have at least one African-American board member.

Most corporate boards perform their work through committees. The executive committee (present in 75 percent of corporate boards) works closely with top managers on important business matters. The audit committee (present in virtually all boards) is normally composed entirely of outside directors; it reviews the company's financial reports, recommends the appointment of outside auditors, and oversees the integrity of internal financial controls. The compensation committee (97 percent), also staffed by outside directors, administers and approves salaries and other benefits of high-level managers in the company. The nominating committee (67 percent) is charged with finding and recommending candidates for officers and directors, especially those to be elected at the annual stockholders' meeting. Since the 1980s, a number of corporations have created an ethics committee (7 percent) or public affairs committee (17 percent) that gives special attention to ethical issues and social responsibility problems.[7]

These committees, which may meet several times each year, give an active board of directors very important powers in controlling the company's affairs. In addition, when the entire board meets, it hears directly from top-level managers and has an opportunity to influence their decisions and policies.

Top Management

Professional managers generally take the leading role in large corporations. These managers might have backgrounds in marketing and sales, or

---

[7]The figures in the preceding two paragraphs are based on data presented in Korn/Ferry International, *Board of Directors: Twenty-First Annual Study*, New York: 1994. All data are for 1993.

in engineering design and production, or in various aspects of financial analysis. The expanding scale and complexity of national and international business calls for management specialists to guide the affairs of most big companies. The source of their power is a combination of their managerial expertise and simply being given organizational responsibility for carrying out the needed work.

Managers increasingly tend to consider their responsibilities as being primarily to the company, rather than just to the stockholders. They perceive themselves to be responsible for (1) assuring the economic survival of the firm; (2) extending its life into the future through product innovation, management development, market expansion, and other means; and (3) balancing the demands of all groups in such a way that the company can achieve its objectives. This viewpoint considers shareholders to be just one of several stakeholder groups that must be given attention. Concerning their specific responsibilities to owners, managers today often express the belief that "what is good for the company in the long run is good for the stockholder." Some observers believe that the power of top managers has declined somewhat in recent years, as boards of directors, institutional stockholders, and other stakeholders have grown more assertive.[8]

Creditors

Since the mid-1990s, creditors have become a powerful influence in the governance of corporations. Traditionally, creditors have lent money to businesses to help them finance the purchase of new buildings, equipment, or the expansion of a business into new areas of activity. In the 1980s, a number of financiers persuaded corporate executives that issuing high-risk, high-yield bonds, known as "junk bonds," could enable them to acquire other firms, reorganize them, sell off unwanted portions, and both meet the debt payments on the bonds and improve total corporate financial performance.

The idea was appealing, and dozens of companies used such financing to build larger and larger corporate empires. The threat of unwanted takeover bids became so serious that many managements sought to find ways of making their companies "private" (i.e., eliminate the public stockholders). This led, in turn, to further use of debt in a series of **leveraged buyouts (LBOs)**. An LBO uses debt financing (bonds or borrowed money) to purchase the outstanding shares of stock from public shareholders. For management, this arrangement replaces impatient shareholders, who are ready to sell their stock to the highest bidder, with a

[8]For an argument for management's expanded obligations to a variety of stakeholders, see James O'Toole, *Vanguard Management: Redesigning the Corporation,* New York: Doubleday, 1985. For an account of the changing role of the chief executive, see "Chief Executives See Their Power Shrink," *Wall Street Journal,* Mar. 15, 1993, pp. B1, B7.

creditor whose view is longer term. As long as the company can continue to pay the high yield on the bonds, management is relatively well protected from hostile takeover action. During the recession of the early 1990s, however, many users of debt financing found that revenues were insufficient to pay bond interest. The result was often bankruptcy or even complete dissolution of the company. This course of action was forced by the creditors, who wanted some return—albeit less than full value—on the money they had loaned. Dealing with creditors has therefore become a major corporate governance issue for companies.[9]

The Process of Corporate Governance

Who will govern the corporation internally is a central issue facing business. There is no easy answer to the question, "Who's in charge?" The current system of corporate governance is the product of a long historical process, dating back to the emergence of the modern, publicly held corporation in the late 1800s. This section presents two contrasting models of corporate governance, against which recent developments may be compared.

According to the traditional, legal model of corporate governance, stockholders hold the ultimate authority in the firm. In this view, stockholders exercise control through their legal right to elect the board of directors. The directors, in turn, hire top management, set overall strategy, and are responsible for making sure stockholders earn a fair return from a well-managed operation. These principles of governance are embodied in corporate law and in the legal rights stockholders enjoy, as shown in Figure 13-2. In the traditional model, stockholders are the group at the "top" of the chain of command within the firm.

Many analysts of the modern corporation, however, have long maintained that the traditional model is not a very realistic picture of how companies really work. In this "revisionist" view, several forces counteract the legal power of stockholders. Most shareholders in the United States historically have been individuals who owned a small number of shares. Typically, shareholders as a group were (and still are) geographically dispersed, and government rules made it difficult for them to contact each other or to organize on behalf of their collective interests. Most owners of stock who disapproved of management were more likely to do the "Wall Street walk"—simply sell their shares and walk away—than they were likely to try to change corporate policy.

By the same token, boards of directors—rather than controlling managers—as the traditional model suggested—were more likely to be controlled by them. Members of the board, in practice, were (and still are in

[9]Michael C. Jensen, "Eclipse of the Public Corporation," *Harvard Business Review,* Sept.–Oct. 1989, pp. 61–74.

many companies) nominated by top managers and served at their pleasure. Contested elections for board seats were rare. Board members, who usually served on a part-time basis, often lacked the information or expertise to challenge full-time managers and were likely to "rubber-stamp" decisions placed before them. In the revisionist view, then, corporate governance was turned on its head, with top managers having the ultimate authority—and with stockholders at the bottom.[10] The traditional and revisionist models are contrasted in Figure 13-3.

Recent trends in corporate governance suggest that neither model may any longer be an accurate description of how corporations are run. In the 1990s, the relative power of stakeholder groups within the firm, both in the United States and in other countries, has changed significantly. Stockholders, particularly large institutions, and boards of directors have both became more assertive relative to top management. Social activist shareholders have exerted influence through the proxy (absentee ballot) election process, and in some cases workers have exercised control through new forms of stock ownership. These important developments are profiled in the next section.

CURRENT TRENDS IN CORPORATE GOVERNANCE

The Rise of Institutional Investors

As shown earlier, institutional investors—pensions, mutual funds, endowment funds, and the like—have enlarged their stockholdings and since the mid-1980s have become more assertive in promoting the interests of their members. This trend has had important implications for corporate governance.

One reason institutions have become more active is that it is more difficult for them to sell their holdings if they become dissatisfied with management performance. Large institutions have less flexibility than individual shareholders, because selling a large bloc of stock could seriously depress its value. Accordingly, institutional investors have a strong incentive to hold their shares and organize to change management policy.

---

[10]A discussion of the legal basis for the roles of stockholders, boards, and managers in the modern corporation may be found in the American Law Institute, *Principles of Corporate Governance*, Philadelphia, PA: 1994. Early statements of the revisionist argument appear in Robert A. Gordon, *Business Leadership in the Large Corporation*, Los Angeles and Berkeley: University of California Press, 1948; and Myles Mace, *Directors: Myth and Reality*, Boston: Harvard Business School Press, 1971. For more recent discussions of corporate governance, see Jay W. Lorsch with Elizabeth MacIver, *Pawns or Potentates: The Reality of America's Corporate Boards*, Boston: Harvard Business School Press, 1989; Robert A. G. Monks and Nell Minow, *Power and Accountability*, New York: Harper Business, 1991; and Murray Weidenbaum, *The Evolving Corporate Board*, St. Louis, MO: Center for the Study of American Business, 1994.

FIGURE 13-3
Traditional and revisionist models of corporate governance.

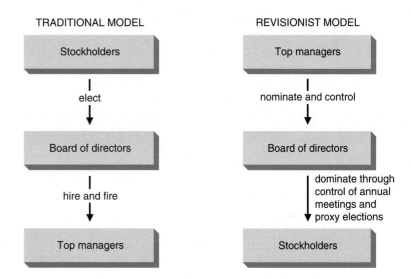

TRADITIONAL MODEL

Stockholders

| elect

Board of directors

| hire and fire

Top managers

REVISIONIST MODEL

Top managers

| nominate and control

Board of directors

| dominate through control of annual meetings and proxy elections

Stockholders

In 1985, the Council of Institutional Investors was formed. Within a decade, the council had grown to eighty-seven members and represented institutions and pension funds with investments totaling more than $650 billion. The council developed a "Shareholder Bill of Rights" and urged its members to view their proxies as assets, voting them on behalf of shareholders rather than automatically with management. The activism of the council's institutional members was facilitated in the early 1990s by new Securities and Exchange Commission rules that made it easier for shareholders to communicate with one another, get access to lists of other shareholders, and circulate proxy campaign material.[11]

The early 1990s witnessed a movement toward **relationship investing.** This occurs when large shareholders—pensions, mutual funds, or a group of private investors—form a long-term, committed link with a company. Often, institutional owners buy a significant stake in a company and acquire a seat on the board, or at least meet frequently with management. The benefits of relationship investing are that companies gain a long-term commitment from key shareholders, who in turn get more say in management. At Sears, for example, Robert Monks, a leading advocate of relationship investing, bought a major share in the company and then convinced managers to spin off its financial units and make other major changes. Monks's partner stated, "Corporate governance is our tool for making money. We are talking about nontakeover takeovers. Like the raiders, we hope to realize value that's buried. We've found a better, earlier way to do it."[12]

[11]"A Lethal Weapon for Shareholders?" *Business Week,* June 15, 1992, p. 40.
[12]"Relationship Investing: A New Shareholder Is Emerging—Patient and Involved," *Business Week,* Mar. 15, 1993, pp. 68–75.

Some observers maintained that by the mid-1990s, the movement for shareholder rights had matured, as many corporations increasingly accepted an enlarged role in corporate governance for institutional owners. "Corporations have changed and are beginning to accept the possibility of a very real partnernship with shareholders," said one researcher. "All out war is no longer needed."[13]

The activism of institutional investors has begun to spread to other countries. These efforts in many cases have been spearheaded by U.S.-based pension and mutual funds that in recent years acquired large stakes in foreign companies. By 1993, American pension funds owned an estimated $140 billion worth of stock in foreign firms—almost triple their overseas holdings just three years earlier. To protect their globalized investments, fund managers have become active in proxy battles in Japan, Britain, Hong Kong, and many other countries. Although these efforts have usually been unsuccessful, in the long run they may influence corporate governance abroad, as the following example shows.

> In Germany, a representative of Calpers, the California state employees' pension fund, stood up at the annual meeting of a major utility company and denounced shareholder voting restrictions, calling them "an embarrassing anachronism which pulls Germany out of step with international norms." The restrictions were not changed, but the German press gave the incident wide coverage, calling the confrontation "unprecedented."

A 1994 study of thirteen nations found that nearly half of the companies surveyed reported growing contact with institutional investors over the past three years.[14]

Movements for shareholder rights often confront formidable obstacles abroad, where stock markets may be smaller and corporate governance is often dominated by networks of allied businesses, creditors, and managers—to the exclusion of stockholders. Many countries do not share the U.S. principle of "one share, one vote" or traditions of open debate at shareholder meetings. Even so, stockholders have successfully ousted top executives in Britain, organized for higher dividends in Japan, and blocked antitakeover provisions in the Netherlands. The movement for the rights of shareholders—like the investments they hold—is becoming increasingly globalized.[15]

---

[13]"Have Activist Shareholders Lost Their Edge?" *New York Times*, Jan. 30, 1994, p. F7; and "Shareholder Rights Movement Sways a Number of Big Companies," *Wall Street Journal*, Apr. 14, 1991, pp. C1, C10.

[14]Ronald E. Bernbeim, "Company Relations with Institutional Investors," New York: The Conference Board, 1994.

[15]"Yankee-Style Activists Strike Boardroom Terror Abroad," *Business Week*, Mar. 15, 1993, p. 74; and "Exporting Shareholder Activism," *New York Times*, July 16, 1993, p. C1–C2. An excellent comparative analysis of corporate governance in different countries may be found in "Corporate Governance: A Survey," *The Economist*, Jan. 29, 1994, pp. 3–18.

Changing Role of the Board of Directors

Like institutional investors, some boards of directors have also become more assertive. At both ailing and healthy companies, boards have stopped "rubber-stamping" management policies and have begun thinking more independently. As the American Express example that opened this chapter illustrated, some boards have fired their chief executives. Others have redirected, reorganized, and generally rethought their companies. The CEO of Dayton-Hudson commented, "[Boards] are thinking through the whole process of corporate governance—what they're responsible for—and going into more detail about it."[16]

The new assertiveness of some boards has several sources. Directors have found themselves pressured by institutional investors anxious to protect their shareholders' interests. Another factor has been an increase in lawsuits against board members. Since 1985, a number of court decisions have held directors personally liable for poor management decisions, making them more sensitive to their responsibilities to stockholders.[17] Organizational reforms of the board have also led to increased independence from management. Growing representation by outside directors is one such trend. When General Motors' board ousted its chairman, Robert C. Stempel, in 1992, the move was masterminded by John G. Smale, former CEO of Procter & Gamble and an outsider on the board. Because of recent reforms, GM's board for the first time had a majority of outside directors, many of whom allied themselves with Smale's position.[18] Another such reform is separation of the duties of the chief executive and the board chairman, rather than combining the two in one person as is done in many corporations. With this split in responsibilities, a board has an improved chance of receiving completely candid reports about a company's affairs.

Social Responsibility Shareholder Resolutions

Another important current trend in corporate governance is the rise of **social responsibility shareholder resolutions.**[19]

The Securities and Exchange Commission (SEC) allows stockholders to place resolutions concerning appropriate social issues, such as environmental responsibility or alcohol and tobacco advertising, in proxy state-

[16]"Taking Charge: Corporate Directors Start to Flex Their Muscle," *Business Week,* July 3, 1989, pp. 66–71.

[17]"A Seat on the Board Is Getting Hotter," *Business Week,* July 3, 1989, pp. 72–73.

[18]"General Motors Chairman Quits After Growing Split with Board," *New York Times,* Oct. 27, 1992, pp. A1, C5.

[19]For general background on the rise of investor social activism, see Lauren Talner, *The Origins of Shareholder Activism,* Washington, DC: Investor Responsibility Research Center, 1983; and David Vogel, *Lobbying the Corporation: Citizen Challenges to Business Authority,* New York: Basic Books, 1978.

ments sent out by companies. These SEC rules reflect a belief that stockholders should be allowed to vote on social as well as economic questions that are related to the business of the corporation. The SEC has tried to minimize harassment by requiring a resolution to receive minimum support in order to be resubmitted in following years—5 percent of votes cast the first year, 8 percent the second year, and 10 percent the third year. Resolutions cannot deal with a company's "ordinary business," since that would constitute unjustified interference with management's decisions in running the company. In the early 1990s, several lawsuits contested the SEC's definition of ordinary business matters, with business seeking to exclude resolutions dealing with such issues as discrimination against homosexual employees, and investor groups seeking to include such issues.[20] Despite continuing controversy, in recent years the number and variety of social responsibility shareholder resolutions has continued to increase markedly.

Shareholder activists in 1994 sponsored almost 300 resolutions dealing with fifteen major social issues at meetings of more than 100 corporations. Nearly 100 church groups were joined by individual shareholders, unions, environmental groups, and a growing number of pension funds. Many of these groups were members of a coalition, the Interfaith Center on Corporate Responsibility (ICCR), that coordinated the activities of the social responsibility shareholder movement. Figure 13-4 summarizes the leading social policy resolutions in 1994.

Since shareholder resolutions not favored by management rarely garner enough votes to be adopted, what is their point? There are several answers. The annual meetings provide a forum for debating social issues. Stockholders have a legal right to raise such issues and to ask questions about how "their" company is responding. Management is questioned about controversial issues and has to justify its policies in public. In order to avoid the glare of publicity, an increasing number of corporations have met with dissident groups prior to the annual meeting and have agreed to take action on an issue voluntarily. For example, in 1994 General Motors agreed to endorse the CERES Principles, a code of environmental conduct described in Chapter 12, after three years of discussion between the company and religious investors who had backed shareholder resolutions in support of the code. The coordinator of the CERES negotiating team said that GM's voluntary agreement "demonstrates the new power of shareholders in corporate America. Shareholders can bring companies and public interest groups together to produce environmental commitments that are both local and global in scope."[21]

[20]"Federal Court Strikes Down SEC Rule Barring Proxy Resolutions on Employment Issues—SEC Appeals," *The Corporate Examiner*, vol. 22, no. 7, 1993, p. 1; and "Investors Sue SEC over Ban in Proxies of Employee Issues," *Wall Street Journal*, Mar. 4, 1993, p. C23.
[21]"General Motors Endorses CERES Principles," *The Corporate Examiner*, vol. 12, no. 10, p. 1.

FIGURE 13-4

Social responsibility shareholder resolutions, 1994.

SOURCE: "Corporate Responsibility Challenges—Spring 1994, Part I: The Sponsors and Companies, and Part II: The Resolutions," *The Corporate Examiner*, vol. 22, no. 8–9, 1993, pp. 1–16.

Area of Resolution	Number of Resolutions Filed
Environmental Responsibility CERES Principles, environmental audits and disclosure, energy conservation, environmental policy committees	55
Corporate Governance Staggered board terms, diversity on board of directors, executive compensation, confidential proxy ballot	48
Alcohol and Tobacco Advertising, sales to minors, marketing to minorities and the poor, warning labels, economic conversion	29
Equal Employment Opportunity Reporting of data and efforts to expand opportunities	22
South Africa Assisting in development of democratic South Africa	22
Northern Ireland MacBride Principles	20
Military Issues Economic conversion, gun sales, arms sales to foreign governments	17
Other Issues Mexican plants (maquiladoras), lending practices, labor and occupational health, human rights abuses, health care, trade issues, nuclear power, infant formula	73
Total	286

Employee Stock Ownership

A final trend, one that affects a small but growing number of U.S. corporations, is the form of stock ownership known as an **employee stock ownership plan (ESOP).** An ESOP is a kind of benefit plan in which a company purchases shares of its own stock and places them in trust for its employees. The idea is to give employees direct profit-sharing interest in addition to their wage and salary income. ESOP advocates claim that this kind of share ownership benefits the company by increasing worker productivity, reducing job absenteeism, and drawing management and employees closer together into a common effort to make the company a success. Not only do ESOP participants receive regular dividends on the stock they own, but workers who quit or retire can either take their stock from the fund or sell their shares back to the company. A major financial benefit to an ESOP company is that its contributions to the plan are tax deductible.

Beginning in the mid-1970s, ESOPs grew at an explosive pace, mainly because of new federal and state laws that encouraged their formation. From less than 500 in 1975, ESOPs grew to about 9,500 by 1993, covering over 10 million employees and controlling $150 billion in corporate stock. Most ESOPs are in private companies, but they have become more popular in publicly-owned firms as well, where employees typically own between 5 and 20 percent of the company's stock.[22]

An example of an employee-owned company is Avis, the rental car firm. The company was purchased by workers in 1987, using borrowed money, after Avis was "spun off" by Wesray Corporation. Avis workers not only own shares in the company, but they also participate in management directly through "employee participation groups." Employees meet with local managers to discuss various problems. Elected employee representatives also meet with regional and national managers. Observers said that Avis workers were, indeed, "trying harder" (a company slogan)—because they owned the company.[23]

Studies have shown that where employee ownership is linked with participative management practices, as at Avis, companies experience significant gains in performance.[24]

In sum, the 1990s have been a period of fluidity and flux in corporate governance. The answer to the question, "Who governs the corporation?" is becoming "Many people and groups." The authority of top managers has been increasingly checked—by powerful groups of institutional investors, newly assertive boards of directors, and, in a smaller number of cases, by activist shareholders and worker owners. It is clear that the process of corporate governance is undergoing significant change, much of it leading to a greater dispersion of power within the firm.

EXECUTIVE COMPENSATION: A SPECIAL ISSUE

An issue of increasing controversy in the 1990s is **executive compensation**. Even as top managers' authority has diminished in some respects,

---

[22]National Center for Employee Ownership, "Employee Ownership Fact Sheet," Oakland, CA: 1994, and personal communication of the author.

[23]"Avis: 100 Percent Employee Ownership," *Business Ethics*, Nov.–Dec. 1992, p. 26.

[24]Michael Quarrey and Corey M. Rosen, *Employee Ownership and Corporate Performance*, Oakland, CA: National Center for Employee Ownership, 1994. For further analysis of the impact of ESOPs, see Joseph Blasi and Douglas Kruse, *The New Owners: The Mass Emergence of Employee Ownership in Public Companies and What It Means to American Business*, New York: HarperCollins, 1991; and Corey M. Rosen, Katherine J. Klein, and Karen M. Young, *Employee Ownership in America: The Equity Solution*, Lexington, MA: Lexington Press, 1986.

their salaries have soared. Are top managers paid too much, or are their high salaries and bonuses a well-deserved reward for their contributions to the companies they lead? This debate has been the focus of much recent attention by boards of directors, shareholders, and government regulators seeking to increase the accountability of top managers.

Executive compensation in the United States, by international standards, is very high. In 1993, according to a survey by *Fortune* magazine, the chief executives of the 200 largest corporations in the United States earned, on average, $4.1 million, including salaries, bonuses, and the present value of stock grants. This was a 28 percent increase over the previous year's total compensation.[25] By contrast, top managers in other countries earned much less. In Japan, for example, chief executives at the leading 50 industrial companies made about $900,000 on average in 1992—less than a third of their U.S. counterparts' earnings; and the *highest* paid Japanese business leader made a "mere" $6 million. Business executives in Germany and Britain made even less than the Japanese.[26]

Another way to look at executive compensation is to compare the pay of top managers with that of average employees. In the United States, CEOs in the mid-1990s made about 150 times what the average worker did; in Japan, CEOs made only 32 times as much.

Why are American executives paid so much? Corporate politics play an important role. Graef S. Crystal, a compensation expert and critic of inflated executive pay, argues in his book *In Search of Excess* that one reason salaries are so high is that they are set by compensation committees of boards of directors. These committees are usually made up of individuals hand-picked by the CEO; often, they are CEOs themselves and sensitive to the indirect impact of their decisions on their own salaries. Moreover, compensation committees rely heavily on the advice of consultants who conduct surveys of salaries in similar firms. Graef argues that since boards usually want to pay their own executives above the median for comparable firms, the median tends to keep going up.[27]

Some observers say that the comparatively high compensation of top U.S. executives is justified. In this view, well-paid managers are simply being rewarded for outstanding performance. For example, Stephen J. Ross, the former CEO of Time Warner and for many years one of the top-

---

[25]"A Knockout Year for CEO Pay," *Fortune,* July 25, 1994, pp. 94–103. For a slightly different computation, see "That Eye-Popping Executive Pay: Is Anybody Worth This Much?" *Business Week,* Apr. 25, 1994, pp. 52–58. By contrast, chief executives at small and mid-size companies make much less. One survey of companies with annual revenues below $400 million found median annual compensation of CEOs to be $312,000. See "Pay Gap Grows for Chiefs of Big Firms and Small Ones," *Wall Street Journal,* Oct. 25, 1994, p. B2.

[26]"What Do Japanese CEOs Really Make?" *Business Week,* Apr. 26, 1993, pp. 60–61.

[27]Graef S. Crystal, *In Search of Excess: The Overcompensation of American Executives,* New York: W. W. Norton, 1991. For a further discussion of executive pay and its impact on society, see Derek Bok, *The Cost of Talent: How Executives and Professionals Are Paid and How It Affects America,* New York: The Free Press, 1993.

paid U.S. executives, delivered a compound return of almost 24 percent annually between 1973 and 1990. To many shareholders, his pay ($78 million in 1991, his last full year in office) was clearly "worth it." Much of the increase in executive compensation in the 1980s can be accounted for by the exercise of stock options (a benefit whose value typically rises with stock prices), reflecting the stock market run-up during the decade—a development that benefited shareholders as well as executives.

Supporters also argue that high salaries provide an incentive for innovation and risk taking. In an era of intense global competition, restructuring, and downsizing, the job of CEO of large U.S. corporations has never been more challenging, and the tenure in the top job has become shorter. Another argument for high compensation is a shortage of labor. In this view, not many individuals are capable of running today's large, complex organizations, so the few that have the necessary skills and experience can command a premium. Today's high salaries are necessary for companies to attract top talent. Why shouldn't the most successful business executives make as much as top athletes and entertainers?[28]

On the other hand, critics argue that inflated executive pay hurts the ability of U.S. firms to compete with foreign rivals. High executive compensation diverts financial resources that could be used to invest in the business, increase stockholder dividends, or pay average workers more. Multimillion dollar salaries cause resentment and sap the commitment of hard-working lower-level employees who feel they are not receiving their fair share. As for the performance issue, critics suggest that as many extravagantly compensated executives preside over failure as they do over success. A study published in the *Harvard Business Review* concluded that "in most publicly held companies, the compensation of top executives is virtually independent of performance."[29]

Some shareholder activists have tried to rein in excessive executive compensation. The New York City Teachers' Retirement System, a major institutional investor, opposed an incentive pay plan for Westinghouse Electric that would have raised the compensation of some top managers. "It's out of control," said an official of the public pension fund, referring to executive pay.

Executive compensation has also been the subject of new government regulations. Under SEC rules introduced in 1992, companies must clearly disclose what their five top executives are paid, and lay out a rationale for their compensation. A separate chart must report the company's stock and dividend performance. These rules expand stockholders' rights by making it easier for them to determine a manager's total compensation and

[28]A defense of high executive pay may be found in Andrew Brownstein and Morris J. Panner, "Who Should Set CEO Pay? The Press? Congress? Shareholders?" *Harvard Business Review,* May–June 1992, pp. 28–38.
[29]Michael C. Jensen and Kevin J. Murphy, "CEO Incentives—It's Not How Much You Pay, But How," *Harvard Business Review,* May–June 1990, pp. 138–149.

whether it is justified by the firm's record. The SEC also for the first time allowed nonbinding shareholder votes on executive and director compensation.[30] Congress passed a rule that would prevent companies from taking a tax deduction on executive salaries in excess of $1 million annually, although many compensation experts said it would make little difference in how much top managers were paid.

Some companies have responded to these stakeholder pressures by changing the process by which they set executive pay. Some have made compensation committees of the board of directors more independent, staffing them exclusively with outside directors and permitting them to hire their own consultants. At American Exploration Co., an oil and gas company, the board voted against extra compensation for top executives after an independent consultant told them it was not necessary to remain competitive. Other companies have sought to restructure compensation to tie top executives' pay more closely to performance. A few top managers have even taken pay cuts—like Merck's CEO Roy Vagelos, whose compensation fell 11 percent in 1993 after the company's profits dropped by that amount. Some firms, including Du Pont and Tandem Computers, have made stock options available to all employees, giving everyone—not just the top executives—a stake in the company's performance. A tiny handful of companies have ruled that top executives cannot earn more than a certain multiple of others' pay.[31]

The active debate in the 1990s over "excess" executive compensation was part of the larger issue of the relative power within the corporation of managers, directors, and stockholders and of the regulation of their roles by government.

GOVERNMENT PROTECTION OF STOCKHOLDER INTERESTS

Securities and Exchange Commission

The major government agency protecting stockholders' interests is the Securities and Exchange Commission (SEC). Established in 1934 in the wake of the stock market crash and the Great Depression, its mission is to protect stockholders' rights by making sure that stock markets are run fairly and that investment information is fully disclosed. The agency—which, un-

[30]"You Can't Bury CEO Treasure Chests Anymore," *Business Week*, Apr. 26, 1993, p. 62; "Higher Profits Fatten CEO Bonuses, But New Pay Packages Come with More Strings Attached," *Wall Street Journal*, Apr. 21, 1993, pp. R1–R2; and "Firms Ordered to Fully Disclose Executive Pay," *Los Angeles Times*, Oct. 16, 1992, p. D1.
[31]For some recommendations on how companies can better structure executive compensation, see Ira T. Kay, *Value at the Top: Solutions to the Executive Compensation Crisis*, New York: Harper Business, 1992.

like most in government, generates revenue to pay for its own operations—has been called "one of government's better agencies."[32] In 1994, the SEC issued a major report, *Market 2000,* that called for major changes in the regulation of securities markets, including rules requiring better training for stockbrokers and investment advisers, more complete disclosure for buyers of mutual funds, and tougher policing of municipal bond markets.[33]

Government regulation is needed because stockholders can be damaged at times by abusive practices. One area calling for special efforts to protect and promote stockholder interests is insider trading.

Insider Trading

Insider trading occurs when a person gains access to confidential information about a company's financial condition and then uses that information, before it becomes public knowledge, to buy or sell the company's stock. Since others do not know what an insider trader knows, it is possible for the insider to make advantageous investments or sell stock well in advance of other stockholders.

Insider trading is illegal under the Securities Exchange Act of 1934, which outlaws "any manipulative or deceptive device." The courts have generally interpreted this to mean that it is against the law to:

- misappropriate (steal) nonpublic information and use it to trade a stock
- trade a stock based on a tip from someone who had an obligation to keep quiet (for example, a man would be guilty of insider trading if he bought stock after his sister, who was on the board of directors, told him of a pending offer to buy the company)
- pass information to others with an expectation of direct or indirect gain, even if the individual did not trade the stock for his or her own account.[34]

The most spectacular insider-trading scandal in Wall Street history occurred in 1986 when several individual investors and a few officers of investment banking firms were revealed to have made millions of dollars illegally through secret insider trading. By sharing confidential information about forthcoming mergers of large corporations, they were able to buy and sell stocks before the mergers were announced to the public. The leading investor in this scandal netted an estimated profit of $203 million

---

[32]"Securities and Exchange Commission," *Financial World,* Oct. 26, 1993, pp. 49–50.

[33]"Head of SEC to Seek New Safeguards for Investors," *Washington Post,* Jan. 2, 1994, pp. A1, A6.

[34]"Insider Trading: There Ought to Be a Law," *Business Week,* Dec. 12, 1994, p. 82.

in 1985 and 1986. In a settlement with the Securities and Exchange Commission, he paid a $50 million fine, returned $50 million in illegal profits, was barred from the securities industry for life, and served a jail term.[35] Although this scandal temporarily put a damper on insider trading, within a year the rate of trading based on inside information was as high as ever.

More recently, the merger wave of the early 1990s, described in Chapter 10, apparently contributed to a new rise in insider trading, as investors with knowledge of pending deals bought or sold stocks in advance of public information. The number of insider trader cases brought by the SEC in 1994 set an all-time record.[36]

Insider trading not only is illegal but also is contrary to the logic underlying stock markets: all stockholders ought to have access to the same information about companies. None should have special privileges or gain unfair advantages over others. Only in that way can investors have full confidence in the fairness of the stock markets. If they think that some investors can use inside knowledge for their own personal gain while others are excluded from such information, the system of stock buying might break down because of lack of trust.

STOCKHOLDERS AND THE CORPORATION

Stockholders have become an increasingly powerful and vocal stakeholder group in corporations. Management dominance of boards of directors has weakened, and shareholders—especially institutional investors—are pressing directors and management more forcefully to serve stockholder interests. Institutional investors also have acquired new power as creditors, using their purchases of corporate bonds as an additional form of leverage on corporate management. Shareholder activists and worker-owners have also changed the contours of corporate governance in the 1990s.

Clearly, stockholders are a critically important stakeholder group. By providing capital, monitoring corporate performance, assuring the effective operation of stock markets, and bringing new issues to the attention of management, stockholders play a very important role in making the business system work. Corporate leaders have an obligation to manage their companies in ways that promote and protect a variety of stakeholders. Balancing these various interests is a prime requirement of modern management. While stockholders are no longer considered to be the only important stakeholder group, their interests and needs remain central to the successful operation of corporate business.

---

[35]For a full account of this scandal, see James B. Stewart, *Den of Thieves,* New York: Simon and Schuster, 1991.
[36]"Insider Trading," *Business Week,* Dec. 12, 1994, pp. 70–81.

SUMMARY POINTS OF THIS CHAPTER

- Individuals and institutions own shares of corporations as a means of economic gain. Social purposes sometimes guide investors, as when certain businesses are avoided because of their negative social impacts. Shareholders are entitled to receive dividends, receive information, select directors, attempt to shape corporate policies, bring lawsuits, and sell their shares.
- The corporate governance system is the relationship among directors, managers, and shareholders. It determines who has legitimate power and how this power can be exercised. Creditors have become an important new factor in this relationship.
- Corporate governance has changed during the 1990s. Newly assertive institutional investors and boards of directors have challenged the authority of top management.
- Activists have influenced corporate actions in some cases through social responsibility shareholder proposals, although such proposals rarely gain enough votes to pass.
- Employee stock ownership programs (ESOPs) give employees a stake in the financial success of a company and may enhance worker commitment and productivity, although they also leave employees vulnerable to declining stock prices.
- Insider trading is illegal and unethical. It benefits those with illicitly acquired information at the expense of those who do not have it. Ultimately, it undermines fairness in the marketplace.

KEY TERMS AND CONCEPTS USED IN THIS CHAPTER

- Stockholders
- Institutional investors
- Shareholder lawsuits
- Corporate governance
- Leveraged buyouts (LBOs)
- Relationship investing
- Social responsibility shareholder resolutions
- Employee stock ownership plan (ESOP)
- Executive compensation
- Insider trading

DISCUSSION CASE

SHAREHOLDERS WALK OUT AT PHILIP MORRIS

On September 21, 1994, a group of irate institutional investors abruptly walked out of a meeting with top managers and board members of

Philip Morris. The New York–based company, a diversified multinational worth $61 billion, made a wide range of consumer products, including such household names as Kraft cheese, Miller beer, and Marlboro cigarettes.

"It was clear to me that we were not going to have a discussion, but rather a canned presentation," said one of the dissidents, the director of corporate affairs for the Teamsters, a union whose pension funds owned $170 million worth of Philip Morris stock. The deputy comptroller for New York City's pension funds, holders of over $336 million of the company's stock, also walked out. "They told us we'd have 45 minutes on the issues and then there would be a cocktail party," he told reporters. "I guess they wanted everyone to go away drunk, fat and happy, but we wanted a meeting of substance." The dissident shareholders were particularly unhappy that so few outside directors had attended the session.

Philip Morris managers and directors, who continued the meeting after the walkout, disputed the charge that the event was stage-managed. "[It] gave us an opportunity to explain firsthand the steps we are taking to grow the company," a spokesman said. Investors who did not walk out included representatives of the pension funds of the states of California, Connecticut, and Ohio.

The disrupted meeting had been called in response to repeated requests by institutional shareholders for a frank discussion with the board—especially its outside members. At issue was whether or not Philip Morris should split off its food and beverage operations from its troubled tobacco units. Some believed that the company would be worth much more if it were broken up, because concerns about liability for the health effects of tobacco and higher taxes on cigarettes had dragged down the stock price. At the time of the meeting, Philip Morris stock was trading at about $59 a share, down from a high of $85 in 1992.

Four months earlier, on May 25, this issue had come to a head at a contentious meeting of the Philip Morris board. According to rumors that circulated later, Chairman and CEO Michael A. Miles had "locked horns" with Hamish Maxwell, a former chairman and head of the board's executive committee. Miles reportedly had supported the idea of splitting the company, while Maxwell—who as chairman had acquired General Foods, Kraft, and other food companies for Philip Morris—had opposed the move. A majority of the board (many of whom had assumed their positions during Maxwell's tenure) sided with Maxwell's position, and no action was taken to divide the company. Miles resigned June 19.

In the wake of the September 21 walkout, Philip Morris's institutional investors considered their next move. Some discussed the possibility of mounting a proxy fight and running their own candidates for the board at Philip Morris's April 1995 annual meeting. Others favored trying to meet directly with the company's outside board members. For its part, Philip

Morris maintained that its investors' "complaint that we won't address their concerns is an empty complaint."[37]

Discussion Questions

1. Was the board of directors acting within its powers when it apparently thwarted Miles's plan to split Philip Morris's tobacco and food units?

2. As an individual shareholder of Philip Morris, would you have been pleased with the board's action? With the subsequent actions of the institutional investors? If not, what could you do about it?

3. Are the shareholders of Philip Morris entitled to know the "full story" of Miles's discussion with the board of directors? Should the company's directors feel a responsibility to explain their behavior to shareholders if asked?

4. Do you believe that the actions of top management, the board of directors, and shareholders in this case are consistent with the trends in corporate governance discussed in this chapter? Why or why not?

[37]"Philip Morris Shareholders in a Walkout," *New York Times,* Sept. 22, 1994, p. D1; "New Pressures on Philip Morris," *New York Times,* Sept. 21, 1994, p. D1; "Big Investors Pressing Philip Morris," *New York Times,* June 21, 1994; "Call for Philip Morris: Don't Stonewall the Shareholders," *Business Week,* Oct. 10, 1994, p. 44; "A Rumor of War in the Philip Morris Boardroom," *Business Week,* June 13, 1994, p. 40.

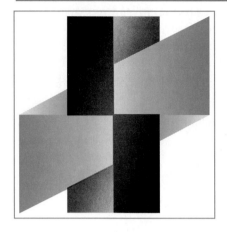

14

Consumer Protection

Safeguarding consumers while continuing to supply them with the goods and services they want is a prime social responsibility of business. Consumers in the 1990s have become increasingly aware of the impact that consumption can have on the environment, on nutrition and health, on the values acquired by children, and on the images of women and ethnic groups that are projected through consumer advertising. Government agencies serve as watchdogs for consumers, supplementing the actions taken by socially responsive corporations.

Key Questions and Chapter Objectives

This chapter focuses on these key questions and objectives:
- Why did a consumer movement develop in the United States?
- What are the environmental impacts of a high-consumption society?
- Why has advertising become a target of consumer activists and government regulators?
- In what ways do government regulatory agencies protect consumers?
- Is there a product liability crisis, and what reforms, if any, should be made?
- How have socially responsible corporations responded to consumer needs?

Knowing that she had a potentially defective heart valve implanted in her chest "has made living a nightmare," declared one of the estimated 60,000 recipients of a Shiley Convexo-Concave heart valve. Her fears stemmed from awareness that 389 similar valves had broken, killing 248 of the recipients. She also had been told that surgery to replace her valve was riskier than leaving it in place. Her peace of mind was not improved by knowing that the U.S. Food and Drug Administration (FDA) had approved sale of the valve in 1979, seeing it as an improvement over earlier models. After repeated valve failures, the manufacturer withdrew it from the market in 1986 when strong pressure was exerted by FDA regulators. In 1992,

Pfizer Inc., parent of Shiley, agreed to pay at least $175 million for research, medical care, and consultations for people with faulty valves.[1]

A Texas man had to have his foot amputated after a hunting rifle he was unloading, the Remington Model 700, accidentally discharged, seriously wounding him. Five years later, in 1994, a jury returned a verdict of $17 million against Remington, including $15 million in punitive damages. The company called the rifle "a safe and reliable sporting firearm" and disputed that it was in any way defective. But the Texan's attorney introduced internal documents showing that Remington had received complaints about the rifle dating back to 1982, and that the company had designed a safer firing mechanism but had decided not to use it. Guns are among the few consumer products for which the government has no authority to regulate safety. Although firearm accidents cause as many as 1,400 deaths a year, the National Rifle Association and gun manufacturers have vigorously opposed federal oversight.[2]

In 1993, after nearly a decade of controversy, the U.S. government approved bovine somatropin (BST), a genetically engineered hormone to boost milk production in cows. Years of testing by the Food and Drug Administration and health organizations showed that milk produced with BST was indistinguishable from milk that was not. But the day before the hormone was released for use, several of the country's largest food companies—including Kroger, Pathmath, and Southland, operator of 7-Eleven convenience stores—announced that they would not buy milk produced by cows given the drug. "Food is an emotional issue," a spokesperson for Southland said. "We felt a responsibility to take this action because of concern expressed by our customers."[3]

These three episodes demonstrate some of the complexities of serving consumers in the 1990s. New standards of business performance are being demanded. Today's consumers are increasingly aware of the broad impact that consumption can have not only on themselves but on society generally. This chapter examines these issues and the various ways that consumers, government regulators, and business firms have dealt with them.

PRESSURES TO PROMOTE CONSUMER INTERESTS

As long as business has existed—since the ancient beginnings of commerce and trade—consumers have tried to protect their interests when they go to the marketplace to buy goods and services. They have haggled over prices,

[1] "Settlement Approved on Pfizer Heart Valves," *New York Times*, Aug. 20, 1992, p. C4; "Heart Trouble at Pfizer," *Business Week*, Feb. 26, 1990, pp. 47–48; and "FDA Says Pfizer Inadequately Warned Heart-Valve Recipients of Risk of Death," *Wall Street Journal*, Dec. 10, 1990, p. B4.
[2] "Remington Faces a Misfiring Squad," *Business Week*, May 23, 1994, pp. 90–91.
[3] "Crying over Unnatural Milk," *Business Week*, Nov. 22, 1993, p. 48; and "Grocers Challenge Use of New Drug for Milk Output," *New York Times*, Feb. 4, 1994, pp. A1, A8.

taken a careful look at the goods they are buying, compared the quality and prices of products offered by other sellers, and complained loudly when they feel cheated by shoddy products. So, consumer self-reliance has always been one form of consumer protection. The Latin phrase, *caveat emptor*—meaning "let the buyer beware"—has put consumers on the alert to look after their own interests. This form of individual self-reliance is still very much in existence today.

However, the increasing complexity of economic life in the twentieth century, especially in the more advanced industrial nations, has led to organized, collective efforts to safeguard consumers. These organized activities are usually called consumerism or the **consumer movement.**

The Anatomy of Consumerism

At the heart of consumerism in the United States is an attempt to expand the rights and powers of consumers. The goal of the consumer movement, which began in the 1960s as part of a broader movement for social change (discussed in Chapter 3), is to make consumer power an effective counterbalance to the rights and powers of business firms that sell goods and services.

Within an advanced, industrialized, private enterprise nation, business firms tend to grow to a very large size. They acquire much power and influence. Frequently, they can dictate prices. Typically, their advertisements sway consumers to buy one product or service rather than another. If large enough, they may share the market with only a few equally large competitors, thereby weakening some of the competitive protections enjoyed by consumers where business firms are smaller and more numerous. The economic influence and power of business firms may therefore become a problem for consumers unless ways can be found to promote an equal amount of consumer power.

Most consumers would feel well protected if their fundamental rights to fair play in the marketplace could be guaranteed. In the early 1960s, when the consumer movement in the United States was in its early stages, President John F. Kennedy told Congress that consumers were entitled to four different kinds of protections:

1. *The right to safety:* to be protected against the marketing of goods which are hazardous to health or life.
2. *The right to be informed:* to be protected against fraudulent, deceitful, or grossly misleading information, advertising, labeling, or other practices, and to be given the facts to make an informed choice.
3. *The right to choose:* to be assured, wherever possible, access to a variety of products and services at competitive prices and in those industries in which competition is not workable and government regulation is substituted, to be assured satisfactory quality and service at fair prices.

4. *The right to be heard:* to be assured that consumer interests will receive full and sympathetic consideration in the formulation of government policy, and fair and expeditious treatment in its administrative tribunals.

The **consumer bill of rights,** as it was called, became the guiding philosophy of the consumer movement. If those rights could be guaranteed, consumers would feel more confident in dealing with well-organized and influential corporations in the marketplace.

Reasons for the Consumer Movement

This consumer movement exists because consumers want to be treated fairly and honestly in the marketplace. Some business practices do not meet this standard, which results in consumer abuses such as unfairly high prices, unreliable and unsafe products, excessive advertising claims for the effectiveness of some consumer goods and services, and the promotion of some products (such as cigarettes, fatty foods, and farm products contaminated with pesticides) known to be harmful to human health.

Additional reasons for the existence of the consumer movement are the following:

- *Complex products have enormously complicated the choices consumers need to make when they go shopping.* For this reason, consumers today are more dependent on business for product quality than ever before. Because many products are so complex—a personal computer or a television set, for example—most consumers have no way to judge at the time of purchase whether their quality is satisfactory. Many of the component parts of such products are not visible to consumers who, therefore, cannot inspect them even if they have the technical competence to do so. Instructions for use or care of products often are so complicated and detailed that buyers cannot understand or remember what to do. First-time computer users may spend weeks or months learning even the simplest software package—and then discover that it is not adequate for their needs. Consumers find that they are almost entirely dependent on business to deliver the quality promised. In these circumstances, unscrupulous business firms can take advantage of uninformed consumers.
- *Services, as well as products, have become more specialized and difficult to judge.* When choosing lawyers, dentists, colleges, or hospitals, most consumers do not have adequate guides for evaluating whether they are good or bad. They can rely on word-of-mouth experiences of others, but this information may not be entirely reliable. Or, when purchasing expensive items such as refrigerators,

householders have not only to judge how well the items will perform but also to know what to do when they break down. The consumer faces a two-tier judgment problem in making purchases: First, is the product a good one? Then, what will good service cost? The uninformed or badly informed consumer is frequently no match for the seller who is in the superior position.

■ *When business tries to sell both products and services through advertising, claims may be inflated or they may appeal to emotions having little to do with how the product is expected to perform.* An example was an ad for a stereo that declared, "She's terrific in bed, she's witty and intelligent and makes her own pasta." But, the speaker continued, she didn't own the advertised sound system, so he married a woman who did. The ad was withdrawn after numerous complaints poured in to the manufacturer.[4] A 1993 survey by *American Demographics* magazine found that nearly a third of adults found sexual references or images in advertising offensive.[5] Ad-industry critics have also frequently found fault with advertisements that air during children's television programs and feature violence, sell sweetened cereals, or promote toys—for example, the Ninja Turtle or G.I. Joe characters—by building program plots around these products, thus taking advantage of young children unable to differentiate between a fictional program and a commercial advertisement.[6] Beer commercials feature "good old boys" relaxing after work, cigarette advertisements that hint at freedom and pleasure for users, or auto advertisements that link male virility with horsepower and speed have come under attack for ignoring the negative impacts of alcohol abuse, tobacco use, and high-speed automobile deaths and injuries.

■ *Product safety has often been ignored.* The symbolic beginning of consumerism in the United States was Ralph Nader's well-publicized charges in the early 1970s about the hazards of driving the Corvair.[7] As public interest in health and nutrition grew during the 1960s and 1970s, many consumers worried about food additives, preservatives, pesticide residues left on fruits and vegetables, diet patterns that contributed to obesity, and the devastating health effects of long-term tobacco use. If the public could not count on business to screen out these possible dangers to consumers, who could they turn to for help? This question was raised more and more often, which led eventually to corrective actions by business, government, and consumer advocacy groups.

[4]"Does Sex Sell? Yes, But . . . ," *The Detroit News*, June 12, 1994.
[5]Doris Walsh, "Safe Sex in Advertising," *American Demographics*, Apr., 1994, pp. 24–30.
[6]"Watch What Your Kids Watch," *Business Week*, Jan. 8, 1990, pp. 50–52.
[7]Ralph Nader, *Unsafe at Any Speed: The Designed-in Dangers of the American Automobile*, New York: Grossman, 1972.

Consumer Advocacy Groups

One of the impressive features of the consumer movement in the United States is the many organized groups that actively promote and speak for the interests of millions of consumers. One organization alone—the Consumer Federation of America—brings together over 250 nonprofit groups to espouse the consumer viewpoint; they represent some 50 million Americans. Two nonprofit organizations—Consumers' Research and Consumers Union—conduct extensive tests on selected consumer products and services and publish the results, with ratings on a brand-name basis, in widely circulated magazines. (*Consumer Reports* is the best known of these magazines.) Consumer cooperatives, credit unions, and consumer education programs in schools and universities and on television and radio round out a very extensive network of activities aimed at promoting consumer interests.

The most-publicized consumer advocate is Ralph Nader, who with his associates formed the organizations shown in Figure 14-1. Public Citizen,

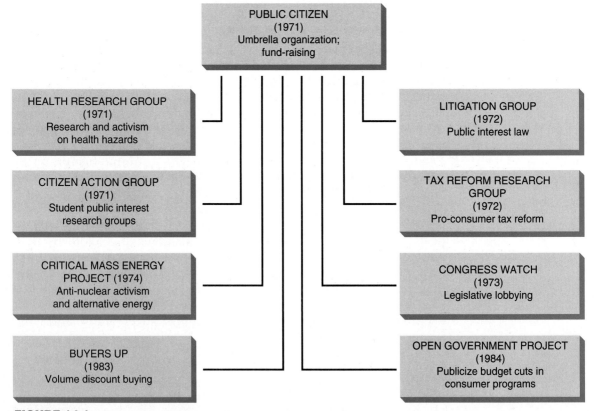

FIGURE 14-1

Ralph Nader's consumer protection network.

SOURCE: Adapted from David Bollier, "15 Years," *Public Citizen,* Oct. 1986, pp. 20–24, 32.

founded in 1971, became the umbrella organization for specialized units, the main fund-raising organization, and a publishing arm for consumer publications. The Health Research Group has taken the lead in urging a ban on harmful color dyes used in various foods, putting warning labels on dangerous products, setting exposure limits on hazardous substances, and alerting the public to possibly dangerous medical products on the market, such as silicone breast implants. Other organizations under the Public Citizen umbrella include the Litigation Group, which gives legal assistance to people who have difficulty in gaining adequate access to the court system, and Congress Watch, which monitors Congress. Nader's organization is also allied with a network of state and local activist groups.[8]

In 1993, Public Citizen published an analysis of government policy on consumer issues in the 1980s, *Who's Protecting Consumers?* This report charged that under the Reagan and Bush administrations, consumers had lost ground, and the consumer movement had failed to accomplish many of its objectives. "The most basic consumer protections have been lost in the last decade," stated Joan Claybrook, president of Public Citizen. ". . . The federal cop has left the regulatory beat, and 'let the buyer beware' has gone from homely motto to government policy."[9]

LEADING CONSUMER ISSUES OF THE 1990s

After three decades, the consumer movement in the early and mid-1990s had begun to concern itself with more than just protecting consumers against poorly made, overpriced goods and services. A broader range of social issues emerged. Three of these issues were (a) the ecological impacts of high consumption; (b) nutritional and safety concerns; and (c) the value-shaping and image-making force of advertising. Each of these issues is discussed next.

Ecological Impacts of Consumption

According to national surveys conducted in the late 1980s and early 1990s, four out of every five U.S. consumers said that a company's environmental reputation would affect whether they would buy its products. By 1996, "green" products were projected to account for 16 percent of all consumer product sales. This intersection of environmentalism (discussed in Chapters 11 and 12) and consumerism is called **green consumerism,** or

---

[8]David Bollier, "15 Years," *Public Citizen*, Oct. 1986, pp. 20–24; and "The Second Coming of Ralph Nader," *Business Week*, Mar. 6, 1989, p. 28.
[9]"Assessing the Damage: 12 Years of Reagan-Bush Anti-Consumerism," *Public Citizen*, Jan.–Feb. 1993, pp. 10–13, 26.

green marketing, which one observer said "may be the most powerful new environmental force to emerge in the past decade."[10]

"Green consumers" focus public attention on the ecological impacts brought on by a high-consumption society. "Each year Americans throw away 16 billion disposable diapers, 1.6 billion pens, 2 billion razors and blades, and 220 million tires. They discard enough aluminum to rebuild the entire U.S. commercial airline fleet every three months."[11] As a result of this mountain of disposable waste, municipal landfills began reaching capacity limits in many parts of the nation. Consumers have become increasingly aware of the need to minimize packaging waste, to cut back on nonbiodegradable or nonrecyclable materials, and to buy products manufactured with environmentally friendly methods.

Many leading producers of consumer goods have felt the pressures of consumers' ecological concerns, as illustrated by the following examples.

Union Camp Corporation, a paper company, started a program at its Franklin, Virginia, mill to use more recycled fiber and to cut down on the use of chlorine, a water pollutant. The company's vice president called the program "a market-driven decision," saying that "customers want recycled products." Union Camp installed new machines that removed ink from used office paper, so it could be recycled, and that whitened paper without chlorine. Consumers and many large companies, including Bank of America, The Gap, and Bechtel Group have committed to purchasing recycled paper. The government has boosted the trend by requiring federal agencies to buy paper with at least 20 percent recycled content.[12]

Mobil and Sunoco Products initiated programs to recycle the 12 billion plastic grocery bags used each year. They hoped to convince environmentally conscious consumers and lawmakers that recycling would be preferable to a ban on the bags, which now account for 60 percent of grocery bags used in the United States. Mobil earlier had been pressured by attorneys general from several states to stop claiming that its plastic garbage bags were biodegradable (would decay naturally). Although the company had added a chemical to the bags that permitted them to decompose when exposed to sunlight, rain, and wind, they would not disintegrate when buried in a sealed landfill. In the wake of this dispute, the Federal Trade Commission issued guidelines

[10]Denis Hayes, "Harnessing Market Forces to Protect the Earth," *Issues in Science and Technology*, Winter 1990–1991, p. 50. Survey data are from *Fortune*, Feb. 12, 1990, p. 50; "So, What Is 'Environmentally Friendly'?" *New York Times*, Jan 26, 1991, p. 50; Hayes, op. cit., pp. 46–47; and "Green Market Alert's Green Product Market Forecasts," *Green Market Alert*, May 1992, p. 1.

[11]*Time*, Jan. 2, 1989, p. 45.

[12]"Union Camp Turns a Cleaner Page," *New York Times*, Oct. 20, 1993, pp. C1, C5; and "How Much Green in 'Green' Paper," *Business Week*, Nov. 1, 1993, pp. 60–61.

for companies, telling when they could use terms like "biodegradable" and "recyclable" to describe their products.[13]

Consumer advocates in several nations have begun programs that label products and packaging considered to be environmentally friendly. In 1977, the Federal Republic of Germany started the world's first environmental labeling program. Canada's Environmental Choice labeling began about the same time, Japan followed in 1988, and Norway, Sweden, France, the Netherlands, Great Britain, and Spain have similar efforts under way. Leaders of the German program claimed that improvements required of producers who use the "Blue Angel" label reduced emissions from oil and gas heaters and also lowered paint solvents entering that nation's waste stream. In the United States, consumer advocates and environmentalists have introduced "Green Seal" and "Green Cross" labels that are awarded to products considered to be environmentally acceptable. The Environmental Protection Agency has introduced its own green label, called the Energy Star.[14] Although many U.S. consumers welcomed environmental labeling, some were confused by the presence of several different labels.

Nutritional and Safety Concerns

Consumers in Western industrial nations tend to favor diets high in protein, animal fats, salt, and sugar. Processed foods that often are low in nutritional quality also are popular, as are the so-called convenience foods and fast foods that match the life-styles of busy people. As greater nutritional awareness and education have spread throughout the general public, food manufacturers have heard increasing demands from their customers who want to know more about the content of the foods they buy. Oversugared and oversalted foods and fatty meats have been at the center of nutritional concern, because too much of these items can contribute to long-term health problems. Many food experts have urged people to rely more heavily on grains, fresh unprocessed vegetables, and diets high in fiber.

To provide better information for consumers, Congress tightened food-labeling requirements. A new law, that went into effect in 1993, requires food manufacturers to adopt a uniform nutrition label, specifying the amount of calories, fat, salt, and other nutrients contained in packaged, canned, and bottled foods. The same kind of information about fresh fruits and vegetables, as well as fish, must be posted in supermarkets.

---

[13]"Mobil to Recycle the Plastic Bags from Groceries," *Wall Street Journal*, May 16, 1990, p. B1; "Mobil Unit to Face Suit on Hefty Bags," *Wall Street Journal*, June 12, 1990, pp. B1, B8; and "Guides on Environmental Ad Claims," *New York Times*, July 29, 1992, p. C3.
[14]Hayes, op. cit., pp. 46–51; and "Uncle Sam Goes on an Eco-Trip," *Business Week*, June 28, 1993, p. 76.

As consumers heeded the advice of food experts and began to eat more fresh vegetables and fruit, they confronted yet another problem—pesticide and herbicide residues left on farm products. Some of these chemicals cause nerve damage if consumed in large quantities; others have produced cancers in test animals; and some consumers have serious allergic reactions to vegetables or fruit treated with chemicals to preserve freshness or color. Children are thought to be especially at risk because they eat proportionately more vegetables and fruit per body weight than adults consume, and the chemicals are thought to do serious damage to developing nerve, digestive, and other systems.

In 1993, an important court decision involving the Delaney Clause forced the consumer movement, business, and government to take a fresh look at the issue of pesticide residue in food. The Delaney Clause, passed by Congress in 1958, is a provision of the Food, Drug, and Cosmetics Act that bans all food additives known to cause cancer in humans or animals. In the early 1990s, citizen groups sued to force the government to treat pesticides as a food additive under this law, and in 1993 the Supreme Court upheld their position. This court decision would require removal from the market of any pesticides that cause cancer and that appear as a residue in flour, juice, baked goods, or other processed foods. The Clinton administration responded by calling for repeal of the Delaney Clause, while also asking for new policies that would gradually phase out the use of dangerous pesticides.[15] Policymakers confronted the challenge of protecting the public's health without causing unnecessary harm to agricultural producers.

Advertising's Social Dimension

"There's a great deal of social consciousness building up among consumers that is to some extent putting restrictions on advertisers. In the '90s, people are going to politicize consumer products. Companies that aren't socially responsible are going to be hearing from consumers."[16] This statement by the head of an advertising agency summed up a new awareness among advertisers and consumers that advertisements do more than simply attempt to sell products. Many advertisements and advertised products carry strong, sometimes controversial social messages, as well. A vivid example is the uproar over explicit sexual terms used by rock music groups, which led to voluntary labeling of records and videotapes containing potentially offensive language. Advertising's social influ-

---

[15]"EPA Plans to Seek Loosening of a Law on Food Pesticides," *New York Times*, Feb. 2, 1993, p. A1; and "Administration's Pesticide Plan Puts Safety First," *New York Times*, Sept. 21, 1993, pp. A1, A12.
[16]"Critics Use New Soapbox to Assail Ads for Infant Formulas, Tobacco," *Wall Street Journal*, Mar. 15, 1990, p. B6.

ence is seen also in the pictures and images of people depicted in ads, in the health claims made for some products, and in the promotion of alcohol and tobacco products—particularly to young people. Some of these broader social dimensions of advertising are discussed next.

Advertising images

It is natural for almost any group in society to want to be fairly and accurately represented when appearing in advertisements. Advertising images, because they are sent out to so many viewers, have the potential to influence the way people think about other people, as well as about the product being advertised. Some advertisers have learned this lesson the hard way, as shown in the following illustrations.

Advertisements by Quaker Oats Company featured a well-known cartoon character called Popeye the Sailor. Popeye had always been known to comics-page readers as a tough fighter who was strong because he ate spinach. However, the Quaker ads showed the sailor eating instant Quaker Oatmeal and then using his legendary strength to batter his enemies, sharks, and other targets. Following these deeds, he would proclaim, "I'm Popeye the Quaker Man!" Quakers, who are members of the religious order known as the Society of Friends, and who have long been known for their peaceful, nonviolent approach to life, objected. Some Quaker schoolchildren wrote the company, saying, "We think anyone calling himself a Quaker should act like one and stick with Quaker philosophy." Others called the advertisements "totally offensive." Following these complaints, the company modified the ads, and a company official said, "Try as we might, we sometimes unwittingly offend particular groups."[17]

How to depict women in advertisements has become another puzzling problem for advertisers. To feature them exclusively in homemaking settings—waxing floors, preparing meals, tending children—runs the risk of offending women who prefer to emphasize the newer professional and working roles being filled by more and more women. Advertisers cannot ignore the two-thirds of all U.S. mothers, and over half of those with very young children, who now work outside the home. How to appeal to women consumers who now fill a variety of social and professional roles challenges advertisers to recognize the opinion-shaping influence of their advertising images. "You can't talk to all women in the same way. By targeting one group, you alienate the other," said the editor of one women's magazine.[18]

[17]"Will Quaker Oats Bow to Friendly Persuasion?" *Business Week,* Mar. 12, 1990, p. 46.
[18]"Grappling with Women's Evolving Roles," *Wall Street Journal,* Sept. 5, 1990, p. B1. Chapter 16 discusses other business changes brought about by the entry of women into the nation's workforce.

The influence of the media in projecting positive or negative images of social groups is further discussed in Chapter 18.

Health-related claims

Even more serious impacts can occur when companies make excessive health claims for their products.

U.S. aspirin makers came under pressure from the Food and Drug Administration to stop promoting aspirin as reducing the risk of a first heart attack. Their claims were based on a scientific study that said taking an aspirin every other day had lowered the risk of heart attacks in middle-aged men. The FDA said that the study's findings were preliminary, were restricted to the test group, and could not be recommended for the general population. After meeting with FDA officials, the companies voluntarily stopped their advertising claims.

Five of the country's largest commercial diet programs, including Weight Watchers International, Nutri/System, and Jenny Craig, were sued by the Federal Trade Commission for making unsubstantiated promises of weight loss. The agency wanted the diet programs to back up their advertising claims and to warn consumers that weight loss was often temporary. A FTC representative stated, "The bottom line is that losing weight is hard work—and keeping it off is harder still. . . . Consumers who buy into these programs need to understand that all too often, promises of long-term weight loss raise false hopes of an easy fix for a difficult problem."[19]

Food manufacturers must also be careful not to make exaggerated claims for their products. Under new food labeling rules, companies must follow strict guidelines when using words such as "healthy," "light," or "low-fat" to describe their products. For example, the FDA ruled that Tang, an orange-flavored drink, could not be called "healthy" because it did not restore nutrients that were originally in fresh oranges. Since 1994, food advertisers have been required to follow these guidelines.[20]

Curbing tobacco and alcohol promotions

Tobacco and alcoholic beverages carry health risks, not just for users but for others as well. For that reason, when tobacco and alcoholic beverage companies advertise their products, they are having an impact on public health that goes beyond a company's goal of persuading smokers and drinkers to use a particular brand.

Awareness of this public health problem is widespread. A survey commissioned by the *Wall Street Journal* found that almost half of U.S. consumers favor banning all television ads for beer and wine, and over half approve bans of cigarette ads in magazines and newspapers. Several other

---

[19]"Five Diet Firms Charged with Deceptive Ads," *Los Angeles Times*, Oct. 1, 1993, pp. A1, A15.
[20]"U.S. Issues Rules for Labeling Food 'Healthy,'" *New York Times*, May 5, 1994, p. B8; and "FTC to Require Food Ads to Follow FDA Label Guides," *Wall Street Journal*, May 16, 1994, p. A6.

nations, including Italy, Portugal, Norway, Sweden, Canada, Singapore, China, and Thailand, have already banished tobacco ads from television and the print media. Even the Moscow City Council passed a resolution barring most cigarette promotions. The Clinton administration proposed funding health care reform, in part, by taxes on cigarettes; and two federal agencies, the National Cancer Institute and the Office on Smoking and Health, have launched programs to fund antitobacco coalitions in every state.[21]

An issue that has been the focus of much recent controversy is advertising for alcoholic beverages and cigarettes that may be aimed at youth. The debate surrounding RJR Nabisco's use of the cartoon character, Joe Camel, to promote cigarettes, is profiled in Exhibit 14-A.

In all of these ways, consumers and their government representatives were sending a strong signal to the manufacturers and their advertising agencies that tobacco and alcohol promotions should be strictly curbed. It is another example, among many mentioned in this book, that business operates within a web of social values and social attitudes that can have a vital impact on how business should be conducted.

HOW GOVERNMENT PROTECTS CONSUMERS

The federal government's involvement in consumer affairs is extensive. During the 1960s and 1970s, Congress passed important laws to protect consumers, created new regulatory agencies, and strengthened older consumer protection agencies. These developments meant that consumers, rather than relying solely on free market competition to safeguard their interests, could also turn to government for protection. During most of the 1980s, a deregulatory attitude by the federal government tended to blunt federal initiatives on behalf of consumers. However, state governments became more active, particularly regarding price-fixing, car insurance rates, and corporate takeovers that threatened jobs and consumer incomes. The mid-1990s have witnessed a revival of government regulatory activism in many areas of consumer protection.

Goals of Consumer Laws

Figure 14-2 lists some of the safeguards provided by **consumer protection laws.** Taken together, these safeguards reflect three goals of government policymakers and regulators.

---

[21]For the survey data, see "Rebelling against Alcohol, Tobacco Ads," *Wall Street Journal*, Jan. 14, 1989, pp. B1, B11. For regulations in other countries, see "A Red Flag in Moscow on Tobacco and Liquor Ads," *New York Times*, July 20, 1993, p. C1.

EXHIBIT 14-A

THE SAGA OF JOE CAMEL

Joe Camel is a well-known cartoon character, launched in the United States in 1988 by the R. J. Reynolds Tobacco Company to promote its Camel brand of cigarettes. Sporting shades, a T-shirt, and a blazer, Joe hangs out at a trendy bar, Joe's Place, where he and his fun-loving crowd shoot pool, dance to the music of the blues quartet Hard Pack, and—of course—smoke Camels.

The Joe Camel advertising campaign has been a major success for Reynolds and its parent firm, RJR Nabisco. The brand's market share has stabilized at around 4 percent, at a time when other premium brands' shares were declining. "The Camel advertising does what we want it to do," an RJR Nabisco spokesperson commented in 1994.

The campaign also stirred a major controversy over the ethics—and even the legality—of cigarette advertising.

In a series of articles published in 1991, the *Journal of the American Medical Association (JAMA)* reported that Joe Camel was as widely recognized by children as Disney's Mickey Mouse, and that Camels had become the brand of choice among many children. The executive director of the AMA stated, "We believe the company is directing its ads to the children who are 3, 6 and 9 years old. This is an industry that kills 400,000 per year, and they have got to pick up new customers."

In 1994, the Federal Trade Commission prepared to act on a recommendation by its staff to force RJR Nabisco to halt its Joe Camel advertising. The American Lung Association, the American Heart Association, and the American Cancer Society joined former surgeons general in urging this course. But some FTC officials believed that the agency did not have the authority to block advertising that was not clearly deceptive.

R. J. Reynolds responded with a vigorous defense of its smooth-talking dromedary. The company increased its Joe Camel ad budget (even introducing a female companion, "Josephine"), attacked *JAMA*'s research, and undertook its own studies aimed at showing that Joe was not as well known among youngsters as previously reported. It also appealed to the public on the grounds of free speech rights.

SOURCE: "That's One Angry Camel," *Business Week*, Mar. 7, 1994, pp. 94–95; Susan Cohen, "Smooth Sell," *Washington Post Magazine*, Feb. 20, 1994, pp. 8–28; and "Top Health Official Demands Abolition of 'Joe Camel' Ads," *New York Times*, Mar. 10, 1992, pp. A1, C5.

First, some laws are intended to provide consumers with better information when making purchases. Consumers can make more rational choices when they have accurate information about the product, thereby making comparison with competing products easier. For example, the Truth in Lending Act requires lenders to inform borrowers of the annual rate of interest to be charged, plus related fees and service charges. The laws requiring health warnings on cigarettes and alcoholic beverages broaden the information consumers have about these items. Knowing the relative energy efficiency of household appliances, which must be posted

FIGURE 14-2

Major consumer protections specified by consumer laws.

Informational Protections

Hazardous home appliances must carry a warning label

Home products must carry a label detailing contents

Automobiles must carry a label showing detailed breakdown of price and all related costs

Credit loans require lender to disclose all relevant credit information about rate of interest, penalties, etc.

Tobacco advertisements and products must carry a health warning label

Alcoholic beverages must carry a health warning label

All costs related to real estate transactions must be disclosed

Warranties must specify the terms of the guarantee and the buyer's rights

False and deceptive advertising can be prohibited

Food and beverage labels must show complete information

Food advertising must not make false claims about nutrition

Direct Hazard Protections

Hazardous toys and games for children are banned from sale

Safety standards for motor vehicles are required

National and state speed limits are specified

Hazardous, defective, and ineffective products can be recalled under pressure from EPA, CPSC, NHTSA, and FDA

Foods contaminated by pesticides and other farm chemicals can be banned from sale

Pricing Protections

Unfair pricing, monopolistic practices, and noncompetitive acts are regulated by FTC and Justice Department and by states

Liability Protections

When injured by a product, consumers can seek legal redress

Other Protections

No discrimination in the extension of credit

by retailers, permits improved choices. False or deceptive advertising is illegal.

A second aim of consumer legislation is to protect consumers against possible hazards from products they may purchase. Required warnings about possible side effects of pharmaceutical drugs, limits placed on flammable fabrics, inspections to eliminate contaminated or spoiled meats, and the banning of lead-based paints are examples of these safeguards. A 1988 federal law requires health-warning labels on alcoholic beverages.

A third goal of consumer laws is to encourage competitive pricing. When competitors secretly agree to divide up markets among themselves, or to rig bidding so that it appears to be competitive, or to fix prices of goods and services at a noncompetitive, artificially high level, they are taking unfair advantage of consumers. Both federal and state laws forbid these practices, as discussed in Chapter 10. Competitive pricing also was promoted by the deregulation of railroads, airlines, intercity bus lines, trucking, telephones, and various financial institutions in the 1970s and 1980s. Prior to deregulation, government agencies frequently held prices artificially high and, by limiting the number of new competitors, shielded existing businesses from competition.

Major Consumer Protection Agencies

Figure 14-3 depicts the principal consumer protection agencies that operate at the federal level, along with their major areas of responsibility. The oldest of the six is the Food and Drug Administration which, along with

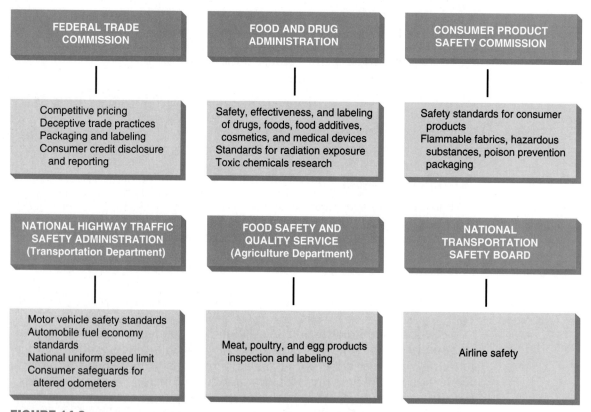

FEDERAL TRADE COMMISSION	FOOD AND DRUG ADMINISTRATION	CONSUMER PRODUCT SAFETY COMMISSION
Competitive pricing Deceptive trade practices Packaging and labeling Consumer credit disclosure and reporting	Safety, effectiveness, and labeling of drugs, foods, food additives, cosmetics, and medical devices Standards for radiation exposure Toxic chemicals research	Safety standards for consumer products Flammable fabrics, hazardous substances, poison prevention packaging
NATIONAL HIGHWAY TRAFFIC SAFETY ADMINISTRATION (Transportation Department)	FOOD SAFETY AND QUALITY SERVICE (Agriculture Department)	NATIONAL TRANSPORTATION SAFETY BOARD
Motor vehicle safety standards Automobile fuel economy standards National uniform speed limit Consumer safeguards for altered odometers	Meat, poultry, and egg products inspection and labeling	Airline safety

FIGURE 14-3

Major federal consumer protection agencies and their main responsibilities.

the Department of Agriculture's meat and poultry inspection programs, dates back to the first decade of the twentieth century. The Federal Trade Commission was established in 1914 and has been given additional powers to protect consumers over the years. Three of the agencies—the Consumer Product Safety Commission, the National Highway Traffic Safety Administration, and the National Transportation Safety Board—were created during the great wave of consumer regulations in the 1960s and early 1970s. Not pictured in Figure 14-3 is the Antitrust Division of the Department of Justice, which indirectly protects consumers by policing monopolistic and anticompetitive practices of business firms. Its functions are described further in Chapter 10.

Of these agencies, the one with perhaps the greatest impact on the business community is the Food and Drug Administration (FDA). The FDA's mission is to assure the safety and effectiveness of a wide range of consumer products, including pharmaceutical drugs, medical devices, foods, and cosmetics. The agency has authority over $960 billion worth of products—about a quarter of all consumer dollars spent each year.

One of the FDA's jobs is to review many new products prior to their introduction—such as the Shiley heart valve, mentioned at the beginning of this chapter. This job requires regulators to walk a thin line as they attempt to protect consumers. On one hand, the agency must not delay beneficial new products unnecessarily; on the other hand, it also must not approve ones that are harmful or do not work. These two types of regulatory "errors" are illustrated by the following examples.

The Sensor Pad is a simple $7 medical device, consisting of two sealed plastic sheets separated by a layer of lubricant, designed to help women conduct monthly breast self-exams. Many doctors praised the product, and its developer was honored as a finalist in an "inventor of the year" contest. The Sensor Pad product was readily approved in Canada and in many European and Asian countries. But its manufacturer in Decatur, Illinois, Inventive Products, Inc., fought unsuccessfully for almost a decade to win FDA approval. Regulators expressed concern that the device would give women a false sense of security, and they demanded that the company conduct exhaustive clinical trials comparing the number of cancers detected with and without use of the Sensor Pad. In 1994, Inventive Products' president laid off all the company's workers except two and stated, "We're at the point of surrender."[22]

In October, 1991, Optical Radiation Corp. abruptly pulled one of its medical products, called Orcolon, off the market. A gel designed to be injected into the eye during cataract surgery, Orcolon had been ap-

[22]"How a Device to Aid in Breast Self-Exams Is Kept off the Market," *Wall Street Journal*, Apr. 12, 1994, pp. A1, A5.

proved by the FDA the previous March. In the following months, numerous patients treated with Orcolon had to have surgery to save their eyes, and at least two became permanently blind. Investigators found that the gel caused a dangerous buildup of pressure in the eye—something that should have been caught during the review process. The FDA admitted that it had made a mistake in approving Orcolon, and initiated an investigation.[23]

The FDA has been criticized both for overly zealous regulation and for lax oversight of consumer safety. In the early 1990s, the agency undertook a major internal reorganization aimed at better serving the public and easing the regulatory burden on business.[24]

All six government regulatory agencies shown in Figure 14-3 are authorized by law to intervene directly into the very center of free market activities, if that is considered necessary to protect consumers. In other words, consumer protection laws and agencies substitute government-mandated standards and the decisions of government officials for decision making by private buyers and sellers.

Product Liability: A Special Problem

In today's complicated economy, consumers' relationships with products they use and their relationships with producers of those products are complicated and abstract. The burden of responsibility for product performance has been shifted to the producer, under the legal doctrine of **product liability**. Although many businesses have attempted to assume much of the responsibility through money-back guarantees and other similar policies, consumers have thought that this is not enough and have demanded that business assume a larger burden of responsibility. The result has been a strengthening of product liability laws and more favorable court attitudes toward consumer claims. Walls protecting producers from consumer lawsuits have crumbled, and there has been a dramatic increase in product liability suits.

Traditionally consumers had little legal recourse against producers of faulty products. The liability (legal responsibility) of manufacturers was limited, and the consumer bore the burden of proving injury. In recent years, however, court decisions have become more favorable to the consumer. The following sections discuss three legal doctrines—privity of contract, warranties, and strict liability—and their significance for consumers' legal rights. These three doctrines are summarized in Figure 14-4.

---

[23]"Amid Lax Regulation, Medical Devices Flood a Vulnerable Market," *Wall Street Journal*, Mar. 24, 1992.

[24]"Getting the Lead Out at the FDA," *Business Week*, Oct. 25, 1993, pp. 96–98; and "Inside FDA: Building New Consensus to Improve Public Safety," *Washington Post*, July 15, 1993, p. A25.

FIGURE 14-4

Three types of legal liability to consumers.

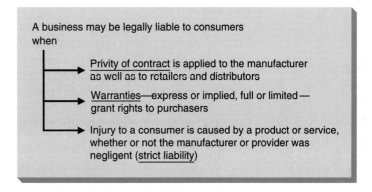

A business may be legally liable to consumers when

Privity of contract is applied to the manufacturer as well as to retailers and distributors

Warranties—express or implied, full or limited—grant rights to purchasers

Injury to a consumer is caused by a product or service, whether or not the manufacturer or provider was negligent (strict liability)

Privity of contract

The doctrine of privity of contract held that producers could avoid responsibility for product failure if a product was purchased from someone other than the manufacturer. This meant that injured consumers could sue only the person from whom they purchased a defective product—not the producer. The dealer could then sue the wholesaler, who could then sue the manufacturer. In a simple business system, this doctrine probably made a great deal of sense. But as the distance between consumer and producer widened and as products passed through longer and more complex channels of distribution, this legal principle began to fade. The landmark court decision was rendered in 1916.

> MacPherson purchased a new Buick from a local automobile dealer. Shortly thereafter defective wooden spokes in a wheel collapsed, and MacPherson was injured as a result. He sued Buick. The company claimed that MacPherson had purchased the car from a dealer and not from Buick and therefore Buick had no obligation to him. The judge ruled that Buick had been negligent because the wheel had not been inspected before it was put on the car. He further ruled that Buick was responsible for defects resulting from negligence, regardless of how many distributive firms were in between.

This legal philosophy has been expanded since the MacPherson decision. Today an injured consumer can sue any or all people in the chain of distribution. In general, the courts have reasoned that through advertising and labeling, manufacturers make a variety of claims about a product. The manufacturer intends and expects the product to be purchased and used in accordance with these performance claims and assurances of quality. Therefore, when a product fails to live up to expectations and causes injury to the purchaser, the consumer has the right to be reimbursed.

Warranties

A warranty is a guarantee or assurance by the seller. There are two kinds—express and implied. When a product is offered for sale, the seller makes claims for its characteristics. Claims that are explicitly stated by the seller are express warranties. Statements on a warranty card that the parts of a product will not fail within ninety days from the time of purchase are examples of express warranties. Not all express warranties are on the warranty card. Statements on labels, wrappers, packages, and in advertising also are express warranties.

More troublesome for sellers is the question of implied warranties. Courts have held that simply by selling a product to a customer the seller implies that the product is fit for the ordinary use for which it is likely to be used. The landmark case in the area of implied warranty occurred in 1960.

> In this case, Claus Henningsen purchased a new automobile that he and his wife drove around town for several days. Then, when driving out of town, the steering mechanism failed, and Mrs. Henningsen crashed into a highway sign and then into a brick wall. She sustained injuries and the car was a total loss. Henningsen went to court. The automobile company claimed that Henningsen had signed a disclaimer when he bought the car and this limited the liability of the company to replacement of defective parts. The court held that the company could not avoid its legal responsibility to make automobiles good enough to serve the purpose for which they were intended.

Congress attempted to clarify warranty provisions by passing the Magnuson-Moss Warranty Act in 1975. The law, administered by the FTC, requires manufacturers, retailers, and importers to specify whether warranties they voluntarily issue are full or limited, says the terms must be spelled out in clear language, and gives consumers the right to sue if warranties are not honored.

Strict liability

Within the last few years courts have increasingly taken the position that manufacturers are responsible for injuries resulting from use of their products. One result has been a rapid rise in the number of personal injury and product liability lawsuits—from about 2,400 in 1975 to 13,400 in 1989 in the federal courts alone—increasing from 2 to about 6 percent of the civil caseload. The cost to industry of general liability insurance during the same period rose from $3.1 billion to $19.1 billion annually.[25] Eighty-three percent of executives in a recent poll felt that their decisions were increasingly affected by the fear of lawsuits, and 62 percent said the civil justice system significantly hampered the ability of U.S. firms to com-

---

[25]W. Kip Viscusi, *Reforming Products Liability*, Cambridge: Harvard University Press, 1991, pp. 17–18.

pete with Japanese and European companies.[26] Small companies are especially vulnerable to lawsuits and may be driven out of business by sky-high liability insurance rates.

Under existing court interpretations, it is not necessary for consumers to prove either negligence or breach of warranty by the producer. Nor is the consumer's own negligence an acceptable defense by the manufacturer. If a product is judged to be inherently dangerous, manufacturers can be held liable for injuries caused by use of the product. This doctrine, known as **strict liability**, extends to all who were involved in the final product—suppliers, sellers, contractors, assemblers, and manufacturers of component parts.

The following case illustrates the extent to which businesses can be held liable:

> In 1994, an eighty-one-year-old woman was awarded $2.9 million by a jury in Albuquerque, New Mexico, for burns suffered when she spilled a cup of hot coffee in her lap. The woman, who had purchased the coffee at a McDonald's drive-through window, was burned when she tried to open the lid as she sat in her car. In court, McDonald's argued that customers like their coffee steaming, that their cups warned drinkers that the contents are hot, and that the woman was to blame for spilling the coffee herself. But jurors disagreed, apparently swayed by arguments that the woman's burns were severe—requiring skin grafts and a seven-day hospital stay—and by evidence that McDonald's had not cooled down its coffee even after receiving many earlier complaints. McDonald's appealed the jury's verdict and later settled the case with the elderly woman for an undisclosed amount.[27]

In this case, McDonald's was held liable for damages even though it provided a warning and the customer's actions contributed to her burns.

Much of the increase in product liability cases over the past two decades can be traced to a rise in the number of cases involving asbestos, a mineral fiber widely used by industry and in consumer products, that is known to cause cancer and other serious illnesses. In 1988, Manville Corporation, the largest maker of asbestos, emerged from bankruptcy after establishing a trust valued at between $2.3 and $3 billion to pay liability claims. The workers and other victims of asbestos who have received compensation from this fund have received an average of $20,000 each after lawyers' fees.[28]

---

[26]"Guilty! Too Many Lawyers and Too Much Litigation: Here's a Better Way," *Business Week*, Apr. 13, 1992, p. 66.

[27]"How a Jury Decided That a Coffee Spill Is Worth $2.9 Million," *Wall Street Journal*, Sept. 1, 1994, pp. A1, A5; and "McDonald's Settles Lawsuit Over Burn from Coffee," *Wall Street Journal*, Dec. 2, 1994, p. A14.

[28]An account of the asbestos litigation may be found in Arthur Sharplin, "Johns-Manville and Riverwood-Schuller," *Case Research Journal*, vol. 13, no. 1, Winter 1993, pp. 15–40.

Business efforts to reform the product liability laws

Faced with increasing liability suits and the costs of insuring against them, business has lobbied for changes in laws and court proceedings. In the 1980s and early 1990s, bills were introduced in Congress that would establish the following principles in product liability suits.

- *Set up uniform federal standards for determining liability.* Companies would not have to go through repeated trials on the same charges in many different states, which would lower legal costs for companies and help them develop a uniform legal strategy for confronting liability charges in court.
- *Shift the burden of proving liability to consumers.* Consumers would have to prove that a manufacturer knew or should have known that a product design was defective before it began producing the item. Under present law and judicial interpretations, a company is considered to be at fault if a product injures the user, whether or not the company was negligent.
- *Eliminate some bases for liability claims.* Products not measuring up to a manufacturer's own specifications—for example, poorly made tires that blow out at normal speeds—could be the basis for a liability claim, but the vast majority of liability cases go further and blame poorly designed products or a failure of the manufacturer to warn of dangers.
- *Require the loser to pay the legal costs of the winner.* If a plaintiff (consumer) refused an out-of-court settlement offer from the company and then received less in trial, he or she would have to pay the company's legal fees—up to the amount of his or her own fees. This would discourage many plaintiffs from proceeding to trial.
- *Limit punitive damages.* (Punitive damages punish the manufacturer for wrongdoing, rather than compensate the victim for actual losses.) Punitive damage awards over the past twenty-five years have averaged $625,000, and some awards in recent years—like the one in the Remington case, mentioned at the beginning of this chapter—have been in the multi-millions of dollars.[29] One proposal would limit punitive damages to $250,000 or three times compensatory damages, whichever was greater.

In 1995, Congress once again took up the issue of product liability law reform. Although supported by many business groups, including the Business Roundtable and the National Association of Manufacturers, these reform proposals faced vigorous opposition from consumers' organizations and from the American Trial Lawyers Association, representing plaintiffs' attorneys. These groups defended the existing product liability system,

---

[29]"Product Suits Yield Few Punitive Awards," *Wall Street Journal*, Jan. 6, 1992, p. B1.

saying that it put needed pressure on companies to make and keep products safe.[30]

POSITIVE BUSINESS RESPONSES TO CONSUMERISM

The consumer movement has demonstrated to business that it is expected to perform at high levels of efficiency, reliability, and fairness in order to satisfy the consuming public. Because business has not always responded quickly or fully enough, consumer advocates and their organizations have turned to government for protection. On the other hand, much effort has been devoted by individual business firms and by entire industries to encourage voluntary responses to consumer demands. Some of the more prominent positive responses are discussed next.

Total Quality Management

In the 1980s and 1990s, many businesses adopted a philosophy of management known as **total quality management (TQM).** This approach, which borrows from Japanese management techniques, emphasizes achieving high quality and customer satisfaction through teamwork and continuous improvement of a company's product or service. TQM businesses seek to "delight the customer," as shown in the following example.

> At the Saturn plant in Spring Hill, Tennessee, TQM methods have been used to produce a car of superior quality. Joint labor-management teams designed the car from the start to compete head-on with popular Japanese imports. Workers can stop the assembly line if they see a defect. Saturn keeps in close contact with car buyers, so it can correct any problems that crop up. The result has been a vehicle that has been extremely popular with customers. Saturn topped all other domestic cars in the 1994 J. D. Power survey of customer satisfaction.[31]

Total quality management is a response to pressure from consumer activists and an attempt by business to address its customers' needs. It is an example of the interactive strategy discussed in Chapter 3, where companies try to anticipate and respond to emerging stakeholder expectations. One of the primary changes created by the TQM movement has been for companies to focus on the customer. This occurs in many different ways.

[30]"First of Three Bills on Legal System Is Passed in House," *New York Times,* Mar. 8, 1995, pp. A1, A13; and "Vast Overhaul of Tort System Fails in Senate," *New York Times,* May 5, 1995, pp. A1, A13. For a discussion of the consumer viewpoint on product liability reform, see Peter Nye, "The Faces of Product Liability: Keeping the Courthouse Door Open," *Public Citizen,* Nov.–Dec. 1992, pp. 16–21.
[31]Barry Bluestone and Irving Bluestone, "Reviving American Industry: A Labor-Management Partnership," *Current,* May 1993, pp. 10–16.

Consumer Affairs Departments

Since the 1970s, many large corporations have operated consumer affairs departments, often placing a vice president in charge. These centralized departments normally handle consumer inquiries and complaints about a company's products and services, particularly in cases where a customer has not been able to resolve differences with local dealers. Some companies have installed consumer "hot lines" for dissatisfied customers to place telephone calls directly to the manufacturer. Experienced companies are aware that consumer complaints received internally by a consumer affairs department can be handled more quickly, at lower cost, and with less risk of losing goodwill than if customers take a legal route or if their complaints receive widespread media publicity.

Arbitration and Consumer Action Panels

Companies have also set up both inside and outside procedures for dealing with consumer complaints. Some have established arbitration panels that are given authority to settle disputes between customers and the company. In these cases, specially appointed arbitrators who are not related to either party in the dispute make final decisions.

General Motors, Ford, Chrysler, and many foreign auto importers "now sponsor some kind of local umpire system that will handle knotty warranty, product, service, or sales problems when the customer cannot get satisfactory redress from the company or dealer."[32] Automakers find that many complaints—from 40 to 85 percent—can be resolved without going to an arbitration panel. They also have learned that these referee programs reduce consumer dissatisfaction and improve the industry's image. Industry groups have also set up consumer action panels (CAPs) to help resolve consumer complaints.

In some cases, companies have taken additional positive actions to address consumer concerns. Following two airplane crashes in 1994 and a drop in bookings apparently caused by travelers' safety concerns, USAir hired a former U.S. Air Force commander to oversee safety procedures and brought in an outside company to review flight operations and procedures.[33]

Product Recalls

Beginning in the mid-1970s, **product recalls** by companies became a more frequent way of dealing with consumer dissatisfaction. A product re-

[32]"Detroit's Tonic for Lemon Buyers," *Business Week*, Apr. 4, 1983, pp. 54–55; and Leslie Maitland, "Arbitration Plan Set for Defects in G.M. Cars," *New York Times*, Apr. 27, 1983, p. 1.
[33]"Polishing Up Air Safety," *Business Week*, Dec. 5, 1994, p. 46; and "USAir's Flight Plan Leaves Little Room to Maneuver," *Business Week*, Oct. 17, 1994, p. 48.

call occurs when a company, either voluntarily or under an agreement with a government agency, takes back all items found to be dangerously defective. Sometimes these products are in the hands of consumers; at other times they may be in the factory, in wholesale warehouses, or on the shelves of retail stores. Wherever they are in the chain of distribution or use, the manufacturer tries to notify consumers or potential users about the defect so that they will return the items. A recalled product may be repaired or replaced or destroyed, depending upon the problem. In 1993, automakers recalled 11 million vehicles, the largest number since 1977, including Ford Taurus, Honda Accord, and GM minivan models. Analysts said that the rise in recalls reflected not a decline in quality, but rather the growing complexity of many vehicles. Companies had also learned that they could build customer loyalty by fixing problems promptly through well-handled recalls.[34]

The four major government agencies responsible for most mandatory recalls are the Food and Drug Administration, the National Highway Traffic Safety Administration, the Environmental Protection Agency (which can recall polluting motor vehicles), and the Consumer Product Safety Commission.

CONSUMERISM'S ACHIEVEMENTS

After thirty-five years of the consumer movement, its leaders could point to some important gains for U.S. consumers. Consumers in the 1990s are better informed about the goods and services they purchase, are more aware of their rights when something goes wrong, and are better protected against inflated advertising claims, hazardous or ineffective products, and unfair pricing. Several consumer organizations serve as watchdogs of buyers' interests, and a network of federal and state regulatory agencies acts for the consuming public.

Some businesses, too, have heard the consumer message and have reacted positively. They have learned to assign high priority to the things consumers expect—high-quality goods and services, reliable and effective products, safety in the items they buy, fair prices, and marketing practices (such as advertising) that do not threaten important human and social values.

All of these achievements, in spite of negative episodes that occasionally occur, bring the U.S. consuming public closer to realizing former President John F. Kennedy's four consumer rights: to be safe, to be informed, to have choices, and to be heard.

---

[34]"In the Year of the Recall, Some Companies Had to Fix More Cars Than They Made," *Wall Street Journal*, Feb. 24, 1994, p. B1.

SUMMARY POINTS OF THIS CHAPTER

- The U.S. consumer movement that began in the 1960s represents an attempt to promote the interests of consumers by balancing the amount of market power held by sellers and buyers.
- By the late 1980s the consuming public was aware that many consumer products and services, whose production and distribution generate much solid waste and hazardous substances, can be harmful to the environment. Public pressures have been exerted on business to correct some of these environmental impacts.
- The general public's growing interest in nutrition and safety, plus the ability of advertising to exert widespread social influence, brought new demands for business to be socially responsible in serving consumers and led to new food-labeling requirements in the 1990s.
- Consumer protection laws and regulatory agencies attempt to assure that consumers are treated fairly, receive adequate information, are protected against potential hazards, have free choices in the market, and have legal recourse when problems develop.
- Business has complained about the rising number of product liability lawsuits and the high cost of insuring against them. But, efforts to reform product liability laws have been opposed by consumer groups and lawyers representing people injured by dangerous or defective products.
- Socially responsible companies have responded to the consumer movement by giving serious consideration to consumer problems, increasing channels of communication with customers, and recalling defective products. They have also pursued total quality management in an effort to meet—and even anticipate—consumers' needs.

KEY TERMS AND CONCEPTS USED IN THIS CHAPTER

- Consumer movement
- Consumer bill of rights
- Green consumerism
- Consumer protection laws
- Product liability
- Strict liability
- Total quality management (TQM)
- Product recalls

DISCUSSION CASE

GENERAL MOTORS' PICKUP TRUCK

On February 4, 1993, Elaine and Thomas Moseley watched as an Atlanta, Georgia, jury returned a verdict of $105 million against General Motors.

The Moseleys had sued GM after their son, Shannon, who was seventeen at the time, burned to death in a fiery crash while driving a GM-made pickup truck. The Moseleys contended that the truck had a deadly design flaw. Because its two gasoline tanks were mounted on the sides of the vehicle, outside the frame, they were vulnerable to explosion and fire in a side-impact crash—the kind Shannon had been in.

The Moseleys' attorney presented testimony from a former GM safety engineer, who told jurors that the company had not conducted proper tests, knew that the side-mounted gas tanks were dangerous, and had failed to fix the problem. The youth's parents refused settlement offers from GM, insisting that the case go to trial. Afterward, his voice breaking with emotion, Thomas Moseley said, "We've given a statement to GM and the government. It's for everybody out there. People I don't know, the son I did know." GM said it would appeal, arguing that the trucks were safe and that its gas tanks exceeded all federal government standards for safety.

The decision—and its attendant publicity—could not have come at a worse time for General Motors. The company had reported a loss for 1992 of $4.5 billion, and in January 1993 Standard and Poor's had downgraded its debt.

The pickup truck at the center of the controversy had been introduced by GM in 1973. The company changed the design in 1988, placing the gas tank inside the frame. The large Chevrolet and GMC pickups were the company's best selling models and among the most profitable. In 1993, almost 5 million of the side-saddle-designed trucks were still on the road in the United States and Canada.

Evidence on the vehicles' safety record was mixed. The Center for Auto Safety, an affiliate of Ralph Nader's Public Citizen, claimed that the design flaw had been responsible for over 1,200 deaths. But an insurance industry study showed that although the GM pickups were more vulnerable to fire in side-impact crashes, they were safer in some other types of crashes, giving them an overall safety record similar to other manufacturers' pickups.

Shortly after the Moseley verdict, GM went on the offensive. In November 1992, *Dateline NBC*, a television newsmagazine show, had aired a fifteen-minute segment on the pickups called "Waiting to Explode?" The episode included video footage—shot by NBC as a demonstration—of a GM truck catching fire after being struck from the side in a simulated crash.

On February 8—the Monday after the Thursday of the Moseley verdict—Harry J. Pearce, GM's general counsel, held a two-hour press conference in which he vigorously disputed NBC's conclusions and presented evidence to show that NBC had staged its video by using small rockets to ignite the fire. "We sure don't build them that way," Pearce stated, meaning pickups with rockets attached.

The company's spirited counterpunch provoked considerable admiration in some quarters. The *Wall Street Journal*, for example, called the press conference a "brilliantly executed rejection of a highly public attack on [GM's] corporate reputation." NBC immediately apologized and agreed to pay GM $2 million to cover the cost of its investigation. The head of NBC's news division resigned soon afterward.

In April 1993, after a lengthy investigation and much pressure from consumer groups, The National Highway Traffic Safety Administration (NHTSA) told General Motors that it should recall and repair its 1973–1987 pickups. Saying a recall would cost between $500 million and $1 billion, GM flatly refused to comply and vowed to fight in court. Government attorneys later acknowledged that they would probably lose a legal showdown, throwing the recall effort into disarray.

In July 1993, General Motors settled all class-action lawsuits involving its pickups by offering owners a $1,000 coupon toward the purchase of a new GM truck. Joan Claybrook, president of Public Citizen, told the press that "This bizarre settlement sounds more like a marketing strategy than a serious resolution of a safety hazard." In announcing the settlement, a GM spokesperson said, "GM has consistently maintained, and continues to maintain, that the fuel systems in these full-size pickup trucks do not have a safety-related defect."[35]

Discussion Questions

1. In your opinion, was the safety of GM's pickup trucks acceptable? Identify all of the stakeholders in this situation, and tell how each would answer this question.
2. Comment on General Motors' response to pressure from the media, government, consumer groups, and individual lawsuits. Did the company react in socially responsible and socially responsive ways? Were its actions and settlement offer reasonable?
3. Using the GM pickup episode as background information, tell who you believe should be mainly responsible for consumer well-being. Should it be the individual consumer, the companies that make consumer products, or consumer protection agencies of government?

[35]Based on news accounts appearing in the *Wall Street Journal, New York Times, Los Angeles Times, Washington Post, Fortune, Business Week,* and Center for Auto Safety newsletters between November 1992 and July 1994.

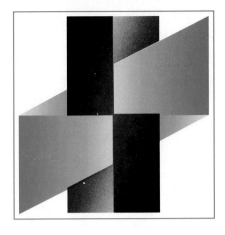

15

The Employee-Employer Relationship

Employees and employers are engaged in a critical relationship affecting the corporation's performance. There is a basic economic aspect to this relationship. Employees provide labor for the firm; employers compensate workers for their contribution of skill or productivity. Yet, also present in the employee-employer exchange are numerous social, ethical, legal, and public policy issues. Attention to the multiple aspects of this association can benefit the firm, its workers, and society.

Key Questions and Chapter Objectives

This chapter focuses on these key questions and objectives:

■ What are employers' duties and obligations within the "employer-employee contract" to provide job security and equal opportunities for employment to their workers?

■ How does greater diversity in the workforce affect a business's obligations to its employees?

■ As governmental intervention into employee safety and health issues increases, what are a business's duties in protecting its workers?

■ Does a business's acquiring information about its workers violate an employee's right to privacy? For example, do drug testing, AIDS testing, and honesty tests violate an employee's privacy?

■ Do businesses have the right to regulate employees' personal activities, like smoking, that are legally permitted?

■ Do employees have a duty to blow the whistle on corporate misconduct, or should employees always be loyal to their employer?

Joseph Hazelwood had a history of drinking. Although his employer knew of his problem, the firm failed to prevent him from working while intoxicated. In March 1989, Hazelwood, who was later tested and found to be legally drunk, grounded the Exxon oil tanker, the *Valdez*, spilling nearly 11 million gallons of crude oil in the pristine Prince William Sound off the coast of Alaska—the largest oil spill in United States. In the first of a series of court trials against Exxon, where over $15 billion in compensatory and punitive damages were sought, a jury awarded $286.8 million to a group of commercial fishermen due to the destruction of salmon and other fish previously living in the Alaskan coastal waters.

Although most U.S. oil companies prohibit alcohol on their U.S.-flag vessels, alcohol is available aboard some foreign tankers as part of a ship crew's labor agreement. Over half of the tankers owned by U.S. oil companies fly foreign flags, where cultural customs approve serving beer and wine at mealtime. Wanting to avoid other environmental disasters linked to alcohol use, but wanting also to keep tanker crews satisfied with working conditions, oil company officials faced a tricky situation.[1]

Flour-mill operators confronted another knotty problem affecting their employees. Research revealed a much higher rate of lymph cancer in flour-mill workers than among others in the grain industry, leading some to believe that chemicals used to combat insect infestations in the grain elevators were carcinogenic. Workers most exposed to these chemicals seemed to contract cancer from three to eight times more frequently than coworkers. Flour-mill managers faced the prospect of having to give up the chemical fumigants that had been widely used since the 1960s. Doing so might greatly increase flour-mill operating costs and result in lower-quality flour for bakers and other consumers.[2]

THE EMPLOYEE-EMPLOYER CONTRACT

Employees and employers are engaged in a stakeholder relationship which includes numerous expectations by both parties. The employer, for example, has assumed various duties and obligations. Some of these responsibilities are economic or legal; others are social or ethical in nature. The relationship is clearly more than simply paying a worker for the labor provided. Cultural values and traditions also play a role. In Europe, em-

---

[1]"Jury Finds Exxon Reckless in Oil Spill; Damages of $16.5 Billion May Be Sought," *Wall Street Journal*, June 14, 1994, p. A3; "Jury Orders Exxon to Pay $286.8 Million," *Wall Street Journal*, Aug. 12, 1994, p. A3; and "Oil Concerns Revising Rules on Drinking Aboard Tankers in Aftermath of Valdez," *Wall Street Journal*, Feb. 23, 1990, p. A7A.
[2]"Flour-Mill Workers Face Increased Risk of Lymph Cancer, Federal Study Shows," *Wall Street Journal*, May 16, 1990, p. B4.

ployers feel they have a duty to include workers on the board of directors to assist in forming company policy. For many years Japanese employers have offered their workers lifelong employment, although this practice is being modified. By contrast, since the late 1800s in the United States the contractual basis for employee labor has been employment-at-will. **Employment-at-will** means that employees are hired and retain their jobs "at the will of," or as decided by, the employer. Recently, this contractual notion has undergone a significant transformation in the United States. An increase in "wrongful discharge claims" by employees has dramatically curtailed American employers' freedom to terminate workers. Workers are assuming greater responsibilities in the employee-employer relationship.[3]

The New Social Contract

The shift toward greater employee responsibility is due in part to employers' actions which have influenced the basic expectations underlying the employee-employer relationship. Beginning in the late 1980s and continuing into the 1990s, fierce global competition and greater attention toward improving the "bottom line" resulted in significant corporate restructuring of the organization and downsizing (termination) of employees. Along with these changes came a new way of thinking about the employee-employer relationship.[4] As described in Figure 15-1, the new **Employer-Employee Social Contract** shifts the focus of employers' obligations away from long-term job security. The new relationship is aimed at satisfying employees at work by emphasizing interesting and challenging work, performance-based compensation, and worker training to become more employable within and outside the company. In return, employees are expected to contribute to the employer-employee social contract by providing a strong commitment to the job task and work team. Employees are expected to share in the responsibility of achieving company success. The new message for employees is: *you* are responsible for your lifetime employment.[5]

Although formally evolving in the United States, evidence of this change of contractual employment can be seen in many countries. In a 1990 U.S. downsizing poll, 43 percent of the companies reported workforce reductions and cited actual or anticipated business downturns as the primary reason for the employee cuts. Companies reduced their

[3]See Marvin J. Levine, "The Erosion of the Employment-at-Will Doctrine: Recent Developments," *Labor Law Journal*, Feb. 1994, pp. 79–89.
[4]See a collection of papers in *Human Resources Briefing: The New Employer-Employee Contract*, New York: The Conference Board, 1994; and "A New Social Contract to Benefit Employer and Employee," *Wall Street Journal*, Nov. 29, 1994, p. B1.
[5]Brian O'Reilly, "The New Deal," *Fortune*, June 13, 1994, pp. 44–51.

FIGURE 15-1

The new employer-employee social contract.

SOURCE: From James E. Post, "The New Social Contract," in Oliver Williams and John Houck, eds., *The Global Challenge to Corporate Social Responsibility* (New York: Oxford University Press, 1995); and Barbara W. Altman and James E. Post, "Challenges in Balancing Corporate Economic and Social Responsibilities," Boston University Working Paper, Boston, MA, 1994.

Emphasizes:

- The burden of maintaining employment shifts from the employer to the employee
- Job security is no longer based on seniority but on job performance
- Worker employability is enhanced by training and development programs

Positive Results for Employers

- Greater ability to move employees from job to job
- Greater ease in removing marginal performers
- Greater ability to recruit and retain high performers
- More flexibility due to temporary workforce
- More self-directed, independent employees
- Development of diversity and work/family programs

Negative Results for Employers

- Lower employee morale
- Reduced productivity
- Employee mistrust of the firm
- Temporary workforce more difficult to manage
- Increase in unplanned turnover
- Uncertainty of job skills possessed by future workforce
- Pressure to develop social programs to replace job security

workforce by an average of 10.7 percent during that year. Fifteen percent of the firms reported additional downsizing to occur within a year. In the first quarter of 1994 employers announced more than 3,100 job terminations *per day.*[6]

> In 1994, Digital Equipment experienced an unexpectedly heavy third-quarter loss and feared that the entire firm could be at risk. The firm's response was to slash 20,000 employees from the organization's 85,000 person workforce. This dramatic layoff was preceded by terminations of nearly 40,000 employees during the previous eighteen months. "Failure to act promptly will result in greater loss of employment," warned Digital's CEO Robert Palmer. "In fact, the entire enterprise could be at risk."[7]

[6]The results from the AMA downsizing survey and other issues involving corporate layoffs are discussed in Eric Rolfe Greenberg, "Downsizing AMA Survey Results," *Compensation & Benefits Review*, July–Aug. 1991, pp. 33–38. See also "The Pain of Downsizing," *Business Week*, May 9, 1994, p. 60.

[7]"Digital Plans at Least 20,000 More Job Cuts," *Wall Street Journal*, May 6, 1994, p. A3.

Government Intervention in the United States

Due to the increasing economic and social impacts of employee layoffs, government intervention in the United States is attempting to aid employees affected by job termination. The Clinton administration proposed amending the **Worker Adjustment Retraining Notification Act,** also referred to as the WARN Act or the Plant Closing Law enacted in 1988. Under this law, companies are required to provide sixty days notice whenever companies lay off a third or more workers at any site of 150 workers, or if they cut 500 employees at any facility. About half of all plant closings are exempt from the law due to size. Under the new proposal, any company that laid off 50 workers would have to give its workers advance notice. In 1991, the Labor Department estimated that there were 3,900 layoffs involving at least 50 workers.[8]

In addition to stricter governmental regulation, President Clinton unveiled an ambitious proposal to increase job-search services, counseling, and training for the jobless. The proposed Re-employment Act of 1994 largely targeted middle-class workers and would have merged six existing federal training programs. Companies are also voluntarily developing worker retraining programs, primarily for blue-collar workers, or extensive job outplacement services, typically targeted at white-collar employees recently laid off. However, these programs are often subject to economic recessions and company cutbacks.

International Alternatives to Employee Layoffs

Employee layoffs are a common by-product of the economic impacts of global competition or changes in corporate strategies. However, companies operating in other parts of the world are finding alternatives to firing employees.

In Japan, where lifelong employment has been a sacred cultural tradition, Matsushita Electric Industrial announced a corporate restructuring in December 1993. In the United States, this type of reorganization usually means massive layoffs. Instead, Matsushita shifted 6,000 administrative jobs to sales and new market development. Similarly, Toyota Motor developed a creative alternative to worker layoffs. The company created a new category of temporary professional workers by offering new employees a limited number of one-year contracts. As an incentive, the firm compensated the employees with a high annual salary

[8]"Clinton Unveils $13 Billion Proposal to Streamline Nation's Jobless System," *Wall Street Journal,* Mar. 10, 1994, p. A2.

based on individual merit, rather than the traditional system of linking pay with seniority and company performance.[9]

European businesses have often resisted employee firings. Air France reduced its workforce in 1993 by 2,100 people, or about 5 percent, through early retirements and natural attrition. A European auto manufacturer, Volkswagen, began an experimental four-day work week to ease its troubled financial picture.[10]

EQUAL JOB OPPORTUNITY

Working to ensure **equal job opportunity** continues to be a socially desirable goal for U.S. business. This area of employee relations calls for positive responses and initiatives if business is to continue its evolution toward social responsiveness and public approval.

Government Policies and Regulations

Beginning on a major scale in the 1960s, U.S. presidents issued directives and Congress enacted laws intended to improve equal treatment of employees. The most important of these are shown in Figure 15-2. These government rules apply to most businesses in the following ways:

- Discrimination based on race, color, religion, sex, national origin, physical or mental handicap, or age is prohibited in all employment practices. This includes hiring, promotion, job classification, and assignment, compensation, and other conditions of work.
- Government contractors must have written affirmative action plans detailing how they are working positively to overcome past and present effects of discrimination in their workforce.
- Women and men must receive equal pay for performing equal work.

The major agencies charged with enforcing federal equal employment opportunity laws and executive orders are the **Equal Employment Opportunity Commission (EEOC)** and the Office of Federal Contract Compliance Programs (OFCCP). The EEOC was created in 1964 and given

---

[9]"Matsushita Plans to Shift Workers in Restructuring," *Wall Street Journal*, Dec. 9, 1993, p. A11; "Tradition Be Damned," *Business Week*, Oct. 31, 1994, pp. 108–110; and "Toyota Creates Work Contracts Challenging Lifetime-Job System," *Wall Street Journal*, Jan. 24, 1994, p. 10.

[10]For a full discussion and contrast of American and European corporate practices regarding layoffs, see "In Employment Policy, America and Europe Make a Sharp Contrast," *Wall Street Journal*, Mar. 14, 1994, pp. A1, A6.

FIGURE 15-2

Major federal equal job opportunity laws and executive orders.

LAWS	
Equal Pay Act Requires equal pay for equal work.	1963
Civil Rights Act Created EEOC. Forbids job discrimination by race, color, religion, and national origin.	1964
Age Discrimination in Employment Act Forbids job discrimination against persons forty to sixty-five years of age.	1967
Equal Employment Opportunity Act Strengthened enforcement powers and expanded jurisdiction of EEOC. Forbids sex discrimination.	1972
Vocational Rehabilitation Act Requires affirmative action for handicapped persons by government contractors and other companies.	1973
Americans with Disabilities Act Bans discrimination against disabled people in employment, public accommodations, transportation, and telecommunications. Provides protection for AIDS-infected workers.	1990
Civil Rights Act Extends punitive liability to employers who discriminate based on sex or disability. Makes it easier for workers to sue employers over alleged job discrimination.	1991

EXECUTIVE ORDERS AND GUIDELINES	
Executive Order 10925, President Kennedy Prohibits job discrimination by government contractors.	1961
Executive Order 11246 and 11375, President Johnson Requires written affirmative action programs by most government contractors.	1965, 1967
Revised Order No. 4, OFCCP, Department of Labor Requires results-oriented affirmative action, with goals, timetables, and statistical analysis.	1970

added enforcement powers in 1972 and 1990. This agency is primarily responsible for enforcing provisions of the Civil Rights Acts of 1964 and 1991, the Equal Opportunity Act, the Equal Pay Act, the Age Discrimination in Employment Act, and the Americans with Disabilities Act. The OFCCP in the Department of Labor monitors compliance of government contractors.

Regulators and courts first used a results-oriented approach to these laws. In other words, a company would be considered in violation of the law if statistical analysis revealed that its jobs were out of line with the proportions of whites and nonwhites or men and women potentially available for such work. Later, other judicial interpretations were handed down. These decisions, in the early 1980s, were seen as "gains" for business because companies were less vulnerable to discrimination lawsuits and freer to make personnel decisions on their own.

In the 1990s, government efforts continued to place additional responsibilities upon businesses and to overturn the effects of the U.S. Supreme Court decisions from the early 1980s. For example, under the 1990 EEOC guidelines, employers faced greater liability for employee conduct involving sexual harassment. EEOC guidelines proposed in 1994 would extend employers' liability to harassment involving race, color, religion, national origin, age, and disability. In addition, employers were obligated to demonstrate that alleged discriminatory practices were "job related" and consistent with practices necessary to operate a business, according to the 1991 Civil Rights Act.

Corporate Responses

Generally, businesses have developed approaches to curb discrimination and equalize employment opportunities. They are shown in Figure 15-3.

One of the most successful approaches has been affirmative action programs. Since the mid-1960s, major government contractors have been required by presidential executive order to adopt written affirmative action plans specifying goals, actions, and timetables for promoting greater on-the-job equality. Their purpose is to reduce job discrimination by encouraging companies to take positive (that is, affirmative) steps to overcome past employment practices and traditions that may have been discriminatory.

Companies that have not responded affirmatively to equality in employment often find themselves facing expensive lawsuits. For example, in 1992 State Farm Insurance Company was accused of sex discrimination

FIGURE 15-3

Alternative methods for reducing job discrimination and promoting greater job equality for excluded groups.

- **Passive Nondiscrimination:** all company hiring and promotion decisions are made without regard to race, sex, age, color, religion, national origin, or handicap

- **Affirmative Action:** company efforts to ensure employment opportunities are highly visible and firm seeks minorities, women, and other excluded groups for employment

- **Preferential Hiring:** company gives preference to minorities, women, and other excluded groups in hiring and promotion decisions

- **Employment Quotas:** company establishes specific numbers or proportions as goals for minorities, women, and other excluded groups to be hired or promoted

and negotiated a $240 million settlement. Hughes Aircraft Company was hit with a $89.5 million race discrimination verdict in 1994.

> Discrimination suits can be very expensive. In a survey of 515 trial verdicts involving wrongful termination lawsuits from 1988 to 1992, successful age-bias claims resulted in an average award of over $300,000, compared with approximately $250,000 awarded for sex discrimination actions. Race bias and disability discrimination claims, on average, received approximately $200,000 per claim.[11]

On the other hand, some large corporations have found that legally required affirmative action programs are helpful in monitoring the company's progress in providing equal job opportunity. General Electric, AT&T, and IBM have said that they would continue to use affirmative action goals and timetables even if they were not required by law.

Americans with Disabilities Act

The Americans with Disabilities Act (ADA) of 1990 requires employers to make accommodations for disabled workers and job applicants and prohibits employers from discriminating on the basis of a person's disability. A more elaborate description of the provisions in the ADA is shown in Figure 15-4.

Even before the law was signed employers began complaining that there was no clear definition of what was a disability. Nonetheless, the act was passed and those with disabilities began to exercise their new rights. The EEOC reported it had received over 16,000 ADA-related complaints by the end of 1993. Nearly half of the charges involved the discharge of a disabled employee. Other complaints accused employers of failing to provide reasonable accommodations for the disabled at work, discriminatory hiring practices, or the harassment of disabled workers.

Corporate responses were generally slow. However, about 175 of the largest corporations and labor unions belong to the Industry-Labor Council of the National Center for Disability Services. The council seeks to promote efforts toward the development and implementation of programs that advocate the hiring and advancement of people with disabilities. Many employers have been encouraged to hire people with disabilities based on the good results others have achieved through this practice.

Reverse Discrimination

Reverse discrimination describes the unintended negative impact suffered by an individual or group as a result of legal efforts to overcome dis-

---

[11]"Age-Bias Cases Found to Bring Big Jury Awards," *Wall Street Journal,* Dec. 17, 1993, pp. B1, B8.

FIGURE 15-4

Provisions of the Americans with Disabilities Act of 1990.

Source: Adapted from The Equal Employment Opportunity Commission, *The Americans with Disabilities Act of 1990*, Washington, DC, 1991.

Prohibits employers when hiring from inquiring about:

- Medical history
- Prior insurance claims
- Work absenteeism due to illness
- Past treatment for alcoholism
- Mental illness

Defines a "qualified disabled worker" as:

- One who can perform the "essential functions" of a job, with or without reasonable accommodations

Requires employers to make "reasonable accommodations" to disabled workers by:

- Modifying work equipment
- Providing readers or interpreters
- Adjusting work schedules
- Making existing facilities accessible

crimination against another individual or group. For example, reverse discrimination occurs if granting job rights to an individual who is a member of a religious or racial group that is legally protected against discrimination directly causes others to be denied such rights and privileges. Reverse discrimination can occur regarding preferential treatment in hiring, training, layoffs, promotions, and other job opportunities.

WORKPLACE DIVERSITY

The sheer diversity of the U.S. workforce spawns many new employee issues and problems. Women, African Americans, Hispanics, Asians, the physically or mentally challenged, and other entrants are changing the nation's labor pool in dramatic ways. According to the Hudson Institute, 85 percent of the growth expected in the U.S. workforce by the year 2000 will come from white and nonwhite women, nonwhite men, and immigrants of both sexes and various races. As the large group of white men now dominant in the labor force ages and retires, they will occupy a smaller share of the total labor pool—only about 39 percent by the year 2000, according to the U.S. Department of Labor.

Businesses adjusting to these changes in the workforce may be in a position to reap the benefits of a well-integrated, yet culturally diverse, work population. These advantages include attracting applicants from a large potential labor pool, a work environment enriched by multiple cultures, and the ability to meet the needs of a culturally diverse customer base.

> For example, Voice Processing Corporation, which manufactures speech-recognition software, has eleven nationalities represented among its forty corporate headquarters' staff members. Combined, these employees speak thirty languages, including Mandarin Chinese, Russian, Hindi, Turkish, Thai, and Serbo-Croatian. The multilingual workforce has enabled Voice Processing to more easily introduce and market its products in countries all over the world.[12]

Immigration

Immigration has complicated the management jobs of many companies. The Immigration Reform and Control Act, passed in 1986, was intended to reduce the flow of *illegal* immigrants into the United States by forbidding their employment. Hiring illegal aliens, or failure of a business firm to keep accurate records of its employees' immigration status, can result in fines and jail sentences. This legal pressure has caused some employers to go beyond the law and refuse to hire anyone who looks or sounds like a foreigner. This kind of job bias against foreigners, or against those merely imagined to be illegal immigrants, is on the increase, according to the General Accounting Office. Job seekers object to this kind of job discrimination, while employers complain that they are made to act as immigration officers for the government.[13]

Language in the Workplace

About one of five workers seeking jobs in the 1990s is expected to be a recent immigrant. That often means relying on employees whose limited knowledge of English can interfere with their work.

> Motorola confronted the problem by offering to "meet employees halfway," said a training supervisor. English communication classes were provided at the company's expense and, increasingly, on company time. By 1992, the company spent $30 million on the program, begun in 1986, which included basic literacy for English speakers. Motorola says about 6,000 employees received language training.[14]

---

[12]"Small Company Goes Global with Diverse Work Force," *Wall Street Journal,* Oct. 12, 1994, p. B2.
[13]"Wide Bias in Hiring Blamed on Immigration Sanctions," *Wall Street Journal,* Mar. 8, 1990, p. B1.
[14]"Firms Grapple with Language Barriers," *Wall Street Journal,* Nov. 7, 1989, p. B1.

The push for on-the-job language efficiency can lead to problems, how-ever, if a company decides that all of its rules and regulations must be ex-clusively in English. These "English-only" rules have been upheld by the U.S. Supreme Court. In 1994, the Court refused to overturn a lower court ruling that permitted a California company to require its employees to speak English on the job.[15] However, according to the U.S. Equal Employ-ment Opportunity Commission, these practices can be used to discrimi-nate against certain groups at work, thereby heightening ethnic tensions. Where non-English-speaking employees make up a large bulk of a com-pany's workforce, employers need to demonstrate a commitment to fair-ness by adopting a flexible language policy.

Managing a Diverse Workforce

Managers have many new lessons to learn if they are to be effective in mo-tivating and directing their multicultural employees. One lesson is to lis-ten—to hear the distinct and often subtle ways of speaking and communi-cating that are routinely used by various ethnic groups, to hear the often submerged voices of women employees, Hispanics, Native Americans, African Americans, Asian Americans, the physically or mentally chal-lenged, and others.

> A group of regional and national companies have formed the Diversity Council. The purpose of the organization is to help member firms man-age diversity issues through cooperative efforts. Through the council, member firms are able to share ideas and participate in group problem solving for workforce diversity management and training. Managing the corporate culture regarding diversity involves providing a work en-vironment that encourages all employees to perform at their best and to feel that they are part of the company. To be successful, firms must adopt cultural diversity as a corporate priority and recognize the dif-ferent ways people think, see, and respond to the world around them.[16]

When employees believe they are respected, rather than ridiculed, for the way they talk, the way they approach business problems, or for their gender or ethnic background, their morale is higher and a company's pro-ductivity tends to be higher.

Corporations in the United States are slowly beginning to acknowledge differences in employee sexual orientation and life-styles. Gay and lesbian employees are becoming a vocal minority, winning important victories in

---

[15]"Court Upholds 'English-only' Rule," *Pittsburgh Post-Gazette,* June 21, 1994, p. A5.
[16]Larry Reynolds, "Companies Will Work Together on Workforce Diversity," *HR Focus,* Dec. 1992, p. 17.

the courts. Gay city employees in New York City and Seattle demanded and received benefits for their domestic partners. Standford and Harvard universities also provide this type of coverage for their employees. Spurred by this mounting pressure, firms are responding.

> By March 1994, more than seventy major U.S. corporations offered domestic-partner benefits, including coverage for the partners of gay employees. Lotus Development, Microsoft, Time Warner's HBO, and MCA are among the firms responding to employee sexual orientation diversity. A few firms also cover heterosexual unmarried couples, including Ben and Jerry's, Levi Strauss, Federal National Mortgage Association, and Borland International.[17]

Addressing issues of cultural or sexual diversity in the workplace is simply another way of saying what other chapters in this book say: business operations always occur within a social and cultural setting, and the best managers are those who recognize this relationship and learn to make their decisions on that basis. The next chapter in this book focuses on the workplace issues that occur as greater numbers of women seek jobs.

JOB SAFETY AND HEALTH

Much industrial work is inherently hazardous because of the extensive use of high-speed and noisy machinery, production processes requiring high temperatures, an increasing reliance on sophisticated chemical compounds, and the nature of such work as construction, underground and undersea tunneling, drilling, and mining. Accidents, injuries, and illnesses are likely to occur under these circumstances. Annually, nearly 10,000 workers are killed, 6 million are injured, and 300,000 become ill while on the job, according to union reports.[18] Despite some decreases in worker fatalities and injuries, "the annual death rate is still radically higher than other industrialized nations," stated Donald Millar, director of the National Institute for Occupational Safety and Health.

Over the past decade new categories of accidents or illnesses have emerged, including the fast-growing job safety problem of office injuries. Stress from rising productivity pressure and escalating job demands can be the cause of cumulative trauma disorders. The number of health problems attributed to the use of video display terminals, keyboard usage, and

[17]"Gay Employees Win Benefits for Partners at More Corporations," *Wall Street Journal,* Mar. 18, 1994, pp. A1, A2.
[18]Helen L. Richardson, "Accept Responsibility for Safety," *Transportation & Distribution,* Aug. 1992, pp. 29–32.

tasks requiring repetitive motion have increased tenfold in the past decade. "Ergonomics" has quickly become the office buzzword of the 1990s. **Ergonomics** means adapting work and work conditions and equipment to suit the worker rather than forcing the worker to adapt to the design of the machine, for example. Office furniture that lacks ergonomic features may be partly responsible for lost time due to illness and injury, as well as poor productivity.

Three decades ago, an aroused and alarmed labor union movement mounted a campaign for stronger federal legislation primarily to protect employees in manufacturing industries. In the 1990s, there was a shift toward protecting employees in service and high-technology industries. Legislation dating from the 1960s—as well as new regulations proposed in the 1990s—thrust the issue of employee safety and health into the forefront of social problems facing employers.

Occupational Safety and Health Administration

The **Occupational Safety and Health Administration (OSHA),** created by Congress in 1970, quickly became one of the most controversial of all the government agencies established in the great wave of social legislation during the 1970s. Congress gave OSHA important powers over employers, requiring them to provide for each employee a job "free from recognized hazards that are causing or likely to cause death or serious physical harm." Employers found in violation of OSHA safety and health standards can be fined and, in the case of willful violation causing the death of an employee, be jailed as well.

OSHA in the 1980s and 1990s

OSHA's relations with business in the early 1980s reflected the Reagan administration's deregulatory philosophy. During this time OSHA proposed to exempt nearly three-fourths of all U.S. manufacturing companies from routine safety inspections. A year later, OSHA proposed a year-long experimental program of self-inspection where companies would take over the agency's safety and health inspections. However, these changes were never made, and labor and other groups continued to call for stricter safety regulations, as they have done for decades.

As a response to these interest groups, OSHA demonstrated renewed vigor as a government watchdog agency in the late 1980s and into the 1990s. The agency re-established its pattern of aggressively pursuing significant safety violations and imposing large fines on violators.

For example, in 1988 Chrysler agreed to pay $1.6 million to settle OSHA charges of worker overexposure to lead and arsenic and other alleged health and safety violations. In 1993, OSHA charged the Wyman-Gordon Company with 149 safety violations at its Massachusetts metal forging plant. Over $1 million in penalties was proposed.[19]

These tougher regulatory actions were accompanied by expanding workplace exposure standards intended to protect employees from hazardous substances. In 1989, the agency declared 376 potentially toxic chemicals dangerous enough to justify greater engineering controls to limit worker exposure. These new rules were expected to reduce on-the-job hazards for over 21 million employees. In March 1990, OSHA issued the Hazardous Waste Operation and Emergency Response Standard. This standard applied to employees involved in routine operations at hazardous waste treatment, storage, and disposal facilities, and in emergency response operations involving a release of a hazardous substance.

Management's Responses

Although some praised OSHA's renewed posture as an aggressive government watchdog, business has generally criticized OSHA as being a too costly way to safeguard employees. Small businesses in particular have a difficult time carrying the paperwork burden required by OSHA's rules. Other companies object to the high cost of redesigning machinery and production processes, saying that these expenses far outweigh any tangible or marginal benefit in increased safety and health for workers. Employees themselves have refused to wear required safety goggles, earplugs, respirators, and other special equipment to protect them from harm, but if they were to be injured while not wearing such items, the employer, not the employee, would be subject to penalty.

One of the more popular and widespread methods businesses have used to reduce employee injuries is **workplace safety teams.**

Safety teams are generally made up of equal numbers of workers and managers. In operation, these teams not only reduce employee accidents, but also lower workers' compensation costs. The effect is particularly dramatic at small companies that typically do not have the financial or human resources to develop the more elaborate and costly safety programs and committees found in large corporations.

Some state legislatures are requiring small firms to form safety teams. For example, in Montana only firms with fewer than six workers are exempt from the mandate for safety teams; in Nebraska, the state re-

---

[19]"Chrysler to Pay Record Penalty in OSHA Case," *Wall Street Journal,* Feb. 2, 1987, p. 20; and "OSHA Asks Safety Penalties of More Than $1 Million," *Wall Street Journal,* Aug. 13, 1993, p. B2.

quirement is applied to all enterprises, rather than the traditional exemption to businesses with less than twenty-five workers.[20]

The experience with employee safety teams is encouraging. Norfolk Southern reduced its number of injuries by two-thirds, while reducing the size of its safety staff by 84 percent. The rise in worker compensation costs at State Fair Foods was reversed after the firm initiated worker-safety teams and gave them the authority to correct problems immediately.[21]

Businesses seem to be responding with cautious cooperation to renewed federal, state, and local involvement to protect employees. Some appear to be complying only with the letter of the law; others are exceeding government standards to avoid regulatory investigation. In spite of these mixed results, many firms accept their responsibility to protect their employees' health and safety. Exhibit 15-A shows Reebok's concern for its workers on a global scale.

Workplace Violence

Employers are being challenged by another social issue affecting their employees' safety: violence in the workplace. Stories of angry or distraught employees, ex-employees, or associates of employees attacking workers, coworkers, or superiors at work are becoming more frequent. For example, there is a growing trend for workers who have lost their jobs to seek vengeance against individuals who terminated them, often in calculated and cold-blooded fashion. An employee fired eight years earlier from James River Corporation, a Pennsylvania paper products manufacturer, faked a family emergency to gain access to the company's executive offices. Brenton F. Halsey Jr., vice president and the son of the company's founder, was shot eight times before the former employee turned the gun on himself.

Nearly one-fourth of the 311 companies surveyed reported that at least one of their employees had been attacked or killed on the job since 1990. Another 31 percent claim threats have been made against workers. Overall, 1,004 Americans were murdered on the job in 1992. Homicide is the second greatest cause of death in the workplace, and the leading cause of workplace fatalities for women.[22]

---

[20]"Businesses Fall in Love with Workplace Safety Teams," *Wall Street Journal,* Mar. 16, 1994, p. B2.

[21]Michael A. Verespej, "Better Safety through Empowerment," *Industry Week,* Nov. 15, 1993, pp. 56–68.

[22]"Disgruntled Workers Intent on Revenge Increasingly Harm Colleagues and Bosses," *Wall Street Journal,* Sept. 15, 1992, pp. B1, B10; "Waging War in the Workplace," *Newsweek,* July 19, 1993, pp. 30–31, 34; "Companies See More Workplace Violence," *Wall Street Journal,* Apr. 12, 1994, pp. B1, B6; and "Murder in Workplace Is a Major Part of the Latest Death-on-the-Job-Statistics," *Wall Street Journal,* Aug. 11, 1994, p. A4.

EXHIBIT 15-A

> ## EXPORTING WORKERS' RIGHTS
>
> Reebok International's long-standing commitment to worker safety and the protection of fundamental human rights was tested in 1994. For two years workers employed under a Reebok contract in the Chinese province of Guangdone had been provided with living quarters on the factory grounds. In the first six months of 1994, 136 workers at the Guangdone factory died in fires; many of the victims were trapped in their upper-floor dormitories. It was common for flammable materials to be stored in the workers' dormitories, a practice specifically prohibited by government regulation but ignored.
>
> Standing by the company's "Human Rights Production Standards," which promises employees reasonable working hours, fair wages, and safe working conditions, Reebok management swung into action. The company ordered its Chinese contractor, Yue Yuen International, to provide safer housing for the workers or else Reebok would cancel its orders. The local company agreed and provided additional compensation to workers due to their new two-hour daily commute.
>
> SOURCE: "Reebok Compels Chinese Contractor to Improve Conditions for Workers," *Wall Street Journal*, Aug. 16, 1994, p. B2.

Unfortunately, many companies are poorly prepared to deal with these situations. Only 24 percent of employers offer any type of formal training to their employees in coping with workplace violence, and just 10 percent offer this type of training to *all* employees. Government intervention in this area of employee safety is also lacking.

CHALLENGING EMPLOYEES' PRIVACY

Privacy rights in the business context refer primarily to protecting a person's private life from intrusive and unwarranted business actions. The employees and customers of business, along with the general public, believe that their religious, political, and social beliefs, as well as personal life-styles, are private matters and should be safeguarded from snooping or analysis. The same view applies to personal acts and conversations in locations such as company lavatories and private homes. Exceptions are permitted grudgingly only when job involvement is clearly proved. For example, it may be appropriate to know that an employee is discussing with a competitor, through electronic mail (e-mail) messages, the specifications of a newly developed product not yet on the market. Other behaviors are not so clear-cut. For example, should a job applicant who is experiencing severe financial problems be denied employment out of fear that the individual may be more inclined to steal from the company? Should an employee be terminated after the firm discovers that the person has a serious medical problem, although it does not affect the employee's job performance, since the company's health insurance premiums may dramatically increase? At what point do company interests weigh more heavily than an employee's right to freedom and privacy?

Computer Data Banks

The development of computers with massive capacity to store and recall information has caused concern about the potential for improper storage and release of personal information. Companies need information about people in order to conduct business, but rights to privacy must be judiciously balanced against the firm's right to know. According to one expert, corporate policies to handle these rights should follow these guidelines:

- Ensure that any intrusions into an employee's private life are job related.
- Provide fair notice when implementing new procedures.
- Be certain that information about an employee is accurate, complete, and relevant before placing it in the employee's personnel file.
- Restrict in-house access to employee records to people with a legitimate need to know.[23]

Several federal privacy laws govern the dissemination of information: the Fair Credit Reporting Act (1970), Privacy Act (1974), Right to Financial Privacy Act (1978), Video Privacy Protection Act (1988), and Computer Matching and Privacy Protection Act (1988). Unfortunately, each of these laws has loopholes. For example, under the Fair Credit Reporting Act, anyone with a "legitimate business need" can gain access to personal information in credit files. The Right to Financial Privacy Act is intended to forbid access to individuals' bank accounts; however, the act makes exceptions for state agencies, law enforcement officials, and private employers.

Monitoring Employee Activity

Besides the collection and storage of employee information, corporations are actively involved in observing workers' activities. Since employers are exempt from the Electronic Communications Privacy Act (1986), they are free at any time to view employees on closed-circuit televisions, to tap their telephones, e-mail, and network communications, and to rummage through their computer files with or without employee knowledge or consent.

The ability of employers to monitor employee activities exploded in the

---

[23]Extracted from Jane Easter Bahls, "Checking Up on Workers," *Nation's Business,* Dec. 1990, pp. 29–31.

1990s due to the greater availability of sophisticated surveillance equipment, the greater affordability of this equipment, and the ease of access to employee activity through technological advances in e-mail and facsimile machines (faxes), as the following example and Exhibit 15-B illustrate.

> Procter & Gamble's (P&G) company practices were exposed in a 1993 book, *Soap Opera: The Inside Story of Procter & Gamble,* by Alecia Swasy. In the book, the company's activities of routinely obtaining medical records of employees, watching them with video cameras, monitoring their telephone calls from P&G offices and their homes, and following them on business trips were described. For years the firm employed former agents from the government's Central Intelligence Agency and Federal Bureau of Investigation, as well as former police officers, as part of a security department that conducted investigations that bordered on harassment and invasions of privacy, according to Swasy's book.[24]

Management justifies the increase in employee monitoring for a number of reasons: to achieve greater efficiency at work, to maintain an honest workforce and protect the firm from employee theft, and to reduce health insurance premiums by reducing employee negligence or failure to comply with safety regulations. Yet employees are becoming more aware of corporate monitoring and are challenging it in court as an invasion of privacy. Judges have ruled that workers must prove that their reasonable expectations for privacy outweigh the company's reasons for secretive monitoring. Employers sometimes satisfy the court's demands by simply

---

[24]"Is Your Boss Spying on You?" *Business Week,* Jan. 15, 1990, pp. 74–75; "P&G Keeps Tabs on Workers, Others, New Book Asserts," *Wall Street Journal,* Sept. 7, 1993, pp. A3, A10; and Alecia Swasy, *Soap Opera: The Inside Story of Procter & Gamble,* New York: Times Books, 1993.

EXHIBIT 15-B

EAVESDROPPING ON EMPLOYEE E-MAIL

Two Nissan Corporation employees discovered managers reading their e-mail. After being warned about using the system for personal messages, they lodged a complaint and were subsequently fired. They sued for invasion of privacy and wrongful termination.

An extensive one-year survey of more than 300 companies by MacWorld magazine revealed that 22 percent of top corporate managers reviewed communications between employees, especially work files and e-mail. Those numbers mean that as many as 30 million American workers may be monitored through their computers.

SOURCE: Frank Jossi, "Eavesdropping in Cyberspace," *Business Ethics,* May–June 1994, pp. 22, 24–25.

informing workers of the company's surveillance policies. Others require job applicants to sign a privacy waiver before being hired.

AIDS Testing

The disease known as acquired immune deficiency syndrome (AIDS) has become a major public health problem. Emerging first among homosexual males and drug users, the AIDS epidemic now affects all segments of the world's population. Children receiving tainted blood during transfusions are vulnerable, as are children born to mothers who are infected with the AIDS virus. Cases of AIDS among heterosexual males in the United States rose from 4,042 in 1992 to 9,288 in 1993, a 130 percent increase. The Center for Disease Control reported that AIDS was spreading at a faster rate among women than men in the early 1990s. Overall, 103,500 cases of AIDS were reported by 1993.

AIDS's rapid spread and resistance to treatment or permanent cure has raised many questions of an ethical nature, especially since initial infection may be a matter of personal life-style. Among those questions is the issue of mandatory **AIDS testing** of employees whose work activities are thought to carry some potential risk of infecting coworkers or customers.

In 1990, the federal government passed the strongest anti-AIDS discrimination legislation embodied in the Americans with Disabilities Act (ADA). As presented earlier in this chapter, the ADA specifically prohibits a company from firing or even reassigning an employee solely because the person has AIDS. Under the ADA, a person with AIDS can sue for punitive damages in bias cases, giving the employee a powerful economic tool against employers who discriminate. More than thirty states have antidiscrimination laws, which bar job discrimination against people with AIDS. Courts in New York and Arizona, in 1990, banned or severely limited insurance companies from requiring AIDS testing; however, the practice of routinely testing city fire fighters and paramedics in Ohio was upheld by a U.S. District Court in 1992.

Opponents of AIDS testing argue that employees should not be tested for the presence of the AIDS virus because it would be an invasion of privacy, the available tests are frequently inaccurate, and the tests do not reveal whether a person having AIDS antibodies will ever develop the disease. According to guidelines issued in 1985 by the U.S. Department of Health and Human Services, since AIDS cannot be contracted by casual and normal workplace contacts, employees with the illness should not be segregated from others nor should they be restricted in performing jobs for which they are qualified.

Many firms believe that information is the best defense against AIDS, and the benefits that may result are listed in Figure 15-5. Even so, AIDS imposes costs on companies, especially through their health benefit programs. Insurance companies favor trying to isolate high-risk applicants by means of AIDS antibody tests, fighting off attempts by some states to ban

FIGURE 15-5
Advantages of an
AIDS information
program.

- ■ Minimizes disruption in the workplace
- ■ Decreases chances of costly litigation
- ■ Establishes consistent company guidelines
- ■ Reduces health care costs
- ■ Enhances employee-employer relations
- ■ Provides up-to-date AIDS information to employees
- ■ Promotes a responsible corporate public image

such blood tests and using substitutes for tests where they are banned. Insurers also favor denying new policies on grounds of the enormous costs to society and aggressively fighting existing policyholders' claims in court. According to the National Commission on AIDS, if this nation is to conquer AIDS then "strong, positive leadership is needed to overcome ignorance and fear, as well as to rectify the serious flaws and deficits in care and prevention strategies."[25]

EMPLOYEES' RIGHTS AND RESPONSIBILITIES

Just as an employer must assume certain duties and obligations in the employee-employer relationship, so must the employee as a corporate stakeholder assume certain responsibilities. Employees have rights that must be protected from violation by the employer, yet workers can lose their privileged rights through irresponsible or illegal activities. In addition, employees must attend to various responsibilities entrusted to them in the employee-employer relationship. These responsibilities include acting in a manner that does not harm coworkers, customers, or other company stakeholders, as well as acting in a way that contributes to overall business performance and mission.

TESTING TO CONTROL EMPLOYEES' ACTIONS

The issues discussed in this section focus upon actions taken by businesses to control particular employee behavior. For example, the rampant increase in employee drug and alcohol use on the job or its affect on job performance prompted companies to institute drug and alcohol testing.

[25]"How Insurers Succeed in Limiting Their Losses Related to the Disease," *Wall Street Journal,* May 18, 1987, p. 12; and "Who Will Pay the AIDS Bill?" *Business Week,* Apr. 11, 1988, p. 71. Quotation by the National Commission on AIDS is from Romuald A. Stone, "AIDS in the Workplace: An Executive Update," *Academy of Management Executive,* vol. 8, no. 3, 1994, pp. 52–64.

Employee theft gave impetus to employers conducting honesty tests of their employees and job applicants.

Employee Drug Use and Testing

Abuse of drugs, particularly hard drugs such as heroin and cocaine, has become an epidemic problem for employers. By the late 1980s, 75 percent of drug users reported that they had used drugs on the job, and 64 percent said that they had sold drugs on the job. Eighteen percent of drug users had drug-related job accidents and 60 percent reported impaired job performance. Nearly one in five said they stole from their employer to pay for drugs. Drug abuse costs the U.S. industry and taxpayers an estimated $176 billion in health claims, compensation, and lost work days, including $99 billion in lost productivity.[26]

One way business has dealt with on-the-job drug abuse is through **drug testing.** Company drug testing increased from 5 percent in 1982 to almost 50 percent in 1988 to 84 percent in 1993. Some of this increase may be attributed to the Drug-Free Workplace Act of 1988, which requires federal contractors to establish and maintain a workplace free of drugs. Tests of job applicants in several different industries revealed that, in 1988, 12 percent of prospective employees tested positive. By 1992 positive drug tests for job applicants dropped to 4.3 percent, and current employees tested positive for drug use only 2.5 percent of the time.[27]

Typically drug testing is used on three different occasions.

- *Preemployment screening.* Some companies test all job applicants or selected applicants before hiring, usually as part of a physical examination, often informing the applicant ahead of time that there will be a drug screening.
- *Random testing of employees.* This type of screening may occur at various times throughout the year. In many companies, a member of a particular job category (for example, an operator of heavy machinery) or job level (for example, a supervisor) is eligible for screening at any time.
- *Testing for cause.* This test occurs when an employee is believed to be impaired by drugs and unfit for work. It is commonly used after an accident or some observable change in behavior.[28]

Small businesses are also becoming more involved in employee drug testing. "The word on the street is that people with drug problems are

---

[26]George E. Stevens, Carol D. Surles, and Faith W. Stevens, "A Better Approach by Management to Drug Testing," *Employee Responsibilities and Rights Journal,* 1989, pp. 61–71; and Kristin Staroba, "The Substance Abuse Maze," *Association Management,* Nov. 1990, pp. 26–32.

[27]For a presentation of the 1993 American Management Association study of workplace drug testing, see "Fewer People Fail as Workplace Drug Testing Increases," *HR Focus,* June 1993, p. 24.

[28]Stevens et al., op. cit., p. 63.

going to small companies because they know that the IBMs and the Xe-
roxes and the GTEs are drug screening and have been for years," said an
operations vice president at Corporate Wellness, a drug consulting firm.[29]
So, employers at small businesses see a growing need to protect themselves from drug abusers.

The debate over employee drug testing is summarized in Figure 15-6.
In general, proponents of testing emphasize the need to control the potential harm to others and the cost to business and society attributed to drug
use on the job. Opponents challenge the benefits of drug testing and its in-
trusion on individual privacy.

Companies are discovering that they must do more than weed out
drug abusers with testing; they must also educate the majority of
nonabusers in the workforce to help manage the problem. At Nalco Chemical employees learn about the physiological and psychological impact of
drugs. Any of the 711 Champion International employees in Roanoke
Rapids, North Carolina, may participate in classes on parenting to help
them manage the threat of drug abuse in their families.[30]

Alcohol Abuse at Work

Another form of employee substance abuse—which causes twice the problems of all illegal drugs combined—is also challenging employers: alcohol
use and addiction. Studies show that up to 40 percent of all industrial fatalities and 47 percent of industrial injuries are due to alcohol abuse. U.S.
businesses lose an estimated $102 billion per year in productivity directly
related to alcohol abuse.[31] The consequences of uncontrolled alcohol use
are clearly evident in the following examples.

> Five people were killed and 133 injured in an August 1991 New York
> City subway crash. The driver disappeared from the scene, and was
> found returning to his home six hours later. He was tested for alcohol
> and had a .21 blood alcohol level—twice the legal standard for driving
> while intoxicated. The Exxon *Valdez* oil spill, mentioned at the begin-
> ning of the chapter, was due in part to the negligence of the intoxicated
> ship captain.

Company programs for drug abusers and alcohol abusers are often
combined. Since the 1980s an increasing number of firms recognized that
they had a role to play in helping alcoholics control or break their habit.

[29]"Small Companies Move to Increase Anti-Drug Programs," *Wall Street Journal,* Nov. 6, 1990,
p. B2.
[30]Bill Oliver, "How to Prevent Drug Abuse in Your Workplace, *HR Magazine,* Dec. 1993, pp.
78–82.
[31]Carl E. King, "When Is a Drug Not a Drug?," *Security Management,* Feb. 1990, pp. 59, 61; and
Jim Carraher, "Progress Report: Drug Tests," *Security,* Oct. 1991, p. 40.

FIGURE 15-6

Pros and cons of employee drug testing.

Arguments Favoring Employee Drug Testing

- Business cooperation with U.S. "War on Drugs" campaign
- Improves employee productivity
- Promotes safety in the workplace
- Decreases employee theft and absenteeism
- Reduces health and insurance costs

Arguments Opposing Employee Drug Testing

- Invades an employee's privacy
- Violates an employee's right to due process
- May be unrelated to job performance
- May be used as a method of employee discrimination
- Lowers employee morale
- Conflicts with company values of honesty and trust
- May yield unreliable test results
- Ignores effects of prescription drugs, alcohol, and over-the-counter drugs
- Drug use an insignificant problem for some companies

As with drug rehabilitation programs, most alcoholism programs work through employee assistance programs (EAPs) that offer counseling and follow-up. In 1994, 84 percent of companies responding to a survey indicated that they provide EAPs for alcohol (and drug) abusers. United Airlines' EAP reported dramatic reductions of absenteeism plus excellent recovery rates during a ten-year period, and it is considered a model for other firms.

Employee Theft and Honesty Testing

Employees can irresponsibly damage themselves, their coworkers, and their employer by stealing from the company. **Employee theft** has emerged as a significant economic, social, and ethical problem in the workplace. A survey of U.S. retail businesses reported that nearly 38 percent of company losses were attributed to employee theft, almost as much as shoplifting. The U.S. Department of Commerce estimates that employee theft of cash, merchandise, and property costs businesses $40 to $50 billion a year. Employee theft accounts for 20 percent of the nation's business failures. In Canada, employee theft costs firms $20 billion a year.[32]

Many companies in the past used polygraph testing as a preemploy-

[32]Lisa Arbetter, "Retail Theft from the Inside Out," *Security Management*, Apr. 1993, pp. 11–12; Joan Delaney, "Handcuffing Employee Theft," *Small Business Reports*, July 1993, pp. 29–36; and Andrew Holt, "Controlling Employee Theft," *CMA Magazine*, Sept. 1993, pp. 16–19.

ment screening procedure or upon discovery of employee theft, although its use was considered an invasion of privacy and a coercive procedure. In 1988, the Employee Polygraph Protection Act became law. This law severely limited polygraph testing by employers and prohibited approximately 85 percent of all such tests previously administered in the United States. Employers were required to post a notice of the prohibition in the workplace. In addition to the 1988 federal law, more than twenty states and the District of Columbia regulate or restrict the use of polygraphs, and the federal law does not preempt any state or local law that is more restrictive.

In response to the federal ban on polygraphs, many corporations have switched to written psychological tests, or **honesty tests,** that seek to predict employee honesty on the job. These pen-and-paper tests rely on answers to a series of questions that are designed to identify undesirable qualities in the test taker. When a British chain of home improvement centers used such tests to screen more than 4,000 applicants, theft dropped from 4 percent to 2.5 percent, and actual losses from theft were reduced from 3.75 million pounds to 2.62 million pounds.[33]

The use of honesty tests, like polygraphs, is not without controversy. The American Psychological Association noted that there is a significant potential for these tests to generate false positives, indicating that the employee probably would or did steal from the company even though this is not true. After extensively studying the validity of honesty tests and the behavior they try to predict, Dan Dalton and Michael Metzger, leading academic researchers in this field, concluded that the tests are only 13.6 percent accurate at best, and only 1.7 percent accurate at their worst. Critics also argue that the tests intrude upon a person's privacy and discriminate disproportionately against minorities.[34]

RESTRICTING EMPLOYEE BEHAVIOR

Companies have tried to restrict or control some legally permitted employee activities, arguing that the welfare of others or the good of the company takes precedence over the rights of the individual. For example,

[33]"Reducing the Cost of Counter Productive Behaviour at Work: The Case for Integrity Testing; Push Button Analysis for Job Seeking," *Journal of Managerial Psychology,* vol. 6, no. 3, 1991, pp. i–iv.

[34]Support for the reliability of honesty tests can be found in Denis S. Ones, Cockalingam Viswesvaran, and Frank L. Schmidt, "Comprehensive Meta-analysis of Integrity Test Validities: Findings and Implications for Personnel Selection and Theories of Job Performance," *Journal of Applied Psychology,* Aug. 1993, pp. 679–703; and H. John Bernardin and Donna K. Cooke, "Validity of an Honesty Test in Predicting Theft Among Convenience Store Employees," *Academy of Management Journal,* Oct. 1993, pp. 1097–1108. The American Psychological Association's challenge to these tests and the opinions noted in this paragraph can be found in Dan R. Dalton and Michael B. Metzger, " 'Integrity Testing' for Personnel Selection: An Unsparing Perspective," *Journal of Business Ethics,* Feb. 1993, pp. 147–156.

firms have tried to restrict employees who would prefer to smoke while at work, or persuade workers to keep quiet when they feel that they have uncovered an incident of company wrongdoing. These issues pit employees' rights against employers' interests.

Smoking in the Workplace

The life-threatening health dangers for smokers have been repeatedly proven in medical research studies. In addition, health officials estimate that **environmental tobacco smoke**—smoke that is emitted from a lit cigarette, cigar, or pipe, or exhaled by a smoker—is related to nearly 50,000 nonsmoker deaths in the United States each year. Concern about the effects of smoking on nonsmokers has led many companies to restrict smoking to designated areas and private offices. Some believed that these measures were inadequate since smoke from these "smoking areas" could be recirculated and have banned all smoking in company buildings, establishing smoke-free workplace environments.

These policies encourage (or force) smokers to join smoking cessation programs, often provided by employers, or to stop smoking on their own. Employers are convinced that nonsmoking employees are generally more productive, incur lower insurance premiums, and are sick less than those who smoke. Economists estimate that smokers cost employers more than $4,000 a year.

> Texas Instruments does not have an outright ban on smoking, but it does have a policy that bans smoking in common areas at work. In addition, the company charges smokers $10 a month more for insurance. If an employee's dependents smoke, they are charged an additional $10 for each, up to $30. The firm increased smokers' premiums after an in-house study revealed that smokers' health costs were 50 percent higher than nonsmokers' costs. The policy of increased health costs affects approximately 20 percent of Texas Instruments' 44,000 employees.[35]

Employees who smoke were divided in their reaction to smoking restrictions or bans at work. Some smokers welcomed the opportunity to stop smoking, and many took advantage of company-paid smoking cessation programs. Others, however, were incensed at what they perceived as a violation of personal rights and freedoms. Some employers have sought government protection from the growing intolerance of workplace smoking and have joined the tobacco industry in appealing to state legislatures. By 1993, twenty-eight states and the District of Columbia had passed laws making job discrimination against smokers illegal. Although the laws do

[35]Nancy A. Lang, "The Last Gasp: Workplace Smokers Near Extinction," *Management Review,* Feb. 1992, pp. 33–36.

not affect office smoking bans or smoke-free areas in the workplace, they do prohibit companies from refusing to hire smokers and from firing employees who choose to continue to smoke.

Whistle-Blowing

Sometimes the loyal bonds between a company and an employee are strained to the breaking point, especially when a worker thinks the company is doing something wrong or harmful to the public. When the employee reports alleged organizational misconduct to the public or to high-level company officials, **whistle-blowing** has occurred. In the 1980s, employee whistle-blowers frequently exposed fraud in the country's defense contracting system. In the 1990s, the health care industry has become increasingly vulnerable to whistle-blowers. For example, Jack Dowden received $15 million for whistle-blowing in 1990 against National Health Laboratories. The medical lab company paid $111.4 million in a settlement over allegations of Medicare fraud.[36]

Whistle-blowing has both defenders and detractors. Generally, employees are not free to speak out against their employers because there is a public interest in allowing companies to operate without harassment from insiders. Company information is generally considered to be proprietary and private. If employees, based on their personal points of view, are freely allowed to expose issues to the public and allege misconduct, the company may be thrown into turmoil and be unable to operate effectively.

On the other hand, there may be situations in which society's interests override those of the company, so an employee may feel an obligation to blow the whistle. According to one expert, certain conditions must be satisfied to morally justify blowing the whistle to outsiders (e.g., informing the media or government officials):

- The unreported act would do serious and considerable harm to the public.
- Once such an act has been identified, the employee has reported the act to his or her immediate supervisor and has made the moral concern known.
- If the immediate supervisor does nothing, the employee tries other internal pathways for reporting the problem.[37]

Only after each of these conditions has been met should the whistle-blower "go public."

Government protection for the whistle-blower has increased at federal and state levels. The federal False Claims Act permits employees to sue

---

[36]"Whistles Blow More Often on Health Care," *Wall Street Journal,* Sept. 2, 1993, pp. B1, B8.
[37]Richard DeGeorge, *Business Ethics,* 4th ed., Englewood Cliffs, NJ: Prentice Hall, 1995, pp. 231–238.

companies suspected of government fraud and then to share in any financial restitution. A 1989 federal law protects federal employees from retaliation by their supervisors when they expose government waste or fraud. Under the growing possibility of similar legal assistance for employees of private companies, employees are more willing to challenge employers' actions in the courts.

> For example, in 1993, Chuck Hamel, an employee at Alyeska Pipeline Service, reportedly tipped off Congress and regulators, claiming environmental wrongdoing along the Trans-Alaskan pipeline. In retaliation to Hamel's whistle-blowing actions, Alyeska secretly tapped his phone calls and rifled through his mail, garbage, phone records, and credit records. The firm even employed attractive female operatives to try to entice Hamel into admissions or actions that might discredit him.[38] After months of legal battles, the company agreed to a multimillion dollar settlement with Hamel.

EMPLOYEES AS CORPORATE STAKEHOLDERS

The issues discussed in this chapter illustrate forcefully that today's business corporation is open to a wide range of social forces. Its borders are very porous, letting in a constant flow of external influences. Many of these social forces are brought inside by employees whose personal values, life-styles, and social attitudes become a vital part of the workplace.

Managers and other business professionals need to be aware of these employee-imported features of today's workforce. The employee-employer relationship is central to getting a corporation's work done and to helping satisfy the wishes of those who contribute their skills and talents to the company. The task of the corporate manager is to reconcile potential clashes between employees' human needs and the requirements of corporate economic production. Acknowledging the important stake that employees have in the successful pursuit of the corporation's economic mission enables business leaders to cope more effectively with the many issues that concern employees.

SUMMARY POINTS OF THIS CHAPTER

- Practices in Europe and Japan provide alternatives to the common U.S. practice of employee layoffs, which has serious negative consequences for all employees and has increased the likelihood of more government intervention in the United States. Equal job opportunities for employees regardless of race, sex, age, physical or mental dis-

[38]"Alyeska Settles Suit by a Whistle-Blower," *Wall Street Journal,* Dec. 21, 1993, p. B8.

ability, or any other nonwork-related factor contain additional ethical and legal challenges for businesses.

- An increasingly diverse workforce requires corporate managers to respect and be able to deal effectively with a wide range of cultures and social attitudes among today's employees.
- Job safety and health concerns have increased due to rapidly changing technology in the workplace. Employers must comply with expanding OSHA regulations and respond to the growing trend toward violence at work.
- Employees' privacy rights are frequently challenged by employers' needs to have information about their health, their work activities, and even their off-the-job life-styles. When these issues arise, management has a responsibility to act ethically toward employees while continuing to work for a high level of economic performance.
- Employees have an obligation to act in a manner that does not needlessly harm others or the company. Testing employees for drug use, alcohol abuse, AIDS, and the probability of dishonest activity is becoming a common business practice. Workers' ability to freely smoke in the workplace is becoming more restricted.
- Blowing the whistle on one's employer is often a last resort way to protest company actions considered to be harmful to others. It can usually be avoided if corporate managers encourage open communication and show a willingness to listen to their employees.

KEY TERMS AND CONCEPTS USED IN THIS CHAPTER

- Employment-at-will
- Employer-Employee Social Contract
- Worker Adjustment Retraining Notification Act
- Equal job opportunity
- Equal Employment Opportunity Commission (EEOC)
- Reverse discrimination
- Ergonomics

- Occupational Safety and Health Administration (OSHA)
- Workplace safety teams
- Privacy rights
- AIDS testing
- Drug testing
- Employee theft
- Honesty tests
- Environmental tobacco smoke
- Whistle-blowing

DISCUSSION CASE

RESPONDING TO AIDS IN THE WORKPLACE

Tim, a service support manager for San Francisco–based Wells Fargo Bank, had been an exemplary employee for several years. A strong leader who had a good reputation, 32-year-old Tim was well liked by upper management and the 15 employees he supervised.[39]

This up-and-coming individual also had a medical condition that was beginning to wear down his body's immune system. Infected with the human immunodeficiency virus (HIV), Tim had developed a form of acquired immune deficiency syndrome (AIDS), which can result in such symptoms as shortness of breath, a lingering dry cough, skin rashes, extreme fatigue, and lightheadedness. Symptoms never surface in many people who are infected, and others develop conditions years after infection.

Extreme fatigue became part of Tim's daily life and was a detriment to his usual top-notch performance. As his health deteriorated, he began to realize his physical limitations. About 15 months earlier, Tim revealed the information about his health to his middle management supervisor, Sandra. He asked her to keep the news confidential. Tim was aware of his condition several months before he informed his manager. Because HIV is not contagious through casual contact, this individual was not a health risk to other bank employees and therefore was under no obligation to share such personal information with his employer. Because he could not keep up with his workload, however, Tim wanted to inform Sandra that the problem was medical. Knowing that Wells Fargo's policy on HIV ensured his confidentiality, Tim believed that the company would accommodate him by not disclosing his illness.

After her discussion with Tim, Sandra consulted Bryan Lawton, the bank's employee assistance director and a clinical psychologist. She asked how to respond to managers and employees who have questions about workers who have HIV. "Sandra was distressed because she was concerned about Tim's health," says Lawton. Tim was showing signs of fatigue and was missing work. His coworkers began to wonder if he was ill. "Sandra was afraid that Tim was wearing himself down," Lawton adds. "She also was concerned about the impact the illness was having on the people he supervised—people who had suspicions about him being infected with the disease, but who didn't know what to say or do."

Sandra was aware of the company's four-point policy:

- Keep confidential all information about the medical condition and medical records of an employee who has AIDS.
- Consult Employee Assistance Services (EAS) immediately after learning that an employee has been diagnosed with AIDS.
- Work with EAS and your personnel officer to arrange job accommodations that are deemed medically necessary for the employee with this condition.

---

[39]This case was adapted from an actual incident reported in Jennifer J. Laabs, "Wells Fargo's and IBM's HIV Policies Help Protect Employees' Rights," copyright April 1990, p. 40. Reprinted with the permission of *Personal Journal*, ACC Communications, Inc., Costa Mesa, CA. All rights reserved. The names of employees have been disguised.

- Help employees learn about AIDS by asking EAS for the AIDS Education Program.

Yet, even though Sandra was aware of the policy, she had never had to implement it or manage its effects. She had several questions and needed assistance in how to implement company policy on Tim's behalf. She also wanted to demonstrate concern and compassion for her fellow employee while staying within the legal boundaries of confidentiality. One particular point of interest for Sandra was possible job-based adjustments that Tim might need in the months ahead. Because Tim was a valued employee, Sandra wanted to minimize his concerns while maximizing his tenure.

Discussion Questions

1. Given the passage of the Americans with Disabilities Act, does the bank's AIDS policy adequately protect the rights of all Wells Fargo employees?
2. Is the protection of Tim's privacy rights more important than, less important than, or equally as important as the bank's need to be efficient in getting its day-to-day work done? Should Tim be removed from his job?
3. If Tim is given special job privileges because of his illness, would other bank employees have a right to complain about unequal and discriminatory treatment?

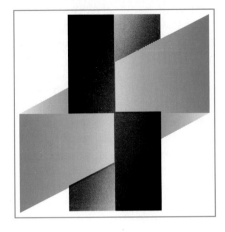

16

Women, Work, and the Family

Developing opportunities for women who work in business has become a major social challenge for corporations. Barriers to women's equal participation in the workplace are yielding to the forces of economic change, greater need for skilled people in all categories, the demands of women to be treated equally, and equal opportunity laws. Achieving full workplace parity remains a goal to be reached. Women's greater participation in the nation's labor force has brought adjustments in family life and social values, requiring changes in corporate practices and policies.

Key Questions and Chapter Objectives

This chapter focuses on these key questions and objectives:

- Why have women entered the workforce in such large numbers, and what problems have women faced as workers?
- What roles do women play as managers and business owners, and do women manage differently from men?
- What role does the government play in securing women's workplace rights and opportunities?
- What can companies do to develop policies and practices that promote women's workplace opportunities and that support both women and men in their efforts to balance work and family responsibilities?

In 1992, Charlotte L. Beers was recruited for the position of chairperson and CEO of Ogilvy and Mather Worldwide, a leading Madison Avenue advertising agency. Beers, who was widely regarded as a charismatic and effective executive, came to Ogilvy from a Chicago firm, where she had quadrupled revenues in ten years. Her promise appeared to be fulfilled when, in 1994, Beers landed the contract for representing all IBM advertising accounts worldwide—considered a major coup in the industry.

In 1993, Lucky Stores, a major grocery chain in California, agreed to pay nearly $75 million in damages to women who had been denied promotion opportunities in its stores—one of the largest settlements ever in a sex discrimination case. Women employees said they were channeled into dead-end jobs, such as working as cashiers or as sales clerks in bakeries and delicatessens. The judge stated that "sex discrimination was standard operating procedure at Lucky's."[1]

These two examples capture some of the contradictions that face women in the business world in the United States in the mid-1990s. Nearly half of all U.S. workers—and over four of every ten managers—are women. For a half century, women have been entering the workforce in larger and larger numbers, finding jobs formerly denied to them. Women have made great strides in the professions, skilled trades, and middle ranks of management. A few, like Charlotte L. Beers, have reached the pinnacle of success in corporate America. Yet, most women, like those who experienced discrimination at Lucky's, still work in relatively low-paying jobs with poor prospects for upward mobility in traditionally female-dominated occupations.

The enormous transition that has occurred as women have entered the workforce in greater numbers has produced new social challenges. In this chapter, we discuss these changes and their implications for business. Understanding the history of women in society is a key to seeing what business can do today to meet these challenges.

THE STATUS OF WOMEN IN SOCIETY: HISTORICAL BACKGROUND

The status of both women and men in society is largely a product of social custom and tradition. These customs evolve over extremely long periods of time, and they resist change. In all societies it is customary for men to perform certain tasks and for women to perform others. Once established, these distinctions between women's tasks and men's tasks—the **sexual division of labor**—tend to be accepted as proper and are reinforced over time by habit and custom. The sexual division of labor exerts a strong influence on the relative amounts of power and influence possessed by men and women within the family, clan, tribe, and larger society. Societies around the world and throughout history have varied greatly in how they arrange this basic division of labor.

Most societies in human history have been both patriarchal—men serve as head of the family or clan—and patrilineal—family lineage is traced through the father's ancestors. Because these male-centered social customs allocate power and privileges mainly to men, women have generally found themselves with relatively less social standing. Matriarchal soci-

---

[1] "Through the Glass Ceiling," *Business Week*, June 8, 1992, p. 78; "Ogilvy's Big Bet on Big Blue," *Business Week*, July 4, 1994, p. 73; and "Big Grocery Chain Reaches Landmark Sex-Bias Accord," *New York Times*, Dec. 17, 1993, pp. A1, B11.

eties—where women are politically, economically, and socially dominant—have occasionally existed but not as frequently. Generally, it has been men, rather than women, who become chiefs, clan heads, tribal elders, shamans and priests, monarchs, presidents, prime ministers, generals, and corporate executives. Women's social standing in these patriarchal (male-dominated) societies has been tied closely to childbearing and family sustenance.[2]

This general pattern of male-female relations continues in modern societies. Sex segregation based on custom has meant that today's women in general possess less economic and political power than men. Until quite recently, leadership positions in politics, government, business, religion, trade unions, sports, engineering, university teaching, military service, space exploration, science, and other fields have been considered off-limits to women. Although today's research demonstrates that women are as well qualified and capable as men to hold these high-level positions, sex discrimination based on custom, social habit, and gender bias has limited their opportunities.

Exhibit 16-A explains how these persistent, gender-based customs have affected the jobs women hold, even long after explicit sex discrimination was outlawed.

[2]For a discussion of the history of patriarchy, see Gerda Lerner, *The Creation of Patriarchy*, New York: Oxford University Press, 1986.

EXHIBIT 16-A

THE LONG SHADOW OF SEX SEGREGATION

"The explicit policies to segregate the workplace and to fire married women that I have uncovered in the historical records of hundreds of firms would be clearly illegal today. . . . Many of these discriminatory policies, at least as the written procedures of firms, were abandoned sometime after 1950. Some were changed in the 1950s as a response to tighter labor supply conditions, while others were altered only later when the policies became clearly illegal. *But their impact remained long after.* If few women worked for extensive periods of time, even fewer would remain when jobs were dead end and when women were barred from promotional ladders. When virtually no woman was an accountant, for example, few would train to be accountants. And if women's work was defined in one way and men's in another, few individuals would choose to be the deviant, for deviance might cost one dearly outside the workplace. Thus change in the economic sphere is slowed not only by the necessity for cohorts (age groups) to effect change, but also by the institutionalization of various barriers and by the existence of social norms maintained by strong sanctions."

SOURCE: From *Understanding the Gender Gap: An Economic History of American Women*, by Claudia Goldin. Copyright © 1990 by Oxford University Press, Inc. Reprinted by permission. Emphasis added.

The Women's Movement

The women's movement that began in the 1960s and has continued into the 1990s is the most recent phase of women's efforts to redress the unequal balance that cultural history has left on contemporary society's doorstep. The fight for equal rights for women in modern times began over a century earlier in England as women sought the right to vote. In the United States, that same right was finally secured in 1920 with the passage of the Nineteenth Amendment to the U.S. Constitution.

The women's movement that renewed itself among American women in the 1960s proved to be a watershed. On one side were customs that cast most women in their traditional roles of homemaker and helpmate to their male companions—loyal sister, dutiful daughter, faithful wife, nuturing mother. On the other side of the watershed, events produced a new attitude toward women's place in society. This attitude supported the liberation of women from customary restraints and stressed the importance of equality, greater choice, and personal control. Without rejecting the vital social contributions women had long made, leaders of the movement nevertheless advocated greater independence for women and a reexamination of long-accepted social habits and attitudes. In this new climate, women began to question their roles, their lives, their relationships, and where it all was leading them.[3]

This questioning ran deeper than had the earlier struggles of women to gain the right to vote, to own and control property, and to regulate family size. None of those earlier campaigns, even when successful, had seriously challenged society's prevailing distribution of power, privileges, and jobs that favored men. Women now were seeking equal rights, equal privileges, and the kind of liberty that would permit them to pursue lives determined largely by options of their own choosing. Their aims were self-determination and social justice, which meant having an equal claim on human rights and an equal standing with others around them.

Some believe that the woment's movement lost ground in meeting these goals during the 1980s, a decade characterized by author Susan Faludi as one of backlash against women. A 1992 survey found that 59 percent of female executives believed that progress by large American companies in hiring and promoting women had slowed down, stopped, or actually gotten worse.[4]

---

[3]The seminal work that energized the U.S. women's movement is Betty Friedan's *The Feminine Mystique,* first published in 1963. For her views of what the movement had accomplished after twenty years, see the foreword of *The Feminine Mystique,* 20th anniversary ed., New York: Norton, 1983.

[4]Susan Faludi, *Backlash: The Undeclared War Against American Women,* New York: Doubleday, 1991; and "The Gains Are Slow, Say Many Women," *Business Week,* June 8, 1992, p. 77.

WHY WOMEN HAVE ENTERED THE WORKPLACE

Women have always "worked," whether paid or not. In farming-based societies—including the United States through the mid-1800s—the family was the primary economic unit. Women's work was essential to the family economy and involved farming, food preparation, the manufacture of household items, and the care of children. In the slave-based system of the Southern states prior to the Civil War, the labor of African-American women made essential contributions to the plantation economy. The advent of the industrial revolution in the early and mid-1800s profoundly altered the nature of women's work by bringing females into the wage labor force. During the late 1800s and the first half of the 1900s—with the exception of periods of wartime—women who worked outside the home were mostly young and single, widowed or divorced, or married to men unable for some reason to support their families.

During the post–World War II period, the proportion of women working outside the home has risen dramatically, as shown in Figure 16-1. In 1950, about a third of adult women were employed. This proportion has risen almost steadily since, standing at 58 percent in 1993. Participation rates (the proportion of women in the workforce) have risen for all groups of women, but the most dramatic increases have been among married women, mothers of young children, and middle-class women—those who had earlier been most likely to stay at home. Men's participation rates declined somewhat during this period; by the year 2005, the proportions of adult women and men at work are projected to be within 7 percentage points of each other (66 percent and 73 percent, respectively). The ex-

FIGURE 16-1

Proportion of women in the labor force, 1950–1993.

SOURCE: U.S. Bureau of Labor Statistics.

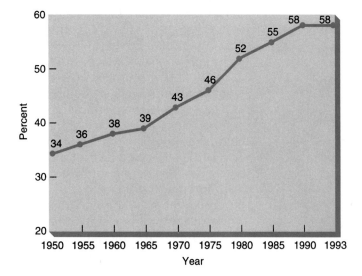

panding participation of women in the workforce has posed many challenges for business.

Women have entered the workforce for many of the same reasons men do. They need income to support themselves, their children, their aging, retired, or sick parents or other close relatives, and their marital partner, and to enjoy a satisfying life-style. A paycheck is a ticket to economic freedom, a symbol of freeing oneself from having to ask others for money to pursue one's own interests. Having a job with pay also gives a woman psychological independence and security. It can open up new vistas of opportunity, permitting and encouraging higher degrees of self-actualization. Being economically productive and contributing to society through paid work contributes as much to women's as to men's sense of self-esteem.

When marriages terminate, through either divorce or the death of one partner, the remaining person usually needs a paying job. Many women who choose not to work outside the home during their married life confront this necessity when joint savings or life insurance are inadequate for their postmarriage life. Research reveals that most women, even those with jobs, suffer a decline in their living standard following divorce. During the 1980s when many corporate takeovers and mergers, along with increased global competition, resulted in massive job layoffs, working women often found themselves the sole breadwinners in their families.

Inflation also puts financial pressure on families, frequently pushing women into the labor force just to sustain an accustomed standard of living or to put children through college or to care for aging parents.The inadequacies and uncertainties of retirement plans and health care programs frequently mean that women, as well as men, need to save, invest, and plan for the future.

The rapid rise of female labor force participation also reflects the expansion of segments of the economy that were major employers of women. In 1940, about one third of all U.S. jobs were white-collar (not requiring manual labor); by 1980, over half were white-collar. Professional, technical, and service jobs also grew relative to the economy. The creation of many new positions in fields traditionally staffed by women produced what economists call a "demand-side" pull of women into the labor force. More "women's jobs" meant more women working.

The widespread entry of women into the labor force has changed the character of many families and some kinds of family life. In 1993, in 55 percent of U.S. married households—28 million families in all—both husband and wife worked, far outnumbering the traditional family in which the husband works while the wife remains at home, which comprised only 13 percent of married households. (In 24 percent, neither husband nor wife worked; and in 8 percent, only the wife or other family member worked.) The decline of traditional family arrangements, as more and more women have entered the labor force, has been responsible for much of the criticism directed toward women who work outside the home. It also has focused attention on the numbers and types of jobs actually held by women, which we examine next.

WHERE WOMEN WORK AND WHAT THEY ARE PAID

Highlights about working women in the United States include the following:[5]

- Over half (58 percent) of all women are employed.
- Women make up nearly half (46 percent) of the entire labor force.
- Three quarters of all working women (75 percent) have full-time jobs.
- A majority (60 percent) of married women with children under the age of six hold jobs outside the home.
- The main jobs held by women are administrative support and clerical work (27 percent of all women's jobs), service work (18 percent), and sales (13 percent). About one of every eight working women (12 percent) is a manager.
- Women hold 42 percent of all executive, administrative, and managerial posts, but most of these are at low and middle levels of organizations.
- Less than 5 percent of top corporate executives are women, according to a 1990 survey.

Although women have become major participants in doing the paid work of U.S. society, their distribution among jobs and industries remains lopsided. They have found more places in the service industries than in manufacturing, mining, or agriculture. They serve more as clerks and low-level administrative helpers than as high-level leaders in organizational life, and as staff workers more than as workers in line jobs with central authority over policies and practices.

One persistent feature of the average working woman's world is receiving lower pay than men. This **gender pay gap** narrowed during the 1980s and the early 1990s, but—as Figure 16-2 shows—women as a group still earned only slightly over three-quarters of men's pay in 1993. The gap is narrower in some jobs that call for more education, or among younger workers, or where the experience of men and women is more balanced. The gender pay gap is smaller between African-American and Hispanic women and men than between white women and men, reflecting the lower wages of nonwhite men.

[5]Bureau of Labor Statistics, Division of Labor Force Statistics, private communication; and Catalyst, "INFObrief: Women in Corporate Management," New York: 1992–93. All data are for 1993, unless otherwise noted.

FIGURE 16-2
The gender pay gap, 1980–1993.

SOURCE: U.S. Bureau of Labor Statistics.

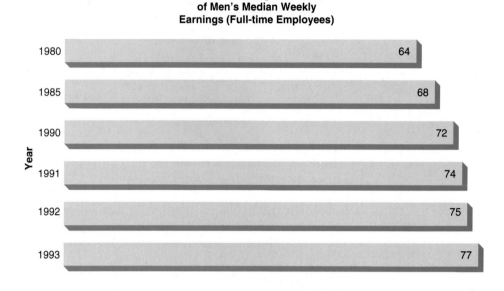

Women's Earnings as Percent of Men's Median Weekly Earnings (Full-time Employees)

Year	Percent
1980	64
1985	68
1990	72
1991	74
1992	75
1993	77

Most observers believe that the pay gap persists because of what is called **occupational segregation,** which concentrates women in traditionally female-dominated jobs. In the early 1990s, almost a third of all working women were employed in what has been called the "pink-collar ghetto" of jobs dominated by women—clerk, waitress, nurse or nursing aide, child-care worker, cashier, elementary school teacher, secretary, retail salesworker, and health technologist (e.g., dental hygienist). Because so many women hold these relatively low-paying jobs, women's average income is pulled down below the average wages of men. The labor market produces this kind of occupational segregation partly because women find better paying jobs less accessible to them when they look for work. In some cases, an entire occupational category such as bank teller or clerical worker will shift from employing all men to hiring virtually all women, as men move on to more attractive and high-paying job opportunities. Occupational segregation frequently means that women cannot get the jobs that could break the cycle of relatively low pay.[6]

WOMEN IN MANAGEMENT

The most prestigious and highest-paying jobs in a corporation are in top management. Because corporations are organized hierarchically, top management jobs are few in number. For that reason, only a minority of

[6]Diana M. Pearce, "Something Old, Something New: Women's Poverty in the 1990s," in Sherri Matteo, ed., *American Women in the Nineties,* pp. 79–97, Boston: Northeastern University Press, 1993.

either men or women can hope to reach the upper levels of management. Men have traditionally filled most of these desirable spots. Business's challenge now is to broaden these high-level leadership opportunities for women.

Where Women Manage

Over 6 million U.S. women were managers by the mid-1990s, doubling their numbers in one decade. In 1993, as Figure 16-3 reveals, more than four out of every ten managers—and a majority of managers in some categories, such as personnel and health care—were women. Clearly, women have broken into management ranks. Women are more likely to be managers, though, in occupational areas where women are more numerous at lower levels, including medicine and health care, personnel, labor relations, and education. They also are concentrated in service industries and in finance, insurance, real estate, and retail businesses. Women managers have also made gains in newer industries, such as biotechnology, where growth has created opportunity.[7]

Where women managers are scarce is in the executive suites of large corporations. Rarely do they represent more than 5 percent of these top jobs. Women are also scarce on corporate boards; only 6 percent of board members of *Fortune* 500 and *Fortune* Service 500 firms were women in 1993. Half of these companies' boards did not have a single female member. Occasional exceptions do occur, as at Wells Fargo Bank, where women held 66 percent of managerial positions in 1992.[8]

Access to management jobs is restricted in most areas of the world, according to a study of women managers in several nations.

> In country after country, the proportion of women holding managerial positions falls short of men's share. Corporations, it appears, have systematically ignored women as a potential resource. In all countries, the higher the rank within the organization, the fewer the women found there. In some countries, the percentages, though small, have increased over the last decade; but in none have they approached equality. This pattern prevails in oriental and occidental cultures, communist, socialist, and capitalist systems, and [in] both economically developed and developing countries.[9]

---

[7]"Biotech Industry Is Bonanza for Women," *Wall Street Journal,* June 6, 1994, pp. B1, B10.
[8]Catalyst, *Women on Corporate Boards: The Challenge of Change,* New York: 1993; "The 'Glass Ceiling': A Barrier in the Boardroom, Too," *Business Week,* Nov. 22, 1993, p. 36; and "Women Make Strides, But Men Stay Firmly in Top Company Jobs," *Wall Street Journal,* Mar. 29, 1994, pp. A1, A8.
[9]Nancy Adler and Dafna N. Izraeli, eds., *Women in Management Worldwide,* Armonk, NY: Sharpe, 1988, pp. 7–8. For a discussion of international aspects, see also Nancy Adler and Dafna N. Izraeli, eds., *Competitive Frontiers: Women Managers in the Global Economy,* Cambridge, MA: Basil Blackwell (in press); and Ariane Berthoin Antal and Dafna N. Izraeli, "A Global Comparison of Women in Management: Women Managers in Their Homelands and as Expatriates," in Ellen A. Fagenson, ed., *Women in Management: Trends, Issues, and Challenges in Management Diversity,* Newbury Park, CA: Sage, 1993.

FIGURE 16-3
Where women
manage.
SOURCE: U.S. Bureau
of Labor Statistics.

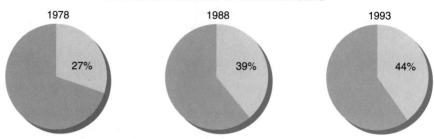

WOMEN AS A PERCENT OF ALL MANAGERS

1978 — 27%

1988 — 39%

1993 — 44%

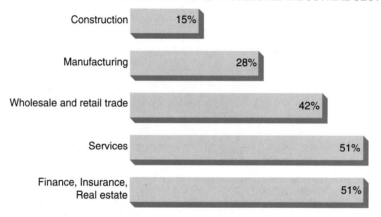

PERCENT OF WOMEN MANAGERS IN SELECTED INDUSTRIAL SECTORS, 1993

Construction — 15%

Manufacturing — 28%

Wholesale and retail trade — 42%

Services — 51%

Finance, Insurance, Real estate — 51%

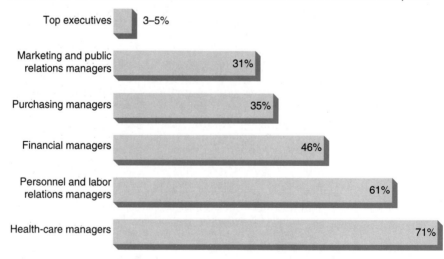

PERCENT OF WOMEN MANAGERS IN SELECTED MANAGEMENT CATEGORIES, 1993

Top executives — 3–5%

Marketing and public relations managers — 31%

Purchasing managers — 35%

Financial managers — 46%

Personnel and labor relations managers — 61%

Health-care managers — 71%

Do Women and Men Managers Manage Differently?

When women do become managers, do they bring a different style and different skills to the job? Are they better, or worse, managers than men? Are women more highly motivated and committed than male managers? Are they accepted by those they manage, or do customary ways of thinking cause both men and women to react negatively to having female managers?

The research evidence strongly favors the "no difference" point of view. According to this research, managers of both sexes do not seem to differ in any significant way in performing their tasks. These results are summarized in Figure 16-4. Women managers do not appear to be more people-oriented than men, nor do they tackle task-oriented jobs less effectively than their male counterparts. Men managers and women managers score about the same on motivation tests, but one study of 2,000 managers, cited by Gary N. Powell, seemed to demonstrate that "female managers were more concerned with opportunities for growth, autonomy, and challenge" and exhibited a "more mature and higher-achieving motivational profile" than the men in the study.

Commitment studies show mixed results, with women sometimes more job-committed and men at other times registering stronger commitment. For both sexes, commitment is always stronger when people have satisfying jobs, believe their work is meaningful, and when their skills are used and appreciated. On-the-job sex discrimination can contribute to lowered job commitment by making the workplace less attractive for women. The amount of time and commitment that anyone brings to a job and career is also affected by the amount of home-based support one receives. Women who bear a disproportionately large share of household tasks and family care may be unable to make as full a commitment to job and career as they would prefer.

Reaction of subordinates to women managers varies, but "once subordinates have worked for both female and male managers, the effects of [traditional sex-role] stereotypes disappear and managers are treated as individuals rather than representatives of their sex."[10]

Some research supports the idea that women bring different attitudes and skills to management jobs, such as greater cooperativeness, an emphasis on affiliation and attachment, nurturance, and a willingness to bring emotional factors to bear in making workplace decisions. These differences are seen to carry advantages for companies, because they expand the range of techniques that can be used to help the company manage its workforce effectively.[11]

[10]Gary N. Powell, "One More Time: Do Female and Male Managers Differ?" *Academy of Management Executive,* Aug. 1990, pp. 68–75. For a discussion of similarities and differences among men and women managers, see Powell's book *Women and Men in Management,* 2d ed., Newbury Park, CA: Sage, 1993.

[11]Jan Grant, "Women as Managers: What They Can Offer to Organizations," *Organizational Dynamics,* Winter 1988, pp. 56–63.

FIGURE 16-4

Sex similarities and differences in management.

SOURCE: Gary N. Powell, "One More Time: Do Female and Male Managers Differ?" *Academy of Management Executive*, Aug. 1990, p. 69. Reprinted by permission of the publisher and author.

SEX DIFFERENCES IN MANAGEMENT: SELECTED RESULTS

Dimension	Results
BEHAVIOR	
Task-oriented	No difference
People-oriented	No difference
Effectiveness ratings	Stereotypical difference in evaluations of managers in laboratory studies: Males favored
	No difference in evaluations of actual managers
Response to poor performer	Stereotypical difference: Males use norm of equity, whereas females use norm of equality.
Influence strategies	Stereotypical difference: Males use a wider range of strategies, more positive strategies, and less negative strategies. This difference diminishes when women managers have high self-confidence.
MOTIVATION	No difference in some studies
	Nonstereotypical difference in other studies: Female motivational profile is closer to that associated with successful managers.
COMMITMENT	Inconsistent evidence regarding difference
SUBORDINATES' RESPONSES	Stereotypical difference in responses to managers in laboratory studies: Managers using style that matches sex role stereotype are favored.
	No difference in responses to actual managers

A study commissioned by the International Women's Forum discovered a management style used by some women managers (and also by some men) that differs from the command-and-control style traditionally used by male managers. Using this "interactive leadership" approach, "women encourage participation, share power and information, enhance other people's self-worth, and get others excited about their work. All these things reflect their belief that allowing employees to contribute and to feel powerful and important is a win-win situation—good for the employees and the organization." The study's director predicted that "interative leadership may emerge as the management style of choice for many organizations."[12]

The Glass Ceiling

Although women are as competent as men in managing people and organizations, they very rarely attain the highest positions in corporations. Their ascent seems to be blocked by an invisible barrier, or what is called a **glass ceiling.**

Failure to attain the topmost jobs in some cases is due to lack of experience or inadequate education. Because gender bias has kept women out of management until recent years, they have not had time to acquire the years of experience that are typical of most high-ranking executives. Also in earlier years, women were discouraged from entering graduate schools of engineering, science, business, and law which have been pathways to corporate management. Even as those barriers have been lowered, though, women remain underrepresented at executive levels. As a group, they have not yet broken through the glass ceiling to become chief executive officers, presidents, or board chairpersons.

What continues to hold women back? Recent studies by the U.S. Department of Labor and others have identified several reasons for the persistence of the glass ceiling. One barrier women face is **glass walls—** fewer opportunities to move sideways into jobs that lead to the top. Female managers are often found in staff positions—such as human resources or public relations—rather than in line positions in such core areas as marketing, sales, or production where they can acquire the broad management skills necessary for promotion. Many women also experience what sociologist Catherine White Berheide in 1992 called the "sticky floor." Her research showed that 55 percent of women in state and local government worked in low-paying jobs with poor prospects for promotion. Only a quarter of all men worked in such positions. In other words, women did not advance because they were concentrated in jobs that did not lead to well-defined career paths. The "sticky floor" was particularly evident for Hispanic, African-American, and Native-American women.[13]

Another problem women face is reliance on word-of-mouth by recruiters for top positions—the "old boys' network" from which women are often excluded. Other causes include a company's lack of commitment to

---

[12]Judy B. Rosener, "Ways Women Lead," *Harvard Business Review,* Nov.–Dec. 1990, pp. 120, 125.

[13]"Study Says Women Face Glass Walls as Well as Ceilings," *Wall Street Journal,* Mar. 3, 1992, pp. B1, B2; and "At Work: And Now the 'Sticky Floor,' " *New York Times,* Nov. 22, 1992, p. F23.

diversity and too little accountability at the top-management level for equal employment opportunity.[14]

The success of a few women, however, has demonstrated that the glass ceiling can be shattered. A 1994 study of a group of highly successful executive women found that most had been helped by top-level supporters and multiple chances to gain critical skills. Some companies have promoted women's mobility by assigning mentors—more senior counselors—to promising female managers and providing opportunities that include wide-ranging line management experience. In 1988, for example, American Airlines initiated a "Supertrack" program, requiring detailed career development plans for all high-potential women in middle management ranks and above. Evaluations of these individuals were accessible to all senior officers. The proportion of women in mid- and upper-management ranks rose from 12 percent in 1986 to 21 percent in 1991.[15]

Women Business Owners

Some women have risen to the top by founding or taking over their own businesses. Female entrepeneurs made major strides in the past decade. The number of businesses owned or controlled by women more than doubled between 1982 and 1992 to around 6.5 million firms, approaching one third of all U.S. companies, according to the National Foundation for Women Business Owners. Many of these businesses are in retail trade, finance, insurance, and real estate. Women are now forming new businesses at roughly twice the rate that men are! Although most female-headed firms are small, collectively they employ more people in the United States than the *Fortune* 500 firms do worldwide.[16]

An example of a successful female entrepeneur is Judy Figge, CEO of In Home Health, a company that provides nursing care to patients in their homes. A registered nurse, Figge bought the company in 1981, when revenues were $300,000 annually. 1993 sales were $104 million, with an annual growth rate of 76 percent over the past five years. "I always

---

[14]Ann M. Morrison, Randall P. White, and Ellen Van Velsor, *Breaking the Glass Ceiling: Can Women Reach the Top of America's Largest Corporations?* updated ed., Reading, MA: Addison-Wesley, 1992; and U.S. Department of Labor, *Pipelines of Progress: A Status Report on the Glass Ceiling,* Aug. 1992.

[15]Lisa A. Mainiero, "Getting Annointed for Advancement: The Case of Executive Women," *Academy of Management Executive,* May 1994, pp. 53–63; and "Corporate Women: Progress? Sure. But the Playing Field Is Still Far from Level," *Business Week,* June 8, 1992, pp. 74–83.

[16]The National Foundation for Women Business Owners (NFWBO), "Women-Owned Businesses: The New Economic Force," Washington, DC: NFWBO, 1992; and "Women Entrepreneurs: They're Forming Small Businesses at Twice the Rate of Men," *Business Week,* Apr. 18, 1994, pp. 104–110.

wanted to run my own business, and this [nursing] is what I knew," Figge said.[17]

Contrary to popular belief, women entrepeneurs are just as successful as men, according to a mid-1980s study of over 400 Midwestern small firms. The study's researchers reported that "the determinants of survival and success operated in much the same way for men and women. . . . Despite the widely shared assumption that women are less apt than men to innovate, for example, we found no evidence of women's being less likely to do this in their businesses. Moreover, we found no evidence that men were more confident of their business abilities."[18]

GOVERNMENT'S ROLE IN SECURING WOMEN'S WORKPLACE RIGHTS

From early in the twentieth century, government laws and regulations—nearly all of them enacted at the state level—were used to protect women from some of the harsh and risky conditions found in factories, mines, construction sites, and other places of business. These protective laws were adopted on grounds that women were weaker physically than men, that their childbearing powers should be shielded from workplace harms, and that whatever work they performed was generally to supplement family income rather than to provide the main income. However, "protection" often meant being excluded from certain jobs and occupations, thus contributing to occupational segregation and unequal pay. Protective laws, however well intentioned, put women at a competitive disadvantage in the labor market.

Equal Pay and Equal Opportunity

The idea that women should be paid the same as men has been around for a long time. In the 1860s, for example, male printers demanded that female printers should receive "equal pay for equal work"—mainly so that their own wages would not be depressed by competition from lower-paid women. The same fear that women workers would lower all wage rates was observed during the First and Second World Wars when women took over jobs formerly held by men, who were in the armed forces. It was not until 1945 that an Equal Pay Act was introduced in Congress; even then, it

---

[17]"Lessons from America's Fastest Growing Companies," *Fortune*, Aug. 8, 1994, p. 59.
[18]Arne L. Kalleberg and Kevin T. Leicht, "Gender and Organizational Performance: Determinants of Small Business Survival and Success," *Academy of Management Journal*, Mar. 1991, pp. 157–158.

was a tactic to defeat or forestall a more comprehensive Equal Rights Amendment to the U.S. Constitution. The Equal Pay Act finally become law almost twenty years later, in 1963.

One year after that, Congress adopted the Civil Rights Act, which prohibits employment discrimination on the basis of race, color, religion, sex or national origin. When the Civil Rights Act was strengthened in 1972 and again in 1991, working women—along with minorities—had additional legal machinery to use in their quest for workplace equality.[19] For more than half a century, an Equal Rights Amendment to the U.S. Constitution has been advocated but never ratified by the necessary number of states. The proposed amendment declares: "Equality of rights under the law shall not be denied or abridged by the United States or any state on account of sex."

Figure 16-5 outlines the major laws and one executive order that are intended to promote women's on-the-job opportunities. These equal opportunity laws and regulations are discussed in more detail in Chapter 15.

---

[19]Claudia Goldin, *Understanding the Gender Gap: An Economic History of American Women*, New York: Oxford University Press, 1990, pp. 201–202. The word "sex" was inserted in the 1964 Civil Rights bill, just one day before Congress voted on it, by a congressional opponent who was said to believe that its inclusion would help defeat the bill.

FIGURE 16-5
Major federal laws and an executive order to protect women's workplace rights.

EQUAL PAY ACT (1963)
Mandates equal pay for equal work

CIVIL RIGHTS ACT (1964, amended 1972, 1991)
Forbids sex discrimination in employment

EXECUTIVE ORDER 11246 (1965)
Mandates affirmative action for all federal contractors and subcontractors

EQUAL EMPLOYMENT OPPORTUNITY ACT (1972)
Increased power of Equal Employment Opportunity Commission to combat sex (and other types of) discrimination

PREGNANCY DISCRIMINATION ACT (1978)
Forbids employers to discharge, fail to hire, or otherwise discriminate against pregnant women

FAMILY AND MEDICAL LEAVE ACT (1993)
Requires companies with fifty or more employees to provide up to twelve weeks unpaid leave for illness, care of a sick family member, or the birth or adoption of a child

Comparable Worth

Equal pay for equal work combats pay discrimination within the same job categories within the same firm—for example, providing equal pay rates for men and women carpenters and equal salaries for men and women managers performing identical work. However, it does little to reduce pay inequities when men and women hold different jobs that require approximately equal skills but are paid at unequal rates. Much of the gender pay gap discussed earlier occurs because many women are employed in jobs and occupational categories that are lower paying than those held predominantly by men. Equalizing pay levels in the same job category does nothing about the unequal rates paid to different jobs or occupations. The problem is especially unfair when these different jobs call for about the same degree of skill, effort, and responsibility. For example, the chief bookkeeper and payroll manager of the city of Princeton, Minnesota—a woman—earned $5,678 a year less than supervisors of road maintenance and sewer repair—typically men. When the state legislature required city governments to equalize the pay of women and men in jobs requiring similar levels of education, skill, and responsibility, the bookkeeper got a raise.[20]

Comparable worth is an attempt to overcome this kind of pay inequity. Jobs are matched with each other in terms of skills, effort, responsibility, and working conditions, and pay is made equal when these factors for the two jobs are about equal or comparable with one another. As of the mid-1990s, pay equity based on comparable worth had been rejected by U.S. federal courts, but some states—like Minnesota, mentioned in the example above—have laws authorizing comparable worth plans for public employees. Canada, Great Britain, and Australia have comparable worth laws that appear to be effective in lessening pay discrimination.[21]

WHAT BUSINESS CAN DO: POLICIES AND STRATEGIES

As women enter the labor force in large numbers, seeking permanent, well-paying, full-time jobs and aspiring to lifelong business careers, and as new laws pass protecting equal workplace rights for women, some changes are bound to take place in the way business organizes and con-

[20]Naomi Barko, "Equal Pay in Your Pocketbook," *Working Mother,* November 1993, p. 42.
[21]For a description and analysis of Canada's comparable worth laws, see Kenneth A. Kovach and Peter E. Millspaugh, "Comparable Worth: Canada Legislates Pay Equity," *Academy of Management Executive,* May 1990, pp. 92–101. Britain's experience is described in Zafiris Tzannatos, "Narrowing the Gap—Equal Pay in Britain 1970–1986," *Long Range Planning,* Apr. 1987, pp. 69–75.

ducts its affairs. The three types of changes most needed in business are (1) reforming personnel policies and production policies to assure equal opportunities, (2) providing support programs that make a working life and a family life possible and rewarding for both men and women, and (3) removing sexist attitudes and behavior toward working women. Gender bias occurs throughout society, not just in the workplace, so these business reforms represent only those steps that business itself can take to provide equal workplace opportunities for women.

Reforming Personnel Policies

If women are to be treated equally in the workplace, all jobs and occupations must be open to them so that they may compete on the same terms as all others. A company's recruiters need to seek out qualified workers and not assume that women are unqualified. Rates of pay and benefits need to be matched to the work to be done, not to the gender of the jobholder. Pay raises for doing one's present job well, along with promotions to more attractive jobs, also require equal treatment. Job assignments should be made on the basis of skills, experience, competence, capability, and reliability—in other words, proven ability to get the job done, not whether women have traditionally worked at one task rather than another. Exhibit 16-B describes a company that fits this pattern remarkably well.

Career ladders, whether short ones going only a few steps or longer ones leading into the higher reaches of corporate authority, should be placed so that both men and women can climb them as high as their abilities can carry them.

Providing Support Programs for Work and Family

No other area of business illustrates the basic theme of this book better than the close connection between work and family life. *Our basic theme is that business and society—in this case the family symbolizes society—are closely and unavoidably intertwined, so that what affects one also has an impact on the other.* When large numbers of women began to enter the ranks of business in the 1940s, 1950s, and 1960s, they did not shed their usual roles in society. Women continued to marry and bear children. The customary roles of wife, homemaker, and child-caretaker did not disappear. Women were still expected to be "feminine" even as they filled what had formerly been "masculine" jobs. So when women came to work, they carried more than a lunch pail or a briefcase; they also bundled their customary family roles on their backs.

Study after study has demonstrated that women continue to do more housework than their male partners. Child care, preparing meals, cleaning house, shopping, and other household functions are still seen to be

EXHIBIT 16-B

> ### HEWITT ASSOCIATES
>
> Hewitt Associates is a leading employee benefits consulting firm, serving an extensive network of corporate clients, including over 70 percent of the *Fortune* 500 companies. Headquartered in a Chicago suburb, Hewitt has a reputation as a desirable place to work. According to *The Best Companies for Women,* sexual harassment and sex discrimination appear to be nonexistent in the company. Of Hewitt's 2,000 employees, 60 percent are women, 10 percent of upper-level managers are women, and women make up 15 percent of the firm's senior partners. About half of those interviewed and hired are female, and the firm is pledged to equal pay for women and men. Family needs of its employees rank high, as shown by the following major benefits:
>
> - Reimbursement for child or parent care when overnight work or travel requires absence from home
> - Financial assistance when an employee adopts a child
> - Financial support for child-care centers near the company's offices
> - Information and counseling for expectant parents
> - Workshops to help employees balance work and family responsibilities
> - Private on-the-job facilities for nursing mothers
> - Maternity leave plus two additional weeks beyond
> - Up to two years extended maternity leave of absence, with equivalent job guaranteed on return
> - Part-time work arrangements and job sharing available
> - A consultant to help working parents solve work-and-family problems
> - A resource library stocked with books, audio- and videotapes, magazines, and other materials on parenting, child development, child care, elder care, and related family issues
>
> SOURCE: Baila Zeitz and Lorraine Dusky, *The Best Companies for Women,* New York: Simon & Schuster, 1988; and Hewitt Associates newsletters.

the responsibility of the mother more than the father, even when both parents work full-time. Many women thus work what has been called a "second shift" before and after their paying job.[22] In the 1960s and 1970s women worked a month longer each year in combined job and housework than men did, and later studies show a continuation of the general pattern.

In other words, many women and men work within a surrounding network of social obligations imposed by tradition. For them and for their employers, business and the family are inseparably intertwined. This close

[22]Arlie Hochschild, *The Second Shift: Working Parents and the Revolution at Home,* New York: Viking, 1989; see esp. the appendix, "Research on Who Does the Housework and Childcare."

relationship between family and work presents business with new kinds of challenges and requires changes in customary routines. Some of these are discussed next.

Child care and elder care

The demand for **child care** is enormous and growing. Some 24 million children need daily care, especially the six out of every ten children whose mothers hold jobs. A major source of workplace stress for working parents is concern about their children; for example, almost half of American Express employees who were surveyed admitted that this kind of worry affected their work, and over one-third were absent from their jobs because of child-care problems.[23]

Business has found that child-care programs, in addition to raising employee morale, reducing absenteeism and tardiness, and improving productivity, also aid recruiting by improving the company's image and helping to retain talented employees. Seventy-eight percent of large U.S. companies provide some type of child-care assistance, including referral services, parent education, dependent care accounts, and vouchers. Slightly under one in ten large companies provides child-care services on-site. An example is Johnson Wax, a consumer products firm that cares for 400 children in a state-of-the-art center at its Racine, Wisconsin, headquarters. "This isn't a benefit," explained a company spokesperson. "It's a good business decision because we want to attract the best."[24]

Other companies have combined child care with **elder care,** since many of today's families must find ways to care for aging parents and other older relatives. This issue will become increasingly important to business in the coming decade as baby boomers pass through their forties and fifties, the prime years for caring for elderly parents. According to the consulting firm Work/Family Directions, the proportion of workers with elder care responsibilities will rise from around 15 percent in 1994 to 37 percent by 2005.[25] Many businesses have found that job flexibility and referrals to services for the elderly can greatly help affected employees. An important collaborative initiative by a group of companies and nonprofit agencies to support both child care and elder care is described in Chapter 3.

Parental leaves

What was once called a maternity leave has become a **parental leave;** or when care of elderly parents is involved, it is called a **family leave.** Both

[23]Richard Levine, "Childcare Inching Up the Corporate Agenda," *Management Review,* Jan. 1989, p. 44. For a status report, see Catalyst, *Childcare in Corporate America,* New York: 1993.
[24]"What Price Child Care?" *Business Week,* Feb. 8, 1993, pp. 104–105.
[25]"The Aging of America Is Making 'Elder Care' a Big Workplace Issue," *Wall Street Journal,* Feb. 16, 1994, p. A1, A8.

parents may need time off from work when children are born and during the important early months of the child's physical and emotional development, and men and women may need time to care for elderly or ill parents or other family members. Under the Family and Medical Leave Act (FMLA), passed in 1993, companies that employ fifty or more people must grant unpaid, job-protected leaves of up to twelve weeks to employees faced with serious family needs, including the birth or adoption of a baby. Smaller companies, not covered by the FMLA, usually do less for expectant and new parents.

How many fathers actually take leave to care for children? Several studies have demonstrated that men are reluctant to take advantage of parental leave programs. Because a man typically makes more money than his spouse, taking a long unpaid job leave may work greater financial hardships on the family. Men also fear—as do women—that being away from the job will interfere with their career. However, there is some evidence that this pattern has begun to shift in the wake of the FMLA. In 1993, for example, thirty-two fathers at Du Pont Corporation took advantage of the company's parental leave policy, up from eighteen the year before.[26]

Work Flexibility

Companies have also accommodated the changing roles of women and men by offering workers more flexibility, through such options as flextime, part-time employment, job sharing, and working at home.

Aetna Life & Casualty, one of America's biggest insurance companies, demonstrates the benefits of the many kinds of work flexibility for both company and employees.[27]

Women make up 70 percent of Aetna's 45,000 employees and nearly two out of every ten Aetna managers, so company officials realized that flexible scheduling would meet the needs of many women employees. In some departments, 40 percent of employees work "flextime" schedules, beginning and quitting at different times of the day. Others share jobs, with each working half a week. Many jobs are held on a part-time basis, leaving the worker time to be at home with children or elderly parents. Several hundred Aetna employees "telecommute"—work with computers—from their homes. The company has a Work/Family Strategies unit to assist employees in using these programs to meet family needs without seriously disrupting company routines. Aetna estimates

[26]"More Dads Take Off to Look After Baby," *Wall Street Journal,* Dec. 17, 1993, p. B1.
[27]"As Aetna Adds Flextime, Bosses Learn to Cope," *Wall Street Journal,* June 18, 1990, pp. B1, B5; and "Work and Family," *Business Week,* June 28, 1993, p. 83.

it saves $1 million a year by not having to train new workers. In 1992, fully 88 percent of workers taking family leave eventually returned to work.

Aetna is not the only corporation introducing these practices. A 1993 survey of over 1,000 large companies revealed that 44 percent had flex-time schedules, 40 percent offered part-time work, and 19 percent permitted job sharing.[28]

Reforming Attitudes in the Workplace

The largest obstacle to equity for working women is conventional attitudes about the place of women in society. Both men and women hold these attitudes. Such views contribute to continued occupational segregation, unequal pay and job opportunities, stymied career paths, and the failure of society to draw fully on all of its human resources for greater productivity and higher living standards. A key problem that symbolizes the need for changed workplace attitudes is sexual harassment.

Sexual harassment

Sexual harassment at work occurs when any employee—woman or man—experiences repeated, unwanted sexual attention, or when on-the-job conditions are hostile or threatening in a sexual way. It includes both physical conduct—for example, suggestive touching—as well as verbal harassment, such as sexual innuendoes, jokes, or propositions. Women are the target of most sexual harassment. Guidelines issued by the U.S. Equal Employment Opportunity Commission give limited legal protection to employees.

Harassment can occur whether or not the targeted employee cooperates. Jobs can be lost or gained by sexual conduct; if such behavior is treated as a requirement or strong expectation for holding a job or getting a promotion, it is clearly a case of unlawful sexual harassment. This kind of sex discrimination is not limited to overt acts of individual coworkers or supervisors. If a company's work climate is blatantly and offensively sexual or intimidating to employees—through prevailing attitudes, bantering, manner of addressing coworkers, lewd photographs, or suggestive behavior—then sexual harassment exists.[29]

---

[28]*Work and Family Benefits Provided by Major U.S. Employers in 1993*, Lincolnshire, IL: Hewitt Associates, 1993.

[29]Catalyst, "INFObrief: Sexual Harassment," New York: 1993. For a discussion of legal issues, see Titus E. Aaron with Judith A. Isaksen, *Sexual Harassment in the Workplace*, Jefferson, NC: McFarland & Co., 1993; for a discussion of workplace strategies for women, see Ellen Bravo and Ellen Cassedy, *The 9 to 5 Guide to Combatting Sexual Harassment*, New York: John Wiley, 1992.

An important legal case decided by the Supreme Court in 1993 made it easier for women to win sexual harassment lawsuits against their employers. In this case, *Harris v. Forklift Systems Inc.*, a woman manager at a truck leasing firm was subjected to repeated offensive comments by the company president. For example, he asked her in front of other employees if she used sex to get a particular account and suggested that the two of them "go to the Holiday Inn to negotiate [her] raise." The manager quit her job and sued.

The Supreme Court upheld her charges, saying that the president's behavior would reasonably be perceived as hostile or abusive, even though it had not caused "severe psychological injury" or caused the woman to be unable to do her job. Some employers' attorneys expressed concern that this decision would open the door to frivolous claims of sexual harassment. Others welcomed the ruling and believed it would encourage many employers to develop policies and training to prevent such incidents.[30]

Women employees regularly report that sexual harassment is common. From 38 to 60 percent of working women have told researchers that they have been sexually harassed on the job. Managers and supervisors are the most frequent offenders, and female office workers and clerical workers are the main targets. As many as 90 percent of incidents of harassment are never reported.

Like most other problems that confront women in the workplace, sexual harassment stems from customary attitudes about women's functions in society. One expert explains these attitudes as **sex-role spillover,** meaning that many men continue to think of women mainly as performing their traditionally defined roles of sex partners, homemakers, and childbearers—and only secondarily as coworkers and qualified professionals. These attitudes "spill over" into the workplace, leading to improper behavior that has no relation to the work to be done. This kind of conduct is most likely to occur where jobs and occupations are sex-segregated and where most supervisors and managers are men.[31]

What can companies do to combat sexual harassment? Exhibit 16-C summarizes four major steps recommended by one authority. The twin keys to success are (a) a written policy, visibly supported by a company's top management, and (b) rewards for sex-neutral behavior (and punishments for harassment). Only then is there a chance that the company's culture and work climate will begin to encourage attitudes that welcome women as full and equal workers and professionals.

---

[30]"Court, 9–0, Makes Sex Harassment Easier to Prove," *New York Times,* Nov. 10, 1993, pp. A1, A15.
[31]Barbara A. Gutek, *Sex and the Workplace,* San Francisco: Jossey-Bass, 1985, chap. 8.

CONTROLLING SEXUAL HARASSMENT

Barbara Gutek, an authority on sexual harassment in the workplace, advocates companies adopt a four-point action program to curb sexual harassment.

1. *Adopt a companywide policy forbidding sexual harassment and communicate it to all employees and others who deal with the company.* Specific actions include orientation of new employees, training films and seminars, posters, a personal statement by top management, and designation of a neutral third party to hear complaints and field questions from employees.

2. *Vigorously investigate all complaints and act on the findings.* Specific actions include giving investigative responsibility to a qualified person who understands the psychological and organizational dimensions of sexual harassment. Follow-up based on the findings is required if the policy is to have meaning for everyone in the company.

3. *Include sexual harassment in performance appraisals of all employees, punishing those who violate company policy.* Treat sexual harassment as a form of unprofessional conduct that lowers the victim's job satisfaction, affects her or his progress and career in the company, and lowers overall company performance and productivity. Promoting or otherwise rewarding a harasser sends the wrong message about sexual harassment.

4. *Create and reinforce a climate of professional behavior that discourages sexual harassment.* Specific steps include frequent reminders of the importance of acting professionally, alerting employees to professional forms of addressing one another (avoiding "girlie," "doll," and "sweetie," for example), and striving for sex-neutral interchanges when men and women work together.

SOURCE: Adapted form Barbara A. Gutek, *Sex and the Workplace: The Impact of Sexual Behavior and Harassment on Women, Men, and Organizations,* San Francisco, CA: Jossey-Bass, 1985, pp. 173–178.

THE GENDER-NEUTRAL, FAMILY-FRIENDLY CORPORATION

As a desirable goal for both business and society, a gender-neutral, family-friendly corporation would be one that has removed sex discrimination from all aspects of its operations and that has supported both men and women in their efforts to balance work and family responsibilities. Job advantages would not be granted or denied on the basis of gender. People would be hired, paid, evaluated, promoted, and extended benefits on the basis of their qualifications and ability to do the tasks assigned. The route to the top, or to satisfaction in any occupational category, would be open to anyone with the talent to take it. The company's stakeholders, regardless of their gender, would be treated in a bias-free manner. All laws forbidding sex discrimination would be fully obeyed. Programs to provide leaves or financial support for child care, elder care, and other family responsibilities would support both men and women employees and help promote an equitable division of domestic work. Corporations themselves would then experience a much-desired and much-needed boost in productivity, as the nation's entire range of potential managerial and professional skills—provided by both men and women—becomes available for use.

By adopting these gender-neutral and family-friendly policies, this kind of corporation would embody such ethical principles as social justice and respect for human rights, express the social responsibilities of enlightened corporate self-interest, demonstrate the kind of social responsiveness that serves the corporation's stakeholders, and align itself with the currents of social change that have brought the issue of women's rights to the fore in the late twentieth century.

SUMMARY POINTS OF THIS CHAPTER

- Women have entered the workforce in large numbers to gain economic security, find satisfying work, and achieve psychological independence. Working women continue to encounter job discrimination, including unequal pay and occupational segregation, but some gains have been registered in the last half of the twentieth century.
- The proportion of women in management has grown, although women continue to face a glass ceiling blocking their access to top executive ranks. The number of women-owned businesses has increased sharply, and women now form businesses at twice the rate men do. Research shows that men and women managers do not differ significantly in their leadership styles.
- Government laws and regulations prohibit employment discrimination on the basis of sex, mandate equal pay for equal work, and require unpaid family and medical leave under some circumstances.
- To provide equal opportunity, corporations need to support the career development of female employees, provide family-friendly programs, and help create positive workplace attitudes about working women. Corporations also need written policies prohibiting sexual harassment.

KEY TERMS AND CONCEPTS USED IN THIS CHAPTER

- Sexual division of labor
- Gender pay gap
- Occupational segregation
- Glass ceiling
- Glass walls
- Comparable worth
- Child care
- Elder care
- Parental leave
- Family leave
- Sexual harassment
- Sex-role spillover

DISCUSSION CASE

JOHNSON CONTROLS AND FETAL PROTECTION IN THE WORKPLACE

In 1983, a thirty-four-year-old mother of two children made a difficult decision to undergo surgical sterilization in order to take a job at Johnson Controls' automotive lead battery plant in Bennington, Vermont. Under a "fetal protection" policy, adopted in 1982, the company had decided not to hire any fertile women for production jobs, because of the possible risks of lead exposure to unborn children.

The United Auto Workers union, which represented most of Johnson Controls' production workers at its fifteen battery plants, believed that the company's policy was illegal. In 1984, it filed suit on behalf of all adversely affected employees, charging sex discrimination under Title VII of the Civil Rights Act. The union argued that because sterility (incapacity to bear children) had nothing to do with a person's ability to make batteries, the policy was clearly discriminatory. Moreover, the union attacked the company for invading employees' privacy and for assuming that women were unable to make intelligent decisions about the conditions under which to bear children.

Johnson Controls vigorously defended its policy, despite its apparently discriminatory impact and the tough decisions it forced many female job applicants and employees to make. Medical evidence clearly showed, the company believed, that maternal exposure to lead could interfere with fetal development, causing neurological damage and other birth defects. "To knowingly poison unborn children," the company reasoned, was "morally reprehensible."

Johnson Controls further argued that it had a legitimate interest in protecting itself from expensive liability lawsuits, if a child were born with impairments traceable to its mother's occupational exposure. The company, which was in compliance with Occupational Safety and Health Administration (OSHA) lead standards for adult exposure, maintained that there was no technologically or economically feasible way to reduce lead levels in the battery-making process sufficiently to eliminate risk to the fetus. An earlier, voluntary policy had failed, according to the company, since several female employees had become pregnant even after they had been warned of the dangers of lead.

After a long journey through the judiciary, the dispute was finally decided by the Supreme Court on March 20, 1991. This decision affected not just female employees and job applicants at Johnson Controls but also the fate of perhaps as many as 20 million other women who also worked in jobs with exposure to substances potentially hazardous to a fetus.

The Supreme Court overturned Johnson Controls' fetal protection policy, ruling that employers may not exclude women from jobs in which exposure to toxic substances could harm a fetus. On the key point of the legality of Johnson's exclusionary policy, the Justices were unanimous. Since the company's policy was discriminatory on its face, the Justices reasoned, the company had to prove that incapacity to bear children was a "bona fide occupational qualification," or BFOQ. This meant that because infertility was not a skill or aptitude related to the job, Johnson's policy of fetal protection violated Title VII of the Civil Rights Act, as amended by the Pregnancy Discrimination Act, and was therefore illegal. The court opinion stated:

> [W]omen as capable of doing their jobs as their male counterparts may not be forced to choose between having a child and having a job. . . . Employment late in pregnancy often imposes risks on the unborn child, . . . but Congress indicated that the employer may take into account only the woman's ability to get the job done. . . . Decisions about the welfare of future children must be left to the parents who conceive, bear, support and raise them rather than to the employers who hire those parents.

Although all agreed that Johnson's policy was illegal, the Justices were divided on whether such protective policies were ever justified. The court majority argued that Title VII prohibited all fetal protection policies. A minority of three, however, maintained that the company's concern with fetal health was legitimate and that employers should be permitted to defend specific fetal protection policies in court.

Following the Johnson Controls decision, businesses were faced with other ways to handle this kind of workplace risk. They could reduce the total amount of dangerous substances in the workplace, thereby giving greater protection to all workers, instead of removing a few women employees from their jobs. Substitute materials might be used in some industrial applications. Employees could be required to use safety devices, such as breathing masks and protective clothing, to lower the risks. What employers could no longer do legally was to bar women or men from these jobs. The most they could do was warn employees of the potential risks to themselves and their families.[32]

Discussion Questions

1. Identify the ethical issues that arose in the Johnson Controls case. How can conflicting rights be reconciled? How can social justice be attained? How can a woman's privacy be preserved while also protecting employees' on-the-job health?
2. What would be the socially responsive course of action for companies that use hazardous materials and also employ workers who may be at risk from those toxic compounds? Refer to the strategies of social responsiveness discussed in Chapter 3.

[32]Adapted from Anne T. Lawrence, "Johnson Controls and Protective Exclusion from the Workplace," *Case Research Journal,* Winter 1993, pp. 1–14.

3. Was the Supreme Court's decision in the Johnson Controls case fair to business? Should the court have given more weight to the high costs involved in making the workplace safer?
4. Should U.S. corporations with operations in other countries apply this new reasoning about the workplace rights of women to those foreign settings, even though U.S. civil rights laws do not officially apply there (as the Supreme Court ruled in early 1991)? What would be the ethical and socially responsible thing for business to do?

PART SEVEN

Social Issues in Management

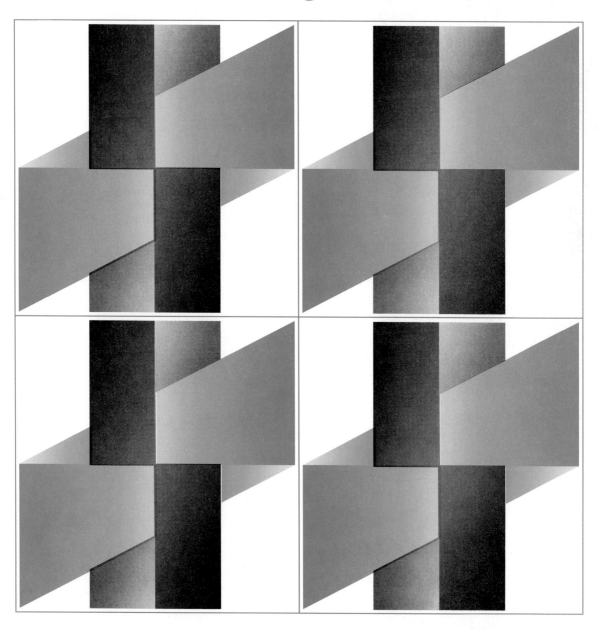

17

The Community and the Corporation

When business has a good relationship with its community, it can make an important difference in the quality of that community's life and in the successful operation of the company. Communities look to business for civic leadership and for help in coping with local problems, while business expects to be treated in fair and supportive ways by the local community. In the 1990s, corporate restructuring is creating special problems to be solved through joint efforts of business and community groups.

Key Questions and Chapter Objectives

This chapter focuses on these key questions and objectives:

- What critical links exist between the community and business?
- How do businesses respond to community problems and needs?
- What goals and objectives are achieved when business contributes to the community?
- How does volunteerism contribute to building strong relationships between business and the community?
- What are the community impacts of corporate restructuring and what strategies do companies and communities use in responding?
- How are social partnerships between business and the community used to address today's pressing social problems?

The Walt Disney Company is one of America's leading entertainment corporations. Founded by Walt Disney, and best known for animated movies such as *Fantasia, The Little Mermaid,* and *The Lion King,* and characters such as Mickey Mouse and Donald Duck, Disney has also created the famous theme parks Disneyland and Disney World in the United States and international theme parks in France and Japan. The company has had unparalleled success integrating its movies, theme parks, and related products into a commercial colossus. Imagination, creativity, and dedicated people have enabled Disney to become a leader in the multibillion dollar entertainment industry.

In the early 1990s, Disney began planning a new generation of theme parks. In November 1993 the company announced that it had purchased an option on a 3,000-acre tract of land in Haymarket, Virginia, on which it intended to build an American history theme park called Disney's America. The land, located in Prince William County, about thirty-five miles southwest of Washington, D.C., is near the Manassas National Battlefield Park, site of the battles of Bull Run, two of the Civil War's bloodiest battles. Plans called for building a theme park, as many as 2,281 homes, 1,340 hotel rooms, and about 1.96 million square feet of retail and commercial space.

Critics immediately argued that the thousands of visitors expected at such a theme park would overwhelm the ability of local communities to absorb and manage side effects. A group calling itself Protecting Prince William County was quickly formed to provide organized opposition to the Disney plan. But local and county officials, working with Disney staff, concluded that the negative effects were being exaggerated and would, in any event, be outweighed by benefits the region would reap, including 19,000 jobs and nearly $50 million in new tax revenues. Both the jobs and the tax revenues were seen as vital to the long-term well-being of the county's communities and residents.

For nearly a year, hearings were held by local, state, and federal government legislatures and agencies. Repeatedly, local opponents presented arguments against the project while Disney executives and local government officials presented positive arguments. According to participants, Disney representatives were always cordial, evidenced a willingness to compromise, and sought to find "win-win" solutions to the concerns being raised. But opponents had no interest in compromise. A group of historians, which included several famous Civil War experts, campaigned against the Disney project through an organization called Project Historic America. They argued that Disney's proposed "virtual reality" battles would trivialize and sanitize the true battles that had occurred at the site. The Piedmont Environmental Council, a coalition of seventy organizations and more than 5,000 families from northern Virginia, took a different approach: they sued Disney, alleging violations of state and federal environmental laws. Lobbying occurred at all levels of government, and it was estimated that hundreds of lawyers, lobbyists, and political advisers were employed on behalf of Disney, its opponents, and interested parties.

In late 1994, Disney announced plans to drop the project. Its option on the land was about to expire, forcing it to either renew the option or buy the land outright. Either would be costly, and in the face of opposition generated since the announcement, it was unlikely that the company could complete the project by its intended completion date in 1998. In announcing the decision, John Cooke, chairman of Disney's America, said: "We are starting afresh and are reaching out to historians who have opposed us to make sure our portrayal of the American experience is responsible." Recognizing that his community would get neither jobs nor new tax revenues, Mayor Jack Kapp of Haymarket, Virginia, spoke more directly: "People around here are devastated. It's an economic blow to Prince William County. I feel like I've been to a funeral today."[1]

Disney's America illustrates some of the complex issues that can arise between a company and the community in which it operates. This chapter examines how companies try to integrate community and citizenship concerns with their financial goals and objectives. Businesses and communities can do much together to create "win-win" solutions to common problems.

COMMUNITY RELATIONS

The **community** discussed in this chapter is an organization's area of local business influence. It includes many individual stakeholders, and may include more than one geographic or political community, for such boundaries do not necessarily follow economic and social impacts. A bank in a large metropolitan area, for example, has numerous stakeholders (see the stakeholder model in Chapter 1) and may define its community as the central city and the towns and cities in which it does business. A local merchant's community may comprise several surrounding cities or towns. A multinational firm may have a separate community for each of the local areas it serves around the world. In all cases, both company and community have a mutual dependence that is significant in economic and social terms.

The involvement of business with the community is called **community relations**. Community relations in the 1990s are quite different from those of 50 or 100 years ago. Technological advances and massive population shifts in the United States and much of the industrialized world are putting great pressures on both business and the community. Community relationships in the United States and abroad are entwined with cultural norms. Business decisions have become more complex, and the impact of those decisions has loomed larger in the life of communities. Keeping community ties alive, well, and relevant is a major task for today's businesses.

Many corporations have established community relations offices to coordinate community programs, manage donations of goods and services, work with local governments, and encourage employee volunteerism in

---

[1]Based on articles in the *New York Times* and *Wall Street Journal* appearing in 1993 and 1994. See especially, Sallie Hofmeister, "Disney Vows to Seek Another Park Site," *New York Times*, Sept. 30, 1994, p. A12; and Michael Janofsky, "Town 'Devastated' by Loss of Project," *New York Times*, Sept. 30, 1994, p. A12.

nonprofit and civic groups.[2] Companies have increasingly become involved with local communities on diverse issues including education reform, environmental risk management, local taxes, and improving the
lives of the homeless. Their aims are to improve local conditions that produce or attract a workforce qualified to meet the company's needs and to
build a positive relationship between the firm and important local groups.
Community relations officers work closely with other corporate offices
that link the corporation to the external world, such as the employee relations, public relations, or public affairs offices (see Chapter 3). These linkages form important bridges between the corporation and community
groups.[3]

Limited Resources Face Unlimited Community Needs

Every community has many social needs requiring far more resources
than are available. Choices must be made and priorities established. In
some instances, the community decides the priorities, but in other instances, business influences community priorities very directly. Further,
in all cases, once management has decided to help serve a need, it still
must decide how its resources can best be applied to that need. This
means that any action management takes will result in some dissatisfaction
from those who get no help and from those who do not get as much help
as they want.

Figure 17-1 illustrates the variety of expectations that communities
have of business. Each year, companies receive requests for artistic, educational, and charitable assistance serving both special groups and the community as a whole. A company may agree to support some, but not all, of
these requests, and its work with these groups will consume hundreds of
days of employee time and thousands of dollars of company resources.
Meanwhile, the company must still meet its business objective of serving
customers competitively throughout the nation.

Community Involvement and Firm Size

Community involvement has become a part of most business life-styles.
Studies show that both large and small businesses, whether they are local
firms or branches of national firms, tend to be active in community af-

[2]See James E. Post and the Foundation for Public Affairs, "The State of Corporate Public Af-
fairs in the United States: Results of a National Survey," in J. Post., ed., *Research in Corporate
Social Performance and Policy*, Vol. 14, Greenwich, CT: JAI Press, 1993, pp. 79–89; and Lee
Burke et al., "Corporate Community Involvement in the San Francisco Bay Area," *California
Management Review*, Spring 1986, pp. 121–141.
[3]See Boston College Center for Corporate Community Relations, "Profile of the Community
Relations Profession," *Community Relations Letter*, March 1993, Chestnut Hill, MA: Boston
College Center for Corporate Community Relations.

FIGURE 17-1
What the community and business want from each other.

Requests Made by the Community to Business

- Assistance for less-advantaged people
- Support for air and water pollution control
- Support for artistic and cultural activities
- Employment and advancement of minorities and women
- Assistance in urban planning and development
- Support of local health care programs
- Donation of equipment to local school system
- Support of local bond issues for public improvements
- Aid to community hospital drive
- Support of local program for recycling
- Executive leadership for United Way fund-raising campaign

Community Services Desired by Business

- A cultural and educational environment that supports a balanced quality of life for employees
- Adequate family recreational activities
- Public services, such as police and fire protection, and sewage, water, and electric services
- Taxes that are equitable and do not discriminate for or against business
- Acceptance of business participation in community affairs
- A fair and open public press
- An adequate transportation system to business and residential areas (e.g., suitable public transportation and well-maintained streets)
- Public officials, customers, and citizens who are fair and honest in their involvement with business
- Cooperative problem-solving approach to addressing community problems

fairs.[4] Business leaders bring knowledge and ability to civic and community matters. Much of this activity involves participation in groups such as local business councils and roundtables, leadership civic task forces, and regional public affairs councils. Through such activities executives become familiar with local needs and issues and the ways in which businesses and communities affect each other.

Large companies usually have more public visibility in community af-

[4]Center for Corporate Public Involvement, *1993 Social Report of the Life and Health Insurance Business*, Washington, DC: American Council of Life Insurance and Health Insurance Association of America, 1993.

fairs. These "name" firms are more established and help to characterize their surrounding towns.[5] Executives, often acting as board members and consultants, tend to participate more actively in philanthropy, volunteerism, and community issues when the headquarters is located in the community.[6]

When a company has numerous *branches*, its community involvements extend into those cities and towns and corporate policy has to be implemented in different local situations. An effective policy has to recognize the unique needs of each community in which the firm is involved. This makes it desirable for corporate headquarters to give local managers broad leeway to make community-related decisions.

> Target Stores is a retailer with more than 600 stores throughout the United States. Community involvement—which Target calls their "Good Neighbor" program—is a basic part of every store's business strategy. Local store managers are expected to develop innovative community outreach programs to reinforce the message that Target is a good neighbor whose deeds make the community a better place for all to live.

Target Stores are not alone in assigning community relations responsibility to local managers. Research studies have found that nearly 60 percent of firms have delegated local community relations responsibilities, including corporate contributions, to managers in local plants, branch offices, and service branches.[7]

Foreign-owned companies also participate in community affairs. As shown in Exhibit 17-A, their profile of activities is quite similar to that of domestic companies.

Small business participation in community activities is just as important as large business involvement. Small business representatives, such as automobile dealers, restaurants, real estate brokers, supermarkets, and other retail merchants, significantly influence the quality of community life. They tend to be personally and professionally involved in community affairs, often expressing a deep commitment to the community based on many years of residence.

> Local businesses are often part of a community's chamber of commerce, Kiwanis, and Rotary clubs. These organizations work on community issues such as parking and traffic, business development, and cooperation with local schools. In one community, for example, a real estate brokerage donated the time of its employees to several local middle schools that needed adult assistance to run a weekly bottle and can recycling collection. Every Friday morning, teams of real estate bro-

---

[5]Ibid.

[6]See Burke et al., op. cit., for a discussion of these involvements.

[7]Target Stores data provided by company. See also, Audris Tillman, *Corporate Contributions, 1993*, New York: The Conference Board, 1994.

EXHIBIT 17-A

COMMUNITY INVOLVEMENT OF FOREIGN-OWNED CORPORATIONS IN THE UNITED STATES

Foreign-owned companies tend to adopt community involvement strategies as part of the cost of doing business in the American market. Communities expect corporations to participate in community programs, and foreign-owned companies are especially sensitive to these expectations, according to David Logan, author of a study on the community activities of foreign-owned companies for the Conference Board, a leading business research organization. Foreign-owned companies tend to favor traditionally accepted forms of community involvement.

Cash giving — 78%
Employee volunteerism — 67%
Sponsorship (e.g., arts or sports events) — 65%
Direct gift to United Fund or United Way — 64%
Product — 59%
Employee matched giving — 48%
Other — 11%

Community programs

Percent of companies participating (n = 108)

SOURCE: David Logan, *Community Involvement of Foreign-Owned Companies in the United States,* Research Report 1089-94, New York: The Conference Board, 1994.

kers worked with students at each middle school to receive the bottles and cans dropped off by residents during the morning commuting hours.

Community Support of Business

The relationship of business and community is one of mutual interdependence. Each has responsibilities to the other because each has social power to affect the other. This power-responsibility equation applies to both parties and reminds that success is a matter of mutual support, rather than opposition. The concept of a "social contract" is very fundamental to the relationship between business and the community.

Business normally expects various types of support from the local communities in which it operates. As shown in Figure 17-1 business expects fair treatment, and it expects to be accepted as a participant in community affairs because it is an important part of the community. It also expects community services such as a dependable water supply and police protection. Companies are encouraged to remain in the community and grow if there are appropriate cultural, educational, and recreational facilities for their employees and, of course, if taxes remain reasonable. Businesses also have come to recognize that they rely heavily on the public school system and other local services to run their businesses efficiently.

This combination of business-community mutual support is illustrated in Figure 17-2. The diagonal line in the diagram illustrates the situation when business receives support from the community that is equal to that which it provides to the community. Sometimes, business will invest more in the community than the community seems to provide to business in return. This is illustrated by the area above the diagonal line. Conversely, communities sometimes provide much more support to business than business seems to contribute to the community. This is shown by the area below the diagonal line. Ideally, business and community provide relatively equal amounts of support to each other and, more importantly, their interaction moves from the lower left end of the box to the upper right. This signifies a high degree of interaction and relatively equal amounts of support for one another. As a company grows, for example, it provides more jobs, tax revenues, volunteers for community projects, support to local charities, and so forth. But positive relationships between a company and a community are sometimes difficult to develop.

Wal-Mart, for example, has encountered serious local objection to its plans to build superstores and distribution centers in a number of local communities. Wal-Mart's founder, Sam Walton, now deceased, was fond of saying that he would never try to force a community to ac-

FIGURE 17-2
Business and the community need support from each other.

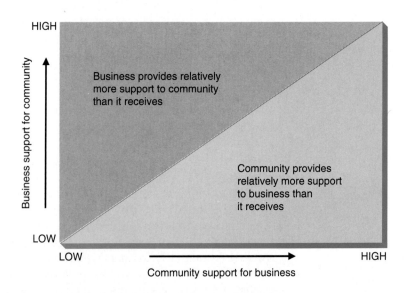

cept a Wal-Mart store. "Better to go where we are wanted," he is reported to have said. In the 1990s, however, that view is less often endorsed by Wal-Mart management. In a series of high-profile local conflicts, Wal-Mart sparked intense local opposition from several communities that were worried about traffic patterns, safety, and negative effects on local small businesses from the opening of giant Wal-Mart facilities.[8]

STRENGTHENING THE COMMUNITY

Business initiatives have helped improve the quality of life in communities in many ways, some of which are listed in Figure 17-3. Although not exhaustive, the list suggests the range of community needs that a corpora-

[8]In a short period of time, Wal-Mart encountered opposition in several Massachusetts and Vermont communities. See "Town Residents Oppose Proposed Wal-Mart Center," *Wall Street Journal*, Aug. 22, 1994, p. B5.

FIGURE 17-3

Community projects of 180 insurance companies.

Source: Center for Corporate Public Involvement, *1993 Social Report of the Life and Health Insurance Business*, Washington, DC: Center for Corporate Public Involvement, 1993.

Types of Projects	Percentage of Reporting Companies Supporting Projects in Each Area
Education	86%
Arts and culture	76
Local health programs	72
Youth activities	69
Neighborhood improvement programs	66
Programs for hunger and the homeless	55
AIDS education and treatment	49
Minority affairs	48
Programs for the handicapped	47
Drug or alcohol abuse programs	46
Activities for senior citizens and retired persons	41
Housing programs	39
Safety programs	33
Environmental programs	32
Day-care programs	31
Prenatal programs	27
Hard-to-employ programs	26
Crime prevention	25
Transportation programs	16
Other	14

tion's executives are asked to address. These community concerns challenge managers to apply talent, imagination, and resources to develop creative ways to strengthen the community while still managing their businesses as profitable enterprises.

Improving Economic Development

Business leaders and their companies are frequently involved in local or regional economic development, which is intended to bring new businesses into an area or to otherwise improve local conditions.[9] Central business districts, unlike older and often neglected poorer residential areas, have benefited from businesses during recent decades. Business has helped transform these business areas in major U.S. cities into a collection of shining office buildings, entertainment facilities, fashionable shopping malls, conference centers, and similar urban amenities. In spite of these developments, many urban areas have become forbidding and inhospitable places, fraught with drugs, violence, and frighteningly high crime rates.[10]

Through extensive cooperative efforts, planners are trying to control development so that the central business districts will again become attractive to all citizens. Some of the ingredients needed are police protection that ensures safety, open spaces devoted to fountains, green grass, and trees, outdoor sitting areas, arcades, a variety of attractive stores, outdoor cafes, theaters, and interesting people.

Sometimes the rush of business development can be a problem as well as an opportunity for a community. For example, when Toyota announced in December 1985 that it would build an automobile manufacturing facility in Georgetown, Kentucky, residents were both pleased and anxious. The plant was expected to add as many as 3,500 jobs, but local people worried about how the community would be able to absorb the influx of outsiders and how their tightly knit community would be affected.

> Acknowledging its responsibility for the expected changes, Toyota gave Georgetown $1 million to build a community center. By working closely with local government officials, acknowledging their responsibility, and communicating openly about expected problems, Toyota helped the community become a more dynamic place to live while expanding its business presence.[11]

[9]George Peterson and Dana Sundblad, *Corporations as Partners in Strengthening Urban Communities*, Research Report 1079-94, New York: The Conference Board, 1994.

[10]Dennis R. Judd and Todd Swanstrom, *City Politics: Private Power and Public Policy*, New York: HarperCollins College Publishers, 1994.

[11]The community involvements of foreign-owned companies are discussed in David Logan, *Community Involvement of Foreign-Owned Companies in the United States*, Research Report 1089-94, New York: The Conference Board, 1994. See also, "Toyota in Bluegrass Country," *Industry Week*, June 5, 1989, pp. 30–33; and "As U.S. Car Makers Cut Back, Toyota Is Expanding Briskly," *New York Times*, Jan. 1, 1991, p. A1.

The congestion and other problems that accompany metropolitan growth are not limited to large cities. Office building has mushroomed in many suburban areas; almost two-thirds of new office space built in the late 1980s was in the suburbs, creating in many metropolitan areas what is called **urban sprawl**. Technological changes permit many business operations to be located away from central headquarters, and suburban building and rental costs are usually much less than those of center city locations. In the San Francisco suburb of Walnut Creek, for example, local citizens voted to bar large-scale office buildings and retail projects until traffic congestion was relieved. The most celebrated case in the 1990s, however, may have been the failed efforts of the Disney Company to build a history theme park in Virginia near Civil War battle sites. (See the opening example in this chapter.) Residents were concerned about traffic from the park, but were also worried about the long-term impact of office and residential construction on their communities.

Housing

Suburban areas appeal to business because of generally less crowded conditions. Many people choose to live in suburban communities which usually feature space and some sense of the "small town" atmosphere that is rooted in American culture. Many suburban communities have grown during periods of prosperity, as families sought to move from apartments to houses or from smaller homes to more spacious dwellings. When communities have been battered by layoffs and plant closings, they are often pleased to have any new businesses open. But rarely will communities ignore public concerns about the type of growth and the type of businesses that locate in a town. To avoid community backlash and an antigrowth attitude, business leaders need to work with community groups in balancing business growth with respect for community values. Community planning efforts by municipal governments, done in cooperation with private industry, represent one of the steps that business can take to achieve this balance.

Life and health insurance companies have taken the lead in programs to revitalize neighborhood housing through organizations such as Neighborhood Housing Services (NHS) of America. NHS, which is locally controlled, locally funded, nonprofit, and tax-exempt, offers housing rehabilitation and financial services to neighborhood residents. Similar efforts are being made to house the homeless. The New York City Coalition for the Homeless includes corporate, nonprofit, and community members. In Los Angeles, Transamerica Life Companies, a founding partner of the Greater Los Angeles Partnership for the Homeless, has provided money and sent trained people to assist the partnership's efforts. Banks are also involved in meeting the housing needs of low income residents. Under the requirements of the federal Community Reinvestment Act, banks are required to demonstrate their commitment to local communities through low-income lending programs and to provide annual reports to the public.

Education Reform

The aging of the post–World War II "baby boom" generation and the subsequent decline in the number of entry-level workers have forced businesses to pay attention to the quality of the workforce. In assessing how the available workforce can be improved, many businesses have recognized that local public schools are a critical resource. Amidst the severe criticism of America's public schools, which began with the publication, *A Nation at Risk*,[12] business has become significantly involved in education reform.

Thousands of local school-business partnerships sprang up during the 1980s. Many of these collaborations, called "adopt-a-school" partnerships, engaged businesses in working with school teachers for the first time. Business leaders began participating on school boards and as advisers to schools and government officials who needed business-specific training. The National Alliance of Business (NAB), for example, developed a social "compact" project in which local businesses pledged their assistance and support to local schools. Demonstration projects in twelve cities led to an improved understanding of the factors required for successful business-education collaboration.[13]

According to one leading research organization, business involvement in education has passed through four stages, or "waves."[14] Beyond business support for programs (first wave). and the application of management principles to school administration (second wave), business has become increasingly committed to public policy initiatives (third wave), and collaboration with all of education's stakeholders to reform of the entire system (fourth wave). An example of this systemic reform is described in Exhibit 17-B.

Efforts at workforce improvement involve direct business participation in worker training and retraining, especially efforts to train the disadvantaged. Much of this participation has come about as a result of federal job legislation, which requires that public sector job training programs be su-

---

[12]National Commission on Excellence in Education, *A Nation at Risk: The Imperative for Educational Reform*, Washington, DC: U.S. Government Printing Office, 1983.

[13]See Sandra A. Waddock, *Not by Schools Alone: Sharing Responsibility for America's School Reform*, New York: Praeger, 1995; and Sandra Waddock, "Understanding Social Partnership: An Evolutionary Model of Partnership Organizations," *Administration and Society*, vol. 21, May 1989, pp. 78–100. The National Alliance of Business project is described in National Alliance of Business, *The Compact Project: School-Business Partnerships for Improving Education*, Washington, DC: National Alliance of Business, 1989.

[14]Sandra A. Waddock, *Business and Education Reform: The Fourth Wave*, Research Report 1091-94, New York: The Conference Board, 1994, p. 13.

EXHIBIT 17-B

KENTUCKY'S EDUCATIONAL REFORM PARTNERSHIP

Kentucky, one of America's five commonwealth states,[1] has become a leader in the nation's efforts to reform public education. The active involvement of the state's largest business corporations, and the personal involvement of chief executives and managers from companies of all sizes, have been key factors in Kentucky's commitment to reforming the entire educational system.

Public education faced a crisis in Kentucky when a court decision declared the system unconstitutional because of discrimination among racially divided schools. The decision was a "wake-up call" for political leaders, many of whom had not been previously involved in education reform. Business leaders recognized that without a functioning school system, Kentucky businesses would not be able to hire new employees with the fundamental skills needed for productive activity in the workplace.

Kentucky has become home to a wide range of manufacturing and service industries. Among the largest and best-known companies headquartered in Kentucky are Ashland Oil, Humana, and United Parcel Service. Financial services have also grown rapidly, including General Electric's credit operations which are located in Louisville. These companies each employ many thousands of people whose skills are vital to the productivity and success of the companies. With such a large stake in an educated workforce, Kentucky's business leaders stepped forward and announced the Partnership for Kentucky School Reform in 1990. At an inaugural meeting in 1991, fifty business leaders formally committed their efforts to the passage of the Kentucky Education Reform Act (KERA)—a state law that would radically restructure the schools—thereby joining with dozens of other political and education leaders to form a powerful coalition for educational improvement.

The Partnership for Kentucky School Reform set forth three goals: (1) to promote support for the implementation of KERA's provisions and goals; (2) to provide an ongoing forum for discussion of problems and concerns; and (3) to serve as a vehicle for securing the technical assistance and expertise needed to facilitate implementation of school reform. Most importantly, the companies that agreed to become Partnership members have made a ten-year commitment. As Kent "Oz" Nelson, chairman and chief executive officer of United Parcel Service, said, "KERA has been recognized by many as the most comprehensive education reform legislation in the nation. . . . It is also a vast undertaking, which requires a serious and deep commitment if it is to be implemented successfully." Kentucky businesses have made that commitment and will be engaged in the cause of improving public education well into the twenty-first century.

[1]The other commonwealth states are Maryland, Massachusetts, Pennsylvania, and Virginia.

SOURCE: Sandra A. Waddock, *Business and Education Reform: The Fourth Wave*, Research Report 1091-94, New York: The Conference Board, 1994, pp. 26–27.

---

pervised by private sector managers through private initiative councils (PICs) in every community where federal funds are used. Businesses have generally welcomed this chance to participate as a way to better match school and community efforts with business workforce opportunities and needs.

Technical Assistance to Government

In a number of cities, business has spearheaded programs to upgrade the quality of local government. It provides special advice and technical expertise on budgeting, financial controls, and other management techniques. Many of the techniques of total quality management pioneered in the private sector are now being adapted to the analysis and improvement of government programs. Business know-how in these matters can inject vitality and efficiency into government systems that are often overburdened, underfinanced, and obsolete.[15]

Aid to Minority Enterprise

In addition to programs to hire and train urban minorities for jobs in industry, private enterprise has extended assistance to minority-owned small businesses that must struggle for existence in the inner cities. These businesses are often at a great economic disadvantage: they do business in economic locations where high crime rates, congestion, poor transportation, low-quality public services, and a low-income clientele combine to produce a high rate of business failure. Large corporations, sometimes in cooperation with universities, have provided financial and technical advice to minority entrepreneurs and have helped launch programs to teach managerial, marketing, and financial skills. They also have financed the building of minority-managed inner-city plants and sponsored special programs to purchase services and supplies from minority firms. In sum, private sector efforts have significantly helped some minority entrepreneurs who otherwise might have failed.

Environmental Programs

The positive impacts of business on the community are balanced by a number of negative effects, including environmental problems. As local landfills near capacity, for example, communities have become concerned about the disposal of solid wastes. Citizen groups using slogans like NIMBY ("not in my back yard") or GOOMBY ("get out of my back yard") have resisted development of additional landfills to handle solid waste disposal, to which businesses contribute in great quantities. So high was public concern about solid waste disposal in Seattle, for example, that Procter & Gamble began a pilot project there to collect and recycle disposable diapers. Seattle's families provided an enthusiastic test case for Procter & Gamble's experiment in recycling and P&G learned important lessons about public perceptions of the environmental impact of its products.

Community perceptions of environmental risk can have a powerful ef-

---

[15]See Peterson and Sundblad, op. cit.

fect on the ability of companies to operate existing facilities and to expand their businesses. Chemical companies are among the industrial manufacturers facing such problems. They have created **community advisory panels (CAPs)** to build communications bridges between managers of their facilities and residents of local communities. These advisory panels have a continuing dialogue with plant managers and bring issues of public concern to the meetings. The chemical industry has formally adopted this approach as part of the Responsible Care Program commitments all its members make to the communities in which they operate.

Disaster Relief

One of the most common forms of corporate involvement in the community is disaster relief. Throughout the world, companies—like individuals—tend to lend assistance when disaster strikes a community. When major flooding occurred in the midwestern United States in 1994, assistance worth millions of dollars poured into affected communities from companies across the country and many overseas. When an earthquake seriously damaged the Japanese port city of Kobe in 1995, individuals and businesses from all over the world sought to provide assistance.

> For example, Abbott Laboratories, a health care products company headquartered near Chicago, Illinois, joined with dozens of other companies to provide needed medical products for Kobe's survivors. Abbott contributed 1,600 cases of sterile water, intravenous solutions, antibiotics, and pharmaceuticals to a coordinated relief effort organized by AmeriCares, a private international relief organization based in New Canaan, Connecticut. A shipment of more than 200,000 pounds of materials was airlifted to Japan where another organization, the Japan International Rescue Action Committee, distributed the products to earthquake victims in Kobe.

Networks of volunteer agencies, such as the American Red Cross and AmeriCares, are instrumental in aligning resources with needs in such instances. International relief efforts are becoming more important, as communications improve and people around the world are able to witness the horror of disasters. Corporate involvement in such efforts, then, is an extension of the natural tendency of people to help one another when tragedy strikes.

CORPORATE GIVING

America is a generous society. Based on information collected by the Internal Revenue Service, it is estimated that individuals and organizations give more than $120 billion each year to churches, charities, and other nonprofit organizations. American businesses are a small but important part of this broad cultural tradition of giving.

One of the most visible ways in which business helps a community is through gifts of money, property, and employee service. This corporate philanthropy, or **corporate giving**, demonstrates the commitment of business to assist the community by supporting such nonprofit organizations as United Way, Community Chest, and individual hospitals, schools, homeless shelters, and other providers of important community services.

The federal government has encouraged corporate giving for educational, charitable, scientific, and religious purposes since 1936.[16] The current Internal Revenue Service rule permits corporations to deduct from their taxable income all such gifts that do not exceed 10 percent of the company's before-tax income. In other words, a company with a before-tax income of $1 million might contribute up to $100,000 to nonprofit community organizations devoted to education, charity, science, or religion. The $100,000 in contributions would then reduce the income to be taxed from $1 million to $900,000, thus saving the company money on its tax bill while providing a source of income to community agencies. Of course, there is nothing to prevent a corporation from giving more than 10 percent of its income for philanthropic purposes, but it would not be given a tax break above the 10 percent level.

As shown in Figure 17-4, average corporate giving in the United States is far below the 10 percent deduction now permitted. Though it varies from year to year, corporate giving has been closer to 1 percent of pretax income since the early 1960s, with a sharp rise in the early 1980s that reached a peak in 1986. A few corporations, including a cluster that are headquartered in the Minneapolis-St. Paul metropolitan area, have pledged 5 percent of their pretax income,[17] although most companies average between 1 and 2 percent of pretax income.[18] Even at the national average of 1 percent giving, substantial amounts of money are channeled to education, the arts, and other community organizations. Corporate giving totaled more than $6 billion in 1993, including more than $2.5 billion for education.[19]

The courts have ruled that charitable contributions fall within the legal and fiduciary powers of the corporation's policymakers. Some critics have argued that corporate managers have no right to give away company

---

[16]The evolution of corporate philanthropy is summarized in Mark Sharfman, "Changing Institutional Rules: The Evolution of Corporate Philanthropy, 1883-1953," *Business & Society*, vol. 33, no. 3, Dec. 1994, pp. 236–269; and, "Charities Tap Generous Spirit of Hong Kong," *Wall Street Journal*, Nov. 3, 1994, pp. B1, B8.

[17]See Maria R. M. Buenaventura, *Corporate Contributions Survey, 1992*, New York: The Conference Board, 1993.

[18]See Audris Tillman, *Corporate Contributions Survey, 1993*, New York: The Conference Board, 1994.

[19]Council for Aid to Education, press release, Sept. 19, 1994; and "Corporate Giving to Charity Increased a Scant 2% in 1993," *Wall Street Journal*, Sept. 19, 1994, p. A7.

FIGURE 17-4

Corporate contributions as a percentage of pretax net income, 1950–1993.

SOURCE: Maria R. M. Buenaventura, *Corporate Contributions Survey, 1992*, New York: The Conference Board, 1993. This chart is derived from Internal Revenue Service data presented in Appendix Table 1, p. 56.

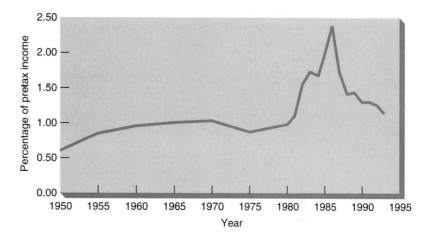

money that does not belong to them. According to this line of reasoning, any income earned by the company should be either reinvested in the firm or distributed to the stockholders who are the legal owners. But the courts have taken the position that corporate contributions are one additional way in which companies link themselves to the broader interests of the community, thereby advancing and strengthening the company rather than weakening it.

Another way a company helps local communities is the substantial number of business gifts donated but not recorded in these figures because they are handled separately. Routine gifts of products and services for local use often are recorded as advertising expenses; gifts of employee time for charity drives and similar purposes usually are not recorded; and the costs of soliciting and processing employee gifts, such as payroll deductions for the United Way, usually are not recorded as corporate giving.

Many large corporations have established nonprofit foundations to handle their charitable contributions programs. This approach permits them to administer contributions programs more uniformly and provides a central group of professionals that handles all grant requests. Foreign-owned corporations use foundations less frequently, although Japanese firms such as Matsushita (Panasonic) and Hitachi do use corporate foundations to conduct their charitable contributions activities in the United States. As corporations expand to more foreign locations, pressures will grow to expand international corporate giving.

Corporate Giving in a Strategic Context

One way to stretch the corporate contributions dollar is to make sure that it is being used strategically to meet the needs of both the recipient and the donor. Creating a strategy of mutual benefits for business and society is one of the major themes of this book, and this type of **strategic philan-**

thropy is a means of achieving such "win-win" outcomes. As shown in Figure 17-5, strategic philanthropy blends traditional corporate philanthropy with giving programs that are directly or indirectly linked to business goals and objectives. In the 1990s, more companies are approaching corporate philanthropic giving in this way.[20]

One example of linking business goals to charitable giving is **cause marketing**. Developed by American Express as a way to promote wider use of its credit cards, many companies have now created formulas for making contributions to nonprofit organizations based on how many of the nonprofit organization members use the credit card, purchase products, or otherwise enhance the revenues of the donor. In 1994, Johnson & Johnson broke new ground when it introduced "Arthritis Foundation" pain relief medicine. It agreed to make a contribution to the Arthritis Foundation for each package of pain reliever sold under the AF name.

One group of scholars pointed out that strategic philanthropy occurs in two forms. One, called "strategic *process* giving," applies a professional business approach to determine the goals, budgets, and criteria for specific grants. The second approach, called "strategic *outcome* giving," emphasizes the links between corporate contributions and certain business-oriented goals such as introducing a new product, providing needed

[20]See Craig Smith, "The New Corporate Philanthropy," *Harvard Business Review,* vol. 72, no. 3, May–June 1994, pp. 105ff; and Myra Alperson, *New Strategies for Corporate Giving,* New York: The Conference Board, 1995.

FIGURE 17-5
Corporate giving and community relations.

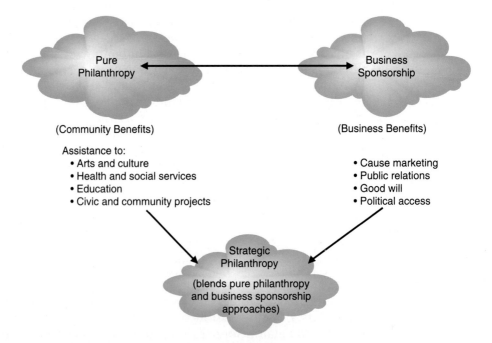

Pure Philanthropy

Business Sponsorship

(Community Benefits)

Assistance to:
- Arts and culture
- Health and social services
- Education
- Civic and community projects

(Business Benefits)

- Cause marketing
- Public relations
- Good will
- Political access

Strategic Philanthropy

(blends pure philanthropy and business sponsorship approaches)

services to employees (e.g., child-care centers), or maintaining positive contacts with external stakeholder groups (e.g., Asian-Americans).[21] Continuing pressures to justify the use of every corporate dollar are leading managers to think about new ways to tie charitable contributions to business goals.

Priorities in Corporate Giving

The distribution of corporate contributions reflects how the business community views major community needs. As shown in Figure 17-6, corporate giving from 1982 to 1992 varied somewhat among categories, but the "pie" was divided in approximately the same way. These percentages are not identical among different companies and industries, however, and some companies tend to favor support for education while others give relatively greater amounts to cultural organizations or community groups.

The actual contributions of an individual company will depend on company goals and priorities. Corporate giving is often justified as a *social investment* that benefits business in the long run by improving the community, its labor force, the climate for business, or other conditions affecting business. An alternative view is that routine local gifts are a *normal expense* of operating a business in the community and should be treated like

[21]Jeanne M. Logsdon, Martha Reiner, and Lee Burke, "Corporate Philanthropy: Strategic Responses to the Firm's Stakeholders," *Nonprofit and Voluntary Sector Quarterly*, vol. 19, no. 2, Summer 1990, pp. 93–109.

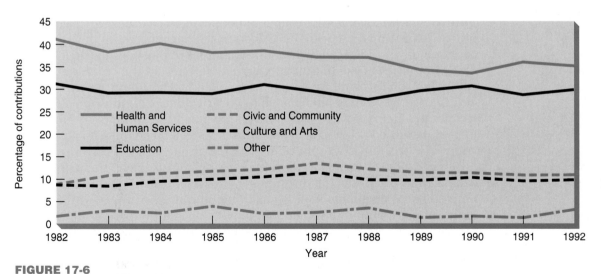

FIGURE 17-6

Distribution of corporate contributions, 1982–1992.

Source: Maria R. M. Buenaventura, *Corporate Contributions Survey, 1992*, New York: The Conference Board, 1993, p. 24.

other public relations expenses. Another view holds that the corporation is a citizen and, as such, has a *citizenship responsibility* to give without regard to self-interest. Some believe that giving should be *linked to business purposes* as exemplified in the cause-related marketing pioneered by American Express. The customer gets the product or service, the charity receives a contribution, and company sales grow.

Another point of view is that some corporate gifts take on the characteristics of taxes. Since it is widely believed that corporations should be good citizens, helpful neighbors, and human institutions, the community's expectations come close to imposing some types of gift giving on the corporation as a form of *unofficial tax*. The gifts are given to retain public approval.

Regardless of whether gifts are considered to be an investment, an expense, philanthropy, or a tax, most of their costs are probably passed on to consumers, because giving in the long run becomes a cost of doing business. Business is then acting partly as agent and trustee for the community, receiving funds and distributing them according to perceived and expressed community needs. In its trusteeship role, business responds to various stakeholder claims in its community, and one of these responses is gifts to those whose claims are perceived as being either legitimate or so powerful that they threaten the business if not satisfied. Thus, both the legitimacy of claim and the power of claimants are considered when making a decision concerning corporate giving.

THE ROLE OF VOLUNTEERISM

Volunteerism involves the efforts of people to assist others in the community through unpaid work. The United States has a long and distinguished tradition of volunteerism, with many examples dating back to the founding of communities as the population moved west across the continent. In the 1980s, the spirit of volunteerism was invoked by Presidents Ronald Reagan and George Bush as an alternative to government programs to solve community problems. In the early 1980s, the business community united to form the Council on Private Sector Initiatives as a mechanism to encourage voluntary business-community activities. Volunteerism received a highly publicized boost when President Bush launched his "1,000 Points of Light" campaign to celebrate 1,000 voluntary efforts by individuals and organizations to solve problems in American communities. In the mid-1990s, the Points of Light Foundation has sought to be a catalyst to continue stimulating voluntary action programs in local communities.[22]

[22]Points of Light Foundation, "Special Report: The 1994 National Community Service Conference," *Newsletter*, Washington, DC: Points of Light Foundation, vol. 2, no. 7, July–Aug. 1994.

Businesses—large and small—are often enlisted as allies in efforts to improve communities. Managers are asked to announce, publicize, and promote such efforts among staff members, employees, and associates. Some companies may also provide money, supplies, T-shirts, transportation, or other resources to these community efforts. Corporate community relations managers are frequently the executives who are asked to coordinate these efforts.

> For example, when Atlanta was awarded the 1996 Summer Olympic Games by the International Olympic Committee, a major element of the city's bid was the commitment by Atlanta-based corporations such as Coca-Cola to provide extensive voluntary support. By the time the games are actually held, Coca-Cola's community relations staff will have coordinated tens of thousands of employee days of volunteer work in support of the games.

Although most companies and communities are involved in activities that are less visible than the Olympic Games, nearly every city and local community has community needs that require the helping hands of volunteers. For business, this means that in addition to providing jobs, paying taxes, and directing charitable contributions dollars to worthy causes, there is a role for companies as catalysts in encouraging volunteerism that helps build local communities.

CORPORATE RESTRUCTURING AND COMMUNITY RELATIONS

Beginning in the 1980s, and continuing through the mid-1990s, American businesses have been going through massive corporate restructuring, reorganization, and reengineering. This change process, which many believe is vital if American firms are to be successful in competitive global businesses, has also become a serious and disruptive fact of life for communities.

Corporate restructuring means that companies are reshaping their business activities in some fundamental way so as to become more competitive. Restructured companies often close down older, less productive facilities, improving the firm's ability to produce goods more efficiently. Sometimes they sell off assets to other corporations that may not have the same relationship to the local community as the previous owner. Restructuring may be voluntarily undertaken by management to avoid being taken over by hostile corporate "raiders" or simply to meet the forces of global competition by introducing labor-saving technology, moving production facilities to low-wage regions of the world, or using new, substitute materials such as plastic and ceramic auto parts.

Social Costs of Restructuring

Whatever the reasons for the restructuring, the effects on the community are similar: local plants close, workers are laid off, jobs are lost, individuals are relocated. Studies show that displaced workers seldom manage to find new jobs as good or as well paying as the ones they lose when a plant closes. Single-income families may be so hard hit that home mortgage payments cannot be met, and homes may be sold to meet back taxes. Sometimes pension benefits and health care insurance are lost. Older workers, minorities, and women suffer more than other groups of displaced workers, taking longer to find new jobs and receiving lower pay when they do. Family tensions build up: divorce rates increase, depression and mental illness increase, suicides become more frequent, alcoholism and drug abuse grow, child abuse and spouse abuse occur more often. The impact was summed up in a *Time* cover story: "We're #1 and It Hurts."[23]

Community Responses

Communities may be unable to adjust as corporate restructuring reshapes the local business community.

> Akron, Ohio, was for many years known as the Rubber Capital. Millions of tires and inner tubes were produced in Akron's massive tire factories until more than 10,000 jobs were lost in the tire industry's intense global competition during the 1980s. Struggling to recover from these devastating losses, Akron's city government worked hard to attract and develop smaller and mid-sized businesses in the city to replace some of the jobs that were lost. While local supporters boast of the "New Akron," economic recovery is slow, requiring many more (and smaller) businesses to provide an equivalent number of jobs to offset those that were lost. The new industries also require more cooperation between public and private sector officials in order to create the conditions for business success.

The human and community problems created by restructuring are not confined to the industrial "Rust Belt" of the midwestern United States. California's Silicon Valley and Massachusetts' high technology belt also have been squeezed by foreign competition in the 1990s. Texas, Louisiana, and other oil-producing states have faced falling oil prices since the 1980s, resulting in dramatic and well-publicized failures of savings and loan institutions, a decline in the local housing markets, and, in the mid-1990s, a wave of job reductions and downsizings by major oil companies. These job

---

[23]George J. Church, "We're #1 and It Hurts," *Time,* Oct. 24, 1994, pp. 50–56.

losses have resulted in the same negative impacts on people and communities that have occurred elsewhere.

The end of the cold war also meant the reduced need for large military forces and for a defense industry that employed millions of workers. California alone suffered the loss of hundreds of thousands of jobs in the early 1990s because of what are called **defense industry conversion** pressures.

> Lockheed was one of Southern California's largest employers for more than thirty years from the 1960s to the early 1990s. The company manufactured airplanes and other aerospace equipment, developing a reputation as one of the American defense industry's most reliable contractors. As defense budgets began to shrink in the post–cold war era, Lockheed began to trim its business operations. From a high of more than 100,000 employees, the company reduced its workforce to less than 30,000 by early 1994. Then, in an announcement that shocked many, Lockheed management announced that the company would be merged into Martin Marietta, another defense contractor.[24]

In the United States, each year during the 1980s, plant closings displaced about 500,000 workers who had more than three years on the job; in the 1990s, corporate restructurings continued to eliminate jobs at the rate of more than 400,000 jobs per year, including more than 600,000 jobs in 1993. As shown in Figure 17-7, job losses have a cascading effect in the community. Job losses were once primarily felt by lower-wage, hourly workers, including members of minority groups. But in the 1990s, the impact has affected workers at all income levels, including professional staffs and managers.

Many stakeholder groups are affected by these restructuring activities. Local, state, and federal governments, company management, employees, labor unions, local businesses, and community organizations all suffer the impact of restructuring-induced job losses. There is no official estimate of the social costs that have resulted from restructuring during the 1990s, but the cumulative costs of unemployments taxes, social assistance to unemployed workers and their families, and economic-adjustment assistance to affected businesses attributable to corporate restructuring is thought to have surpassed $100 billion from 1990 to 1994. In 1994 alone, corporate America spent more than $10 billion on restructuring while communities spent much more.[25]

As the number of plant closings grew, and their impact became better

---

[24]"Aerospace: Swords into Satellites," *The Economist,* Sept. 3, 1994, pp. 60–61.
[25]"When Slimming down Is Not Enough," *The Economist,* Sept. 3, 1994, pp. 59–60; "Downsizing Government," *Business Week,* Jan. 25, 1995, pp. 34–41; and, "Defense Improvement," *Business Week,* Feb. 6, 1995, pp. 144–145.

FIGURE 17-7

The cascading effects of job losses on a community.

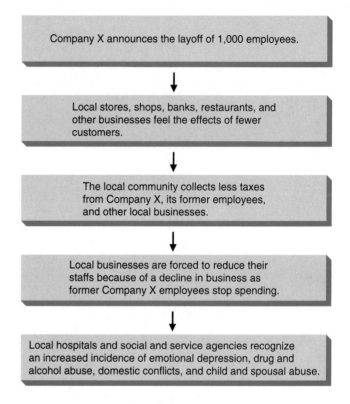

Company X announces the layoff of 1,000 employees.

Local stores, shops, banks, restaurants, and other businesses feel the effects of fewer customers.

The local community collects less taxes from Company X, its former employees, and other local businesses.

Local businesses are forced to reduce their staffs because of a decline in business as former Company X employees stop spending.

Local hospitals and social and service agencies recognize an increased incidence of emotional depression, drug and alcohol abuse, domestic conflicts, and child and spousal abuse.

understood, state and federal governments stepped up their efforts to protect workers and communities. In the 1980s, many state legislatures created **plant closing laws** that required a company to give advance warning before closing a plant. Then, in 1988, the U.S. Congress enacted the Worker Adjustment and Retraining Notification (WARN) Act. WARN required employers to give sixty days' advance notice of plant closings and major layoffs that result in permanent job losses.

Business argued that the need for companies to become more efficient in the face of competition required faster action than these laws would permit. Some research suggests, however, that most of the negative impacts on business were temporary[26] and there is little evidence that such laws have deterred corporate restructuring in the 1990s.

Much of the current U.S. worker legislation is modeled on western European government requirements that employers provide notice to employees, job training, and job search assistance when layoffs are necessary. European laws often require compensation payments to the

[26]See Sylvia Nasar, "Layoff Law Is Having Slim Effect," *New York Times*, Aug. 3, 1993, pp. C1, C2; and Ronald G. Ehrenberg and George H. Jakubson, "Advance Notification of Plant Closing: Does It Matter?" *Industrial Relations*, Winter 1989, pp. 60–71.

community as well. The European Union (EU), for example, has tried to create common standards of compensation and has provided EU funds to communities and regions that have lost jobs to the new competition of the international marketplace.[27]

Company Responses

Management practices vary from company to company when corporate restructuring occurs. In some cases, advance notice is given and management makes an effort to find new jobs for displaced workers and to work with local citizens' groups and municipal officials to ease the impact of a closing. At other times, only the minimum legal requirements are met by a company that does not want to be pressured to reverse its decision. It may offer little aid to employees, local government, or the community.

Restructuring does not always work as planned: some companies have discovered that employees they wished to retain have taken advantage of early retirement or other voluntary programs. Others have learned that employees who remain with the company are disillusioned, unhappy, and fearful of the next round of layoffs. This can result in lack of loyalty and low morale among remaining employees, making it more difficult for the company to respond effectively to the competitive pressures that forced the restructuring in the first place.[28]

The Age of Anxiety

Employees faced with job loss suffer a variety of fates. Some may move to another job with the same company but in a different location. Some are retrained and enter a new skill or craft. Others hang on to false hopes: one steel mill worker with twenty years of experience at one company simply refused to accept reality, saying, "I think the mill is going to open again." Those who find new jobs often end up with lower pay, have less desirable jobs, and lose their seniority. In the 1990s, U.S. Secretary of Labor Robert Reich has led a highly visible campaign to convince employees and employers that lifelong learning and continued development of job skills are the only real security that people can have in a world of rapid competitive change. As Secretary Reich delivered his message around the nation, he began referring to the 1990s as "The Age of Anxiety."[29]

[27]See, for example, "Steel Region Wins £36 Million EU Funds," *The Financial Times,* Oct. 14, 1994, p. 9. The EU's rules on plant closing are reported in *European Labor Law,* Washington, DC: BNA Research, 1994.

[28]See William Bridges, "The End of the Job," *Fortune,* Sept. 19, 1994, pp. 62–74.

[29]Robert Reich, Address to the National Alliance of Business, Sept. 25, 1994, Washington, DC. See also Catherine S. Manegold, "Reich Urges Executives to Aid Labor," *New York Times,* Sept. 25, 1994, p. 25.

The era of corporate restructuring has led some corporations to downsize and reevaluate activities, including corporate giving. As the following example shows, even charitable contributions are no longer a "sacred cow" in the competitive environment of the 1990s.

In 1994, the senior management of ARCO, one of the world's largest petroleum companies, informed the senior executive of the ARCO Foundation that a decision had been made to reduce its funding and eventually eliminate the foundation. ARCO had been a highly visible and much-admired corporate citizen in its headquarters community of Los Angeles. The company provided important leadership in Los Angeles in such efforts as education reform, community development, and Rebuild LA, a major attempt to address the city's complex social and racial issues after the 1992 riots. Through the ARCO Foundation, millions of dollars were targeted at community needs. Still, persistently low prices for oil forced oil companies to reduce staffs, trim expenses, and reengineer operations. A consulting firm was called in by ARCO's top management and concluded that no lasting damage would be done to ARCO's image or profits by cutting out its contributions program. Despite its record of good works, the ax fell on the ARCO Foundation in 1994.

THE NEED FOR PARTNERSHIP

In few areas of society is the need for a **public-private partnership** between business and government more apparent than in dealing with community problems. The idea of partnership is not new. As one group of business executives said in 1982:

Whether growing or contracting, young or old, large or small, in the Frost Belt or Sun Belt, America's urban communities possess the resources of an advanced and affluent society: highly educated and skilled individuals, productive social and economic institutions, sophisticated technology, physical infrastructure, transportation and communications networks, and access to capital. Developing this potential will require cooperation. . . . Public-private partnerships are a source of energy and vitality for America's urban communities.[30]

Corporate restructuring and refocusing has underscored the importance of this point nearly fifteen years later. Many community problems are "people problems" involving hopes, attitudes, sentiments, and expectations for better human conditions. Neither government nor business can simply impose solutions or be expected to find quick and easy answers to

---

[30]Committee for Economic Development, *Public-Private Partnership: An Opportunity for Urban Communities*, New York, 1982, p. 1.

problems so long in the making and so vast in their complications. Moreover, neither government nor business has the financial resources to solve these issues. Grassroots involvement is needed, where people are willing and able to confront their own needs, imagine solutions, and work to fulfill them through cooperative efforts and intelligent planning. In that community-oriented effort, government and business can be partners, contributing aid and assistance where feasible and being socially responsive to legitimately expressed human needs. Exhibit 17-C describes such an effort in communities along the U.S.-Mexico border.

A study by the Conference Board and the Urban Institute identified three distinct strategies that corporations can use to become effective "partners" with urban communities.[31] One is to become *directly involved* in addressing specific problems in specific neighborhoods or communities. A second approach is to develop *partnerships* with the community wherein the community's needs and priorities guide the form and type of corporate activity. The third strategy is for the corporation to be involved in the community through an *intermediary organization,* such as a citywide umbrella organization that helps to coordinate the efforts of many local businesses and nonprofits. An example of such an organization is discussed in the profile of The Atlanta Project (TAP) in "Save Our Cities," a case study at the end of this book.

Communities need jobs, specialized skills, executive talents, and other resources that business can provide. Business needs cooperative attitudes in local government, basic public services, and a feeling that it is a welcome member of the community. Under these circumstances much can be accomplished to upgrade the quality of community life. The range of specific business-community involvements is extensive, giving business many opportunities to be socially responsible. Corporate restructurings, erratic growth patterns, and an explosion of community needs challenge business involvement with the community. Still, by using management skills, corporate philanthropy, employee volunteerism, and other creative means, companies can have a positive impact on the quality of community life.

SUMMARY POINTS OF THIS CHAPTER

- Business and the community have a mutual dependence that is both economically and socially significant. Thus, business works to be accepted as a participant in community affairs by supporting community interests as well as its own.
- Many corporations have established a community relations office which links the company's activities to local needs and community

[31]George Peterson and Dana Sundblad, *Corporations as Partners in Strengthening Urban Communities*, Research Report 1079-94, New York: The Conference Board, 1994.

EXHIBIT 17-C

BUSINESS MEETS THE MAQUILADORAS[1]

The South Texas border with Mexico is not the usual hotbed of corporate community affairs. It is, however, a hotbed of commercial expansion as companies from around the world establish manufacturing and assembly operations called "maquiladoras." In-expensive Mexican labor and easy access to American markets make the maquilado-ras the vehicle for boomtown development.

The boomtowns are growing in areas where social problems—including no schools, no housing, and no social infrastructure to hold together the community—abound. In El Paso, for example, low wages and the prestige of a "Made in the USA" label have helped keep employment high, with more than 20,000 jobs in the apparel industry in 1994. More than 100 million pairs of jeans are made in El Paso each year. But the stiff competition also helps account for the fact that El Paso is the poorest metropolitan region in the United States, with personal incomes only 59 percent of the national average. Patricia Fogerty, a former NYNEX community affairs officer who lives in McAllen, Texas, says: "Some (companies) are finding they have to develop the entire social infrastructure in the towns."

A model for doing so is being developed by the El Paso Community Foundation. It organizes Hispanic wives of workers to do community work and serves as a bridge between employers and social problems in the border communities. Among the leadership companies that have "partnered up" with community groups are Levi Strauss, General Electric, Sierra West, and Alcoa. Yet the maquiladora conditions are so bad that many church groups in the United States are campaigning to press companies to do much more in dealing with these poor and needy communities on both sides of the border.

[1]There are two accepted spellings for this word. We have chosen to use "maquiladora" rather than "machi-ladora," which also appears in published materials.

SOURCE: Allen R. Myerson, "Jeans Makers Flourish on Border," *New York Times*, Sept. 29, 1994, pp. D1, D9; and "Machiladora Blues," in Craig Smith, ed., *Corporate Philanthropy Report*, vol. 5, no. 1, August–Sept. 1989, p. 12. See also, "Doing Business in the Maquiladoras," a case study in this book.

---

groups and develops strategies for creating "win-win" approaches to solving community problems.

■ Corporate contributions to educational, charitable, scientific, and community programs help sustain vital community institutions while benefiting business in a variety of ways. Strategic philanthropy represents a way of linking corporate giving and business goals.

■ Corporate volunteerism involves encouraging employees to partici-pate in projects that address a wide range of community needs. Some companies have made volunteerism an explicit part of their strategy.

■ Corporate restructuring and layoffs can affect many community groups—merchants, employees, school systems, local government, and charitable organizations. Successful strategies for coping with the social consequences and pressures that restructuring can place on community life involve cooperation among business, govern-ment, employees, labor unions, and community organizations.

■ The development of public-private partnerships has proven to be effective in tackling some problems in education, economic development, and social service needs. Partnerships and volunteerism provide models of a shared responsibility in which business and communities address social problems. Many businesses and communities are creating new strategies based on these models.

KEY TERMS AND CONCEPTS USED IN THIS CHAPTER

- Community
- Community relations
- Urban sprawl
- Community advisory panels (CAPS)
- Corporate giving
- Strategic philanthropy

- Cause marketing
- Volunteerism
- Corporate restructuring
- Defense industry conversion
- Plant closing laws
- Public-private partnership

DISCUSSION CASE

ABBOTT LABORATORIES HELPS HABITAT FOR HUMANITY

Habitat for Humanity is a worldwide organization that builds homes and sells them to low-income families on a no-profit, no-interest basis. Habitat was founded in 1976 and has built more than 30,000 homes throughout the world. It has more than 1,000 affiliates in its worldwide network.

Among Habitat's many affiliates are groups of people who are employed by companies such as Abbott Laboratories, a pharmaceutical and health care products manufacturer which employs more than 50,000 people. About 15,000 Abbott employees and retirees live in Lake County, Illinois, where Abbott's world headquarters is located.

Employees of Abbott Laboratories are involved in many types of volunteer activity in their local communities, so it was no surprise when a group decided to form the Abbott Chapter of Habitat for Humanity. The Abbott Chapter has worked closely with Lake County's Habitat organization to identify needs and plan a construction project. Local government officials have also been instrumental in identifying sites for Habitat projects and for obtaining needed permits. Since its formation, the Abbott Chapter has helped renovate several buildings in North Chicago and Waukegan, Illinois.

In 1994, Ms. Robin Coleman and her four children learned that they had been selected as the family to work with the Abbott Chapter in building a new house in North Chicago. Habitat families are selected on the basis of need, ability to make a low mortgage payment, and a willingness to help construct the homes of others as well as their own. With the help of more than 200 Abbott employee volunteers, a $38,000 grant for materials from the Abbott Laboratories Fund, and more than 500 hours of "sweat equity" by the Coleman family, Habitat volunteers built the house in less than one year. In August 1994, Ms. Coleman and her family received the keys to their new home.

A dedication ceremony was held at the new Coleman family home, and Abbott officials, the mayor of North Chicago, Habitat officials, and many of the volunteers attended. Jim Donovan, an R&D quality manager in Abbott's diagnostic division and president of the Abbott Chapter of Habitat, said: "All the people involved in this project have felt a great sense of pride in contributing to the future of the Coleman family as well as to the community."[32]

Discussion Questions

1. What is the motivation for Abbott employees to participate in the Habitat project? What is the motivation for Abbott to provide charitable contributions to the project?
2. What do you believe the Abbott/Habitat project means to the long-term relationship between the company and the North Chicago community? Use Figure 17-2.
3. What are the elements of community partnership that are essential to the success of this effort?
4. If you were an employee of Abbott Laboratories, what would attract you to participate in such a project?

[32]Information provided by the corporate communications department, Abbott Laboratories, Abbott Park, Illinois.

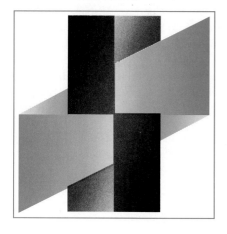

18

Technology and the Media

As we prepare to enter the twenty-first century, civilization is in its greatest age of technological change. Both business and society are in the midst of the massive task of absorbing technology on a scale never before experienced. At the focal point of the "age of information technology" are the media and their enormous powers of influence and persuasion. Modern technology has given business new capacities but also the responsibility to use technology in a way that enhances the quality of life.

Key Questions and Chapter Objectives

This chapter focuses on these key questions and objectives:
- What are the major features of technology?
- Which phase of technology describes our society's current state of development?
- What are the social and ethical consequences of technological change?
- How do government and business influence technological change?
- What major social issues are raised by the emergence of media technology?
- How can corporations effectively and responsibly interact with media?

Architecture, the arts, and history have all come to our homes. Apple Computer Corporation has unveiled a revolutionary technological breakthrough which allows computer users to take "realistic 'tours' of places and buildings." QuickTime VR represents the first of what may become a long line of virtual reality software for use on personal computers. The software contains a collection of photographs and assembles them into an integrated scene. The result is a museum room, for example, where a classic painting can be closely examined. Through computer technology, objects can appear to be held and turned around for enhanced viewing. When this technology was introduced to 150 multimedia developers and

Hollywood entertainment executives in June 1994, the audience erupted in applause as they viewed the image of an ancient Indian statue from the Asian Art Museum in San Francisco. "People are going to be both impressed and inspired by it," said Jonathan Seybold, chairman of a software consulting firm.[1]

Technological breakthroughs occur in areas other than arts education. In September 1994 AT&T introduced PersonaLink, a highly sophisticated on-line network system that acts as an "electronic assistant" or "agent." PersonaLink can sort through an individual's electronic mail and order the messages according to importance. The "agent" can also save messages, fax messages, and dispose of "junk mail" messages. Through a national communications network, PersonaLink allows one "agent" to communicate with other "agents" or with merchants, publishers, stockbrokers, and others.[2]

If someone is looking for a more elementary use of modern technology they may want to turn to PizzaNet, a pilot program using software developed for Pizza Hut, a pizza food chain. The software program allows customers to call up a computerized menu, select the desired toppings and the preferred size of the pizza, and then place the order—all by simply clicking the mouse device connected to a computer linked to the Internet.[3]

These technological breakthroughs are changing the way people learn, work, or live their lives. As we enter the twenty-first century, we are facing more and more life-style and work transformations due to the emergence of technology.

TECHNOLOGY AS A SOCIAL FORCE

Throughout history technology has had an enormous effect. It has pressed onward like a glacier, slowly and steadily exerting its influence. It appears virtually impossible to stem the advancement of technology. In early nineteenth century England, for example, a band of unhappy workers known as Luddites challenged the industrial revolution by roaming the countryside smashing machinery and burning factories. From their narrow viewpoint, machines were enemies taking away jobs and freedom and harming people. But the Luddites were soon overcome by the benefits brought by the same machinery they opposed. Though the industrial

---

[1]"Apple Unveils Technology That Lets Users Take 'Tours' of Places, Buildings," *Wall Street Journal,* June 8, 1994, p. B6.

[2]"Electronic 'Agents' Bring Virtual Shopping a Bit Closer to Reality," *Wall Street Journal*, Sept. 27, 1994, pp. A1, A6; and "Finding an 'Agent' to Bag Your E-Mail," *Business Week*, Nov. 14, 1994, p. 18.

[3]"PepsiCo Unit Takes Orders for Pizza via the Internet," *Wall Street Journal*, Aug. 22, 1994, p. A5A.

revolution created new and serious human problems for some people in society, it was a great advance in the history of civilization. New jobs and skills replaced older ones, living standards were raised, and economic abundance extended life expectancy for millions of people.

Technology continues to grow because of people themselves. Human beings have sampled and embraced the fruits of knowledge. It seems that people have acquired an insatiable desire for it. They forever seek to expand knowledge of their environment, probably because of the excitement of learning and their belief that more knowledge will help them adapt to their environment.

Features of Technology

The dominant feature of technology is *change* and then more change. Technology forces change on people whether they are prepared for it or not. In modern society it has brought so much change that it creates what is called *future shock*, which means that change comes so fast and furiously that it approaches the limits of human tolerance and people lose their ability to cope with it successfully. Although technology is not the only cause of change, it is the primary cause. It is either directly or indirectly involved in most changes that occur in society.

Some years ago, right after the start of the personal computer revolution, industry experts observed that if automobiles had developed at the same rate as the computer business, a Rolls Royce would cost $2.75 and go 3 million miles on a gallon of gasoline. Today's microcomputers cost less than those of 1983 and offer ten times the power and many more times the speed of their predecessors.

Another feature of technology is that its effects are *widespread,* reaching far beyond the immediate point of technological impact. Technology ripples through society until every community is affected by it.[4] For example, **telecommunications**, the transmission of information over great distances via electromagnetic signals, has played a historically significant and positive role in our society's development. This innovation enhanced international commerce, linked relatives living great distances apart, and enabled us to discover many of the mysteries of outerspace. Yet, along with these advances come the potential for a greater invasion of privacy through wiretapping and telemarketing practices. The "human touch" in our communication with others through the convenience of electronic voice mail is diminished.

The shock waves push their way into even the most isolated places. People cannot escape it. Even if they travel to remote places like the Grand Canyon, technology is still represented by vapor trails from airplanes fly-

---

[4]For a discussion on the impact of technology, see Harold A. Linstone and Ian I. Mitroff, *The Challenge of the 21st Century: Managing Technology and Ourselves in a Shrinking World*, Albany: State University of New York Press, 1994.

ing overhead, microwave communication signals from satellites moving at the speed of light, and a haze from air pollution often preventing a view of the other side.

An additional feature of technology is that it is *self-reinforcing.* As stated by Alvin Toffler, "Technology feeds on itself. Technology makes more technology possible."[5] This self-reinforcing feature means that technology acts as a multiplier to encourage its own faster development. It acts with other parts of society so that an invention in one place leads to a sequence of inventions in other places. Thus, invention of the microprocessor led rather quickly to successful generations of the modern computer, which led to new banking methods, electronic mail, bar-code systems, and so on.

Business Applies Technology

As soon as new knowledge exists, people want to apply it in order to reap its benefits. At this point business becomes important, because business is the principal institution that translates discovery into application for public use. Printing, manufacturing, housing, information processing, transportation, and television are all dependent on business activities to make them work productively. Society depends on business to keep the stream of discovery flowing into useful goods and services for all people. Less-developed nations have learned that scientific discoveries mean very little to them unless they have competent business systems to produce for their people what science has discovered. In a similar manner, developed nations have learned that an innovative business system helps translate technological developments into useful goods and services for their people.

Phases of Technology in Society

Looking at technology in a very general way, five broad **phases of technology** have developed, as shown in Figure 18-1. In history, nations have tended to move sequentially through each phase, beginning with the lowest technology and moving higher with each step, so the five phases of technology roughly represent the progress of civilization throughout history. Although one phase of technology tends to dominate a nation's activities at a particular time, other phases often will be practiced at the same time. Some societies move very rapidly from one phase to another; others may be forced to skip a phase when an intruding culture overturns a long-established society.

The current phase of technology is the **information society**. This phase emphasizes the use and transfer of knowledge and information, rather than manual skill. It dominates work and employs the largest pro-

[5]Alvin Toffler, *Future Shock,* New York: Bantam, 1971, p. 26.

FIGURE 18-1
Phases in the development of technology in the United States.

Technology Level	Phases in the Development of Technology	Approximate Period of Dominance in U.S.	Activity	Primary Skill Used
1	Nomadic-Agrarian	Until 1650	Harvests	Manual
2	Agrarian	1650–1900	Plants and harvests	Manual
3	Industrial	1900–1960	Builds material goods	Manual and machine
4	Service	1960–1975	Focuses on providing services	Manual and intellectual
5	Information	1975–1990s	Abstract work	Intellectual and electronic

portion of the labor force. Work becomes abstract, the electronic manipulation of symbols. Businesses of all sizes, including the smallest firms, are exploring the benefits of the "information age."[6] Examples of people in information jobs are news editors, accountants, computer programmers, and teachers. Even a transplant surgeon, who must use a delicate manual skill, is primarily working from an information or intellectual base. Examples of information industries are newspaper publishing, television, education, book publishing, telecommunications, and consulting.

An information society's technology is primarily electronic in nature and is heavily dependent on the computer and the semiconductor silicon chip. The power of these devices rests on their ability to process, store, and retrieve large amounts of information with very great speed. With the arrival of the 1990s, the information age exploded into nearly every aspect of business and society. Civilization had never experienced that much change that fast. The information age is radically transforming the way people learn, think, conduct business, and live their lives. The technology developed in this new age has provided the mechanisms for more information to be produced in a decade than in the previous thousand years.[7]

Entry-level employees are now trained to better understand computer systems and to use computers to support many work functions. The tech-

[6]Shoshanah Zuboff, *In the Age of the Smart Machine,* New York: Basic Books, 1988; and "Mom and Pop Go High Tech," *Business Week,* Nov. 21, 1994, pp. 82–90. See also Ronald Henkoff, "Make Your Office More Productive," *Fortune,* Feb. 25, 1991, pp. 72–84.
[7]April Dymtrenko, "The Information Age Has Arrived or 'Much Ado About Everything,' " *Records Management Quarterly,* Oct. 1992, pp. 20–25.

nological expertise possessed by entry-level and other employees in business supports the development of more sophisticated telecommunications systems. More than 65 percent of the workforce processes information through telecommunication systems in order to do their jobs. In addition, telecommunications has changed where workers perform their jobs. At BC TEL, a Canadian telecommunications firm, employees report for work at a satellite office located in a suburb rather than commuting to the downtown Vancouver office. At IBM, workers report to a central office once or twice a week for meetings and messages; otherwise employees are linked by telecommunication networks to other employees, suppliers, or customers while working at home.[8]

Economic Effects of Technology

Perhaps the most fundamental effect of technology is *greater efficiency* in terms of quality and quantity. Seeking a more efficient method or means of production or process is the main reason that most technology is adopted. In a hospital the objective may be qualitative, such as maintaining a life with electronic monitoring equipment regardless of costs. In a factory the goal may be quantitative in terms of more production for less cost. Numerous scientific studies support the claim that using computers increases employee productivity. For example, at Allegheny Ludlum a computerized cost-measurement system helped management achieve a 45 percent improvement in productivity. Various technological advances in inventory control and materials flow provided increased productivity and lower costs at Apple Computers.[9]

Technology places more emphasis on *research and development* (R&D). Research concerns the creation of new ideas, and development is their useful application. Effective management of R&D is important because it brings social benefits through increased productivity. By spending nearly $2 billion in 1993 on R&D programs, Bayer AG has pioneered numerous breakthrough in their life sciences divisions: pharmaceutical and agricultural chemicals.[10] With the world's exploding population and the needs of less-developed nations, society requires the material and social gains that R&D can provide. Society also depends on R&D to find ways to reduce pollution and otherwise improve the quality of life.

An emphasis on R&D also benefits business. In a study of 727 companies in the 1980s, a strong correlation was found between average busi-

---

[8]Jocelyne Cote-O'Hara, "Sending Them Home to Work: Telecommuting," *Business Quarterly,* Spring 1993, pp. 104–109.

[9]Other examples of improved corporate productivity while using technological advancements can be found in L. William Seidman and Steven L. Skancke, "Making It Happen: Case Studies in Productivity," *Modern Office Technology,* June 1991, pp. 12, 14; and Howard Gleckman, "The Technology Payoff," *Business Week,* June 14, 1993, pp. 56–68.

[10]David Rotman, "As Its R&D Budget Nears $2 Billion, Bayer Rethinks Priorities," *Chemical Week,* Mar. 17, 1993, p. 28.

ness R&D expenditures per employee and subsequent company profit margin and sales per employee. A positive relationship between R&D expenditure and company productivity was also found. Firms have begun to discover that R&D investment, particularly in information technology, can lead to greater productivity and increases in company profitability.[11]

The third economic effect of technology is its *insatiable demand for capital.* Large capital investments are required to build the enormous production systems that save labor time and provide other benefits of technology. At the turn of the century, an investment of $1,000 for each worker often was adequate in a factory, but modern investments in pipelines and petroleum refining exceed $200,000 for each worker.

Technology is costly but essential for business, thereby creating a problem for managers. The failure to maintain current, up-to-date technology can mean a loss of competitiveness, as occurred in the U.S. steel industry in the 1980s. Both productivity and product quality can suffer. Such expenditures do not tell the entire story however. New technology requires other expenditures to keep the labor force up to date with the machinery and technological changes. This in turn requires managers to select their technology carefully, train people properly, and encourage the continuous improvement of employees' understanding about the best ways to make use of technological capability. These demands also require business to generate large amounts of capital and engage in more long-range planning and budgeting for capital use. It also is desirable for government to establish public policies (e.g., the U.S. government's commitment of Defense Department funds for civilian use) that encourage business to generate capital for needed jobs. Global competitiveness requires each nation to invest heavily in its technological future.[12]

SOCIAL CONSEQUENCES OF TECHNOLOGICAL CHANGE

Technological advances bring both benefits and costs to society. A balanced judgment about technology will consider the pluses and minuses.

Social Costs

Although economic growth—driven by the engine of technological progress—has conferred wide benefits on humankind, technology also

---

[11]Graham K. Morbey and Robert M. Reithner, "How R&D Affects Sales Growth, Productivity and Profitability," *Research-Technology Management*, May–June 1990, pp. 11–14. See also Gerald M. Hoffman, *Technology Payoff: How to Profit with Empowered Workers in the Information Age,* Burr Ridge, IL: Richard D. Irwin, 1994.

[12]See, for example, Michael L. Dertouzos, Richard K. Lester, and Robert M. Solow, *Made in America,* Cambridge, MA: MIT Press, 1989 which was influential in public discussion of this issue in the early 1990s.

has had social side effects. When they are negative, they become social costs. For example, high-tech producers of microprocessors have contaminated groundwater supplies with chemical production wastes, and high-powered weapons designed for warfare have been used by urban street gangs. Many environmental pollution problems occur when sophisticated technology is carelessly used.

While a nation's political system lacks the capability to monitor and pass judgment on the overall good or bad impact of every scientific advancement, societal values may provide mechanisms that evaluate new technologies. On the political front, courts and legislatures can regulate the use of certain technologies. When coupled with a mobilization of public constituencies, political forces have checked and curbed the use of technology in business, for example, requiring pollution controls and seat belts in vehicles. Technology assessment is a useful technique that seeks to provide feedback about technology's effects and to anticipate the unintended, indirect, and possibly harmful effects of new technology. The Office of Technology Assessment was created by Congress to undertake studies of this type in projects involving government funding. Since its creation in 1972, it has conducted thousands of studies of all types of technologies.

Individually and collectively our society has begun to address quality of life questions such as whether to keep comatose patients alive on life support machines when there is no hope of recovery. The challenge is one that technological advancement has put squarely on both business leaders' shoulders and on each of us as individuals.[13]

Genetic Engineering—A New Frontier

Another good example of the problems and opportunities associated with new scientific and technological breakthroughs is the modern era of **genetic engineering**, a component of the **biotechnology** field. Genetic engineering has a history over a century old, rooted in agriculture. In the nineteenth century the botanist, Gregor Mendel, pioneered the science of genetics. Ever since, genetic scientists have cloned and reproduced crops that have helped farmers produce more food per acre that is of better quality and less labor-intensive.

The new era of genetic engineering includes new techniques that enable scientists to combine knowledge from various areas of science, such as biochemistry, genetics, microbiology, and ecology. Scientists can now identify and manipulate molecules in genetic material with revolutionary applications in agriculture, medicine, and industry. Some of the results are truly startling, as the following example illustrates.

---

[13]Many of these challenges are addressed in Georg Aichholzer and Gerd Schienstock, eds., *Technology Policy: Towards an Integration of Social and Ecological Concerns*, Berlin: de Gruyter, 1994.

Since 1982, Mitsui Toatsu Chemicals, a Japanese petrochemical company, has organized an In-House Plant Biotechnology Research Group, conducting research using various crops such as rice, soybeans, and tomatoes. Success involving the regeneration of rice cultures gave the group an opportunity to utilize new breeding technologies: cell fusion and recombinant DNA. Since rice is the main food crop for the Japanese people, the domestic seed market is estimated to be as large as 30 billion yen.[14]

No one doubts the end-use benefits of these new scientific and technological advances. The trouble comes when the economic, ethical, and social consequences are considered. Boosting milk production by using growth hormones is fine, but it may force from 10 to 25 percent of dairy farmers out of business since fewer farms will be able to produce all the milk needed. The Congressional Office of Technology Assessment predicted in 1986 that about 1 million farms—nearly half of the total in the United States—would disappear by the end of the century, leaving only 50,000 large farms to produce three-quarters of the foodstuffs. So the small farmer, including dairy farmers, may vanish from the social scene, the victim of a scientific revolution intended to improve the quality of life for all.

During the past twenty-five years, professionals involved in the field of genetic engineering have become more aware of their ethical responsibilities, through pressures by consumers, employees, and environmentalists. The International Federation for Medical and Biological Engineering, for example, identified the following moral concerns: the determination of the effectiveness of biotechnology, fetal research and its methods, and the influence of medical technology on the physician-patient relationship. As the industry affects more and more people, its managers will have to give more attention to the social and ethical responsibilities and impacts of genetic engineering.

Information Technology

As described earlier in the chapter, society is in the midst of the information phase of technology. Embedded in this phase is the new "information age." The lives of every member of our society, including workers in businesses around the world, have changed. Information has become more abundant, available faster, more accessible to countless people, and cheaper to acquire. Accompanying the great technological advancement are fears of serious social costs and violations of ethical principles.

---

[14]Tetsuichi Shinozawa, "Plant Biotechnology Projects at Mitsui Toatsu Chemicals, Inc.," *Japan 21st,* Aug. 1993, pp. 40–41. See also Julie Pitta, "Biosynthetics," *Fortune,* May 10, 1993, pp. 170–171.

Social and ethical concerns

As the information age increases its impact on people's lives, individuals fear that some strands of our social network are unraveling. Although technology is often applauded for its contributions to the modern age, its benefits are unevenly distributed and the lack of access to technology has contributed to a gap between socioeconomic classes of people. The technologically rich are getting richer, while the technologically deprived are falling farther behind. The increasing use of technology in the workplace also has sparked objections, despite its apparent economic advantages. For example, thirty studies conducted during the 1980s were analyzed and a common conclusion was found: programmable manufacturing technology led to organizational growth, but also contributed to employee stress and perceptions of reduced job security and mobility.[15]

Various ethical concerns and their importance are magnified as the information age becomes a more dominant force in our lives. Are there safeguards against criminal misconduct due to the ease of access to confidential information? What are the safety risks facing individuals due to the presence of information technology (e.g., exposure to emissions from computer monitors)? What happens to personal privacy when so many businesses and individuals have access to confidential credit, health, family, and criminal records? What if the data in the information record is inaccurate and those accessing and using the information cannot verify its accuracy? These and other ethical questions are voiced as information technology becomes an established social force in our society.

Global interaction and development

The widespread impact of information technology is evident in its quick expansion into the global marketplace. One authority on electronic networks said,

> What is occurring is no less than the creation of the first global, interactive, human network—a network that will provide information and communication in all its forms, collapse time and space in a way that has never been accomplished before, place control fully in the hands of the user, and do it all in a way that is so intuitive that the technology behind it will go virtually unnoticed.[16]

Such developments present business with many opportunities and hold great promise for making fundamental improvements in the quality of human life. Society could change for the better. People living in developing countries could be the greatest beneficiaries of this information

---

[15]Jeffrey K. Liker, Ann Majchrzak, and Thomas Choi, "Impacts of Programmable Manufacturing Technology: A Review of Recent Studies and Contingency Formulation," *Journal of Engineering & Technology Management*, Sept. 1993, pp. 229–264.

[16]Raymond W. Smith, CEO, Bell Atlantic, "The Global, Interactive, Human Network," *Vital Speeches*, Sept. 1, 1993, pp. 691–695.

revolution. The Association of Southeast Asian Nations (ASEAN), which unites the most rapidly evolving economic region in the world, has quickly grasped this business opportunity. Malaysian businesses are actively joining the telecommunications industry, aligning themselves with many regional and international opportunities. The government of Indonesia pushed forward an ambitious telecommunication satellite development program. TELECOMS Singapore developed a highly sophisticated telecommunications system and has continued to lead in technology adoption and innovation within the ASEAN community.[17]

Countries whose businesses have traditionally been technological leaders have also excelled in information technology. Innovative Japanese companies have pioneered a "total technology management" system. The thrust is on a team approach, with middle management playing the key role. The system has been characterized as a "middle-up-down" process, where middle managers assume much of the responsibility and top management provides the grand vision and creates an environment for innovation.[18]

However, taking advantage of a "technologically connected" world requires adequate understanding of potential consequences and the rigorous adoption of appropriate countermeasures, for example, against serious losses of data confidentiality, system integrity, and resource availability.

Stakeholder Reactions

Challenges to advances in technology arise from corporate stakeholders when people perceive that the full productive potential of technology is inconsistent with social values and institutions.

> The marketing of dairy products containing the synthetic bovine growth hormone (BGH), came under attack by consumer groups. A boycott of fast-food restaurants that sold milk containing BGH was organized in 1994 by the Pure Food Coalition, led by Jeremy Rifkin, an environmentalist and consumer activist.
>
> Over 200 scientists gathered at Rice University in February 1994 to discuss the social challenges posed by biotechnology. A commitment was made by the group to take their concerns to scientists and health care professionals involved in biotechnology development. Other aca-

---

[17]These programs are discussed in Mark A. Hukill and Meheroo Jussawalla, "Telecommunications Policies and Markets in the ASEAN Countries," *Columbia Journal of World Business,* Spring 1989, pp. 43–57.

[18]See S. K. Subramanian, "Managing Technology—The Japanese Approach," *Journal of Engineering & Technology Management,* May 1990, pp. 221–236.

demics, such as New York University professor Neil Postman, have called for an ethical and social evaluation of technological impacts on schools, family life, and society's values and life-styles.[19]

Many societies, perhaps most of those that adopt modern technology, encounter similar but less dramatic problems in arriving at a fit between their traditional social institutions and the new trends of technological development.

ROLE OF GOVERNMENT AND BUSINESS IN TECHNOLOGICAL CHANGE

As technological growth infiltrates every aspect of our society, governments throughout the world are becoming increasingly involved in guiding, promoting, and regulating the development and use of technology in business activities. A variety of governmental strategies are shown in Figure 18-2 and described more fully below.

Government Involvement

During the 1980s, the U.S. government implemented a set of international trade policies in an effort to protect U.S. dominance in high technology. Unfortunately, these policies severely restricted U.S. businesses' competitiveness in the global technology arena. Fearful that the United States was

[19]For a discussion of the various challenges to technological change by stakeholder groups, see Dale Buss, "Don't Sell the Milk: Why? We'll Boycott You," *Restaurant Business,* Jan. 20, 1994, p. 24; Pamela S. Zurer, "Scientists Confront Ethical Challenges Posed by Progress in Biotechnology," *Chemical & Engineering News,* March 14, 1994, pp. 20–21; and Lew McCreary, "Postman's Progress," *CIO,* Nov. 1, 1993, pp. 74–84.

FIGURE 18-2
A sample of government's involvement in technological development.

Government's Role in Technological Change	
United States	Commitment of vast research and development network and Department of Defense research funds to business alliances and partnerships
European Union	Support for industry projects, but resistance toward involvement in business-government partnerships
Japan	Use of public policy incentives to support business enterprises with the objective of improving the quality of life for the Japanese people
South Korea	Limited government support for business partnerships, but attempts to encourage citizens to become interested in advanced technological developments by businesses

losing its technological advantage to foreign competition, the federal government placed a high-profile emphasis on forging an alliance between the federal government's vast R&D apparatus and business. The cornerstone of the technology campaign was the shifting of billions of Defense Department research funds into civilian agencies for the development of critical cutting-edge commercial technologies, including the development of advanced supercomputers, biotechnology, artificial intelligence, robotics, and the so-called digital electronic superhighway.[20]

In contrast, western European governments, represented in the European Union (EU), had a mix of policies which evolved in the early 1990s. The issues explored by the EU focused on the nature of technology and the means by which it was transmitted between firms and between countries. The EU was concerned with the increasing internationalization of production and the degree to which technology was dominated by international collaboration and multinational companies. In general, the EU took a position of supporting industry-based projects for technological advancement, but unlike its U.S. counterparts, failed to adopt a position of promoting government-business partnerships.[21]

Governments in Asian countries have a strong tradition of government-business cooperation. This practice was also evident in the area of technology development. The Japanese approach was to portray technology innovation as more than merely a business opportunity. The Japanese government used its public policy tools to provide incentives for firms to focus attention on technology-based developments which benefited Japanese businesses and the Japanese people.

In South Korea, the government encouraged the development of economically successful technologies without government aid, and government support was limited in the early 1990s. Government attention was more apparent in the promotion of Taejon Expo '93, an international exposition dedicated to future technologies. The event was an attempt by the government to impress South Koreans that their economy is lacking in advanced technology, having relied on labor-intensive exports while neglecting research.[22]

Business Responsibility for Technological Change

Although government involvement in technological development has increased in the 1990s, traditionally business has served as society's desig-

---

[20]Examples of $170 million in U.S. government research grants are described in "Research Grants Given to 42 Firms by the Government," *Wall Street Journal*, Oct. 25, 1994, p. B6.

[21]Margaret Sharp and Keith Pavitt, "Technology Policy in the 1990s: Old Trends and New Realities," *Journal of Common Market Studies*, June 1993, pp. 129–151.

[22]See Michael M. Crow and Shrilata A. Nath, "Technology Strategy Development in Korean Industry: An Assessment of Market and Government Influences," *Technovation*, Mar. 1992, pp. 119–136.

nated agent responsible for developing new technology. Whether one thinks of Henry Ford's Model-T car or Bill Gates's microprocessor chip, private enterprise has led the way in introducing new technology for human use. The public has expected and wanted business to perform this function. It has praised business for enriching and elevating human life and experience in all the material ways made possible by technology: high living standards, the creation of jobs, greater leisure time, and an apparently inexhaustible flow of new products and services. For taking the technological lead, business has been rewarded with profits, growth, and general social approval.

At times, these technological advances have appeared unfettered, with little foresight for long-term consequences. For example, when new surface mining equipment made coal recovery in the western regions of the United States more profitable than the deep mining that was typical in the southern and eastern regions, many parts of Appalachia were thrust into deeper poverty than they had ever known. At the same time, unplanned urban sprawl can accompany rapid economic buildup brought on by the newer forms of electronic technology. California's Silicon Valley, home of the revolutionary computer chip, is a good example of headlong economic development that presses hard on environmental resources and brings on many serious urban problems.

These problems may seem unique to today's technological age but they are not. Adjusting society's institutions and people to new technology is an ancient problem. Long ago, many farmers resisted the use of iron plows instead of wooden ones, believing that the metal would contaminate the soil and ruin the crops. Many people have expressed fear and hostility concerning the computer, just as others did years ago when telephone companies switched home dialing systems to digits from a combination of letters and digits. Not only were people forced to change their habits, they also feared a loss of individual identity and being regimented to an impersonal technological system.

The major difference today in adjusting technology and institutions is in the scale, magnitude, and speed of needed adjustments. Worldwide competition and enormous productivity gains pose the possibility of massive unemployment in industrial nations unless retraining programs are developed for workers whose skills are outdated. The risk of economic and social dislocation appears to be more painful, more long-lasting, and more resistant than satisfactory solutions.

What are business's responsibilities in a time of rapid and sometimes disruptive technological change? Now that technology has extensively permeated our society, there is no turning the technological clock back. Instead, society seems to be sending three kinds of signals to the business community.

- One message is that society wants new technology to be introduced with greater care and more foresight. For example, premarket testing of drugs, safety guidelines for genetic engineering projects, and

government regulation of chemical waste disposal can safeguard individuals and society.

- Another emerging development is the idea of a compensatory payment or other type of support by business that would help individuals, groups, or communities readjust their lives when damaged by
technological changes. Examples of such help include industrial retraining programs for technologically displaced employees and acceptance by multinational firms of some sacrifice in economic efficiency in order to strengthen national security and preserve jobs at
home instead of shifting operations to the lowest-cost foreign location.

- Perhaps less clearly perceived—but vitally necessary—is an emerging
understanding that technology is far too central, far too important,
and far too complex in its consequences to be entrusted to any single
institution in society. Business has pioneered the creative development of much technology, just as government has led the way in
sponsoring the technology of national defense. However, universities, labor unions, nonprofit institutions, professional groups, and
many local communities have made distinctive contributions to technological advance. All of these groups and institutions are technological stakeholders, each with an interest in the outcome of society's
great adventure in technological achievement.[23]

The idea of a broad institutional partnership for humane technological
advance belongs in the thinking of business leaders, as well as in the
minds and actions of all those in society who have a stake in the technological future.

EMERGENCE OF THE MEDIA AS A TECHNOLOGICAL FORCE

Role of the Media in an Information Society

The **media**, taken together, create a vast communication network responsible for sending millions of messages to the public on a daily basis. Most
people have multiple, overlapping media exposure because they view television, read daily newspapers, listen to the radio, view videotapes, subscribe to magazines, read books, attend the theater, see films, and enjoy
listening to a wide range of musical recordings. The power of the media in
our current technological phase of development, the information society,
can be overwhelming. For example, television's ability to touch the lives of
its viewers, perhaps briefly through a single program or through sustained average viewing time, is of great significance in the media world.

[23]This issue is discussed in U. Franklin, *The Real World of Technology,* Toronto: CBC, 1990.

Media researchers have known from early in the television age that the intertwining of sight and sound in the convenience of one's home reaches and affects more people more effectively and more lastingly that other media forms. Having been extended widely throughout the world, television has achieved the creation of a "global village," as described in Exhibit 18-A.[24]

Critical Media Issues

The nature, size, and influence of the media have created several pivotal and highly controversial issues. All of these issues raise questions about business's social and ethical responsibilities. The media themselves are businesses, and they are expected to adhere to the same social responsibility principles (e.g., the principles of charity and stewardship, presented in Chapter 2) that apply to all other businesses. The same is true of companies that buy advertising time in the media for their commercial messages and the advertising agencies and production companies that design and produce the advertisements. They are not exempt from social and ethical obligations to the general public. Perhaps in no other area of the business-society relationship does it become so clear that business actions and policies can have such an enduring and significant impact on quality of life

[24]This point was first made by Marshall McLuhan, *Understanding Media: The Extensions of Man,* 2d ed., New York: McGraw-Hill, 1964.

EXHIBIT 18-A

WELCOME TO THE GLOBAL VILLAGE

Information is power, technologists proclaim. Until recently, power had been firmly grasped by those in developed countries. However, in the 1990s, power seeped out of the tightly clenched fists of the economic superpowers: Japan, Germany, the United States. Power began to be transmitted through the technology of satellite telecommunications to millions of people across Asia, with more information available than a human being could possibly process in a lifetime.

In April 1990, AsiaSat I, a telecommunications satellite, began to orbit the globe. Shortly thereafter, satellite dishes, costing a few hundred dollars, began to dot the Asian countryside. Remote villages, once cut off from economic prosperity and social development, were inextricably linked with distant cities. Access to news, sports, music, and soap operas loosened government's grip on information. People from Burmese villages, to the bustling city of Calcutta, India, to Jordanian towns could tune in and watch CNN, World Cup Soccer, or *Lifestyles of the Rich and Famous.* By 1994, it was estimated that nearly 45 million viewers had access to the cable network linked to AsiaSat I.

Source: Based on "A Satellite TV System Is Quickly Moving Asia into the Global Village," *Wall Street Journal,* May 10, 1993, pp. A1, A8.

and on a society's fundamental values. Four of the most critical media issues are discussed next.

The image issue

The *image issue* is about the way people and social groups, including business, are depicted by the media. Although all media—for example, tabloids and talk radio—are capable of projecting false or misleading images of people and social groups, much of the criticism is directed at television.

One of business's strongest complaints about the media is that business activities and business people frequently are portrayed in unflattering, negative ways. For example, businesspeople portrayed on TV are often depicted as greedy, foolish, or criminal. They often are shown committing illegal acts or acquiring large sums of money or power at the expense of the powerless or naive. Unfortunately for business, silence may be the common response to the question, "What TV show best depicts the role of business or a corporate executive in American society?" This negative media view is also seen in the slant of the news coverage of corporate actions. In a recent study of twenty-nine companies, a researcher discovered that the *tone* of media exposure was an important factor in changing the firm's reputation and influencing the strategic response taken by the firm.[25]

Some companies have fought back when shown in a negative light by media presentations. For example, after *NBC Dateline* showed GM trucks bursting into flames after a collision from the side, the truck manufacturer quickly investigated these tests. GM discovered and announced to the press that the tests were rigged—model rocket engines were ignited by radio transmissions at the point of impact. Another classic example of a firm fighting back is the following incident.

> Illinois Power was featured in a *60 Minutes* program that emphasized cost overruns in the construction of nuclear power plants, especially in a plant being built by Illinois Power. The company claimed that the *60 Minutes* presentation was grossly unfair and damaging to the company's reputation. A public affairs official said, "The show was simply devastating to us. . . . We began getting hate telephone calls minutes after the broadcast. The next day, Monday, more than three times as many shares of our stock were traded in a single day than ever before, and the stock price dropped by more than one dollar. And our employee morale hit rock bottom. We knew we had to do something, and fast."[26]
>
> Fortunately, the company had made its own videotapes as *60 Min-*

---

[25]See Steven L. Wartick, "The Relationship between Intense Media Exposure and Change in Corporate Reputation," *Business & Society,* Spring 1992, pp. 33–49.

[26]Quoted in Frank M. Corrado, *Media for Managers: Communications Strategy for the Eighties,* Englewood Cliffs, NJ: Prentice-Hall, 1984, p. 86.

utes interviewed its executives. It used these tapes and additional facts taken from official government records to answer the *60 Minutes* charges. Entitled *60 Minutes/Our Reply,* the videotape compared what was shown on network television with the complete tapes made of the interviews. One *60 Minutes* interview that lasted ninety minutes was edited to show only two-and-one-half minutes that told Illinois Power's side of the story. Several statements *60 Minutes* made about the company and its cost structure were revealed by the full videotape to be false and misleading. The Illinois Power videotape was widely distributed and became a well-known symbol of corporate efforts to offset negative and unfavorable media images of business.

Numerous research studies have shown that U.S. women are numerically underrepresented in television programming; are shown mainly in roles as wives and/or parents rather than as professionals; and are depicted as more emotional than men, subordinated to men, and less likely to control events in their lives than are men. This trend extends beyond the United States.

In Singapore, female managers are depicted in the media as constantly facing dilemmas and role conflicts at work. The managerial abilities to resolve common business problems typically are exhibited by male managers. Female managers are shown to rely on male mentors, a supportive husband, and a mother or maid to help with the household chores. Male managers depend wholly on themselves.[27]

An *Advertising Age* survey on racial issues found that more than half of media executives believed that advertising has played a role in the current racial problems in America.[28] African Americans have long criticized films, radio, and television for ignoring blacks almost entirely or for presenting negative images of black behavior. During the 1950s and 1960s, African Americans were rarely seen on television and practically never in commercials. Later, when they began to appear, the characters they played tended to reflect traditional racial stereotypes. African-American actors appeared less frequently than whites, and the roles they played were minor and involved less time on-screen than others. Three decades after the civil rights movement began prodding the media industry to improve and diversify its portrayal of minorities, African Americans, His-

---

[27]A recent study contrasting the images of U.S. females and males is reported in Debra Gersh, "Promulgating Polarization," *Editor & Publisher,* Oct. 10, 1992, pp. 30–31, 48. The Singapore portrayal of managers in the press was taken from S. K. Jean Lee and Tan Hwee Hoon, "Rhetorical Vision of Men and Women Managers in Singapore," *Human Relations,* Apr. 1993, pp. 527–542.

[28]Adrienne Ward, "What Role Do Ads Play in Racial Tension?," *Advertising Age,* Aug. 10, 1992, pp. 1, 35.

panics, Asian Americans, and Native Americans remain nearly invisible or assume subservient roles in advertisements, movies, or television programming.

> Asian-American and African-American communities raised strong objections regarding the media coverage of the Los Angeles riots in 1992. Opinion polls following the Rodney King beating trial tended to lump all minorities' responses together. Criminal activities during the riots often showed African Americans and Hispanics stealing from stores and vandalizing neighborhoods. Korean storeowners, armed with rifles to protect their shops from looters, were portrayed as typical Asian Americans living in Southern California.

Hispanic Americans, the fastest-growing ethnic group in the United States, are only marginally visible to national television audiences. Hispanic men have been usually cast as funny or crooked, or as cops. Helping to offset this negative image are the several Spanish-language television stations in large urban centers whose programming includes Hispanic cultural content as well as truer and more positive images.

One of the most vulnerable groups in our society, children, has also been a media victim. Half of all television shows and 40 percent of newspaper stories about children also involve crime and violence. Conversely, 3 to 4 percent of stories about children emphasize concern for their poverty and even fewer deal with health care issues.[29]

The values issue

The *values issue* is about the power of the media to shape social attitudes and values. This issue is closely related to the image issue just discussed, but more is involved because values are one of the basic determinants of human behavior and social attitudes. Most of us acquire our values from early family experiences, from friends and authority figures (parents, teachers, and other role models), and from the trial-and-error process of growing up and learning to live with other people. The media, especially compact and laser disks, videotapes, radio, films, and television, are now recognized as new value-shaping forces in society. As a value source, the electronic media tend to act as parent, school, church, and peers all rolled into one.

Many diverse stakeholders have challenged the values advocated by or reflected in the media. For example, the American Family Association, a group boasting of 1 million supporters in fifty states, launched an attack against the television industry for its portrayal of nudity, violence, and raw language. In the fall of 1993, the attack focused squarely on the season premiere of the television show *NYPD Blue,* although most TV stations aired

---

[29]"Children Say Media Give Negative View of Youth," *Los Angeles Times,* Mar. 1, 1994, p. 3.

the show, resisting the threat of advertisers' boycotts, and the show became one of the season's most watched series.

Violence, especially on television, has been a constant target. In 1952, Congress held its first hearings on television violence and its relationship to juvenile delinquency. Twenty years later, the U.S. Surgeon General issued a five-volume report which linked violence on TV with aggressive behavior in our society. And the debate rages on. After a five-year-old boy set a trailer on fire, killing his sister in 1993, the boy's mother blamed his behavior on scenes from MTV's *Beavis and Butthead* show. MTV officials denied any responsibility, but removed references to fire from its show and began airing the program later in the evening. Later that year, U.S. Attorney General Janet Reno endorsed advertisers' boycotts of television shows depicting excessive violence. Congress introduced the Children's Television Violence Protection Act, which would require violent shows to carry parental warnings. The Canadian government instituted in 1993 a self-regulating code to monitor violence on television. The code banned all "gratuitous and glamorized violence" and confined all other violent scenes to programming aired after 9:00 in the evening.[30]

Materialism is another value that has received extensive coverage in the media. Commercial messages bombard listeners, viewers, and readers with opportunities to live "the good life" if only they will buy the advertised products. The effect (and purpose) of this steady drumbeat of material display is to attract a viewing audience and to stimulate consumer demand for these and similar goods and services. While the media do not necessarily *initiate* or *begin* the cycle of consumer materialism—which, as noted previously, is probably a combination of family influence, peer pressure to conform, and learning the traditional pathways to adulthood in our society—the media surely encourage and support the value of material consumption. Their programs, films, and commercial images show materialism to be a desirable social value, embraced by those who have succeeded in life.

Aware of the value-shaping power of television, some educational groups have experimented with programs that teach socially acceptable "prosocial" values and attitudes. The popular children's programs *Sesame Street* and *Mr. Rogers' Neighborhood* are examples. The development of the educational cable television market has dramatic potential as a positive force and educational tool. Programs featuring the sciences, languages, political issues, and other topics are available every schoolday in every classroom—all that is required is a television set and a cable television hookup. High school students tuned into *Channel One,* a cable news program, in 1993 performed 5 percent better on current event tests than non-

---

[30]The Canadian code is discussed in Sean Scully, "Canadians Come Down Hard on Television Violence," *Broadcasting & Cable,* Nov. 8, 1993, p. 12; and Mark Clayton, "Canadian Broadcasters Set Violence Standards for TV," *Christian Science Monitor,* Dec. 20, 1993, p. 15.

viewing students. Middle-school students demonstrated an 8 percent better mark on similar tests.[31]

The fairness and balance issue

The *fairness and balance issue* is about how the news media report events, including business activities.

Central to the fairness and balance issue is the Fairness Doctrine, created by the Federal Communications Commission (FCC) in 1949. The Fairness Doctrine required all licensed broadcasters to cover important or controversial issues of broad public interest and give the opportunity for contrasting viewpoints to be aired. In the deregulation climate of the 1980s, the head of the FCC advocated elimination of the Fairness Doctrine, and a 1986 federal court ruling stated that the doctrine was not required by law but was only a discretionary power of the FCC. In August 1987, the FCC voted to abolish the Fairness Doctrine, but the doctrine's supporters hoped that Congress would reinstate the rule by making it a law.

Businesses have repeatedly attacked the media industry for unfair reporting of business activities. A 1994 poll of business executives and media personnel highlighted their differences in opinion and is shown in Figure 18-3. At the core of the tension between business and the media lie questions of technical competency, a belief that the relationship is necessarily adversarial, and a basic difference of opinion regarding the proper role of the media in society. Is the media a public servant, entrusted to report all the facts to the public, or a business enterprise seeking to satisfy its customers and maintain a profit? At times it appears that the media lose their objectivity in their coverage of events.

In 1994, Sadayoshi Tsubaki, head of the Asahi National Broadcasting Company, ordered his staff to cover the Lower House political elections in a way that would help oust the Liberal-Democratic party from power. Later, he was summoned to appear before the Japanese judiciary to explain his actions. This situation demonstrated the close relationship between the media industry and the government in Japan. Efforts there have been made to shift the media's attention toward serving the public. Journalists are required to seek feedback from citizens. The typical appointment of senior journalists to government advisory panels has also been challenged.[32]

In the United States, Japan, and other countries, the media industry is constantly being challenged to maintain its objectivity in collecting and

---

[31]"Study Finds Channel One Boosts Pupils' Knowledge," *Wall Street Journal*, Feb. 3, 1994, p. B6.

[32]Kyoto Sato, "Media's Role in Society, Ties to Establishment Examined," *Japan Times Weekly International Edition*, Mar. 7–13, 1994, pp. 10–11.

FIGURE 18-3

Business-media opinion poll.

SOURCE: Mike Haggerty and Wallace Rasmussen, *The Headline vs. the Bottom Line: Mutual Distrust between Business and the News Media,* Arlington, VA: The Freedom Forum First Amendment Center, 1994, pp. 9–20.

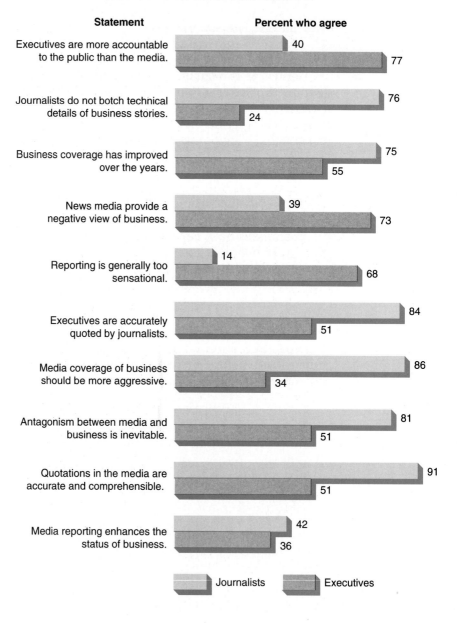

The Media versus Business: Differences in Opinion of 385 Journalists and 111 Executives, 1994

Statement	Percent who agree
Executives are more accountable to the public than the media.	Journalists 40 / Executives 77
Journalists do not botch technical details of business stories.	Journalists 76 / Executives 24
Business coverage has improved over the years.	Journalists 75 / Executives 55
News media provide a negative view of business.	Journalists 39 / Executives 73
Reporting is generally too sensational.	Journalists 14 / Executives 68
Executives are accurately quoted by journalists.	Journalists 84 / Executives 51
Media coverage of business should be more aggressive.	Journalists 86 / Executives 34
Antagonism between media and business is inevitable.	Journalists 81 / Executives 51
Quotations in the media are accurate and comprehensible.	Journalists 91 / Executives 51
Media reporting enhances the status of business.	Journalists 42 / Executives 36

Journalists   Executives

broadcasting newsworthy events to a public that is increasingly dependent on the media for information.

The free speech issue

The *free speech issue* is about how to find a balance between the media's constitutional right to free expression and business's desire to be fairly and accurately depicted in media presentations, as well as how to present business's views on controversial public issues. (Of course, the free speech issue also affects other groups in society, but our discussion focuses on business.)

The press in the United States is a "free press," meaning that it operates under explicit constitutional protections. The First Amendment to the Constitution says, in part, "Congress shall make no law . . . abridging the freedom of speech, or of the press." State governments also are prohibited, under the due process clause of the Fourteenth Amendment, from passing laws that impair free speech or interfere with a free press. Constitutional free-press guarantees mean that the privately owned, profit-seeking media are free to print, broadcast, and distribute messages to the general public without getting authorization from government officials.

Defenders of the media say that freedom of expression, even when the result is negative or unfavorable to business, is a vital part of maintaining a free and open society.

> If business could conduct its affairs in a society that had a controlled press, the only news that would be made public would be that presently found in house organs, annual reports, company brochures, and speeches by executives. Management could comfortably go about its business without revealing anything that might in any way be legally damaging. But the qualities of our society and the protection of public interest which all of us—business executives as well as reporters—hold especially dear would be jeopardized.[33]

The contrasting business point of view is that the media's right to free speech is not the same as an ordinary citizen's right of expression. The media are enormously influential in shaping public attitudes toward business. When the media disseminate messages to the public, those messages cannot be called back. They enter the public domain where they create impressions, encourage certain attitudes, and inculcate various values. Therefore, business says, the media have an overarching responsibility to be fair, balanced, and accurate in their portrayals of business if they are to be justified in retaining their constitutional rights to freedom of expression. The same could be said, of course, about business's own media advertising messages, which may also lack balance and accuracy.

---

[33]David Finn, "The Media as Monitor of Corporate Behavior," in Craig E. Aronoff, ed., *Business and the Media,* Santa Monica, CA: Goodyear, 1979, p. 125.

CORPORATE MEDIA STRATEGIES

To be effective in communicating with the public—which means getting the corporation's viewpoint across to key stakeholders—companies can take action on four fronts.

Public Relations

The most fundamental media strategy for any corporation is to design and manage an effective public relations program. Chapter 3 describes the major features of the public affairs function in today's socially responsive corporations. Briefly, a good **public relations** program sends a constant stream of information from the company to stakeholders, and the company keeps its doors open for dialogue with stakeholders whose lives are affected by company operations. Public relations should be proactive, not reactive. Channels of communication with the media should be established on a continuing basis, not just after a problem has arisen. Once this step has been taken, a company can then view the media as a positive force that can help the company communicate with the public. The Public Relations Society of America (PRSA) recognizes successful and creative public relations efforts. For example, PepsiCo's reaction to unfounded and exaggerated reports of syringes found in cans of Diet Pepsi was honored by the PRSA in 1994. (This incident is recounted in the discussion case at the end of the chapter.) Other PRSA award winners for 1994 include: CARE, a nonprofit organization, for raising public awareness of the Somalian civil war and drought conditions in the region and organizing a $2 million relief campaign; Consumer Aerosol Products Council, for its educational program to correct myths about the use of aerosol products and its effects on the ozone layer; and the City of San Jose, for increasing citizen support to expand a recycling project.

Crisis Management

Media relations are a vital part of crisis management. **Crisis management** occurs during any period when a company faces a serious disruption in its operations, such as a massive oil spill or a large-scale industrial accident. A specially chosen crisis management task force devotes full time to coping with the problem and trying to find solutions. In the best-managed companies, a media-contact person is a key member of this group, and contingency plans are made beforehand on how media relations are to be handled during any emergency period. In highly visible emergencies, an outside public relations firm may be called in to develop an ongoing plan for dealing with the media and assuring that the company's point of view is included in media presentations. A classic example of an exemplary crisis management response is described in the Johnson & Johnson

Tylenol case in the case studies section of the book. Contrasting examples of how two tire manufacturers managed their "crises" are shown in Exhibit 18-B.

Advocacy Advertising

A third proactive media strategy involves **advocacy advertising,** which is another way to get a corporate viewpoint into the media. A well-known example is Mobil Corporation's vigorous and sometimes provocative advocacy ads on a broad range of public issues; they appear in national-circulation newspapers as statements of the company's views which frequently are at odds with editorial opinions and government policies. Another example comes from cigarette manufacturers.

EXHIBIT 18-B

GOODYEAR/FIRESTONE:
TRAVELING TWO DIFFERENT ROADS IN CRISIS MANAGEMENT

"Two tire companies in the same city. Two problems, two different corporate approaches.

". . . The Firestone 500—Firestone's benchmark product—was discovered to be faulty. Tires were blowing out on the highway, and some drivers died. The company clammed up and for seven years fought the government's claim that the tires were to blame. . . . Firestone was [eventually] forced to recall 7.5 million radial tires, an effort that cost the corporation an estimated $150 million. Firestone no longer exists as an independent company. It is part of Bridgestone, the Japanese company that has become one of the largest tire manufacturers and distributors in the world.

". . . Goodyear found itself the center of local and national attention when it became a [takeover] target. . . . Anglo-French financier and corporate raider Sir James Goldsmith began buying shares in Goodyear and accumulated an 11.5 percent stake in the company. . . . Sir James wanted control of the company. Goodyear wanted to remain independent.

"Goodyear fought hard against Goldsmith, opening up lines of communication to rally shareholders, the media, the community and the government behind its cause. Goldsmith was painted as the bad guy, the intruder who would hurt the city and its workers. State and local officeholders rallied to the cause, passing legislation to protect Goodyear.

"Goodyear paid a high price for its independence. A charge against earnings of $150 million was required to reduce the company's attractiveness to Goldsmith. Goodyear bought him out for more than $618 million in . . . 'greenmail' and rolled up $2 billion in debt. It sold the aerospace division for $640 million and reduced employment from 114,000 to 95,000. But Goodyear today is independent and returning to prosperity."

SOURCE: Reprinted from *The Headlines vs. The Bottom Line: Mutual Distrust Between Business and the News Media,* co-authored by Mike Haggerty and Wallace Rasmussen while serving as Visiting Professional Scholars at The Freedom Forum First Amendment Center at Vanderbilt University. Reprinted with permission.

In 1994, the tobacco industry, led by R. J. Reynolds Co., utilized advocacy advertising to confront the growing trend of prohibiting smoking in public areas and office buildings in this country. The campaign featured full-page advertisements in numerous newspapers, with headlines seeking to combat antismoking sentiments. Four healthy-looking individuals were pictured, with the caption below stating, "We have never smoked. But it was our choice, not the governments." Another ad depicted an apparent arrest by police officers, who announced, "Come out slowly, sir, with your cigarette raised above your head." In a third ad, an intelligent-looking woman was featured, with the statement, "The smell of cigarette smoke annoys me, but not nearly as much as the government telling me what to do."[34]

Media Training of Employees

A fourth media strategy corporations can follow is to give media training to executives and employees who are likely to have contact with the media.

Media training is necessary because communicating with the media is not the same as talking with friends or coworkers. As a company representative, an employee is normally assumed to be speaking for the company or is expected to have special knowledge of company activities. Under these circumstances, the words one speaks take on a special, "official" meaning. In addition, news reporters sometimes "ambush" an executive, asking penetrating or embarrassing questions and expecting instant answers. Even in more deliberate news interviews, the time available for responding to questions is limited to a few seconds. Moreover, facial expressions, the tone of one's voice, and body language can convey both positive and negative impressions.

Many large corporations, such as Mobil, General Motors, and Bank of America, routinely send a broad range of their employees to specific courses to improve their media skills. Media communication experts generally give their clients the following advice.

- Resist the temptation to see reporters and journalists as the enemy. Business media representatives should build bridges with the media. Employees should resist avoiding the media and not withdraw into a shell of silence which tends to generate suspicion that the company has something to hide.
- Employees should be instructed to keep the long-term reputation of the company in mind.
- Being open and honest is a successful media strategy. "Honesty is the best policy," especially since media personnel will investigate to con-

---

[34]Captions taken from issues of the *Wall Street Journal,* July 26, 1994, p. B3, Aug. 9, 1994, p. C26, and Aug. 23, 1994, p. C24.

firm all information business provides and the truth will be uncovered.

■ Businesses should make communications a priority, and the training of the company spokesperson a critical and ongoing program.[35]

SOCIAL RESPONSIBILITY GUIDELINES FOR THE MEDIA AND MEDIA SPONSORS

The public expects the media to exhibit a high level of social responsibility for many reasons. One reason is the awesome power of the media to influence culture, politics, business, social groups, and individual behavior. Media technology reaches into every corner of society and into the inner recesses of human consciousness. No other form of technology is so subtle yet forceful in influencing human affairs.

Social and ethical responsibilities also arise from the potential clash of commercial motives and society's traditional values. The media's need for high ratings and large circulation figures may at times allow cherished human and social values to be overridden, ignored, or diminished.

The media's great potential for being a positive force in society is most likely to be realized if the media and their commercial sponsors try to observe the following social responsibility guidelines.[36]

■ Balance media power with an equal amount of responsibility in all presentations because the media wield such potentially great influence on social values and individual behavior.

■ Seek and present the truth accurately and professionally, while striving for a balanced view of controversial issues and events.

■ Protect and preserve the privacy and dignity of individuals who are the subject of media coverage. The public's "right to know" needs to be balanced against the price paid by individuals whose privacy and personal dignity may be threatened by media presentations.

■ Portray professional, social, and ethnic groups accurately, avoiding unfavorable stereotypical images that damage such groups' social acceptability. This principle applies to media images of business, as well as to those of ethnic minorities, religious groups, and others.

■ Present the full spectrum of human values typical of a society, rather than emphasizing a narrow band of values that tends to distort social reality. Choices among a society's values can then be made with

[35]These guidelines and other suggestions are discussed in Mike Haggerty and Wallace Rasmussen, *The Headlines vs. The Bottom Line: Mutual Distrust Between Business and the News Media,* Arlington, VA: The Freedom Forum First Amendment Center, 1994, pp. 89–92.
[36]Numerous examples of professional codes of ethics governing the media field exist, for example, the *Associated Press Managing Editors' Declaration of Ethical Standards* appears in *Ethics: Easier Said Than Done,* Marina del Rey, CA: Josephson Institute of Ethics, Issue 25, 1994, pp. 49–52.

greater intelligence by the people themselves, instead of the media substituting their judgment for the public will.

SUMMARY POINTS OF THIS CHAPTER

- Technology involves change, reaching far beyond the immediate point of technological impact. Technology is self-reinforcing, acting as a multiplier to foster more technological development.
- In the 1990s, advanced societies are immersed in the "information age" phase of technology. This age supports greater efficiency and demands a large commitment of R&D and capital expenditures.
- Accompanying the economic benefits of technological change are many social and ethical consequences: negative social side effects, new ethical questions associated with advances in biotechnology and information technology, and challenges raised by corporate stakeholders.
- Governments have assumed different degrees of participation in technological development. Some are actively involved in cooperative partnerships with business; others are more passive in their role. Businesses, due to their significant role in technological change, must assume responsibility for the consequences of technological development.
- The most important social issues resulting from the media as a technological tool are the kinds of images of people and institutions projected by the media, the values emphasized by media presentations, whether fairness and balance characterize media programming, and the balance that must be found between free speech and social responsibility.
- The media can be an important resource as corporations develop public relations, crisis management, and advocacy advertising strategies. Media training of employees is essential to foster positive business-media relations.

KEY TERMS AND CONCEPTS USED IN THIS CHAPTER

- Telecommunications
- Phases of technology
- Information society
- Genetic engineering and biotechnology
- Media
- Public relations
- Crisis management
- Advocacy advertising
- Media training

DISCUSSION CASE

MEDIA WOES AND A TRIUMPH

Burroughs Wellcome's Sudafed

Burroughs Wellcome, maker of a decongestant product called Sudafed 12-Hour Capsules, recalled the product nationwide in March 1991 when two people died and a third became gravely ill after taking cyanide-contaminated Sudafed capsules. The company acted less than 24 hours after learning of the two deaths. Network television, radio, and national newspapers carried the recall announcement. Notices were sent to pharmacies, doctors, retailers, wholesalers, and warehouses. Worried customers could call a toll-free number for information. Burroughs Wellcome's CEO held a news conference four days after the recall to offer a reward for information about the tampering. A week later, he appeared in a nationally televised 60-second commercial, alerting viewers to the problem and explaining the company's actions to avoid further deaths and illness.

In spite of these prompt steps, Burroughs Wellcome came under fire for not doing enough soon enough. Speaking of the ten-day delay in airing the CEO's TV spot, one public relations official said, "The basic rule of crisis communication is to tell it all and tell it fast. Sudafed is awfully late. They have a big-time communication problem." A marketing expert faulted the company for not reassuring customers earlier and arranging exchanges and refunds for capsules they had purchased prior to the recall. He said, "It's important to have thought through your strategy. Not two weeks later. By this time, people have found alternatives. It's much too late to wait." And a corporate image consultant, aware that Burroughs Wellcome had been widely criticized earlier for the high price it charged for AZT, an AIDS drug, added, "Who is Burroughs Wellcome? They haven't attended to their image concerns. . . . When a tragedy happens to a company that hasn't maintained its image as a high priority, you've got a problem."[37]

Source Perrier's Bottled Water

Another company that stumbled in its media relations was Source Perrier, the French company that sells Perrier bottled water. Perrier was recalled from world markets when U.S. government officials found traces of benzene—three times the amount allowed under U.S. law—in bottles of the famous spring water. As one source said, "Perrier's explanation for the recall has changed as quickly as a trendy Yuppie's drink of choice." Perrier's

---

[37]The quotations are from the *Wall Street Journal,* Mar. 12, 1991, p. B6.

officials first said that a worker had contaminated a bottling line when cleaning it with a benzene-based fluid and that only bottles sold in the United States had been affected. Then, to everyone's astonishment, the company admitted that benzene is a naturally occurring ingredient of the spring water, which had always been promoted for its purity. Workers, according to the company, had failed to clean the filters often enough, which allowed small amounts of the toxic chemical to remain in the bottled product. A month later, it was reported by Perrier consultants that the *real* problem was failure to change gas filters in a special holding tank used to boost the natural bubble content of the spring water. This latter disclosure only added to the company's image problems because Perrier water had always been advertised as "naturally sparkling," a designation that the U.S. Food and Drug Administration said would now have to be removed since some of the carbonation was artificial.

In what was described as "a raucous news conference in Paris," Perrier's president declared that "all this publicity helps build the brand's renown," a remark that dumbfounded some marketing experts. "That's unbelievable," said one. "No publicity is a lot better than bad publicity. It's extraordinarily hard to believe that benzene will be good for the brand."[38] By June 1993 Perrier had failed to recover its lost market share, causing the firm to launch a new advertising campaign emphasizing the product's "simplicity" and "naturalness."

Diet Pepsi-Cola Hoax

In June 1993 two cases of Diet Pepsi cans were reported to contain syringes. This initial report from Tacoma, Washington, mushroomed to more than fifty claims from twenty-three states within a week. PepsiCo's public relations response during this crisis was considered by many to be exemplary.

At the core of the firm's strategic response were coordination and communication. Soon after the reports of alleged product contamination were made, PepsiCo assembled a twelve-person crisis management team at corporate headquarters in Somers, New York. The crisis management team faced a difficult challenge: no one had been reported injured so a recall of the product or the closing of production facilities was unwarranted. The company decided to attack the problem through the media. Within a few days, Craig Weatherup, president of PepsiCo, appeared on ABC's *Nightline*, each of the three major networks' morning shows, the *Larry King Live* radio show, and the *McNeil-Lehrer News Hour*. "We've gone through

---

[38]The quotations are from *Newsweek,* Feb. 26, 1990, p. 53; and the *Wall Street Journal,* Feb. 15, 1990, pp. B1, B8.

every can line, every plant, numerous records," Weatherup stated in his interviews. "All the evidence points to syringes going into the cans after they were opened." He concluded that since "there is no health issue," there was no need for a product recall.

Some consumer advocates criticized PepsiCo's lack of precautions—such as an immediate product recall—but many applauded the company's actions. "Fear is a consumer-sensitive issue," commented Bill Southland, president of a New York-based public relations firm. "It's very important . . . to position yourself as a company that is concerned." Weatherup's extensive public relations blitz conveyed that message to PepsiCo's consumers. While some customers were leery of the product's safety, the firm reported no noticeable impact on sales.

Following an investigation of the numerous reports of contaminated Pepsi cans, PepsiCo was never accused of any wrongdoing. The Food and Drug Administration reported that the initial tampering claim in Tacoma was caused by a diabetic relative disposing of a syringe in an elderly couple's can of Diet Pepsi. The couple rejected this report, but other copycat tampering incidents were proven to be hoaxes. In Pennsylvania a man was arrested on federal charges of making a false report for claiming to find a syringe in his Diet Pepsi can. The "Diet Pepsi Hoax," as the public relations industry refers to the ordeal, was over in a few weeks. PepsiCo convincingly communicated through the media to its customers and the general public that its production methods and quality control systems were effective. The firm assured people that the problem, if it was real at all, was not due to any company negligence. PepsiCo's summer sales in 1993 were the highest in five years. Reputation and public confidence were reported to be at an all-time high, causing an industry observer to comment, "they might even get a sympathy backlash because they'll be viewed as a victim."[39]

Discussion Questions

1. For each of the three companies, identify the central media issue that led to poor or good public relations for the firm. What aspects of media strategy were overlooked by Burroughs Wellcome or Perrier? What aspects of media strategy were successfully used by PepsiCo?
2. Identify the social and ethical responsibilities of the media in each of these episodes. Did they have an obligation beyond merely getting the

---

[39]All quotations are from "Pepsi Faces Problem in Trying to Contain Syringe Scare," *Wall Street Journal,* June 17, 1993, pp. B1–B2. Additional facts for the cases are from "Media Blamed in Pepsi Hoaxes," *Pittsburgh Post-Gazette,* June 19, 1993, p. A5; and the Public Relations Society of America's 1994 Anvil Awards, p. 2.

facts and reporting them to their readers? What ethical principles from Chapter 5 of this book apply?

3. When a company's image is threatened or damaged by media stories, do the media bear any of the responsibility? Should media reporters and editors soften the impact of their news stories in order to protect business's image?

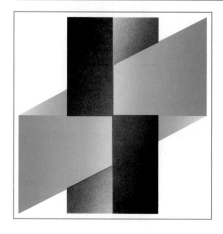

19

Business and the Twenty-First Century

As the twenty-first century approaches, individuals and organizations are challenged to think about critical trends in population, globalization, the environment, political relationships, technology, and more. Social issues such as violence, immigration, the socioeconomic underclass, and racism present extremely complex and important challenges to the long-term health of society and, of course, business. Businesses and individuals cannot avoid being involved in these issues. Creating a society that provides opportunities for companies and for people requires that business, government, and nonprofit organizations work together in designing systems to meet the challenges.

Key Questions and Chapter Objectives

This chapter focuses on these key questions and objectives:

- How will the new social contract affect the outlook for jobs, prosperity, and national well-being in the next decade?
- What fundamental questions will the five factors of social change raise for business and society in the next decade?
- What factors contribute to the apparent rise in violence? What does this mean for society and for businesses?
- Do increases in immigration lead to improved or worsened economic conditions for business and a nation's citizens?
- What is meant by "socioeconomic underclass"? How does the growth of an underclass affect a nation's economic future?
- Why is racism an issue of importance to business? How does business affect public attitudes toward racism?

Bell Atlantic and Ben & Jerry's are both preparing for the twenty-first century. Leadership has been one of the top priorities at both companies. In 1995, Bell Atlantic selected two promising executives to head critical parts of its business. Observers believe that one of the two managers will likely succeed Raymond Smith as the company's chief executive officer by the end of the 1990s. Ben & Jerry's selection of Robert Holland Jr. to succeed co-founder Ben Cohen as chief executive officer also looked to the future. The company needed an experienced and savvy leader to manage a business that wished to maintain its strong ethic of social responsibility, but had run into hard economic times. Mr. Holland, an African American, was a proven expert on "corporate turnarounds." A seasoned business consultant, he had also been CEO of Gilreath Manufacturing Inc. in Howell Michigan, a manufacturer of plastic injection-molds, and a beverage company in Detroit. Importantly, Mr. Holland was a strong believer in the kind of social commitments to people, communities, the environment, and world peace that have characterized Ben & Jerry's from its inception.

Technology and the marketplace was also on the minds of people in both companies. Bell Atlantic has invested heavily in new, state-of-the-art technologies. Although the proposed merger with cable television giant TCI collapsed (see Chapter 1), Bell Atlantic has made big investments in cellular technology, fiber optics, photonics, and other communications technologies. The company has also invested in its people: employees, shareholders, community neighbors, and customers. Education and training are part of each employee's regular activities, and more efforts than ever have been directed at volunteer activities, community improvement, and customer service. At Ben & Jerry's, business growth has created needs for new manufacturing facilities, with improved product quality, environmental safety, and delivery systems. New markets for superpremium ice cream exist in Central and South America, Europe, and Asia. The idea of "Cherry Garcia" ice cream being sold in Brasilia or Bangkok may surprise some people, but many believers—including Robert Holland—think the world is just waiting for Ben & Jerry's ice cream!

These two companies—one an example of traditional "big business," the other an example of "socially conscious" entrepreneurship—illustrate a central theme in this book: the need to integrate a company's economic strategy with its social strategy.

As earlier chapters have shown, it is widely recognized that all organizations—large and small, for-profit and not-for-profit—have stakeholders whose interests must be incorporated into the organization's mission, strategy, and operations. This chapter builds on that premise and examines some of the key issues and relationships that will challenge business, government, and society in the twenty-first century. They are the challenges that today's students (and tomorrow's managers) will have to meet and resolve.

CORPORATE STRATEGY FOR THE TWENTY-FIRST CENTURY

The turbulence that will challenge business firms in the future stems from many sources. Growth in the world's population, from 5 billion people in the early 1990s to as many as 10 billion people in the year 2050—within the lifetime of today's students—will create enormous strains on natural resources such as land, water, and clean air, and such human-made resources as food and housing. Services such as health care and education will be under enormous strains as well.

Population, Technology, and Workforce

Every nation on the globe faces the challenge of developing capabilities on which to build the economy of the future. Some will capitalize on natural resources, others on financial wealth, still others on human resources. Virtually all nations will see the need to vastly improve the education of their populations. In the mid-1990s, we can already see clearly the direct linkage between education and economic prosperity. Economists from around the world are nearly unanimous in endorsing the importance of knowledge as a vital economic resource in the economy of the twenty-first century. Knowledge, skills, and job opportunities will go together as never before.

Revolutions in science and technology will expand the scope of human activity for both good and evil, allowing us to prolong human life through miracle drugs and health care, and to destroy it through more powerful and effective military weapons. These developments, and the directions they take, obviously depend on people, knowledge, and political direction.

Human aspirations for fulfillment and happiness will also grow. No aspect of the business environment is more important than the workplace. Productivity depends greatly on the skills and talents of human workers. Knowing how to effectively organize, motivate, and focus the energies of others continues to be the defining and central task of managers and management.

Because work is done by people, as well as machines, an enormous number of complex human issues occur in the workplace. These include the desire of employees to be recognized as the unique individuals they are and to be treated with personal dignity on the job. Safeguarding employees' privacy has become more important, especially since computer data banks contain personal medical records, job performance evaluations, and other sensitive materials. Safety and health at work are given higher priority because on-the-job injuries are more likely through the use of complex machinery, toxic chemicals, and electronic equipment with unknown side effects. Employees, unions, activist groups, and government officials have demanded an end to workplace discrimination against ethnic minorities, women, disabled persons, and older employees. Retirement security and pension benefits are important to an aging workforce, especially since competitive pressures and corporate takeovers sometimes threaten employee pension plans. Economic security has become a major social concern for millions of workers whose jobs are neither secure nor as rewarding as in the past.[1]

Adding to this complex picture is globalization of business and the growing cultural diversity of the workforce. Worker migration across national boundaries has been common in Europe for many years, and enterprises there have learned to cope with the social changes it introduces into the workforce.[2] Experts and business executives foresee new social pressures developing as companies—large and small—expand their worldwide operations and integrate workforces whose attitudes, cultural views, and values are quite different.

Inequality of income—within and among nations—will pose serious challenges. More people live in poverty in the United States in the 1990s than have ever lived in poverty in the nation's history. A 1993 study by the U.S. Department of Labor Statistics showed that more than 15 percent of households had incomes below the official poverty level. It is doubtful that business can continue to prosper in a society that poses such ominous conditions for so many of its citizens. The gap between the income levels of the rich and poor is widening, and it undermines the concept of community to have substantial portions of a society with too few skills and too little opportunity to effectively engage in the economic life of the society. In the view of some experts, the existence of such a social and economic underclass is one of the most potent long-term social issues in the United States and other industrialized nations.[3] Income inequality among nations also has serious social ramifications for societies and for business. Immigration can worsen these pressures, as people from poor and politically unstable nations seek to enter industrial societies where jobs and political freedom are more abundant. The United States, Germany, Canada, and many other industrial societies have faced serious immigration issues because of global wealth gaps among nations. These issues are discussed in greater detail later in this chapter.

The New Social Contract

The relationship between business and society is continuously changing. People, organizations, and social activity change; new social issues arise

---

[1]Katherine S. Newman, *Declining Fortunes: The Withering of the American Dream*, New York: Basic Books, 1993.

[2]Andrew Caranfil, *Immigration in Europe*, Global Business White Paper No. 14, New York: The Conference Board, Dec. 1994.

[3]Paul Krugman, *The Age of Diminished Expectations*, rev. ed., Cambridge, MA: MIT Press and The Washington Post Company, 1994, especially chapters 2 and 3.

and challenge managers to develop new solutions. To be effective, corporate strategy must respond to the biggest and most central questions in the public's mind. As the twentieth century closes, people everywhere expect businesses to be competitive, to be profitable, and to act responsibly by meeting the reasonable expectations of stakeholders. This is the essence of the social contract between business and society (see Chapters 1 and 15). The corporation of the twenty-first century is certain to be affected by global economic and political trends, powerful new technologies, and a global population of stakeholders who expect their interests to be integrated into the business strategies and thinking of the companies from which they buy goods and services, to which they contribute labor and ideas, and to which they extend the hospitality and support of local communities. These pressures and forces will influence and continuously reshape the social contract between individual companies and the communities in which they operate, between business and national governments, and between the free market system and the world's population.

BUSINESS AND SOCIETY IN THE TWENTY-FIRST CENTURY

Throughout this book, five major themes have been interwoven into a coherent picture of business-society relations. Corporate strategy, ethical values, global change, the role of government, and ecological concerns all interact on a daily basis affecting individuals, families, businesses, and communities. Each of these factors presents possibilities for change that will affect lives, careers, and organizational futures. Most importantly, these factors, and the underlying elements of change each represents, pose critical questions for business and society. These are the questions that business and political leaders everywhere will have to address in the years ahead.

Corporate Strategy

Historians are likely to see the last decade of the twentieth century as an era in which there occurred a remarkable redefinition of business. Many companies struggled to reengineer operations, making them highly efficient but often less dependent on people than in the past. Waves of restructuring produced massive dislocation of people from all levels of companies. Many of the middle- and upper-level managers who lost their jobs founded new companies after failing to find comparable jobs at other large firms. The 1990s saw a great burst of new business formation, often guided by values that differed sharply from those of the big companies where these entrepreneurs had worked. The effects of restructuring and layoffs affected a new generation of employees too. As Exhibit 19-A shows, many talented people who might have once flocked to large companies

EXHIBIT 19-A

WORKFORCE 2000: WHAT KIND OF OPPORTUNITY ARE YOU LOOKING FOR?

Are you looking for a job in a large company, a hospital, a nonprofit community organization, or a small business that is just getting started? For Americans born after
1970, there is a good reason to believe that big business is lower on the list of priorities than it was for their parents and grandparents. A study done by *Fortune* in 1995
drew the following comments from some former business students:

> "At a big company your ideas about how to change things are usually not very
> welcome. You try to question people—and you're out."
> —Barbara Doran (age 41), general partner, Doran Capital Management

> "I really want to be in a situation where your growth is limited only by your own tal-
> ent, your own energy—and that usually means an entrepreneurial situation."
> —Tim McDonald (age 31), president, Interactive Management Institute

> "To succeed in a large organization, you've got to put on a mask and tuck part of
> your true self away. I'm not willing to do that."
> —Daniel Grossman (age 37), Wild Planet Toys

> "I have no interest in a blue-suit, traditional corporate life. I have much more pro-
> gressive views about what a job should be."
> —Melanie Dulbecco (age 33), chief operating officer, R. Torre & Co.

Fortune concluded that there are five things the current generation of business
women and men hate about organizational life:

- The best bureaucrats, not the best performers, are more likely to get ahead.
- It's too easy to get pigeonholed or stuck in a dead-end job with no way out.
- It takes too long to get enough responsibility, authority, and rewards.
- There's not enough flexibility about where and when you work.
- Top managers say they want risk takers, but they don't.

These views may or may not be representative of students in college in the late
1990s. They do suggest that values—the things that matter most to people—are shifting when it comes to work and the way we live. Among the findings by researchers is
the importance that young adults place on a company's approach toward the community. The integration of economic and social goals isn't a choice for many people; it's
a demand that life make sense in social and economic terms.

SOURCE: Quotations appear in "Kissing Off Corporate America," *Fortune,* Feb. 20, 1995, pp. 44–52.

have found better opportunities and more happiness in smaller, independent businesses of their own.

These trends in business direction suggest a number of basic questions for business and political leaders. Foremost among these, business leaders need to consider whether, and how, their companies can integrate commitments to employees with the changing needs and demands of customers for products and services. The U.S. Labor Department has studied trends in employment brought about by modern competitive pressures and concluded that what is emerging in many companies is a **high-performance workplace,** defined as one that provides "workers with the information, skills, incentives, and responsibility to make decisions essential for innovation, quality improvement, and rapid response to change."[4]

To achieve such results, companies must invest in employee education, skill development, and process changes to effectively empower employees. Some companies have made significant efforts to do so, but others have been more cautious in creating these high-performance workplace environments. Among the strategic issues for managers is how beneficial these changes will be relative to the costs involved. The Department of Labor study pointed to many examples of success. Many labor unions and institutional investors have tried to encourage such change directly, by working with management, and indirectly, by offering shareholder resolutions asking companies to create high-performance workplace environments.[5]

Ethics and Public Values

As business is conducted in conditions that are changing, the ability of companies to adhere to core values and principles is tested. The commitment to ethical principles of action need not be subject to shifting fortunes. However, circumstances do change and individual managers are naturally challenged to apply ethical concepts to those new circumstances. Changes in technology, for example, are creating a host of new issues regarding the ownership, use, and distribution of intellectual property. Systems such as the Internet, for example, raise many new issues about the use of ideas that are available through World Wide Web resources. Should utilitarian, rights, or fairness principles define how the system adjusts, balances, and reconciles different interests?

Ethical issues are bound to grow more complicated for managers. Many will involve problems of global business activity. As discussed in Chapters 4 and 5, these issues will culminate in one central question for business leaders: *How can business be conducted within a framework of*

---

[4]U.S. Department of Labor, *Road to High-Performance Workplaces,* Washington, DC: U.S. Government Printing Office, 1994, p. 1.
[5]Investor Responsibility Research Center (IRRC), "The High Performance Workplace," *Social Issues Service: 1995 Background Report H,* Washington, DC, 1995.

ethical ideals, norms, and standards that are understood and accepted by people throughout the world?

Global Challenges

As the twentieth century closes, historians are assessing the central changes that have taken place: industrialization, the expanded scale of warfare, the creation of weapons capable of destroying the planet itself, urbanization, nationalism, population growth, ecological damage, and more. While it is speculative to consider what the list might look like in another one hundred years, it seems likely that "global" will be added to each of the aforementioned changes. Industrialization will become truly global by the early part of the twenty-first century. Warfare has gone global twice before, and may again. The manufacture and sale of weapons is already a global business. Urban growth, with all of its problems and opportunities, is occurring worldwide, as are population growth and ecological damage. Nationalism, with its implicit relationships to racial, economic, and religious values, is likely to remain a threat to global peace. And communications are becoming so completely global that within the next few decades there will be few, if any, places on earth that cannot be reached instantaneously from any other place on earth.

Within these trends are the new avenues of global commerce that will create business opportunities, markets, demand for goods and services, and expectations as to how businesses will relate to society. Many questions of business responsibility will be redefined in the world of global commerce that many experts foresee.

One central question for business leaders is likely to be: *How can business operate in a global marketplace in ways that serve societal objectives by meeting real needs, yet accommodate the diverse demands made by stakeholders whose interests will sometimes conflict?* This issue arises in narrow and specific ways for individual managers and companies. But the frequency with which the issue arises, and the need for rethinking the balance to be struck among conflicting demands, will surely keep this question alive for many years to come.

Political Revolutions of the 1990s

The relationship between business and government is always changing. The many demands and needs of both businesses and governments guarantee that ideas about how to change existing arrangements will always be percolating in the minds of business managers, government officials, and policy experts.

Rethinking the role of government is a form of the "continuous improvement process" thinking that has swept through management in the past decade. Prompted by difficult economic problems, including a huge federal deficit and voter anger at the high taxes that followed, many political leaders have recognized the inevitability of the need to rethink government's appropriate role. This has occurred at several levels and in many nations, including the United States. First, the role of the federal government is the primary focus of attention. The growth of government in numbers of personnel, budget, and as a percentage of gross domestic product suggests to many that it is now too large (see Chapter 8). A related problem in the United States involves the tendency of federal officials to mandate that state governments provide services or meet standards without providing any budget resources to meet the costs involved. These rules and requirements, which are known as **unfunded mandates,** have been viewed as extremely unfair by state and local government officials. Unfunded mandates effectively force state and local taxes higher in order to fund projects and programs that federal officials—often far removed from the communities involved—have ordered. In 1995, Congress passed a law to restrict the federal government from creating more unfunded mandates.

Another item on the agenda of reform-minded politicians in the 1990s is a **balanced budget amendment** to the Constitution. Congress has long failed to balance the national budget, with annual deficits growing rapidly thereby requiring increased borrowing from foreign investors. In the 1990s, the political will finally emerged to require that the budget be balanced except in times of war and other emergency. The Republican party's "Contract with America" promised an effort to force Congress to operate with a balanced budget.[6]

Many state governments operate on a balanced budget because their state constitutions require it. The problems of a balanced budget for the federal government are numerous, especially because of such issues as national defense, disasters, and national emergencies. It is usually proposed that such issues be among the limited exceptions that would permit a short-term deficit to be created.

As discussed in Chapters 6 and 8, governments around the world are in the throes of redefining—and reinventing—their role in the global economy of the twenty-first century. Many factors will influence the choices of individual nations, including the new reality of global financial markets that react instantaneously to financial news in any part of the globe. When Mexico's government devalued the peso in late 1994, the financial markets reacted immediately. Investments were pulled out of Mexico and a series of financial support measures were discussed by national governments. Each announcement affected financial markets with unparalleled speed. Governments that do not follow what are thought to be sound economic policies will be pressured by the global financial market to adjust rapidly. The valuation of global currencies is one way investors signal the strength of a nation's economy. As the twentieth century closes, it is re-

[6]Ed Gillespie and Bob Schellhas, eds., *Contract with America,* New York: Random House, 1994, p. 3.

markable to note how government policy making of earlier times was noticeably free of the kinds of pressure global communications create today. The next century promises to produce even more pressures of this type as communication expands and it becomes even more difficult to "keep secrets" in government or business.

Ecological Challenges

In the view of many experts, ecological challenges will emerge as the most important vector of change in the twenty-first century. Historian Paul Kennedy, for example, says that understanding the interconnectedness of economic and demographic conditions is crucial to preparing for the twenty-first century. As Kennedy defines it,

> the greatest test for human society as it confronts the twenty-first century is how to use the "power of technology" to meet the demands thrown up by the "power of population"; that is, how to find effective global solutions in order to free three-quarters of humankind from the growing Malthusian trap of malnutrition, starvation, resource depletion, unrest, enforced migration, and armed conflict—developments that will also endanger the richer nations, if less directly.[7]

This contest between the power of technology and the power of population reveals a number of central ecological policy questions for business and society.

- How will the world's wealthy nations, with populations that consume disproportionately large amounts of resources (e.g., fossil fuels), adjust expectations and behavior to more sustainable levels? What will businesses do to reduce overconsumption or to adapt to declining consumption?
- How will the world's poorest nations reconcile their need for economic development and improved social welfare with global environmental requirements that may conflict with national goals? Can the global commons—the atmosphere, oceans, Arctic, and space—be preserved without discriminating against the poorest?
- How will environmental risks be assessed and weighed against the benefits to business and society of economic activities? Can scientific assessments be made that people will trust and act upon?
- What obligations do business and society have to preserve endangered species and the integrity of ecosystems, and how should these rights be balanced against property rights?

[7]Paul Kennedy, *Preparing for the Twenty-First Century,* New York: Random House, 1993, p. 12.

These questions are very basic to meeting the challenge of creating a world in which economic activities are compatible with an ecologically sustainable universe. If human beings fail to achieve such a sustainable balance, students in the future may well look upon the 1990s as an era in which business and government had an opportunity but failed to take the bold actions necessary.

PROBLEMS OF COMMUNITY

One of the foremost issues facing people in the next century is how to find moral purpose in the face of so many crumbling institutions while others are not yet built or rebuilt.[8] There is little doubt that the United States which today's students know differs markedly from that of their parents or grandparents. The difficulty is that the world has not yet created all—or even most—of the institutions it will need to meet the requirements of 2025. Worse, there are deep ideological divisions among people as to what institutions are needed and what roles those institutions should play in the future.

Four social issues illustrate the gap between "what is" and "what needs to be." As students become active and involved citizens in the new century, their careers and families will lead them to think about problems of a sort not resolved by today's business, governmental, or university leaders. They will have to create solutions or live with the consequences of some extraordinarily complex social issues, including the four discussed below: immigration, violence, the socioeconomic underclass, and racism.

IMMIGRATION

International migration has been a major global issue since the end of World War II. Since the end of the cold war, the issue has become even more intense and more challenging to national governments. The free movement of people is now expected to have major consequences for eastern Europe, the former Soviet Union, and the Mediterranean basin on the European continent. Similar effects are anticipated in North America, where immigrants to the United States from Mexico have precipitated backlash policies in states such as California. In Africa, the Middle East, and the Asia-Pacific region workers are often recruited as **guest workers** (i.e., migrant workers) from nations with abundant populations but few

[8]Philip Selznick, *The Moral Commonwealth: Social Theory and the Promise of Community*, Berkeley and Los Angeles: The University of California Press, 1992, p. 3.

work opportunities to nations with economic opportunity but too few low-wage workers. In other words, there is virtually no place on earth that is not likely to change—and be affected profoundly—by the influx of different cultural traditions and moral values brought about through immigration.

Figure 19-1 shows the root causes of immigration as a mixture of **"push" and "pull" factors.** For example, many Mexican citizens have entered the United States in search of economic opportunity. A second wave of family members often follows, as relatives seek to be reunited. According to one research study, about 85 percent of all legal immigration in Europe during the late 1980s and early 1990s has been on social and humanitarian grounds, including family reunion and qualification as refugees.[9]

Barriers to Immigration

Nations are not open to all would-be immigrants. Governments often tightly control the number and nationality of those entering the country. Although some countries wish to attract immigrants as settlers, guest workers, bearers of rare skills, or owners of financial resources, many of the most economically advanced nations—including the United States—have established barriers to immigration. Foreign workers need work permits; students need visas and identification papers; political refugees are not permitted to take jobs and may be prevented from exercising travel

[9]Caranfil, op. cit., p. 12.

FIGURE 19-1
The "push" and "pull" causes of immigration.

"Push" Factors	"Pull" Factors
■ War and civil strife	■ Economic opportunity
■ Economic decline, rising unemployment, poverty	■ Family reunion with workers already in another nation
■ Population pressures	■ Freedom from fear of violence, persecution, hunger, and poverty
■ Human rights violations	■ Freedom of expression (speech, publication)
■ Natural disasters	■ Education
■ Government resettlement policies which threaten ethnic integrity	■ Advances in communication technology
■ Resurgent nationalism	■ Maintenance of ethnic identity
■ Escape from oppressive religious rule	

rights granted to citizens; visitors must apply for visas and may not stay past their approved time. These restrictions are created to protect domestic workers from competition that would lower wages or take away jobs; to protect social services systems from being overwhelmed with needy newcomers; and, in some instances, to preserve the racial, ethnic, cultural, and religious features of a society.

Throughout history, there have been ethnic and racial obstacles to free movement of the world's peoples.[10] When economic fortune is entwined with these traditional biases, it is little surprise that barriers to mobility are perpetuated for generations. In Italy, for example, there are believed to be more than 800,000 illegal immigrants from the Maghreb (an area of northwest Africa including Morocco, Algeria, Tunisia, and Libya). In the United States, officials have estimated that more than 2 million illegal immigrants live in California, costing the state an estimated $3 billion per year for education, medical treatment, and incarceration. Most are from Mexico despite an extensive border control effort by U.S. immigration authorities.[11]

According to an expert on European migration, there are five distinct types of immigrants in Europe in the 1990s.[12] These are shown in Figure 19-2 for several years preceding and following the collapse of the Soviet Union. In this period, the total number of immigrants rose sharply, and several categories—registered immigrants, asylum seekers, illegal immigrants—increased sharply.

U.S.-Mexico Immigration Issues

Along the U.S.-Mexico border, immigration has produced numerous pressures and problems for government and for the business community. Many industries have a need for inexpensive labor, such as restaurants, lawn care services, low-technology assembly operations, maintenance services, car washes, and agriculture. States such as Florida, Texas, and California have hundreds of thousands of immigrants working in these industries. Because U.S. wages—even for the lowest paying jobs—are still higher than those in Mexico, millions of Mexicans have sought to cross the border and enter the United States. Legal immigration is restricted and U.S. laws do not permit unrestricted entry from Mexico. The result is predictable: many Mexican citizens seek to enter the United States illegally.

---

[10]Arthur M. Schlesinger Jr., *The Disuniting of America*, New York: W. W. Norton, 1992, pp. 119–138.

[11]"What Proposition 187 Was All About," *Tampa Times*, Nov. 27, 1994, p. 2; Corporation for Public Broadcasting, "Persona Non Grata?" *The MacNeil/Lehrer News Hour*, Transcript 5079, Oct. 19, 1994.

[12]Jonas Widgren, "Shaping a Multilateral Response to Future Migrations," in K. Hamilton, ed., *Migration and the New Europe*, Washington, DC: Center for Strategic and International Studies, 1994, pp. 40–41.

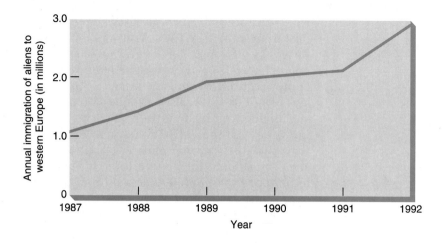

FIGURE 19-2
Total annual immigration of aliens to western Europe, 1987–1992.
SOURCE: Jonas Widgren, "Shaping a Multilateral Response to Future Migrations," in K. Hamilton, ed., *Migration and the New Europe,* Washington, DC: Center for Strategic and International Studies, 1994, pp. 40–41.

Type of Immigrant	1987	1988	1989	1990	1991	1992
Immigrants registered for residence	760,000	910,000	1,080,000	980,000	1,020,000	1,240,000
Constitutional immigration rights	101,000	217,000	392,000	417,000	239,000	252,000
Asylum seekers	170,000	220,000	310,000	430,000	550,000	680,000
War refugees (from Yugoslavia)	—	—	—	—	42,000	370,000
Illegal immigrants (estimated)	55,000	90,000	150,000	210,000	280,000	370,000
Total	1,086,000	1,437,000	1,932,000	2,037,000	2,131,000	2,912,000

Once in the country, they often find jobs in businesses that violate immigration laws by hiring illegal aliens and pay less than minimum wage to desperate job seekers.

Businesses may be affected by illegal immigration in several ways. First, they may be competing against companies that achieve an unfair labor cost advantage by paying lower wages to illegal immigrant workers. Second, companies that abide by the law are also paying taxes to meet the social service needs of the illegal immigrants. This cost of doing business leaves them disadvantaged against competitors from other states that do not face such tax burdens or from overseas competitors whose home nations do not provide comparable social benefits to illegal immigrants.

California has faced especially large and complex issues with regard to immigration. The state has long been a destination for immigrants from Mexico, providing a wide range of economic and social opportunities. A generous system of social welfare has extended educational, health, and family support benefits to residents, irrespective of legal status. The cost of social benefits has been substantial, however. As California's economy slipped into a deep and extended recession during the early 1990s, politicians sought to curb the escalating costs of social services. Illegal immigrants became a target of voter anger and political wrath: a ballot referendum (citizen's initiative), Proposition 187, was drafted that would cut off social service benefits to illegal immigrants. Bumper stickers read, "Save Our State. No Funding Illegals." Proposition 187 also became a central issue in California's gubernatorial, U.S. Senate, and state legislative races. Despite strong opposition to the measure from a wide array of interests and political leaders, including some who argued that the state's agricultural industry would collapse without the workers, the referendum passed. In November 1994, California's voters adopted the proposition by a wide margin, thereby creating a law that restricts state benefits to illegal immigrants.

California's action was immediately challenged in court as unconstitutional and many legal battles loom. Immigration pressures grew steadily worse, especially in 1995 following Mexico's devaluation of the peso. This action further reduced the purchasing power of the peso and created yet another incentive for Mexicans to move to the United States in search of economic opportunity.[13]

VIOLENCE

Of all the issues and problems in American communities, that which produces more fear among citizens of every age is violence. The elderly fear muggings and robberies; young people fear shootings and stabbings; homeowners and tenants fear burglaries; women fear rape; children fear abduction and molestation. Crime and violence are inextricable companions of American life in the 1990s.

For teenagers and younger children, violence is associated with school,

[13]"Clinton Plan Aims to Curb Illegal-Alien Employment," *Wall Street Journal*, Feb. 8, 1995, p. A5.

community, and peers. Most often, the violence is by one juvenile against another. According to a *New York Times* report:

> Young criminals strike all age groups and emotionally scar parents, spouses, siblings and friends. But most victims of juvenile crime are . . . children themselves. The Justice Department reported in 1992 that 55 percent of all crimes against people 12 to 19 years old were committed by people in the same age group. Juvenile attackers also accounted for 64 percent of all gang assaults, gang rapes and gang robberies committed against the young.[14]

Violence is a social problem that presents many different faces in the modern world. The causes are numerous and very complex; some say the only thing more complicated than the causes of violence are the solutions to violence. Businesses are affected in direct and indirect ways by violent behavior. Conflicts among employees in the workplace, for example, can be physically dangerous, even life-threatening, and are certainly damaging to employee morale (see Chapter 15).

Murder, assault, rape, and other forms of physical harm have become more frequent and more serious problems in the 1990s. Statistics collected by the U.S. Justice Department reveal a number of clear trends and causal connections:

- Violent crimes are rising in number and severity, in part because there are more weapons found in households across the nation.
- Violence often begins early in a child's life, thereby triggering a **cycle of violence** that may eventually involve school, peers, family, gangs, and guns. Crime, injury, and death are frequent consequences of violent beginnings.
- Crimes against young people—children, teens, young adults—are caused by peers. In other words, youth are the most frequent perpetrators of crimes against other youth. Much of this occurs in or near schools.
- Theories abound as to the connection between violence in television, film, and the media and violence in homes, schools, and the workplace. There is little consensus among experts regarding this relationship.

Metropolitan Life Insurance Company (MetLife) has had a long-standing interest in the views and attitudes of teachers in American schools.

---

[14]Joe Sexton, "Young Criminals' Prey: Usually Young," *New York Times*, Dec. 1, 1994, pp. A1, B14.

[15]Metropolitan Life Insurance Company, *The Metropolitan Life Survey of the American Teacher, 1993, Violence in America's Public Schools*, New York: Louis Harris and Associates, Inc., 1993; and Metropolitan Life Insurance Company, *The Metropolitan Life Survey of the American Teacher, 1994, Violence in America's Public Schools: The Family Perspective*, New York: Louis Harris and Associates, Inc., 1994.

EXHIBIT 19-B

VIOLENCE IN AMERICAN SCHOOLS

Among the key findings of Metropolitan Life Insurance Company's survey on violence in American schools are the following:

- A majority of students and parents believe their schools provide a safe environment in the school building. However, more than one-third of junior high (36 percent) and high school (34 percent) students believe their school does only a fair or poor job of providing a safe environment in the school building.
- More than half (58 percent) of students in grades 3–12 believe their school has a problem with vandalism such as graffiti or broken windows and doors.
- Students who believe their school provides only a fair or poor education also believe that vandalism is a significant problem in their school.
- Situations that could provoke violence occur frequently and affect the lives of most high school students. Forty-four percent of students surveyed said they had "personal experiences with angry scenes or confrontations" in the month prior to the survey; 24 percent said they had had personal experience with physical fights.
- Students who have been victims of violence uniformly believe that sometimes teachers in their school think of students as numbers. The exact opposite is true among students who have not been victims—only 15 percent believe teachers sometimes think of them as numbers.
- Nearly three-fourths (72 percent) of students who have been victims think there would be less violence if there were more things for students to do.
- Students and parents believe that because of violent incidents, students are likely to distrust one another. More than 40 percent of the students surveyed in grades 7–12 say that because of violence or threats of violence they do not trust others.

SOURCE: These points are drawn from Metropolitan Life Insurance Company, *The Metropolitan Life Survey of the American Teacher, 1994, Violence in America's Public Schools: The Family Perspective*, New York: Louis Harris and Associates, Inc., 1994, pp. 3–9.

Since 1984 the company has commissioned large-scale surveys of American teachers and students to learn more about issues of concern. The company undertook its first study of violence in America's public schools in 1993 and has conducted additional research studies on the topic (see Exhibit 19-B).[15]

The prevalence of violence in schools and the workplace mirrors broad trends in society that cannot help but affect business. People bring social attitudes into the workplace and inevitably act on those views and beliefs. To believe, for example, that violence is an approved way of responding to conflict, is to create a heightened potential of workplace violence and violence toward customers, Similarly, acceptance of vandalism and deterioration of physical facilities is a serious problem because it is associated with a lack of safety and lack of communication. The fact that students who have been victims of violence become distrusting is very significant to workplace dynamics: building teams, for example, simply will not be as easily done when victims of violence are part of the team. Crime also affects business costs, including security, surveillance, police protection, and employee protection.

Many businesses support community projects to reduce crime and violence. MetLife, for example, has contributed money, volunteer time, and research to support school-based initiatives aimed at responding to issues raised by students and teachers in the surveys. CIGNA, an insurance company with headquarters in Philadelphia, has worked extensively with the police department, mayor's office, educators, and community groups in that city to combat youth violence. These efforts usually require cooperation among community, government agencies, and businesses. Partnerships are virtually required for violence prevention to be successful.

The impact of violence is felt in all nations, not only the United States. For example, in the years following the breakup of the Soviet Union, a crime wave swept Russia and the other republics and deterred many foreign companies from investing. Reports on Russia often focused on crime as one of the country's three most important uncertainties, the others being the instability of the ruble and the political fate of Russian leaders.[16] Bribery, corruption, and violence are often connected. In some nations, business cannot be conducted without resorting to extensive security arrangements, including private guards, armored vehicles, and special living quarters for employees and families.

THE UNDERCLASS

The population of every nation has both rich and poor citizens. The distribution of income—i.e., what percentage of the population has what percentage of a nation's income (gross domestic product)—is an indicator of the relative equality or inequality in a society. In some nations, a small number of people hold enormous amounts of national wealth—this has been the case in Central America, for example, where a small number of landowners often controlled the agricultural resources of countries such as El Salvador and Nicaragua. Whether ruled directly by an "oligarchy" of ruling families or by a political dictator, military and political power is often used to crush resistance and reinforce the distinctions between the rich and the poor. Haiti was dominated by colonial landowners for generations, leading to a series of tyrannical political regimes including those of

---

[16]Stephen Sestanovich, *Russia: Land of Opportunity?* Global Business White Paper No. 12, New York: The Conference Board, 1994.

"Papa Doc" Duvalier, "Baby Doc" Duvalier, and in the 1990s, General Cedras. Only after the United States threatened to invade Haiti to restore de-
mocratically elected President Jean Paul Aristide, did Haiti's military
rulers relinquish their power.

A nation's **socioeconomic underclass** refers to those people who
are kept in poverty, usually over several generations of families. The term
is used by many experts to describe people who are caught in conditions
of chronic poverty with little or no real hope of moving into a better standard of living. In the United States, about 30 million people are considered
to be part of this economic underclass. About 15 percent of all Americans
live below an official poverty line defined by the federal government as
the income needed to support a family of two adults and two children.
Since the 1980s, the number of people in this group has grown despite
general economic prosperity in the country. How has this happened? Experts cite several factors as contributing to the growth of the underclass.[17]
First, as the economy has changed, many low-wage jobs have been eliminated. This creates fewer opportunities for unskilled workers with limited
education. Second, there are more people competing for the jobs which
do exist, including those which do not require high-skill levels. So, there
are more unskilled workers competing for a smaller pool of unskilled
jobs, producing an inevitable increase in unemployment among the unskilled population. Third, segments of the population are afflicted with
other social problems—poor health, disabilities, drug dependence, alcoholism—that make employment a near impossibility. As welfare support
declines, or fails to grow, these people slip further below the poverty line.

Businesses are affected by the existence of an economic underclass in a
number of ways. First, businesses are affected by labor market conditions.
Companies that employ unskilled workers find a large number of such
people. Agricultural businesses, for example, especially farms that grow
seasonal fruits and vegetables, employ large numbers of migrant workers,
most of whom are unskilled. Second, businesses pay taxes and the costs of
supporting the underclass are growing. This inevitably poses the question: Who shall pay? Third, the economic underclass represents a part of
the population that cannot afford to purchase the goods and services that
companies want to sell. In most countries, welfare support is designed to
meet minimal food, shelter, clothing, and related needs. Rarely does it provide the money for purchases of luxury goods or expensive services. Businesses that are looking to expand their markets must consider whether it
makes business sense to ignore as much as 15 percent of the American
public.

Businesses are divided about how to respond to these issues. In 1995,
for example, President Clinton proposed an increase in the minimum
wage from $4.25 to $5.00 per hour. For workers with a 40-hour work

---

[17]Krugman, op. cit., pp. 23–29.

week, this would amount to about $30.00 before taxes. This may not seem like a large increase in salary, but in some businesses the cumulative effect could be quite substantial.

> For example, one restaurant owner calculated that to raise the minimum wage by even $.50 per hour would add $500.00 to the weekly wage costs. These costs would have to be passed on to the consumer in the form of price increases. Of course, this owner's competitors would have to meet the provisions of the new law too. The owner's greatest concern was that customers would simply visit the restaurant less often because prices were higher.[18]

There are no easy answers to the question of how to reduce the size of the underclass. Experts are concerned that as the economy of the twenty-first century takes shape, more skills will be required of every worker, eliminating virtually all of the unskilled jobs now in existence. Work will become more and more of a privilege in such a future, and the underclass is likely to grow, not shrink. Education seems to be a key to improving the life of people caught in the underclass, but problems exist with this solution as well. Schools in low-income communities are often less well-equipped and staffed than those in wealthy communities, suggesting that the poor will be less well-served than the rich. Many businesses are working with schools and school districts to improve the effectiveness of all education. Once again, the results are quite uneven and no easy solution is at hand.

The problems of the economic underclass are deep-rooted and often entwined with other social issues. Young black men under the age of 21, for example, are a segment of the population that has the highest unemployment rate, several times higher than that of any other population group. This segment of the population also has a high dropout rate from school. Crime statistics are also correlated with lack of education and persistent unemployment. The fact that race is correlated with certain kinds of advantage and disadvantage in society poses important policy issues for government, business, and other institutions. Equal opportunity is a core social value in America, yet such opportunity is systematically eroded for segments of the population when an underclass continues to grow. At the political level, leaders are then forced to decide how the distribution of national wealth shall occur—what taxes shall be paid and by whom; what welfare payments shall be made and to whom; and what social services shall be provided and to whom. Each decision, in turn, has ramifications for individual businesses, citizens, and taxpayers. The choices are easier when a economy is growing, because the amount of wealth to be distributed is growing. But when an economy is stagnant, or even shrinking, the

[18]Peter T. Kilborn, "A City Built on $4.25 an Hour," *New York Times*, Feb. 12, 1995, pp. F1, F4, F5.

choices become much more difficult. No one can get something without others giving up something. The questions of how to support America's underclass, and how to create pathways out of poverty for those people in the underclass, are very central issues for business and society as the twentieth century comes to a close.

RACISM

The publication of *The Bell Curve* set off a wave of debate in the United States in the mid-1990s about the relationship of race to many of America's social problems.[19] Its subject—the genetic and alleged intellectual inferiority of blacks—has been taboo for many years and is indicative of the racial issues that threaten to erupt again in the late 1990s. The volatility of the topic is demonstrated by an example.

> At Rutgers University, the president, Francis L. Lawrence, gave a speech to faculty in November 1994 that discussed the academic challenges facing students. In speaking about evaluation and the need for accountability, he cited the SAT scores of black students—which average 750—as an example of the issue facing the university. He then asked, "Do we set standards in the future so we don't admit anybody with the national test? Or do we deal with a disadvantaged population that doesn't have the genetic, heredity background to have a higher average?"[20]

The comments proved explosive once they were leaked to the press in early 1995. During the half-time break at a basketball game between Rutgers and the University of Massachusetts men's teams (February 7, 1995), 150 students sat down on the floor and refused leave in protest of Lawrence's remarks. The game, which was being broadcast on national television, could not be resumed. After negotiations failed to end the protest, the basketball game was suspended. Despite the president's apology and efforts to clarify what he said was the true meaning of his comments, critics demanded that president Lawrence resign or be fired by Rutgers University trustees.

Business both affects and is affected by racism in society. **Racism** exists when social institutions are used to enforce or perpetuate practices that emphasize racial differences. In South Africa during apartheid, for example, public restrooms were restricted to people of different colors—"Whites Only," "Blacks Only," "Coloreds Only." In the United States, public

---

[19]Richard J. Herrnstein and Charles Murray, *The Bell Curve: Intelligence and Class Structure in American Life,* New York: The Free Press, 1994.
[20]Joe Burris, "UMass-Rutgers Game Suspended," *Boston Globe,* Feb. 8, 1995, pp. 53, 58.

Parks to ride in the back of a bus that prompted a series of demonstrations and a lengthy boycott of public transportation by black citizens of Selma, Alabama, in 1964; it was the pervasive segregation of restaurants that prompted lunch counter sit-ins at Woolworth stores and led to boycotts, marches, and other pressures that finally forced these businesses to open their doors to all customers.

Racism does not end when such institutional restrictions are changed. Less obvious forms of racial discrimination may exist and businesses are often involved in perpetuating these as well. Consider the following example:

> Denny's is a chain of restaurants that operates across the United States. The restaurants have been successful by offering a large selection of meals at reasonable prices. The restaurants depend on a high volume of sales per outlet and a rapid turnover of patrons at tables. Speedy service is therefore expected by customers and necessary for profitable operations. In many communities, Denny's is a popular lunch stop for a wide range of business people. Quality, prices, and service create customers whose loyalty and regular business is important to the restaurant. In some Denny's restaurants, however, not all customers were treated alike. Having concluded that a high proportion of black customers would deter white customers from patronizing their restaurants, some Denny's store managers deliberately tried to dissuade black customers from frequenting their restaurants. The tactics were predictable: long waits for tables, slow service by staff members, serving food that was too cold, failure to refill coffee cups, and so on.[21]

It was not until a group of black FBI agents were victimized by such practices that an organized effort was launched to challenge Denny's policies and practices. Individual lawsuits were filed; others who had been treated similarly joined in a "class action" lawsuit against the restaurant chain; and former managers came forward to describe the corporate policies that encouraged such action. Rather than risk continued protest and legal liability, Denny's settled the lawsuits and paid a large sum of money to patrons who had been victimized by the practices. The company's management agreed to a vigorous program designed to change internal standards of acceptable and unacceptable behavior and to enhance nondiscriminatory ways of doing business.

All industries face the challenge of dealing with race relationships. Banks and insurance companies have been suspected of discriminating against particular racial groups—African Americans, Hispanics, Asians—in lending mortgage money and other forms of credit to communities.[22]

---

[21]Howard Kohn, "Service with a Sneer," *The New York Times Magazine,* Nov. 6, 1994, pp. 42ff.
[22]Albert R. Karr, "Federal Drive to Curb Mortgage-Loan Bias Stirs Strong Backlash," *Wall Street Journal,* Feb. 7, 1995, pp. A1, A10.

Racism also affects the relationships among those who are most closely associated with the company. Relationships among employees, associates, customers, suppliers, and others can all be tainted by racist attitudes.

The importance of racial attitudes will grow in the decades ahead. As businesses of all types deal with customers and suppliers from around the world, the idea that some of the people involved in these relationships are "second-class citizens" is not sustainable. There are many ethical reasons to treat all people equally. There are economic reasons as well: as economic wealth is shared more widely and among more people of diverse racial backgrounds, it will become increasingly unacceptable for a business to say that it will refuse to deal with customers having particular racial characteristics. Such attitudes will make neither ethical nor economic sense.

BUSINESS MUST BE INVOLVED

A central theme in this book is the idea that business *is* involved in many forms of social change occurring in the world, and *must be* involved in designing solutions or responses to the issues of our times. This means, in turn, that each of us, as managers and as citizens, also have a responsibility to understand the issues, reflect on those steps that can be taken to respond, and then actually do so. This is a managerial responsibility, a citizen's responsibility, and, ultimately, a human responsibility.

Each generation has a **stewardship responsibility**—a duty to care for society and pass it on to others—to the next generation (see Chapter 2). This idea is very popular among those who are concerned with ecological and environmental risks (see Chapters 11 and 12). But it also applies more generally to people's responsibilities to one another. If we fail to act as stewards of the earth's resources, for example, there may be too little water, pure air, or forest resources for our children. Similarly, if we fail to protect and strengthen institutions of effective government, honest business practice, and community service to others, we jeopardize the foundations of civil society. Michael Brown, co-founder of City Year, the youth service program that was the model for the AmeriCorps program of national service, has said that the greatest battle in the 1990s is between the forces of *cynicism* and *idealism* (see Exhibit 19-C). If the "perpetual scoffing" of the cynics prevails, society will suffer because people will fear taking risks, being positive, trying to solve problems. If idealism prevails, people will try new things, tackle difficult problems and issues, and build institutions, including businesses, that are profitable and meet social needs.

Whether it is designing the high-performance workplace, creating global supply and marketing networks, configuring new technologies to share information faster, or working with others in business, government,

EXHIBIT 19-C

CITY YEAR: A NEW KIND OF VOLUNTEERISM

City Year is a national youth service organization which provides young people, ages seventeen to twenty-three, a demanding year of full-time community service, leadership development, and civic involvement. Started in Boston in 1988, City Year was begun as a private venture by two young entrepreneurs, Alan Khazei and Michael Brown. Their concept was simple: provide an opportunity for young people from diverse backgrounds to learn, work in teams, and develop leadership skills through activities that tackle real problems and real needs in the community. But who would support such a concept?

The two young founders discovered that there were lots of interested sponsors. Companies such as Digital Equipment Corporation, The Timberland Company, and Bank of Boston were early supporters. Some money was raised from governmental and nonprofit agencies to assist specific projects, and individual donors also provided support. Many of the companies supporting City Year provide in-kind support including boots, jackets, computers, fax machines, consulting support, and audit services.

City Year volunteers start each day with a program of physical exercise, usually in a highly visible place such as Boston's City Hall Plaza. Wearing distinctive red shirts and ski jackets with a clearly visible "City Year" emblazoned on them, the group does a brisk 30-minute workout. They are then formed into teams that leave for a day's work in the city's schools, housing developments, parks, or other places of need. City Year members are paid $100 per week plus a $5,000 public service grant for college at the end of nine months of service. Teams may be assigned to work with teachers in schools in support of reading programs, repair run-down housing, clean up parks and vacant lots in the city, or meet dozens of other community needs. The teams that are formed to work on these projects involve male and female members who may be drawn from the poorest inner-city neighborhoods as well as the wealthiest suburban

and the community to develop a youth violence prevention program, managers have a vital role to play in creating both the businesses of the future and the communities of the future. That is why business and business people cannot—should not—stand on the sidelines. The stakes are nothing less than the future of business and society. Peter Drucker, the famous management writer and adviser, summed up his review of the "age of social transformation" in these terms: "If the twentieth century was one of social transformations, the twenty-first century needs to be one of social and political innovations, whose nature cannot be so clear to us now as their necessity."[23]

In 1966, when the first edition of this book was published, Professors Keith Davis and Robert Blomstrom wrote about the "iron law of responsibility." This law, they said, requires that those institutions with wealth and power in a society bear a responsibility to use those assets in ways that are socially beneficial. Thirty years later, looking ahead to the new century and new millennium in which today's students will develop their careers

[23]Peter F. Drucker, "The Age of Social Transformation," *Atlantic Monthly,* Nov. 1994, p. 80.

communities. They are racially mixed and culturally diverse, and this diversity helps demonstrate the principle that people have different abilities and strengths that don't depend on race, gender, or economic background.

As project teams tackle more complicated problems, everyone has an opportunity to bring their best talents to bear on solving the problem. As one City Year participant said, "My team mates were awesome. . . . Every one of them had something special to give to others and to our team."

City Year has caught the attention of national leaders. In 1992, during the Bush administration, City Year was selected to be a National Demonstration Project and received its first federal grant. In 1991, presidential candidate Bill Clinton visited City Year, met corps members, and was so impressed that he began referring to it as a model for national service. All City Year sites became part of the AmeriCorps National Service Program when that program was created. The additional funding allowed the City Year model to be expanded with new projects started in Chicago, Illinois, Columbia, South Carolina, Columbus, Ohio, Providence, Rhode Island, and San Jose, California. Plans are underway to continue expanding City Year to some of the other communities that have requested City Year involvement.

City Year's founders describe the program as an "action tank"—part program, part think tank—for the idea of national voluntary service. Members believe this commitment of young people to service improves communities by creatively tackling problems that matter and by doing it in a way that breaks down discrimination based on race, gender, or economic circumstance. The City Year concept is summed up in the bright red bumper stickers often seen in the communities where the program operates. They read, "City Year: Putting Idealism to Work."

SOURCE: Based on interviews with current and past participants in the City Year program and materials provided by City Year, including *City Year: Putting Idealism to Work*, Boston, MA, 1995.

and live their lives, that law remains a valid principle to guide people, business, and society.

SUMMARY POINTS OF THIS CHAPTER

- The new social contract between business and society will emphasize less of the security that existed in earlier times and more of the necessary individual responsibility to build skills, be prepared for change, and be capable of creating new organizations that are effective in meeting needs and efficient in delivering valued goods or services to others. The twenty-first century is more likely to be a century of small rather than large organizations as long as information, capital, and human intelligence are free to move around the world without barriers.
- Business and society will be challenged by changes in the strategies of companies; shifting ethical climates and public values; a new glob-

alism; an altered balance between the responsibilities of government, the private sector, and the social sector; and ecological imperatives produced by global population growth and rising levels of consumption.

- Immigration occurs for many reasons. New immigrants are attracted to countries that provide opportunity and security. Factors that prompt people to leave their home country include many forms of hardship, repression, or change. Well-educated and talented immigrants can benefit a country by adding to the skill base that business needs. If they are unskilled, however, immigrants may end up competing for unskilled jobs while working for low wages. This may benefit some businesses, but places social costs on taxpayers and the community. In recent years, illegal immigration has become a major problem in the United States.

- Violence contributes to the worsening of many social issues and creates serious problems for business and other institutions. Developing effective teams is more difficult when violence has affected peoples' lives. Relationships that require trust are more difficult to establish when violence has affected other relationships. Violence erodes the foundation of cooperation and trust necessary to build sound organizations.

- The "socioeconomic underclass" refers to that portion of a population that is structurally "locked in" to chronic poverty, poor education and training, and heavy dependence on public welfare assistance. A society suffers when the underclass is large, growing, and when those within it are unable to escape through honest effort, hard work, and adherence to the law.

- Racism reflects a view that some racial (or ethnic) groups are superior to others. Biases about the behavior, attitudes, intelligence, and worth of other people in a society are characteristic of racist thinking. Businesses give direct support to racism when they discriminate against segments of society on racial grounds. They give indirect support by tolerating employees, customers, or others who harbor racist attitudes. Racism is self-defeating for business because it erodes relations with employees, customers and suppliers, and with communities that are often quite diverse.

KEY TERMS AND CONCEPTS USED IN THIS CHAPTER

- High-performance workplace
- Unfunded mandates
- Balanced budget amendment
- Guest workers
- Immigration: "push" and "pull" factors
- Cycle of violence
- Socioeconomic underclass
- Racism
- Stewardship responsibility

DISCUSSION CASE

THINKING ABOUT THE FUTURE

Business leaders are rarely guaranteed their positions. One of the traits that helps them stay in office is to be accurate in charting their company's course through competitive pressures and through macroeconomic, social, and political change. This "vision" of how companies should get ready for the future is built on the foundation of understanding and knowledge.

According to a report by The Conference Board, chief executives in the United States and Europe are generally optimistic about the outlook for their companies as we approach the twenty-first century. More than 350 U.S. chief executives and 170 European business leaders were asked to consider a range of economic and social developments and to assess their significance. Here's how they rated these drivers of change:

- U.S. chief executives reported that several developments would have "very serious" negative consequences for their company's growth and profitability in the future: (1) more governmental regulations, (2) higher taxes, and (3) higher health care costs. European business leaders ranked the "very serious" developments this way: (1) more governmental regulations, and (2) and (3) (a tie) currency instability and rising wage demands. Overall, the European leaders were much less prone to score developments in the "very serious" category than American counterparts.
- When asked to rate a series of specific issues as to their impact on the growth and stability of the national economy, U.S. chief executives differed from their European peers. Among the European business leaders, only one issue—national budget deficits—was ranked by 20 percent or more of the leaders as having a "very serious" effect on the future of their economies. According to U.S. executives, however, no less than five issues were foreseen by at least 20 percent of the respondents as having "very serious" effects on national growth and stability: (1) crime, (2) national budget deficits, (3) inadequately trained workers, (4) drug abuse, and (5) immigration. Interestingly, four of the five categories involve what most people would identify as social issues, not economic issues.

Both U.S. and European chief executive officers are very positive about their countries' prospects for economic growth and development through the remainder of the twentieth century. They also expressed positive views about the effects of trade agreements such as GATT and NAFTA. European executives were very positive about the effects of the European Union (EU), although only a small group of American executives saw the EU as providing benefits to the United States. Both European and American executives expressed concern about potential competitive threats from Japan and emerging Asian/Pacific nations and trade groups.

Discussion Questions

1. Does the data described above add up to a coherent picture of the future? Describe it in your own words.
2. Among the social issues evaluated by these groups, pollution ranked rather low as a "very serious" problem for national economies. Is it possible that pollution costs have largely been internalized into modern economies?
3. Three of four U.S. executives said crime would probably have a negative impact on the nation's economic growth and stability in the remaining years of the 1990s. Discuss possible reasons these executives might have for such a strong view.

Case Studies
in Corporate Social Policy

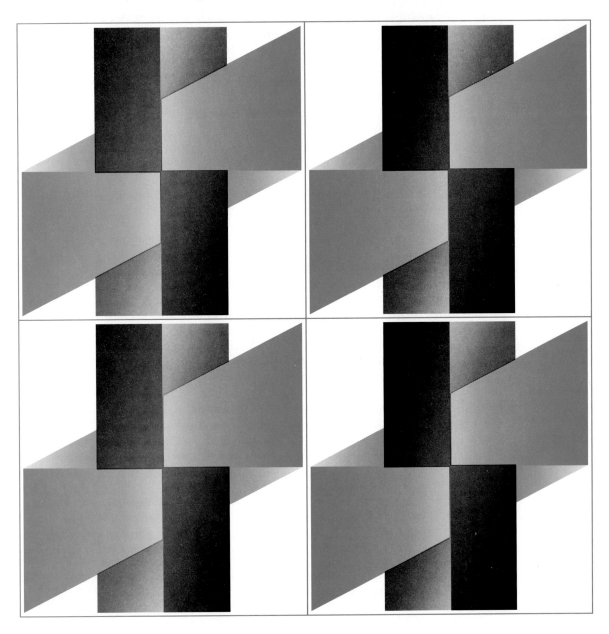

Twice within a four-year period, one or more poisoners placed cyanide in capsules of Extra-Strength Tylenol sold as over-the-counter (o-t-c) medications for pain relief. These tainted capsules killed seven persons in 1982 and one person in 1986. Tylenol's manufacturer, Johnson & Johnson, is a leading health care products firm, and at the time of both poisonings Tylenol was one of the company's major and most successful products.

When these two poisoning episodes occurred, the company faced crises of enormous ethical and financial proportions. With human lives at stake, swift decisions were needed to prevent further deaths. But with millions of dollars also at stake, company officials realized that a false step or a bad judgment could jeopardize not only Tylenol but also the company's financial future and the jobs of its employees. Few management challenges have been so filled with frightening possibilities as the ones that unfolded in Chicago in September 1982 and in New York's Westchester County in February 1986.

When it was all over, most observers praised Johnson & Johnson officials for the way they handled the two crises. Their actions were widely accepted as "the way to do it."

Johnson & Johnson: A Brief History

Johnson & Johnson began operations in 1886 in New Brunswick, New Jersey, and was incorporated in 1887. The company pioneered the concept of an antiseptic surgical dressing, based on the work of Sir Joseph Lister, an English surgeon. Over the years the company grew in size by broadening its array of products for the health care market. BAND-AID, one of its best known and most widely used products, was introduced in 1921.

The company pursued a vigorous strategy of growth by acquisition as well as internal development of new products and businesses. New product lines included baby care, feminine protection, birth control, ethical surgical products, hypodermic needles and syringes, prescription drugs, veterinary drugs, kidney dialysis products, and other health care items.

Simultaneously with product line expansion and diversification, the company began to expand internationally. Johnson & Johnson in 1982

[1]Prepared with the assistance of Vasudevan Ramanujam. Sources include articles in the *Wall Street Journal*, the *New York Times*, *Advertising Age*, *Chemical Week*, *Business Week*, *Newsweek*, *Fortune*, and *Chemical Marketing Reporter* during October and November 1982 and several months in 1986. These sources are cited in the case narrative only when used for verifying specific figures or quotations, company information, and similar items. Two Johnson & Johnson publications were used: "Brief History of Johnson & Johnson" and "The Tylenol Comeback," both available from the company.

was a worldwide group of 150 companies, based in 50 countries, whose products were sold in 149 nations.

In 1959, the company acquired McNeil Laboratories, a producer of prescription pharmaceuticals. In keeping with the spirit of decentralization generally prevalent in the company, McNeil was operated as an autonomous division. McNeil was the manufacturer of the Tylenol line of o-t-c analgesics.

The parent company was known as a maker of quality products serving the needs of society. Its commitment to quality products and its strong consumer orientation were handed down from the company's early founders. The following legend appears on a large bronze plaque in the company's New Brunswick headquarters:

> We believe our first responsibility is to the doctors, nurses, and patients, to mothers and all others who use our products and services. In meeting their needs, everything we do must be of high quality.

The above quotation was a part of what the company called its "credo" philosophy. In looking back over their own conduct in the face of the Tylenol tragedy, company officials credited this "credo" for guiding their actions and decisions during the 1982 crisis.[2]

The First Tylenol Crisis: 1982

The first five Tylenol-related deaths occurred on Thursday, September 30, 1982, in three Chicago suburbs. That morning Johnson & Johnson learned of three of the deaths from a reporter of the *Chicago Sun-Times,* who, in turn, had heard about them from the Cook County (Illinois) medical examiner's office. Within forty-eight hours, the roster of victims rose to seven, all from the Chicago area.

The company's response

Johnson & Johnson's response to the bad news was swift and direct. Within hours of learning of the Chicago deaths, the company announced a recall of all 93,400 bottles of Extra-Strength Tylenol in the implicated MC2880 lot, which had been manufactured in McNeil's Fort Washington, Pennsylvania, plant and distributed to thirty-one Eastern and Midwestern states. This decision was made quickly, even though tests on samples of the same lot did not reveal any contamination, suggesting that the poisoning may not have occurred in manufacture. By noon that day, the firm had dispatched nearly half a million mailgrams to physicians, hospitals, and wholesalers, alerting them to the danger. A press staff member and several scientific and security people were flown to Chicago by corporate jet to assist in the investigations. A laboratory was set up outside Chicago and

---

[2]"The Tylenol Comeback," New Brunswick, NJ: Johnson & Johnson, p. 4.

staffed with thirty chemists to help the authorities analyze samples of Extra-Strength Tylenol.[3] It placed an additional 500 salespersons from two of its pharmaceutical divisions on call to help recall the Tylenol shipments. By late evening the company also offered a $100,000 reward to anyone who could give information leading to the arrest and conviction of "the person or persons responsible for the murders." All advertising and promotion of Tylenol was suspended. One of the company's two plants that manufactured Tylenol capsules was idled.

The recall was expanded by the following day to include one more batch of 171,000 bottles that had been manufactured in Round Rock, Texas, since the death of the latest victim was traced to a capsule from that batch. However, the worst was yet to come. An apparently unrelated case of strychnine-contaminated Tylenol that almost killed a man in Oroville, California, prompted the company to extend the recall to *all* Tylenol capsules, both regular and extra-strength. Production of the capsules was temporarily halted. On October 5, 1982, within a week of the first of the Tylenol deaths, the company was beginning to pull back the product and was considering destroying the entire stock. Some 31 million bottles with an estimated retail value of $100 million were involved. The decision to recall all Tylenol was considered by the company for four days and was no doubt hastened by the California incident. The after-tax impact was expected to be approximately $50 million. On the following morning, cyanide was discovered in Tylenol capsules in the apartment of a Philadelphia student who was thought to have committed suicide some seven months earlier.

The company stated that its first reaction was to protect the public and inform them about rapidly unfolding developments. The recalls seem to have been decided on almost as a matter of course. In fact, according to *Fortune,* James E. Burke, the chairman of Johnson & Johnson, had wanted to announce a total recall of all Extra-Strength Tylenol from the very beginning, but, surprisingly, the FBI and the Food and Drug Administration (FDA) had advised him against premature recall on the grounds that such an action might "cause more public anxiety than it would relieve."[4] Early during the crisis, Burke said, "It's important that we demonstrate that we've taken every single step possible to protect the public, and that there's simply nothing else we can do."[5] At that point, the company said they were not thinking about the future of the brand. Another Johnson &

---

[3]However, local authorities appeared to have been reluctant to release the suspected samples to the company, leading to one of the few skirmishes between the company and the investigators. In another instance, an attorney for McNeil objected when Chicago authorities broadened the recall to include other forms of Tylenol in addition to extra-strength capsules. See the *Wall Street Journal,* Oct. 4, 1982, pp. 3, 16.

[4]"The Fight to Save Tylenol," *Fortune,* Nov. 29, 1982, p. 48.

[5]*Wall Street Journal,* Oct. 4, 1982, p. 16.

Johnson executive declared, "We've been trying to put out the fire. We really haven't thought about how to rebuild the house."

In its effort to protect and inform the public, the company undertook a number of other voluntary steps. A conscious decision was made not to place any warning ads in newspapers but to respond only to press calls. In the first week of the crisis, toll-free lines were established to respond to inquiries concerning the safety of Tylenol. Through November, more than 30,000 phone calls had been handled through this medium. The company made it a policy to respond to every letter from consumers about Tylenol. By late November, some 3,000 responses had been sent.

Rebuilding the Tylenol name

While the above steps were of a firefighting nature, the company soon began to plot a strategy for reestablishing the embattled Tylenol name. A seven-member crisis management team of key Johnson & Johnson and McNeil executives began to meet twice daily to make decisions on rapidly developing events and to coordinate companywide efforts.

At the time of the crisis, Tylenol was the leading o-t-c analgesic, with an estimated 37 percent share of the $1.2-billion-a-year market. From modest beginnings in the mid-seventies, when it held a 10 percent share of a much smaller market, Tylenol was carefully nurtured to its dominant position by shrewd and sometimes hard-hitting marketing techniques. By 1982 Tylenol had far outdistanced its nearest competing brands. Figure 1 gives estimated market share data for those brands.

FIGURE 1

ESTIMATED MARKET SHARES OF THE OVER-THE-COUNTER ANALGESIC INDUSTRY PRIOR TO THE TYLENOL CRISIS

Company	Product	Market Share (%)
Johnson & Johnson (McNeil Consumer Products Company Division)	Tylenol	37
American Home Products	Anacin	13
	Anacin-3	1
Sterling Drug	Bayer Aspirin	11
Bristol-Myers	Excedrin	10
	Bufferin	9
	Datril	1
All others		18

SOURCE: *Chemical Week*, Nov. 3, 1982, p. 30.

Tylenol had been positioned as a safe and effective alternative to aspirin, and the company claimed it to be free of the unpleasant side effects that some aspirin users experienced. For many years it was promoted heavily among doctors and hospitals before a concerted program of advertising and promotion directly aimed at the end user was begun. This change of approach was mainly in response to the heavy advertising and promotion campaigns launched by competitor Bristol-Myers for its own nonaspirin painkiller, Datril. In the marketing battle that ensued, Tylenol emerged the clear winner. Tylenol's spectacular success over the years was attributed to its image as a safe and effective product and to the trust and support it received from the medical community, the retail trade, and, of course, the final consumer. Advertising had clearly played a major role in the process of building up this overwhelming level of trust and support. In 1981, Tylenol alone accounted for an estimated $43 million of advertising expenditures, the largest in the analgesics field.[6]

The critical question facing Johnson & Johnson and McNeil in the days immediately following the crisis was, "To what extent had the Chicago incidents damaged the product's image, and how long would it take to repair that damage, if it was at all possible to do so?" To many experts the brand's prospects appeared very dim, in view of its association with death. But the company remained strongly committed to the Tylenol name. The options of dropping the line or reintroducing it under another name were never seriously considered.

To gauge the shifting public perceptions in the weeks following the crisis, the company commissioned a series of opinion polls. The polls revealed that both the brand and the company were getting a lot of potentially negative publicity, the effects of which could not be estimated with confidence. However, a large proportion of the respondents did not appear to be blaming the company for the poisonings, and as time passed, more and more of the regular users were expressing a willingness to return to the fold. By the fifth week after the tragedy, this figure rose to 59 percent. When asked if they would buy Tylenol in a tamper-resistant package, as many as 77 percent of regular Tylenol users answered positively.[7]

In the wake of the crisis, sales of Tylenol fell sharply, by as much as 80 percent, according to some estimates. At the same time, sales of aspirin and other competing brands of nonaspirin pain relievers were beginning to surge. In the face of such adverse circumstances, the company mounted a carefully planned campaign of communication and packaging modifications in an effort to win back the public trust it was losing. It began by sending some 2 million pieces of literature to doctors, dentists, nurses, and pharmacists, the groups that had most contributed to making Tylenol the success it was. The fact that the company had not been the source of the poisonings was strongly emphasized in the communications.

[6]*Chemical Week,* Nov. 3, 1982, p. 33.
[7]See *Advertising Age,* Nov. 15, 1982, p. 78, and Oct. 11, 1982, p. 78.

Throughout the crisis, employees of the company had shown a strong sense of commitment and high morale. Hundreds of them volunteered to work around the clock without extra pay, and many were staffing the phone lines to answer as many calls as possible. To help maintain that morale, the company also undertook an internal communications program. This included writing letters to all employees and retirees, keeping them updated on important information and thanking them for their continued support and assistance. Four videotaped special reports were prepared and distributed or shown to employees.

Before the crisis, the company had generally been known for its low-key profile and tight-lipped approach to dealing with press and public inquiries. The crisis changed that policy. The press became a close ally of the company, especially in the first frenzied days, providing the company with its most accurate information on various developments. The company praised the efforts of the broadcast community, which had been instrumental in getting Tylenol commercials off the air in a matter of hours after news of the first deaths.[8] In a reversal of the company's traditional policy, company executives made several appearances on television, including *60 Minutes, The Phil Donahue Show, ABC Nightline, Live at Five,* and others. Interviews were freely granted to business journals and periodicals, such as *Fortune* and the *Wall Street Journal.* In short, every effort was made to "get the word out," to use the company's own phrase.

The press praised Johnson & Johnson's quick action, citing it as an example of corporate responsibility. The *Wall Street Journal* declared:

> Johnson & Johnson, the parent company that makes Tylenol, set the pattern of industry response. Without being asked, it quickly withdrew Extra-Strength TYLENOL from the market at a very considerable expense . . . the company chose to take a large loss rather than expose anyone to further risk. The anticorporation movement may have trouble squaring that with the devil theories it purveys.

The *Washington Post* equally admired the company's actions in the face of adversity:

> Johnson & Johnson has efficiently demonstrated how a major business ought to handle a disaster. From the day the deaths were linked to the poisoned TYLENOL . . . Johnson & Johnson has succeeded in portraying itself to the public as a company willing to do what's right regardless of cost.[9]

While Tylenol advertising still remained off the air, Johnson & Johnson beamed a series of trust-building messages to the American public during October and early November. These sixty-second messages featured Dr. Thomas Gates, medical director of McNeil, who assured consumers that the company would do everything possible to maintain the

---

[8]*Advertising Age,* Oct. 11, 1982, p. 78.
[9]Both press passages are quoted in Johnson & Johnson, "The Tylenol Comeback," p. 8.

trust and support of the public, and it also alerted them to the fact that the company planned to reintroduce Tylenol capsules in new tamper-resistant packaging.

The company hastened to be the first in the market with improved tamper-resistant packaging for its Tylenol products, even though new regulations on the packaging of o-t-c products were still being debated by the FDA and the Proprietary Association, the trade association of the o-t-c products industry. On November 11, 1982, a new safety package, with three separate safety seals, was demonstrated at a video conference, broadcast via satellite, and simultaneously aimed at thirty cities and attended by some 1,000 reporters and news media representatives. In that conference the chairman of Johnson & Johnson reaffirmed his company's continuing commitment to the Tylenol name, referring to the commitment as a "moral imperative."

The company's polls had revealed that 35 percent of Tylenol users had thrown away their supplies of the product when news of the crisis broke. To make good their loss and to help overcome their reluctance to use the product again, the company placed special coupons in newspapers nationally that could be exchanged for a free bottle of any Tylenol product. A toll-free number also was established for this purpose. Consumers could call and a coupon would be sent in the mail for a free bottle of Tylenol.

The company was fully aware that while a beginning had been made, restoring Tylenol's market share to its precrisis level of 37 percent was still a formidable task. In one interview, the chairman of McNeil stated that he expected Tylenol's share for the next reporting period to be in the 5 to 10 percent range.[10] In that interview, it also was revealed that in a four-city survey where Tylenol had a 27 percent market share before the tragedy, grocery scanning data showed that the brand's share fell to 6.5 percent the week after the poisonings but had rebounded to 18 percent. By the end of 1982, Tylenol had regained first place among analgesics, with 29 percent market share.

The cost impact

In addition to the toll of human lives, the Tylenol tragedy had a profound cost impact on the company in the short term. Just prior to the crisis, Johnson & Johnson's stock had been trading on the market at $46.125. Immediately following the crisis, it fell by as many as 7 points before eventually stabilizing in the mid-40s.

The costs directly associated with the recall of the capsules translated into a $50 million write-off against the company's third-quarter profits. In percentage terms, this represented a 26 percent drop in net income. Fourth-quarter domestic income declined by more than $25 million compared with the same period in 1981, and industry observers believed the drop was due to the Tylenol incident.

[10]*Advertising Age,* Nov. 15, 1982, p. 78.

The company decided to absorb the costs of the improved packaging, estimated to be 2.4 cents a bottle. Since price increases were ruled out as a matter of company policy and may not have been practical anyway, these costs would continue indefinitely. The costs of the coupon campaign were estimated between $20 million and $40 million. The dealer discount program also added to the overall costs. Johnson & Johnson estimated that the cost of all these actions could run as high as $140 million.

The company also was faced with three lawsuits shortly after the deaths in Chicago. However, some observers believed that since it appeared that the company was not responsible for the poisonings and could not reasonably have foreseen them, no damages could be won in court.[11]

Other intangible costs to the company were difficult to estimate. For many weeks the Tylenol crisis occupied the key executives of the company on a full-time basis. The day-to-day operations of the other divisions of the company were left to others. What effect this had on their performance, if any, remains uncertain.

Government regulatory responses

The first actions of a regulatory nature were taken by local and state officials, who issued warnings and orders of their own. Stores began to remove stocks of Tylenol in response to these warnings. At first the FDA issued a warning related only to the first implicated lot, but as news of more deaths followed, implicating other lots, the warnings were extended to Tylenol capsules in general. The FDA also sent its inspectors to McNeil's Fort Washington, Pennsylvania, plant, to collect samples, review batch records, and to investigate manufacturing processes. The agency's nineteen laboratories began collecting and testing some 40,000 Tylenol samples. It was expected at that time that some 2,100 FDA employees would assist in the testing. Over the weeks that followed, some 8 million capsules were analyzed, of which 75 were found to contain cyanide. The major question for the agency was to determine quickly if the cyanide had been introduced into the capsules during the manufacturing process, at a later point in the distribution chain, or at retail stores.

Chicago's mayor went on the air to urge citizens not to take any Tylenol. The sale of Tylenol was banned in the state of North Dakota, and Colorado ordered stores to withdraw all Tylenol capsules, while Massachusetts retailers were directed to remove all Tylenol products. Warnings also were issued by health officials in New York. Similar actions were taken in foreign countries as well.[12]

Soon initiatives for regulating safety packaging of all o-t-c products were taken. On October 4, the Cook County Board voted unanimously to re-

[11]*New York Times*, Oct. 7, 1982, p. B12; and *Chemical Week*, Oct. 13, 1982, p. 17.
[12]*New York Times*, Oct. 2, 1982, p. 21, and Oct. 6, 1982, p. A24.

quire all o-t-c drugs and medicines to carry manufacturers' seals. The ordinance was to take effect in ninety days, and required a seal of plastic, paper, metal, or cellophane, which restricts air into the product, and when broken, would be evident to an observer or consumer. Mayor Byrne also proposed an ordinance to the City Council that would, after hearings, require protective sealings on all o-t-c products.

There was some concern that piecemeal local and state regulations would proliferate. The federal government was irked by the precipitate actions of local authorities in Chicago, which some believed had been politically motivated because county legislators were facing reelection soon. The FDA was ordered to enact an emergency packaging code that would require manufacturers to introduce interim bottle seals within ninety days. Industry and government officials had announced earlier that they would work together to develop federal regulations requiring tamper-resistant packaging for all drugs sold without a prescription. It was anticipated that such regulation would take time to draft and implement, since no single, simple solution would be uniformly applicable to all products. Also, the industry association believed that individual companies should have sufficient flexibility in choosing packaging methods or options. A later meeting of industry representatives concluded that tamper-resistant packaging was feasible for drug items. As a first step, a tamper-resistant package was defined as "one that can reasonably be expected to provide visible evidence to consumers if the package is tampered with or opened."[13]

While the industry association and the FDA both appeared to favor some form of packaging regulation, one economist expressed doubts about the costs and benefits of such regulation. In an article in the *New York Times,* he argued that the costs of such regulation would far exceed the benefits, and the consumer would pay more for drugs.[14] Some expressed more pragmatic concerns, namely, that seals and other elaborate protective measures might render the package harder to open by arthritics, who were among the major users of pain relievers.

Competitor and industry responses

Competitive reactions varied. Many competitors attested that they had no intentions of exploiting the company's misfortunes. However, the actions of some told a different story. Major retail chains such as Walgreen in Chicago were approached by the representatives of Johnson & Johnson's competitors with offers to fill the shelf space vacated by Tylenol.[15] American Home Products, maker of Anacin, Anacin-3, and Arthritis Pain Formula, and normally low-key and press-shy, called a rare press conference

---

[13]*Chemical Week,* Oct. 13, 1982, p. 16; *New York Times,* Oct. 6, 1982, p. A1; *Wall Street Journal,* Oct. 8, 1982, p. 17.

[14]Paul W. MacAvoy, "F.D.A. Regulation—At What Price?" *New York Times,* Nov. 21, 1982, p. F3.

[15]*Wall Street Journal,* Oct. 5, 1982, p. 22; and *Chemical Week,* Nov. 3, 1982, p. 30.

to announce plans for increased production of its nonaspirin pain relievers. The company also announced plans for newer formulations of its Anacin-3 brand.[16] Although American Home Products declined to disclose whether it planned to step up advertising support for its products, one report alleged that the company was trying to pick up the air time released by Tylenol. The company responded with a statement that it was not AHP's policy to capitalize on the misfortunes of its competitors.[17]

At Bristol-Myers, whose Datril had suffered badly when Johnson & Johnson battled it head-on with heavy advertising of Tylenol, company officials would not discuss any plans. It acknowledged a surge in demand for Datril and stated that the company was looking into new packaging for all its analgesic products. The company ran coupons for Bufferin and Excedrin in a number of national newspapers during the first week of the Tylenol crisis. What made these advertisements unusual was their placement on late-news pages, not in the usual food-shopping sections. A company representative claimed that the company was simply doing "business as usual."[18] Seemingly opportunistic moves also were made by Richardson-Vicks, which ran consumer ads for the first time for its newly acquired Percogesic brand.

The search for the killer

Finding the Tylenol poisoner was not easy. One suspect was convicted and given a ten-year jail term for trying to extort $1 million from Johnson & Johnson after the poisonings took place; his wife had formerly worked for Tylenol's maker. Another person who had been employed in a store where some of the poisoned capsules were found was imprisoned for the 1983 slaying of a man he believed had identified him to the police as a Tylenol suspect. Authorities were not convinced that either of these suspects was the actual Tylenol killer. A police official said, "This is an unusually tough case. There's little physical evidence. The victims and the tainted bottles show no pattern. And the motive is unclear. It's enormously frustrating."[19]

The Second Tylenol Crisis: 1986

By early 1986, Tylenol was once again the premier over-the-counter (o-t-c) pain reliever, with a 35 percent share of the annual $1.5-billion market. It was Johnson & Johnson's most profitable single brand, bringing in $525 million in revenues. Extra-Strength Tylenol, the type that had been in-

[16]*Advertising Age,* Oct. 18, 1982, p. 82.
[17]*Advertising Age,* Oct. 11, 1982, p. 78; *Chemical Week,* Nov. 3, 1982, p. 30; and *Fortune,* Nov. 29, 1982, p. 49.
[18]*Advertising Age,* Oct. 11, 1982, p. 78.
[19]*New York Times,* Feb. 21, 1986, p. A11.

volved in the Chicago killings, accounted for about one-third of those revenues. Overall, the company's recovery had been remarkable.

The poisoning and early management response

On the evening of February 8, 1986, a 23-year-old woman living in Yonkers, New York, took two Extra-Strength Tylenol capsules from a brand-new package and went to bed. When she did not appear for breakfast and lunch the next day, relatives went to her room and found her dead. The cause of death was cyanide poisoning. Investigating police found three other cyanide-tainted Tylenol capsules in the same bottle. The bottle had been purchased at a nearby A&P grocery store.

The first public reaction was, How could this have happened again, since all Tylenol containers had been triple-sealed after the Chicago experience? The mystery only deepened when it was learned that the Yonkers bottle had indeed been triple-sealed in the approved manner. The finding led to an early theory that the poison had been put in the capsules during the manufacturing process, but this theory apparently would not hold up under more careful investigation that was to come later.

When the cause of death was announced on February 10, Johnson & Johnson's chairman, James Burke, who had guided the company through the 1982 crisis, ordered continuous monitoring of consumer sentiment about Tylenol products. He also cancelled all Tylenol capsule advertising after seeing an ad for the capsules on the same newscast that announced the cause of the victim's death. Although shocked by the reappearance of poison, this time in the safety-sealed packages, company officials tended to believe that it was an isolated incident.

Then came the real shocker. On February 13, Frank Young, head of the FDA, whose staff had been examining Tylenol that was pulled from stores in the Yonkers area, told Burke that a second container of cyanide-laced Extra-Strength Tylenol had been found in a Woolworth's store only two blocks from the A&P store where the first bottle had been bought. Burke replied, "Frank, that is the worst news you could give us."[20] The poisoned capsules in the second container showed evidence of tampering—the logo printed on the capsule halves was misaligned—but the outer and inner seals appeared to be intact. Again, it seemed that the cyanide must have been introduced during manufacture before the safety seals were secured.

To make things even more complicated, investigators discovered that the two containers were produced in different locations at different times. After the safety seals were affixed, the two bottles had been stored at the same storage facility but at different times. Within a day, the FDA revealed that the cyanide in both of the contaminated bottles appeared to have come from the same source, but it did not match the cyanide found in Tylenol capsules during the 1982 crisis.

[20]*Newsweek,* Mar. 3, 1986, p. 52.

The recall

Spreading public alarm caused the FDA to warn consumers not to use Tylenol capsules for the time being, and ten states banned their sale. Inside Johnson & Johnson, officials were reading the results of polls showing that customer loyalty was beginning to fade as the "single local incident" theory looked less plausible. Other market research revealed that 36 percent of the public believed the tampering came from inside the company, which was a contrast with the 1982 episode when the vast majority concluded that an outsider had been to blame.

Burke created a six-member crisis management team. It included the two top managers from Johnson & Johnson and from McNeil Consumer Products Company (the maker of Tylenol) plus Johnson & Johnson's general counsel and its vice president for public relations. The team was advised by the public relations firm of Burson Marsteller.

The day following the FDA chief's phone call to Burke, the crisis management team decided to suspend production of Tylenol capsules. Saying that "[t]his is an act of terrorism, pure and simple," Burke offered a $100,000 reward for information leading to the arrest and conviction of the poisoner. The company also announced that it would give a refund or a new bottle of Tylenol tablets or caplets to customers wishing to exchange their Tylenol capsules. More than 200,000 people responded to the offer. Simultaneously, Johnson & Johnson's stock price fell $4 per share to $47.75.

With capsule advertising and production suspended and public confidence waning, a spirited debate broke out among top company officials about next steps to take. Burke himself told reporters later that some of the meetings were punctuated with "yelling and screaming." Managers from McNeil Consumer Products Company, the maker of Tylenol, argued that the company should try to ride out the storm since only two tainted bottles had been found and since surveys showed that 52 percent of capsule users wanted the company to keep producing them. They also feared the financial impact on the McNeil division if more drastic action were taken. However, Burke concluded that "there is no tamperproof package [and there] is never going to be a tamperproof package." If a third poisoned package were to turn up, "Not only do we risk Tylenol, we risk Johnson & Johnson."[21]

Eight days after the Yonkers death, on February 16, the company decided to recall all Tylenol capsule products and to abandon the use of capsules entirely for all its o-t-c products. The decision was announced to the public the next day. These actions would cost the company an estimated $150 million in 1986.

The case took another puzzling turn in late February when the FBI reversed an earlier opinion that the tampering probably occurred in the manufacturing process. An FBI official said, "Previously undetected signs

---

[21]Ibid.

of tampering have now been discovered using sophisticated scientific examinations. Our examinations have further determined it was possible to invade the bottles after packaging was complete without detection through conventional means of examination." This finding applied to both bottles containing the poisoned capsules.[22]

Tylenol's recovery

"To date [mid-1986], our recovery looks very strong," said McNeil's vice president of marketing. Just five months after the second tampering, Tylenol had recovered 90 percent of its previous market share. In fact, discontinuing the capsule form apparently had not damaged the company as much as some had feared. Immediately after the poisoning death, Tylenol sales dropped by $128 million, but $48 million of these sales had been regained by late April. One reason for the quick recovery was the availability of caplets as an alternative to capsules. Johnson & Johnson's caplets had been on the market since 1984 and already accounted for nearly one-fourth of all Tylenol sales. When the capsules were recalled, McNeil's plants went on a crash program to increase production of caplets, spending $20 million for new equipment. In the switchover from capsules to caplets, which caused the encapsulating machinery to be idled, no McNeil employees were furloughed.

Doctors and hospitals continued to recommend Tylenol to their patients, and McNeil's sales force managed to convince 97 percent of their top accounts to maintain shelf space for Tylenol products. One year after the Yonkers poisoning, Johnson & Johnson claimed it was once again the leading seller of o-t-c analgesics.[23]

Copycat tampering

A major reason why public authorities are wary of nationwide recalls of suspect drugs is the fear of encouraging further tampering and creating consumer panic. It did not take long for "copycat" episodes to emerge.

A Nashville, Tennessee, man was found dead on February 23 of a massive dose of cyanide. A bottle of Extra-Strength Tylenol containing one capsule was found under his bed. Investigators said the bottle and capsule revealed traces of cyanide, but they were unwilling to say that his death was caused by taking poisoned Tylenol.

One of the most bizarre episodes occurred in March when Smithkline Beckman Corporation withdrew Contac, Teldrin, and Dietac capsules from the market after rat poison was found in some of these products. Police then arrested a former stock brokerage clerk who allegedly hoped that the poisoning threat would force down the price of Smithkline stock,

---

[22]*New York Times*, Feb. 27, 1986, p. 20.
[23]"Tylenol Begins Making a 'Solid Recovery,'" New Brunswick, NJ: Johnson & Johnson, 1986; and *New York Times*, Feb. 8, 1987, p. 35.

thus enabling him to make a profit by trading in stock options. He was convicted and jailed in October.

Other copycats followed. In May, the Walgreen drugstore chain removed all Anacin-3 capsules from its shelves, following the death of an Austin, Texas, man whose body contained cyanide. An opened bottle of Anacin-3 that had been bought at Walgreen's Austin store showed signs of tampering. Bristol-Myers ordered a nationwide recall of Excedrin capsules after two deaths in the Seattle area were linked to the cyanide-tainted painkiller. Like Johnson & Johnson, Bristol-Myers was expected to replace capsules with caplets at an estimated cost of $10 million.

The tampering was not limited to drugs. IC Industries' Accent flavor enhancer had to be removed from Texas stores after someone claimed that he had placed cyanide in six cans. A similar call forced General Foods to clear the shelves of sugar-free Jello in four supermarket chains in four states.

Nor was tampering confined to the United States. In Japan eight people had died in 1985 after drinking juice that had been mixed with weedkiller, and boxes of chocolate had to be recalled after being dusted with cyanide. The previous year, animal-rights activists in Britain who were opposed to using animals for tooth-decay research forced a recall of Mars candy bars after claiming some were poisoned.[24]

Gerber Foods dug in its heels and refused to recall baby food after receiving a rash of reports that glass shards were found in over 200 bottles in at least thirty states. In fact, Gerber sued the state of Maryland for ordering retailers in that state to withdraw Gerber's strained peaches from sale. As with Johnson & Johnson, it was Gerber's second contamination crisis; in 1984 it had voluntarily recalled over a half million bottles of juice at a considerable financial loss. Believing the company was being victimized by fraudulent claims of contamination, Gerber's CEO said, "When we tried to quiet the press with an unjustified recall [in 1984], it didn't work. So why should we do it again? It's our decision not to keep this media event going. We have found no reason to suspect our product. I suppose we could get on television and make that statement every day. But generally, the sensational gets covered, and the unsensational does not."[25]

The industry response

Where capsules were concerned, sentiment throughout the o-t-c analgesic industry tended to favor Gerber's hard-nosed stand rather than Johnson & Johnson's more cautious approach of banning capsules. American Home Products, maker of Anacin-3, decided to stick with capsules. So did Smithkline Beckman, whose Contac cold capsules had been contaminated with rat poison. Smithkline's consumer products division president said,

[24]*Fortune,* Mar. 31, 1986, p. 62.
[25]*Business Week,* Mar. 17, 1986, p. 50.

"We looked for a way to improve the relative safety of the capsule and found one; the others decided they couldn't. One of us could be wrong, or we could both be right. It will be interesting to watch. We take our responsibility for public safety very seriously." However, the company also offered Contac customers a choice of caplets or capsules.[26]

Both the FDA and the Proprietary Association, a trade association for non-prescription drug makers, opposed a general ban on capsules. The FDA's chief officer said, "If we banned capsules the problem of tampering wouldn't go away. It would probably occur in other product forms which are just as vulnerable."[27] Some consumerists disagreed, citing the spate of capsule contamination cases already on the record as evidence of the need for even greater caution. They wondered if the FDA, as one of the federal government's main consumer protection agencies, might be working too closely with an industry that it was supposed to be regulating in the public interest.

The issue arose again in early 1991 when two people died and another became gravely ill after taking cyanide-contaminated capsules of Sudafed 12-Hour Capsules, manufactured by Burroughs-Wellcome. The triple-sealed packages had been opened, and cyanide had been placed in some of the capsules. A Burroughs-Wellcome official said, "Nobody would put their hand on their heart and say that any package was tamper-proof." The CEO of a consumer consulting firm added, "This proves once more that no consumer product is tamper-resistant. The over-the-counter health products makers have done more than any other consumer category to make tamper-resistant packages, and yet it is their products that people bent on poisoning take on as a challenge."[28]

One defensive tactic favored by the Proprietary Association was to offer rewards for information about tamperers. More than $1 million was set aside for this purpose, and it paid a $200,000 reward to a stockbroker who reported the trading activities of the clerk who had put rat poison in Contac capsules.

Federal antitampering laws were strengthened after the 1982 Tylenol episode; tampering with food, drugs, or cosmetics can lead to a maximum penalty of life imprisonment and a $250,000 fine, and a hoax can land a person in jail for five years. However, of more than 100 tampering investigations undertaken by the FBI from 1984 to early 1986, only four convictions were obtained; sentences were relatively light, ranging from five years' probation to five years in jail.[29]

In May 1991, Tylenol's manufacturer reached a confidential out-of-court settlement with the families of the 1982 victims. Some observers speculated that the company feared more bad publicity and additional

---

[26] *Wall Street Journal,* July 31, 1986, p. 23.
[27] *Wall Street Journal,* May 30, 1986, p. 2.
[28] *Wall Street Journal,* Mar. 5, 1991, p. B1.
[29] *Fortune,* Mar. 31, 1986, p. 62.

copycat poisonings if the case had gone to trial. A company official said, "Though there is no way we could have anticipated a criminal tampering with our product or prevented it, we wanted to do something for the families and finally get this tragic event behind us."[30]

Tylenol in the 1990s

On September 30, 1992, the tenth anniversary of the original Tylenol-related deaths passed quietly.[31] A decade after the deaths of seven people, the murders remained unsolved but actions taken in the aftermath of the tragedy affect millions of people each day. First, tamper-resistant packaging has been expanded to use on a wide range of consumer products, including pharmaceuticals. Second, criminal penalties have been established for illegal tampering with consumer products and federal regulations now require protective seals over nonprescription drugs.

Another effect has been the improvement of police intelligence systems to provide surveillance of stores, packages, and retail distribution systems. While still far from "foolproof" police experts say, the public is now much better protected from such product tampering crimes.

In the mid-1990s, Tylenol remains one of America's most popular and trusted brand names.[32] The product commands nearly one-third of the $3 billion brand name analgesic market. No other brand approaches even 50 percent of Tylenol's market share.

A New Threat?

Tylenol's continuing market success was clouded by a new development in 1995. Acetaminophen, the generic drug compound, had been proven to be an enormously effective and safe nonprescription drug. According to McNeil Consumer Products, Tylenol's manufacturer, more than 185 billion acetaminophen tablets have been consumed, roughly one pill per week per U.S. adult for twenty years. But the product's safety has been questioned. Dr. David Whitcomb, a physician at the University of Pittsburgh Medical Center, studied the medical records of nearly 127,000 patients and found 21 who suffered serious liver damage after taking acetaminophen (Tylenol) while fasting or drinking alcohol. The label limit of acetaminophen is 4 grams (eight extra-strength tablets) per day. Dr. Whitcomb discovered that exceeding the limit even a little (5 grams or ten tablets per day) could injure a person's liver. So, if a sick patient isn't eating

---

[30]*Wall Street Journal,* May 14, 1991, p. B5; and *New York Times* News Service, May 14, 1991.
[31]Only a few newspaper stories commemorated the event. See "Tylenol Deaths Change Food, Drug Packaging; In The Decade Since Seven People Died After Taking the Pills, Companies Have Made Coverings Tamper-Resistant," *Orlando Sentinel Tribune,* September 29, 1992, p. 1.
[32]Emily DeNitto, "100 Leaders Monopolize Pain Relievers," *Advertising Age,* September 29, 1993, p. 1ff.

properly, or a person is drinking heavily, excessive use of Tylenol could be dangerous to that person's health.

A second study focused on 716 kidney-dialysis patients and 361 healthy people. Chronic users of acetaminophen had more than double the risk of kidney failure, a finding that McNeil Consumer Products immediately challenged as flawed because it wasn't clear whether the kidney damage occurred before or after the drug use started. Still, the research helped support a lawsuit by an Alexandria, Virginia, man who combined the recommended dose of Tylenol with three or four glasses of wine per day and suffered severe liver damage. A federal court awarded the man $8.8 million; Johnson & Johnson, McNeil's parent company, said it would appeal the verdict.

What can a company do if consumers don't read the product label? Anthony Temple, McNeil's executive director of medical affairs, pointed to the widespread misperception that over-the-counter drugs are risk free. "They're sold over the counter because they're safe enough to be selected and used by consumers according to the label," he explained, not because they are without risk. But if consumers ignore label warnings, should companies be responsible for the unintended effects? At McNeil Consumer Products, that had become a question of importance and concern.[33]

Discussion Questions

1. Do you consider Johnson & Johnson's voluntary recall decisions to be acts of corporate social responsibility? Why or why not?
2. Product tampering has been called "corporate terrorism." What corporate strategies can you recommend for reducing this kind of terrorist attack?
3. Identify the ethical issues involved in product-tampering episodes. To what extent are companies such as Johnson & Johnson obliged to take ethical actions to protect their customers, even if doing so causes financial losses to stockholders or threatens employees' jobs?
4. What is the role for public policy in the area of product tampering? Assess the actions of government authorities—local, state, and federal—in the Tylenol poisonings. Did they act properly and in the public interest?
5. Relations between the news media and business are not always congenial, but they were in both of the Tylenol episodes. What factors produced this good relationship? Do those factors provide a basis for improving media-business relationships in general? Discuss the possibilities.
6. More than ten years have passed since the Tylenol poisonings. Do these episodes have any value to today's managers at Johnson & John-

[33]Marilyn Chase, "Health Journal: Acetaminophen Is Safe—Provided You Follow Instructions," *Wall Street Journal*, Feb. 6, 1995, p. B1.

son? Nearly all of the executives involved in the Tylenol decisions are retired or working elsewhere. What can Johnson & Johnson do, if anything, to teach its new managers about the credo and how it was applied in the Tylenol situations?

7. Dr. Sidney Wolfe, head of Public Citizen Health Group, a public watchdog group that follows health issues closely, has said that Tylenol needs a new label. His suggested warning label reads: "Don't mix Tylenol and alcohol. If you drink regularly, even in moderate amounts, don't take Tylenol. If you take Tylenol, stay away from alcohol." What is your assessment of Dr. Wolfe's suggestion? Would you urge McNeil Consumer Products or Johnson & Johnson to place Dr. Wolfe's warning on its Tylenol label?

It began without public warning at 12:56 A.M., December 3, 1984. As 900,000 people slept in and around the city and slums of Bhopal, India, a cloud of toxic gas consisting of methyl isocyanate (MIC) leaked from a storage tank at a Union Carbide pesticide plant. The evening's brisk winds pushed the cloud, within minutes, through the nearby dwellings, and within an hour agony had engulfed the lives of tens of thousands of Indians. Hundreds died in their beds, most of them children and the elderly weakened by hunger and frailty. Thousands more awoke to a nightmare of near suffocation, blindness, and chaos. They stumbled into the streets, choking, vomiting, sobbing, their eyes burning. Dogs, cows, and buffalos were stricken. Chaos filled the city, as death and panic spread.

By week's end more than 2,500 people were dead. Over 150,000 received medical care in the first week, and twice that many were treated by year's end. It was the world's worst industrial disaster. Lingering effects of the poisonous gas were felt for months after the leak. Many residents suffered shortness of breath, eye irritation, and depression, and continued to flock to hospitals, clinics, and rehabilitation centers. As many as 40,000 were estimated to be permanently injured from inhaling the poisonous fumes; many of these were so weakened as to be incapable of working or earning their livelihood.

Union Carbide Corporation

At the time of the accident, Union Carbide was the nation's third largest chemical producer, after Du Pont and Dow Chemical. The firm earned revenues of over $9 billion in 1982 and in 1983, though its net income fell from $310 million in 1982 to $79 million in 1983, which was its poorest performance in over a decade. One year before the disaster, Union Carbide had assets exceeding $10 billion, 99,506 employees worldwide, and a book value per share of $69.95.

In 1984, its strategic focus shifted away from the big cash generators of basic petrochemicals, which were swamped by global overcapacity, and metals and carbon products, which were hurt by poor conditions in the beleaguered steel industry. The firm announced in October 1984 an increased concentration of investment in three other lines of business—consumer products, industrial gases, and technology services and specialty

[1]Information for this case was drawn from the following sources: the *Wall Street Journal; Business Week; Time; Newsweek;* the *New York Times;* Union Carbide Corporation news releases and annual reports; Paul Shrivastava, *Bhopal: Anatomy of a Crisis,* Cambridge, MA: Ballinger, 1987; and R. Clayton Trotter, Susan G. Day, and Amy E. Love, "Bhopal, India and Union Carbide: The Second Tragedy," *Journal of Business Ethics,* 1989, vol. 8, pp. 439–454.

products—all earmarked as growth areas. Just as this new corporate strategy was unfolding, the Bhopal disaster struck.

Union Carbide's operations in India go back to the beginning of this century, when it began marketing its products there. In 1934, an assembly plant for batteries was opened in Calcutta. By 1983, Union Carbide had fourteen plants in India that manufactured chemicals, pesticides, batteries, and other products. The plant in Bhopal was built in 1969 to formulate a range of pesticides and herbicides derived from a carbaryl base. In 1979, the company commissioned the Bhopal plant to manufacture MIC. At the time of its construction, the plant stood well away from most of Bhopal's population, but in intervening years many poor people had settled near the plant.

Union Carbide was one of a few foreign firms in India in which the parent company was permitted to hold a majority interest. Normally foreign investors are limited to minority ownership of equity in Indian companies, but the Indian government waived this requirement in the case of Union Carbide because of the sophistication of its technology and the company's potential for export. Union Carbide Corporation owned 50.9 percent of the Indian subsidiary (known as Union Carbide India), with the remaining 49.1 percent distributed among Indian shareholders. However, the direct involvement of the parent company in the Bhopal plant was limited, and the operations were supervised and staffed by Indian workers.

The Chemical Industry and Public Safety

Every day in the United States the chemical and petroleum industries produce about 275 million gallons of gasoline, 2.5 million pounds of pesticides and herbicides, and nearly 723,000 tons of dangerous wastes. Many of these hazardous materials, chiefly petrochemicals, are shipped across the country. Yet, in spite of the high potential for disastrous consequences, the safety record of these industries in the United States is exceptionally good. The chemical industry's safety record in the year prior to the Bhopal disaster showed 5.2 reported occupational injuries per 100 workers versus a 7.5 average for all manufacturing.

Although chemical companies insisted that they applied the same standard of safety and environmental protection in foreign facilities as at home, leading chemical industry executives were aware that, when operating in a third world country, they faced many problems in attempting to reach the same standard of safety achieved in the United States. Most experts agreed that chemical companies building plants in the third world rarely were seeking to dodge environmental rules at home. Nevertheless, weaker regulations and enforcement abroad when combined with difficulties in maintaining quality control posed worrisome possibilities for disaster.

Host governments' efforts to respond to the growing need for safety and environmental safeguards had been minimal. The number of environmental control agencies in developing countries had soared from 11 in

1972 to 110 in 1984. However, many of these were small, underfinanced, and only meagerly supported by their governments. In India, for example, the federal environmental department had a staff of about 150 persons, compared with the U.S. Environmental Protection Agency's headquarters staff of 4,400. A study by the International Labor Organization found that labor inspectors in developing countries had little status, poor pay, and huge territories to cover.

These conditions had contributed to disasters prior to the Bhopal tragedy. In Mexico City in November 1984, liquefied-gas tanks exploded in a storage facility. The resulting fire took 452 lives and injured 4,248, and 1,000 people were reported missing. In Cubatao, Brazil, in February 1984, gasoline from a leaky pipeline exploded into a giant fireball that killed at least 500 people. Near San Carlos de la Rapita, Spain, in July 1978, an over-loaded 38-ton tank truck carrying combustible propylene gas skidded around a bend in the road and slammed into a wall. Flames shot 100 feet into the air, engulfed a tourists' campsite, and killed 215 people.

These and other incidents demonstrated the broad potential for danger since few of the developing nations had the elaborate system of safety regulations and inspections found in the United States. Yet workplaces in the third world were fast acquiring many of the same kinds of complex industrial processes present in the United States. An environmentalist commented, "We're thrusting 20th-century technology into countries which aren't yet ready to deal with it. We've gotten away with it so far because there have been only minor tragedies. But the Union Carbide accident has really torn apart the whole cover on this, and things will never be the same again."[2]

Union Carbide's Response

As soon as the wire services carried news of the spreading tragedy in Bhopal, Union Carbide called an immediate halt to worldwide production and shipment of MIC. A company official explained that the firm took this precautionary step to determine if safety processes and devices were fully operational at their plants worldwide. To offset community fears near one of its MIC-producing plants in West Virginia, the company launched a public relations campaign that stressed the plant's excellent safety record and efficient safety equipment and procedures. On the day following the tragedy, Warren M. Anderson, Union Carbide's chairman, flew to India to provide relief and compensation to the victims. On December 6, Union Carbide employees around the world stopped work at noon to join in a moment of silence to show their grief and sorrow for those afflicted in the Bhopal disaster.

According to a Union Carbide fact sheet, the company responded to the

---

[2] *Wall Street Journal,* Dec. 13, 1984, p. 1.

Bhopal accident in three phases: immediate reponses, intermediate responses, and long-term relief efforts.

Immediate relief efforts included Warren Anderson's trip to Bhopal on December 4; sending internationally recognized pulmonary and eye experts to treat survivors; dispatching a five-person medical relief and technical investigation team to Bhopal; offering a $1 million contribution to the Bhopal Relief Fund; contributing (through Union Carbide India) medicine, medical equipment, blankets, and clothing; and treating 6,000 persons at the plant's dispensary immediately after the incident.

Following these initial steps, the corporation focused on "intermediate" needs. These included collecting $120,000 through the firm's Employee Relief Fund; donating $5,000 toward a Bhopal eye center; sending additional donations of food, medicine, and clothing; and offering financial support for community rebuilding projects. However, the Indian subsidiary found its offers—of fully equipped medical care and research centers; facilities for rehabilitation, vocational education, and job training; a mobile medical van; and educational scholarships—rejected or ignored by the state government of Madhya Pradesh where Bhopal was located. It was at this time that Union Carbide Chairman Anderson commented that the company was in a "negotiation mode."

According to Union Carbide the company's long-term relief efforts were aimed at meeting health and welfare needs. U.S. Federal District Court Judge John Keenan, who held temporary legal authority over Bhopal matters, ordered the firm to disburse $5 million of Union Carbide's funds to assist survivors. Union Carbide began working with American investors to establish a prototype factory in Bhopal to manufacture low-cost prefabricated housing, but this project was later abandoned. Union Carbide India proposed to build dwellings for 500 residents, plus a job training center, a school, and a community center. In conjunction with Arizona State University, the U.S. firm developed a project to establish a Bhopal Technical and Vocational Training Center; this effort was not welcomed by the Madhya Pradesh state authorities, who subsequently accused the project's management of fraudulent use of Union Carbide funds.

In addition, a pledge of $10 million was made by Union Carbide to establish a hospital in Bhopal, modeled on U.S. Veterans Administration hospitals that had been initially created to care for war-injured personnel. Some observers believed that this gesture was part of Union Carbide's efforts to establish a stronger negotiation position regarding legal settlements.

Explanations and Causes of the Gas Leak

The safety of the plant's design and operations was the subject of an internal report by Union Carbide (U.S.A.) in May 1982, two and a half years before the accident. Ten major deficiencies were reported. They included a potential for materials to leak from storage tanks, the possibility of dust explosions, problems with safety valves and instruments, and a high rate of personnel turnover at the Bhopal plant.

Union Carbide India responded to this report with an "action plan" to correct the deficiencies. Progress in upgrading the plant was described in three separate reports. The final report, dated June 1984, six months prior to the disastrous leak, said that virtually all the problems at the plant had been corrected. The two remaining deficiencies, however, involved the operation of a safety valve used in the methyl isocyanate manufacturing process and the possibility that the tank storing MIC could be mistakenly overfilled. The report concluded that work on these two deficiencies was almost complete and depended on delivery of a control valve which was expected in July.

Human factors may have played a role. Employee morale was said to be low; some believed there were not enough staff, that training was inadequate, and that managerial experience was insufficient.

Various strategic factors and operating policies and procedures may have contributed to the accident and its aftermath. The Bhopal plant represented less than 3 percent of the parent firm's worldwide profits and thus was not critically important. Union Carbide's top management endorsed a plan in July 1984 to sell the plant because of the declining and increasingly competitive pesticides market. The facility had had eight plant managers in fifteen years, and it lacked contingency plans for dealing with major accidents. Indian insistence, like that in other developing nations, on placing operational control in the hands of host-country nationals may have worked perversely to reduce home-country headquarters control of the plant.

Finally, technological factors may have been involved. Various experts pointed to flaws in plant or equipment design, defective or malfunctioning equipment, the use of contaminated or substandard supplies and raw materials, and reliance on incorrect operating procedures. These failures might have been inadvertent, deliberate, or caused by negligence.[3]

Several investigations were conducted, and accusations surfaced regarding the cause of the accident.

On December 20, 1984, Union Carbide researchers arrived in Bhopal and conducted a three-month-long effort to reconstruct the sequence of events leading to the accident. They began by drilling into the remains of the MIC storage tank. Samples were sealed in 20 small glass vials and carried by courier to a West Virginia Union Carbide laboratory. The team's report was released in March 1985. It concluded that multiple systems failure and lapses, themselves linked to neglect of safety, maintenance, and operating procedures, appeared to have combined to cause the accident.

---

[3]For a discussion of these human, organizational, and technological possibilities, see Paul Shrivastava, *Bhopal: Anatomy of a Crisis,* Cambridge, MA: Ballinger, 1987, pp. 48–57.

The report stated that a safety valve opened as a result of a chemical reaction in the storage tank that contained 90,000 pounds of MIC. The valve remained open for nearly two hours before it resealed. During that period over 50,000 pounds of MIC in vapor and liquid form were discharged through the safety valve.

Other experts thought that the plant's scrubber system was not functioning or that the MIC gas leaked into the air through a loosened valve or ruptured tank without ever reaching the scrubber. The scrubber, a cylinder which washed the MIC with a caustic soda solution and converted it into safer substances, was the main safety device for preventing MIC gas from getting into the atmosphere.

In August 1985, Union Carbide suggested yet another possible cause of the disaster: sabotage. The company called attention to a wire service report that a group of Sikh extremists had claimed credit for the disaster. Sikh factions were pitted against the Gandhi government in a bitter political struggle that earlier had included armed repression of the Sikhs and the assassination by Sikhs of Prime Minister Indira Gandhi, whose son, Rajiv Gandhi, succeeded her as prime minister. The company said that it did not necessarily endorse the report, and a Union Carbide representative later said that the company now believed that a large volume of water had been deliberately introduced into the storage tank, perhaps by a disgruntled employee. Previously the company had said the water could have been inadvertently allowed into the tank. But a three-year investigation by Arthur D. Little, Inc., a U.S.-based engineering consulting firm hired by Union Carbide, confirmed Carbide's claim that a disgruntled employee may have tampered with the storage tank, causing a chemical reaction which led to the gas leak.

The Role of the Indian Government

The Indian government, like Union Carbide, was active in responding to the anguish and devastation following the tragedy. In his first official pronouncement regarding the disaster Prime Minister Rajiv Gandhi called the incident "horrifying" and established a $400,000 government emergency relief fund. A year later the Indian government had spent nearly $40 million on food and medical care for the 300,000 victims.[4]

Besides this direct assistance the Indian government took an active legal role. Responding to the earliest reports of the tragedy, police arrested five plant officials on negligence charges and sealed off the factory. More arrests followed. On December 7, 1984, as Chairman Warren Anderson stepped out of the plane at the Bhopal airport, police arrested him on charges of death by negligence, criminal conspiracy, causing air pollution, and killing livestock. Two of the firm's top Indian executives were seized

[4]*Business Week,* Nov. 25, 1985, p. 96.

when they arrived at the airport intending to investigate the disaster. After Anderson posted $2,500 bail, he was ordered to leave the country.

On December 6, the Indian government, on behalf of the Indian people stricken by the tragedy, filed a criminal complaint against Union Carbide's Indian unit over the poisonous gas leak. Pursuant to the complaint, Indian police conducted an investigation to determine whether to prosecute. State authorities closed the plant in December 1984, declaring that it would never be allowed to reopen.

In March 1985, Union Carbide began talks with the Indian government in an attempt to resolve the growing number of liability claims against the firm which totaled over $15 billion in compensation and punitive damages. In an interview published in the *Financial Times of London,* Rajiv Gandhi said his government had rejected as inadequate a settlement offer by Union Carbide. The offer included an immediate payment of $60 million and an additional $180 million over the next thirty years. Three days later the Indian government filed suit against Union Carbide (U.S.A).

Other negotiations also were under way between Union Carbide and lawyers for the Bhopal victims. On March 23, 1986, they agreed to settle the litigation claims, with Union Carbide paying $350 million. When the Indian government heard of this agreement they proclaimed, "It has to be pointed out that there cannot be any settlement without agreement by India."[5] The Indian response further clarified that Union Carbide's proposed settlement was simply inadequate. There was pressure upon the government to push hard with its demands. A group of activists, the Poison Gas Episode Struggle Front, was calling for the nationalization of Union Carbide's Indian factories and for punitive damages equal to the total assets of the parent Union Carbide Corporation.

A critical legal question emerged shortly after the Bhopal tragedy. Should the claims be heard in United States courts, since Union Carbide was a U.S.-based corporation and the majority owner of the plant where the disaster occurred? Or should the claims be settled in Indian courts, since the disaster occurred on India's territory?

The lawyers for the victims and the Indian government favored a trial in U.S. courts, presumably because these courts traditionally delivered larger awards to accident victims and delivered them faster than their Indian counterparts. The landmark decision handed down in May 1986 by U.S. Federal District Judge John F. Keenan, which had significant implications for all U.S.-based multinational corporations, ruled that the claims were to be decided in India, not in the United States.

Judge Keenan stated that to retain the litigation in the United States would be an example of imperialism, where an established sovereign inflicts its rules, its standards, and its values on a developing nation. The In-

---

[5]*Business Week,* Apr. 7, 1986, p. 39.

dian courts, according to Keenan, have the proven capacity to mete out fair and equal justice.

After this court decision was handed down, the Indian government found itself in a weakened negotiating position. As settlement talks dragged on, the government took another bold step. On September 8, 1986, it sued Union Carbide in a Bhopal district court for an unspecified amount of damages arising from the poison gas leak. The suit said the firm failed to provide the required standard of safety at its Bhopal plant. It also blamed the company for highly dangerous and defective plant conditions. Two months later the Indian government disclosed that it would seek at least $3 billion from Union Carbide. Criminal charges of homicide were later filed against former Union Carbide chairman Warren Anderson and eight other Carbide officials.

In 1987, Judge Deo, in an Indian court, ordered Union Carbide to pay $270 million in damages. This decree surprised the business community since, without a trial and presentation of evidence, responsibility for the deaths and injuries attributed to the gas leak had not been established. Carbide won their appeal of this decision and Judge Deo was later dismissed from the case because of bias.

Over four years after the accident, in February 1989, a settlement between Carbide and the Indian government was reached and approved by India's Supreme Court. Carbide agreed to pay $470 million in compensation to the Bhopal victims, with $5 million already having been distributed at the time of the accident. Since the settlement was reached before a trial was held, no blame for the Bhopal gas leak was legally assigned.

Worldwide Ramifications

Following the tragedy in Bhopal, fears spread through the community near Union Carbide's West Virginia plant, producer of MIC and other potentially hazardous chemicals. Three days after the Bhopal tragedy a gas bomb explosion rocked a Union Carbide plant in West Germany. The words "Poison Killer" and "Swine" were sprayed-painted on the plant's walls. A shipment of MIC, bound for France, was barred by the French Environment Ministry. Several European government agencies balked at continuing negotiations with Union Carbide over proposed plant construction plans.

Initially, the Union Carbide employees showed their sympathy and support for the tragedy's victims by contributing $150,000. Two years after the tragedy, a survey of Union Carbide employees in the United States discovered that many did not know how much was collected or what was done with the funds. Few knew, or seemed to care, about the progress of lawsuits or negotiations with the Indian government. They seemed to feel no personal responsibility for the tragedy and believed that the company was a victim of circumstances. "India forced the company not only to build a plant there but also to give control to its local subsidiary. We're bitter. A few incompetent, casual Indians put a black mark on my name," claimed one U.S. Union Carbide employee.[6]

The "black mark" also extended to the chemical industry and to U.S.-based multinationals operating in developing countries. "If I were a corporate manager, I would reexamine my profile of global activities, and in some cases I might pull out some products or processes where the risk is great and the profit marginal," said Ingo Walter, a professor at New York University's Graduate School of Business.[7]

These thoughts were echoed throughout the chemical industry. Ray R. Irani, president of Occidental Petroleum, said that the Bhopal incident meant that corporations must evaluate the reasons for establishing such operations in underdeveloped nations and search their souls as to the benefits to the corporation and to the country. Both Du Pont and Dow Chemical noted difficulties in conducting hazardous operations abroad, and many chemical companies reviewed their safety operations and emergency response procedures, reduced the storage of some toxic chemicals, reevaluated the risks of operating in developing countries, and initiated programs for informing area residents about hazards. Union Carbide announced in March 1985 that it was tripling the number of safety inspections of all its plants.

These changes in corporate operations were a result of various external pressures. The insurance industry sharply reduced coverage for toxic waste sites, while increasing premiums. This placed the chemical industry in a bind since the law required them to buy insurance, but the insurance companies either would not sell it or its cost was prohibitive.

Governments of several third world countries imposed new curbs on chemical firms. For example, in Brazil, the world's fourth-largest user of agricultural chemicals, state authorities immediately restricted use of the deadly methyl isocyanate. The European Economic Community's regulation, developed as a response to a 1976 dioxin accident in Italy, required chemical plant operators to demonstrate that they had adequate safety measures and emergency plans and to inform residents in danger zones of the potential perils of accidents. In Germany new demands were made for stricter controls or even for plant closures.

Thousands of Americans living near chemical plants worried about their safety. The push for chemical right-to-know laws increased. These laws require companies to list and label all toxic or potentially hazardous workplace chemicals, so that employees, transport companies, and public safety officials are informed about actual and potential risks. The city of Akron, Ohio, passed such a law just one week after the Bhopal disaster, and similar measures were considered in hundreds of other communities

[6] *Business Week,* Nov. 25, 1985, p. 45.
[7] *Business Week,* Dec. 24, 1984, p. 27.

and in nineteen state legislatures. Studies to develop federal legislation were begun shortly after the tragedy. "There's definitely heightened awareness," said Sandy Buchanan, director of the Toxic Action Project in Ohio. "Bhopal made it difficult for anyone to argue against people needing to know."[8]

Long-Term Impact on Union Carbide

Bhopal weakened Union Carbide in a number of ways. In the week following the accident, the company's stock dropped to $35 per share from $49, wiping out 27 percent, or almost $1 billion, of its market value. Eighteen months later, Union Carbide announced a massive restructuring plan. The plan involved a wave of plant closings and the dismissal of 4,000 employees, about 15 percent of the company's white-collar workforce.

Analysts were divided on whether the restructuring was primarily due to the massive Bhopal lawsuit claims filed against the company or to an attempted takeover by GAF Corporation. Some observers thought Union Carbide's lowered stock value had increased its attractiveness as a takeover target. In August 1985, GAF increased its stake in Union Carbide to 7.1 percent and rumors of a takeover circulated on Wall Street. In January 1986, GAF formally offered $5 billion for Union Carbide.

Union Carbide suppressed the hostile takeover with a defense that was upheld in the courts. The company's defense included putting on the selling block one of the firm's prime assets, the $2 billon Consumer Products Division, doubling Union Carbide's debt to $4.5 billion, and cutting the company's equity value to one-fourth of what it had been. Though Union Carbide claimed victory in this fight, the company emerged as a shadow of its former self.

Continued Rumblings

The settlement for $470 million was appealed by the new Indian government of Prime Minister V. P. Singh, which was still seeking $3 billion in civil damages and criminal charges against Carbide officials. Some Bhopal victims, wanting additional compensation, continued to target Union Carbide. Protestors at Carbide's annual stockholders meeting in 1989 were arrested for unlawfully distributing a report critical of Union Carbide's performance in Bhopal since the accident. At a protest commemorating the fifth anniversary of the gas leak in Bhopal, 800 people were arrested when they tried to hold a meeting inside the vacant pesticide plant. Carbide spent over $24 million in legal fees, substantially changed its safety precautions at its plants worldwide, and has restructured its worldwide holdings as a result of the accident in Bhopal.

[8]*Business Week,* Feb. 18, 1985, p. 36.

Discussion Questions

1. Assess the corporate social strategy of Union Carbide both before and after the Bhopal accident. Identify the company's strategic goals prior to the accident, and tell how they were changed after the accident. Were these goals appropriate for the company and for its stakeholders?

2. Develop a stakeholder map for Union Carbide, based on the Bhopal incident. Include each stakeholder's major interest, and rank the stakeholders in terms of their relative power. How would such information help Union carbide management in dealing with this crisis?

3. Of the various possible causes of the accident, which one do you believe to have been the most important? What could Union Carbide management have done to reduce or eliminate this causal factor? In your opinion, why did the company not take such action before the accident?

4. Over 2,500 deaths and 300,000 injuries are attributed to the effects of the gas leak. Is the $470 million settlement paid by Union Carbide "fair compensation" to the survivors of the Bhopal accident? If not, what would be a "fair settlement?"

5. What are the main ethical issues of this case? Show how you would use utilitarian reasoning, rights reasoning, and justice reasoning to analyze these ethical issues.

PAT JONES

Pat Jones was an engineer at the Hamilton Company, a manufacturer of power transmission products. Hamilton was a highly respected company, offering a quality product with a reputation for ethical business practices. The company had developed and widely distributed a formal code of ethics and regularly provided ethics training for its employees.

Hamilton's management recently introduced a policy of "participative management." Management believed that decision-making responsibility should rest with those closest to the decision. Participative management was intended to allow the company to respond quickly to changing market conditions. It was a deliberate move toward a decentralized organizational structure.

Hamilton's sales were running 20 percent below last year's level and were expected to continue to decline. Management attributed the slump to poor economic conditions. Hamilton's president had recently sent a memo to the sales and engineering personnel. The memo expressed concern regarding incoming orders, recommending cost cutting measures and alluding to possible layoffs. The president also pointed out market niches that Hamilton managers should pursue more aggressively and indicated that all orders should be reviewed for potential sales of additional accessory products. Most of the accessories offered attractive profit margins.

While working on a recent order, Pat Jones noticed that the order included three oil pumps. Oil pumps were not necessary for the intended application for this order. Oil pumps were normally used on variable speed or inclined drives where the standard splash lubrication system was not adequate. For this application the oil pumps offered no advantage to the customer. The oil pump accessories were sold for $5,000 each and were to be provided on each of three gearboxes.

Pat contacted Kelly Long, the sales agent for the order. Kelly indicated that the oil pumps were included in the order because they were often needed and the customer had insisted on a quick quote. Sales agents typically did not have sufficient information to determine when oil pumps would be required.

Kelly was reluctant to approach the customer to discuss removing the oil pumps from the order. Kelly said, "Look Pat, this customer is very difficult to work with. The purchase order specified oil pumps. Unless it has a

[1]The organizations and individuals portrayed here are fictional. They are based on the author's discussions of common ethical dilemmas with corporate managers.

detrimental effect on the gearbox, let's give the customer what was ordered. Besides, I'd rather put my efforts toward increasing sales than reducing sales." It was Hamilton's policy to have the sales agent handle all communications with the customer.

Pat discussed the matter with two colleagues at Hamilton. One coworker indicated that the oil pumps should be provided as ordered. The other coworker suggested that oil filters should be included with the oil pumps in the order. The oil filters would provide additional value-added to the customer by providing an oil filtration system ordinarily not furnished, although it was not clear that this additional system was essential for the customer's needs.

Discussion Questions

1. Since the Hamilton Company has introduced a "participative style of management," decision-making responsibility rests with Pat Jones. In light of the firm's economic troubles, should Pat approve the order for the oil pumps? What is Pat's responsibility to Hamilton? to the customer? to the sales agent?

2. Is Hamilton's reputation as an ethical business compromised by the sales agent including oil pumps in the order, or by Pat approving the order? What ethical safeguards at Hamilton are being challenged in the case or should be developed by Hamilton to ensure ethical behavior by its employees?

3. The oil pumps provide an additional, although unnecessary, function for the customer. Is it wrong to provide this benefit to the customer? One of Pat's coworkers suggested an additional accessory: oil filters. Should they be added to the order as well?

4. Using the ethical decision-making framework presented in Chapter 5, what is the proper ethical response to the question confronting Pat? Which is a better guide for ethical conduct in this situation: utilitarianism, rights, or justice?

CHRIS BROWN

Lee Samson and Chris Brown had worked for fifteen years as entry-level system programmers for Runner Manufacturing, a leading manufacturer of automotive ride control products. Runner was a large, centralized firm with a traditional, formal hierarchy marked by multiple levels of supervision. Typically, important decisions were made by top management. Respect for authority and being a "team player" were highly valued by the organization's senior management team.

While working at Runner's corporate headquarters, Lee and Chris slowly worked up through the ranks of the large systems department. In the process, they developed a close friendship. As system analysts, Lee and Chris designed, tested, and brought to operational status software that automated payroll, inventory, finance, and operations management.

Eight months earlier, both had been promoted to a supervisory level upon the retirement of their predecessors. Lee became supervisor of the systems group responsible for operations (inventory controls and product plans), while Chris became supervisor of the functional systems group responsible for program maintenance and development for administration and finance areas. While both were pleased with their promotions, they both felt uneasy at giving up hands-on work with software. They also believed that they had reached the upper limit of career growth given the rigid cultural climate at Runner.

It was Lee Samson who broached the topic of going off "on their own." At first, it was simply a little off-duty talk. Eventually, both Lee and Chris recognized they had skills in software programming that could have a real "outside" demand. The idea took shape of starting an information systems storage and consulting service for small and medium-sized firms. They decided to take the plunge and resign from the firm as soon as they had acquired the necessary hardware.

This new venture required Lee and Chris to convert space in Lee's home into an office for their computer. While recently inspecting new file servers (data storage equipment), Chris was surprised to find sophisticated software already loaded onto their personal systems at the new office. Closer scrutiny proved the software was similar to the operations, payroll, and accounting systems currently in use at Runner's corporate headquarters. When questioned, Lee at first tried to hedge but finally admitted to systematically copying Runner's system programs and routines that would be useful in their new business. Copying was a simple matter since the office in Lee's home was connected by a modem to the company's mainframe computer. Lee assured Chris that great care had been taken to avoid copying any actual data, as this would have been theft of company proprietary information and a violation of Runner's code of ethics. Seeing Chris's dismayed look, Lee said, "Look Chris, we've worked our tails off for fifteen years installing, testing and making every one of these systems run. If anyone 'owns' these systems and the right to their use, it's you and me. Runner loses nothing in this, no product or customer data, absolutely nothing."

Discussion Questions

1. From an ethical perspective, who owns the computer software—the developers of the software (Lee and Chris), or the firm that hired the developers (Runner Manufacturing)? What ethical principles support your position?
2. What kinds of ethical problems, discussed in Chapter 4, are involved in this case: face-to-face ethics? corporate policy ethics? functional-area ethics?

3. What action alternatives are available to Chris in this case? Using each of the six stages of moral development and ethical reasoning discussed in Chapter 5, what action do you think Chris will select? What is the "best" action for Chris?

JESSE GREEN

Jesse Green worked in the accounting department for Premier Jewelry, Incorporated. Premier Jewelry had been in existence for over 100 years. The company had a written mission statement that emphasized the value of respecting its employees. The company was highly regarded throughout the industry, operating stores in seventeen states.

Jesse Green had worked with the company for five years and had been quite successful. The company was going through a time of change in the past three years with many departments downsizing and restructuring to cut costs. It was increasingly important for Premier Jewelry to manage expenses so that profit margins were equivalent or better than other similar companies in the jewelry industry. The accounting function for the company recently had been decentralized and Jesse was in charge of the accounting area for a business unit of Premier Jewelry.

Jesse was given a specific personnel target size during an interim reorganization period. Several permanent positions were decided, but it was determined that several positions should be filled with temporary employees until the organization would know definitely its long-term needs for permanent staffing.

Premier Jewelry had stated in its policy manual that it would hire people permanently or let them go after one year. This policy had generally not been in conflict with everyday business practices in the past, as temporary employees were usually able to complete their work in less than a year. Temporary employees were not typically told that they had no chance of permanent employment with the company.

Jesse's department had two temporary employees. Alex, a secretary, had been an employee for just over one year. Leslie, an accounting clerk, had been employed for just under a year. Both contracts had been extended for an additional six months by the controller for Jesse's business and the director of finance for Jesse's division. The controller told Jesse that making a personnel hiring decision was a million dollar decision for every employee. The controller and director were in favor of limiting the number of permanent employees for cost reasons. Jesse was told that managing division expenses was something considered in the annual employee performance review.

Jesse felt that the current situation was in violation of the company's stated policy not to hire temporary employees for extended periods of time. Additionally, Jesse felt the company was being unfair and deceptive to the individuals involved, as they had not been told they had no opportunity for long-term employment.

Jesse worked with two other managers in the financial accounting area. Both had been in similar situations and suggested that if Jesse wanted to continue on a successful career path that the two temporary employees should be hired for an additional six months and Jesse should not worry about it. "Besides," they said, "everybody is doing it."

Discussion Questions

1. Assess the ethical basis for Premier Jewelry's policy regarding the hiring of temporary employees. Is the policy "fair"? Does it respect the employees' "rights"? Does it achieve the "greatest good for the greatest number affected"?
2. Which of the nine ethical climates, discussed in Chapter 5, reflects Premier Jewelry's ethical climate? Is this climate ethically acceptable? If not, how could it be improved?
3. Assume that Jesse finds it "ethically objectionable" to extend Alex and Leslie's contracts for an additional six months. What company ethical safeguards could Jesse use or create to avoid taking this action?

by **Jeanne M. Logsdon**   *University of New Mexico*

Lorraine Ross lived in Los Paseos, a neighborhood in San Jose, California. Her year-old daughter had been born with a heart defect, and she had heard of a high number of other birth defects, miscarriages, and serious illnesses suffered by neighbors living in the area. She wondered, as she read the *San Jose Mercury News* in early 1982, whether she might have discovered a clue to these health problems. The paper reported that hazardous chemicals were contaminating groundwater. A well had been closed six weeks earlier because of high concentrations of a potentially carcinogenic (cancer-causing) chemical, TCA (1,1,1-trichloroethane). The well provided drinking water to 16,500 residents of Los Paseos. The TCA had leaked from an underground chemical storage tank at the Fairchild Semiconductor plant, which was located about half a mile from the well.

Over the next few weeks, four other large high-technology companies announced that they had discovered leaking underground chemical tanks or pipes during the previous two years. These reports triggered public concerns and fears that tap water was dangerous. Since 50 percent of the drinking water in the region comes from deep underground aquifers, chemical contamination was potentially a very serious public health problem. The companies and local public officials were under pressure to ensure that the water was safe and that no more leaks would occur.

High-Tech and Chemical Use

High-technology electronics firms provide many useful consumer and industrial products. Computers, compact disk players, calculators, video equipment, cars, and many other products contain semiconductor chips that process information at phenomenal speed and accuracy. In order to manufacture chips and high-tech products, companies use a wide variety and high quantity of hazardous chemicals. Some of these chemicals are known or suspected carcinogens or cause other serious health problems if stored or used improperly. For example, a widely used solvent, trichloroethylene (TCE), was phased out in the late 1970s because scientific studies found that it caused cancer in laboratory animals. Many firms switched voluntarily to a substitute solvent, TCA. TCA's carcinogenic status was not established, but it was considered to be much less hazardous.

Companies stored large quantities of chemicals in tanks located underground with connecting pipes to their plant facilities. Local fire codes re-

[1]This case study is based upon interviews with key participants and archival research, especially news reports by the *San Jose Mercury News*.

quired that the tanks be placed underground to protect against the danger of fires and explosions. During the 1960s and 1970s, companies complied with existing fire regulations when they installed the standard single-walled steel tanks. No one had foreseen that the tanks and pipes might corrode and leak the contents.

Early Discoveries of Tank Leaks

IBM was the first Silicon Valley electronics firm to discover that its underground storage tanks had leaked TCE and other chemicals into the soil. IBM was conducting a voluntary companywide survey after tank leaks had been found at one of its east coast facilities. When soil contamination was confirmed at the South San Jose plant in April 1980, IBM notified the regional office of the state agency responsible for regulating surface water quality. This agency had no formal jurisdiction over underground water or chemical tanks—no regulatory agency did at that time. But the agency had the closest connection to underground water quality, and it assumed an oversight role.

IBM recommended that it install monitoring wells to investigate whether any chemicals had migrated through the soil to reach water levels. After several months of monitoring, tests confirmed that some contamination in parts per billion was occurring at water levels near the surface, but it was not endangering any drinking water supplies that come from deep aquifers. Geological experts thought that the aquifers were protected from contamination by a clay layer that would stop the chemicals. Since there were no dangers to public health, IBM and the agency agreed that no public announcement was necessary. The company removed the leaking tanks, transported contaminated soil to approved hazardous waste sites, and installed more monitoring wells to continue investigating the extent of contamination.

Over the next year, Hewlett Packard, Intel, and Advanced Micro Devices also discovered leaking tanks and voluntarily notified the state agency. Each firm stopped using the tanks immediately, installed monitoring wells to identify the magnitude of contamination, and removed contaminated soil. As with the IBM leaks, no publicity accompanied these voluntary disclosures and cleanup efforts. The agency was satisfied that the companies were handling the leaks responsibly.

Fairchild Semiconductor discovered its tank leak in mid-November 1981. This time, however, the consequences were quite different. The company's environmental consultants conducted studies for several weeks and then informed Fairchild that the chemicals had migrated off-site into the drinking water well for the Los Paseos neighborhood. Fairchild, in turn, informed the water company in early December, and the well was closed immediately. Six weeks later, citizens read about the well closure in the local newspaper. The prevailing geological opinion had proved to be wrong—it had not taken into account the presence of abandoned agricultural wells that connected near-surface waters with deep aquifers. These old wells had punctured the clay layer long ago and became conduits for the chemical contaminants.

Public Fears and Demands

Lorraine Ross began to talk to her neighbors about her suspicions that the drinking water was causing medical problems. When this possible linkage was reported in the media along with the reports about the leaks found at the other large firms, citizens throughout the region became alarmed. Industry leaders shared their concerns. According to one knowledgeable manager, executives were as surprised as the general public at these announcements. Companies had not shared with each other the information about leaks they had discovered in their own tanks. Nor had any government agency told them that other companies were experiencing similar problems with chemical storage tanks. Since most leaks had occurred in tanks installed within the previous five years, each firm had believed that its leak was a fluke and each worked independently and quietly to handle the problem. But now it appeared that the leaking-tank problem might be more pervasive.

The high-tech firms, which had enjoyed a good public image and community support in the past, faced a suspicious and angry public for the first time. Many people were shocked when they learned about the hazardous nature of the chemicals that were routinely used by the industry. Previously, chipmakers were known for the surgical-operating-room cleanliness of their operations, and these new disclosures put them in a new unfavorable light. Since the companies had not disclosed these problems earlier, some citizens accused them of being negligent and irresponsible.

High-tech executives and public officials both were blamed for not protecting the public from contaminated water. Many angry public meetings were held over the next two months to force immediate action to clean up existing sites and prevent any future chemical leaks. Los Paseos residents attended meetings carrying signs that said, "Who's got the leak of the week?" and "Water, water, everywhere, not a drop we'd drink." The regional water quality agency took the lead role for the first task of investigation and cleanup. The second task of preventing future leaks was left to local governmental jurisdictions.

Over the next two years, 136 sites where chemicals had contaminated the soil or groundwater were reported to the agency. About 40 percent of the sites were operated by electronics firms. Firms in other industries, such as chemical processing and distribution, chemical waste recycling, metal plating, printing, and pharmaceuticals, found chemical tank leaks too.

The Model Ordinance Task Force

Santa Clara County, the center of the Silicon Valley, is composed of 15 cities, including San Jose, the locale of the Los Paseos neighborhood. These cities often zealously guard their independence, even when dealing with interdependent regional problems. Several cities aggressively compete with one another for industrial development. Other cities prefer to remain quiet residential areas and sometimes resent the costs of regional growth, including overcrowding, traffic congestion, air pollution, and noise. However, in the spring of 1982 it was widely perceived that prevention of chemical tank leaks was not just each industrial city's problem. Underground aquifers extend under political boundaries. Nor could each city solve the problem individually without incurring costs in lost economic base if less responsible firms sought out cities with weak regulations. In short, local government officials quickly identified the presence of a collective interest in establishing uniform standards throughout the county.

Most electronics firms also perceived a collective interest in addressing the prevention issue quickly. Negative publicity was threatening the relatively good rapport that these companies had developed with local governments and citizens. They needed a way to demonstrate responsiveness to public concerns. The risk of potential future liability for health and environmental damage was another incentive to support prudent prevention standards. In addition, certainly most if not all executives were genuinely concerned about the possible health risks to communities—after all, they and their families also drank the local water—and they supported reasonable prevention rules that would apply equally to all firms. Thus high-tech companies backed the concept of uniform storage tank standards.

The common interests of local government and industry stimulated the formation of a task force to develop a Model Hazardous Materials Storage Permit Ordinance. The goal of the task force was to create a uniform set of requirements and then convince each city council in the Silicon Valley to pass and implement them.

The convening group was the Santa Clara County Fire Chiefs' Association. This somewhat surprising choice for sponsorship of the task force was actually quite logical and even brilliant. The fire chief of the city of Santa Clara had sponsored a very innovative chemical hazards program in 1980 to inventory chemicals for fire safety protection. Palo Alto's fire department had copied Santa Clara's program. Thus some experience with chemicals, but not with storage tank leaks, had developed within two local fire departments. In addition, the fire chiefs' association was perceived as oriented toward public safety but neutral about the economic impacts of tank regulations on firms and cities. It was widely respected by all parties as fair and professional.

The process of collaboration began in spring 1982 when Lt. Charles

Rice of the Sunnyvale Public Safety Department was appointed to head the Model Ordinance Task Force. He was advised to create a uniform ordinance that would satisfy everyone and to do it quickly. Rice recruited participants, eventually numbering one hundred, from both the public and private sectors. He believed that success depended on including as many groups and individuals as possible. While diverse membership would be difficult to manage, it would pay off in the long run with easier passage and implementation of new regulations. All cities in Santa Clara County, the county government, and appropriate state and local public agencies were represented. On the business side, high-technology firms were represented through the Industry Environmental Coordinating Committee (IECC).

The IECC was itself a collaborative group of five trade associations: the Semiconductor Industry Association, Santa Clara County Manufacturing Group, American Electronics Association, Electronics Association of California, and the Peninsula Industry and Business Association. The IECC was formed shortly after public disclosure of the Fairchild leak. Leaders of the Semiconductor Industry Association (SIA) and the Santa Clara County Manufacturing Group championed the formation of IECC in order to coordinate the public policy positions and activities of individual companies and trade associations.

Larry Borgman of Intel was selected to head IECC because he was then serving as chair of the Facilities and Buildings Standards Subcommittee of SIA's environment and health committee. His subcommittee was working on building and fire code recommendations for semiconductor manufacturing plants. Since trade association executives initially viewed the issue as a building or fire code problem, Borgman's experience with codes would be valuable. In addition, he had worked with public officials in many jurisdictions in his Intel assignment as the worldwide manager of facilities engineering and planning. He was widely regarded as not only technically knowledgeable but also politically astute.

Some high-tech companies felt apprehension in turning over responsibility for representing their individual interests to IECC. The firms and associations had not worked together before. In fact, many of the companies were very tough marketplace competitors with one another. In spite of these tensions, Borgman and leaders of the trade associations were effective in convincing individual companies of their collective interest in supporting reasonable tank standards, the necessity of a joint approach, and the competence of the managers who served on IECC. This trust was essential in creating a mechanism for collaborative industry participation.

Borgman quickly realized that the problem could not be solved through changes in building or fire codes. Codes were not automatically binding on cities, and environmental agencies did not recognize these codes as legitimate environmental regulations. Borgman evaluated several initiatives that were being suggested at various governmental levels for dealing with chemical tank standards. He decided that the Model Ordinance Task Force was the most likely to succeed and offered to have industry executives serve as members on all seven subcommittees that Lt. Rice had established.

The government-industry task force worked for three months on the first draft of the model ordinance. Weekly meetings of the central committee were held, with more frequent subcommittee meetings. Very little legal precedent was available for use by the task force. The only existing U.S. environmental regulations for tanks had been developed for fuel storage tanks in Suffolk County, New York, and Dade County, Florida. Many task force members initially believed that their task was to devise legal standards for each separate industry. But IECC representatives stressed that the issue was hazardous materials storage across all types of businesses. The ordinance should not target specific industries but should apply more generally to all chemical tanks. This view was quickly accepted by other task force members, and the subcommittees began their work on topics such as materials to be regulated, tank technology, disclosure issues, insurance requirements and availability, and legal wording.

The leadership role played by Lt. Rice was critical in establishing ground rules and keeping the process open for new participants. Rice made it clear that all information would be known by all participants and there would be "no dealing around people." He perceived his role as facilitator, peacekeeper, diplomat, and in a few instances decision maker. On several occasions when a point could not be resolved by consensus, Rice decided what the draft ordinance would state and indicated to the other side that they could take the issue to the next round of public debate if they felt strongly about their position.

IECC chair Borgman's style also helped the early discussions to be productive and lead quickly to consensus. He identified simple points that were irrefutable. For example, he continually said, "What goes into the tank is supposed to stay in the tank." This position established the principle that no leak, however small or slow-moving, was permissible. So the members did not have to get bogged down in deciding what levels of various chemical leaks might be safe. When enough of these simple points were accepted by the participants, consensus formed fairly easily around specific tank regulations.

The first draft of the ordinance was presented to the public in July 1982. The draft proposal reflected electronics industry support for generally strong and effective regulation. The draft's major provisions included the following requirements:

■ Permits for using any underground chemical storage tank.
■ A monitoring system for existing tanks and replacement of leaking tanks.
■ Secondary containment (such as double-walled construction) and a monitoring system for new tanks.

- An inventory of chemicals used at each site and a comprehensive management plan for handling them.
- Insurance coverage for each firm to pay for cleanup in case of accidental leaks.
- Permit fees, set by each city, to cover regulatory costs.
- Fines for noncompliance up to $500 per day.
- Information that companies were to give to regulatory authorities to comply with the ordinance would be protected from public disclosure, and disclosure of this information would be penalized as a misdemeanor.

The response at the first public meeting was generally favorable. However, criticisms were voiced by several labor leaders and public interest activists. They focused on the lack of public disclosure and the anti-whistle-blower bias in the draft. An industry member of IECC defended the confidentiality provision, saying it would protect trade secrets and ensure security from thefts and terrorist attacks. However, the activists had identified and capitalized on an issue that captured public and media attention.

The Silicon Valley Toxics Coalition

Shortly after this public meeting, the Silicon Valley Toxics Coalition was formed as a focal organization for citizen concern. The coalition sought to become a party to the collaborative process in its call for membership: "Together we can work with the industry to ensure appropriate control of toxic substances. We all live and work in Silicon Valley and ultimately we all have the same survival interests." The Toxics Coalition was a collaboration of established environmental and labor organizations as well as individual citizens. Local attorney and activist Ted Smith became its director. Since Lt. Rice was committed to open participation, Smith and other members of the Toxics Coalition were invited to join in the second round of task force meetings. So now the task force was expanded beyond government and business to include public activists.

The next series of task force meetings was somewhat more discordant at first. Skeptical new public interest participants tested their ability to influence the process. However, an industry member notes that some tension had occurred each time any new participant joined because "it takes time to adjust norm states." On a number of issues, IECC and Toxics Coalition representatives agreed and worked together. The respect that developed among the participants helped to generate consensus on most of the issues, and it was crucial in sustaining the process when differences on other issues could not be resolved. With public concern accelerating throughout the period of task force meetings, participants were highly motivated to search for consensus. When conflicting positions could not be compromised, task force members did not resort to delaying tactics but chose instead to keep to the timetable and address conflicts in the appropriate forums for public debate.

The most controversial issue during this second drafting period involved public disclosure. Toxics Coalition members viewed it as the public's right to know about hazards and pushed for 100 percent disclosure of all chemical quantities. Industry members stressed the paperwork burden of including small quantities, as well as the trade secret problem. Manufacturing processes are an important source of competitive advantage, and knowledge of the exact quantities of particular chemicals used by a firm would reveal this proprietary secret. Task force participants could not reach a consensus about how to deal with this issue. Industry's argument about trade secret confidentiality was persuasive to Lt. Rice, who ultimately decided to retain limits on reporting and no public disclosure in the final draft.

Negotiating the Final Ordinance

The arena in which the final provisions of the model ordinance were to be negotiated was the Intergovernmental Council (IGC), a regional advisory group of city, county, and public agency representatives. Their review of the model ordinance took place from November 1982 to February 1983. IGC's main concern was to settle all major differences so that every city would adopt the model without modification. During this period, a series of public meetings was held to gather input from various constituencies. Members of the task force, now including the Toxics Coalition, attended these meetings to explain and speak in favor of a uniform countywide approach. The often large citizen attendance, in part the result of grassroots organizing by the Toxics Coalition, indicated continuing public concern and support for the ordinance. The meetings also gave opponents an opportunity to raise objections and provided the IGC with an indicator of the opposition's strength.

While favoring the uniform approach and most of the model provisions, the Toxics Coalition and the IECC tried to gain support for some changes in the ordinance. The coalition pushed for full public disclosure, protection of whistle-blowers, and an expanded list of chemicals for reporting. The key issues for IECC were to protect trade secrets against public disclosure and limiting required reports for stored chemicals to quantities over 55 gallons.

During the second round of public meetings, opposition to the ordinance was expressed by three individual high-tech firms, several local chambers of commerce, and one powerful industry, petroleum retailing. National Semiconductor, GTE Sylvania Systems, and Lockheed objected to the ordinance because of its high cost, red tape, and potential for delays that might disrupt important defense work. The major criticism made by the chambers of commerce was the cost and paperwork impact on small firms such as dry cleaners, auto repair shops, and gas stations.

Chevron, Shell Oil, and the petroleum retailers trade association concentrated on getting an exemption for fuel tanks. Petroleum interests had not participated significantly in the collaborative task force effort. While a number of petroleum executives had attended several meetings, they maintained no continuity of participation and did not work actively on the subcommittees. They only belatedly discovered that the ordinance would apply to fuel tanks. So they began their effort to influence the ordinance late in the process but with the use of considerable resources.

Their position was that gasoline was not a major groundwater contamination problem and that gasoline storage was already heavily regulated as a flammable material. Another argument they used was the absence of available technology for double containment of very large gasoline tanks, while promising future availability of stronger single-walled fiberglass tanks that would not leak. Some gas stations were already converting from steel to fiberglass tanks to reduce gasoline leaks caused by corrosion. The fundamental issue was cost. Industry representatives said that double containment would cost $30,000 per tank, raising gasoline prices by 4 to 5 cents a gallon.

The major threat to uniformity was the city of Santa Clara. A large number of high-technology firms are located there, and it already had developed a successful chemical hazards program. However, its program did not deal with underground chemical tank leaks but only with inventory reporting requirements and inspection visits. Other cities were watching carefully for Santa Clara's response. If it did not support the major provisions of the ordinance, prevention of groundwater contamination in the entire region was in jeopardy, and Santa Clara would continue to get a large portion of new electronics facilities. It was feared that the entire task force effort was at stake. Amidst extensive media coverage, the Santa Clara City Council indicated in late January 1983 that it would accept in principle almost all of the major provisions of the ordinance. Supporters claimed this was a major victory and a signal to the IGC that the drive for uniformity was working.

Final hearings before the IGC in early February 1983 provided one last opportunity to voice support and objections. Hundreds of people attended the hearings. By chance, a network television camera crew was in town and came to tape the proceedings, and its presence added to the feeling that this was a momentous event. Larry Borgman and other electronics industry representatives expressed firm support for the Model Ordinance in principle and for almost all of its provisions. They requested one change to exempt small quantities of chemicals from required reports. Ted Smith and Toxics Coalition members also expressed support for the ordinance but asked for three changes: full public disclosure, whistleblower protection, and an expanded list of covered chemicals. High-tech executives opposed these changes. The petroleum industry made a particularly strong showing with representatives flown in from around the country. It pressed for a complete exemption from the ordinance.

The final wording of the Model Ordinance revealed the fine art of compromise. The electronics industry got limited trade secret protection through short-form reporting of competitively significant chemicals stored only in small quantities. More extensive public disclosure of large quantities of competitively neutral chemicals would be revealed in long-form reporting. Labor and public interest activists got full whistle-blower protection and public disclosure with restrictions when trade secrets were declared by a firm. The petroleum industry lost a motion to delete double containment for fuel tanks but did get agreement for an additional three-month study of its proposed substitute regulations. The unanimous vote by the IGC, while only advisory, signaled strong support for uniformity when the ordinance was submitted to each city council.

Passage and Implementation

Acceptance of the Model Ordinance was virtually unanimous by every city council in the county. Three large industrial cities acted almost immediately to incorporate the ordinance into their city regulations. By the end of 1983, the other cities, except for Santa Clara, had acted to pass the complete ordinance or have the county government administer the tank permit program.

The only exception to complete uniformity was taken by the city of Santa Clara. On the recommendation of the fire chief, it modified its existing chemical hazards program to incorporate the model's major provisions for secondary containment and monitoring. However, it did not support public disclosure. The fire chief explained later why he did not recommend the model's disclosure provisions. In 1980, he had received the cooperation of the Chamber of Commerce for the chemical hazards inventory and inspection program with the understanding that the information would remain confidential. He felt obliged to continue to honor that agreement. With this relatively minor exception in Santa Clara, the Model Ordinance quickly became the uniform standard throughout Silicon Valley.

Regarding implementation of the ordinance, some companies began to install monitoring systems and double-walled tanks even before final passage of the new ordinance. By February 1986, nearly 85 percent of the 5,546 covered facilities in the county had applied for permits, and 74 percent had received them. In addition, 22 percent of the single-walled tanks that were used in 1982 had been removed, and 618 double-walled tanks had been installed. By 1986, the major criticism of implementation was that city resource constraints had slowed permit processing and inspections.

The hazardous materials ordinance was never challenged by companies in court. In fact, the ordinance that was developed in Silicon Valley became the basis for California and eventually federal tank regulations. Thus high-tech firms and the Toxics Coalition influenced not only the local regulatory approach but set a precedent that affected many different industries all over the nation. While none of the participants claimed that the ordinance was the ideal solution from their group's perspective, they said after it was all over that the Model Ordinance was the best that could have been devised and passed under the circumstances.

Discussion Questions

1. Develop a stakeholder map for the participants in this episode, identifying both primary and secondary stakeholders, along with the major interests and powers of each stakeholder grouping. How could this kind of map contribute to the development and adoption of a Model Ordinance?

2. Assess the social responsibility of each of the corporations and industries involved. In your opinion, did these companies and industries demonstrate skills in social responsiveness? How would you characterize the corporate social strategies they used?

3. Government-business relations are rarely without tension and controversy, but in this case government officials, business representatives, and community activists seemed to get along remarkably well. What factors were responsible for the successful collaboration they achieved? Can those reasons be extended to other kinds of problems?

CASE STUDY **THE LINCOLN SAVINGS AND LOAN SCANDAL[1]**

Shortly after two o'clock in the morning on November 16, 1989, sixty FBI agents, Federal Deposit Insurance Corporation officers, and other plain-clothes police strode into the pink marble lobby of the opulent Phoenician resort hotel in Scottsdale, Arizona. Moving quickly and coordinating their actions by walkie-talkie, the agents informed the startled night clerks that the resort was being seized by order of the federal government. As proceedings were videotaped for possible later use in court, agents posted severance notices on the doors of some thirty managers and ushered on-duty employees out of the building. Across a walkway, agents quickly secured executive offices, including those of Charles H. Keating, Jr., the head of Lincoln Savings and Loan, majority owner of the Phoenician. By the time dawn broke, the 605-room, 130-acre luxury hotel in the Valley of the Sun, from its 18-hole golf course to its seven swimming pools, was firmly in the hands of the federal government.

The predawn raid on the Phoenician severed the final connection between Charles H. Keating, Jr., and Lincoln Savings and Loan, which seven months earlier had been put in receivership by the government. Of the 600 or so S&Ls seized by government regulators at that time in the growing savings and loan crisis, Lincoln was by far the most expensive. The *New York Times* called the Lincoln case a "microcosm—in the extreme to be sure—of the failure of hundreds of other thrift institutions," and an illustration of the forces that contributed to a financial scandal whose eventual cost to taxpayers could exceed $350 billion.

Some read into the Lincoln case a story of political influence and corruption in high places, others a story of deregulation out of control. Others saw simply the consequences of the decline of an overinflated sun belt real estate market, which threatened loans made by the thrift. As for Keating, some saw him as a villain, an immoral and even criminal "financial Blackbeard" who wantonly misused federally insured deposits of a thrift he controlled for his own enrichment. Others saw him as a morally upright, successful real estate developer and financier who was improperly harassed and driven out of business by overzealous and incompetent regulators. Whoever or whatever the villains were, the collapse of Lincoln Savings and Loan had many victims, from the U.S. taxpayers who paid for

---

[1]Sources for this case include articles appearing in the *Wall Street Journal, New York Times, Washington Post, Los Angeles Times, Business Week, Barrons, Forbes, San Francisco Examiner, San Francisco Chronicle, Time, Newsweek,* and *U.S. News and World Report* in 1989 and 1990. These sources are cited in the case narrative only to reference direct quotations by individuals or attributions of opinion. The history of the savings and loan industry is based primarily on Paul Zane Pilzer, *Other People's Money: The Inside Story of the S&L Mess* (New York: Simon and Schuster, 1989); and Stephen Pizzo, Mary Fricker, and Paul Muolo, *Inside Job: The Looting of America's Savings and Loans,* New York: McGraw-Hill, 1989.

the $2.5 billion failure to the 23,000 savers, many of them elderly, who were left holding worthless paper when the company collapsed.

Charles H. Keating, Jr., Sun Belt Developer

Charles H. Keating, Jr., was born in 1923 into the family of a prominent industrialist in Cincinnati. He attended the University of Cincinnati, earned a law degree, and set up a business law practice in his home town with two associates. As a young attorney, he caught the eye of Cincinnati-based corporate financier Carl Lindner, who after a long informal association brought Keating on board as an executive vice president of his firm, American Financial, in 1972. In 1975, Keating moved to Phoenix, Arizona, to run Lindner's home construction subsidiary there. Two years later, Keating bought out Lindner's share in the company for $300,000 and pushed to develop American Continental Corporation (ACC) as a major real estate development firm. Within a decade, Keating had taken ACC to annual revenues of $857 million, developing a reputation both as a builder of upscale homes and commercial properties and as a financial operator with a penchant for creative financing.

By the early 1980s, Keating had established himself, by most measures, as a very successful sun belt real estate mogul. But already, a darker underside of his career had surfaced. In 1979, the Securities and Exchange Commission (SEC) issued a complaint against Keating, Lindner, and another associate based on their activities at American Financial. The complaint charged that the three men had caused several federally insured Ohio financial institutions they controlled to make loans on "wildly preferential terms" to various associates. Keating himself had borrowed $4.5 million, largely unsecured. In settlement of the SEC complaint, Keating "consented" to the charges (although without admitting guilt) and formally agreed to refrain from any further violations of securities laws.

It's a Wonderful Life

The savings and loan industry, as it evolved historically, seemed an odd match for a man of Charles Keating's temperament and business inclinations. For years, S&Ls were jokingly referred to as the "3-6-3" industry; its executives borrowed money from depositors at three percent, loaned it out for home mortgages at six percent, and arrived at the golf course at three P.M. The image of savings and loans as staid, "pillar of the community" institutions was perhaps best captured in Frank Capra's classic 1946 film, "It's a Wonderful Life," in which Hollywood star Jimmy Stewart played the part of an understanding S&L executive who stopped a run on the bank by reminding the community that the thrift had provided mortgage funds to a young couple just starting out.

Savings and loans, or thrifts as they are known, emerged historically in the early 1800s as voluntary associations designed to pool and safeguard their members' savings. Unlike commercial banks, which invest in commercial real estate and other business ventures, savings and loans historically have invested mainly in home mortgages and public bonds. During the Great Depression of the 1930s, many thrifts (as well as commercial banks) failed, and hundreds of thousands of Americans lost their life savings. As part of a larger program of depression-era New Deal banking reforms, Congress in the mid-1930s passed a series of laws governing the thrift industry. Legislators established the Federal Savings and Loan Insurance Corporation (FSLIC), funded by an assessment on deposits at insured institutions, that guaranteed each S&L deposit up to a maximum of $5,000. Over time, this limit was gradually increased; by the time of Lincoln's failure, the maximum stood at $100,000.[2]

In exchange for these guarantees, Congress also tightened up federal control of the industry. It authorized the Federal Home Loan Bank Board (FHLBB) to regulate thrifts and placed restrictions on their activities. Savings and loans were limited in the rate of interest they could pay depositors and could lend only for residential mortgages in their home communities. In effect, the U.S. government told the thrift industry: we will shore up public confidence by guaranteeing your depositors' savings; in exchange, you must act conservatively so as not to put taxpayer's money at risk. For almost half a century, this New Deal "deal" worked without a hitch. Public confidence returned, and at the industry's height one-third of Americans had their savings in their local S&Ls. Returning these funds to the communities they served in the form of residential mortgages, thrifts permitted many Americans to realize their dreams of home ownership.

Undoing the New Deal "Deal"

By the late 1970s, however, the New Deal "deal" had begun to unravel. The entire system rested on a base of stable, low rates of interest and a low inflation rate. When the Vietnam War, followed by the Arab oil embargo of 1973, set off an inflationary spiral, savers saw the value of their S&L fixed-rate accounts rapidly erode. Many depositors pulled out, moving their savings into money market accounts and other new financial vehicles paying higher rates. By 1980, fully 85 percent of thrifts were losing money.

[2]The Federal Deposit Insurance Corporation (FDIC), the insurance fund covering commercial banks, is legally backed by the "full faith and credit" of the U.S. government. In other words, if the FDIC fails, the U.S. government and taxpayers are required to cover the shortfall. By contrast, the FSLIC does not provide such a guarantee; if it fails, deposits are insured only to the extent that Congress can be persuaded to appropriate funds. This is why the "bailout" of the savings and loan industry in the late 1980s and early 1990s was not automatic but had to be debated by Congress. In practice, it is highly unlikely that Congress would permit savings and loan depositors to lose insured funds, since this would cause a massive loss of faith in the nation's banking system. (Pilzer, *Other People's Money*, pp. 52–53.)

Congress's response to the growing crisis was to ease government controls over savings and loans. This political reaction to the thrift industry's troubles was consistent, of course, with the broad movement toward economic deregulation in the 1970s and early 1980s. In the airline, trucking, telecommunications, and other industries, policymakers had moved to reduce government oversight and permit a freer play of market forces. Their objectives were to increase competition, improve efficiency and productivity, and lower prices to the consumer. Now, Congress reasoned, the same approach might help the faltering S&L industry by permitting thrifts to compete freely with other financial institutions.

The deregulation of savings and loans proceeded in several steps. First, the federal government permitted thrifts to pay higher interest rates on deposits. This cure was almost worse than the disease, however, for S&Ls still had their assets locked up in long-term, low-interest home loans and were therefore caught in a vicious "squeeze" between high rates paid to attract depositors and low rates on old loans. The solution, the lawmakers determined, was to allow S&Ls to move into more lucrative (and higher-risk) investments. In 1982, Congress passed the Garn–St. Germain Act, which permitted S&Ls not only to offer money market rates but also to invest up to 40 percent of their assets in nonresidential real estate loans. The federal government also eased accounting standards and lowered net worth requirements. During this period, several states also changed their rules (most thrifts are subject to both state and federal regulation). Texas, California, and Florida, in particular, moved to permit investment in a wide range of nontraditional areas.

At the same time that industry rules were loosened, the federal government reduced its support for regulatory agencies. The Reagan administration cut the frequency of field examinations and stabilized the number of bank board examiners just as the industry was deregulated. At the height of the savings and loan crisis, only 750 FHLBB examiners were charged with regulating the nation's 5,500 savings and loans. Critics have charged, moreover, that federal examiners, who earned an average salary of $25,000 and half of whom had been on the job for less than two years, were ill-equipped to understand the complex financial transactions typical of the high-flying thrift operators of the 1980s.

The regulation of the industry in the 1930s had rested on two foundations: federal deposit insurance and tight government controls. The deregulation of the 1980s effectively decoupled the two by loosening controls, while still retaining federal insurance. In this respect, the deregulation of S&Ls differed from that of other industries of the period, where no such insurance protected players from the downside of market competition. To its supporters, the deregulation of S&Ls was a formula for bailing out a faltering industry by permitting it to compete fairly with other financial institutions. To its critics, it was an invitation to the unscrupulous to speculate widely with the full backing of U.S. taxpayers.

Operating in a Nontraditional Manner

Many entrepreneurs previously unassociated with the savings and loan industry were quick to seize on the opportunities presented by deregulation. Among them was Charles Keating. In February 1984, American Continental purchased Lincoln Savings and Loan of Irvine, California, for $51 million. Keating and his associates found Lincoln attractive because California had recently changed its rules governing thrifts, for the first time permitting direct investment in real estate and securities. Apparently, regulators who approved the sale failed to notice Keating's prior entanglements with the SEC; they later said this "would have made a difference."[3] At the time, Lincoln was a traditional, 29-branch S&L with a loan portfolio consisting mainly of home mortgages. Although the thrift earned $3 million the year before its purchase by ACC, many—including Keating's critics—agree with his assessment that Lincoln was fundamentally a troubled institution, caught like many S&Ls of that era in the squeeze between low-interest home loans and high-interest deposits.

Although he promised the bank board he would retain Lincoln's top-management team, Keating quickly fired the S&L's conservative lending officers and internal auditors and installed his son, Charles Keating III, then a 24-year-old college dropout most recently employed as a country-club busboy, as chairman of the board. "We declared from the beginning," Keating later said, "our intention to operate Lincoln in a nontraditional manner."[4] Lincoln quickly sold off its portfolios of home loans. In addition, the thrift moved to attract deposits. Like many other aggressive S&Ls in the deregulated 1980s, Lincoln sought out, in regulators' lingo, "hot money." By offering high interest rates, thrifts were able literally overnight to raise large sums by selling federally insured $100,000 certificates of deposit (CDs) through various fund brokers. Of course, this practice increased risk, since these deposits were fickle and often withdrawn in search of higher rates when the CDs expired.

Keating promptly moved to invest depositors' fund and the proceeds from the sale of home mortgages into a wide range of high-risk, speculative ventures. The S&L invested $100 million, for example, in Wall Street financier Ivan Boesky's arbitrage fund; $132 million in Gulf Broadcasting Corporation during a hostile takeover attempt; and $12 million in the "junk bonds" of Circus, Circus, a Las Vegas casino. Lincoln also made loans for the purchase of large tracts of undeveloped desert land and bankrolled several commercial real estate projects by ACC and other Keating associates, including the lavish Phoenician hotel. Between 1984, when Keating purchased Lincoln, and 1988, the thrift's assets (loans and other investments) increased fivefold from $1.1 billion to $5.5 billion. In defense

---

[3] *Wall Street Journal*, Nov. 20, 1989, p. 1.
[4] *New York Times*, Nov. 9, 1990, p. C6.

of these investment practices, Keating and his attorneys later argued that he had done exactly what federal and state policymakers in the early 1980s had permitted—indeed, encouraged—thrift operators to do, namely, move their assets into highly risky but also potentially highly profitable ventures.[5]

Keating's investment practices, although highly speculative, were in some respects consistent with much other financial activity of the 1980s, a decade that celebrated the pursuit of money, even if by means of an unproductive exchange of assets and accumulation of debt. The deal making that characterized many of Keating's investments was reminiscent of that of many other "players" of the 1980s, including Michael Milken of Drexel Burnham, himself a Keating associate who helped raise the funds to purchase Lincoln, and who was later indicted in a separate case for racketeering and securities fraud.[6]

Making Out Handsomely

Keating maintained that under his stewardship, these deposit and investment practices generated high profits. By his account, Lincoln earned $17 million in 1984, $100 million in 1985, $80 million in 1986, and $60 million in 1987. He attributed the falloff in earnings after 1985 to regulatory harassment. Even in the wake of government seizure, Keating continued to maintain that Lincoln was a phenomenally successful business. He testified in federal court in January 1990, that "if they [federal regulators] would have left us alone, we'd still be making $100 million a year."[7]

Lincoln did, in fact, earn some big windfalls on its unusual investments. The thrift earned $30 million on its Gulf Broadcasting stock; in effect, Lincoln used federally insured depositors' money to "greenmail" a private firm. Regulators later charged, however, that most, if not all, of the gains Keating cited were bogus, the result of intricate schemes to boost paper profits. In a typical transaction, Lincoln might purchase a tract of desert land. Keating would then arrange for its sale—at a much higher price—to an associate, with the purchase financed by a loan from Lincoln. On paper, the S&L would post a tidy profit on the sale. Eventually, of course, if the borrower defaulted, the loan would be worth much less than its book value, since the inflated price could not be supported on the open market. By the time government regulators seized Lincoln, it had millions of dollars' worth of such bad loans on its books.

In an arrangement that regulators later found particularly worrisome, Keating also siphoned federally insured Lincoln funds directly to Ameri-

---

[5] *Washington Post*, Apr. 10, 1990, p. A23.

[6] For more on the "money culture" of the 1980s, see John Taylor, *The Circus of Ambition* (New York: Warner Books, 1989) and Kevin Phillips, *The Politics of Rich and Poor: Wealth and the American Electorate in the Reagan Aftermath* (New York: Random House, 1990).

[7] *Los Angeles Times*, Jan. 6, 1990, p. D1.

can Continental. Under bank board rules, Lincoln was permitted to "upstream" to the parent firm funds for tax liabilities due on Lincoln's earnings. Keating apparently abused this rule, however, upstreaming to ACC some $95 million in funds that were never paid to the IRS. After ACC declared bankruptcy in April 1989, the government's only access to these funds was through the bankruptcy court, where it had no priority over other creditors.

Whether or not Lincoln was making or losing money—still a matter of dispute—it is clear that Keating and his associates were making out handsomely. In the three years before Lincoln was seized by regulators, Keating and members of his family received $34 million in salaries, bonuses, and payments for their stock in American Continental. As chairman of ACC, Charles Keating himself earned $1.7 million annually during the period ACC owned Lincoln. His son, Charles Keating III, in 1988 received a salary of $1.6 million as chairman of Lincoln S&L. Keating defended the young man's compensation on the grounds that "my son ran an extraordinarily profitable real estate company, probably the largest in the United States."[8]

A Ticking Time Bomb

In 1984, around the time Keating took control of Lincoln, Edwin J. Gray, then chairman of the Federal Home Loan Bank Board, became increasingly concerned about aggressive lending practices some S&Ls had begun in the wake of deregulation. In May, he proposed a new "equity" rule, limiting direct investment in real estate to 10 percent of a thrift's assets. This rule, of course, conflicted directly with Keating's plans for Lincoln. Not long after, the bank board's San Francisco office, which had jurisdiction over Lincoln, began a routine audit of the Irvine thrift. Examiners found direct investments exceeding the 10 percent limit. Over the next three years, the San Francisco office continued to turn up irregular practices, including millions of dollars worth of loans made without proper appraisals or credit checks on borrowers and direct investments far over the mandated limits. Although, in retrospect, it is clear that San Francisco regulators missed much—including the $95 million upstreamed to ACC—by 1987 they had seen enough. In May of that year William Black and Michael Patriarca of the San Francisco FHLBB sent their Washington superiors a 285-page report that recommended federal seizures of Lincoln and also made a "criminal referral," that is, recommended federal investigation for fraud.

Keating countered the mounting challenge from regulators with typical aggressiveness. One approach was simply to offer jobs at lucrative terms to regulators or their relatives. Keating actually offered to hire his nemesis at

[8] *Time*, Apr. 9, 1990, p. 20.

the bank board, Edwin Gray, at a salary of $300,000 a year. Gray refused. He also offered a position to Patriarca's wife, a banking attorney. She also turned him down. Taking another approach, Keating pushed for the nomination of Lee Henkel, a lawyer with whom he had close ties, to the three-member bank board, apparently to counter Gray's influence. Henkel received an interim appointment but withdrew his nomination in the face of intense criticism after he proposed a rule that would have exempted Lincoln from direct investment limits.

Keating also sought the support of prominent intellectuals. In 1985, he hired Alan Greenspan, then a well-respected private economist and later chairman of the Federal Reserve Board, to prepare an analysis of Lincoln. Greenspan provided a letter, which Keating widely distributed, that called Lincoln "a financially strong institution that presents no foreseeable risk." Greenspan later said that "I never anticipated the types of problems Lincoln would ultimately create."[9]

The Keating Five

Keating's most effective effort, by far, was his campaign to influence political figures to intervene on his behalf. In explaining his practice of making contributions to politicians, Keating said, "We support and campaign for the political leaders we believe will represent the best of American virtues. In the contract between the voter and the politician, we have the right to seek their help when needed and demand it when justified. This I have done."[10]

In making contributions, Keating eschewed the use of political action committees (PACs), which are limited by law to donations of $5,000 per candidate per election. Instead, he preferred direct, individual gifts.[11] Federal election laws limit individual contributions to $1,000 per candidate per election and to a total of no more than $25,000 annually. Federal authorities believed Keating may have circumvented this limit by overpaying his employees with the expectation that they would contribute to desig-

---

[9]*U.S. News and World Report,* Nov. 27, 1989, p. 20; and *Wall Street Journal,* Nov. 20, 1989, p. A8.
[10]*Los Angeles Times,* May 30, 1989, p. 11.
[11]Political action committees (PACs) are organizations of like-minded individuals who join together to raise money and donate it to candidates for public office. Under federal election law, companies may not donate directly to a PAC, but they may use corporate funds to create and administer a PAC and may solicit contributions from employees and stockholders. PAC contributions are limited to $5,000 per candidate per election. Although the companies controlled by Keating—American Continental Corporation and Lincoln Savings and Loan—did not use PACs as a vehicle for campaign contributions, many savings and loans during this period did. For example, in the 1988 congressional election, PACs affiliated with savings and loans gave $680,000 to members of the Senate and House Banking Committees, who helped oversee the federal government's regulatory policies. U.S. Representative Jim Leach (Republican-Iowa) has said that S&L's "historically have gotten their way with Congress as much as any group on the hill." (*Los Angeles Times,* Feb. 15, 1989, p. 16.)

FIGURE 1

CONTRIBUTIONS BY CHARLES KEATING AND CLOSE ASSOCIATES, AND AMERICAN CONTINENTAL CORPORATION, TO FIVE U.S. SENATORS

	Direct	Indirect	Total
Cranston	$ 47,000	$ 935,000*	$ 982,000
Glenn	34,000	200,000†	234,000
McCain	112,000	—	112,000
Riegle	76,000	—	76,000
DeConcini	55,000	—	55,000
TOTAL	$324,000	$1,135,000	$1,459,000

*To three political organizations controlled by Cranston and to the California Democratic party.
†To a political organization controlled by Glenn.
SOURCE: *New York Times*, Nov. 18, 1989, p. 12.

nated candidates.[12] On a single day in March 1986, for example, 51 contributions were made to Senator John McCain by Keating, members of his family, and ACC employees. A second method of political influence favored by Keating was known as the "soft money channel": corporate contributions to political parties or other political organizations for nonpartisan activities, such as voter registration. Such indirect donations are not limited by law. During the mid-1980s, Keating and American Continental Corporation gave slightly over a million dollars to targeted political organizations.

Most favored as objects of Keating's largess were five U.S. senators—Alan Cranston (Democrat-California), John Glenn (Democrat-Ohio), John McCain (Republican-Arizona), Dennis DeConcini (Democrat-Arizona), and Donald W. Riegle, Jr. (Democrat-Michigan). The "Keating Five," as these senators later became known, received over $1.4 million in both direct and indirect contributions, as shown in Figure 1. Keating, personally an archconservative, had little in common politically with most of these senators, but they had potential influence on banking regulators. Riegle, for example, served as chairman of the political Senate Banking Committee; Cranston, Senate whip, was next in line for the same post.

Of the Keating Five, Cranston received the most contributions, including $850,000 in 1987 and 1988 to three tax-exempt, nonpartisan political organizations he founded—USA Votes, Forum Institute, and the Center for Participation in Democracy (CPD). Although Cranston drew no salary from them, these groups paid for sixteen trips by him in 1988. They also

[12]*New York Times,* Nov. 9, 1989, p. C6.

provided his son Kim, who served as the unsalaried director of the CPD, with visibility in state political circles. In addition, all three organizations were involved in extensive voter registration activity, mostly aimed at such traditionally Democratic constituencies as minorities and the poor. In the final days of the close 1986 election—which Cranston won by a razor-thin 1 percent—Keaton also gave $85,000 to a California Democratic party get-out-the-vote drive that Cranston acknowledged helped put him over the top.

Both defenders and critics of the Keating Five agree that the high cost of running a senatorial campaign—which can top $10,000 per day for every day of a senator's six-year term in populous states—puts tremendous pressure on elected officials to accept contributions, even from those whose motives may be suspect. In defense of his acceptance of substantial sums from Keating, Cranston told an interviewer in February 1990 that "I have to think in large numbers because I have to raise so darn much money. I did not see anything wrong in doing it. In retrospect, I see how people can read things into that that are not there. That I regret."[13]

On Behalf of Their Friend and Contributor

On April 2, 1987, Senator Riegle summoned FHLBB chief Gray to a meeting with Senators DeConcini, Cranston, Glenn, and McCain. Participants later disagreed over what transpired. Gray recalled that the senators proposed a deal "on behalf of their friend and contributor," in which Lincoln would make more traditional home loans if regulators would withdraw restrictions on direct investments by the thrift. Gray reported that the senators "came at me like lawyers arguing for the client" and called their intervention "an attempt to subvert the regulatory process."[14]

The senators present at the meeting flatly denied this interpretation of events. DeConcini later wrote Gray that "your recollection of the meeting is so distorted as to bear no resemblance to fact." Cranston recalled that he and his colleagues had simply told Gray that "if a case could not be made against Lincoln, [regulators should] bring a halt to what appeared to be . . . harassment."[15]

A week later, all five senators convened again, this time to meet with examiners summoned from the FHLBB's San Francisco office. The content of the second meeting also is in dispute. James Cirona, a top regulator in the San Francisco office, informed the senators that Lincoln was a "ticking time bomb." He and the other examiners stated that Lincoln was "flying blind on all of their different loans and investments" and that their loan practices "violated the law, regulations, and common sense." One examiner later testified at a congressional hearing that "the meeting with five

---

[13]*San Francisco Chronicle*, Feb. 22, 1990, p. A4.
[14]*Time*, Nov. 6, 1989, p. 27; and *Newsweek*, Nov. 6, 1989, p. 36.
[15]*Los Angeles Times*, Nov. 8, 1989, p. A15.

senators was an extraordinary example of political influence—the most extraordinary I've ever seen."[16]

Cranston, disputing this account, later told reporters that the senators met with federal regulators on April 9, 1987, simply to say: "What's going on here? Why don't you bring this to a conclusion one way or the other? That's one of the things a senator is expected to do. We were elected to write laws, but also to go to bat for constituents, at least if it seems they are getting the run-around from the government."[17] On another occasion, Cranston added that he also was motivated by concern that if Lincoln were seized by regulators several hundred Californians would lose their jobs and depositors would be "shaken up."[18]

When asked at a press conference after Lincoln was seized if his financial support had influenced political figures to take up his cause, Keating responded, "I want to say in the most forceful way I can: I certainly hope so."[19]

Cutting the Legs Out from Under the Troops

While the content of the meetings between regulators and the "Keating Five" is in dispute, what then happened is not. The seizure of Lincoln and criminal prosecution recommended by the San Francisco examiners several weeks later did not go forward. Instead, M. Danny Wall, a former aide to Senator Jake Garn (coauthor of the Garn–St. Germain Act that deregulated S&Ls), who succeeded Gray as head of the FHLB in the summer of 1987, transferred the Lincoln case from San Francisco to Washington, where it would be under his direct supervision. The San Francisco examiners interpreted this move as evidence that "political influence" had been used to prevent them from shutting down the savings and loan. Wall, however, strenuously denied that politics played any part in his decision to transfer the case and later told a reporter that "my responsibility was to see that this is not a lynch mob after Keating. The San Francisco office [of the FHLBB] has a history of being hysterical, overzealous, swept away by smoke where there is no gun."[20] U.S. Representative Henry Gonzales (Democrat-Texas) later offered a different interpretation, when he stated at a House hearing that Wall had "cut the legs out from under his . . . troops in the middle of battle."[21]

Rather than closing Lincoln down, as recommended by his local examiners, Wall entered into private negotiations with Lincoln that went on for almost two years, aimed at resolving the thrift's difficulties without a government takeover. Wall and his allies in the Washington FHLBB office

[16]*Time*, Nov. 6, 1989, p. 27; and *Newsweek*, Nov. 6, 1989, p. 36.

[17]*San Francisco Examiner*, Nov. 29, 1989, p. 2.

[18]*San Francisco Chronicle*, Feb. 22, 1990, p. A4.

[19]*Wall Street Journal*, Oct. 16, 1989, p. B10.

[20]*Time*, Nov. 27, 1989, p. 29.

[21]*San Francisco Chronicle*, Oct. 27, 1989, back page.

were concerned that they lacked specific documentation of wrongdoing that would hold up to certain court challenge. Wall specifically said later that if he had known of the $95 million improperly upstreamed to ACC, he would have moved sooner.[22] Washington regulators also wanted to avoid the cost of shutting Lincoln down, hoping instead that the case might be resolved either through Keating's cooperation or by the sale of the thrift to a qualified buyer.

In delaying action against Lincoln, Wall and his associates said they were also influenced in part by reports filed by Lincoln's independent auditor, Arthur Young and Co., which gave the company a clean bill of health in 1986 and again in 1987. Keating later hired Jack Atchison, the Arthur Young & Co. partner who had headed these audits, at a salary of $900,000. Kenneth Leventhal and Co., an auditor later hired by regulators, reported that Lincoln had booked bogus gains for 1986 and 1987 by counting bad loans as profitable. Leventhal said that "seldom . . . have we encountered a more egregious example of the misapplication of generally accepted accounting principles."[23] Keating disagreed, later testifying in federal court that the government auditors simply did not understand complex real estate syndication procedures.

William Seidman, later chairman of the Federal Deposit Insurance Corporation, testified before House Banking Committee hearings in October 1989 that Lincoln should have been seized by regulators as early as 1986, based on his staff's retrospective study of the thrift's records. He estimated that between 1987, when the San Francisco examiners first recommended action, and the April 1989 shutdown, the cost of the Lincoln debacle to the taxpayers rose from approximately $1.3 billion to $2.5 billion, as the thrift continued to make bad loans and investments with depositors' insured funds.

The two-year delay was especially costly for 23,000 small investors, many of them retirees, who purchased uninsured bonds at Lincoln branch offices in the final months of the thrift's existence. In 1988, as regulators were closing in, American Continental sold through Lincoln's branch offices $250 million worth of its own high-yield, short-term subordinated debentures, or "junk bonds." Internal memos revealed that Lincoln employees were paid bonuses for convincing customers to invest, leading them to believe that the uninsured bonds were just as safe as federally insured CDs. The ACC bonds subsequently became worthless.

Finally, American Continental itself forced the government's hand. On April 13, 1989, ACC filed for bankruptcy, apparently to protect its assets from seizure by regulators should Lincoln be shut down. The following day, U.S. government agents seized Lincoln and ousted its top management. The bank board gave a terse reason for the takeover, saying that Lin-

[22] *Los Angeles Times*, Nov. 7, 1989, p. D9.
[23] *Wall Street Journal*, Nov. 20, 1989, p. A8.

coln's management "appeared to operate Lincoln mainly for the benefit of American Continental Corp. at the expense of the institution [and] has repeatedly violated regulations relating to transactions with affiliates, used poor underwriting and has refused to follow supervisory directives." Seven months later, in seizing the Phoenician hotel, the government severed Charles Keating's final relationship with Lincoln.

Four Miles of Legal Documents

The case of the Lincoln Savings and Loan quickly became mired in multiple lawsuits that promised to take years, if not decades, to resolve. At least twenty-four civil lawsuits were filed both by individuals and government agencies, and at least seven state and federal agencies launched investigations of criminal wrongdoing. By early 1990, a records depository in Phoenix had accumulated no less than 20 million pages of documents files in connection with Lincoln litigation—enough file boxes that, if set end to end, would stretch four miles.

Among the highlights of these lawsuits and investigations were the following ones:

- On September 15, 1989, the federal government filed a $1.1 billion civil racketeering lawsuit against Keating, charging that he engaged "in numerous fraudulent, illegal, and imprudent transactions [and] . . . used [Lincoln's] resources to promote his own personal, financial, political, ideological, and religious convictions."[24] The FBI also undertook a criminal investigation.
- On November 17, 1989, the Senate Ethics Committee initiated an investigation into allegations that the Keating Five improperly interfered with regulators' oversight of Lincoln Savings and Loan.
- Bondholders filed several class action suits, charging that Lincoln employees falsely represented ACC bonds as federally insured and seeking recompense from ACC, its auditors and attorneys, and the government.
- As for Keating, he in turn filed multiple lawsuits of his own, charging the government with illegally seizing his assets and blackening his reputation. He continued to maintain that taxpayers would be best served if the government returned Lincoln to him. "I'd love to have Lincoln back," Keating told an interviewer in April 1990. If I got Lincoln back, it would not cost the U.S. taxpayers one dollar, and all my bondholders would get paid off. . . . Give us our assets back and let us work them out, see what happens."[25]

[24]*Washington Post,* Mar. 5, 1990, p. D6.
[25]*Time,* Apr. 9, 1990, p. 20.

Discussion Questions

1. Who or what in your view bears primary responsibility for the Lincoln Savings and Loan scandal: Keating and his associates, Keating's attorneys and accountants, federal regulatory agencies, Congress, the Keating Five, economic conditions, or the public? Tell why you think so.

2. What steps might the federal government, the thrift industry, or the public take to lessen the likelihood of a repetition of the Lincoln Savings and Loan debacle?

3. Do you believe political action committees (PACs) and contributions to candidates and political organizations played a role in the Lincoln Savings and Loan incident? What reforms in campaign financing laws, if any, would reduce the influence-peddling illustrated by this case?

4. Did deregulation cause the savings and loan crisis? What other steps might policymakers have taken in the early 1980s to address the impending crisis in the industry at that time?

5. Conduct a stakeholder analysis of this case. How were various stakeholders of Lincoln Savings and Loan (such as employees, depositors, stockholders, and taxpayers) affected by Keating's actions? Do you feel Keating acted ethically toward these stakeholder groups?

by **Margaret J. Naumes and William Naumes**   *University of New Hampshire*

The announcement on July 28, 1993, set the pharmaceutical industry buzzing. Already operating under uncertainty due to President Clinton's intention to introduce health care reforms, the industry was stunned by the prospect of the merger of two of its largest companies. How would this affect competition among the drug companies? Would Merck, a leading manufacturer, gain an unfair advantage by joining with Medco Containment, a large discount and mail order distributor of prescription drugs? Could Merck, highly respected, coexist with Medco's less savory reputation?

The CEO of Merck shared these concerns. The merger would have to face approval by the Justice Department, given the size of the two companies involved. There was the threat of lawsuits by shareholders and pharmacists. At the same time, he knew that he could not lose sight of possible retaliation, including mergers and acquisitions, by his competitors. It was going to be an interesting few months.

The Merger

Under the terms of the merger, which were subject to approval by the Federal Trade Commission and the Justice Department, Merck agreed to purchase Medco for a combination of cash and Merck stock. Medco stockholders could accept a price of $39.00 in cash, or trade each share of Medco stock for 1.21401 shares of Merck. Completion of the deal depended on at least 60 percent of Medco's 155 million shares being converted to Merck stock. On July 27, the day before the merger was announced, Medco stock had closed at $29.75, and Merck at $32.125. Merck announced that it would pay for the acquisition through $2.4 billion in new debt and by issuing 112 million new shares of stock. The total cost to Merck was estimated at $6 billion.

Shareholders at Medco would have to approve the deal in a special meeting, although Merck shareholders would not. Medco would be incorporated into Merck as an independent, wholly owned subsidiary, to be run by Martin Wygod, its current CEO. Mr. Wygod would also become a member of Merck's board of directors. Mr. Wygod would trade his 2 million shares of Medco for Merck stock. In addition, Mr. Wygod said that he would personally invest about $32 million to acquire Merck stock. The money would come from the after-tax proceeds of a $60 million fee that he would receive for successfully negotiating the sale of Medco. James Manning, Medco's chief financial officer, explained that this fee structure had been approved by Medco's board of directors several years earlier, as a form of incentive pay and "to recognize the tremendous increase in value [Wygod] had created for shareholders."[2]

Merck & Co.

Dr. P. Roy Vagelos, chairman and CEO of Merck, began his 1993 report to the stockholders with a summary of his view of the future: "As health-care systems worldwide struggle to deliver quality care at affordable prices, we believe that Merck's greatest contribution to society is discovering effective medicines for the most serious and costly diseases of our time. This is the foundation of our business success—and our defining vision." He stressed that innovative products were "the linchpin of our success—a fact that is driving Merck's ever-stronger commitment to research." Research and development (R&D) spending had grown at an annual compounded rate of over 15 percent during the 1990s, and was projected at over $1.2 billion for 1993. This was a continuation of the company's longtime emphasis on the importance of new products, and new uses for existing products.

As a result of its commitment to new and innovative product development, Merck had many industry-leading drugs. These included Mevacor (to help control cholesterol), Prilosec (an anti-ulcer medication), and, in 1992, Proscar, first of a new family of drugs to treat prostate enlargement. Also in 1992, Vasotec, already on the market to control hypertension, was approved by the Food and Drug Administration (FDA) for use in treating congestive heart failure. Twelve products were in the large-scale testing phase or further along in the FDA approval process. In 1992, Merck's sales were $9,662 million, of which $2,096 million had been spent for production costs and materials, $2,963 million for marketing and administration, and $1,112 million for research and development.[3]

The company's other main industry segment was Specialty Chemical Products, with sales of $594.9 million and assets of $580.3 million in 1992. Specialty chemicals were used in products ranging from health care to water treatment, food processing to textiles. The company considered its R&D as providing a strong competitive position in these areas.

Merck's pharmaceutical products were sold through a variety of drug wholesalers and retailers. These included hospitals, clinics, and managed care providers such as health maintenance organizations (HMOs), as well as pharmacies. Individual consumers purchased pharmaceuticals through one or more of these outlets. However, since the products were

[2]*Wall Street Journal,* July 30, 1993, p. B5.
[3]Medco Containment Services, Proxy Statement, Oct. 1993, p. 18.

available by prescription only, promotional activities were traditionally aimed at the prescribers, mainly doctors. This consisted of direct mail and ads in medical journals, and a force of 5,500 sales representatives who made personal calls on doctors. While expensive, this sales mix was typical for the industry. CEO Vagelos complained: "From the day I took over, I've looked for ways to stop it. The problem is, whenever you increase sales reps, you increase sales. My people never stop pointing that out to me."[4]

Merck saw several challenges emerging in the human health products industry. Many of the company's leading products were "annuity drugs," medicine that had to be taken every day to control a chronic condition such as heart disease. These products were facing increasing competition. Rising health care costs had created public pressure to reduce prescription prices, sending consumers in search of lower-cost alternatives such as generic drugs or lower-cost sources, such as discount chains (WalMart's pharmacies, for example) or mail order companies. Many doctors and health care providers were also under pressure from government and private medical plans to reduce costs. Companies which spent heavily on research and development, such as Merck, found themselves at the center of intense debate on the ethics of high prescription drug prices, even though their high margins were traditionally set to recover the costs of basic as well as developmental research. Merck had responded by limiting drug price increases to the cost of living index,[5] and by creating a separate business unit specifically to market generic drugs. The company had also temporarily lowered prices on two of its main products.

Another challenge was the uncertainty surrounding health care reform. President Clinton had been elected in 1992 on the basis, in part, of a proposal for health care reform. While the specifics of such a plan were still being debated, Merck management, in the 1993 annual report, declared that the company

> supports a reform system of national cost management that includes outcomes research, responsible individual cost sharing, appropriate managed care, medical liability reform, reduced administrative costs and reduced cost shifting. We believe such initiatives, in conjunction with increased competition and redirected incentives, will constrain costs without severely limiting our ability to innovate.

The company had also signed contracts to be on the approved drugs list ("formulary list") of a number of managed care providers throughout the United States. Managed care providers were businesses that provided a complete health care package which other companies could purchase as part of a benefit program for their employees. This would include medical care, and often also included prescription drugs at low prices, but might only pay or reimburse consumers for products on a pre-approved list.

---

[4]*Fortune,* Sept. 20, 1993, p. 62.
[5]Merck, SEC Form 10-K, 1992, p. 96.

Despite the fact that such managed care and cost containment programs already existed and the major drug companies participated in them, the entire pharmaceutical industry, including Merck, had suffered fluctuations in stock prices based on legislative uncertainty and the prospect of future drug price ceilings. Dr. Vagelos told stockholders, "We saw that 'business as usual' would be a formula for failure."[6] He reassured them that "the strategies that are driving Merck's growth today were conceived in the 1980's when we became convinced that rising health-care costs, structural changes in major markets, and the need to globalize would cause fundamental changes in the pharmaceutical industry."

In response to these pressures, the company had actively developed strategic alliances, aimed at both current and long-term growth. Since 1982, Merck had marketed AB Astra's pharmaceutical products in the United States. In 1992, sales had reached the level that triggered formation of a joint venture between the two companies, to replace the previous marketing arrangement. In 1990, E. I. DuPont de Nemours and Company and Merck established a joint venture, DuPont Merck Pharmaceutical Company, for worldwide research, manufacturing, and marketing of pharmaceuticals and imaging products. Merck had established a joint venture with Johnson & Johnson in 1989 that by 1993 was extending a line of over-the-counter products to Europe. The venture was also seeking approval for an over-the-counter version of Merck's Pepcid ulcer medication. Merck had also introduced new marketing techniques, particularly targeting HMOs in addition to the company's traditional focus on doctors.

Merck's reputation within its industry and the general business community was outstanding. In 1990, the company was named a winner in the first Business Enterprise Trust awards. The Trust cited Merck's donations of treatment for river blindness, a disease affecting 600,000 victims in the Third World. The Trust commended the company's pledge to continue this program "wherever and for as long as needed."[7] In 1993, Merck was named America's most admired corporation in *Fortune*'s annual poll for the second straight year. This was based on the votes of 8,000 senior executives, corporate directors, and security analysts, who compared and rated 311 companies. The survey also identified Merck as having the best reputation in the areas of total return to investors, financial soundness, quality of products, and ability to attract, develop, and keep talented people. On a ten-point scale, Merck's score of 8.74 led its industry by nearly a full point, outranking second-place Johnson & Johnson's 7.83. The pharmaceutical industry in general ranked as the most admired of the 32 industries studied.[8]

[6]Merck & Co., 1993 *Annual Report.*
[7]James O'Toole, "Do Good, Do Well: The Business Enterprise Trust Awards," *California Management Review,* vol. 33, Spring 1991, p. 11.
[8]Jennifer Reese, "America's Most Admired Corporations," *Fortune,* Feb. 8, 1993, pp. 44–46, 59.

Medco Containment Services, Inc.

Medco Containment Services was a young, fast-growing company which was engaged in the marketing and sale of pharmaceutical products. Chartered in 1983, it had sales of $1.8 billion in fiscal 1992. The company defined its business as providing "health care cost containment services, principally managed prescription drug programs, to corporations, labor unions, retirement systems, health and welfare trust, insurance programs, Blue Cross and Blue Shield organizations, federal and state employee plans, health maintenance organizations (HMOs), third-party administrators and other organizations."[9] Its managed prescription care services helped subscribing organizations limit the cost of providing prescription drugs as part of an employee health benefit program. Medco's services included mail-order sales of prescription drugs to members of subscribing companies and organizations. It managed programs that allowed customers to fill prescriptions at low cost in retail pharmacies. The company provided managed mental health care services and employee assistance programs, through its PPC subsidiary. Medco also was the principal owner of two other subsidiaries, Medical Marketing Group, Inc. (MMG), which assisted drug companies in marketing their products more effectively, and Synetic, Inc., which provided pharmaceutical services to institutions.

Throughout 1992, Medco actively pursued growth opportunities. During the fall, it had acquired American Biodyne. This complemented the activities of one of Medco's existing divisions. Both offered employee assistance programs to employers and unions. These programs enabled their members to seek advice, counseling, short term referrals, and emergency mental health care without directly going through their employers, thus allowing them to remain anonymous. Medco also attempted a merger agreement with a competitor, Diagnostek, which sold prescription drugs by mail to members of contracting health plans, and provided management services under contract to retail pharmacies. Medco withdrew from this agreement when Diagnostek revised its statement of earnings downward.

Medco's managed prescription drug programs were designed to help organizations, typically large corporate health plans, control their costs for pharmaceuticals. Organizations could select plans where employees' prescriptions would be filled only at participating retail pharmacies, or could mix services to include mail-order home delivery. They could also choose plans that limited the acceptable prescriptions to the most cost-effective versions of a drug, or to the products of companies with which Medco had a cost-limiting agreement. MMG, of which Medco owned 54 percent, provided marketing services to pharmaceutical companies, en-

[9]Medco Containment Services, SEC Form 10-K, 1992, p. 2.

abling them to learn how their products were being prescribed and to target individual physicians with their marketing efforts. MMG had built an extensive computer data base covering nearly 600 million prescriptions, using its own prescription records and licensing data from other sources, supplemented by surveys and interviews with doctors.[10] The data base also enabled Medco to track prescription costs for its customers, including information on the rate at which particular doctors called for various products. Medco kept information on specific patients confidential, however.

Medco's ability to control costs for its customers depended on its ability to buy pharmaceuticals from their manufacturers at favorable prices. At a meeting in May 1993, Medco's chairman, Martin Wygod, told investors that 80 percent of the company's sales were supplied by twenty-five companies. He predicted that, within five years, five or fewer companies would supply 80 percent of Medco's products. Mr. Wygod described Merck's products as "underrepresented" in Medco's sales mix.[11] He was actively looking for opportunities for strategic alliances with major drug companies.

Medco's growth had been accompanied by some controversy. Prescriptions must be written by a doctor and must be filled exactly as written, unless the doctor allows for the substitution of the generic equivalent. If there is any question concerning the prescription, or to change the prescription to another product, only a pharmacist is authorized to contact the doctor to "interpret" the prescription. Medco and other mail-order prescription services were investigated by a U.S. Senate subcommittee in 1987 following claims that the companies used technicians, who were were not as highly paid as pharmacists, to make calls. Early in 1993, several pharmacists in California filed suit against Medco and several other firms, charging price discrimination and unfair trade practices. One example given, an inhaler system, retailed for $33.00 through independent pharmacies but was available for $2.58 by mail.[12]

Controversy Over the Merger

Through the merger with Medco, Merck stood to gain access to a wide range of information, in addition to acquiring a new distribution system with access to new customers. Dr. Vagelos said, "Merck needs to have closer links to health-care providers, patients, and to bill payers."[13] Merck's board of directors stated that it believed "that the merger will enhance Merck's strategy to remain close to patients and customers in the

[10]Ibid., pp. 8–9.
[11]*Wall Street Journal*, July 13, 1993, p. A3.
[12]*Medical Marketing & Media*, Sept. 1993, p. 90.
[13]*Business Week*, Aug. 9, 1993, p. 28.

rapidly changing and highly competitive health care market."[14] Medco provided access to 33 million potential customers, enrolled with its more than 2,500 major institutional clients. In addition, it had the data base of millions of prescriptions. These could be used to increase sales of Merck products, by identifying doctors who prescribed competing products and having company pharmacists contact them to recommend a switch. The company could also contact patients directly, to urge them to refill expiring prescriptions. Robert Hills, vice president of business strategy and policy, felt that the Medco acquisition would provide much more data than could be obtained through other means. He elaborated, saying that "the free flow of information between the two organizations, subject to patient confidentiality and the interests of other vendors to Medco, is likely to result in the rapid identification of opportunities."[15]

Criticism about the merger came from several different sources. Some observers felt that, in offering $6 billion for Medco, Merck had overspent. At the time of the merger offer, Medco had total assets of $1.6 billion, and sales of $2.6 billion. Company forecasts called for Medco's sales to reach $4.8 billion in 1995 and $6 billion by 1996. Elliot Schneider, a Wall Street analyst, stated, "I doubt that it could really take $6 billion for the reputedly brilliant management of Merck to build their own discount sales operation, particularly after Medco and others have already shown them how to do it."[16]

Access to confidential patient information was a source of concern to pharmacists and physicians. The CEO of Diversified Pharmaceutical Services, a Medco competitor, felt that "what tarnishes [Merck's claims of improved health service] is that it's being stated by a manufacturer of the drug. People wince at that and have a hard time deciphering the scientific value versus the marketing."[17]

Independent retail druggists were particularly concerned with recent trends in the pharmaceutical industry. They felt that managed care organizations, representing the buying power behind thousands of prescriptions, could win price concessions from the manufacturers. They feared that deals such as Merck-Medco would intensify the problem by linking manufacturers more closely with managed care providers.[18] Bill Weinert of Garden State Pharmacy Owners Inc. cited a Medco subsidiary's recent contract with Blue Cross & Blue Shield of New Jersey, which reimbursed pharmacists at a rate so low as to make it unprofitable for smaller, independent pharmacies.[19] In California, several drug companies and wholesalers filed suit against Medco, charging illegal price discrimination, and

---

[14]Medco Containment Services, Proxy Statement, Oct. 1993, p. 30.
[15]*Wall Street Journal,* Aug. 4, 1993, p. B5.
[16]*Barron's,* Aug. 9, 1993, p. 35.
[17]*Wall Street Journal,* Aug. 4, 1993, p. B5.
[18]*Modern Healthcare,* Nov. 29, 1993, p. 16.
[19]*Drug Topics,* Sept. 20, 1993, p. 15.

an independent pharmacy filed a class action suit on behalf of all U.S. community pharmacies, charging that the merger inherently was a "built-in violation of price fixing."[20]

The merger faced other legal challenges. Three shareholder lawsuits were filed, charging a range of violations of fiduciary duty including failure to adequately explore other forms of business alliance, unfairness in the merger's structure, and improper fees paid to certain executives. Medco's shareholders wanted a "meaningful choice between cash and Merck Stock."[21] Medco was also facing a suit by Medical Marketing Group Inc. shareholders, who charged that Medco had made an inadequate offer for the shares of Medical Marketing that it did not already own.

Competition and Antitrust Issues

Another set of concerns related to the impact on competition in the pharmaceutical industry. The president of National Prescription Administrators, Inc., in a letter to the editor of the *Employee Benefit Plan Review*, called for readers to mark their calendars:

> On July 28, 1993, the world of ethical drug marketing, managed health care, and employee prescription drug benefits was turned on its head, never again to be quite what it was. On that date, an 800 pound gorilla swallowed a 600 pound gorilla, leaving the rest of us waiting to see which way the banana peels will fly.[22]

Mr. Wygod, Medco's CEO, agreed: "Some manufacturers are going to look at this as a strong competitive move, and they will perhaps tie up with other pharmacy management companies."[23]

The proportion of prescriptions that were paid for by a third party, such as a prescription plan or an HMO, had risen to 50 percent. However, both manufacturing and distribution of prescription drugs were still considered fragmented industries; in 1990, there were 13 U.S. pharmaceutical manufacturers, of which 6 had between 8.5 and 16 percent of the market.[24] In 1990, Merck ranked third in the United States in market share with 10.82 percent, behind Johnson & Johnson and Bristol-Myers Squibb, and was first among ethical pharmaceuticals producers worldwide, with 4.0 percent of the market.[25]

Distribution of prescription drugs appeared to be even more fragmented. Medco was described in the *Wall Street Journal* as "by far the

---

[20]*Medical Marketing & Media,* Oct. 1993, p. 36.

[21]*Wall Street Journal,* Aug. 12, 1993, p. B4.

[22]Richard O. Ullman, "Merck Acquisition of Medco: Meaning & Concerns," *Employee Benefit Plan Review,* Oct. 1993, p. 10.

[23]*Business Week,* Aug. 9, 1993, p. 28.

[24]Arsen J. Darney and Marlita A. Reddy, *Market Share Reporter, 1992,* Detroit: Gale Research Inc., 1992, p. 179.

[25]Ibid., pp. 174, 178.

largest of about half a dozen prescription-drug packagers,"[26] distributing to between 10 and 20 percent of prescription drug users.[27] Medco felt that its major competitors in mail-order prescription drugs were Express Pharmacy Services (a subsidiary of J. C. Penney Company), Preferred Prescription Services (a division of Baxter International), and Walgreen Co., but "the Company believes that it is the largest for-profit mail service prescription drug provider in the United States."[28] It acknowledged one larger competitor, PCS, Inc. (a subsidiary of McKesson Corporation), in retail drug benefit management. This market also included insurance companies which processed prescription claims as part of their medical insurance plans, as well as many small independent claims processors. Medco sold its prescription drug benefit plans in what it described as a "competitive" market, with alternatives offered by "pharmacy benefit managers, retail prescription drug claim processors, mail service prescription drug companies, insurance companies, certain chain pharmacies, preferred provider networks, HMOs and others."[29]

Initially, antitrust lawyers did not see the merger as causing legal problems. Antitrust lawyer Garrett Rasmussen stated: "The government wouldn't want to send a signal at this time that efforts which could have a significant chance of lowering prices could be subject to strict antitrust scrutiny."[30] However, competitors were concerned that Medco would favor Merck products, and that they themselves would be adding to Merck's profits by continuing to sell through Medco. One competitor asked, "Why would any [drug] maker do business with Medco now that Medco is Merck?"[31] Richard Vietor, a drug industry analyst, saw the nature of competition changing: "I'm not certain most other drug companies yet fully understand what a revolutionary step Merck has taken to control the marketing. . . . Merck, as usual, is just way ahead of where the rest of the industry is going to have to go."[32]

However, in early September, the Federal Trade Commission requested more information from the two companies concerning their proposed merger. The Merck-Medco combination would make Merck, in the words of the *Wall Street Journal*, "by far the biggest, and perhaps only, integrated producer and distributor of pharmaceuticals."[33] It would provide one leading pharmaceutical manufacturer with the most extensive ethical

[26]Michael Waldholz and George Anders, "More Alliances in Drug Field Are Expected," *Wall Street Journal,* July 30, 1993, p. B1.

[27]Edward Felsenthal, "Antitrust Woes Aren't Seen for Merck," *Wall Street Journal,* July 30, 1993, p. B2.

[28]Merck, SEC Form 10-K, 1992, p. 7.

[29]Ibid.

[30]*Wall Street Journal,* July 30, 1993, p. B2.

[31]Ibid., p. B1.

[32]Ibid.

[33]Lourdes Lee Valeriano, "Merck, Medco Say FTC Wants Additional Data," *Wall Street Journal,* Sept. 7, 1993, p. B4.

drug distribution system in the country. It would give Merck, already number three in U.S. sales, access to the most sophisticated data base on doctors' prescribing patterns and drug preferences. It could create a conflict of interest, since Medco currently carried almost exclusively products made by other pharmaceutical companies. Merck could learn the intricacies of competitors' pricing from Medco's supplier records. Because of the formulary lists, drugs preapproved for a particular prescription benefit plan, the merger could limit patients' choices. It could also reduce the choices available to retail pharmacies and even to HMOs and hospitals, if insurers refused to pay for products not on their list. Merck and Medco argued that a more vertically integrated company would make it easier to develop new cost-effective drugs, to monitor how they were prescribed and used, and to track their effectiveness. This would, in turn, benefit subscribing companies by providing improved patient care and lower prescription drug costs.[34]

Management Responds

On Monday, August 2, Merck and Medco ran a full page ad in major newspapers throughout the United States. Under the headline, "The Right Medicine for America," the two companies stated their case for the merger. They defined the problem as "a disconnected drug delivery system" in which "many people don't receive the most cost-effective drugs, don't take what they are prescribed—or take too many medicines." Their prescription: coordinated pharmaceutical care, in which everyone, from patients, to doctors, to pharmaceutical companies, worked together. They concluded:

> Merck and Medco will provide the most appropriate and cost-effective medicines—whether they are patented, generic or non-prescription—regardless of which company makes them.
>
> The result will be improved quality of life, lower drug therapy costs, and real savings for the healthcare system. That's why we believe Coordinated Pharmaceutical Care is the right medicine for America.[35]

Discussion Questions

1. What were Merck's reasons for wanting to merge with Medco? What were Medco's reasons for wanting to merge with Merck? In answering these questions, please consider changes in the macroenvironment of business discussed in Chapter 3 that may have affected these companies' willingness to enter into a merger agreement.

---

[34]Medco Containment Services, Proxy Statement, Oct. 1993, p. 20.
[35]*Boston Globe,* Aug. 2, 1993, p. 7.

2. In your opinion, what stakeholder groups would benefit from this merger? What stakeholder groups would be hurt by it? Why do you think so?
3. In your opinion, would this merger violate any antitrust laws? If so, which law(s), and why?

THE SPOTTED OWL, THE FOREST PRODUCTS INDUSTRY, AND THE PUBLIC POLICY PROCESS[1]

On April 2, 1993, an extraordinary day-long conference opened at the Portland Convention Center in Portland, Oregon. Convened and chaired by President Bill Clinton, the conference was designed—as Clinton had promised during his campaign—to bring together key parties to a long-running dispute over protection of the threatened spotted owl and the logging of old-growth forest in the Pacific Northwest. The conference represented a key, early test of Clinton's position that economic growth and environmental protection are compatible and of his administration's ability to solve difficult problems through open, multiparty discussions.

The importance of the event was underscored by the many top government officials in attendance, including the vice president; the secretaries of Commerce, Labor, Agriculture, and the Interior; the administrator of the Environmental Protection Agency; and the governors of the states of Oregon, Washington, California, Idaho, and Alaska. Arrayed at three roundtables were some fifty invited speakers—scientists, industry officials, timber workers, and environmentalists—many of them longtime antagonists in the controversy.

In addition to the hundreds of observers in the convention center itself, perhaps thousands more rallied noisily outside, where industry groups passed out tree seedlings, environmentalists demonstrated to rock music, and loggers rumbled down the street in their trucks. Although some expressed apprehension about the potentially volatile mixture of groups gathered face to face, expectations ran high that the conference might break the gridlock that had gripped the Pacific Northwest since the late 1980s.

THE SPOTTED OWL AND OLD-GROWTH FOREST

At the center of the controversy was the survival of a reclusive bird that few present at the conference had ever even seen: the northern spotted

[1]This is an edited version of a case presented at the North American Case Research Association (NACRA) annual meeting, New Orleans, Louisiana, November 2, 1994: Anne T. Lawrence, "The Forest Conference: The Pacific Northwest Forest Products Industry, the Spotted Owl, and the Public Policy Process." The case is based on articles appearing in the *New York Times, Washington Post, Seattle Post-Intelligencer,* and other daily newspapers. A full account of the events leading up to the Forest Conference may be found in William Dietrich, *The Final Forest: The Battle for the Last Great Trees of the Pacific Northwest* (New York: Penguin Books, 1992); an analysis of the public policy aspects of the spotted owl controversy may be found in Steven Lewis Yaffee, *The Wisdom of the Spotted Owl: Policy Lessons for a New Century* (Washington, DC: Island Press, 1994).

owl. This small, brown and white predator—just 22 ounces when full-grown—lives mainly in old-growth forests west of the Cascade Mountains from British Columbia to Northern California. As once vast, ancient forests were logged from the Pacific Northwest, the spotted owl's habitat declined; by 1993, only about 3,600 breeding pairs of spotted owls remained, scientists estimated.

The survival of the northern spotted owl is closely linked with the fate of the Pacific Northwest's old-growth forest. Old-growth forest is one in which trees are at least 150 to 200 years old. The majestic stands of old growth in the Pacific Northwest are typically dominated by mature Douglas fir and coastal redwood, often spanning 15 feet in diameter at the base and towering as high as 300 feet. Below these "climax" species grow smaller trees, creating a dense, multilayered canopy in which a great diversity of plant and animal species thrives.

Old-growth forest provides an ideal habitat for the northern spotted owl. The bird typically nests in snags, trees with broken tops. Fallen, decaying logs on the forest floor support abundant prey; and the multilayered canopy protects the spotted owl from extreme temperatures and from its own predators such as the goshawk and the great horned owl. Because of its close association with old-growth forest, ecologists refer to the northern spotted owl as an *indicator species,* meaning that its survival is a kind of "warning light" for the survival of the old-growth ecosystem as a whole and for numerous less well-known species of plants and animals that flourish there.

THE FOREST PRODUCTS INDUSTRY

The old-growth forest on which the spotted owl depends is also a critical resource to a large and powerful industry: the Pacific Northwest forest products industry.

When pioneers first settled the Pacific Northwest in the mid-1800s, somewhere between 17 and 19 million acres of old-growth forest covered the landscape. Much of this land was eventually accumulated by big timber companies such as Weyerhaeuser, Georgia-Pacific, Boise-Cascade, and International Paper, and by holding companies such as railroads and insurance firms.

Throughout the twentieth century and accelerating in the postwar years, old-growth forests were harvested for their high-quality wood. By the 1980s, somewhere between 80 and 90 percent of the ancient forest had been logged. Virtually all privately owned timber, and most on state-owned lands, had been cut; fully 86 percent of remaining spotted owl habitat was in federally owned national forests and 8 percent on national parks. Just a few patches of private old growth remained, including some owned by Plum Creek Timber Company, a firm divested by Burlington Northern Railroad during a reorganization in the late 1980s.

Beginning in the 1960s, many of the bigger timber companies, led by Weyerhaeuser, began a transition to "managed forestry," the practice of growing genetically superior seedlings on massive "tree farms" carved from previously clearcut forest. These firms introduced mechanical harvesting machines and developed new, high-tech mills designed to process the much smaller second-growth logs. They also pursued strategies of vertical integration, building or acquiring facilities for making pulp and paper and manufactured wood products.

A second segment of the forest products industry consisted of independent sawmills and manufacturers that processed old-growth logs and fashioned them into various finished wood products. In the early years, the independents were supplied mainly by private landowners. Later, as private reserves were exhausted, they turned to national forests as their main source of old-growth logs. Although prohibited from selling timber from *national parks,* the U.S. Forest Service was permitted—in fact, encouraged—to sell timber from *national forests,* since these sales provided revenue to the U.S. Treasury. Although some independents switched to processing second-growth timber, capital costs of this transition were high, and many remained dependent on federal old growth for their timber supplies.

THE ENVIRONMENTALISTS' CAMPAIGN TO PROTECT THE ANCIENT FOREST

Environmentalists seeking to preserve remaining ancient forests were quick to seize on the potential value of the spotted owl. "The northern spotted owl is the wildlife species of choice to act as a surrogate for old growth protection," one environmentalist observed. "I've often thought that thank goodness the spotted owl evolved in the Northwest, because if it hadn't, we'd have to genetically engineer it."

In 1986, environmentalists petitioned the Department of the Interior to list the spotted owl as an endangered species.[2] The petition was initially refused, but in 1990 the department reversed its position, listing the spotted owl as "threatened."

In May 1991, in response to further lawsuits brought by environmentalists, U.S. District Court Judge William Dwyer ruled that the evidence re-

[2]The Endangered Species Act (ESA) is the most recent of a series of laws protecting wildlife dating back to 1890. Enacted in 1973, the ESA aims to conserve species of animals and plants whose survival is endangered or threatened. The government is required to make a list of such species and to designate critical habitat. Federal agencies must develop programs to conserve listed species and must not do anything that would destroy or modify critical habitat. One of the most important features of the ESA is that, once a species is listed, economic factors may not be considered in deciding what action to take—or not to take. In their lawsuits, environmentalists also relied on the National Forest Management Act of 1976, which requires that national forests be managed as total ecosystems.

vealed "a deliberate and systematic refusal by the [U.S.] Forest Service and the Fish and Wildlife Service to comply with the laws protecting wildlife." Judge Dwyer issued an injunction blocking timber sales in spotted owl habitat in seventeen national forests in Washington, Oregon, and Northern California until the Forest Service could develop an acceptable plan for protecting the threatened species.

IMPACT ON THE ECONOMY OF THE PACIFIC NORTHWEST

The injunction effectively brought federal timber sales to a halt. In 1992, only 0.7 million board feet of timber were sold from national forest lands in the Pacific Northwest (down from a peak of 5 *billion* board feet during the peak year of 1987). (A board foot is equal to one foot square by one inch thick; a typical single-family house uses about 10,000 board feet of lumber.)

The consequences for the rural economy in many areas of the Pacific Northwest were devastating. By 1993, as many as 135 mills had closed, pushing unemployment up to 25 percent in some small communities. Cutters, loggers, truck drivers, and those in businesses serving them were thrown out of work. Tax receipts declined, affecting social services; the incidence of family problems, alcoholism, and other social problems increased. The intense frustration felt by many in rural Washington and Oregon was reflected in such slogans as "Support your local spotted owl— from a rope" and "Save a logger, shoot an owl."

President Clinton appeared fully aware of the intense controversy that had preceded the Forest Conference as he opened the event—and of the difficulty of reaching a resolution. "The process we begin today will not be easy," he observed. "Its outcome cannot possibly make everyone happy. Perhaps it won't make anyone completely happy. But the worst thing we can do is nothing."

TESTIMONY BEFORE THE FOREST CONFERENCE, APRIL 2, 1993[3]

Participants were seated at three large roundtables. As the conference proceeded, each roundtable was addressed in turn. Participants were asked to make a three-minute statement; the table was then opened for

---

[3]The balance of this case consists of edited excerpts from the verbatim transcript of the Forest Conference, held at the Portland Convention Center, Portland, Oregon, April 2, 1993. Not all speakers are included; however, the speakers represented here appear in the same order in which they spoke at the conference. The original transcript runs 123 pages, single spaced, and is available from the library of the University of Oregon, Eugene, Oregon.

questions and discussion among those seated at the table and officials in attendance.

The First Roundtable

The first roundtable was designed to give, in President Clinton's words, a "diverse, but . . . representative group of people in the Pacific Northwest the chance to say what they have seen or experienced personally about the impact of the present set of conditions."

Diana Wales, attorney (family law), Roseburg, Oregon

"Historically, federal forests in the Northwest have been managed essentially as though they were an inexhaustible raw material stockpile. The result is an ecosystem on the verge of collapse. It strikes me that past policies have been like buying a car and then never changing the oil, checking the water, or replacing the tires. Sooner or later, there's going to be a major problem.

for environment

"The environmental protection laws we have, such as the Endangered Species Act, are like the red idiot lights going on simultaneous with something terrible happening to your car. The spotted owl, marbled murrelet, and numerous wild fish stocks now at risk are the equivalent of all the lights coming on at once.

"When that happens, it's too late to think about a tune-up. You simply have to stop. And the answer is not disconnecting the idiot lights, just as the answer to the forest management dilemma is not suspending or disobeying the laws that let us know we have a serious problem. . . .

"The bottom line is that the 'who' most affected by environmental decisions of this decade will be the grandchildren of our grandchildren. Difficult as it may be, it is vital that all of our vision extends significantly beyond our own lifetimes. We must also recognize that we are simply a part of and dependent upon an ecosystem we do not fully comprehend, but are systematically destroying."

Ken Marson, Marson & Marson Lumber Company

". . . I'm speaking here on behalf of 9,000 lumber dealers, . . . the lumber prices have gone up substantially since last October, nearly have doubled, and a $5,000 increase or more in the cost of a house eliminates approximately 127,000 people from the housing market every year. In many cases, the increases in prices have gone up much more substantially than just $5,000.

For lumber business

"Housing . . . is an essential component of the economic development and growth of this country, and we're really concerned that we're starting to see areas of the country have a slowdown in housing because the builders can't afford it. . . . I really think lumber is truly the most compatible building material we have with the environment. Aluminum, steel, even masonry, they're never going to be renewable. . . ."

Buzz Eades, Eades Forest Products

For forest

"I cut trees for a living, just like my father did before me, and my grandfather. I represent a family that has been working actively in the logging and lumbering business for almost 200 years.

"Two hundred years is a long time. . . . That's how long it takes one of these trees to reach that point we call old growth. I like to think that some of those trees that started life when my ancestor first worked in the timber might be old growth someday, and the trees I am so careful to leave might be my grandchildren's old growth. . . . We're getting old growth, some every day. . . ."

Bill Arthur, Sierra Club

For environment

"It's not an accident that this conference is taking place on the edge of the Pacific Ocean. We have cut our way west from the Atlantic to the Pacific. It took a little bit over a generation to wipe out the great woods of Wisconsin and Michigan and for the logging to move west.

"We are blessed with bigger, larger, vaster forests here in the Northwest. It took a couple of generations to eliminate 90 percent of the once vast ancient forests that we have here. We have only 10 percent left. We're at the edge of the Pacific Ocean, and the timber frontier is over. We have to learn to protect and work with and revive what we have.

"Balance is important, and that's something that we should strive for. But balance means saving the 10 percent we have left. . . . We don't hunt buffalo, we no longer kill whales, and we can't sacrifice the last 10 percent of a remaining ancient forest for the future."

Nat Bingham, commercial fisherman

For environment

"This problem is more than just spotted owls. . . . There is another industry that is dependent on a healthy forest, the salmon fishing industry. . . . If we don't do something right now to protect the remaining habitats, we're going to see listings of salmon that will be of an order of magnitude under the Endangered Species Act that will make the spotted owl situation pale by comparison. I don't think that's something any of us want to see happen."

Meca Wawona, New Growth Forestry

For forest

"I founded New Growth Forestry in 1976 because I was so appalled at the destruction of the magnificent redwood forests in northern California. . . . I thought then that . . . if we figured out a way to make second-growth forestry sustainable, that would extend the nation's wood supply. So we started the company with a vision of helping small, private landowners practice sustainable forestry.

"Sustainable forestry is guided by natural selection and biological criteria, not short-term profiteering. . . . We've discovered over the years that we're up against a number of economic disincentives. For example, sustainable forestry requires more skills and time in the woods to get the wood out. This means it's more job-intensive, so there's more costs. Since the majority of logging operations on corporate timberlands are quick and dirty extractions, the playing field for sustainable forestry is not level. . . . Wood is simply too cheap, even at today's prices, to afford the practice of sustainable forestry."

John Hampton, Willamina Lumber Company

"I . . . have experience in second-growth forests. . . . Our company hasn't cut an old-growth log since 1950. We have high technology. . . . The cost of modern technology is extraordinary. It takes a leap of faith, under these conditions, to invest the kind of money that one does to modernize a plant. Last year, at our Tillamook Lumber Company plant alone, we invested 5 million private dollars in the renovation of that plant, which was in pretty good shape before that, to get the highest value and quality and volume out of those second-growth logs. It's laser technology; it's scanning; it's computerized positioning, all run by skilled workers who make [an average wage of] $39,000 a year."

Larry Mason, Western Commercial Forest Action Committee

"I can speak as an individual who owned a small sawmill. . . . Our mill was an old-growth mill. The reason it was an old-growth mill was because the only available timber supply that was accessible to us was off of federal lands, and the federal lands where I live, on the Olympic Peninsula [in Washington], are managed on a 100-year rotation, much longer than on some [privately owned land]. And we were 50 years into that rotation. . . . What would have happened . . . was a gradually declining volume of old-growth timber access and a gradually increasing volume of second growth. And we built our mill to make that transition.

"But you don't make those transitions overnight when your timber supply is disrupted by a court injunction. You don't make those transitions overnight when your American dream has turned into a nightmare."

Unidentified participant

"Stop looking at it as a little loaf of bread that can be neatly sliced and passed out to special interest groups, one piece for the spotted owl, one piece for the salmon, one piece for the marbled murrelet, and one piece for the people. That doesn't work. That's like drawing lines on maps with arbitrary disregard for what's really best for the forest.

"How about taking a step back and concentrating on overall forest health? How do the forest ecosystems work best? . . . That's a comprehensive approach that will take us to a road where the future will be more stable."

Phyllis Strauger, mayor of Hoquiam, Washington

"This conference is too late for my city. My city got hit on November 12th with the closure of a three-unit mill, and our unemployment rate is now 19.5 percent and climbing. We expect it to go over 20 percent."

Margaret Powell, Hoopa Valley Indian Tribe

"I . . . serve as a member of the tribe's Integrated Resources Management Committee. It seems ironic that we are required to manage within the parameters of a complex federal legal and regulatory management scheme that [is] intended to protect the environment when, in reality, we have practiced the principles of conservation for thousands of years. In fact, even before the present-day environmental regulations on timber and related development, our tribe imposed similar restrictions on ourselves as a matter of tribal law. . . . I respectfully submit that Indian tribes such as Hoopa may serve as useful models of the problems confronting this conference."

The Second Roundtable

The second roundtable was designed, President Clinton stated, to present "the range of scientific opinions about where we are and where we might go."

John Gordon, Yale University

"Ecosystem management, based on sound integrated knowledge of the whole forest, allows us to do many things at the same time, rather than saving one or two species at a time, and has the potential, I think, to remedy this old-growth deficit.

"It focuses on maintaining the health and productivity of the entire forest asset, rather than on isolating parts of processes. But it's important to recognize that it will probably not anywhere result in the optimization of yield of any single resource commodity or species. . . .

"When we talk about vision, foresters and other professionals can't do a good job unless we have a clear idea of what our clients want. . . . What does society want for and from their forests? How do they want to make a living? How do they want the Pacific Northwest to look? How much assurance do they want that endangered species will survive and flourish?"

Lorin Hicks, Plum Creek Timber Company

". . . We are applying new forestry techniques to spotted owl habitat. For example, at the Frost Meadows site on the east side of the Cascades in Washington, I have worked with our foresters to design a timber sale that would maintain spotted owl habitat after harvest. We harvested 55 percent of merchantable timber in this unit, while retaining 80 percent of the trees and maintaining functional old-growth habitat characteristics such as snags, large down-logs, and healthy green trees representative of the original stands. Our radio tracking data revealed that owls continue using the Frost Meadows unit following the harvest."

Charles Meslow, U.S. Department of the Interior, Fish and Wildlife Service

"During the course of developing a recovery plan for the northern spotted owl, biologists determined that some 480 other species of plants and animals were importantly associated with old forests. The recovery team identified 36 other species of birds associated with old forests, 22 species of mammals, 17 amphibians, 43 mollusks.

"In addition, more than 200 stocks of fish are considered at risk within the range of the owl. Thus, the northern spotted owl and marbled murrelet are perhaps only the tip of the iceberg. At least 480 other species may be following in their wake."

Jerry Franklin, University of Washington

"What I've been trying to do during the last decade is . . . to try to produce approaches that do a better job of integrating both ecological and economic values. That's fundamentally what new forestry is all about. . . . We can, with the new forestry, grow structurally complex forests. We probably can grow spotted owl habitat. But we do not know, and it's unlikely we're going to know anytime soon, how to grow old-growth forest, because the complexity of these systems is beyond imagination."

Unidentified participant

"My understanding is that folks who deal in mediation say that sometimes when you're dealing with a can of worms, the trick is to open a larger can of worms. Maybe that's what we need to do with this issue, is start taking the big picture, take our focus off the remaining old growth and really start dealing with the forest landscape."

Louise Fortman, University of California, Berkeley

"We need community-initiated and locality-based planning and management units that make ecological sense and social sense. Locally based management will involve local people and others of their choosing in gathering scientific evidence about local social and economic conditions and about local ecosystems. It will involve community members and others meeting to establish community goals and planning and implementing actions to achieve them. . . .

"Two examples from Northern California: the Plumas Corporation in Plumas County has organized an ecosystem restoration and is working on an economic transition strategy. Trinity Alps Botanicals produces nontimber forest products for export and is developing a forest stewardship program. . . .

"I think that the success of . . . community-based experiments in change tell us that facilitating local process is going to be the most important product of this conference."

Bob Lee, University of Washington

". . . We're moving into a process which looks an awful lot like what happened to the inner city. We're seeing the collapse of families, disintegration of families, disintegration of communities, loss of morale, homelessness, stranded elderly people, people whose lives are in disarray because of substance abuse. It's a very difficult situation."

Ed Whitelaw, University of Oregon

". . . Timber [is] no longer driving the Northwest economies. . . . We have accumulating evidence . . . that many of those jobs—including jobs in manufacturing that are paying substantially higher than the timber industry is paying—many of those jobs are quite sensitive to the environmental amenities here in the Northwest."

The Third Roundtable

The third roundtable was designed, President Clinton said, "to lay out some very specific suggestions about what we ought to do."

Julie Norman, Headwaters

"We must disturb no more of the last remaining centers of biodiversity. These are the refuges and the seed sources for tomorrow's forests, tomorrow's wildlife, and tomorrow's economy. Therefore, we must establish a permanent forest and watershed reserve system based on the best scientific knowledge.

"We must also establish interim protection for additional areas to preserve our options, while thorough scientific studies are completed. All suitable habitat for threatened species, all roadless areas, key watersheds for salmon, riparian zones, and large blocs of intact forest must serve as our scientific controls during this research period."

Unidentified participant

"When I come to this issue of [log] exports, I always feel there's something fundamentally wrong if we're hauling items of that magnitude and weight across the Pacific."

Jim Geisinger, Northwest Forestry Association

"The first step is to break the legal gridlock that has essentially kept our federal forest agencies from selling any timber during the last two years. If we don't reinstate some federal timber sale program this year, our industry is going to be forced to lay off thousands of workers and curtail production very significantly. Some type of interim ecosystem protection and timber production plan is essential to try to get us from where we are today to when Congress can act on a long-term solution. The alternative is to do nothing and experience economic catastrophe in the Pacific Northwest. . . .

"I want to make one final comment about the allegation that . . . only 10 percent is left. . . . [T]he Forest Service, the Bureau of Land Management, and the National Park Service say that they have about 8 million acres of old-growth forest on their ownerships today. Mathematics would tell you then that at some point in time there was 80 million acres of old growth in existence. Yet I have to tell you there's only 42 million acres of commercial forest in all of Washington and Oregon. So we don't buy that figure. . . ."

Gus Kostopulos, Woodnet

"Woodnet is a nonprofit organization . . . it's a network of over 300 very independent wood products manufacturers. . . . Our goal is to get our members to work together in loosely formed networks. They are sometimes called flexible manufacturing networks, and they engage in activities that, by their nature, can be done better in larger groups than they can undertake on their own. It gives them economies of scale that they otherwise wouldn't have."

Roslyn Heffner, vocational counselor

"I found that these workers [unemployed loggers and millworkers] were rugged individuals and proud of their skills and livelihood. . . . [I]n my professional opinion, . . . formal schooling—I'm going to get some flak for this—even in a community college setting does not work well with this group of people. They're not used to sitting in a classroom, and they haven't done it in years. . . . So that in my opinion, [we should be] giving them on-the-job training, even in a new skill, but placing them at the work-site, giving lots of incentives, including targeted jobs [and] tax credit for the employer. . . ."

Rich Nafziger, deputy insurance commissioner, State of Washington

". . . [W]e must adjust our trade policies. Landowners cannot be expected to stop exporting logs when our trading partners put up barriers to finished products but not to raw logs."

Charles W. Bingham, Weyerhaeuser Corporation

"Weyerhaeuser [has] been in business for ninety-three years. I think if there's one thing that we have learned, it is that we must manage large-scale change. . . . And I would suggest—and this is the big dilemma we're all engaged in—we're going to have to ride the bicycle here for a while, while we repair the tire. We can't just throw everybody out of work."

Andy Kerr, Oregon Natural Resources

". . . [E]nvironmentalists such as myself were very wary about this event today because, in a situation like this, all the parties are often called upon to compromise a little and give and take and something like that, like a labor-management negotiation, and then everybody splits the difference and says there's a deal. But when so little of the virgin forest is left—that 10 percent—environmentalists are not in a position to compromise that, compromise the forest any further . . . the forest has been compromised all it can stand.

"[P]eople do make money off of forests without cutting them down. My organization has appealed a few timber sales in its day, and one of the timber sales that we appealed is a sale where we tried to show the Forest Service that . . . the annual harvest of gourmet mushrooms from that stand of trees each year was worth more than the standing value of the timber."

Irv Fletcher, Oregon AFL-CIO

"We . . . need . . . adequate assistance for displaced workers . . . both wood products workers and those workers that are going to be displaced because of the wood products jobs that are gone. . . . [W]e also need some guaranteed level in place of the timber receipts . . . [and we need] a release of timber now."

Bob Dopplet, Pacific Rivers Council

"[Programs to protect and restore rivers will create] jobs back up in the woods doing things that many of the rural community people have done in the past, like use bulldozers and excavators to treat road systems."

Jack Ward Thomas, U.S. Department of Agriculture Forest Service

". . . [T]he first paragraph in the Endangered Species Act says it's not the species that's listed, it's the ecosystem on which it depends. . . . [I]t appears, to me at least, that we have a de facto policy of biodiversity protection, particularly for national forest lands. It becomes an overriding objective."

Walter Minnick, TJ International

". . . We've worked very hard on these reconstituted wood products. This is an example. This is a product that is made out of laminated veneer lumber. . . . [T]he wood fiber can come out of second-growth trees and, because it's got a very high labor content, probably creates twice as many jobs as sawing a round log into rectangular lumber. . . . Essentially, what we need the government to do is to get out of the way, let the market system work, because we don't know whether to build another plant here or to go to Canada or even whether we should be hiring folk for a month from now, because we can't be assured that our veneer suppliers are going to have the raw material we're going to need. . . .

"[T]here is a pretty straightforward and simple answer conceptually. . . . [W]e've got to set aside . . . some forest preserves. . . . We've got to surround these areas with some buffer areas that are managed with Jerry Franklin's new forestry. . . . Then, we've got to release the balance—and some of it's old growth—into the commercial timber base."

Jim Coates, International Woodworkers of America

"I represent the voice of those who haven't been heard through most of this, and that's the workers—those of the unemployed. . . . I hear Andy and some of the others talking about the beauty of the forest. When I go into the beauty of the forest in the Capital Forest and in the Park Service and in the rock quarries, we have people living there. They have no home; they have no water; and they have no power. If I was to divulge where these people were, they wouldn't have their children either."

Ted Strong, Columbia River Inter-Tribal Fish Commission
"In actuality, tomorrow we go out and build coalitions across all ideological lines. We unite as a family, and we begin to do the work that lets us leave behind a legacy of love for our natural resources, to be enjoyed in perpetuity by all humans yet to walk this Earth."

Bill Clinton, president of the United States
". . . One of the things that has come out of this meeting to me, loud and clear, is that you want us to try to break the paralysis that presently controls the situation—to move and to act. I hope that, as we leave here, we are more committed to working together to move forward than perhaps we were when we came. . . .

"I intend to direct the cabinet and the entire administration to begin to work immediately to craft a balanced, a comprehensive, a long-term policy; and I will direct the cabinet to report back to me within sixty days to have a plan to end this stalemate."

Discussion Questions

1. Conduct a stakeholder analysis of this case. Who are the primary and secondary stakeholders, and what are the major concerns of each? Draw a stakeholder map, showing the major lines of expected coalition formation.
2. If you were a member of the interagency task force assembled by the president to devise a solution to this problem, what *goals* or *principles* would you establish to guide development of a plan?
3. What key ideas mentioned by participants in the conference provide a basis for an integrative solution to the controversy faced by public policymakers in this case—a solution that would address both economic and ecological concerns? Do you support these ideas? Why or why not?
4. The Endangered Species Act has been criticized for being too extreme and for not permitting policymakers to balance ecological and economic considerations. Do you agree? If so, in your opinion, what other approach to species protection would work better?

DOING BUSINESS IN THE MAQUILADORAS:
A SHAREHOLDER CHALLENGE

In the early 1990s the Coalition for Justice in the Maquiladoras, an international association of over sixty environmental, religious, community, labor, women's, and Latino organizations, emerged as an important shareholder activist group. The coalition's goal was to convince U.S. multinational corporations to adopt socially responsible business practices in their factories along the northern Mexican border. Many large U.S. corporations had plants in this region, including Allied-Signal, Chrysler, Du-Pont, Eastman Kodak, IBM, and Xerox. Both the region and the factories in the Mexican border area were known as the "Maquiladoras."

Specifically, the coalition urged the adoption of standards of conduct for firms operating in the Maquiladora region. These standards emphasized responsible practices for hazardous waste handling, environmental protection, worker health and safety, fair employment practices, and a concern for the impact of the Maquiladora factories on the surrounding communities. These standards were addressed in a number of social activist shareholder resolutions voted on by company stockholders on annual proxy ballots or at companies' annual stockholder meetings. The resolutions called for comprehensive investigation of companies' Maquiladora operations, public reporting of the findings of the investigations, and correction of unacceptable company practices if discovered.

"We want to send a message into corporate boardrooms," explained Sister Susan Mika, president of the Benedictine Sisters and of the Coalition for Justice in the Maquiladoras. "Moral behavior knows no borders. What is wrong in the United States is wrong in Mexico, too."[1]

Economic and Social Conditions Along the Border

The Maquiladoras development represents the fruits of a Mexican government program begun in 1965. In order to attract capital investment and address high unemployment in the northern border towns, the Mexican government offered lucrative incentives such as preferential tariffs and tax breaks for foreign firms operating plants there. Maquiladora factories would pay no tariffs on materials and semifinished products imported into Mexico. When Maquiladora plants shipped finished products out of Mexico, they would pay tariffs only on the value added in Mexico, not on the value of the entire product.

Since the 1980s, companies have flooded to this region, establishing factories which produced a variety of goods. By 1994, more than 2,150 fac-

---

[1]All quotations are from "Environmental, Religious and Labor Organizations Promote Corporate Social Responsibility in the Maquiladora Industry," *The Corporate Examiner,* vol. 20, no. 1, 1991, pp. 1–8.

tories were located along the northern Mexican border, 90 percent of them owned by U.S. corporations. These plants produced electronic goods, auto parts, chemicals, furniture, machinery, and clothing and employed nearly 550,000 workers.[2]

The Mexican government saw the development project as an economic success. In 1992, it is estimated that the Maquiladora industries contributed $4.74 billion in value-added worth to the products manufactured or assembled in these factories. The Maquiladora region became identified as an attractive site for manufacturing facilities, particularly for companies whose products required labor-intensive assembly. Various businesses associated with the construction and maintenance of manufacturing plants—raw materials suppliers, eateries and grocery stores, and so on—provided an additional boost to the region's economy. In addition to the employment of over a half million people, billions of dollars of investment capital gave the Mexican government a stronger bargaining position when negotiating trade agreements with the United States, Canada, and other trade partners.

Some believed that the benefits of the Maquiladora development did not justify the costs incurred by Mexican workers, local communities, and the natural environment, however. Timothy Smith, executive director of the Interfaith Center on Corporate Responsibility explained,

> We find a range of corporate behavior in the Maquiladoras . . . from the irresponsible polluter and exploiter of labor to companies which are working to live up to standards of fairness. Though many company and plant officials proudly point to their high standards for wages, health and safety, and environment, until now [1991] most companies seem to be involved in a race to the bottom.

Social watchdog organizations documented abhorrent conditions in the Maquiladora area. For example, contamination of the water supply affected both U.S. and Mexican residents. Raw sewage from plants located in Mexicali, Mexico, was dumped into the New River, a waterway extending 120 miles into California. In 1991, more than 20 viruses and bacteria were identified in the river along with over 100 industrial chemicals. People in San Elizario, Texas, were at risk of exposure to hepatitis. Ninety percent of thirty-year-olds in this border town had contracted the disease. On the Mexican side of the border, the 85,000 residents of the town of Juarez had no running water and stored their water supply in 55-gallon drums which previously contained dangerous chemical compounds used at Maquiladora plants. As little as 20 percent of the toxic wastes generated by Maquiladora plants were returned to the United States for proper disposal as required by U.S. and Mexican law.[3]

[2]Joshua A. Cohen, "The Rise of the Maquiladoras," *Business Mexico*, vol. 4, no. 1–2, 1994, pp. 52–55.

[3]Roberto A. Sanchez, "In the Maquiladora Industry, Health Is Also at Risk: Maquiladora Masquerade," *Business Mexico*, vol. 3, no. 1, 1993, pp. 13–15; and "A Maquiladora Case Study: Hazardous Waste Issues," *IRRC News for Investors*, Nov. 1994, pp. 20–23.

The Coalition for Justice in the Maquiladoras charged that multinational corporate owners of Maquiladora factories had failed to improve the living standards of their workers, often migrants from the inland regions of Mexico. According to a *Wall Street Journal* report in 1991, the average hourly wage for Maquiladora workers was $.88 per hour. In comparison, workers averaged $2.46 per hour in Korea, $2.67 in Singapore, and $13.90 in the United States. *Business Week* noted that the average daily wage in the Maquiladoras—$5.00—was the same wage paid to American Ford Motor Company workers in 1914!

Hazardous working conditions in Maquiladora plants were blamed for a 300 percent increase in the annual low birth weight of babies born to female workers in the early 1990s.[4] Medical records showed that children of mothers who worked at an electronics plant were more vulnerable to being born mentally retarded than other Mexican children. Those women were exposed to highly toxic polychlorinated biphenyl (PCB) compounds for long hours, often reaching into deep vats of the chemicals wearing only rubber gloves for protection.

Since Maquiladora plants paid virtually no taxes in Mexico, local governments did not receive sufficient revenue from the corporations to defray the costs for city roads, sewer systems, utility lines, and other public services incurred from the plants' operations. Corporations operating Maquiladoras were accused of ignoring the deteriorating public services in border towns from Matamoros, Mexico (near Brownsville, Texas), to Tijuana (across the border from San Diego, California). Although plants in the region had electricity, water, sewage disposal, and green grass, only a short distance away, residents in nearby towns had—at best—limited access to such basic services and amenities. Research was conducted by the U.S. National Toxics Campaign in the early 1990s to investigate accusations of careless or illegal transportation or disposal of hazardous waste by-products by the Maquiladora factories. The investigation found a "clear and consistent pattern . . . of widespread and serious contamination [of the Maquiladora region] by U.S. owned firms. They are turning the border into a two thousand mile long Love Canal [an area in New York contaminated by long-term underground disposal of toxic wastes]."

Social Issues Enter Corporate Boardrooms

In 1990 the Coalition for Justice initiated the Maquiladora campaign by sponsoring social responsibility shareholder resolutions. These resolutions called on twelve U.S. corporations to describe in detail their environmental practices, health and safety standards, and workers' standard of living in and around their Maquiladora plants. Ten companies—including AT&T, Ford Motor, Johnson & Johnson, and PepsiCo—agreed to provide

---

[4]See "Low Birth Weights at Maquiladoras," *Occupational Hazard*, Feb. 1994, p. 23.

the information or allow inspection of their facilities by interested investors. The shareholder resolutions were then withdrawn.

The campaign escalated a year later when the coalition proposed that corporations operating in the Maquiladora region adopt the "Maquiladora Standards of Conduct." These standards called for companies operating Maquiladora plants to comply with Mexican and U.S. environmental regulations; to observe fundamental workers' rights, including fair wages, a safe and healthy workplace, reasonable hours of work, and decent living conditions; and to support community public service needs, including a commitment to community economic development. The coalition's philosophy and an excerpt from a sample shareholder resolution are presented later in this case study.

Companies Respond to the Shareholders

Some U.S. corporations were quick to respond to the shareholder resolutions filed by coalition members. These firms were already in compliance with or exceeded Mexican laws and regulations. Some firms were committed to applying environmental and employee policies and practices worldwide. The same policies governing U.S. operations were used at the Maquiladora plants. Therefore, some firms already were addressing the various issues emphasized in the shareholder resolutions. A number of these firms drafted statements in response to the shareholder challenges and made these documents available to interested company stakeholders. Highlights from these documents are presented next.

AT&T's report on their Mexican operations

AT&T compiled "A Report for AT&T Shareowners: Manufacturing in Mexico." The report, made available to all interested company stakeholders, addressed numerous issues raised by the coalition, such as human resource, environmental, and worker safety policies and practices.

AT&T was committed to "maintain[ing] consistent, equitable and fair human resources policies at all its locations worldwide." The company policies included paying a competitive wage to all employees, participating in salary surveys in each country where it operated to determine what was a "fair wage," and providing each employee with benefits comparable to what other companies in that country were offering their employees.

AT&T complied with the legal expectations in Mexico regarding the maximum number of hours an employee could work in a week, scheduled rest periods within each workday, and vacation benefits provided for employees. For example, AT&T workers at the Maquiladora plant were paid for 56 hours per week, although the workweek consisted of only 48 hours or less. In addition, the company provided quality of work benefits and programs for its workers. Comprehensive medical care available to AT&T employees exceeded Mexico's legal requirements. Employees were offered educational assistance programs, sports programs, and, in some lo-cations, subsidized plant cafeterias, food and clothing allowances, and free transportation.

AT&T pledged its commitment to support the Mexican government's efforts toward environmental responsibility. The corporation established the following goals for its Maquiladora operations: reducing manufactur-ing emissions of chlorofluorocarbons (CFCs), reducing toxic air emissions, reducing amounts of manufacturing process waste sent for disposal, re-ducing paper use, and increasing recycling efforts.

The company was actively involved in various environmental initia-tives, such as the Industry Cooperative for Ozone Layer Protection, Global Environmental Management Initiative, and International Environmental Health and Safety Conference, which was held in 1992. AT&T went be-yond legal requirements in Mexico when it established a self-contained water supply and waste water systems at its Guadalajara plant.

Worker safety was also a key emphasis for AT&T at its Maquiladora op-erations. In compliance with Mexican regulation, each manufacturing unit formed a safety committee with representation from the workers' union, management, production, and medical departments. New workers at AT&T's Maquiladora plants participated in an orientation program which focused on safety procedures, in compliance with Mexican law.

Ford Motor Company's Maquiladora facilities report

Ford Motor Company's report, "Environmental Practices, Health and Safety Standards and Employee Welfare at Ford Motor Company's Maquiladora Facilities in Mexico," was issued on March 19, 1991, and re-sponded to many of the coalition's various concerns. The report stated that Ford required its Maquiladora operations to meet high standards for responsible environmental, health, safety, personnel, and community re-lations policies and, whenever possible, to follow the same policies and practices as did Ford operations in the United States.

For example, although not required by Mexican law or regulation, Ford applied its U.S. environmental policies to the Maquiladora facilities. These policies required the plants to monitor the handling and disposal of any hazardous materials used in manufacturing processes, which included solvents, cleaners, lubricants, and various metals. The Waste Management Program, launched in 1985 and strengthened in 1990 at Ford's U.S. plants, was applied to its Maquiladora operations. Cross-functional teams within manufacturing, plant engineering, environmental quality, research, occu-pational safety and health, and others met regularly to explore safety is-sues and recommend solutions if necessary. In compliance with Mexican regulation, enforced by SEDUE (the Mexican equivalent to OSHA) and the Mexican Department of Labor, random audits of Ford's Maquiladora facili-ties were conducted. In addition, "self audits" were often conducted at the plants to ensure compliance with Mexican law as well as company policies.

One of Ford Motor Company's basic values is embodied in the statement: "Our people are the source of our strength." This value was manifested in the policies and practices affecting the employees at Ford's Maquiladora plants. In order to establish a "fair wage" scale for its employees, Ford utilized the services of two international compensation consultants who advised the company regarding competitive wages and fringe benefits for each plant location. The company took pride in being able to offer employment to over 10,000 Mexican citizens, providing them with competitive wages and benefits that they could not receive elsewhere, according to the company's report on its Maquiladora operations. Ford Motor Company had been a part of Mexico and the Mexican people for over sixty-five years. According to the Maquiladora facilities report, "Ford has actively participated in the economic, social, and cultural growth of Mexico in many ways. Our active cultural, educational and community participation is a matter of public record of which we are proud."

PepsiCo's Maquiladora report

Evidence of corporate social responsiveness to the social activist shareholder resolutions was reflected in PepsiCo's report:

> PepsiCo is committed to making a real contribution to Mexican economic, technological and social development. PepsiCo operations are guided by these basic principles.

> - PepsiCo companies are committed to the communities they serve, in terms of providing employment opportunity, fair and equitable working conditions and working with local industry suppliers.
> - PepsiCo businesses believe in investing in the future, including establishing employee training and research programs and supporting educational and charitable organizations.
> - PepsiCo believes in full cooperation with the Mexican government, to ensure that our objectives are in the nation's best interest.
> - Finally, PepsiCo is committed to Mexico for the long term and we are projecting continued expansion.[5]

The Future for the Maquiladora Region

With the signing of the North America Free Trade Agreement (NAFTA) by the United States and Mexico in 1994, many observers predicted that the Maquiladora program would diminish as an attractive investment opportunity. They believed the expansion of U.S. plants along the northern Mexican border would lessen over the next decade or two as economic incentives, once unique to this program and region, were blended into a united, free trade economic zone encompassing North America. However, the Coalition for Justice in the Maquiladoras remained committed to challenging U.S. companies to establish safe, healthy, and environmentally sound

[5]"Maquiladoras PepsiCo, Inc.," reprinted courtesy, © PepsiCo, Inc.

business operations in the Maquiladora region. The number of companies receiving shareholder resolutions and requests for entering into dialogue with the coalition doubled from 1992 to 1993. In 1993 and 1994, the coalition requested adherence to their standards of conduct and/or disclosure reports from thirty-eight companies with Maquiladora operations.

Mission Statement and Standards of Conduct of the Coalition for Justice in the Maquiladoras

In 1991, the Coalition for Justice in the Maquiladoras adopted the following mission statement:

> We are an international coalition of religious, environmental, labor, Latino and women's organizations seeking to pressure U.S. transnational corporations to adopt socially responsible practices within the Maquiladora industry in order to ensure a safe environment on both sides of the border, safe work conditions inside the Maquiladora plants and a fair standard of living for the industry's workers.
>
> A central vehicle for achieving these goals is the establishment of the "MAQUILADORA STANDARDS OF CONDUCT." This document provides a code through which we demand that corporations alleviate critical problems created by the industry.
>
> Our efforts are grounded in supporting worker and community struggles for social, economic and environmental justice in the Maquiladora industry. Moreover, by supporting these struggles, we believe our efforts will serve the interests of workers and communities on both sides of the border.
>
> We dedicate ourselves to democratic process and unity of action, maintaining sensitivity to the diverse representation within our coalition.

The following is a summary of the issues proposed in the "Maquiladora Standards of Conduct."[6]

Introduction: Purpose and scope of the standards of conduct

The "MAQUILADORA STANDARDS OF CONDUCT" are addressed to all U.S. corporations which operate subsidiaries, have affiliates, or utilize contractors or shelter plants in Mexico. The objective of these Standards is to promote socially responsible practices, which ensure a safe environment on both sides of the border, safe work conditions inside Maquiladora plants and an adequate standard of living for Maquiladora employees.

United States citizens, who urge U.S. transnational corporations to adhere to these standards, recognize that both Mexico and the U.S.

---

[6]The "Maquiladora Standards of Conduct" is reprinted in a condensed form by permission of the Coalition for Justice in the Maquiladoras, San Antonio, Texas.

have the inherent right to regulate commerce within their own boundaries. These Standards are designed to help promote international efforts to secure a safe workplace for Maquiladora employees, the protection of the environment and the promotion of human rights and economic justice on both sides of the border.

All company disclosures associated with these Standards should be provided in Spanish and English.

Section I: Responsible practices for handling hazardous wastes and protecting the environment

Pollution from the Maquiladora industry is a binational problem which threatens the health of citizens both in Mexico and the United States. Illegal dumping of hazardous wastes pollutes rivers and aquifers and contaminates drinking water on both sides of the border. In addition, accidental chemical leaks from plants or transportation vehicles carrying hazardous materials impact both sides of the border.

In general, corporations operating Maquiladoras will be guided by the principle that they will follow Mexican and United States environmental protection regulations as established by SEDESOL and EPA (the Mexican and United States' environmental regulatory agencies). . . . Corporations operating Maquiladoras, including corporations which utilize contractors or shelter plants, will: [1.] Act promptly to comply with Mexican environmental laws (*Ley General del Equilibrio Ecológico y la Protección al Ambiente*. . . . [2.] Annually, provide full public disclosure of toxic chemical discharges and releases into the air, water and land and amounts of hazardous materials stored and utilized. . . . [3.] Provide full public disclosure of hazardous waste disposal methods, including the final location of waste disposal. . . . [4.] Use state-of-the-art toxics use reduction, chemical accident prevention and pollution control technologies. . . . [5.] Ensure safe and responsible transportation of all hazardous materials in Mexico and the United States. . . . [6.] Provide public verification of all hazardous materials being returned to the country of origin. . . . [7.] Ensure proper disposal of all spent containers used for chemicals and take necessary initiatives to assure that these containers are not used for the storage of drinking water. . . . [8.] Take remedial action to clean up any past dumping which threatens to release hazardous materials into the environment. . . . [9.] Provide fair damage compensation to any community or individual, which has been harmed by pollution caused by the corporation or its subsidiary. . . . [10.] Discuss environmental concerns with the community. . . .

Section II: Health and safety practices

In general, corporations operating Maquiladoras will be guided by the principle that they will follow regulations established by the *Secretaria del Trabajo y Previsión Social* (Secretary of Labor and Social Provision) and the U.S. Occupational Safety and Health Administration (OSHA).

Corporations operating Maquiladoras will: [1.] Disclose to employees, their designated representatives and the public the chemical identity of all chemicals used, as well as amounts of chemical materials and wastes stored on premises. Ensure that all chemical containers will have appropriate warning labels in Spanish as well as English. . . . [2.] In accordance with Mexican law, provide employees with written explanation of risks associated with the use of toxic materials. . . . [3.] Use chemicals that are the safest and least toxic for employees. . . . [4.] Design work operations and tasks to limit repetitive strain injuries and other ergonomic problems. . . . [5.] As required by Mexican law, each plant will establish worker/management health and safety commissions. . . . [6.] Provide all employees with health and safety training using a qualified instructor approved by the Joint Health and Safety Commission. . . .[7.] Provide an adequate ventilation system including local exhaust for all point sources of air contamination, as well as provide employees with appropriate protective equipment and clothing. . . . [8.] Arrange health and safety inspections by qualified outside consultants (approved by the Joint Health and Safety Commission) at least once every six months and provide public disclosure of inspection reports. . . . [9.] Provide fair damage compensation to any worker who suffers an occupational injury or illness. . . . [10.] In accordance with Mexican law and the OSHA Medical Records Rule, provide all employees and their designated representatives access to medical records. . . .

Section III: Fair employment practices and standard of living

U.S. corporations will respect basic workers' rights and human dignity. [1.] U.S. corporations will not engage in employment discrimination based on sex, age, race, religious creed or political beliefs. Equal pay will be provided for equal work, regardless of sex, age, race, religious creed or political beliefs. . . . [2.] In general, workers will be provided with a fair and just wage, reasonable hours of work and decent working conditions. . . . [3.] U.S. corporations will not interfere with workers' rights to organize and to reach collective bargaining agreements. . . . [4.] U.S. corporations will not employ or utilize child labor and will exercise good faith in ensuring that employees are of legal working age. . . . [5.] U.S. corporations will distribute profit sharing to employees as required by Mexican law. . . . [6.] U.S. corporations will print and distribute a written handbook on company employment policies to all employees as required by Mexican law. . . . [7.] In the workplace, U.S. corporations will take positive steps to prevent sexual harassment. . . .

Section IV: Community impact

U.S. transnational corporations recognize that they have social responsibilities to the local communities in Mexico and the United States where they locate facilities. These responsibilities include a commitment to community economic development, and improvements in the quality of life. Facilities will not be abandoned to avoid these responsibilities. [1.] U.S. corporations will not promote barracks-style living arrangements for employees. Where these living arrangements already exist, U.S. corporations will take immediate action to improve living conditions and ensure that workers are provided with basic human rights. . . . [2.] Corporations operating Maquiladoras will work to establish special trust funds to finance infrastructure improvements in communities near Maquiladora plants.

Discussion Questions

1. Assume that the Coalition for Justice in the Maquiladoras has introduced a shareholder resolution at a firm where you are on the board of directors. Would you recommend that your firm adopt the practices outlined in the "Maquiladora Standards of Conduct?" What values or reasons underlie your recommendation? What is your firm's responsibility to your shareholders?

2. The "Maquiladora Standards of Conduct" also ask companies to disclose operations information. Should your firm agree to make public information about your Maquiladora operations, as requested by the coalition? Why or why not?

3. If you were a shareholder, would you vote for or against the resolution? Why?

4. Some believe that the SEC should permit stockholders to vote on social as well as economic questions related to the business of the corporation, while others do not. Do you believe that the issues raised by the "Maquiladora Standards of Conduct" are appropriate ones for stockholders to consider, or should these issues be better left up to management or public officials?

5. Laws governing such matters as environmental policy, labor standards, and gender and race discrimination often differ among nations. Do you believe that multinational corporations have an obligation to apply standards consistently among all their operations, or simply to follow the law in the country or countries in which they are operating?

DOW CORNING AND THE SILICONE BREAST IMPLANT CONTROVERSY[1]

The corporate jet lifted off from Washington's National Airport, en route to Dow Corning Corporation's headquarters in Midland, Michigan. February 19, 1992, had been a grueling day for Keith R. McKennon. Named chairman and chief executive officer of Dow Corning less than two weeks earlier, McKennon had just testified before the Food and Drug Administration's (FDA) Advisory Committee on the safety of the company's silicone gel breast implants. Although not the only manufacturer of breast implants, Dow Corning had invented the devices in the early 1960s and had been responsible for most of their medical testing. Now, the company was faced with the task of defending the product against numerous lawsuits and a rising tide of criticism from the FDA, Congress, the media, and many women's advocacy organizations.

The company's potential liability was large: as many as 2 million American women had received implants over the past three decades, perhaps 35 percent of them made by Dow Corning. In December 1991, a San Francisco jury had awarded a woman who claimed injuries from her Dow Corning implants an unprecedented $7.3 million in damages. Although the company believed its $250 million in product liability insurance was adequate to meet any possible claims, some felt that the company's liability exposure could be much, much larger.

The hearings had been contentious. Critics had repeated their allegations, heard often in the press in recent weeks, that the implants could leak silicone into the body, causing pain, scarring, and—most seriously—debilitating autoimmune diseases such as rheumatoid arthritis and scleroderma. The silicone prostheses could also interfere with detection of breast cancer by mammography, they charged. In response, McKennon had testified that implants served an important public health need and did not pose an unreasonable risk to users. On the job less than a month, however, McKennon had had little time to sort through the thousands of pages

[1]This is an abridged version of a longer case: Anne T. Lawrence, "Dow Corning and the Silicone Breast Implant Controversy," *Case Research Journal*, vol. 13, no. 4, Winter 1993, pp. 87–112. Abridged by the author by permission of the *Case Research Journal*. Sources include articles appearing in the *New York Times, Wall Street Journal, Business Week, Newsweek, Time, Chemical and Engineering News, American Bar Association Journal, Journal of the American Medical Association, New England Journal of Medicine*, the Public Citizen Health Research Group *Health Letter*, The Command Trust Network *Newsletter*, press reports of the *Federal News Service*, and U.S. congressional hearings. The history of Dow Corning and the development of silicones is based on Don Whitehead, *The Dow Story: The History of the Dow Chemical Company* (New York: McGraw-Hill, 1968) and Eugene G. Rochow, *Silicon and Silicones* (Berlin: Springer-Verlag, 1987). The case also draws on internal Dow Corning documents released to the public in February 1992. A full set of footnotes is available in the *Case Research Journal* version.

of relevant documents or to talk with the many managers who had been involved with the product's development over the past thirty years.

The breast implant controversy would surely be a litmus test of McKennon's crisis management skills. Recruited from Dow Chemical Corporation, where he had been executive vice president and head of domestic operations, McKennon came to his new position with a reputation as a "seasoned troubleshooter." At Dow Chemical (which owned 50 percent of Dow Corning), McKennon had earlier managed his firm's response to charges that its product Agent Orange, a defoliant widely used during the Vietnam War, had caused lingering health problems for veterans. Later, he had managed Dow Chemical's problems with Bendectin, an antinausea drug alleged to cause birth defects. At the time of his appointment as chairman and CEO, McKennon had served on Dow Corning's board of directors for nearly six years.

The unfolding breast implant crisis showed every sign of being just as difficult—and potentially damaging—as any McKennon had confronted in his long career. Would Dow Corning become known as another Johnson & Johnson, renowned for its skillful handling of the Tylenol poisonings in the 1980s? Or would it become another Manville or A. H. Robins, companies that had declared bankruptcy in the wake of major product liability crises? McKennon was well aware that the future of the company, as well as his own reputation, might well hinge on decisions he and his top managers would make within the next weeks and days.

Dow Corning, Inc.

Dow Corning was founded in 1943 as an equal joint venture of Dow Chemical Company and Corning Glass Works (later known as Corning, Inc.) to produce silicones for commercial applications. The term "silicone" was coined to describe synthetic compounds derived from silicon, an abundant element commonly found in sand. In the 1930s, Corning researchers working on possible applications of silicone in glassmaking developed a number of resins, fluids, and rubbers that could withstand extremes of hot and cold. In 1940, Corning approached Dow Chemical with a proposal for a joint venture, and by 1942 a small plant in Midland, Michigan (Dow's hometown), had begun production of silicones for military applications. At the close of World War II, Dow Corning moved successfully to develop multiple commercial applications for silicone. Within a decade, the company had introduced more than 600 products and doubled in size three times, making it one of the fastest growing firms in the booming chemical industry. Its varied product line included specialty lubricants, sealants, and resins as well as a variety of consumer items—ranging from construction caulk, to adhesive labels, to Silly Putty.

Although most uses of silicone were industrial, by the mid-1950s Dow Corning scientists had become interested in possible medical applications and developed several implantable devices. In the early 1960s, Dow Corning engineers developed the first prototype of a breast implant by encapsulating a firm-density silicone gel within a silicone rubber bag. First marketed in 1963, this device—known as the Cronin implant—was used initially almost exclusively in reconstructive surgery performed on breast cancer patients following mastectomies (surgical removal of the breast).

When Dow Corning first developed and marketed breast implants (as well as its other medical products), the company was operating with virtually no government oversight. Unlike pharmaceutical drugs, regulated since 1906 under the Pure Food and Drug Act and its several amendments, medical devices—even those designed for implantation in the body—were for all practical purposes unregulated. Under the Food, Drug, and Cosmetics Act of 1938, the FDA had the authority to inspect sites where medical devices were made and could seize adulterated or misbranded devices. The agency could not require premarket approval for safety or effectiveness, however, and could remove a product from the market only if it could demonstrate that the manufacturer had broken the law.

Although not required to prove its implants safe by law, Dow Corning—in accord with standard "good manufacturing" practices at the time—attempted to determine the safety of its own medical products before releasing them for sale. In 1964, Dow Corning hired an independent laboratory to undertake several studies of the safety of medical-grade silicones, including those used in breast implants. No evidence was found that the silicones caused cancer, but two studies found that silicone fluid injected in experimental animals spread widely—becoming lodged in the lymph nodes, liver, spleen, pancreas, and other organs—and created "persistent, chronic inflammation." The company appeared unconcerned, noting that it did not advocate the direct injection of silicone fluid.

In the early 1970s, Dow Corning's breast implant business for the first time experienced a serious competitive threat. In 1972, five young men—all scientists or salesmen at Dow Corning—left the company to work for Heyer-Schulte, a small medical devices company in California, where they used their experience with silicones to develop a competing breast implant. Two years later, the group left Heyer-Schulte to form their own company, McGhan Medical Corporation. Their idea was to modify the basic technology developed over the past decade by Dow Corning to make a softer, more responsive implant that more closely resembled the natural breast. By 1974, both Heyer-Schulte and McGhan Medical had competing products on the market.

The Heyer-Schulte and McGhan implants quickly gained favor with plastic surgeons, and Dow Corning's market share began to erode. By 1975, Dow Corning estimated its market share had declined to around 35 percent, as plastic surgeons switched allegiance to products offered by the small company start-ups. Dow Corning managers became alarmed.

The Mammary Task Force

In January 1975—responding to the challenge from its California competitors—Dow Corning dedicated a special cross-functional team, known as the mammary task force, to develop, test, and bring to market a new generation of breast implants. The group's main goal was to reformulate the silicone gel to create a softer, more pliable implant competitive with the new products recently marketed by McGhan and Heyer-Schulte. The group of about twenty—all men—hoped to have the new implants ready for shipment by June 1975. The company believed it was justified in bringing the new implant to market quickly, without extensive medical testing, because the new product would be based on materials substantially similar to those used in the older Cronin implants. The safety of the existing line, management maintained, had already been satisfactorily documented on the basis of earlier studies and the history of their use.

One of the questions that quickly arose in the task force's deliberations—as reported in the minutes of its January 21, 1975, meeting—was: "Will the new gel . . . cause a *bleed through* which will make these products unacceptable?" (emphasis in original). Dow Corning scientists clearly recognized that a more watery gel (dubbed "flo-gel")—while softer to the touch—might also be more likely to permeate its envelope and "bleed" into surrounding tissue. Two product engineers were assigned to investigate this issue. Three weeks later they reported that their experiments "*to date* indicate that the bleed with new gel is no greater than what we measure from old gel controls." They also added, however, that they viewed their early results as inconclusive, and they remained concerned about "a possible bleed situation."

Biomedical tests were contracted out to an independent laboratory, which proceeded with tests in which the new gel was injected into experimental rabbits. Early reports back from the lab on February 26 showed "mild to occasionally moderate acute inflammatory reaction" in the test animals around the injected gel, but the pathologist concluded it was probably due to the trauma of insertion, not the product itself. The task force also ordered biomedical testing of migration of gel into the vital organs of monkeys. The laboratory results showed "some migration of the [flo-gel] formulation." However, the task force agreed that the bleed was still not any more or less than standard gel.

Development proceeded so rapidly that, by March 31, 10,000 new flo-gel mammaries were ready for packaging. The task force minutes reported that the products were "beautiful, the best we have ever made." Now six weeks ahead of schedule, the company was able to ship some samples of the new product to the West Coast in time for the California Plastic Surgeons meeting on April 21. However, early demonstrations did not go flawlessly. The task force got back the following report: "In Vancouver, and elsewhere on the West Coast introduction, it was noted that after the mammaries had been handled for awhile, the surface became oily. Also, some were bleeding on the velvet in the showcase." The task force ordered samples from the West Coast for examination, but no further discussion of this issue appeared in subsequent minutes.

As the flo-gel implants came on line, the focus of the task force's discussion shifted from production issues to marketing strategy. The task force debated various aggressive marketing approaches, such as rebates, distribution by consignment, price breaks for "big users," and free samples for surgeons known to perform breast enlargement operations. Noting that June and July were the "peak months" of the "mammary season," managers called for a big push to regain some of Dow Corning's eroding market share. The group felt that their market share, which they estimated had eroded to around 35 percent, could be lifted back to the 50 to 60 percent range if they moved aggressively.

By September, Dow Corning was producing 6,000 to 7,000 units per month and aimed to phase out the older models by early 1976. However, many bugs in the production process remained to be ironed out. The reject rate at inspection was high—as high as 50 percent on some lots. Among the problems: floating dirt, weak bags, and thin spots in the envelopes. Doctors had returned some unused mammaries, citing breakage and contamination. Overall, however, plastic surgeons liked the product. One task force member later recalled that when plastic surgeons saw and felt the new material, "their eyes got big as saucers." Besides feeling more natural to the touch, the new softer devices were easier to insert and were more suitable for small-incision, low-trauma cosmetic procedures.

A Boom in Busts

Although breast implants first became available in the 1960s, it was only in the late 1970s and 1980s that the rate of implant surgery took off. The increase was due entirely to a fast rise in the number of so-called cosmetic procedures; by 1990, fully 80 percent of all implant surgeries performed in the United States were to increase the size of normal, healthy breasts, rather than for reconstruction following mastectomy.

One cause of the rise in cosmetic augmentations, of course, was the availability of the softer, more pliable implants, which could be inserted through smaller incisions with less trauma to the patient in less expensive, outpatient procedures. In 1990, 82 percent of all breast augmentation procedures were performed on an outpatient basis. Other, broader trends within the medical profession and the wider culture also played important roles, however.

One factor behind the boom in breast augmentation surgery was the growth of the plastic surgery profession. Although procedures to graft tissue from a healthy part of the body to another that had been damaged or mutilated were developed early in the century, plastic surgery as a distinct subdiscipline within surgery did not emerge until the 1940s. During

World War II, military surgeons struggling to repair the wounds of injured soldiers returning from the front pioneered many valuable reconstructive techniques. Many of these surgeons reentered civilian life to start plastic surgery programs in their home communities. Within a couple of decades, plastic surgery had become the fastest growing specialty within American medicine. Between 1960 and 1983, the number of board-certified plastic surgeons quintupled, during a period when most other medical specialties were growing much less quickly (and the U.S. population as a whole grew by just 31 percent). The draw for the newly minted MDs was regular hours, affluent customers, and high incomes—averaging $180,000 per year after all expenses in 1987.

As their numbers soared, plastic surgeons faced an obvious problem—developing a market for their services. Demand for reconstructive surgery was not fast growing, and cosmetic procedures were often elective and typically not fully covered by medical insurance. In 1983—following approval by the Federal Trade Commission—the American Society for Plastic and Reconstructive Surgery (ASPRS), a professional association representing 97 percent of all board-certified plastic surgeons, launched a major advertising (or, as the society called it, "practice enhancement") campaign. Other ads were placed by individual surgeons. In one appearing in *Los Angeles* magazine, a seductive, well-endowed model was shown leaning against a sports car. The tag line: "Automobile by Ferrari. Body by [a prominent plastic surgeon]."

Plastic surgeons also campaigned to redefine female flat-chestedness (dubbed "micromastia" by the medical community) as a medical disease requiring treatment. In July 1982, the ASPRS filed a formal comment with the FDA that argued:

> There is a substantial and enlarging body of medical opinion to the effect that these deformities [small breasts] are really a disease which in most patients results in feelings of inadequacy, lack of self-confidence, distortion of body image and a total lack of well-being due to a lack of self-perceived femininity. The enlargement of the under-developed female breast is, therefore, often very necessary to insure an improved quality of life for the patient.

The ASPRS later officially repudiated this view.

By 1990, breast augmentation had become the second most common cosmetic procedure performed by plastic surgeons, exceeded only by liposuction (fat removal). Since it was a more expensive procedure, however, breast augmentation was the top money maker for plastic surgeons in 1990. That year, ASPRS members collected almost $215 million in fees from women for breast implant surgery.

Another factor contributing to the rise in cosmetic augmentation may have been changing cultural standards of feminine beauty in the 1980s, a decade characterized by social conservatism and, according to some commentators, by a backlash against feminism and female liberation. In the

1970s, women appearing in the glossy pages of fashion magazines were often tall and lanky, with long, straight hair tied at the nape of the neck, menswear "dress-for-success" suits, and distinctly boyish figures. The 1980s ideal woman was very different: the typical fashion model by this time was more likely to sport 1940s retro-look fashions, thick, full curls, sweetheart lips—and lots of bosom. In a special 100th anniversary edition, published in April 1992, *Vogue* magazine summed up current standards of female beauty in this sentence:

> And in women's bodies, the fashion now is a combination of hard, muscular stomach and shapely breasts. Increasingly, women are willing to regard their bodies as photographic images, unpublishable until retouched and perfected at the hands of surgeons.

Ironically, the same issue also ran an ad, placed by trial attorneys, in which "silicone breast implant sufferers" were invited to come forward with legal claims.

A Stream of Sick and Injured

As the rate of implant surgeries rose in the 1980s, so did the number of women who were sick, injured, and in pain from their breast surgery. Their stories began to be told at medical conferences, in legal briefs, and by women's and consumers' advocacy organizations. As they were, Dow Corning and other implant makers were forced to respond to a growing crisis of confidence in their products.

The most common adverse side effect of implant surgery was a phenomenon known as "capsular contracture," a painful hardening of the breast that occurs when the body reacts to the implant by forming a wall of fibrous scar tissue around it. The FDA estimated that severe contracture occurred in about 25 percent of all patients; some hardening may have occurred in up to 70 percent. Implants could also rupture, spilling silicone gel into the body and often necessitating repeat surgery to replace the damaged implants. Dow Corning's data, based on voluntary reporting by surgeons, showed a rupture rate of only 1 percent. These figures were challenged by researchers who pointed out that ruptures often did not show up on mammograms; some individual doctors reported rupture rates as high as 32 percent. Once the device had broken, silicone could and did travel via the lymphatic system throughout the body, lodging in a woman's spleen, liver, and other internal organs. Also worrisome was the tendency of silicone implants to obscure cancerous tumors that otherwise would be revealed by mammography.

More controversial and less-well documented were allegations that silicone implants could lead to so-called autoimmune disorders—diseases in which the body's immune system attacks its own connective tissues. According to the FDA, by 1991 around 600 cases of autoimmune disorders—

such as rheumatoid arthritis, scleroderma, and lupus erythematosus—had been reported in women with implants. Some scientists speculated that some women were, in effect, allergic to silicone, and that their bodies had attacked their own tissues in an attempt to rid itself of the substance. Such reactions were most likely in the presence of ruptures, but even small amounts of gel bleeding through the envelope—or silicone in the envelope itself—could provoke an autoimmune response.

Other physicians believed, however, that the appearance of autoimmune disorders in women with implants was wholly coincidental. In any substantial population—and 2 million women with implants was clearly substantial—a certain number would develop autoimmune disease purely by chance. In an interview published in the *Journal of the American Medical Association,* one prominent plastic surgeon called the association between autoimmune disorders and breast implants a "crock of baloney. . . . People get immunological diseases and they just happen to have breast implants."

Unfortunately, no long-term controlled studies of the incidence of autoimmune disorders in populations of women with and without implants were initiated—or even contemplated—until 1991. In fact, no comprehensive registries of women with implants existed. The question about the relationship between implants and autoimmune disease was, on the basis of existing data, wholly unanswerable. Representative Ted Weiss (Democrat-New York), who reviewed data submitted to the FDA in 1991, later angrily concluded: "For thirty years, more than one million women have been subjects in a massive, uncontrolled study, without their knowledge or consent."

Victims Seek Redress

Some women who had suffered from breast implants sued. In 1984, a Nevada woman was awarded $1.5 million by jurors in a San Francisco court, who concluded that Dow Corning had committed fraud in marketing its implant as safe; the case was later settled for an undisclosed amount while on appeal, and the court records were sealed. In a post-trial ruling, a federal judge who had reviewed the case records called Dow Corning's actions "highly reprehensible." In the wake of this case, Dow Corning changed its package insert to include a warning that mentioned the possibility of capsular contracture, silicone migration following rupture, and immune system sensitivity.

As other cases slowly made their way through the courts, victims began to speak out publicly—and to organize. Sybil Goldrich and Kathleen Anneken founded the Command Trust Network, an advocacy organization that became instrumental in providing information, support, and legal and medical referrals to implant victims. Other women's and public health advocacy groups also played a role in publicizing the risks of breast implants. One of the most active was the Health Research Group (HRG), a Washington, DC–based spin-off of Ralph Nader's Public Citizen. The HRG in 1988 began a systematic effort to pressure the FDA to ban silicone breast implants. The group petitioned the FDA, testified before Congress and other government agencies, issued regular press releases, and distributed information to consumers. The HRG also initiated an information clearinghouse for plaintiffs' attorneys. Another active advocacy organization was the National Women's Health Network, a public-interest group that widely distributed information on silicone-related issues.

Devising Regulation for Devices

The agency in charge of regulating implants—and thus the object of these and other advocacy organizations' pressure—was the Food and Drug Administration. In 1976—the year after Dow Corning's mammary task force developed its new generation of flo-gel implants—Congress passed the Medical Amendments Act to the Food and Drug Act. Enacted in the wake of the Dalkon Shield controversy—in which thousands of women claimed they had been injured by a poorly designed intrauterine device—the amendments for the first time required that manufacturers of new, implantable medical devices be required to prove their products safe and effective before release to the public. Devices already on the market were ranked by risk, with the riskiest ones—designated "Class III"—being required to meet the same standards of safety and effectiveness as new devices.

In January 1989, after an extensive internal debate, the FDA identified silicone breast implants as Class III devices and gave their manufacturers 30 months—until July 1991—to submit safety and effectiveness data to the agency. Four breast implant manufacturers submitted the required documents to the FDA: Dow Corning, INAMED (formerly McGhan Medical), Mentor (formerly Heyer-Schulte), and Bioplasty. Surgitek, a unit of Bristol-Myers Squibb, withdrew from the implant business, saying it was unable to meet the FDA's deadline. On August 12, the head of the FDA Breast Prosthesis task force submitted a review of Dow Corning's studies, stating that they were "so weak that they cannot provide a reasonable assurance of the safety and effectiveness of these devices."

Finally, on November 13, the FDA convened an advisory panel of professionals to consider the most recent evidence and to take further testimony. The hearings were highly contentious. The panel heard, once again, arguments concerning the dangers of implants. But the hearings also generated intense support for implants from plastic surgeons, satisfied implant recipients, and breast cancer support and advocacy organizations. Among the most vocal defenders of the implants were women who had experienced successful reconstruction following mastectomies, including representatives of such peer support organizations as Y-Me and

My Image After Breast Cancer. Several spoke of the positive psychological benefits of reconstruction and warned that if the FDA took implants off the market, some women—knowing that reconstructive surgery was unavailable—would delay regular checkups for breast cancer, endangering their lives. Other witnesses argued that women should be free to choose implants, so long as they were fully informed of the benefits and risks of the devices.

The advisory panel debate was, by all accounts, heated. In the final analysis, the panel split hairs: it voted that although breast implants "did not pose a major threat to the health of users," the data submitted by manufacturers was "insufficient to prove safety." However, citing "a public health need," the panel recommended that the devices be left on the market.

The regulatory decision, at this point, passed to the FDA Commissioner, Dr. David A. Kessler. Appointed just a few months earlier, Kessler had brought a new commitment to regulatory activism to an agency marked by what some viewed as a pattern of weak government oversight during the Reagan administration. Now, the fledgling commissioner had two months—until mid-January—to rule on the panel's recommendation on breast implants.

Unauthorized Leaks

Unfolding events, however, forced Kessler's hand sooner. In December, a San Francisco jury returned a verdict in *Hopkins v. Dow Corning*, awarding Mariann Hopkins $7.3 million—by far the largest victory ever for a plaintiff in a breast implant suit. Hopkins' attorney claimed that his client's implants (made by Dow Corning in 1976) had ruptured and spilled silicone gel—causing severe joint aches, muscle pain, fatigue, and weight loss—and told the jury that "this case is about corporate greed and outright fraud." Dow Corning immediately moved to have the legal records in the case—which included hundreds of pages of internal company memos Hopkins' attorney had subpoenaed—sealed.

Somehow, however, the documents from the Hopkins trial ended up in Commissioner Kessler's hands. Their contents evidently alarmed him. On January 6, 1992, Kessler abruptly reversed the FDA's November decision and called for a 45-day moratorium on all sales of silicone gel breast implants, pending further study of their safety, and he recalled the advisory panel to consider "new evidence." Both the plastic surgeons and Dow Corning were furious. The president of the American Society of Plastic and Reconstructive Surgeons took the unusual step of calling a press conference to brand Kessler's action as "unconscionable—an outrage" and called on Kessler to reconstitute the advisory panel, which he called unqualified to judge the safety of the devices. For its part, Dow Corning demanded publicly to know what "new evidence" Kessler had obtained and restated the company's intention to block any release of "non-scientific" internal memoranda. The chief of Dow Corning's health care business called a press conference to repeat the company's contention that "the cumulative body of credible scientific evidence shows that the implants are safe and effective."

Dow Corning's efforts to block release of the Hopkins documents, however, failed. On January 13, *New York Times* reporter Philip J. Hilts—saying only that he had obtained the material from "several sources"—broke the Hopkins case memos in a page-one article, under the headline "Maker Is Depicted as Fighting Tests on Implant Safety." In a summary of the contents of several hundred internal company memos, Hilts charged that Dow Corning's safety studies were "inadequate" and that serious questions raised by its own scientific research and by doctors' complaints had not been answered.

More damaging revelations were yet to come. Over the next several weeks, newspaper readers learned of the following incidents, drawn from the company's internal documents:

- In a 1980 memo, a Dow Corning sales representative had reported to his marketing manager that he had received complaints from a California plastic surgeon who was "downright indignant" because the implant envelopes were "greasy" and had experienced "excessive gel bleed." "The thing that is really galling is that I feel like I have been beaten by my own company instead of the competition. To put a questionable lot of mammaries on the market is inexcusable," the sales representative wrote his manager. "It has to rank right up there with the Pinto gas tank."
- A marketing manager had reported in a memo that he had "assured [a group of doctors], with crossed fingers, that Dow Corning had an active study [of safety issues] under way." (The marketing manager later angrily disputed the interpretation given his remarks by the media, saying in a letter to the Associated Press that he had meant the term "crossed fingers" in a "hopeful" rather than a "lying" sense.)
- A Las Vegas plastic surgeon had had an extensive correspondence with the company reporting his dissatisfactions with the product. In one letter, he charged that he felt "like a broken record" and told of an incident in which an implant had ruptured and spilled its contents—which he described as having the "consistency of 50 weight motor oil"—onto the operating room floor.

Whether wholly justified or not, the memos created a strong impression that Dow Corning had been aware of safety concerns about its implants for many years and had failed to act on this knowledge. The press moved in aggressively, attacking Dow Corning for its "moral evasions"; a widely reprinted cartoon depicted a Dow Corning executive apparently deflating as silicone gel oozed from his body.

A Model Ethical Citizen

That Dow Corning was being labeled publicly as "a company adrift without a moral compass"—as one *New York Times* columnist put it several days after the internal memos broke in the press—struck many in and around the company as deeply unjust. Ironically, Dow Corning Corporation was widely regarded in the business community as a model for its efforts to institutionalize ethical behavior.

At the center of Dow Corning's efforts was a formal code of conduct and an unusual procedure for monitoring compliance. In 1976—the first full year of sales for its new generation of breast implants—the company's board of directors had appointed a three-person Audit and Social Responsibility Committee and charged it with developing a corporate code of ethical conduct. Top managers were motivated, in part, by a breaking scandal at that time in which several large companies had been accused of questionable payments to foreign heads of state to secure contracts. With a substantial portion of its operations overseas, Dow Corning wanted its behavior to be above reproach.

In 1977, the company published its first corporate code of conduct, laying out a comprehensive statement of ethical standards. In order to ensure compliance, the company initiated a series of annual audits, in which top managers would visit various cities around the globe to evaluate corporate performance against code standards. In addition, the company held training programs on the code, and its semi-annual employee opinion survey included a section on business ethics.

Yet, for whatever reason, the company's widely admired procedures had failed to flag the safety of breast implants as an ethical concern. A routine 1990 ethics audit of the Arlington, Tennessee, plant that manufactured silicone implants, for example, did not reveal any concerns about the product's safety. When later questioned about the apparent failure of the audit procedure, the chairperson of the conduct committee pointed out that normally product safety issues would come before the relevant management group, not the ethics review.

A "Hardball" Strategy

As the controversy widened, Dow Corning's response, in the words of one *Wall Street Journal* reporter, was to "play hardball." On January 14—eight days after the FDA had announced its moratorium on implant sales and one day after the first leaked documents appeared in the press—Dow Corning took a $25 million charge against fourth quarter, 1991, earnings to cover costs of its legal liability, unused inventory, and efforts to prove implants safe. The company also suspended implant production and placed workers at the company's manufacturing facilities on temporary layoff, with full pay and benefits. Investors, apparently alarmed by this turn of events, knocked down the stock price of both Corning, Inc., and Dow Chemical as they contemplated the parent firms' potential liability.

Implant recipients and trial lawyers also were contemplating the liability question. By March, as many as 600 lawsuits had been filed against Dow Corning and other breast implant makers, according to a representative of the Association of Trial Lawyers of America. The National Products Liability Database estimated that Dow Corning had been sued at least 54 times in federal court and possibly more than 100 times in state courts. Dow Corning's attorney disputed these figures, saying that there were far fewer than 200 cases pending against his client.

The unauthorized leaks created tremendous pressure on Dow Corning to release its own documents to the public. The FDA publicly called on the company on January 20 to release the material so that women and their doctors could evaluate the new evidence for themselves, rather than simply relying on news reports. (The agency, although in possession of the documents, could not release them because they were still protected under court order.) The company responded two days later by releasing a group of scientific studies—but not the infamous "Pinto" memo and other internal materials that the company dubbed "unscientific."

Suspension of breast implant sales and release of the scientific studies did not slow down the crisis engulfing the company. On January 29, in an apparent acknowledgment of the severity of the situation, the company hired former Attorney General Griffin B. Bell—who had performed a similar role at Exxon Corporation following the *Valdez* oil spill and at E. F. Hutton following the check-kiting scandal—to investigate its behavior in making implants.

Finally, on February 10—following a top-level intervention by the chairmen of Corning, Inc. and Dow Chemical, both of whom sat on Dow Corning's board—the board of directors executed a stunning management shakeup. Dow Corning demoted Chief Executive Lawrence A. Reed to the position of chief operating officer and forced longtime board chairman, John S. Ludington, to retire. Keith R. McKennon was named chairman and CEO. Simultaneously, the board announced that it would release to the public 15 scientific reports and 94 nonscientific memos or letters from company files, including the "Pinto" and "crossed fingers" memos, as well as other potentially damaging materials that had not yet been reported by the media.

Several top executives of Dow Corning met the press the same day to present the company's perspective. One defended the company's decision not to release the documents earlier, saying:

> Our motives are simple. First and foremost, these memos do not answer fundamental questions and concerns that women have about breast implants. And by focusing attention on the memos rather than the science that supports the device, we do nothing but further raise the anxiety level of women and physicians and scientists.

He added that "while we are not happy with the memos, we have nothing to hide, and we believe that each memo put in its proper context can be understood and explained." Many of the memos, he said, were best understood as part of the normal give and take that occurs within a technical organization, "one part of a multi-faceted dialogue or communication or discussion that goes on," and did not reflect fundamental problems. By pulling various statements out of context, he implied, the press had misrepresented questions scientists might legitimately raise in the course of their inquiry as final conclusions. The Dow Corning executives closed the press conference by denying categorically that implants could cause autoimmune disease or cancer.

Facing a Crucial Decision

On February 20, the day after his testimony before the FDA, McKennon received word from Washington. After three hours of tense debate, the FDA advisory panel had voted just after 5:00 P.M. to recommend that implants be taken off the market, except for women needing reconstruction following mastectomies or to correct serious deformities. All implant recipients would be required to enroll in clinical studies. Cosmetic augmentations would be strictly limited to those required by the design of the clinical trials. Commissioner Kessler would have sixty days to rule on the panel's recommendation.

McKennon would have to lay a plan of action before his board soon—he certainly could not wait another two months for the FDA's next move. The breast implant business, he had learned, had not made any money for Dow Corning for the past five years. Even in its heyday, it had contributed no more than 1 percent of the company's total revenues. Some of his top executives had urged him just to get out of the implant business altogether and let the attorneys mop up the liability problems. Many in the company felt that the huge settlement in the Hopkins case would be greatly reduced on appeal, and the company's $250 million in insurance would be sufficient to cover their liability. McKennon reflected on these issues as he contemplated his next actions. Certainly, he needed to act decisively to stem Dow Corning's financial losses. But, he pondered, did the company not also have—as he had put it to a reporter a few days earlier—an "overriding responsibility . . . to the women who have our implants"? And what of the company's reputation, so carefully nurtured, for always upholding the highest standards of ethical behavior?

Discussion Questions

1. What internal and external factors contributed to the emergence of the silicone breast implant crisis for Dow Corning?
2. What should CEO McKennon do as of February 20, 1992?
3. What steps can Dow Corning (or other companies) take to prevent this kind of situation from occurring in the future?

The portrait of urban violence, crime, drugs, and poverty displayed in newspapers and on television reflects a frightening reality for millions of Americans. Myriad social problems afflict thousands of neighborhoods in hundreds of American communities. To many observers, these problems have worsened considerably in the past twenty years. Despite millions of dollars and endless political rhetoric, the problems of America's cities seem to be escalating. Many efforts have been launched to save our cities. Often, they have failed; some may have even made the situation worse.

Fear grows as reality worsens. The city has become an even more fearful place as media attention highlights the bizarre, the insane, the dangerous. Perception often is reality, and some who can avoid the city do so, in an effort to immunize themselves from society's problems. But some people fight back, continuing to find new ways of combating the terror of fear. In many cities, volunteer community groups, local government, and law enforcement continue the struggle to make cities safe for citizens.

Businesses are also involved in the struggle to save America's cities. Most businesses do not have the luxury of relocating to "safe harbor" locations where crime does not happen and social ills do not exist. Most businesses, like most people, have to find ways to cope with their problems, face challenges, and continue their daily activities.

Law enforcement, vigilant neighbors, active community groups, and economic development are all needed if communities are to win the fight to save our cities. Big cities like Atlanta, Cleveland, and Boston, as well as small and medium-sized cities and towns, are undertaking new experiments and forging new approaches. Business is a critical part of these efforts. Although it is too early to know if there are best practices that can be imitated in every community, there is reason to believe that some of the new efforts being undertaken are making an impact.

How Businesses Are Involved

The Urban Institute, a research "think tank" based in Washington, DC, has studied business involvement in cities and concluded that while individ-

[1] Sources for discussion of The Atlanta Project include: Archie B. Carroll and Gerald T. Horton, "Do Joint Corporate Social Responsibility Programs Work?" *Business and Society Review*, no. 90, Summer 1994, pp. 24–28; and Archie B. Carroll and Gerald T. Horton, "The Atlanta Project: Corporate Social Responsibility on a Mega Scale," in Steven Wartick and Denis Collins, eds., *1994 Proceedings of Fifth Annual Conference, International Association for Business and Society*, Hilton Head, NC, Mar. 17–20, 1994, pp. 261–266. Primary sources include: *The Atlanta Project*, Atlanta, GA: The Carter Center, 1992; *Improving the Quality of Life in Our Neighborhoods: The Atlanta Project, Strategic Plan*, Atlanta, GA: The Carter Center, Mar. 1992; and J. Carter, "Preface," in *Because There Is Hope: Gearing Up to Renew Urban America*, Atlanta, GA: The Carter Center, 1993. Additional data provided by The Atlanta Project. We are grateful for the assistance of Mr. Richard Watson and Mr. Jason Foss of TAP.

ual companies are involved in a wide variety of community activities in cities across the nation, three distinct strategic approaches have dominated corporate involvement in rebuilding and strengthening urban communities.

Direct involvement

The concept of "hands on" business activities with neighborhoods is a relatively new form of direct involvement. Traditionally, business has made somewhat "passive" charitable contributions to arts, educational, and community groups. Investments have rarely been neighborhood-focused, except for those in downtown redevelopment projects. Increasingly, however, businesses have made direct investments in urban neighborhoods for the purpose of stabilizing, even reclaiming, areas that were once thought to be in hopeless decline. There are a few models worth studying. One is a landmark effort, the Crown Center Redevelopment Project in Kansas City. The neighborhood around its corporate headquarters was becoming surrounded by abandoned buildings and empty lots when Hallmark Cards Inc. began a neighborhood redevelopment effort. Twenty-five years after the initiative began, Hallmark has invested more than $500 million in what is considered a "jewel" in Kansas City's development.

In the 1990s, neighborhood needs are being addressed in a more complete or holistic manner. This has led to direct investments that attack a range of community-based problems. Upjohn, a pharmaceutical company based in Kalamazoo, Michigan, recognized the importance of housing as a stabilizing force in the local community. "Citizen ownership" of a community begins with home ownership, which is seen as critical to convincing residents that they have a stake in the neighborhood. To restore housing and improve home ownership in neighborhoods near its facilities, Upjohn recruited and supported the Local Initiative Support Corporation (LISC)— a nonprofit development corporation—to help build home ownership by making mortgage loans to local residents in Kalamazoo. The long-term effect of Upjohn's efforts appears favorable: home ownership has increased in the target neighborhoods, and other social indicators—crime rates, drug use—have declined.

Community partnership around a business core

Some companies have found it possible to integrate community development objectives into their normal business operations. The company pursues its profit-making business but takes on as a partner a comprehensive community organization. For example, Ben & Jerry's Homemade Inc. has collaborated with Larkin Street Youth Center in San Francisco to open an ice cream shop that provides job training to youths (ages 12 to 17) who are mostly runaways. The company helps meet the education, training, and self-esteem needs of youth with the center's staff. Profits from the ice cream store are shared with the Larkin Center.

Ben & Jerry's has expanded this partnership concept to many other cities and locations. In New York City, for example, the company has part-nered with the Harlem Ark of Freedom. The organization runs a homeless shelter and is engaged in a range of community development activities. Again, the store partnership helps to train people who lack education and job skills, to stabilize the neighborhood, and to attract additional busi-nesses.

Some retail businesses with large workforces and connections to the community lend themselves to this approach. A number of supermarkets such as Pathmark, Kroger, and First National have created similar commu-nity "anchors" by building stores, employing previously unemployed peo-ple, and serving as a magnet for other economic investment.

Use of intermediary institutions

In some cities, community leaders have created a separate institution to serve as an umbrella vehicle for development efforts. In Cleveland, for ex-ample, the Cleveland Foundation convened a Commission on Poverty in 1990 to devise a long-term comprehensive strategy for bringing together business, government, and community resources to connect the city's poor neighborhoods to mainstream economic opportunity.

Business leaders were recruited to work with the commission, to study its findings, and to devise alternative responses to the problems. Leaders from Cleveland-based businesses such as White Consolidated Industries, The Higbee Company, Reliance Electric, and several leading law firms par-ticipated and saw the linkage between "altruism and self-interest." Eco-nomic revitalization was critical to community improvement and to build-ing Cleveland into a community that could support a modern base of service and manufacturing industries. It required that action be taken in school reform, housing, and community services. In short, a long-term business goal—a well-trained workforce—was intimately connected to com-prehensive community involvement. The Cleveland Foundation has played a central role in aligning projects, sponsors, and corporate partici-pation in what are called "villages" or neighborhoods in the city. Four core areas of community need were defined: education, investment, family de-velopment, and health. The foundation, and its Community-Building Initia-tive Council, helped to coordinate the focusing, funding, and delivery of programs to address these needs in each village. In the course of five years, the entire project has begun to achieve measurable improvement in meeting these core needs using a variety of social and economic indica-tors.

Building Better Communities: Contrasting Approaches

Businesses often become involved in the social issues affecting cities be-cause they are asked to play a role or work with others to tackle a critical problem. Two examples of corporate involvement are discussed next. One

is The Atlanta Project, a broad sweeping approach to Atlanta's complex social issues. The macro or comprehensive approach developed in Atlanta
contrasts with the narrower, more selective (micro) approach of Boston
Against Drugs, which has enlisted companies to tackle drug issues
throughout that city.

The Atlanta Project: A Macro Approach to Social Issues

The Atlanta Project (TAP) is one of the best-known and widely studied recent efforts to save America's cities. Atlanta, like many other American
cities, displays contrasting faces: one is the face of wealth, prosperity, a
positive spirit, and an optimistic view of life; the other is a face of despair,
poverty, and fear. Dr. Johnetta Cole, president of Spelman College in Atlanta, said it this way: "We have two cities . . . one rich, one poor." In Atlanta, civic leaders such as Dr. Cole are in the vanguard of a broad effort to
turn two cities into a single, prosperous, safe community for all. The Atlanta Project is a coalition of Atlanta-based organizations—businesses,
churches, community groups, government agencies, universities—formed
to attack the poverty, crime, and community conditions that contribute to
the "second city."

The Atlanta Project was launched on October 25, 1991, by a former
president of the United States, Jimmy Carter. Carter, a Georgia native,
whose presidential library and "home base" for continuing activities—the
Carter Center at Emory University—are located in Atlanta, had been persuaded by Atlanta's civic leaders to lead the campaign to address the city's
poverty and related social problems. Carter's natural interest in such an
effort was coupled with his own "action theory" of how social change occurs in any community: *through the full participation of those affected.* It
is an approach Carter has put into practice in global affairs as well: his mediation in Haiti helped to peacefully remove General Cedras and restore
President Aristide to power; his efforts helped defuse a crisis over North
Korea's nuclear capability; and his efforts helped to negotiate a cease-fire
agreement to slow ethnic warfare in Bosnia. Carter has called The Atlanta
Project the domestic centerpiece of the Carter Center's work. And, as in
his international mediation efforts, fear of failure does not deter the former president. "The real failure, for Atlanta and cities like it, would be not
to try," according to Carter.

Collaborative empowerment

Atlanta has a large, successful professional population. But the city also
has a much larger (500,000) inner-city population that suffers the problems of chronic poverty, crime, drugs, joblessness, illiteracy, teenage pregnancy, and substandard housing. To tackle these problems, Carter was determined to engage a broad cross-section of community resources. The
former president called together leaders from business, local government, and community organizations and created a consortium to engage

the issues. The leaders pledged their cooperation and the involvement of their organizations. As one executive said, "Mr. Carter is very persuasive and a good arm-twister." The former president solicited substantial pledges from such Atlanta-headquartered businesses as Marriott, Coca Cola, Delta Airlines, and BellSouth. Each would become an important partner in TAP. As of 1994, Atlanta businesses had contributed more than $30 million.

TAP was organized around Atlanta's local neighborhoods. The idea was to find a natural community around which an integrated approach to social services and economic assistance could be built. The focus turned to Atlanta's high schools which, it was discovered, served as natural focal points for Atlanta's neighborhoods. Each area was designated a *cluster community.* These twenty clusters became the unit of analysis and action for the project, although they often span political boundaries (e.g., parts of three counties are included in TAP's clusters).

The concept of local empowerment is vital to every aspect of TAP. Within each TAP cluster, for example, is a cluster coordinator and assistant coordinator who live in the neighborhood they represent. These coordinators are employed by TAP to work with a cluster steering committee composed of residents, service providers, and representatives from cluster schools, churches, businesses, and community groups. Cluster coordinators are not "bosses" in this process; rather, they are facilitators who help the community identify its needs, find the tools for tackling the issues, and create possible solutions to the cluster's problems. TAP has a central "resource center" to which all coordinators can turn for help, but the emphasis is on community-based solutions to community needs. Each cluster coordinator has to be skillful at using corporate partners, local government agencies, and other community resources to address the agenda of issues, needs, and concerns that the cluster community shares. Imagination is crucial to achieving success.

Business involvement in TAP operates at several levels. The chief executives of Atlanta companies met with former president Carter and leaders of other Atlanta organizations to map out strategies and initiatives in broad terms. Individual companies have been paired with one of the clusters, assigning at least one full-time manager to work with the cluster coordinator and his or her team. (TAP requested that the companies commit a full-time manager for up to *five* years in order to build real expertise at community problem solving.) Some companies have taken the lead in specific city-wide projects that span the clusters: BellSouth, for example, has had a companywide commitment to improving adult literacy. The company took the lead in creating a program to bring thousands of books to Atlanta's clusters, coupling the book donations with a volunteer program to teach reading throughout the city. Hundreds of BellSouth employees have participated in this adult literacy education effort.

Thousands of employees in TAP companies have volunteered to help in the clusters, undertaking tasks as diverse as providing computer instruction for teachers and students in local schools; offering small business forums to help residents turn ideas into community enterprises; organizing basketball camps; helping students prepare college financial aid applications; and providing local residents with technical training in electrical wiring, plumbing, secretarial skills, and how to meet commercial driver's license requirements.

Collaboration among all of Atlanta's racial, demographic, and economic segments is the essence of the process. That doesn't happen immediately in most situations because trust must be built, a common vision must be developed, and an understanding of how to work together needs to emerge. Once a diverse community starts to work together, however, new ideas emerge, action follows ideas, and visible progress begins to occur. That is the essence of former president Carter's notion of collaborative empowerment.

Problems

The Atlanta Project is not without its problems and its detractors. Some say the project is too ambitious, too costly, and too closely tied to Carter's unique vision of empowerment. Most observers, however, point to Carter's role as one of being a *catalyst,* not a director. TAP's problems, in their view, have to do with the day-to-day challenges of getting people, who may have never been involved in community processes, to participate and trust the cluster approach. There are also the problems of sustaining the "fire" in cluster coordinators and others who show signs of physical and emotional burn-out after several years of hard work and of continuing to find new ways to leverage limited resources against a very formidable list of community issues and needs. In early 1995, as the fifth year of the five-year TAP program began, several clusters were still operating with acting coordinators.

Business involvement has also suffered some problems. Loaned executives from Atlanta companies, for example, have sometimes sought to return to their companies for personal career reasons. Five years on leave in a community job may be too long away from the mainstream of a telecommunications or banking career. And business representatives have sometimes been frustrated by the slow decision-making processes that accompany the empowerment approach. Discussion takes time, and endless meetings of community representatives may be necessary before a consensus is reached on what to do and how to do it. Still, this is an investment in community decision making that supporters believe will be repaid many times over as more complex problems are tackled by the clusters.

Atlanta's businesses seem likely to stay involved for several reasons. First, former president Carter has made it quite clear that he will not let them walk away from so vital a process. The Atlanta Project is scheduled to continue for a full five years, through 1996, and it has drawn such interest from other cities that Carter announced a national "rollout" of the concept to other cities starting in 1995. Second, the presence of the 1996 Olympic Summer Games in Atlanta has meant that businesses, government agencies, and community groups have to cooperate to meet the city's commitments as host city. TAP objectives and needs mesh nicely into some aspects of Atlanta's Olympic planning efforts. Third, the entire process is reinforcing an ethic in the Atlanta business community that was summarized by former Atlanta mayor and United Nations ambassador, Andrew Young, in this way: "At the end of the day, the success of business depends not on profit and loss, but on the quality of life." Quality of life cannot mean two cities, one rich and one poor; it must mean one community, with opportunity and hope for all.

Boston Against Drugs: A Micro Approach to Social Issues

Illegal drugs have been a part of America's social problems for many years. Since the 1970s, federal, state, and local governments have tried to combat drug distribution and sale through vigorous enforcement efforts. Many experts believe the nation is still losing its battle against drugs and that renewed efforts must be made to address drug sale and use.

Private sector initiatives have also been undertaken to deal with drugs. Many companies have instituted drug testing programs in the workplace to identify workers whose drug abuse may be harmful to others. To the extent drugs undermine workforce productivity, they threaten the competitiveness of companies. Worse, by far, drugs impair a person's judgment and physical actions. This can be fatal for coworkers and innocent bystanders if the impaired employee is operating mechanical equipment, motor vehicles, or airplanes. Public safety and workplace safety considerations have made drug testing and substance-abuse education common among many companies.

A second type of private sector antidrug effort has involved public education campaigns to persuade people, especially young adults, not to experiment with illegal substances. One of the best-known programs is the advertising campaign sponsored by Partnership for a Drug-Free America. Media companies, advertisers, and advertising agencies have teamed up to raise millions of dollars to broadcast the creative, sometimes shocking Partnership ads. (In one, the camera focuses on an egg as a voice says, "This is your brain." The next scene shows a cracked egg frying on a hot griddle as the voice says, "This is your brain on drugs.") The objective is to deter people from ever trying drugs.

Business has also become involved in grassroots, community-based efforts to tackle drug use. In Boston, such a program is called Boston Against Drugs (BAD). BAD is a partnership of businesses, nonprofit organizations, and government agencies formed in 1987 when former mayor Ray Flynn called on local businesses to assist in dealing with the city's drug and substance abuse issues. A number of corporate chief executives were willing to become involved because they believed drugs to be a social "scourge" which their companies were already addressing through drug testing, education, and prevention programs. Others concluded it was not politically smart to say "no" to a popular mayor who seemed likely to hold political office for years to come.[2]

As in The Atlanta Project, Boston Against Drugs adopted a neighborhood focus. The city was divided into sixteen neighborhoods. For each, a team was formed consisting of government officials, community leaders, and a business that had connections to the area. For example, in South Boston, Gillette, the consumer products giant, signed on as the corporate team member. Among the other companies were Bank of Boston; New England Telephone (NYNEX); Group Bull, a computer manufacturer; Boston Edison, an electric utility; and Blue Cross and Blue Shield, a health insurer. The Boston Herald (daily newspaper), MassPort (public authority which operates the airport and harbor), the MBTA (subway and bus system), and several law firms also were involved.

Business leadership was key to BAD's activities. The first challenge was to get the cooperation of community groups, government officials, and businesses to actually form the community teams. Because each of these organizations faces many demands on their time, considerable persuasion was necessary to get the proper players on board. An even greater challenge was to get the team members talking in a constructive and positive way. What were the problems in each neighborhood? What could and should be done? How could obstacles be overcome? Would any of their efforts really make a difference? Months passed before the teams developed enough trust and sense of common purpose for initiatives to begin taking shape. Once they did, however, things began to change in the community. In one neighborhood, the need was for a basketball program; in another, classes were offered at a community center; in yet another, a job counseling project was started. By the end of a year, there were signs of progress.

Boston Against Drugs started small but had potential. In 1990, the program received a federal grant to expand the program to all of the city's neighborhoods and to begin a systematic evaluation process to see whether such efforts ultimately influenced drug use by the population of a neighborhood. An evaluation team was created to work with neighborhood teams, to track results, neighborhood by neighborhood, and to facilitate sharing lessons learned. Boston became a model for other antidrug programs throughout the United States.

---

[2] Victor Forlani, "Boston Against Drugs: An Analysis of Business in the Community," in Steven Wartick and Denis Collins, eds., *1994 Proceedings of Fifth Annual Conference, International Association for Business and Society*, Hilton Head, NC, Mar. 17–20, 1994, pp. 300–304. Boston Against Drugs, *Annual Report*, Boston, Office of The Mayor, 1994.

A narrow focus

Drugs are often at the center of a city's social problems. Many experts believe that by focusing sharply on antidrug activities, "leverage" can be created for addressing issues such as crime, education, and poverty. Some BAD leaders believe it is crucial to keep a clear focus on drugs if anything is to be accomplished. These people fear a loss of focus if other community problems are added to the agenda.

Business played an important role in Boston Against Drugs. By providing leadership, human resources, financial leverage, and demonstrated commitment, the business community has helped make the program an important part of the city's commitment to saving its neighborhoods. When Mayor Flynn resigned in 1993 to assume the position of U.S. ambassador to the Vatican, a city council member named Thomas Menino became acting mayor. Several months later, Menino was elected to a full term as mayor of Boston. Among his early actions, the new mayor endorsed the concept and reinforced the importance of the Boston Against Drugs partnership: "If we are to build a safe city that serves all of our people, we need partnerships like BAD."

The Future

Not all public-private partnerships succeed in solving the problems of America's cities. Some observers believe that many of these efforts fall short of their goals and objectives. Since program evaluation is often weak, however, the truth is hidden.

Given the complexity of the social ills being addressed, and the challenge of coordinating private sector, public sector, and voluntary sector organizations, it is not surprising that saving the cities is a very difficult task. One role business can play is to insist on careful evaluation of programs in a continuing effort to figure out what works best and what works least well. The business community knows a great deal about program evaluation, total quality management concepts, benchmarking, and quantifying the costs, benefits, and value-added of activities. This expertise needs to be brought to bear on saving our cities. As the authors of the Urban Institute report state:

> The difficulty of measuring such abstract concepts as "improved community spirit" and "increased leadership potential," coupled with the fact that many grassroots organizations do not have access to measurement tools, has made comprehensive evaluation infrequent. However, this trend is slowly changing, partly as a result of increased corporate involvement in distressed communities. As corporations move away from pure philanthropic donations and look at their contributions as investments, they are demanding to see some return on that investment and have increased the demand for measurement of outcomes.[3]

[3]George Peterson and Dana Sundblad, *Corporations as Partners in Strengthening Urban Communities,* Research Report 1079-94, New York: The Conference Board, 1994, p. 43.

Discussion Questions

1. What factors have helped to make The Atlanta Project a success? Which are unique to Atlanta and which are common to all communities?

2. What factors have helped to make Boston Against Drugs a success? Which are unique to Boston and which are common to all communities?

3. Consider the problems in your own community. Compare the *comprehensive* approach suggested by The Atlanta Project with the *selective* approach of Boston Against Drugs. Which approach has the best potential for success in your community?

4. Dr. Johnetta Cole, president of Spelman College, has been an active participant in TAP. She has said, "If we focus, if we cooperate, if we sacrifice, . . . we can do it." Are focus, cooperation, and sacrifice enough to save our cities? What else is needed? Is there a role for the federal government? the state government?

5. In some states, there are one or two large cities and many small and medium-sized communities. Should businesses that are located in the large cities, but draw employees and customers from smaller communities as well, participate in projects to strengthen all of these communities? How can they decide which ones not to support?

6. Consider the community in which your college or university is located. What kind of community involvements does it have? How does it participate in projects to improve the community? What organizations provide the leadership?

GLOSSARY

This glossary defines technical or special terms used in this book. It may be used by students as a quick and handy reference for terms that may be unfamiliar without having to refer to the specific chapter(s) where they are used. It also can be a very helpful aid in studying for examinations and for writing term papers where precise meanings are needed.

Acid rain. Rain that is more acidic than normal; occurs when emissions of sulfur dioxide and nitrogen oxides from utilities, manufacturers, and vehicles combine with water vapor in the air.

Acquisition. (See **Corporate merger.**)

Administrative costs. The direct costs incurred in running government regulatory agencies, including salaries of employees, equipment, supplies, and other such items. (See also **Compliance costs.**)

Administrative learning. A stage in the development of corporate social responsiveness during which managers and supervisors learn the new practices necessary for coping with social problems and pressures.

Advocacy advertising. A strategy used by companies to promote their social, political, or economic viewpoint through the media.

Affirmative action. A positive and sustained effort by an organization to identify, hire, train if necessary, and promote minorities, women, and members of other groups who are underrepresented in the organization's workforce.

Air pollution. When more pollutants, such as sulfur dioxide or particulates, are emitted into the atmosphere than can be safely absorbed and diluted by natural processes.

Altruism. Acting for the benefit of others at the risk of sacrificing one's self-interest.

American dream. An ideal goal or vision of life in the United States, usually including material abundance and maximum freedom.

Annual meeting. A yearly meeting called by a corporation's board of directors for purposes of reporting to the company's stockholders on the current status and future prospects of the firm.

Anticompetitive merger. A merger of two or more companies that reduces or eliminates competition in an industry or region; usually illegal under U.S. antitrust laws.

Antitrust laws. Laws that promote competition or that oppose trusts, monopolies, or other business combinations that restrain trade.

Biodiversity. The variety of living organisms and the range of their genetic makeup.

Biotechnology. The use and combination of various sciences, including biochemistry, genetics, microbiology, ecology, recombinant DNA, and others, to invent and develop new and modified life forms for applications in medicine, industry, farming, and other areas of human life.

Blowing the whistle. (See **Whistle-blowing.**)

Board of directors. A group of persons elected by shareholder votes to be responsible for directing the affairs of a corporation, establishing company objectives and policies, selecting top-level managers, and reviewing company performance.

Bottom line. Business profits or losses, usually reported in figures on the last or bottom line of a company's income statement.

Bubble concept. A pollution control plan that determines compliance by measuring combined total emissions from an entire industrial installation, rather than from each of the plant's individual pollution sources.

Business. The activity of organizing resources in order to produce and distribute goods and services for society.

Business and society. The study of the relationship of business with its entire social environment.

Business Council for Sustainable Development (BCSD). A group of corporate executives from around the world formed in 1990 to encourage the participation of the international business community in the Earth Summit and to develop a global business perspective on economic development and the environment.

Business ethics. The application of general ethical ideas to business behavior.

Business legitimacy principle. The view that a company must comply with the law and conform to the expectations of its stakeholders in order to be a corporate citizen in good standing.

Carrying capacity. The maximum population that an ecosystem can support. (See also **Limits to growth hypothesis.**)

Cause marketing. A form of philanthropy in which contributions to a nonprofit organization are tied to the use of the donor organization's products or services by the recipient organization's members.

Central state control. A socioeconomic system in which political, social, and economic power is concentrated in a central government that makes all fundamental policy decisions for the society.

CERES Principles. A corporate code of conduct, developed by the Coalition for Environmentally Responsible Economies (CERES), that commits signers to sound environmental policies and sustainable use of natural resources. (Formerly known as the Valdez Principles.)

Charity principle. The idea that individuals and business firms should give voluntary aid and support to society's unfortunate or needy persons, as well as to other (nonprofit) organizations that provide community services.

Child care. The care or supervision of another's child, such as at a day-care center; offered as a benefit by some employers to working parents.

Chlorofluorocarbons (CFCs). Manufactured chemicals, used as refrigerants, insulation, solvents, and propellants in spray cans, that are believed to react with and deplete ozone in the upper atmosphere. (See also **Montreal Protocol, Ozone.**)

Coalitions. Groups of organizations or corporate stakeholders who work together to achieve a common goal.

Codetermination. A system of corporate governance providing for labor representation on a company's board of directors.

Collaborative partnerships. Companies joining with their key stakeholders to respond better to an important issue or problem by pooling resources.

Command and control regulation. A regulatory approach where the government "commands" companies to meet specific standards (such as amounts of particular pollutants) and "controls" the methods (such as technology) used to achieve these standards. This approach is often contrasted with market-based regulatory approaches where the government establishes general goals and allows companies to use the most cost-effective methods possible to achieve them.

Commons. Traditionally, an area of land on which all citizens could graze their animals without limitation. The term now refers to any shared resource, such as land, air, or water, that a group of people use collectively. (See also **Global commons.**)

Community advisory panels (CAPs). Groups of citizens from a local community who meet with corporate officials to discuss issues of common interest about a company's operations, such as plant safety, traffic patterns, and emergency planning.

Community relations. The involvement of business with the communities in which it conducts operations.

Comparable worth. The idea that different kinds of jobs can be equated with each other in terms of difficulty, training required, skills involved, effort made, responsibility involved, and working conditions, for the purpose of equalizing wages paid to people holding jobs approximately equal in these ways.

Competition. A struggle to survive and excel. In business, different firms compete with one another for customers' dollars.

Competition policies. A term used to describe antitrust laws or policies in some nations and trading groups.

Compliance costs. The costs incurred by business and other organizations in complying with government regulations, such as the cost of pollution control machinery or the disposal of toxic chemical wastes. (See also **Administrative costs.**)

Comprehensive Environmental Response, Compensation, and Liability Act (CERCLA). (See **Superfund.**)

Concentration (corporate, economic, industrial, market). When relatively few companies are responsible for a large proportion of economic activity, production, or sales.

Conglomerate merger. The combination, or joining together, of two or more companies in unrelated industries into a single company. (See also **Horizontal merger, Vertical merger.**)

Consumer movement. A social movement that seeks to augment the rights and powers of consumers. (Also known as *consumerism.*)

Consumer protection laws. Laws that provide consumers with better information, protect consumers from possible hazards, or encourage competitive pricing.

Consumer rights. The legitimate claims of consumers to safe products and services, adequate information, free choice, a fair hearing, and competitive prices.

Consumerism. (See **Consumer movement.**)

Contingent valuation. A method of determining the value of a public good, such as clean air or water, based on public opinion surveys.

Corporate crime. Illegal behavior by company employees that benefits a corporation.

Corporate culture. The traditions, customs, values, and approved ways of behaving that prevail in a corporation.

Corporate giving. (See **Corporate philanthropy.**)

Corporate governance. Any structured system of allocating power in a corporation that determines how and by whom the company is to be governed.

Corporate legitimacy. Public acceptance of the corporation as an institution that contributes to society's well-being.

Corporate merger. The combination, or joining together, of two or more separate companies into a single company. (See also **Conglomerate merger, Horizontal merger, Vertical merger.**)

Corporate philanthropy. Gifts and contributions made by corporations, usually from pretax profits, to benefit various types of nonprofit community organizations.

Corporate policy ethics. Companywide ethics problems and situations that require top-management policy decisions.

Corporate political agency. A theory that holds that politicians are the agents of those who elect or appoint them to office.

Corporate power. The strength or capability of corporations to influence government, the economy, and society, based on their organizational resources and size.

Corporate restructuring. The reorganization of a corporation's business units and activities which often involves the closing of current facilities and reduction of workforce.

Corporate social involvement. The interaction of business corporations with society.

Corporate social policy. A policy or a group of policies in a corporation that define the company's purposes, goals, and programs regarding one or more social issues or problems.

Corporate social responsibility. The idea that businesses are accountable for the effects of their actions and should seek socially beneficial results as well as economically beneficial results.

Corporate social responsiveness. The way firms address social demands initiated by their stakeholders, or actions taken by firms that affect their stakeholders.

Corporate social strategy. The social, political, and ethical parts of a company's plans and activities for achieving its goals and purposes.

Corporate stakeholder. A person or group affected by a corporation's policies and actions.

Corporate strategic management. Planning, directing, and managing a corporation for the purpose of helping it achieve its basic purposes and long-term goals.

Corporate strategic planning. A process of formulating a corporation's basic purpose, long-term goals, and programs intended to achieve the company's purposes and goals.

Corporate takeover. The acquisition, usually by merger, of one corporation by another.

Corporation. Legally, an artificial legal "person," created under the laws of a particular state or nation. Socially and organizationally, it is a complex system of people, technology, and resources generally devoted to carrying out a central economic mission as it interacts with a surrounding social and political environment.

Cost-benefit analysis. A systematic method of calculating the costs and benefits of a project or activity that is intended to produce benefits.

Council of Institutional Investors. An organization founded in 1985 that represents the interests of institutional investors.

Crisis management. The use of a special team to help a company cope with an unusual emergency situation that may threaten the company in serious ways.

Cross-media pollution. Pollution that migrates across several different media, such as air, land, or water. For example, hazardous wastes disposed in a dump might leak out, contaminating groundwater, or evaporate, causing air pollution. (Also known as *multi-media pollution.*)

Culpability score. Under the U.S. Corporate Sentencing Guidelines, the degree of blame assigned to an executive found guilty of criminal wrongdoing.

Cultural distance. The amount of difference in customs, attitudes, and values between two social systems.

Cultural shock. A person's disorientation and insecurity caused by the strangeness of a different culture.

Delaney Clause. An amendment to the Food, Drug, and Cosmetics Act of 1958 that bans all food additives know to cause cancer in humans or animals. (Also known as the *Delaney Amendment.*)

Deregulation. The removal or scaling down of regulatory authority and regulatory activities of government.

Directors. (See **Board of directors.**)

Discrimination (in jobs or employment). Unequal treatment of employees based on *non-job-related* factors such as race, sex, age, national origin, religion, color, and physical or mental handicap.

Diversity (global and cultural). A concept that describes an organization or community composed of people of many racial, cultural, ethnic, religious, and other distinguishing characteristics.

Divestment. Withdrawing and shifting to other uses the funds that a person or group has invested in the securities (stocks, bonds, notes, etc.) of a company. Investors sometimes have divested the securities of companies doing business in countries accused of human rights abuses.

Dividend. A return-on-investment payment made to the owners of shares of corporate stock at the discretion of the company's board of directors.

Downsizing. The reduction of a company's workforce; often part of a corporate restructuring program designed to reduce costs.

Earth Summit. An international conference sponsored by the United Nations in Brazil in 1992 that produced several treaties on global environmental issues. (Also known as the *Conference on Environment and Development.*)

Ecology. The study, and the process, of how living things—plants and animals—interact with one another and with their environment.

Ecosystem. Plants and animals in their natural environment, living together as an interdependent system.

Egoist. (See **Ethical egoist.**)

Elder care. The care or supervision of elderly persons; offered as a benefit by some employers to working children of elderly parents.

Electoral politics. Political activities undertaken by business and other interest groups to influence the outcome of elections to public office.

Emissions charges or fees. Fees charged to business by the government, based on the amount of pollution emitted.

Employee stock ownership plan (ESOP). A benefit plan in which a company purchases shares of its own stock and places them in trust for its employees.

Employment-at-will. The principle that workers

are hired and retained solely at the discretion of the employer.

Enlightened self-interest. The view that social responsiveness and long-run economic return are compatible and are in the interest of business.

Entitlement. A view that a person or group is guaranteed an economic or social benefit by virtue of being a member of the designated group. (See also **Right [human].**)

Environmental audit. A company audit, or review, of its progress toward meeting environmental goals, such as pollution prevention.

Environmental labeling. When government agencies or private organizations label products or packaging judged to be environmentally acceptable.

Environmental Protection Agency (EPA). The United States federal government agency responsible for most environmental regulation and enforcement.

Environmental scanning. Examining an organization's environment to discover trends and forces that could have an impact on the organization.

Environmental standards. Standard amounts of particular pollutants allowable by law.

Equal-access rule. A legal provision that requires television stations to allow all competing candidates for political office to broadcast their political messages if one of the candidates' views are broadcast.

Equal job opportunity. The principle that all persons otherwise qualified should be treated equally with respect to job opportunities, workplace conditions, pay, fringe benefits, and retirement provisions.

Ergonomics. Adapting work tasks, working conditions, and equipment to minimize worker injury or stress.

Ethical climate. The prevailing, often unspoken ethical attitudes and beliefs of an organization that tend to guide the behavior of organization members when confronted with an ethical dilemma.

Ethical egoist. A person who puts his or her own selfish interests above all other considerations, while ignoring or denying the ethical needs and beliefs of others.

Ethical relativism. A belief that ethical right and wrong are defined by various periods of time in history, a society's traditions, the special circumstances of the moment, or personal opinion.

Ethics. A conception of right and wrong conduct, serving as a guide to moral behavior.

Ethics audit. A systematic effort to discover actual or potential unethical behavior in an organization.

Ethics code. A written statement that describes the general value system and ethical rules of an organization.

Ethics committee. A high-level group of executives who provide ethical guidance for employees and are often empowered to investigate and punish ethical wrongdoing at the firm.

Ethnocentric business. A company whose business standards are based on its home nation's customs, markets, and laws.

European Union (EU). The political and economic coalition of European countries.

Executive compensation. The compensation (total pay) of corporate executives, including salary, bonus, stock options, and various benefits.

Export of jobs. A loss of jobs in a business firm's home nation, and a creation of new jobs in a foreign nation, caused by relocating part or all of the business firm's operations (and jobs) to the foreign nation.

Expropriation. (See **Nationalization.**)

Face-to-face ethics. The personal interactions people have with each other at work that involve ethical issues; the human, individual dimension of ethics that is part of most working relationships.

Family leave. A leave of absence from work, either paid or unpaid, for the purpose of caring for a family member.

Fiduciary responsibility or duty. A legal obligation to carry out a duty to some other person or group in order to protect their interest.

Fiscal policy. The patterns of spending and taxation adopted by a government.

Flextime. A plan that allows employees limited control over scheduling their own hours of work, usually at the beginning and end of the workday.

Foreign direct investment (FDI). The investment

and transfer of funds by investors in one nation into business activities or organizations located in another nation.

Foreign investment review board. A national government body that is empowered to review and approve or disapprove proposed investments by foreign owners in a nation.

Fraud. Deceit or trickery due to the pursuit of economic gain or competitive advantage.

Free enterprise ideology. A set of beliefs about one way to organize economic life that includes individualism, freedom, private property, profit, equality of opportunity, competition, the work ethic, and a limited government.

Free enterprise system. A socioeconomic system based on private ownership, profit-seeking business firms, and the principle of free markets.

Free market. A model of an economic system based on voluntary and free exchange among buyers and sellers. Competition regulates prices in all free market exchanges.

Full-cost pricing. Pricing goods to account for their full environmental costs.

Functional-area ethics. The ethical problems that typically occur in the various specialized operational areas of business, such as accounting, marketing, and finance.

Functional regulation. Regulations aimed at a particular function or operation of business, such as competition or labor relations.

Future shock. A human reaction to rapid technological change whereby individuals experience difficulty in coping with the new conditions of life brought on by new technology.

Gender pay gap. The difference in the average level of wages, salaries, and income received by men and women.

Genetic engineering. (See **Biotechnology.**).

Geocentric business. A company whose business standards and policies are worldwide in outlook including multinational ownership, management, markets, and operations.

Glasnost. A Russian term used to describe "openness" during the late 1980s and early 1990s when the Soviet Union began to collapse as a political entity.

Glass ceiling. A barrier to the advancement of women, minorities, and other groups in the workplace.

Glass wall. A barrier to the lateral mobility of women, minorities, and other groups in the workplace, such as from human resources to operations.

Global commons. The idea that certain types of natural resources, such as the earth's atmosphere, tropical rain forests, and oceans, are vital for all living organisms. (See also **Commons.**)

Global village. The most remote places on earth are linked together—like a single village—through technological advances that allow faster and more widespread communications.

Global warming. The gradual warming of the earth's climate, believed by some scientists to be caused by an increase in carbon dioxide and other trace gases in the earth's atmosphere resulting from human activity, mainly the burning of fossil fuels.

Government and business partnership. A subtype of socioeconomic system in which government and business work cooperatively to solve social problems. (See also **Public-private partnerships.**)

Grassroots politics. Political activity directed at involving and influencing individual citizens or constituents to directly contact government officials on a public policy issue.

Green consumerism. An attitude of consumers that considers the ecological effects of their purchase, use, and disposal of consumer goods and services.

Green management. An outlook by managers that emphasizes the importance of considering ecological factors as management decisions are made.

Green marketing. A concept that describes the creation, promotion, and sale of environmentally safe products and services by business.

Greenhouse effect. The warming effect that occurs when carbon dioxide, methane, nitrous oxides, and other gases act like the glass panels of a greenhouse, preventing heat from the earth's surface from escaping into space.

Greenmail. The practice of paying a premium over the market price of a company's stock as part of a settlement with investors who wish to take over a company.

Hazardous waste. Waste materials from industrial, agricultural, and other activities capable of causing death or serious health problems for those persons exposed for prolonged periods. (See also **Toxic substance.**)

Home country. The country in which a multinational corporation has its headquarters.

Horizontal merger. The combination, or joining together, of two or more companies in the same industry and at the same level or stage of production or sales into a single company. (See also **Conglomerate merger, Vertical merger.**)

Host country. A foreign country in which a multinational corporation conducts business.

Human rights code of conduct. An organization's statement regarding acceptable and unacceptable types of behavior with respect to people's rights to life, liberty, and well-being.

Human rights reasoning. (See **Right [human].**)

Ideology. A set of basic beliefs that define an ideal way of living for an individual, an organization, or a society.

Individualism. A belief that each individual person has an inherent worth and dignity and possesses basic human rights that should be protected by society. Each person is presumed to be a free agent capable of knowing and promoting his or her own self-interest.

Industrial ecology. Designing factories and distribution systems as if they were self-contained ecosystems, such as using waste from one process as raw material for another.

Industrial policy. Government action to encourage the growth and development of specific industries.

Industrial resource base. The minerals, energy sources, water supplies, skilled labor force, and human knowledge necessary for industrial production.

Industrial society. A society in which the building and mechanical processing of material goods dominates work and employs the largest proportion of the labor force.

Industry-specific regulation. Regulations aimed at specific industries, such as telephone service or railroad transportation, involving control of rates charged, customers served, and entry into the industry.

Inflation. Decline in the purchasing power of money.

Information society. The current phase of technology; emphasizes the use and transfer of knowledge and information.

Insider trading. The illegal practice of buying or selling shares of corporate securities based on fiduciary information which is known only to a small group of persons, such as executives and their friends ("insiders"), and which enables them to make profits at the expense of other investors who do not have access to the inside information.

Institutional investor. A financial institution, insurance company, pension fund, endowment fund, or similar organization that invests its accumulated funds in the securities offered for sale on stock exchanges.

Institutionalized activity (ethics, social responsiveness, public affairs, etc.). An activity, operation, or procedure that is such an integral part of an organization that it is performed routinely by managers and employees. (See also **Organizational commitment.**)

Intellectual property. Ideas, concepts, and other symbolic creations of human intelligence that are recognized and protected under a nation's copyright, patent, and trademark laws.

Interactive model of business and society. The combined primary and secondary interactions that business has with society.

Interactive system. The closely intertwined relationships between business and society.

Intergenerational equity. A term describing the unfairness of one generation's accumulation of debt and tax burdens that will have to be borne by future generations.

Interlocking directorate. A relationship between two corporations that is established when one person serves as a member of the board of directors of both corporations simultaneously.

International regulation. A form of regulation in which more than one nation agrees to establish and enforce the same rules of conduct for international business activities.

Issues management process. The systematic identification, analysis, priority setting, and response to public issues.

Justice reasoning. A mode of ethical reasoning that calls for the fair distribution of benefits and burdens among the people in a society, according to some agreed-upon rule.

Labor force participation rate. The proportion of a particular group, such as women, in the paid workforce.

Labor standards. Conditions affecting a company's employees or the employees of its suppliers or subcontractors.

Laissez faire. A French phrase meaning "to let alone," used to describe an economic system where government intervention is minimal.

Laws. A society's formally codified principles that help define right and wrong behavior.

Leveraged buyouts (LBOs). The acquisition of a corporation by a group of investors, often including top executives, that relies on debt financing to pay the purchase price. The value of the company's assets is used as a "lever" to borrow the necessary amount for the purchase.

Life-cycle analysis. Collecting information on the lifelong environmental impact of a product in order to minimize its adverse impacts at all stages, including design, manufacture, use, and disposal.

Limits to growth hypothesis. The idea that human society is now exceeding the carrying capacity of the earth's ecosystem and that unless corrective action is taken soon, catastrophic consequences will result. (See also **Carrying capacity.**)

Lobbying. The act of trying to directly shape or influence a government official's understanding and position on a public policy issue.

Market failure. Inability of the marketplace to properly allocate costs to the parties responsible (e.g., of air pollution emissions) or to achieve the benefits associated with free market economics.

Megacorporation. One of the very largest business corporations.

Merger. (See **Corporate merger.**)

Microenvironment of business. The interrelated social, economic, political, and technological segments of society which influence and are affected by a company's actions.

Mixed state-and-private enterprise. A socioeconomic system in which government owns some key industrial and financial enterprises but most businesses are owned and operated by private individuals and corporations.

Monetary policy. Government actions to control the supply and demand of money in the economy.

Montreal Protocol. An international treaty limiting the manufacture and use of chlorofluorocarbons and other ozone-depleting chemicals. (See also **Chlorofluorocarbons, Ozone.**)

Moral development stages. A series of progressive steps by which a person learns new ways of reasoning about ethical and moral issues.

Morality. A condition in which the most fundamental human values are preserved and allowed to shape human thought and action.

Most favored nation (MFN). The foreign policy term used to describe any nation with whom the United States has a relationship that is designed to encourage trade by minimizing trade barriers.

Multi-media pollution. (See **Cross-media pollution.**)

Multinational corporation. A company that conducts business in two or more nations, usually employing citizens of various nationalities.

National competitiveness. The ability of a nation to compete effectively with other nations in international markets through the actions of its privately and publicly owned business firms.

National sovereignty principle. A nation is a sovereign state whose laws, customs, and regulations must be respected by people, organizations, and other nations.

Nationalization. Government taking ownership and control of private property with or without compensation. (Also known as *expropriation.*)

New social contract. An evolving view of how a corporation and its stakeholders should act toward one another in light of modern economic and social changes. (See also **Social contract.**)

New World Order. The phrase used to describe relationships among nations following the end of the cold war in the late 1980s.

Nonpoint source. A source of water or air pollution that cannot be easily identified, such as the source of toxic runoff from urban storm drains. (See also **Point source.**)

Nonrenewable resources. Natural resources, such as oil, coal, or natural gas, that once used are gone forever. (See also **Renewable resources.**)

Occupational crime. Illegal activity by a business employee intended to enrich the employee at the expense of the company.

Occupational segregation. The practice of employing predominantly men or women in a particular job category.

Opportunity costs. The various opportunities that cannot be realized because money is spent for one purpose rather than for others.

Organizational commitment. A stage in the development of social responsiveness within a company when social responses have become a normal part of doing business. Therefore, the entire organization is committed to socially responsible actions and policies. (See also **Institutionalized activity.**)

Ozone. A gas composed of three bonded oxygen atoms. Ozone in the lower atmosphere is a dangerous component of urban smog; ozone in the upper atmosphere provides a shield against ultraviolet light from the sun. (See also **Chlorofluorocarbons, Montreal Protocol.**)

Parental leave. A leave of absence from work, either paid or unpaid, for the purpose of caring for a newborn or adopted child.

Paternalistic. Caring for others in need, as a father cares for a child.

Patriarchal society. A society in which men hold the dominant positions in organizations, the society's values reflect and reinforce male-oriented privileges, and women tend to hold subordinate positions.

Perestroika. A Russian term used to describe economic reform and reconstruction during the late 1980s and early 1990s when the Soviet Union began to collapse as a political entity.

Performance-expectations gap. The perceived distance between a corporation's actual performance and the performance that is expected by the corporation's stakeholders.

Perpetual political campaign. The continuous process of raising money, communicating with constituents, and running for reelection.

Philanthropy. (See **Corporate philanthropy.**)

Plant closing laws. Legislation that requires employers to notify employees in advance of the closing of a facility in order to allow time for adjustment, including negotiations to keep the plant open, to arrange an employee buyout, to find new jobs, and so forth.

Pluralism. A society in which numerous economic, political, educational, social, cultural, religious, and other groups are organized by people to promote their own interests.

Point source. A source of water or air pollution that can be easily identified, such as a particular factory. (See also **Nonpoint source.**)

Policy decision. A stage in the public policy process when government authorizes (or fails to authorize) a course of action, such as by passing (or failing to pass) a law, issuing a court opinion, or adopting a new regulation.

Policy evaluation. The final stage in the public policy process when the results of a public policy are judged by those who have an interest in the outcome.

Policy formulation. A stage in the public policy process when interested groups take a position and try to persuade others to adopt that position.

Policy implementation. A stage in the public policy process when action is taken to enforce a public policy decision.

Political action committee (PAC). A committee organized according to election law by any group for the purpose of accepting voluntary contributions from individual donors and then making contributions in behalf of candidates for election to public office.

Political cynicism. A climate of public distrust of politics and politicians.

Polluter pays principle (PPP). A principle that states that a polluter should be responsible for paying for the full costs of its pollution, such as through taxes.

Pollution charge. A fee levied on a polluting source based on the amount of pollution released into the environment.

Pollution prevention. (See **Source reduction.**)

Pollution rights. A legal right to emit a specified amount of pollution; such rights may be bought, sold, or held for future use with approval of government regulators.

Polygraph. An operator-administered instrument used to judge the truth or falsity of a person's statements by measuring physiological changes that tend to be activated by a person's conscience when lying.

Populism. A political philosophy that favors grassroots democracy and an economy based on small businesses and farms, and that opposes big business concentration.

Predatory pricing. The practice of selling below cost for the purpose of driving competitors out of business; usually illegal under U.S. antitrust laws.

Preferential hiring. An employment plan that gives preference to minorities, women, and other groups that may be underrepresented in an organization's workforce.

Price-fixing. When two or more companies collude to set—or "fix"—the price of a product or service; usually illegal under U.S. antitrust laws.

Primary interactions or involvement. The direct relationships a company has with those groups that enable it to produce goods and services.

Primary stakeholders. The people and groups who are directly affected by a corporation's economic activities and decisions.

Principle of national sovereignty. The idea that the government of each nation is legally entitled to make laws regarding the behavior of its citizens and citizens of other nations who are acting within the nation.

Priority rule. In ethical analysis, a procedure for ranking in terms of their importance the three ethical modes of reasoning—utilitarian, rights, and justice—before making a decision or taking action.

Privacy. (See **Right of privacy.**)

Private property. A group of rights giving control over physical and intangible assets to private owners. Private ownership is the basic institution of capitalism.

Privately held corporation. A corporation that is privately owned by an individual or a group of individuals; its stock is not available for purchase by the general investing public.

Privatization. The process of converting various economic functions, organizations, and programs from government ownership or government sponsorship to private operation.

Privity of contract. A legal doctrine that holds that producers can avoid responsibility for product failure if the product was purchased from someone else, such as a dealer. This principle has been weakened by a series of court decisions.

Product liability. A legal responsibility of a person or firm for the harmful consequences to others stemming from use of a product manufactured, sold, managed, or employed by the person or firm.

Product recall. An effort by a business firm to remove a defective or sometimes dangerous product from consumer use and from all distribution channels.

Productivity. The relationship between total inputs and total outputs. Productivity increases when the outputs of an organization increase faster than the inputs necessary for production.

Profit maximization. An attempt by a business firm to achieve the highest possible rate of return from its operations.

Profit optimization. An attempt by a business firm to achieve an acceptable (rather than a maximum) rate of return from its operations.

Profits. The revenues of a person or company minus the costs incurred in producing the revenue.

Proxy. A legal instrument giving another person the right to vote the shares of stock of an absentee stockholder.

Proxy statement. A statement sent by a board of directors to a corporation's stockholders announcing the company's annual meeting, containing information about the business to be considered at the meeting, and enclosing a proxy form for stockholders not attending the meeting.

Public affairs function. An organization's activities intended to perceive, monitor, understand, communicate with, and influence the external environment, including local and national communities, government, and public opinion.

Public issue. A problem or concern of corporate stakeholders that has the potential to become a politicized matter, leading to legislation, regulation, or other formal governmental action.

Public issues life cycle. The sequence of phases through which a public issue may pass.

Public policy. A plan of action by government to achieve some broad purpose affecting a large segment of the public.

Public policy agenda. All public policy problems or issues that receive the active and serious attention of government officials.

Public policy process. All of the activities and stages involved in developing, carrying out, and evaluating public policies.

Public-private partnerships. Community-based organizations that have a combination of businesses and government agencies collaborating to address important social problems such as crime, homelessness, drugs, economic development, and other community issues. (See also **Government and business partnership.**)

Public referendum. A citizen's initiative to place a question or resolution on the election ballot for a popular vote.

Public trustee. A concept that a business owner or manager should base company decisions on the interests of a wide range of corporate stakeholders or members of the general public. In doing so, the business executive acts as a trustee of the public interest. (See also **Stewardship principle.**)

Publicly held corporation. A corporation whose stock is available for purchase by the general investing public.

Questionable payments. Something of value given to a person or firm that raises significant ethical questions of right or wrong in the host nation or other nations.

Quotas (job, hiring, employment). An employment plan based on hiring a specific number or proportion of minorities, women, or other groups who may be underrepresented in an organization's workforce.

Rain forest. Woodlands that receive at least 100 inches of rain a year. They are among the planet's richest areas in terms of biodiversity.

Reengineering. The concept of redesigning work systems and organizations in ways that enhance productivity and efficient work activities.

Regulation. The action of government to establish rules by which industry or other groups must behave in conducting their normal activities.

Reinventing government. A phrase used to describe efforts to reengineer, restructure, and reduce the cost of government.

Relationship investing. When large stockholders, usually institutions, form a long-term, committed link with a company.

Renewable resources. Natural resources, such as fresh water or timber, that can be naturally replenished. (See also **Nonrenewable resources.**)

Re-regulation. The imposition of regulation on activities that were deregulated earlier.

Reverse discrimination. The unintended negative impact experienced by an individual or group as a result of legal efforts to overcome discrimination against another individual or group.

Right (human). A concept used in ethical reasoning that means that a person or group is entitled to something or is entitled to be treated in a certain way. (See also **Entitlement.**)

Right of privacy. A person's entitlement to protection from invasion of his or her private life by government, business, or other persons.

Rule of cost. The idea that all human actions generate costs.

Secondary interactions or involvement. The relationship a company has with those social and political groups that feel the impact of the company's main activities and take steps to do something about it. These relationships are derived from the firm's primary interactions.

Secondary stakeholders. The people and groups in society who are indirectly affected by a corporation's economic activities and decisions.

Sex role spillover. When men continue to think of women mainly as performing traditional roles as sex partners, homemakers, and childbearers, rather than roles as coworkers and qualified professionals.

Sexual division of labor. The traditional or accepted allocation of jobs or roles in a society between men and women.

Sexual harassment. Unwanted and uninvited sexual attention experienced by a person, and/or a workplace that is hostile or threatening in a sexual way.

Shareholder. (See **Stockholder.**)

Shareholder resolution. A proposal made by a stockholder and included in a corporation's notice of its annual meeting that advocates some course of action to be taken by the company.

Shareholder suit (individual). A lawsuit initiated by one or more stockholders that attempts to recover damages *they* (as stockholders) *personally* suffered due to alleged actions of the company's management.

Shareholder's derivative suit. A lawsuit initiated by one or more stockholders that attempts to recover damages suffered *by the company* due to alleged actions of the company's management.

Social accountability. The condition of being held responsible to society or to some public or governmental group for one's actions, often requiring a specific accounting or reporting on those activities.

Social audit. A systematic study and evaluation of an organization's social performance. (See also **Social performance evaluation.**)

Social Charter. Social policy developed by countries in the European Union.

Social contract. An implied understanding between an organization and its stakeholders as to how they will act toward one another. (See also **New social contract.**)

Social forecasting. An attempt to estimate major social and political trends that may affect a company's operations and environment in the future.

Social overhead costs. Public and private investments that are necessary to prepare the environment for effective operation of a new business or other major institutions.

Social performance evaluation. Information about an organization's social performance, often contained in a company's annual report to stockholders and sometimes prepared as a special report to management or the general public. (See also **Social audit.**)

Social regulation. Regulations intended to accomplish certain social improvements such as equal employment opportunity or on-the-job safety and health.

Social responsibility. (See **Corporate social responsibility.**)

Social responsibility shareholder resolution. A resolution on an issue of corporate social responsibility placed before stockholders for a vote at a company's annual meeting, usually by social activist groups.

Social responsiveness. (See **Corporate social responsiveness.**)

Society. The people, institutions, and technology that make up a recognizable human community.

Socioeconomic system. The combined and interrelated social, economic, and political institutions characteristic of a society.

Solid waste. Any solid waste materials resulting from human activities, such as municipal refuse and sewage, industrial wastes, and agricultural wastes.

Source reduction. A business strategy to prevent or reduce pollution at the source, rather than to dispose of or treat pollution after it has been produced. (Also known as *pollution prevention.*)

Special economic zones. Industrial areas in the People's Republic of China that are reserved for foreign companies to establish business operations.

Specialized learning. A stage in the development of corporate social responsiveness within a company during which managers and supervisors, usually with the help of a specialist, learn the new practices necessary for coping with social problems and pressures.

Stakeholder. (See **Corporate stakeholder.**)

Stakeholder coalitions. Temporary unions of a company's stakeholder groups in order to express a common view or achieve a common purpose on a particular issue.

Stakeholder power. The ability of one or more stakeholders to achieve a desired outcome in their interactions with a company.

State-owned enterprise. A government-owned business or industry (e.g., a state-owned oil company).

Stateless corporation. A multinational corporation whose activities are conducted in so many nations as to minimize its dependence on any single nation and enable it to establish its headquarters' activities virtually anywhere in the world.

Stewardship principle. The idea that business managers should act in the interest of all members of society who are affected by their business decisions, thus behaving as stewards or trustees of the public welfare. (See also **Public trustee.**)

Sticky floor. When women, minorities, or other groups are unable to advance in the workplace because they become "stuck" in entry-level, low-paying jobs.

Stockholder. A person, group, or organization owning one or more shares of stock in a corporation. (Also known as *shareholder.*)

Strategic philanthropy. A form of philanthropy

in which donor organizations direct their contributions to recipients in order to achieve a direct or indirect business objective.

Strategies of response. (See **Corporate social strategy.**)

Strict liability. A legal doctrine that holds that a manufacturer is responsible (liable) for injuries resulting from the use of its products, whether or not the manufacturer was negligent or breached a warranty.

Superfund. A U.S. law, passed in 1980, designed to clean up hazardous or toxic waste sites. The law established a fund, supported mainly by taxes on petrochemical companies, to pay for the cleanup. (Also known as the *Comprehensive Environmental Response, Compensation, and Liability Act [CERCLA].*)

Sustainable development. A concept that describes current economic development that does not damage the ability of future generations to meet their own needs.

Technology. The tools, machines, skills, technical operations, and abstract symbols involved in human endeavor.

Telecommunications. The transmission of information via electromagnetic signals.

Telecommuting. Performing knowledge work and transmitting the results of that work by means of computer terminal to an organization's central data bank and management center, while the employee works at home or at some other remote location.

Tender offer. An offer by an individual, group, or organization to buy outstanding shares of stock in a corporation, frequently in an effort to gain control or otherwise benefit themselves.

Term limits. Limits on the maximum number of terms in office that an elected official can serve.

Third world nations. Developing nations relatively poorer than advanced industrial nations.

Total quality management (TQM). A management approach that achieves high quality and consumer satisfaction through teamwork and continuous improvement of a product or service.

Toxic substance. Any substance used in production or in consumer products that is poisonous or capable of causing serious health problems for those persons exposed. (See also **Hazardous waste.**)

Tradable allowances. A market-based approach to pollution control in which the government grants companies "rights" to a specific amount of pollution (allowances) which may be bought or sold (traded) with other companies.

Trade association. An organization that represents the business and professional interests of the firms or persons in a trade, industry, or profession, such as medical doctors, chemical manufacturers, or used car dealers.

Trade-offs, economic and social. An attempt to balance and compare economic and social gains against economic and social costs when it is impossible to achieve all that is desired in both economic and social terms.

Trade policy. Actions by government to encourage or discourage commerce with other nations.

Unanimity Rule. In ethical analysis, a procedure for determining that all three modes of ethical reasoning—utilitarian, rights, and justice—provide consistent and uniform answers to an ethical problem or issue.

Utility (social). A concept used in ethical reasoning that refers to the net positive gain or benefit to society of some action or decision.

Values. Fundamental and enduring beliefs about the most desirable conditions and purposes of human life.

Vertical merger. The combination, or joining together, of two or more companies in the same industry but at different levels or stages of production or sales into a single company. (See also **Conglomerate merger, Horizontal merger.**)

Volunteerism. The uncompensated efforts of people to assist others in a community.

Wall Street. A customary way of referring to the financial community of banks, investment institutions, and stock exchanges centered in the Wall Street area of New York City.

Warranty. A guarantee or assurance by the seller of a product or service.

Water pollution. When more wastes are discharged into waterways, such as lakes and rivers, than can be naturally diluted and carried away.

Whistle-blowing. An employee's disclosure to the public of alleged organizational misconduct, often after futile attempts to convince organizational authorities to take action against the alleged abuse.

White collar crime. Illegal activities committed by corporate managers, such as embezzlement or fraud.

Women's movement. A social movement for the rights of women.

Workplace safety team. A group of workers and managers who seek to minimize the occurrence of workplace accidents.

BIBLIOGRAPHY

In addition to references cited in the footnotes of each chapter, readers may find the following publications of special value in expanding concepts discussed in this book. Among the many journals serving the business and society field, readers will find relevant articles in the following: *Business and Society* (International Association of Business and Society), *Business and Society Review* (Management Reports, Inc.), *Business Ethics, Journal of Business Ethics, Business Horizons, Columbia Journal of World Business, Harvard Business Review,* and *California Management Review.* See also the journals of the Academy of Management: *The Academy of Management Review, Academy of Management Journal,* and *Academy of Management Executive.* Also, see *Research in Corporate Social Performance and Policy* (Greenwich, CT: JAI Press), an annual research series.

PART ONE (Chapters 1–3)

Academy of Management Review, Special Topic Forum on Shifting Paradigms: Societal Expectations and Corporate Performance, vol. 20, no. 1, Jan. 1995.

Ackerman, Robert, *The Social Challenge to Business,* Cambridge, MA: Harvard University Press, 1975.

Bowen, Howard R., *Social Responsibilities of the Businessman,* New York: Harper, 1953.

Bradshaw, Thornton, and Vogel, David, eds., *Corporations and Their Critics,* New York: McGraw-Hill, 1981.

Chamberlain, Neil W., *The Limits of Corporate Social Responsibility,* New York: Basic Books, 1973.

————, *Social Strategy and Corporate Structure,* New York: MacMillan, 1982.

Dertouzas, Michael L., Lester, Richard K., and Solow, Robert M., *Made in America: Regaining the Productivity Edge,* Cambridge, MA: MIT Press, 1989.

Dickie, Robert S., and Rouner, Leroy S., eds., *Corporations and the Common Good,* Notre Dame, IN: Notre Dame University Press and School of Management Boston University, 1986.

Donaldson, Thomas J., and Freeman, R. Edward, *Business as a Humanity,* New York: Oxford University Press, 1994.

Drucker, Peter, *The New Realities,* New York: Harper & Row, 1989.

Etzioni, Amitai, and Lawrence, Paul R., eds., *Socio-economics: Toward a New Synthesis,* Armonk, N.Y.: M. E. Sharpe, 1991.

Freeman, R. Edward, *Strategic Management: A Stakeholder Approach,* Marshfield, MA: Pitman, 1984.

Harrison, Bennett, *Lean and Mean: The Changing Landscape of Corporate Power in the Age of Flexibility,* New York: Basic Books, 1994.

Heath, Robert L., et al., *Strategic Issues Management: How Organizations Influence and Respond to Public Interests and Policies,* San Francisco: Jossey-Bass, 1988.

Kuhn, James W., and Shriver, Donald W. Jr., *Beyond Success: Corporations and Their Critics in the 1990's,* New York: Oxford University Press, 1991.

Miles, Robert, *Managing the Corporate Social Environment: A Grounded Theory*, Englewood Cliffs, NJ: Prentice-Hall, 1987.

Mitchell, Neil J., *The Generous Corporation: A Political Analysis of Economic Power*, New Haven, CT: Yale University Press, 1989.

Mitroff, Ian, and Pauchant, Thierry, *We're So Big and Powerful, Nothing Bad Can Happen to Us*, New York: Carroll Publishing Group, 1990.

Post, James E., *Corporate Behavior and Social Change*, Reston, VA: Reston, 1978.

Post, James E., ed., *Research in Corporate Social Performance and Policy*, "The Corporation and Public Affairs," Vol. 14, Greenwich, CT: JAI Press, 1993.

Preston, Lee E., and Post, James E., *Private Management and Public Policy*, Englewood Cliffs, NJ: Prentice-Hall, 1975.

Scott, Mary, and Rothman, Howard, *Companies with a Conscience: Intimate Portraits of Twelve Firms That Make a Difference*, New York: Citadel Press Book/Carroll Publishing Group, 1994.

Sethi, S. Prakash, and Falbe, Cecelia M., *Business and Society: Dimensions of Conflict and Cooperation*, Lexington, MA: Lexington Books, 1987.

Vogel, David, *Lobbying the Corporation: Citizen Challenges to Business Authority*, New York: Basic Books, 1978.

Werhane, Patricia H., *Adam Smith & His Legacy for Modern Capitalism*, New York: Oxford University Press, 1990.

PART TWO (Chapters 4–5)

Cavanagh, Gerald F., *American Business Values*, 3d ed., Englewood Cliffs, NJ: Prentice-Hall, 1992.

Colby, Anne, and Damon, William, *Some Do Care: Contemporary Lives of Moral Commitment*, New York: The Free Press, 1992.

Colby, Anne, and Kohlberg, Lawrence, *The Measurement of Moral Judgment: Volume I, Theoretical Foundations and Research Validation*, Cambridge, MA: Harvard University Press, 1987.

DeGeorge, Richard T., *Business Ethics*, 4th ed., Englewood Cliffs, NJ: Prentice-Hall, 1995.

Donaldson, Thomas, *The Ethics of International Business*, New York: Oxford University Press, 1989.

Etzioni, Amitai, *The Moral Dimension: Toward a New Economics*, New York: Free Press, 1988.

Freeman, R. Edward, and Gilbert, Daniel R. Jr., *Corporate Strategy and the Search for Ethics*, Englewood Cliffs, NJ: Prentice-Hall, 1988.

Freeman, R. Edward, ed., *Business Ethics: The State of the Art*, New York: Oxford University Press, 1991.

Guy, Mary E., *Ethical Decision Making in Everyday Work Situations*, New York: Quorum Books, 1990.

Jackall, Robert, *Moral Mazes: The World of Corporate Managers*, New York: Oxford University Press, 1988.

Kidder, Rushworth M., *How Good People Make Tough Choices*, New York: William Morrow and Co., 1995.

Mills, Claudia, *Values and Public Policy*, New York: Harcourt Brace, 1991.

Nash, Laura L., *Good Intentions Aside: A Manager's Guide to Resolving Ethical Problems*, Boston: Harvard Business School Press, 1990.

———, *Believers in Business*, Nashville, TN: Thomas Nelson Publishers, 1994.

O'Toole, James, *The Executive's Compass*, New York: Oxford University Press, 1993.

Rawls, John, *A Theory of Justice*, Cambridge, MA: Harvard University Press, 1971.

Stone, Christopher D., *Where the Law Ends: The Social Control of Corporate Behavior*, Prospect Heights, IL: Waveland Press, 1975.

Toffler, Barbara Ley, *Tough Choices: Managers Talk Ethics*, New York: Wiley, 1986.

PART THREE (Chapters 6–7)

Harding, Harry, *China's Second Revolution: Reform After Mao*, Washington: Brookings, 1987.

Kennedy, Paul, *The Rise and Fall of the Great Powers*, New York: Random House, 1987.

———, *Preparing for the Twentieth Century*, New York, Random House, 1992.

Krugman, Paul, *The Age of Diminished Expectations: U.S. Economic Policy in the 1990s*, Washington, DC: The Washington Post Co., 1994.

Laaksonen, Oiva, *Management in China During and After Mao in Enterprises, Government, and Party*, Berlin: Walter de Gruyter, 1988.

Lenway, Stefanie Ann, *The Politics of U.S. International Trade: Protection, Expansion and Escape*, Marshfield, MA: Pitman, 1985.

Reich, Robert B., *The Next American Frontier*, New York: Penguin Books, 1983.

Savas, E. S., *Privatization*, Chatham, NJ: Chatham House, 1987.

Stross, Randall, *Bulls in the China Shop and Other Sino-American Business Encounters*, New York: Pantheon Books, 1991.

Vachani, Sushil, *Multinationals in India*, New Delhi: Oxford & IBH Publishing Co., 1991.

Veljanovski, Cento, *Selling the State: Privatisation in Britain*, London: Weidenfeld & Nicholson, 1987.

PART FOUR (Chapters 8–10)

Ayres, Ian, and Braithwaite, John, *Responsive Regulation: Transcending the Regulation Debate*, New York: Oxford University Press, 1992.

Berry, Jeffrey M., *The Interest Group Society*, Boston: Little, Brown, 1985.

Cranston, Ross, *Law, Government and Public Policy*, New York: Oxford University Press, 1987.

Dewey, Donald, *The Anti-Trust Experiment in America*, New York: Columbia University Press, 1990.

Eagleton, Thomas F., *Issues in Business and Government*, Englewood Cliffs, NJ: Prentice-Hall, 1991.

Epstein, Edwin M., *The Corporation in American Politics*, Englewood Cliffs, NJ: Prentice-Hall, 1969.

Fugate, Wilbur L. (assisted by Lee Simowitz), *Foreign Commerce and the Anti-Trust Laws*, 4th ed., Boston: Little, Brown, 1991.

Galambos, Louis, and Pratt, Joseph, *The Rise of Corporate Commonwealth: United States Business and Public Policy in the 20th Century*, New York: Basic Books, 1988.

Garvey, George E., and Garvey, Gerald J., *Economic Law and Economic Growth: Anti-Trust, Regulation, and the American Growth System*, New York: Greenwood Press, 1990.

Lipset, Seymour Martin, and Schneider, William, *The Confidence Gap: Business, Labor, and Government in the Public Mind*, Baltimore: Johns Hopkins University Press, 1987.

Lodge, George C., *The New American Ideology*, New York: Alfred A. Knopf, 1978.

———, *Comparative Business-Government Relations*, Englewood Cliffs, NJ: Prentice-Hall, 1990.

———, *Perestroika for America: Restructuring Business-Government Relations for World Competitiveness*, Boston: Harvard Business School Press, 1990.

Maitland-Walker, Julian, ed., *Toward 1992: The Development of International Anti-Trust*, Oxford, England: ESC Publishing, 1989.

Marcus, Alfred A., Kaufman, Allen M., and Beam, David R., *Business Strategy and Public Policy: Perspectives from Industry and Academia*, Westport, CT: Quorum Books, 1987.

Oxford Analytica, *America in Perspective: Major Trends in the United States Through the 1990's*, Boston: Houghton Mifflin, 1986.

Peters, B. Guy, *American Public Policy: Promise and Performance*, 2d ed., Chatham, NJ: Chatham House, 1986.

Porter, Michael, *The Competitive Advantage of Nations*, New York: Basic Books, 1991.

Reich, Robert B., *The Work of Nations*, New York: Free Press, 1991.

Reich, Robert B., ed., *The Power of Public Ideas*, Cambridge, MA: Ballinger, 1988.

Scherer, F. M., *Competition Policies for an Integrated World Economy*, Washington, DC: The Brookings Institution, 1994.

Vietor, Richard H. K., *Strategic Management in the Regulatory Environment*, Englewood Cliffs, NJ: Prentice-Hall, 1989.

Weidenbaum, Murray, *Business, Government and the Public*, 4th ed., Englewood Cliffs, NJ: Prentice-Hall, 1990.

Wolf, Charles, *Markets or Government: Choosing Between Imperfect Alternatives*, Cambridge, MA: MIT Press, 1988.

PART FIVE (Chapters 11–12)

Brown, Lester R., et al., *State of the World, 1994: A Worldwatch Institute Report on Progress Toward a Sustainable Society,* New York: W. W. Norton, 1994.

Buchholz, Rogene, *Principles of Environmental Management,* Englewood Cliffs, NJ: Prentice-Hall, 1993.

Buchholz, Rogene, Marcus, Alfred, and Post, James E., *Managing Environmental Issues: A Casebook,* Englewood Cliffs, NJ: Prentice-Hall, 1992.

Collins, Denis, and Starik, Mark, eds., *Research in Corporate Social Performance and Policy,* "Sustaining the Natural Environment: Empirical Studies on the Interface Between Nature and Organizations," Vol. 15, Supp. 1, Greenwich, CT: JAI Press, 1995.

Ehrlich, Paul R., and Ehrlich, Anne H., *The Population Explosion,* New York: Simon & Schuster, 1990.

Fischer, Kurt, and Schot, Johan, eds., *Environmental Strategies for Industry: International Perspectives on Research Needs and Policy Implications,* Washington, DC: Island Press, 1993.

Gore, Al, *Earth in the Balance: Ecology and the Human Spirit,* Boston, MA: Houghton Mifflin, 1992.

Hoffman, W. Michael, Frederick, Robert, and Petry, Edward S., eds., *The Corporation, Ethics and the Environment,* Westport, CT: Quorum Books, 1990.

Kolluru, Rao V., ed., *Environmental Strategies Handbook: A Guide to Effective Policies and Practices,* New York: McGraw-Hill, 1994.

Lee, Henry, ed., *Shaping National Responses to Climate Change,* Washington, DC: Island Press, 1994.

Mann, Charles C., and Plummer, Mark L., *Noah's Choice: The Future of Endangered Species,* New York: Alfred A. Knopf, 1995.

Meadows, Donella H., Meadows, Dennis L., and Randers, Jorgen, *Beyond the Limits: Confronting Global Collapse, Environing a Sustainable Future,* Post Mills, VT: Chelsea Green Publishing Co., 1992.

Schmidheiny, Stephan, *Changing Course: A Global Perspective on Development and the Environment,* Cambridge, MA: MIT Press, 1992.

Stead, W. Edward, and Stead, Jean Garner, *Management for a Small Planet,* Newbury Park, CA: Sage Publications, 1992.

Stone, Christopher, *The Gnat Is Older Than Man: Global Environment and Human Agenda,* Princeton, NJ: Princeton University Press, 1993.

PART SIX (Chapters 13–16)

Adler, Nancy, and Israeli, Dafna N., eds., *Competitive Frontiers: Women Managers in the Global Economy,* Cambridge, MA: Basil Blackwell, 1995.

Bloom, Paul, and Smith, Ruth Belk, eds., *The Future of Consumerism,* Lexington, MA: Lexington Books, 1986.

Fagenson, Ellen A., ed., *Women in Management: Trends, Issues, and Challenges in Management Diversity,* Newbury Park, CA: Sage, 1993.

Faludi, Susan, *Backlash: The Undeclared War Against American Women,* New York: Doubleday, 1991.

Goldin, Claudia, *Understanding the Gender Gap: An Economic History of American Women,* New York: Oxford University Press, 1990.

Gray, Barbara, *Collaborating: Finding Common Ground for Multiparty Problems,* San Francisco: Jossey-Bass, 1989.

Gunderson, Martin, Mayo, David J., and Rhame, Frank S., *AIDS: Testing and Privacy,* Salt Lake City: University of Utah Press, 1989.

Gutek, Barbara A., *Sex and the Workplace: The Impact of Sexual Behavior and Harassment on Women, Men, and Organizations,* San Francisco: Jossey-Bass, 1985.

Herman, Edward S., *Corporate Control, Corporate Power,* Cambridge, England: Cambridge University Press, 1981.

Hochschild, Arlie, *The Second Shift: Working Parents and the Revolution at Home,* New York: Viking, 1989.

Kester, Carl W., *Japanese Takeovers: The Global Contest for Corporate Control,* Boston: Harvard Business School Press, 1991.

Kuenne, Robert E., *Economic Justice in American Society*, Princeton, NJ: Princeton University Press, 1993.

Linowes, David F., *Privacy in America: Is Your Private Life in the Public Eye?* Urbana, IL: University of Illinois Press, 1989.

Lorsch, Jay William, *Pawns or Potentates: The Reality of America's Corporate Boards*, Boston: Harvard Business School Press, 1989.

Matteo, Sherri, ed., *American Women in the Nineties*, Boston: Northeastern University Press, 1993.

Morrison, Ann M., White, Randall P., and Velsor, Ellen Van, *Breaking the Glass Ceiling: Can Women Reach the Top of America's Largest Corporations?* updated ed., Reading, MA: Addison-Wesley, 1992.

Powell, Gary N., *Women and Men in Management*, 2d ed., Newbury Park, CA: Sage Publications, 1993.

Puckett, Same B., and Emery, Alan R., *Managing AIDS in the Workplace*, Reading, MA: Addison-Wesley, 1988.

Rix, Sara E., *The American Woman 1990–91: A Status Report*, New York: Norton, 1990.

United Nations, *The World's Women, 1970–1990: Trends and Statistics*, New York: United Nations Publications, June 1991.

PART SEVEN (Chapters 17–19)

Barcus, F. Earl, *Images of Life on Children's Television: Sex Roles, Minorities, and Families*, New York: Praeger, 1983.

Corrado, Frank M., *Media for Managers: Communications Strategies for the Eighties*, Englewood Cliffs, NJ: Prentice-Hall, 1984.

Dates, Jannette L., and Barlow, William, eds., *Split Image: African-Americans in the Mass Media*, Washington, DC: Howard University Press, 1990.

Dertouzas, Michael L., Lester, Richard K., and Solow, Robert M., *Made in America: Regaining the Productivity Edge*, Cambridge, MA: MIT Press, 1989.

Etzioni, Amitai, *The Spirit of Community: Rights, Responsibilities, and the Communitarian Agenda*, New York: Crown Publishers, 1993.

Hernstein, Richard J., and Murray, Charles, *The Bell Curve: Intelligence and Class Structure in American Life*, New York: Free Press, 1994.

Kuenne, Robert E., *Economic Justice in American Society*, Princeton, NJ: Princeton University Press, 1993.

Linowes, David F., *Privacy in America: Is Your Private Life in the Public Eye?* Urbana, IL: University of Illinois Press, 1989.

Oskamp, Stuart, ed., *Television as a Social Issue*, Newbury Park, CA: Sage Publications, 1988.

Schlesinger, Arthur M. Jr., *The Disuniting of America: Reflections on a Multicultural Society*, New York: Norton, 1993.

Steele, Shelby, *Content of Our Character: A New Vision of Race in America*, New York: St. Martin's Press, 1990.

Ten Berge, Dieudonne, *The First 24 Hours: A Comprehensive Guide to Successful Crisis Communications*, Cambridge, MA: Basil Blackwell, 1990.

Wilson, James Q., Petersilia, Joan, eds., *Crime*, Cambridge, MA: ICS Press, 1994.

Name Index

Aaron, Titus E., 458*n*.
Abellard, Delphine A., 39*n*.
Abrams, Frank W., 43*n*.
Ackerman, Robert W., 76*n*.
Adler, Nancy, 445*n*.
Aichholzer, Georg, 504*n*.
Akers, John, 9
Altman, Barbara W., 342*n*., (fig.) 408
Anders, George, 625*n*.
Anderson, John, 256
Andrews, Edmund L., 228*n*.
Antal, Ariane Berthoin, 81*n*., 445*n*.
Aramony, William, 23
Arbetter, Lisa, 428*n*.
Aristide, Jean Paul, 547
Arlow, Peter, 119*n*.
Armstrong, Susan J., (exh.) 314
Aronoff, Craig E., 519*n*.
Aupperle, Kenneth E., 53*n*.
Auster, Ellen R., (fig.) 341
Avolio, Bruce J., 116*n*.

Baguet, Dean, 103*n*.
Bahls, Jane Easter, 422*n*.
Balmer, Thomas A., 293*n*.
Bannon, Lisa, 106*n*.
Bardige, Betty, 121*n*.
Barko, Naomi, 453*n*.
Barnett, Carole, 144*n*.
Barnett, Richard J., 184*n*., 185*n*.
Bartlett, Christopher, 178*n*.
Bear, Larry Allen, 99*n*.
Beauchamp, Tom L., 102*n*.
Beers, Charlotte L., 437, 438
Behr, Peter, 196*n*., (exh.) 196
Bell, Alexander Graham, 4
Berenbeim, Ronald E., 90*n*., (fig.) 91, 133*n*., 138*n*., 364*n*.
Berheid, Catherine White, 449
Bernardin, H. John, 429*n*.
Biddle, David, (exh.) 329
Billenness, Simon, 355*n*.
Bird, Frederick, (exh.) 97, (fig.) 117, (fig.) 131, 131*n*.
Birnbaum, Jeffrey, 255*n*., 263*n*.
Black, Amy, 92*n*.

Blackwell, Basil, 445*n*.
Blank, Helen, 60
Blasi, Joseph, 368*n*.
Blomstrom, Robert, 552
Bluestone, Barry, 400*n*.
Bluestone, Irving, 400*n*.
Blumberg, Philip I., 38*n*., 276*n*.
Boerner, Christopher 347*n*.
Boesky, Ivan, 288
Boje, David, (fig.) 40
Bok, Derek, 369*n*.
Bollier, David, (fig.) 382, 383*n*.
Borgman, Larry, 596–597, 600
Botzler, Richard G., (exh.) 314
Bowie, Norman E., 102*n*.
Bradsher, Keith, (exh.) 220
Bravo, Ellen, 458*n*.
Bridges, William, 491*n*.
Brooke, James, 212*n*.
Brooks, Leonard J., 133*n*.
Brown, Lester R., 304*n*.
Brown, Michael, 551, (exh.) 552
Brownstein, Andrew, 370*n*.
Bruyn, Severyn T., 20*n*.
Buchholz, Rogene A., 50*n*., 56*n*., 324*n*.
Buenaventura, Maria R. M., 482*n*., (fig.) 483, (fig.) 485
Burke, Francis, 92*n*.
Burke, Lee, 470*n*., 472*n*., 485*n*.
Burris, Joe, 549
Bush, George, 28, 144, 227, 256, 383, 383*n*., 486, (exh.) 553
Buss, Dale, 508*n*.
Butterfield, Fox, 75*n*.
Buzzeli, David, 238

Caranfil, Andrew, 532*n*., 540*n*.
Carnegie, Andrew, 41
Carraher, Jim, 427*n*.
Carroll, Archie B., 53*n*., 77*n*., 118*n*., 665
Carter, Jimmy, 227, 256, 668–671
Carville, James, 234
Casey, John L., 99*n*.
Cassedy, Ellen, 458*n*.
Castro, Fidel, 157
Cavanagh, Gerald F., 156*n*.

Cavanaugh, John, 184*n*., 185*n*.
Cedras, General, 547
Champy, James, 20*n*.
Chant, Peter D., (exh.) 97
Chapman, Christi, 135*n*.
Chase, Marilyn, 574*n*.
Chavez, Cesar, 242
Choi, Thomas, 506*n*.
Chonko, Lawrence B., (fig.) 98
Chung, Kwang S., 290*n*.
Church, George J., 488*n*.
Ciulla, Joanne B., 108*n*.
Clark, Lindley H., Jr., 29*n*.
Clausen, A. W., 136
Claybrook, Joan, 383, 404
Clayton, Mark, 516*n*.
Clinton, Bill, 28, 144, 211, 233–234, 256, (exh.) 260, 261, (exh.) 289, 386, 409, 409*n*., 543*n*., 547, (exh.) 553
Clinton, Hillary Rodham, 234–235, 261, (exh.) 289
Cobb, Roger W., 244*n*.
Cochran, Philip L., 102*n*.
Cohen, Ben, 530
Cohen, Joshua A., 642*n*.
Colby, Anne, 120*n*.
Coleman, Robin, 495, 496
Collins, Denis, 665*n*., 672*n*.
Conte, Lisa, 315
Cooke, Donna K., 429*n*.
Cooke, John, 468
Corrado, Frank M., 513*n*.
Cote-O'Hara, Jocelyne, 502*n*.
Coughlin, Richard M., 122*n*.
Crow, Michael M., 509*n*.
Crystal, Graef S., 369, 369*n*.
Cullen, John B., (fig.) 123, 123*n*.
Curran, Tim, 255*n*.

Dalton, Dan R., 93*n*., 429*n*.
Darney, Arsen J., 624*n*.
Davis, Keith, 552
Day, Susan G., 576*n*.
Deal, Terrence E., 122*n*.
DeBenedetti, Carlo, 106
de Butts, John, 10*n*.
DeGeorge, Richard, 431*n*.

Delaney, Joan, 93n., 428n.
Dell'Apa, Frank, 283n.
Denison, Richard, 324n.
DeNitto, Emily, 573
DePalma, Anthony, 212n.
Dertouzos, Michael L., 215n., 503n.
Dickie, R. B., 80n.
Dierkes, Meinolf, 81n.
Dill, William, 10n.
Dillon, Patricia S., 342n.
Disney, Walt, 467
Donaldson, Thomas, 108, 108n.
Donovan, Jim, 496
Dowd, Maureen, 249n.
Dowden, Jack, 431
Drucker, Peter F., 552, 552n.
Dukerich, Janet M., 119n.
Dulbecco, Melanie, (exh.) 534
Dusky, Lorraine, (exh.) 455
Duvalier, "Baby Doc", 547
Duvalier, "Papa Doc", 547
Dymtrenko, April, 501n.

Eagleton, Thomas J., 255n.
Eells, Richard, 43n.
Ehrenberg, Ronald G., 490n.
Eirinberg, Keith, 167n.
Eisner, Robert, 220n.
Elder, Charles D., 244n.
Elm, Dawn R., 119n.
Epstein, Edwin M., 251n., 275n., 276n.
Etzioni, Amitai, 6n.
Evans, William D., 56n.

Facchinetti, Ronald, (exh.) 265
Fagenson, Ellen A., 445n.
Fahey, Liam, 70n.
Falbe, Cecilia M., 50n.
Faludi, Susan, 440n.
Feinstein, Diane, (exh.) 260
Festervand, Troy A., 95n.
Figge, Judy, 450
Finn, David, 519n.
Finn, Don W., (fig.) 98
Fischer, Kurt, 342n.
Florsheim, Renee, 100n.
Fogerty, Patricia, (exh.) 494
Ford, Gerald, 227
Ford, Henry, 41, 204, 510
Ford, Henry, II, 204
Ford, William Clay, 203–204
Forlani, Victor, 672n.
Foss, Jason, 665n.

Foulkes, Fred, 192n.
Franklin, U., 511n.
Frederick, William C., 120n., (fig.) 107, 232n.
Freeman, R. Edward, 14n., 43n., 67n.
Fricker, Mary, 603n.
Friedan, Betty, 242, 440n.
Friedman, Milton, 29, (exh.) 155

Gaebler, Ted, 229n.
Gaedeke, Ralph M., 99n.
Gaertner, Karen N., 122n.
Galamos, Louis, 205n., 280n.
Garfield, Charles A., 52n.
Gates, Bill, 294, 510
Gentile, Mary C., 119n.
Gersh, Debra, 514n.
Getz, Kathleen A., (fig.) 107, 260n.
Ghoshal, Sumantra, 178n.
Gillespie, Ed, 235n., 537n.
Gilligan, Carol, 121, 121n.
Gingrich, Newt, 242, 256
Gleckman, Howard, 502n.
Glen, James R., Jr., 119n.
Glenn, James, 118
Goldin, Claudia, (exh.) 439, 452n.
Goldman, Merle, 150n.
Goldsmith, Sir James, (exh.) 521
Gong, Gerrit W., 167n.
Gorbachev, Mikhail, 28
Gordon, Robert A., 362n.
Gore, Al, 229, 229n., 300n.
Grant, Jan, 447n.
Graves, Samuel B., 53n.
Greenberg, Eric Rolfe, 408n.
Greeno, J. Ladd, 342n.
Grillo, John P., 100n.
Grossman, Daniel, (exh.) 534
Gumbel, Peter, 106n.
Gutek, Barbara, 459n., (exh.) 460
Guy, Mary E., 122n.

Haas, Barbara, (exh.) 67
Hagerty, Mike, (fig.) 518, (exh.) 521, 523n.
Hair, Jay, (exh.) 67
Hamel, Chuck, 432
Hamilton, K., 541n., (fig.) 542
Hammer, Michael, 20n.
Hanson, David, 335n.
Hanson, Kirk O., 122n., 136n.
Hardin, Garrett, 301n.
Harrington, Susan J., 135n.
Hatfield, John D., 53n.

Hayes, Denis, 384n., 385n.
Hazarika, Sanjoy, 184n.
Hazelwood, Joseph, 406
Heald, Morrell, 41n.
Heath, Robert L., 260n.
Henkoff, Ronald, 501n.
Henningson, Claus, 396
Henriques, Diane B., 103n.
Herrnstein, Richard J., 549n.
Heyman, Philip B., 244n.
Hill, Anita, (exh.) 258
Hill, John W., 93n.
Hochschild, Arlie, 455n.
Hoffman, Gerald M., 503n.
Hofmeister, Sallie, 469n.
Holland, Robert, Jr., 530
Holt, Andrew, 428n.
Honey, William, 109n.
Hoon, Tan Hwee, 514n.
Hornsby, Jeffrey S., 109n.
Horton, Gerald T., 665n.
Hosmer, LaRue Tone, 88n.
Houck, John, (fig.) 408
Houston, Jane E., 133n.
Howell, Jane M., (fig.) 116
Howenstine, Ned G., (fig.) 187, (exh.) 189
Howlett, Debbie, 240n.
Hoy, Frank, 77n.
Huffington, Michael, (exh.) 260
Hukill, Mark A., 507n.
Hunt, Christopher B., (fig.) 341
Hunt, Shelby D., (fig.) 98
Hussein, Saddam, 206

Inoue, Yasuo, (exh.) 39
Isaksen, Judith A., 458n.
Izraeli, Dafna N., 445n.

Jackall, Robert, 121n.
Jacques, Tony, 247n.
Jakubson, George H., 490n.
Janofsky, Michael, 469n.
Jensen, Michael, C., 361n., 370n.
Johnson, Robert, 56n.
Jones, Peter, 80, 80n.
Jorgenson, Dale W., 338n.
Josephson, Matthew, 41n.
Jossi, Frank, (exh.) 423
Judd, Dennis R., 476n.
Jussawalla, Meheroo, 507n.

Kalleberg, Arne L., 451n.
Kallman, Ernest A., 100n.
Kaplan, Jeffrey M., 93n.

Kapp, Jack, 469
Karr, Albert R., 550*n.*
Kaus, Mickey, 220*n.*
Kay, Ira T., 371*n.*
Kelley, Craig A., 99*n.*
Kelley, Patricia C., 252*n.*
Kennedy, Allan A., 122*n.*
Kennedy, John F., 379, 402
Kennedy, Paul, 538, 538*n.*
Khazai, Alan, (exh.) 552
Kilborn, Peter T., 548*n.*
King, Carl E., 427*n.*
King, Larry, 261
King, Martin Luther, Jr., 242
King, Rodney, 515
Klein, Katherine J., 368*n.*
Kohlberg, Lawrence, (fig.) 120, 120*n.*
Kohls, John, 135*n.*
Kohn, Howard, 550*n.*
Kolluru, Rao V., (exh.) 318, 324*n.*, 342*n.*
Koppel, Ted, 261
Kovach, Kenneth A., 453*n.*
Kram, Kathy E., 131*n.*
Krugman, Paul, 532*n.*, 547*n.*
Kruse, Douglas, 368*n.*
Kuratko, Donald F., 109*n.*

Laabs, Jennifer J., 434*n.*
Labich, Kenneth, 228*n.*
Laczniak, Gene R., 99*n.*
Lambert, Thomas, 347*n.*
Lang, Nancy A., 430*n.*
Langlois, Catherine C., 133*n.*
Lawrence, Anne T., 309*n.*, 342*n.*, 463*n.*
Lawrence, Francis L., 549
Lee, S. K. Jean, 514*n.*
Leicht, Kevin T., 451*n.*
Lenway, S., 214*n.*
Leopold, Aldo, (exh.) 314
Lerner, Gerda, 439*n.*
Lester, Richard K., 215*n.*, 503*n.*
Levin, Doron P., 103*n.*
Levine, Dennis, 228
Levine, Marvin J., 407*n.*
Levine, Richard, 456*n.*
Liebig, James E., 43*n.*, 118*n.*
Liker, Jeffrey K., 506*n.*
Likierman, Andrew, 98*n.*
Limbaugh, Rush, 261
Linstone, Harold A., 499*n.*
Little, Arthur D., 319*n.*
Lodge, George C., 156*n.*, 205*n.*

Logan, David, 174*n.*, (exh.) 473, 476*n.*
Logsdon, Jeanne M., 485*n.*
Lorenzo, Frank, 65
Lorsch, Jay W., 362*n.*
Love, Amy, 576*n.*
Lynn, Matthew, 339*n.*

MacAvoy, Paul W., 566*n.*
McCreary, Lew, 508*n.*
McCuddy, Michael K., 102*n.*
McDonald, Tim, (exh.) 534
Mace, Myles, 362*n.*
McGowan, Richard, 222*n.*, 241*n.*, 242*n.*
McGuide, Jean B., 53*n.*
MacIver, Elizabeth, 362*n.*
McLuhan, Marshall, 512*n.*
McNealy, Scott, 296
Mahon, John, 260*n.*
Mainiero, Lisa A., 450*n.*
Maitland, Leslie, 400*n.*
Majchrzak, Ann, 506*n.*
Maldonado-Bear, Rita, 99*n.*
Malone, John, 4
Mandela, Nelson, 174
Manegold, Catherine S., 218*n.*, 491*n.*
Marcus, Alfred A., 324*n.*
Marx, Thomas G., 68*n.*
Mason, Marcy, 134*n.*
Mathews, M. Cash, 132*n.*
Mathieu, Casey, 135*n.*
Mathison, David L., 37*n.*, 39*n.*, (fig.) 40
Matteo, Sherri, 444*n.*
Maxwell, Hamish, 375
Meadows, Dennis L., 304*n.*, 308*n.*
Meadows, Donella H., 304*n.*, 308, 308*n.*
Mendel, Gregor, 504
Metzger, Michael B., 93*n.*, 429*n.*
Michaels, Patrick J., (exh.) 312
Miles, Michael A., 375
Miles, Robert H., 52*n.*, 66*n.*, 77*n.*
Milken, Michael, 228
Millar, Donald, 417
Miller, Krystal, 103*n.*
Millspaugh, Peter E., 453*n.*
Minow, Nell, 362*n.*
Mintz, Steven M., 98*n.*
Mitnick, Barry M., 260*n.*, 262*n.*
Mitroff, Ian I., 499*n.*
Miyazaki, Kuniji, (exh.) 39
Modic, Stanley J., 100*n.*

Monks, Robert A. G., 362*n.*, 363
Moore, John R., 66
Morebey, Graham K., 503*n.*
Morell, David, 342*n.*
Morrison, Ann M., 450*n.*
Morrison, Robert, (exh.) 44
Moseley, Elaine, 403
Moseley, Shannon, 403
Moseley, Thomas, 403
Moyers, Bill, 300*n.*
Moynihan, Patrick, 205
Mufson, Steve, 111*n.*
Muller, Ronald E., 184*n.*
Mullins, Morton L., (exh.) 318
Muolo, Paul, 603*n.*
Murphy, Kevin J., 370*n.*
Murphy, Patrick E., 99*n.*
Murray, Charles, 549*n.*
Murray, Edwin A., (exh.) 51
Myers, Norman, 313
Myerson, Allen R., (exh.) 494

Nader, Ralph, 62, 242, 242*n.*, 381, 381*n.*, 382, (fig.) 382, 383, 383*n.*, 403
Naess, Arne, (exh.) 314
Naj, Amal Kumar, 104*n.*
Narayanan, V. K., 70*n.*
Nasar, Sylvia, 490*n.*
Nash, Laura L., 132*n.*
Nash, Roderick, (exh.) 314
Nath, Shrilata A., 509*n.*
Neil, Alfred C., 275*n.*, 277*n.*
Nelson, Donald, 119*n.*
Nelson, Oiva, 150*n.*
Nelson, Richard Alan, 260*n.*
Nelson, Ronald, 135*n.*
Newman, Katharine S., 532*n.*
Nichols, Mary Lippitt, 119*n.*
Nigh, Douglas, 102*n.*
Nomani, Asra O., 196*n.*
Novak, Michael, 6*n.*
Nulty, Peter, 66*n.*
Nye, Peter, 399*n.*

Obremski, Tom E., 119*n.*
Oliver, Bill, 427*n.*
Ones, Denis S., 429*n.*
O'Reilly, Anthony J. F., 35
O'Reilly, Brian, 407*n.*
Oreskes, Michael, 258*n.*, (fig.) 267
Osborne, David, 229*n.*
O'Toole, James, 46*n.*, 360*n.*, 620*n.*
Oz, Effy, 100*n.*

Paderon, Eduardo S., 100n.
Palmer, Robert, 408
Panner, Morris J., 370n.
Parks, Sharon Daluz, 119n.
Pavitt, Keith, 509n.
Pearce, Diana M., 444n.
Pearce, Harry J., 404
Perlez, Jane, 27n., 76n., 200n.
Perot, Ross, 28, 256, (exh.) 260
Perry, William K., 93n.
Peterson, George, 476n., 480n.,
    493n., 673n.
Petrick, Joseph A., 131n.
Phillips, Kevin, 255n., 608n.
Pilzer, Paul Zane, 603n., 605n.
Piper, Thomas R., 119n.
Pitta, Julia, 505n.
Pizzo, Stephen, 603n.
Popoff, Frank, 324n.
Posner, Barry Z., 117n., 124n.
Post, James E., 66n., 68n., (fig.) 69,
    241n., 252n., 264n., 324n.,
    342n., (fig.) 408, 470n.
Postel, Sandra, 300n., 304n.,
    306n.
Postman, Neil, 508
Powell, Gary N., 447, 447n., (fig.)
    448
Prater, Nick H., 36
Pratt, Joseph, 205n., 280n.
Prince, Jackie, 324n.
Pucik, Vladimir, 144n.
Pullins, Ellen B., 131n.

Quarrey, Michael, 368n.

Rabe, Barry G., 331n.
Ramanujam, Vasudevan, 558n.
Randers, Jorgen, 304n., 308n.
Randolph, W. Alan, 117n.
Rappaport, Alfred, (exh.) 51
Rasmussen, Wallace, (fig.) 518,
    (exh.) 521, 523n.
Reagan, Ronald, 28, 227, 256, 383,
    383n., 486n.
Reddy, Marlita A., 624n.
Reed, Gary E., 131n.
Reese, Jennifer, 620n.
Rehbein, K., 214n.
Reich, Robert B., 144n., 244n.,
    291n., 491, 491n.
Reichardt, Karl E., 102n.
Reidy, Chris, 264n.
Reiner, Martha, 485n.
Reinhardt, Forest, 322n.

Reithner, Robert M., 503n.
Reno, Janet, 295, 516
Repetto, Robert C., 317n.
Reynolds, Larry, (exh.) 47, 416n.
Ricci, David M., 248n.
Richardson, Helen L., 417n.
Rifkin, Jeremy, 315n., 507n.
Riggle, David, 316n.
Robinson, Eugene, 88n.
Rochow, Eugene, 651n.
Roddick, Anita, 21, 22n.
Rolston, Holmes, (exh.) 314
Rose, Frederick, 262n.
Rosen, Corey M., 368
Rosener, Judy B., 449n.
Ross, Lorraine, 592, 594
Ross, Stephen J., 369
Rotman, David, 502n.
Rouner, Leroy S., 80n.

Samuelson, Robert J., 20n.
Samuelson, Susan S., 293n.
Sanchez, Roberto A., 642n.
Sandroff, R., (fig.) 95
Sanger, David E., 165n.
Sapsford, Jathon, 103n.
Sarni, Vincent A., 104n.
Sato, Kyoto, 517n.
Schacht, Henry B., 57
Schellhas, Bob, 235n., 537n.
Schienstock, Gerd, 504n.
Schlegelmilch, Bodo B., 133n.
Schlesinger, Arthur M., Jr., 256n.,
    541n.
Schmidheiny, Stephen, 316n.,
    319n., 320n., 324n.
Schmidt, Frank L., 429n.
Schmidt, Warren H., 117n., 124n.
Schneeweis, Thomas, 53n.
Schneider, Stephen H., 310n.,
    (exh.) 312
Schnot, Johan, 342n.
Scully, Sean, 516n.
Seidman, William L., 502n.
Selznick, Philip, 539n.
Sesser, Stan, 322n.
Sestanovich, Stephen, 546n.
Sethi, S. Prakash, 50n., 231n.,
    275n.
Sexton, Joe, 544n.
Seybold, Jonathan, 498
Sharfman, Mark, 482n.
Sharp, Margaret, 509n.
Sharplin, Arthur, 398n.
Sherer, Paul, 106n.

Sherman, Rorie, 133n.
Shinozawa, Tetsuichi, 505n.
Shrivastava, Paul, 576n., 580n.
Singer, Andrew, 138n.
Skancke, Steven L., 502n.
Smale, John G., 365
Smith, Adam, 152
Smith, Craig, 77n., 484n., (exh.)
    494
Smith, Hedrick, 246n.
Smith, Raymond, 4, 506n., 530
Smith, Timothy, 642
Solow, Robert M., 215n., 308n.,
    503n.
Southland, Bill, 527
Staples, Marion M., 92n.
Starks, L., 214n.
Staroba, Kristin, 426n.
Stasch, Julia, 46
Steinem, Gloria, 242
Stempel, Robert C., 365
Stevens, Faith W., 426n.
Stevens, George E., 426n.
Stevenson, Richard W., 88n.
Stewart, James B., 99n., 373n.
Stewart, Terence P., 39n.
Stewart, Thomas A., 293n.
Stoever, William A., 190n.
Stone, Christopher D., (exh.) 312
Stone, Peter H., 255n.
Stone, Romuald A., 425n.
Strauss, Levi, 293
Strong, Maurice, 301
Subramanian, S. K., 507n.
Sullivan, Dianne, 76
Sundblad, Dana, 476n., 480n.,
    493n., 673n.
Sundgeon, Alison, 53n.
Sung, Kim I. L., 161
Surles, Carol D., 426n.
Swanson, Carl L., 275n.
Swanstrom, Todd, 476n.
Swasy, Alecia, 423, 423n.
Swiss, Samantha, 40n.

Talner, Lauren, 365n.
Taylor, Jill M., 121n.
Thomas, Clarence, (exh.) 258
Thomas, Tom, 264n., 265, 265n.
Tichy, Noel, 144n.
Tillman, Audris, 472n., 482n.
Toffler, Alvin, 500, 500n.
Toffler, Barbara, 131n.
Tolchin, Martin, 175n.
Toner, Robin, 269n.

Tootelian, Dennis H., 99n.
Toscano, Guy, 109n.
Trotter, R. Clayton, 576n.
Troy, Katherine, 20n.
Tsubaki, Sadayoshi, 517
Tung, Rosalie L., 192n.
Tyson, Rae, 240n.
Tzannatos, Zifiris, 453n.

Ullman, Richard O., 624n.
Ulrich, Thomas A., 119n.

Vagelos, Roy, 371, 618, 620, 622
Valeriano, Lourdes Lee, 625n.
Van Velsor, Ellen, 450n.
Vatikiotis, Michael, 322n.
Velasquez, Manuel, 122n., 136n.
Verespei, Michael A., 420n.
Victor, Bart, (fig.) 123, 123n.
Viscusi, W. Kip, 396n.
Viswesvaran, Cockalingam, 429n.
Vitelli, Scott J., 95n.
Vogel, David, 246n., 365n.
Vollrath, David A., 119n.
von Hayek, Friedrich, (exh.) 155
Votaw, Dow, 276n.
Vyakarnam, Shailendra, (fig.) 40

Waddock, Sandra A., 53n., 478n.,
   (exh.) 479
Wagley, Robert A., 56n.
Waldholz, Michael, 625n.
Walsh, Doris, 381n.
Walton, Clarence C., 48n., 118,
   118n.
Walton, Sam, 474
Ward, Adrienne, 514n.
Ward, Ganie V., 121n.
Ward, Matthew L., 104n.
Warren, Melinda, 227
Wartick, Steven L., 513n., 665n.,
   672n.
Wartzman, Rick, (exh.) 258
Waters, James A., (exh.) 97, (fig.)
   117, (fig.) 131, 131n.
Watson, Richard, 665n.
Watson, Thomas J., Jr., 9
Watson, Thomas J., Sr., 9
Weatherup, Craig, 526, 527
Weber, James, (fig.) 115, 121n.
Weidenbaum, Murray L., 223n.
Welch, Jack, 200
Wendt, Harry, 185n.
Werhane, Patricia H., 127n.
Weston, J. Fred, 290n.
White, Helen E., 112n.
White, Randall P., 450n.

Widgren, Jonas, 541n., (fig.) 542
Wilcoxen, Peter J., 338n.
Williams, Michael, 266n.
Williams, Oliver, (fig.) 408
Wilson, Edward O., 313, 313n.
Windau, Janice, 109n.
Wokutch, Richard, 39n.
Woolard, E. S., 80, 80n.

Xiaoping, Deng, 162

Yaffe, Steven Lewis, 628n.
Yeager, Peter C., 102n., 131n.
Yeltsin, Boris, 28
Yergin, Daniel, 185n.
Young, Andrew, 147
Young, Karen M., 368n.

Zachary, G. Pascal, 195n.
Zedillo Ponce de Leon, Ernesto,
   212
Zedong, Mao, 157, 162
Zeile, William J., (fig.) 187, (exh.)
   189
Zeitz, Baila, (exh.) 455
Zhiranovsky, Vladimir, 28
Zimbalist, Andrew, 283n.
Zimmerman, Janet B., 331n.
Zuboff, Shoshanah, 501n.
Zurer, Pamela S., 508n.

Subject Index

Abbott Laboratories, 284, 481, 495

ABC Nightline, 526

Acid rain, definition of, 328

Acquired immune deficiency syndrome (AIDS); testing, 424–425, (fig.) 425 (*See also* Employee privacy)

Adobe Systems, 295

Advocacy advertising, 521–522 (*See also* Corporate Media strategies)

AEL Industries, 113–114

Aetna Life & Casualty, 457

Affirmative action, (fig.) 412 (*See also* Equal job opportunity)

Aflac, (exh.) 176

African Americans for Environmental Justice, 346

Age Discrimination in Employment Act, 411, (fig.) 411

Agenda 21, (exh.) 303 (*See also* Earth Summit)

AIDS (*See* Acquired immune deficiency syndrome)

Air France, 410

Air pollution, 325–326

Alaska Airlines, 278

Alcoa, (exh.) 494

Alcohol abuse, 427

Altruism, 102

Alyeska Pipeline Service, 432

America Works, (fig.) 47

American Airlines, 278, (exh.) 329

American Business Ethics Award (ABEA), 136

American Exploration Company, 371

American Express (AMEX), 60, (exh.) 176, 351–352, 365, 484, 486

American Family Association, 515

American Home Products, 561, 566–567, 571

American Institute of Certified Public Accountants, 97

American Lung Association, 326

American politics:
  critical problems of, 256–265, (exh.) 260
  1990s overview, 254–256

American Psychological Association (APA), 429

American Red Cross, 481

American Telephone and Telegraph (AT&T), 4, 10, (fig.) 47, 60, 134, 271–273, (fig.) 273, 281, 288, 290, (fig.) 344, 413, 498, 643–645

American Trial Lawyers Association, 399

Americans with Disabilities Act (ADA), 411, (fig.) 411, 413, (fig.) 414, 424 (*See also* Equal job opportunity)

AmeriCares, 481

Amoco, (fig.) 273, (exh.) 333

Anderson, Warren M., 578, 579, 581, 583

Antitrust:
  exemptions, 283–284
  and health care reform, (exh.) 289
  key issues of, 285–286
  laws, enforcement of, (fig.) 281, 284–285
  major laws of, 280–284, (exh.) 282
  objectives of, 278–280

Antitrust Improvements Act, (fig.) 281, 283, 285

Apartheid, 174

Apple Computer, 7, (fig.) 344, 497

Arthritis Foundation, 484

Asahi National Broadcasting Company, 517

Asea Brown Boveri, 254

Ashland Oil, (exh.) 479

Asian Pacific Economic Council (APEC), (fig.) 177

Association of Southeast Asian Nations (ASEAN), 167, (fig.) 167, 507

Atlanta, 665, 668–672 (*See also* The Atlanta Project)

Atlantic Richfield (ARCO), (exh.) 67, 81, 492

Aurora Healthcare, 60

Aveda Corporation, (fig.) 47

Avis, 368

Avon Products, (fig.) 47

Balanced Budget Amendment, 537

Bank of America, 81, 384, 522

Barland International, 417

Bayer AG, 502

BC Tel, 502

Beatrice Foods, 15

Bechtel Group, 384

Bell Atlantic, 4–8, 530

Ben & Jerry's, (exh.) 47, (fig.) 47, 417, 530, 666–667

Bhopal, 576–586

Biodiversity, 313–316, (exh.) 314 (*See also* Environmental issues)

Biotechnology, 504

Body Shop International, 21

Boston Against Drugs (B.A.D.), 671

Breast implant controversy, 652–664

Bristol Myers, 284, 561–562, 566–567, 571

British Airways, 191

British Petroleum, 182

Brooklyn Union Gas, (fig.) 47

Browning-Ferris Industries, (exh.) 329

BTR, 9–10

Bubble concept, 332

Burger King, (exh.) 44

Burke, James E., 560, 568

Burroughs Wellcome, 525

Business abroad, political and social challenges, 188–193

Business and society in twenty-first century:
  corporate strategy, 533–535, (exh.) 534
  ecological challenges of, 538–539

Business and society in twenty-
    first century *(continued)*
ethics and public values,
    535–536
global challenges, 536
political revolutions of,
    536–538
Business Council for Sustainable
    Development (BCSD),
    316–317, 320
Business Enterprise Trust, 46
Business ethics, 90–105, (fig.) 91,
    (fig.) 92 *(See also* Ethics)
Business for Social Responsibility,
    43, (exh.) 47
Business–Government–Society
    Relations:
forces shaping, 18–30, (fig.) 19
systems perspective, 6–8, (fig.) 7
Business legitimacy, principle of,
    22, 184
Business politics:
global responsibility of,
    265–267, (exh.) 265, (fig.) 267
and political involvement,
    252–253, (fig.) 252, (fig.) 253
and political system, 253–254
Business Roundtable, 244, 399
Buy Recycled Business Alliance,
    (exh.) 329
Buyer Up, (fig.) 382 *(See also*
    Consumer protection
    agencies)

California Public Employees
    Retirement System (Calpers),
    352, 364
Campus Circle Project, 60, 70–72
Canon, 291
Capital Investment, 8
Carter, Jimmy, 668–671
CARE, 520
Catholic Knights Insurance
    Company, 60
Cause marketing, 484
Caveat emptor, 379
Center for Auto Safety, 403
Center for business ethics, 131
Center for the Study of American
    Business, 227
Central state control, (fig.) 149,
    156–159, (fig.) 158
CERES principles, 345, 366, (fig.)
    367

Chamber of Commerce of the
    United States, 109
Champion International, 427
Channel One, 516
Charity principle, 41–42, (fig.) 44
    (See also Corporate social
    responsibility)
Chemical Manufacturers
    Association (CMA), (exh.) 318,
    343
Chevron Corporation, 20–21, 28,
    (exh.) 176, (fig.) 273, 282
Child care, 456 *(See also* Women)
Children's Defense Fund, 60
Chrysler Corporation, 174, 243,
    (fig.) 273, 291, 400, 418
Church and Dwight, (fig.) 47, (fig.)
    344
CIGNA, 546
Citicorp, (exh.) 176
Citizen Action Group, (fig.) 382
City Year, (exh.) 552 *(See also*
    Volunteerism)
Civil Aeronautics Board (CAB),
    227, 243
Civil Rights Act, 411, (fig.) 411, 412,
    452, (fig.) 452, 462–463
Clayton Act, 281–282, (fig.) 281
    (See also Antitrust)
Clean Air Act Amendments, (fig.)
    326
Clean Air Act of 1970, (fig.) 326,
    328
Clean Air Act of 1990, 50, (fig.)
    326, 328, (exh.) 333, 334
Clearinghouse for Corporate
    Social Involvement, 81
Cleveland Foundation, 667
Clinton, Bill, 628, 631–633,
    635–640
Clorox, (fig.) 47, (fig.) 344
Coalition for Environmentally
    Responsible Economies,
    345
Coca-Cola, (exh.) 176, 184, (fig.)
    273, (exh.) 329, 487
Collaborative empowerment,
    668–670
Collaborative partnerships, 59–
    61
Command and Control
    Regulation, 332
Committee for Economic
    Development (CED), 43, (fig.)
    45, 218

Common Market *(See* European
    Economic Community;
    European Union)
Community:
business involvement,
    551–553, (exh.) 552–553
definition of, 469
problems of, 539–546, (fig.)
    540, (figs.) 542, (exh.) 545
strengthening of, 475–481, (fig.)
    475, (exh.) 479
Community Advisory Panels
    (CAPs), 481
Community Chest movement, 482
Community Reinvestment Act,
    477
Community relations, 469–475,
    (fig.) 471, (exh.) 473, (fig.) 474
Community Right to Know Law,
    334
Comparable worth, 453 *(See also*
    Women)
Competitiveness, national,
    290–292
Comprehensive Environmental
    Response Compensation and
    Liability Act (CERCLA) *(See*
    Superfund)
Computer matching and Privacy
    Protection Act, 422
Conference Board, (exh.) 473,
    493, 555
Conference on Environment and
    Development, *(See* Earth
    Summit)
Conglomerate merger, 287, (fig.)
    288
Congress Watch, (fig.) 382, 383
    (See also Consumer
    Protection agencies)
Consumer action panels, 400
Consumer advocacy groups,
    382–383, (fig.) 382
Consumer Aerosol Products
    Council, 520
Consumer Bill of Rights, 380 *(See
    also* Consumer movement)
Consumer movement:
achievements, 401–402
advocacy groups, 382–383,
    (fig.) 382
agencies, for protection,
    392–394, (fig.) 392
anatomy of, 379–380
business response to, 399–401

Consumer movement *(continued)*
  government protection for,
    389–392, (fig.) 391
  issues of, 383–389, (exh.) 390
  product liability, 394–399, (fig.)
    395
  reasons for, 380–381
Consumer Product Safety
  Commission, 230, (fig.) 392,
  393, 401
consumer protection agencies,
  392–394, (fig.) 392 *(See also*
  Consumer movement)
Consumer protection laws,
  389–392, (fig.) 391
Consumerism *(See* Consumer
  movement)
Continental, 278
Contingent valuation, 339 *(See
  also* Environmental
  regulation; Pollution control)
Convention on Biological
  Diversity, 316 *(See also* Earth
  Summit)
Copycat tampering, 570–571,
  573
Corporate Conversion Council
  (CCC), (exh.) 67
Corporate culture, 121–122
Corporate Environmental
  Advisory Council, 342
Corporate environmental
  responsibility, 340–345
  elements of effective
    management, 342–344
  proactive companies for, (fig.)
    344
  stages of, 340–342, (fig.) 341
Corporate giving:
  definition of, 482, (fig.) 483
  priorities in, 485–486, (fig.) 485
  in strategic context, 483–485,
    (fig.) 484
Corporate governance, 358–365,
  (fig.) 363
  current trends in, 362–365
  employee stock ownership
    plans (ESOP), 367–368
  executive compensation,
    368–371
  process of, 361–362, (fig.) 363
  social responsibility
    shareholder resolutions,
    365–367, (fig.) 367
Corporate legitimacy, 273

Corporate media strategies:
  advocacy advertising, 521–522
  crisis management, 520–521,
    (exh.) 521
  media training of employees,
    522–523
  public relations, 520
    (See also Media)
Corporate mergers, 286–290
  types of, (fig.) 288
  value of, (fig.) 287
Corporate policy ethics, 95, (fig.)
  95 *(See also* Ethics)
Corporate political agency
  theory, 262 *(See also*
  American politics)
Corporate power, 273–277
  multinational, (fig.) 274
  in U.S., (fig.) 273
Corporate restructuring:
  community response to,
    488–491, (fig.) 490
  company response, 491–492
  partnership, 492–493, (exh.)
    494
  social costs of, 488
Corporate social responsibility,
  35–38, (fig.) 63
  charity principle, 41–42, (fig.)
    44
  costs of, 48
  and law, 49–53
  limits of, 46–49
  modern forms of, 43–46
  origin of, 41
  in other nations, 38–40
  and profits, 53–55
  shareholder wealth, (exh.) 51
  stakeholders, (exh.) 51
  stewardship principle, 42–43,
    (fig.) 44
Corporate social responsiveness,
  68–81, (fig.) 63
  corporate culture of, 77–81,
    (fig.) 78
  corporate social strategy, (fig.)
    78
  formulating strategies for,
    69–73
  inactive strategy, 64–65, (fig.) 64
  interactive strategy, (fig.) 64,
    66–67
  model of, 74–77, (fig.) 74
  proactive strategy, (fig.) 64,
    65–66

Corporate social responsiveness
  (continued)
  public affairs, 67
  reactive strategy, (fig.) 64, 65
Corporate social strategy, 197
Corporate strategy for twenty-
  first century, 531–532
Cost-benefit analysis, 225
Cost limiting agreement, 621–622
Council of Institutional Investors,
  363
Council on Economic Priorities,
  46, (fig.) 47
Council on Private Sector
  Initiatives, 486
Crisis management, 520–521,
  (exh.) 521, 562 *(See also*
  Corporate media strategies)
Crisis management team, 569
Critical Mass Energy Project, (fig.)
  382 *(See also* Consumer
  protection agencies)
Cross-media pollution, 331
Crown Center Redevelopment
  Project, 666
Cultural conflicts, 193
Cultural distance, 192
Cummins Engine Co., (fig.) 47,
  56–58, 135, (exh.) 135
Cycle of violence, 544 *(See also*
  Violence)

Dai-Ichi Kangyo Bank, (exh.) 39,
  (fig.) 274
DAKA International, 46
Dalkon shield controversy, 659
Dayton Hudson, (fig.) 47
Defense industry conversion, 489
Defense Protection Act of 1950,
  36
Delany Clause, 386
Delta Airlines, 278
Democratic National Committee
  (DNC), (exh.) 260
Deregulation, 28, 227–229, 616
Digital Equipment Corporation,
  (fig.) 47, (fig.) 344, 408, (exh.)
  552
Dioxin, 584
Disaster relief, 481
Diversity, 147–149
Diversity Council, 416
Dong Ah Company, 39
Donnelly Corporation, (fig.) 47,
  134

Dow Chemical, 144, 237–239, 250, 324, 342, (fig.) 344, 576, 584

Dow Corning Corporation, 651–664

Drug-Free Workplace Act, 426

Drug testing, 426–427

Dunn and Bradstreet, 134

Du Pont, (exh.) 67, 80, (exh.) 176, 309, 371, 457, 576, 584

Earth Summit, 301, (exh.) 303, 308, 313, 315–316

Eastern Airlines, 64

Eastman Kodak, 60

Ecological challenges, 301–308

Ecological impacts, 15, 29–30

Ecology, definition of, 302

Economic development, 476–477 (*See also* Community)

Ecosystem:
  forces of change to, 305–307, (fig.) 305, (fig.) 307
  limits to growth of, 307–308
  threats to, 303–305

Eddie Bauer, 48

Edison Project, 75

Education reform, 478–479, (exh.) 479

E. I. Du Pont de Nemours and Company (*See* Du Pont)

Elder care, 456 (*See also* Women)

Electronic Communications Privacy Act, 422

Electronic mail, 421, (exh.) 423

Eli Lilly, 289–290

El Paso Community Foundation, (exh.) 494

E-Mail (*See* Electronic mail)

Emissions charges or fees, 334 (*See also* Environmental regulation; Pollution control)

Employee Assistance Programs (EAPs), 428

Employee layoffs:
  international interventions, 409–410
  U.S. government intervention, 409

Employee Polygraph Protection Act, 429

Employee privacy, 421–425

Employee Stock Ownership Plan (ESOP), definition of, 367–368

Employee testing:
  drugs, 425–428, (fig.) 428
  honesty, 428–429

Employee theft, 428

Employer-employee social contract, 407, (fig.) 408, (*See also* New social contract)

Employment-at-will, definition of, 407

Employment quotas, (fig.) 412, (*See also* Equal job opportunity)

Endangered Species Act, (fig.) 326, 630*n.*, 639

Enlightened self interest, 51–52

Entitlements, 219–220

Environmental analysis, 72–73
  issue analysis, 73
  stakeholder analysis, 73
  trend analysis, 73

Environmental audits, 343 (*See also* Corporate environmental responsibility)

Environmental Defense Fund (EDF), 66, 323–324

Environmental ethics, (exh.) 314

Environmental issues:
  global biodiversity, 313–316, (exh.) 314
  global warming, 310–313, (fig.) 311, (exh.) 312
  international community response to, 316–320, (exh.) 318
  management of, 323–324
  ozone depletion, 309–310

Environmental protection, 29–30

Environmental Protection Agency (EPA), 243, 312–313, 325, (fig.) 327, (exh.) 333, 334–335, 337–338, 346–347, 385, 401

Environmental protection laws, 326

Environmental regulation:
  agencies of, federal, 325–337, (fig.) 327
  alternative policy approaches, 331–337, (fig.) 336
  civil and criminal enforcement, 335–337
  cost and benefits of, 337–340, (fig.) 337, (fig.) 340
  laws of, (fig.) 326
  major areas of, 325–331, (exh.) 329

Environmental scanning, 72–73

Environmental standards, 332

Environmental tobacco smoke, 430

Equal employment opportunity (*See* Equal job opportunity)

Equal Employment Opportunity Act, (fig.) 367, 411, (fig.) 411, (fig.) 452

Equal job opportunity:
  Americans with Disabilities Act, 411, (fig.) 411, 413, (fig.) 414
  corporate response, 412–413, (fig.) 412
  government policies and regulations, 410–412, (fig.) 411
  reverse discrimination, 413–414

Equal Opportunity, principle of, 154

Equal Pay Act, 411, (fig.) 411, 451–452

Equal Rights Amendment, 452

Ergonomics, definition of, 418, (*See also* Job safety and health)

Ethic audit (*See* Ethics)

Ethic codes (*See* Ethics)

Ethic committee (*See* Ethics)

Ethic officer (*See* Ethics)

Ethical climate, 122–124, (fig.) 123

Ethical egoist, 102

Ethical principles, 22–23, (fig.) 24

Ethical problems in business, 124–130, (fig.) 129

Ethical reasoning, 125–130, (fig.) 125

Ethical reform:
  comprehensive programs and awards, 136–137
  in corporations, 130–132, (fig.) 131
  ethical safeguards, 132–136
  manager's goals and values, 115–118, (fig.) 115
  manager's moral development, 119–121, (fig.) 120
  manager's moral standards, (fig.) 117
  qualities of ethical leaders, (fig.) 116

Ethical relativism, 89

Ethics:
  in accounting, 97–98

Ethics *(continued)*
  audits, 135–136
  in business, 90–105, (fig.) 91,
    (tig.) 92, (fig.) 101
  codes, 132–133
  committees, 133
  corporate policy, 95, (fig.) 95
  cross-cultural, 104–105
  face to face, 94, (fig.) 95, (fig.) 96
  financial, 99
  functional-area, (fig.) 95, 96
  global, 105–108, (fig.) 107
  information systems, 100
  and law, 108–109
  managers quotes of, (fig.) 97
  marketing, 98–99
  meaning of, 89–94
  officer, 133
  training programs, 134, (exh.)
    135
Ethnocentric perspective, 146
European Commission, (exh.)
  265, 294
European Economic Community,
  25 (*See also* Common
  Market; European Union)
European Union (EU), 22, 25–26,
  39, 165, (fig.) 166, 167, 176,
  (fig.) 177, 230, (exh.) 265, 266,
  291, 491, 509, 555
Executive compensation, 368–371
Exxon, 144, (exh.) 176, (fig.) 180,
  182, 273, (fig.) 273, 339
Exxon *Valdez*, 339, 406, 427

Face to face ethics, 94, (fig.) 95,
  (fig.) 96 (*See also* Ethics)
Fair Credit Reporting Act, 422
Fairchild Semiconductor,
  592–593
Fairness doctrine, 517
False Claims Act, 431
Family and Medical Leave Act,
  (fig.) 452, 457
Family leave, 456 (*See also*
  Women)
Federal Communications
  Commission (FCC), 4, 517
Federal Contract Compliance
  Programs, 410–411
Federal Election Commission,
  257
Federal Express, (fig.) 47
Federal National Mortgage
  Association, 417
Federal Reserve Bank, 212

Federal Trade Commission (FTC),
  (fig.) 281, 283–284, 384, 388,
  (fig.) 392, 393, 396
Federal Trade Commission Act,
  (fig.) 281, 282
  breast implant controversy,
    656
  (*See also* Antitrust)
Fiscal policy, definition of, 210
Foldcraft, (fig.) 47
Food and Drug Administration
  (FDA), 560–575, 651–664
Food, Drug, and Cosmetics Act,
  386, 653
Ford Motor Company, 58, (exh.)
  176, (fig.) 180, 203, 243, 273,
  (fig.) 273, 291, 400, 643,
  645–646
Foreign Corrupt Practices Act, 98,
  266
Foreign investment review
  boards, 187
Free enterprise, (fig.) 149,
  151–156, (fig.) 158
Free market system, (fig.) 151
Frito-Lay, 174
Fuji Bank, (fig.) 274
Full-cost pricing, 317
Functional-area ethics, (fig.) 95,
  96 (*See also* Ethics)
Future shock, definition of, 499

Gates, Thomas, 563
Gender pay gap, 443–444, (fig.)
  444 (*See also* Women)
General Accounting Office, 346,
  415
General Agreement on Tariffs
  and Trade (GATT), 26, (exh.)
  168, 177, (fig.) 177, 231, 555
General Dynamics, 138–139
General Electric, 103, 144, 195,
  199, (fig.) 273, 413, (exh.) 479,
  (exh.) 494
General Electric Plastics, 46
General Foods, 375
General Motors, 81, (exh.) 176,
  178, (fig.) 180, 243, 273, (fig.)
  273, 291, 365, 366, 400,
  403–404, 522
Genetic engineering, 504
Geocentric perspective, 146
Gerber Foods, 571
Gillette, (exh.) 176
Gilreath Manufacturing Inc., 530
Givaudan Far East, Ltd, 164

Glass ceiling, 449–450 (*See also*
  Women)
Glass wall, 449 (*See also* Women)
Global commons, 301–302
Global corporation, (exh.) 179
Global economic change, 23–26
Global Environmental Facility
  (GEF), (exh.) 303
Global Environmental
  Management Initiative
  (GEMI), (exh.) 318
Global population growth, (fig.)
  148
Global warming, 310–313, (fig.)
  311, (exh.) 312 (*See also*
  Environmental issues)
Goodyear/Firestone, (exh.) 521
Government regulation:
  costs of, 225–227, (fig.) 226
  federal agencies of, (fig.) 224
  overview of, 221–229
  size of, 238–241
  types of, 221–223
  (*See also* Regulation)
Government relations (*See*
  Business politics)
Grand Metropolitan plc, 174–175
Grassroots programs, 260
Greater Los Angeles Partnership
  for the Homeless, 477
Green consumerism, 383
Green management, 341 (*See also*
  Corporate environmental
  responsibility)
Green marketing, (exh.) 47, 384
Group Against Smoking Pollution
  (GASP), 243
GTE, 427
Guardian Industries, 272, 291
Guest workers, 539
Gulf & Western, 287

Habitat for Humanity, 495
Hallmark Cards, Inc., 666
Hanna Andersson, 137
Harris Corporation, 135
Hazardous Materials Transport
  Act, (fig.) 326
Hazardous Waste Operation and
  Emergency Response
  Standard, 419
H. B. Fuller, (fig.) 47, 136, (fig.)
  344
HBO, 417
Health Insurance Association of
  America (HIAA), 268–269

Health maintenance organizations (HMO), 618, 620–621, 624–626

Health policy, 216–218, (fig.) 217 (*See also* Social welfare policy)

Health Research Group, (fig.) 382, 383 (*See also* Consumer Protection Agency)

Heinz Company, 35–36

Herman Miller, (fig.) 47, 136, 344, (fig.) 344

Hershey Foods, (exh.) 44

Hewlett Packard, 20–21, 122, 135, 291

High-performance workplace, 535

Hitachi, 291

Honda Motor Company, 103–104

Honesty tests (employee), 429

Honeywell, 135, 195

Hopkins v. Dow Corning, 660

Horizontal merger, 287, (fig.) 288

Housing, 477–478

Hudson Institute, 414

Hughes Aircraft Company, 135, 413

Hughes Environmental Systems, 346

Human rights, 67, 126–127, 144 codes of conduct, 196

Humana, (exh.) 479

IBM, 7, 9, 60, 146, (exh.) 176, (fig.) 180, 273, (fig.) 273, 295–296, 309, 593

Ideology: free enterprise, 152 U.S. business, (fig.) 154

Immigration: barriers to, 540–541, (figs.) 542 causes of, 539–540, (fig.) 540 U.S.-Mexico, issues of, 541–543 (*See also* Community)

Immigration Reform and Control Act, 415

Inactive strategy, 64–65, (fig.) 64, (*See also* Corporate social responsiveness)

Industrial Bank of Japan, (fig.) 274

Industrial ecology, 318–320

Industrial policy, 215, (fig.) 215 (*See also* Fiscal policy)

Industry-Environmental Coordinating Committee (IECC), 596–599

Industry-Labor Council, 413

Information society, 500

In Home Health, 450

Insider trading, 372–373

Institutional investors, 353–354 (*See also* Stockholders)

Intel, (fig.) 273

Intellectual property, definition of, 292–293

Interactive Digital Software Association, 108

Interactive social system, 8

Interactive strategy, (fig.) 64, 66–67 (*See also* Corporate social responsiveness)

Interfaith Center on Corporate Responsibility (ICCR), 642

Intergenerational equity, 219, (exh.) 220 (*See also* Social welfare policy)

Internal Revenue Service, 481–482

International business, 175–178 foreign sales in U.S. corporations, (exh.) 176

International Chamber of Commerce (ICC), 22, (exh.) 318

International Federation for Medical and Biological Engineering, 505

International Olympic Committee, 487

International Standards Organization (ISO), (exh.) 318

International Tropical Timber Organization (ITTO), 322

International Women's Forum, 448

Interstate Commerce Commission, 221

Inventive Products, 393

Issues Management Process (*See* Public issues)

James River Corporation, 420

Jenny Craig, 388

Job safety and health, 417–421, (exh.) 421

Johnson Controls, 462–463

Johnson & Johnson, 53, 60, 136, 163, 192, 324, 484, 520, 558–575, 620, 624, 643, 652

Johnson Wax, 456

J. P. Morgan (bank), 351–352

Justice, 127–128

Keating, Charles H., Jr., 603–616

"Keating Five, The," 610–612

Keidanren, (exh.) 318

Kellogg, (fig.) 47

Kennecott Corporation, 339

Kentucky Education Reform Act (KERA), (exh.) 479

Kessler, David A., M.D., 660

Kraft, 285, 375

Kroger, 378

Kubota, 58

Labor standards, 195

Laissez faire, principle of, 154

Larry King Live, 526

Law, 108–109 (*See also* Ethics)

Leather Development Centre, 319

Leveraged buyouts (LBOs), 360 (*See also* Stockholders)

Levi Strauss, 80, 134, 136, 195, 293, 417, (exh.) 417

Life cycle analysis, 317–318

Limited government, 154

Limits to growth hypothesis, 308 (*See also* Ecosystem)

Lincoln Savings and Loan, 603–616

Litigation Group, (fig.) 382, 383 (*See also* Consumer protection agencies)

Lobbying, 260, (exh.) 265 (*See also* American politics)

Local Initiative Support Corporation (LISC), 666

Lockheed Missiles and Space Corp., 343, 489

Lotus Development, (exh.) 47, 417

Love Canal, 643

LTV, (fig.) 273

Lucky stores, 437

MacBride principles, (fig.) 367

Macroenvironment of business, 70–74, (fig.) 71 economic segment, 71, (fig.) 71 political segment, 71, (fig.) 71 social segment, 70, (fig.) 71 technological segment, 72, (fig.) 72

MacWorld, (exh.) 423

Magnuson-Moss Warranty Act, 396

Manville Corporation, 397

Maquiladora, 641–650

March of Dimes, 48

Market failure, definition of, 221
(*See also* Government
regulation)
Marlboro, 375
Marquette University, 60
Massachusetts Institute of
Technology (MIT), 282
Matsushita Electric Industrial,
409, 483
Mattel Incorporated, 213
MCA, 417
McCaw Cellular
Communications, 271, 281,
288, 290
McDonald's, 66, (exh.) 176, 324,
397
McNeil Laboratories, 559–575
McNeil-Lehrer News Hour, 526
Medco Containment Services,
289, 617–627
Media:
corporate media strategies,
520–523
critical issues of, 512–519, (fig.)
518
definition of, 511, (exh.) 512
social responsibility guidelines,
523–524
Media training, 522–523 (*See also*
Corporate media strategies)
Merck & Company, 46, (fig.) 47,
136, (fig.) 273, 289, 371,
617–627
Mergers, corporate (*See*
Corporate mergers)
Mexico, 641
Microsoft Corporation, 284,
294–296, 417
Midas International, 65
Miller, 375
Mitsubishi, (fig.) 180
Mitsubishi Bank, (fig.) 274
Mitsui & Company, (fig.) 180
Mitsui Toatsu Chemicals, 505
Mixed state-and-private
enterprise, (fig.) 149, 159–
160
Mobay Corporation, 36
Mobil, (exh.) 176, (fig.) 273, 282,
384, 521, 522
Monetary policy, definition of,
211
Monsanto, 136
Montreal Protocol, 49*n.,* 65, 309
(*See also* Environmental
issues)

Most Favored Nation (MFN)
trading status, 144
Motorola, 60, 192, 415
Mr. Rogers' Neighborhood, 516
Multinational Corporation (MNC),
178–183, (exh.) 179, (fig.) 180
(*See also* International
business)
Multinational Enterprise (MNE),
(exh.) 179

Nalco Chemical, 427
National Alliance of Business
(NAB), 478
National Association of Attorneys
General, 285
National Association of
Manufacturers, 251, 399
National Association of
Purchasing Management,
100
National Center for Disability
Services, 413
National Commission on AIDS,
425
National competitiveness,
290–292
National Cooperative Research
Act of 1984, 283
National Environmental Policy
Act, (fig.) 326
National Federation of
Independent Business, 244,
251
National Foundation for Women
Business Owners, 450
National Health Laboratories, 431
National Highway Traffic Safety
Administration (NHTSA),
(fig.) 392, 393, 401, 404
National Semiconductor Corp.,
343
National sovereignty, principle of,
183
National Transportation Safety
Board, (fig.) 392, 393
National Wildlife Federation
(NWF), (exh.) 67
Natural Resources Defense
Council (NRDC), 18
NBC Dateline, 513
NCR Corporation, 193
Neighborhood Housing Services
of America, 477
Nestle, 182
Nestle/USA, 284

New social contract, 20, 407–408,
(fig.) 408, 532–533
New world order, 165–168
New York City Coalition for the
Homeless, 477
New York City Teacher's
Retirement System, 370
Nippon Steel, 319
Nippon Telegraph & Telephone,
(fig.) 274
Nissan Corporation, (exh.) 423
Norfolk Southern, 420
North American Free Trade
Agreement (NAFTA), 23, 26,
165, (fig.) 166, 167, 176, (fig.)
177, 555, 646
North American Treaty
Organization (NATO), 165
Northern Ireland, (fig.) 367
Northern spotted owl, 628–640
Northern Telecom, 291
Northrup, 135
Northwest Airlines, 278
Norton Company, 9–10
Novell, 295
Nuclear Regulatory Commission,
325
Nutri/System, 388
NYNEX, 134, (exh.) 494

Occupational Safety and Health
Administration (OSHA), 325,
418–420, 462
Occupational segregation, 444
Office of Technology Assessment,
504–505
Office on Smoking and Health,
389
Ogilvy and Mather Worldwide,
437
Olivetti, 106
Open Government Project, (fig.)
382 (*See also* Consumer
protection agencies)
Opinion Research Corporation,
52
Optical Radiation Corp., 393
Ozone depletion, 309–310 (*See
also* Environmental issues)

Pacific Bell, 134
Parental leave, 456 (*See also*
Women)
Park Plaza Hotel, 343
Participative management, 587

Partnership for Kentucky School Reform, (exh.) 479

Passive nondiscrimination, (fig.) 412 (*See also* Equal employment job opportunity)

Patagonia, 136

Pathmark, 378

Pepsi Cola, 174

PepsiCo, 164, 174, 520, 526, 643, 646

Perestroika, 27

Performance-expectation gap, 61, (fig.) 62

Perpetual political campaign, 257

Pesticide Control Act, (fig.) 326, 329

Phases of technology, 500, (fig.) 501 (*See also* Technology)

Philanthropy, corporate, 43–46, (fig.) 44 (*See also* Corporate giving)

Philip Morris Co., 112, 182, 241, 249, (fig.) 273, 375

Pitney Bowes Co., (fig.) 47

Pizza Hut, 498

Plant closing laws, 490

Plum Creek Timber Company, 629

Points of Light Foundation, 486

Polaroid Corp., 136, 180

Political Action Committee (PAC), 257–258, (exh.) 258, (fig.) 259, 610

Political cynicism, definition of, 254–256 (*See also* American politics)

Politics and business (*See* Business politics)

Polluter Pays Principle (PPP), 317

Pollution (*See* Environmental regulation)

Pollution control:
  agencies, federal, (fig.) 327
  civil and criminal enforcement, 335–337
  cost and benefits of, 337–340, (fig.) 337, (fig.) 340
  laws, (fig.) 326
  policy approaches to, 331–337, (fig.) 336

Pollution Prevention Act of 1990, (fig.) 326, 330

Pollution Prevention Committee, 343

Population growth, 305–306, (fig.) 305

Poverty, world, 306–307

Preferential hiring, (fig.) 412 (*See also* Equal job opportunity)

Pregnancy Discrimination Act, (fig.) 452, 463

Priority rule, 130

Privacy Act, 422

Privacy rights, 421

Private Initiative Councils (PICs), 479

Privatization, 27, 179

Proactive strategy, (fig.) 64, 65–66 (*See also* Corporate social responsiveness)

Proctor & Gamble, 163, (exh.) 176, 192, 318, 352, 365, 423, 480

Product liability, 394–399
  laws, reforming of, 398–399
  privity of contract, 395, (fig.) 395
  strict liability, 396, (fig.) 395
  warranties, 396, (fig.) 395 (*See also* Consumer movement)

Product recalls, 401

Project Historic America, 468

Profit:
  long-run, 54
  maximum, 54
  optimum, 54
  short-run, 54

Project Baby Safe, 65 (*See also* Midas International)

Protecting Prince William County, 468

Prudential Corporation, (fig.) 47, 324

Public affairs, function of, 67–69, (fig.) 69, (fig.) 70

Public citizen, 382–383, (fig.) 382, 403–404 (*See also* Consumer protection agencies)

Public issues:
  evolution of, 239–249
  life cycle, (fig.) 239, 240–246
  management of, (fig.) 239, 246–250, (fig.) 247

Public policy:
  and business, 208–215
  definition of, 205–207
  elements of, 207–208, (fig.) 207

Public-private partnership, 492, 673

Public referendum, 264 (*See also* American politics)

Public relations, 520 (*See also* Corporate media strategies)

Public Relations Society of America (PRSA), 520

"Push" and "pull" factors, 540, (fig.) 540

Quad Graphics, (fig.) 47

Quaker Oats Company, 387

Quarex Industries, 64

Questionable payments, 194

Racism, 549–551 (*See also* Community)

Reactive strategy, (fig.) 64, 65 (*See also* Corporate social responsiveness)

Reebok International, 196, (exh.) 196, 420, (exh.) 421

Reengineering, 20

Regulation:
  all-industry social, 222–223
  functional, 223
  growth of, 223–229
  industry-specific economic, 222
  international, 229–232, (fig.) 230
  (*See also* Government regulation)

Reinventing government, 229

Relationship investing, 363 (*See also* Stockholders)

Renault, 174

Republican National Committee (RNC), (exh.) 260

Reregulation, 228

Rescue Action Committee, 481

Resource Conservation and Recovery Act of 1976, (fig.) 326, 330

Responsible Care, 344 (*See also* Chemical Manufacturers Association)

Responsible Care Program, 481

Reverse discrimination, 413–414 (*See also* Equal job opportunity)

Right-to-know laws, 584

Rights to Financial Privacy Act, 422

R. J. Reynolds Company, 112, 241, 522

RJR Nabisco, 112, 285, 389

Royal Dutch/Shell Group, (fig.) 180, (fig.) 274

Rubbermaid, (exh.) 329

Rule of cost, definition of, 225
Rutgers, 549

Safe Drinking Water Act of 1994, (fig.) 326, 329
Sakura Bank, (fig.) 274
Samsung, 291
Santa Clara County, 594–602
Sanwa Bank, (fig.) 274
SAS Institute, (fig.) 47
Saturn, 399
S. C. Johnson, (fig.) 47
Scott Paper Company, 18
Securities and Exchange Commission, 363, 365–366, 370–371
Sesame Street, 516
Sex differences in management, 447–449
Sex role spillover, 459
Sex segregation (See Occupational segregation)
Sexual harrassment, 458–460, (exh.) 460 (See also Women)
Shaman Pharmaceuticals, 315
Shareholder (See Stockholders)
Shareholder lawsuit, 357
Shell Netherlands, 182
Shell Oil Company, (exh.) 273
Sherman Act, 280–281, (fig.) 281 (See also Antitrust)
Shore Bank Corporation, (fig.) 47
Sierra West, (exh.) 494
Silicon Valley Toxics Coalition, 598–600
60 Minutes, 513, 514
Social Action Programme, 40
Social charter, 39
Social contract, 20–21
Social investment, 47
Social issues, corporate executives' opinions, (fig.) 40
Social responsibility shareholder resolutions, 365–367, (fig.) 367 (See also Stockholders)
Social Security, 218–219, (exh.) 220 (See also Social welfare policy)
Social welfare policy, 216–220, (fig.) 216
Society of Friends, 387
Socioeconomic system:
  basic types of, 149–150, (fig.) 149
  Chinese, changes in, 161–165
  militarized nondemocratic, 160–161

Socioeconomic underclass, 547
Sony Corporation, 195, 291
Source Perrier, 525
Source reduction, 330
South Africa, 54, 174, (fig.) 367
Southland, 378
Special economic zones, 163
  in China, 163, (fig.) 163
Sprint, 187
Stages of moral development, 119, (fig.) 120 (See also Ethical reform)
Stakeholder:
  analysis, 640
  coalitions, 15–18
  concept of, 8–18
  employees as, 432
  interactive model of business and society, 12, (fig.) 13
  power, 14–15, (exh.) 16–17
  primary, 10–14, (fig.) 11, (fig.) 13, (exh.) 16–17, (fig.) 16
  secondary, 10–14, (fig.) 14, (exh.) 16–17
Starkist Seafood Company, 35–36
State Farm Insurance Co., 412
State of Wisconsin Investment Board, 352
State Street Bank, (exh.) 44
Stateless corporation, 184–185
Sterling Drug, 561
Stewardship principle (See Corporate social responsibility)
Stewardship responsibility, 551 (See also Volunteerism)
Stockholders:
  corporate governance, 358–365, (fig.) 363
  and the corporation, 373
  employee stock ownership plan (ESOP), 367–368
  government protection of, 371–373
  legal right and safeguards of, 356–358, (fig.) 356
  objectives of ownership, 354–356
  types of, 353–354, (fig.) 354
Stonyfield, (fig.) 47, 136
Strategic philanthropy, 483, (fig.) 484
Strict liability, 396–398
Stride Rite Corporation, (exh.) 47, 82
Sumitomo Bank, (fig.) 274

Sun Company, 345
Sunoco Products, 384
Superfund, (fig.) 326, 330
Supermarkets General Holdings, (fig.) 47
Sustainable development, 302–303
Sustainable forestry, 633
Symantec, 295
Systems theory, 6, 30

Takeovers, corporate (See Corporate mergers)
Tandem Computers, 371
Target Stores, 472
Tax Reform Research Group, (fig.) 382 (See also Consumer protection agencies)
Taxation policy, 211–213 (See also Fiscal policy)
TCI, 4, 530
Technological change:
  business responsibility for, 508–511
  genetic engineering, 504–505
  government involvement in, 508–509, (fig.) 508
  information technology, 505–507
  social costs, 503–504
  stakeholder reaction to, 507–508
Technology:
  business application of, 500
  economic effects of, 502–503
  features of, 499–500
  phases of, 500–502, (fig.) 501
Telecom New Zealand, 4
Telecommunications, 499
Tenneco, 58
Tennessee Valley Association (TVA), 333
Term limits, 263 (See also American politics)
Texaco, (exh.) 176, (fig.) 273
Texas Instruments, 430
The Atlanta Project (TAP), 493, 665n., 668–672
The Gap, 384
Tiananmen Square, 143–144
Timberland Company, (exh.) 552
Time Warner, (fig.) 47, 324, 369, 417
Tom's of Maine, (fig.) 47
Total quality management (TQM), 399–400

Toxic Release Inventory (TRI), 334
Toxic Substance Control Act of
  1976, (fig.) 326, 330
Toyota, (fig.) 180, (fig.) 274, 291,
  409, 476
Trade policy:
  definition of, 213
  trade barriers to, 214
  (*See also* Fiscal policy)
Tradeable allowances, 333
Transamerica Life Companies,
  477
Transnational Corporation (TNC),
  (exh.) 179
Truth in Lending Act, 390
TRW, 249
Tubos de Acero de Mexico, 352
Tungsram, 199
TWA, 278
Tylenol, 52, 521, 558–575

Unanimity rule, 128–139
Unfunded mandates, 537
Unilever, 182, 188
Union Camp Corporation, 384
Union Carbide, 181, 242, 576–
  586
Union Pacific Railroad, 134
United Airlines, 191
United Automobile Workers,
  462
United Church of Christ, 346
United Nations, 231, (exh.) 303,
  306
United Nations Security Council,
  144
United Parcel Service, (exh.) 479
United States:
  foreign manufacturing
    businesses in, (fig.) 187
  foreign ownership in, 186–188,
    (exh.) 189
  foreign sales in, (exh.) 176
U. S. Air, 191, 400
U. S. Chamber of Commerce,
  251–252, (exh.) 265, 266
U. S. Corporate Sentencing
  Guidelines, 134
U. S. Department of Agriculture,
  393
U. S. Department of Commerce,
  36, 428
U. S. Department of Defense, 46,
  509

U. S. Department of Health and
  Human Services, 424
U. S. Department of Justice, 109,
  271, (fig.) 281, 284, 291
  Antitrust Division of, 393
U. S. Department of Labor, 409,
  411, 414, 449, 535
U. S. Department of Labor
  Statistics, 532
U. S. Food and Drug
  Administration (FDA),
  377–378, 388, 392–394,
  (fig.) 392, 401, 527
U. S. Foreign Corrupt Practices
  Act, 98
U. S. Forest Service, 630–631
U. S. National Cancer Institute,
  315, 389
U. S. Sentencing Commission,
  335
U. S. West, (fig.) 47
United Way, 23, 48, 482–483
University of Massachusetts, 549
Upjohn, 666
Urban Institute, 493, 665, 673
Urban sprawl, 477
USPCI, 346
USX (formerly U.S. Steel), (exh.)
  67
Utilitarian reasoning, 125–126

Valdez principles (*See* CERES
  principles)
Vertical merger, 287, (fig.) 288
Video Privacy Protection Act, 422
Violence, 543–546, (exh.) 545 (*See
  also* Community)
Vocational Rehabilitation Act,
  (fig.) 411
Voice Processing Corporation,
  415
Volkswagen, 319, 410
Volunteerism, 486–487, (exh.)
  552–553

Walgreen, 566, 571
Wal-Mart, 178, (fig.) 180, 272, 279,
  474
Walt Disney Company, 467, 477
Warsaw Pact, 165
Waste Management Inc., (exh.)
  329

Water Pollution Control Act
  (Clean Water Act), (fig.) 326,
  338
Weight Watchers International,
  388
Wells Fargo Bank, 433–434, 445
Wesray Corporation, 368
Westinghouse Electric, 352, 370
Weyerhauser, (exh.) 67, 630, 638
Whistle-blowing, 431–432
Wisconsin Bell, 60
Wisconsin Energy Corp., 60
Wisconsin Power and Light,
  333–334
Women:
  and government's role in
    workplace rights, 451–453,
    (fig.) 452
  historical background,
    438–440, (exh.) 439
  in management, 444–451, (fig.)
    446, (fig.) 448
  policies and strategies for,
    452–457, (fig.) 455
  and sexual harrassment,
    458–460, (exh.) 460
  and work flexibility, 457–458
  and workplace, 441–444, (fig.)
    441, (fig.) 444
Work ethic, 155
Workers Adjustment Retraining
  Notification Act (WARN),
  409
Working assets, (exh.) 44
Workplace diversity, 414–417
Workplace safety teams, 419 (*See
  also* Job safety and health)
Workplace smoking, 430–431
World Bank, 165, 217, (exh.) 303
World Commission on
  Environment and
  Development, 302
World Health Organization
  (WHO), 216, 231
World Trade Organization
  (WTO), 232
W. R. Grace Company, 15
Wyman-Gordon Company, 418

Xerox, (fig.) 46, (fig.) 273, (fig.) 344,
  345, 427

Yokogawa, 291